# Vacation Places Rated

Rand McNally

# Vacation Places Rated

## Finding the best vacation places in America

Sylvia McNair

**Rand McNally & Company**

Chicago • New York • San Francisco

## Acknowledgments

Many people contributed time, ideas, and constructive criticism during the preparation of this book. My special gratitude goes to Editorial/Research Service and to Patricia Wishart for her unflagging encouragement as well as for many hours of help gathering data.

From the onset, Anna Idol and Peggy Leith Anderson urged me to undertake this project, gave me assurance that it really could be done, and helped me get started; I appreciate their support.

Richard Boyer and David Savageau originated the *Places Rated* series; I thank them for giving me permission to follow in their footsteps. David and Karyl Savageau not only helped me find sources and plan this volume, they also opened their home to me and gave me several days of invaluable consultation.

Thanks are due Patrick J. Tyson, author of the climate data; Karen Greene for assistance in preparing the manuscript; and Deborah Jacobs for her contributions.

Rand McNally's geographic research and editorial staff made countless contributions over many months. If errors have crept in despite their best efforts to keep me out of trouble, the responsibility lies with me, not with them or with any of the dozens of sources consulted.

# Contents

# Sidebars, Tables, and Maps

# Introduction

A couple of intrepid anglers were in a boat on a frigid day in early spring. They sat shivering for several hours, not getting a single bite and hardly speaking to one another. As it got close to noon, they pulled a simple lunch from under a tarp and chewed on the frosty bologna sandwiches until one of them broke the silence, saying, "If this was half as much fun as it was plannin' it and will be, tellin' our friends about it when we get home, we'd be havin' a ball."

Unfortunately, vacations are often like that—more fun in the anticipation and the reminiscence than in the experience.

Where did you spend your last vacation? What did you do? Was it as pleasant and fun filled as you expected it to be? Did you have any arguments with your traveling companions about where to go and what to do?

Choosing a vacation destination is an important decision; a poor choice can have an important impact on your bank account, your morale, and your relationships with those who vacation with you. The object of a vacation is to build up a store of happy memories; an unhappy holiday can leave you disappointed and angry with yourself, your friends and family, or your travel agent for months on end.

The purpose of this book, the third title in the Rand McNally *Places Rated* series, is to rate 107 popular vacation destinations and furnish useful information that can help you make the best possible choices for your next vacation—not only for your destination but for what you will see and do once you are there.

The success of the first two titles, *Places Rated Almanac* and *Retirement Places Rated,* is evidence of the fascination ratings have for many of us. You don't have to look far to find other signs of this fascination. The Sunday papers are full of ratings of one kind and another. Movies are given a score of one to ten by nationally known critics. New restaurants are star rated by local restaurant reviewers. The latest Nielsen ratings of television shows are reported regularly. Public-opinion polls inform voters as to current popularity ratings of national political leaders.

Selecting the right vacation destination requires accurate information—not only about the place you are planning to visit but about your own preferences and needs. Do you look forward to a vacation as a time for lots of rest and relaxation, perhaps on a warm and sandy beach? Are you an active outdoors person? Are you curious to see different scenery and hear accents

---

### Finding Your Way in *Vacation Places Rated*

This *Places Rated* volume contains thousands of useful facts and many descriptive sections, and it is organized so that readers can find specific items that interest them. Each of its first six chapters has five parts:

- The **Introduction** gives basic information on the chapter's topic and discusses specific examples of the kinds of activities or attractions to be found in various places.
- **Scoring** explains the method used in each chapter to arrive at point scores for the Vacation Places.
- **Place Profiles** is an alphabetic list of all 107 Vacation Places with much information about what vacationers will find to see and do in each one. At the end of each profile the score and rank for that chapter are given.
- **Rankings** presents two lists of the Vacation Places. The first is in rank order, from 1 to 107, for the scores for that chapter; the second is an alphabetic list showing the rank for each place.
- **Top Ten** is a description of the Vacation Places that were ranked in the top ten for that chapter, giving more detail than could be included in the Place Profiles about the attractions of these top-ranking places. This section also contains a list of the author's personal favorites. Not all of these favorites happen to be within the boundaries of the Vacation Places.

The chapter entitled Putting It All Together adds up the ranks to identify the best all-around Vacation Places and describes in some detail the advantages of the top ten.

The final chapter, Ranking Your Own Vacation Places, shows readers how to manipulate the data in *Vacation Places Rated* to come up with their own rankings.

### The Most Popular Leisure-Time Activities

A survey by the U.S. Bureau of the Census reflects major leisure-time activities. Half or more of the 5,657 persons aged 12 and over that were questioned reported walking for pleasure, swimming, and visiting zoos, fairs, or amusement parks. Many of the activities listed were used as elements in scoring the Vacation Places.

|  | Participants (in percentage of total) |
|---|---|
| Swimming | 53 |
| Walking for pleasure | 53 |
| Visiting zoos, fairs, or amusement parks | 50 |
| Driving for pleasure | 48 |
| Picnicking | 48 |
| Sightseeing | 46 |
| Attending sports events | 40 |
| Fishing | 34 |
| Bicycling | 32 |
| Boating | 28 |
| Motorboating* | 19 |
| Canoeing or kayaking | 8 |
| Sailing | 6 |
| Running or jogging | 26 |
| Attending concerts, plays, or other events | 25 |
| Camping | 24 |
| Backpacking | 5 |
| Participating in outdoor team sports | 24 |
| Playing tennis | 17 |
| Day hiking | 14 |
| Golfing | 13 |
| Bird-watching or studying nature | 12 |
| Hunting | 12 |
| Off-road vehicle driving (includes motorcycles, does not include snowmobiles) | 11 |
| Sledding | 10 |
| Horseback riding | 9 |
| Snow skiing | 9 |
| Waterskiing | 9 |
| Ice-skating | 6 |
| Other activities | 4 |

Figures reflect September 1982–June 1983 data.

*Indented items are subcategories of the preceding activities.

*Source:* U.S. Bureau of the Census, *Statistical Abstract of the United States: 1985.*

different from those that surround you every day? Do you want the excitement, the nightlife, and the rich variety of activities available in a major city?

*Vacation Places Rated* does not try to judge which popular U.S. destinations are the best for everyone. What really appeals to you might be not merely boring but downright unpleasant for someone else. What this book does is take a look at certain kinds of things vacationers generally like to see and do and determine which of the 107 selected Vacation Places have the most to offer in those categories. In the process of defining vacation categories and rating the 107 Vacation Places, the book also presents a great deal of other information about vacationing in the United States.

Special forms at the back of the book let you determine your own rankings based on the *Vacation Places Rated* system.

## VACATIONING IS NOT NEW

The word *vacation* is derived from a Latin word meaning "freedom" or "release from occupation," and to just about everyone it implies a time to have fun, a chance to rest, and an opportunity to recharge one's inner batteries. Travel—to have a change of scenery, to explore new places, and to escape everyday cares and responsibilities for a while—has been associated with vacationing since the days when Cleopatra sailed up the Nile in a barge, and probably longer.

Styles in vacation activities and destinations change from time to time. All over the world mineral springs were an early attraction—the ancient Romans built elaborate baths, and in North America Native Americans knew about "taking the waters" long before Europeans sailed across the Atlantic. George Washington was fond of visiting springs in the mountains of western Virginia. In Europe wealthy aristocrats of the late 19th century gathered and partied at fashionable spas. A glance at a map of the United States shows many place-names derived from these natural assets. Hot Springs, Warm Springs, Palm Springs, and Mineral Springs are a few of the names given to localities in various states that have been, and in many cases still are, popular resort communities.

Most people look forward to a vacation with excitement. However, it is a well-known fact of psychology that an approaching vacation arouses anxiety in many people; they feel they are shirking their responsibilities if they take any time off without a good excuse. One popular summertime activity provided this excuse for earlier generations of Americans—the camp meeting. Religious revivals were held outdoors in such pleasant and attractive spots as Martha's Vineyard, Massachusetts, and Ocean City, New Jersey. Families could enjoy the ocean breezes, the fellowship of like-minded people, and the spiritual uplift of evangelistic preaching without suffering from guilty consciences about leaving their workaday worlds behind. In time, many of these spots originally developed by church groups evolved into popular resorts.

An outgrowth of the camp meeting tradition was the Chautauqua Institution, founded in 1874 on a lakeshore in western New York State. Here religious lectures were augmented by a wide-ranging program of cultural and educational presentations. Imitations of the Chautauqua proliferated around the country and were popular well into this century. The original institution still exists and attracts thousands of visitors each summer. The addition of a bit of culture and education to the rest and relaxation of a vacation is important to many people.

Outdoor vacations with a lot of physical activity are

popular today—but so are many other types. The seashore has always drawn vacationers, whether they want to sail, swim, surf, or simply lie on the sand and perfect their tans, while people who live in hot, humid places are often attracted by the cool, fresh air of mountain regions. City dwellers who feel hemmed in by concrete canyons may seek wilderness areas where they can camp, hike, fish, or watch wildlife. Residents of small towns sometimes want to spend time among the bright lights of a major metropolis, enjoying the entertainment opportunities, cultural facilities, and variety of activities not available at home.

## SELECTING VACATION PLACES TO BE RATED

The first task in rating the Vacation Places was to determine what the Vacation Places were—and which ones to rate. Obviously, any place at all can be a good spot for a vacation—for someone. Slightly more than half the pleasure trips taken in 1984 were for the primary purpose of visiting friends or relatives, according to a survey published by the U.S. Travel Data Center, and obviously not all those friends and relatives lived in prime vacation destinations. Tourism is an important source of income in every one of the 50 states—which means that every state has vacation places worthy of consideration.

Through Editorial/Research Service, the tourist offices of all 50 states were surveyed. Among other questions, respondents were asked which places within their state were the most popular with vacationers. The results of this survey, along with my experience and knowledge of tourist destinations in the United States, were used to compile a long list of potential places to investigate. I then met with a panel of Rand McNally editors, and after many hours of discussion, the list was shortened to the 107 Vacation Places now included. In the course of paring down the list to a manageable length, a great many delightful and popular vacation spots in the United States fell by the wayside; this is deeply regretted. But the remaining 107 are, in our opinion, the ones most widely recognized as vacation destinations worth traveling long distances to visit. There are no losers, no "bad" places on the list, but some have more to offer than others—in the variety, quantity, and quality of opportunities for enjoyable vacation activities. These were the considerations on which the ratings were based.

Vacation Places do not come in neat geographic packages. Only a few on the list have precisely definable boundaries: Providence–Newport, Rhode Island, includes the whole state, as does Hawaii, and Door County, Wisconsin, is a neat little peninsula reaching into Lake Michigan. In some cases, however, it was not feasible to use only county or state boundaries to define a Vacation Place.

Some popular Vacation Places are metropolitan areas, but many others are in lightly populated parts of the United States. Therefore it was possible in only a few cases to use the boundaries of standard metropolitan areas, as the authors of *Places Rated Almanac* did.

Many Americans look at travel itself as an integral part of vacation enjoyment. If they are trekking across the country from New York to California to see the Big Trees of Sequoia National Park, they feel the few extra hours of driving time needed to include Death Valley and Yosemite are worth it. For this reason, it was decided that in some instances a rather large area could reasonably be treated as one Vacation Place. The 107 places vary a great deal in size: Yosemite–Sequoia–Death Valley, California, covers nearly 20,000 square miles; Cape Cod–The Islands, Massachusetts, has only 549. In all cases, the boundaries were drawn to include the important sightseeing attractions, both natural and man-made, that vacationers to that area would be most likely to consider visiting.

Certain statistical information, such as numbers of hotels and golf courses, is readily available only by county. Therefore, county figures were used to compile this kind of information. These counties are approximated on the *Vacation Places Rated* map and the list entitled The Places We Rate. In the case of sightseeing attractions, accessibility by highway was given more importance than county borders; the boundaries include some areas not within the counties but just as easily reached as many of those within the counties. County lines are useful to statisticians; sightseers are often unaware of them.

Some of the Vacation Places are centered around major cities; some are in remote, but usually quite well-known, wilderness areas. Many of them contain national parks or other major pieces of land administered by federal agencies.

Each Vacation Place has certain outstanding assets that draw many vacationers each year, such as the excitement of a major city, a balmy winter climate, water for fishing and swimming, or world-famous natural or man-made tourist attractions. The table entitled What Each Destination Has to Offer indicates the major attributes that bring visitors to each place.

## ELEMENTS FOR RATING VACATION PLACES

The next task, after the selection of the Vacation Places to be rated, was to determine what elements would be used as a basis for comparing and scoring them. To do this, I looked for data on what vacationers do. Detailed statistics on this subject, I found, are hard to come by and often conflicting. The authors of *Places Rated Almanac* commented that the task of putting their data together was like trying to take "a snapshot of a moving target; metro areas are dynamic and won't always sit still for their statistical portraits." Vacationers not only will not sit still for their portraits, they wear camouflaged clothing that makes it difficult to distinguish them from their backgrounds.

For example, one government source tells us that 42 million Americans aged 16 and over went fishing in 1980; another reports nearly 66 million aged 12 and over in 1983 were fishers. Since there are only about 15 million in the 12 to 16 age group, one of two things must be true—either fishing increased considerably in popularity in three years, or the figures represent quite rough estimates. The latter conclusion is more probable.

Certain statistics are available concerning patterns of pleasure travel, certain others about leisure-time activities, but there is a glaring lack of accurate and useful information about just what people on vacation do with their free time.

Nevertheless, with these limitations in mind, I went ahead, using whatever information I could find and drawing conclusions from it. The table entitled The Most Popular Leisure-Time Activities resulted from a survey conducted by the Bureau of the Census. The survey was not limited to what people reported doing when on vacation, but it was assumed that favorite vacation activities did not differ widely from those popular at other times of leisure. Opportunities for engaging in these activities were a prime ingredient of the ratings.

A further limitation to the absolute accuracy of the findings was the unfortunate fact that Vacation Places, like vacationers, refuse to sit still for their statistical portraits. Information presented in the Place Profiles in each chapter was the latest available at the time the research was done, but changes are always occurring.

Most vacation activities fall into one of four general groups—sightseeing; participating in active sports; being entertained; and restful, sedentary pursuits such as sunbathing, reading, and eating. Sightseeing takes many different forms—admiring and studying the wonders of nature, exploring exciting cities, visiting historic sites, going to museums.

After the many aspects that go into an enjoyable vacation were considered, it was decided to group the various elements to be scored into the following six categories, each of which is treated in a separate chapter: Blessings of Nature, Fun in the Great Outdoors, Basic Necessities, Discovering Our Heritage, Feeding the Mind and Spirit, and Entertainment for All.

## Blessings of Nature

Ratings in this chapter are based on the assumption that several aspects of nature are assets for vacationers: a terrain that offers variety to the landscape; open space, or a low population density; forests; inland bodies of water; a shoreline on the ocean or one of the Great Lakes; rivers; nature preserves; and the presence of widely famous natural spectacles.

Also discussed in this chapter, but not used as a part of the ratings because of the variation in what different vacationers prefer, is climate.

The geographic research and editorial staff of Rand

## Winter Getaways

It's January. Buffalo, New York, had more than 50 inches of snow in December. In Boston the temperature has dipped below zero every day for the past two weeks. Chicagoans haven't seen the sun in ten days. Former northerners who have migrated to Dallas are homesick for snow and mountains. It's time to think about a winter vacation.

Three kinds of destinations appeal to winter vacationers: the warm sands and surf of seaside winter resorts, the dry heat of desert climes, and snowy spots where skiing, snowmobiling, and other winter sports are enjoyed. Vacation Places that appeal to winter vacationers because they offer one of these three advantages are listed here.

Seaside Vacation Places listed are those with an average afternoon temperature in January of 60 degrees Fahrenheit or above, indicating that numerous winter days are well above that average and therefore warm enough for beachcombing, sunbathing, and swimming.

Vacation Places characterized as hot and dry are those with an average humidity of 55 percent or less and an average temperature of 60 degrees Fahrenheit or above in January.

The list of Vacation Places with a special appeal for skiers and lovers of other winter sports includes those with an average January snowfall of ten or more inches.

Many Vacation Places include an area large enough to have considerable variety in terrain and climate. Yosemite–Sequoia–Death Valley, California, for example, has excellent areas for cold-weather winter sports in the Yosemite area and a desert climate in Death Valley.

### Salt Water and Warm Weather

| | Average January Afternoon Temperature (in degrees Fahrenheit) |
|---|---|
| Brownsville–Rio Grande Valley, TX | 70 |
| Corpus Christi–Padre Island, TX | 67 |
| Hawaii | |
|    Hilo and Honolulu | 80 |
| Hilton Head, SC | 60 |
| Houston–Galveston, TX | 62 |
| Los Angeles, CA | 67 |
| Miami–Gold Coast–Keys, FL | |
|    Miami–Gold Coast | 75 |
|    Keys | 72 |
| Mobile Bay–Gulfport, AL–MS | 61 |
| Monterey–Big Sur, CA | |
|    Monterey | 60 |
| New Orleans, LA | 62 |
| Orlando–Space Coast, FL | 72 |
| Panhandle, FL | 64 |
| St. Augustine–Northeast Coast, FL | 68 |
| San Diego, CA | 65 |
| Santa Barbara–San Simeon, CA | |
|    Santa Barbara | 63 |
| Savannah–Golden Isles, GA | |
|    Savannah | 60 |
|    Golden Isles | 61 |
| Tampa Bay–Southwest Coast, FL | |
|    Tampa Bay | 70 |
|    Fort Myers–Southwest Coast | 74 |

## Hot and Dry Climates

| | Average January Humidity (in percentage) | Average January Afternoon Temperature (in degrees Fahrenheit) |
|---|---|---|
| Palm Springs–Desert Playgrounds, CA | 55 | 69 |
| Phoenix–Valley of the Sun, AZ | 50 | 65 |
| Tucson, AZ | 48 | 64 |
| Yosemite–Sequoia–Death Valley, CA | | |
| Death Valley National Monument | 46 | 65 |

## Plenty of Snow

| | Average January Snowfall (in inches) | Average January Afternoon Temperature (in degrees Fahrenheit) |
|---|---|---|
| Adirondack Mountains, NY | 27.6 | 25 |
| Anchorage–Kenai Peninsula, AK | | |
| Anchorage–Upper Cook Inlet | 10.0 | 20 |
| Kenai Peninsula | 11.5 | 19 |
| Kenai Fjords National Park | 16.0 | 29 |
| Aspen–Vail, CO | | |
| Aspen | 25.8 | 34 |
| Vail | 18.6 | 33 |
| Bar Harbor–Acadia, ME | 16.1 | 32 |
| Bend–Cascade Mountains, OR | | |
| Bend Northern Cascade | 11.5 | 41 |
| Mountains (Eastern Slopes) | 71.8 | 33 |
| Berkshire Hills–Pioneer Valley, MA | 16.9 | 32 |
| Black Hills, SD | 10.1 | 34 |
| Blue Ridge Mountains, VA | | |
| Shenandoah National Park | 10.9 | 36 |
| Boise–Sun Valley, ID | | |
| Sun Valley | 33.4 | 31 |
| Boston, MA | 12.4 | 36 |
| Catskill Mountains, NY | 14.9 | 30 |
| Chicago, IL | 10.5 | 33 |
| Crater Lake–Klamath Falls, OR | | |
| Crater Lake | 109.1 | 33 |
| Klamath Falls | 14.6 | 39 |
| Denver–Rocky Mountain National Park, CO | | |
| Rocky Mountain National Park | | |
| Eastern Slope | 14.0 | 38 |
| Grand Lake Area | 26.6 | 30 |
| Door County, WI | 10.7 | 25 |
| Finger Lakes, NY | 14.8 | 33 |
| Glacier National Park–Flathead Lake, MT | | |
| Glacier National Park | 35.4 | 28 |
| Flathead Lake | 11.2 | 31 |

| | Average January Snowfall (in inches) | Average January Afternoon Temperature (in degrees Fahrenheit) |
|---|---|---|
| Grand Canyon Country, AZ | | |
| Grand Canyon National Park | | |
| North Rim | 31.0 | 36 |
| South Rim | 15.8 | 41 |
| Green Mountains, VT | | |
| Green Mountains | 23.4 | 27 |
| Burlington | 18.5 | 25 |
| Holland–Lake Michigan Shore, MI | 20.8 | 31 |
| Lake Tahoe–Reno, NV–CA | | |
| Lake Tahoe | 45.5 | 38 |
| Mackinac Island–Sault Ste. Marie, MI | 28.0 | 21 |
| Niagara Falls– Western New York, NY | 13.0 | 33 |
| North Woods–Land O'Lakes, WI | 14.9 | 21 |
| Pocono Mountains, PA | 13.6 | 32 |
| Portland, ME | 19.0 | 31 |
| Portland–Columbia River, OR | | |
| Mount Hood | 62.2 | 36 |
| Portsmouth– Kennebunk, NH–ME | 16.3 | 32 |
| Rangeley Lakes, ME | 26.9 | 21 |
| Redwoods–Shasta– Lassen, CA | | |
| Whiskeytown-Shasta-Trinity National Recreation Area | 30.6 | 42 |
| Lassen Volcanic National Park | 48.2 | 40 |
| Salt Lake City, UT | | |
| Salt Lake City | 13.3 | 37 |
| Wasatch Range Area | 65.1 | 31 |
| Seattle–Mount Rainier–North Cascades, WA | | |
| Mount Rainier | 122.1 | 31 |
| Mount Baker | 88.0 | 33 |
| Spokane–Coeur d'Alene, WA–ID | 17.6 | 31 |
| Traverse City–Petoskey, MI | 20.7 | 26 |
| White Mountains, NH | 35.4 | 26 |
| Wisconsin Dells, WI | 10.3 | 24 |
| Yellowstone–Jackson–Tetons, WY–ID–MT | | |
| Yellowstone National Park | 18.0 | 28 |
| Jackson Hole | 18.8 | 27 |
| Grand Teton National Park | 32.4 | 25 |
| Yosemite–Sequoia– Death Valley, CA | | |
| Yosemite National Park | 25.4 | 48 |
| Sequoia-Kings Canyon National Parks | 35.3 | 43 |
| Zion–Bryce Canyon, UT | | |
| Bryce Canyon National Park | 19.7 | 36 |

McNally and Company contributed much of the research, scoring, and discussion contained in this chapter.

## Fun in the Great Outdoors

The great out-of-doors is appreciated not only for its beauty, grandeur, and the relaxation it affords but also for the challenge of vigorous outdoor sports and activities. From mountain climbing to sunbathing, from canoeing down white-water rapids to strolling down a country lane—the opportunity for outdoor play is a key part of vacationing for many people.

This chapter discusses many types of outdoor activities available and rates the Vacation Places on the basis of the available space and facilities for some of the most popular ones.

## Basic Necessities

Food, shelter, and transportation are three basic necessities for any vacationer. Of course explorers and adventurers have sallied forth into unknown places since the birth of humankind, but most of today's travelers expect to arrive at their vacation destination with a minimum of effort and once there to find a good bed and decent food to eat. Even backpackers, who use their own legs for transportation, take these elements into consideration and plan for them ahead of time: they carry their own bedrolls and a supply of food (plus, perhaps, fishing gear to enable them to acquire more along the way).

This chapter compares the various destinations on the basis of availability of hotels, campgrounds, and eating and drinking places. Quality ratings determined by several organizations are considered as well.

## Discovering Our Heritage

It seems to be almost a universal human trait to want to know about our roots. Interest in the history of the United States has increased a great deal during this century, especially since the observance of the American Revolution Bicentennial in 1976. All over the country cities are marking out their historic districts, documenting their history, and taking steps to preserve and restore buildings and other landmarks.

This chapter lists hundreds of historic landmarks as well as many types of historical museums and rates the Vacation Places on the basis of how much enjoyable time can be spent by vacationers interested in exploring America's past.

## Feeding the Mind and Spirit

"Wilderness is the raw material out of which man has hammered the artifact called civilization," said Aldo Leopold, an eminent conservationist and ecologist who is credited with establishing the profession of wildlife management.

Man-made attractions often imitate nature. Botanic gardens, zoos, aquariums, planetariums, and natural history museums are creations of civilization derived directly and specifically from the raw materials of nature. These and other types of museums, always popular with sightseers, are listed and scored in this chapter.

## Entertainment for All

Entertainment comes in many forms, and some type of entertainment is a part of vacationing for nearly everyone. This chapter discusses the kinds of entertainment that most often influence vacation decisions.

Those used as a basis for scoring were family entertainment parks, music and theater, professional spectator sports, and special events.

## CONCLUSIONS

Two concluding chapters follow the six mentioned above. Putting It All Together combines all the rankings determined previously in the same manner used by the two previous volumes in the *Places Rated* series. The top ten Vacation Places—the ones with the most to offer according to the elements used for scoring—are identified and briefly described.

The final chapter, Ranking Your Own Vacation Places, is a new feature for the series which, it is hoped, will give you, the reader, some additional enjoyment while planning your next vacation. Step-by-step, the chapter describes how you can use the information in this book to arrive at your own rankings, weighting the various factors according to your own needs and preferences.

## HOW THE VACATION PLACES ARE RATED

Evaluation of the Vacation Places has been done with both quantity and quality in mind. In some cases, such as the number of hotels in a given area, quantity measures are available and have some meaning. The more hotels there are, the better chance a vacationer usually has of finding suitable accommodations. There are exceptions to this, of course; every place has peak seasons when it is difficult to find any place to stay without reservations, but in general, the more plentiful, the better. Competition usually works to the benefit of the consumer.

Added to the quantity measurement, wherever possible, was an evaluation of quality. For example, in the case of hotels and restaurants, the number of awards given by certain well-known rating organizations was a part of the score.

For many institutions, the size of the annual budget was assumed to be a measure of both size and quality. The zoos with the most money to spend have, in general, the largest collections of animals and best facilities for caring for them. To the vacationer, this means that there is more to see and more enjoyable time can be spent at the attraction.

Subjectivity was an unavoidable part of the selection process (what elements were to be used in scoring); it was also, in some chapters, a part of the comparative evaluations. Quality evaluations published by national membership and accrediting organizations were consulted whenever possible. However, such evaluations were not available on a comparable basis, nationwide, for all types of tourist attractions and facilities. Thus it became evident early in the process of research for this book that it would not be possible to use outside sources exclusively for evaluation. Therefore, in consultation with Rand McNally editors, I used a variety of sources to come up with sufficient data on which to base judgments of the relative merits of various attractions for the average vacationer. The following assumptions were made.

First, the more (of almost any kind of attraction, such as mountains, restaurants, or museums), the better, for the vacationer. Availability of all the elements that attract tourists is a plus factor. Second, the more time an average vacationer is apt to spend at an individual attraction is also a plus. Thus, for example, the larger entertainment parks with more numerous rides, performances, and other amenities are scored higher than small neighborhood amusement parks. For details on how point values were assigned, see the scoring section in each chapter.

**BON VOYAGE**

In conclusion, let me add a personal message. Wherever you go, may you truly enjoy all your next Vacation Place has to offer you. As Thomas Jefferson said to a friend in London in 1788, "I have been planning what I would shew [sic] you: a flower here, a tree there; yonder a grove, near it a fountain; on this side a hill, on that a river. Indeed, madam, I know nothing so charming as our own country."

# Editors' Note

Sylvia McNair's impressive credentials make her a natural for *Vacation Places Rated*. She has behind her a lifetime of extensive travel in all parts of the United States and has lived in nine states and the District of Columbia. For nearly twenty years she has been an editor and writer of U.S. travel and tourism, especially of material related to sightseeing, historic sites, and resort accommodations. McNair has a voluminous library of travel books, brochures, press releases, and other types of travel information, which is continuously updated. But her words sum up perhaps her greatest qualification as author of *Vacation Places Rated*: "I love all that this country offers to travelers—its natural assets, its heritage, and its countless fine man-made attractions."

It is the hope of the editors and author that the readers of this book will concentrate on the useful information it contains and enjoy developing their own rankings. Enough material has been presented to be of help to those making decisions about where to go on vacation. It is expected that many people will find something important, charming, and delightful that has been overlooked, and we encourage them to contact us and tell us about it so future ratings can benefit.

## What Each Vacation Place Has to Offer

**Area:** 1980 U.S. census data
**Population:** 1980 U.S. census data
**Bright Lights:** Vacation Place boundaries contain one or more cities with a population of more than 500,000
**Warm Winters:** Average afternoon temperatures of 60 degrees Fahrenheit and above in December and January
**Seacoast:** Frontage on ocean, gulf, or bay
**Lakes:** Abundance of freshwater lakes within Vacation Place boundaries

**Mountains:** Score of 200 or above for terrain in Blessings of Nature chapter
**Plenty of Snow:** Average snowfall of 10 inches or more in January
**Open Space:** Fewer than 40 persons per square mile living within Vacation Place boundaries
**Special Attractions:** Vacation Place has other attractions that draw many tourists

| | Area (in square miles) | Population | Bright Lights | Warm Winters | Sea-coast | Lakes | Moun-tains | Plenty of Snow | Open Space | Special Attrac-tions |
|---|---|---|---|---|---|---|---|---|---|---|
| **Adirondack Mountains, NY** | 10,119 | 345,000 | — | — | — | ✔ | ✔ | ✔ | ✔ | — |
| **Albuquerque–Santa Fe–Taos, NM** | 11,728 | 588,000* | — | — | — | — | ✔ | — | — | ✔ |
| **Anchorage–Kenai Peninsula, AK** | 17,788 | 199,713* | — | — | ✔ | — | ✔ | ✔ | ✔ | ✔ |
| **Asheville–Smoky Mountains, NC** | 3,250 | 277,537 | — | — | — | ✔ | ✔ | — | — | — |
| **Aspen–Vail, CO** | 3,644 | 41,336 | — | — | — | — | ✔ | ✔ | ✔ | — |
| **Atlanta, GA** | 10,667 | 2,607,300 | — | — | — | ✔ | ✔ | — | — | ✔ |
| **Atlantic City, NJ** | 831 | 276,385 | — | — | ✔ | — | — | — | — | ✔ |
| **Austin–Hill Country, TX** | 5,953 | 607,521 | — | — | — | ✔ | — | — | — | ✔ |

| | Area (in square miles) | Population | Bright Lights | Warm Winters | Sea-coast | Lakes | Mountains | Plenty of Snow | Open Space | Special Attractions |
|---|---|---|---|---|---|---|---|---|---|---|
| Baltimore–Chesapeake Bay, MD | 3,156 | 2,241,796 | ✔ | — | ✔ | — | — | — | — | ✔ |
| Bar Harbor–Acadia, ME | 2,637 | 103,136 | — | — | ✔ | — | — | ✔ | ✔ | — |
| Bend–Cascade Mountains, OR | 7,798 | 86,832 | — | — | — | — | ✔ | ✔ | ✔ | — |
| Berkshire Hills–Pioneer Valley, MA | 1,853 | 365,600* | — | — | — | ✔ | ✔ | ✔ | — | — |
| Black Hills, SD | 10,716 | 128,900* | — | — | — | — | ✔ | ✔ | ✔ | ✔ |
| Blue Ridge Mountains, VA | 5,260 | 430,012 | — | — | — | — | ✔ | ✔ | — | — |
| Boise–Sun Valley, ID | 12,932 | 348,000* | — | — | — | — | ✔ | ✔ | ✔ | — |
| Boone–High Country, NC | 2,726 | 280,117 | — | — | — | ✔ | ✔ | — | — | — |
| Boston, MA | 2,429 | 3,662,888 | ✔ | — | ✔ | ✔ | — | ✔ | — | ✔ |
| Brownsville–Rio Grande Valley, TX | 3,063 | 510,545 | — | ✔ | ✔ | — | — | — | — | — |
| Cape Cod–The Islands, MA | 549 | 161,954 | — | — | ✔ | ✔ | — | — | — | — |
| Catskill Mountains, NY | 7,611 | 1,190,762 | — | — | — | ✔ | ✔ | ✔ | — | — |
| Charleston, SC | 2,621 | 430,346 | — | — | ✔ | — | — | — | — | ✔ |
| Chattanooga–Huntsville, TN–AL–GA | 5,865 | 826,176 | — | — | — | ✔ | ✔ | — | — | — |
| Chicago, IL | 2,356 | 6,500,780 | ✔ | — | — | ✔ | — | ✔ | — | — |
| Cincinnati, OH–KY | 2,290 | 1,938,876 | — | — | — | — | — | — | — | ✔ |
| Colorado Springs, CO | 6,603 | 472,106 | — | — | — | — | ✔ | — | — | — |
| Coos Bay–South Coast, OR | 3,285 | 91,000* | — | — | ✔ | ✔ | ✔ | — | ✔ | — |
| Corpus Christi–Padre Island, TX | 3,444 | 383,135 | — | ✔ | ✔ | — | — | — | — | — |
| Crater Lake–Klamath Falls, OR | 12,083 | 298,000* | — | — | — | ✔ | ✔ | ✔ | ✔ | — |
| Dallas–Fort Worth, TX | 6,998 | 2,930,530 | ✔ | — | — | ✔ | — | — | — | — |
| Denver–Rocky Mountain National Park, CO | 4,931 | 1,601,772* | — | — | — | — | ✔ | ✔ | — | — |
| Door County, WI | 492 | 25,029 | — | — | — | ✔ | — | ✔ | ✔ | — |
| Eastern Shore, VA | 702 | 45,893 | — | — | ✔ | — | — | — | — | — |
| Finger Lakes, NY | 6,730 | 1,082,310 | — | — | — | ✔ | ✔ | ✔ | — | — |
| Flaming Gorge, UT–WY–CO | 7,967 | 46,000* | — | — | — | ✔ | ✔ | — | ✔ | — |
| Glacier National Park–Flathead Lake, MT | 9,552 | 81,648 | — | — | — | ✔ | ✔ | ✔ | ✔ | — |
| Grand Canyon Country, AZ | 24,607 | 113,000* | — | — | — | — | ✔ | ✔ | ✔ | ✔ |
| Green Mountains, VT | 2,553 | 218,713 | — | — | — | ✔ | ✔ | ✔ | — | ✔ |
| Hawaii | 6,427 | 964,691 | — | ✔ | ✔ | — | ✔ | — | — | — |
| Hilton Head, SC | 579 | 65,364 | — | ✔ | ✔ | — | — | — | — | — |
| Holland–Lake Michigan Shore, MI | 3,590 | 683,907 | — | — | — | ✔ | — | ✔ | — | — |
| Houston–Galveston, TX | 8,704 | 3,369,418 | ✔ | ✔ | ✔ | — | — | — | — | — |
| Jersey Shore, NJ | 1,113 | 849,211 | — | — | ✔ | — | — | — | — | — |
| Knoxville–Smoky Mountains, TN | 4,719 | 814,917 | — | — | — | ✔ | ✔ | — | — | — |
| Lake of the Ozarks, MO | 4,363 | 99,200 | — | — | — | ✔ | ✔ | — | ✔ | — |
| Lake Powell–Glen Canyon, AZ–UT | 22,494 | 40,000* | — | — | — | ✔ | ✔ | — | ✔ | — |
| Lake Tahoe–Reno, NV–CA | 8,867 | 290,000* | — | — | — | ✔ | ✔ | ✔ | ✔ | ✔ |
| Las Vegas–Lake Mead, NV–AZ | 12,309 | 507,000* | — | — | — | ✔ | ✔ | — | — | ✔ |
| Lexington–Bluegrass Country, KY | 5,330 | 1,310,744 | — | — | — | — | — | — | — | ✔ |
| Long Island, NY | 1,199 | 2,605,813 | — | — | ✔ | — | — | — | — | — |
| Los Angeles, CA | 6,730 | 9,939,516 | ✔ | ✔ | ✔ | — | ✔ | — | — | — |
| Mackinac Island–Sault Ste. Marie, MI | 3,335 | 59,856 | — | — | — | ✔ | — | ✔ | ✔ | — |
| Memphis, TN–AR–MS | 2,308 | 913,472 | ✔ | — | — | — | — | — | — | ✔ |

| | Area (in square miles) | Population | Bright Lights | Warm Winters | Sea-coast | Lakes | Mountains | Plenty of Snow | Open Space | Special Attractions |
|---|---|---|---|---|---|---|---|---|---|---|
| Miami–Gold Coast–Keys, FL | 5,197 | 3,227,000* | — | ✔ | ✔ | — | — | — | — | — |
| Minneapolis–St. Paul, MN–WI | 7,157 | 2,277,064 | — | — | — | ✔ | — | — | — | ✔ |
| Mobile Bay–Gulfport, AL–MS | 4,617 | 743,712 | — | ✔ | ✔ | — | — | — | — | — |
| Monterey–Big Sur, CA | 6,430 | 1,798,661 | ✔ | ✔ | ✔ | — | ✔ | — | — | ✔ |
| Myrtle Beach–Grand Strand, SC | 1,965 | 143,880 | — | — | ✔ | — | — | — | — | ✔ |
| Mystic Seaport–Connecticut Valley, CT | 1,042 | 367,420 | — | — | ✔ | ✔ | ✔ | — | — | ✔ |
| Nashville, TN | 4,060 | 850,505 | — | — | — | ✔ | ✔ | — | — | ✔ |
| New Orleans, LA | 4,580 | 1,365,200 | ✔ | ✔ | ✔ | ✔ | — | — | — | |
| New York City, NY | 914 | 8,197,768 | ✔ | — | ✔ | — | — | — | — | |
| Niagara Falls–Western New York, NY | 3,942 | 1,475,448 | — | — | — | ✔ | — | ✔ | — | ✔ |
| North Woods–Land O'Lakes, WI | 3,749 | 63,525 | — | — | — | ✔ | — | ✔ | ✔ | — |
| Oklahoma City–Cherokee Strip, OK | 6,642 | 961,578 | — | — | — | ✔ | — | — | — | — |
| Olympic Peninsula, WA | 7,164 | 289,375 | — | — | ✔ | ✔ | ✔ | — | — | ✔ |
| Orlando–Space Coast, FL | 5,873 | 1,354,411 | — | ✔ | ✔ | ✔ | — | — | — | ✔ |
| Outer Banks, NC | 3,409 | 182,138 | — | — | ✔ | — | — | — | — | — |
| Ozarks–Eureka Springs, AR–MO | 12,061 | 648,170 | — | — | — | ✔ | ✔ | — | — | — |
| Palm Springs–Desert Playgrounds, CA | 12,230 | 1,470,000* | — | ✔ | — | — | ✔ | — | — | ✔ |
| Panhandle, FL | 5,004 | 529,400 | — | ✔ | ✔ | — | — | — | — | — |
| Pennsylvania Dutch Country, PA | 5,236 | 1,612,352 | — | — | — | — | ✔ | — | — | ✔ |
| Philadelphia, PA–DE–NJ | 3,928 | 4,716,590 | ✔ | — | — | — | — | — | — | ✔ |
| Phoenix–Valley of the Sun, AZ | 14,470 | 1,600,180 | ✔ | ✔ | — | — | ✔ | — | — | — |
| Pocono Mountains, PA | 5,287 | 1,458,759 | — | — | — | ✔ | ✔ | ✔ | — | — |
| Portland, ME | 2,944 | 479,673 | — | — | ✔ | ✔ | — | ✔ | — | — |
| Portland–Columbia River, OR | 8,744 | 1,460,779 | — | — | ✔ | ✔ | ✔ | ✔ | — | — |
| Portsmouth–Kennebunk, NH–ME | 2,077 | 415,492 | — | — | ✔ | ✔ | — | ✔ | — | — |
| Providence–Newport, RI | 1,054 | 947,154 | — | — | ✔ | ✔ | — | — | — | — |
| Put-in-Bay–Lake Erie Shore, OH | 2,293 | 799,862 | — | — | — | ✔ | — | — | — | — |
| Rangeley Lakes, ME | 4,496 | 23,900* | — | — | — | ✔ | ✔ | ✔ | ✔ | — |
| Redwoods–Shasta–Lassen, CA | 17,843 | 294,047 | — | — | ✔ | ✔ | ✔ | ✔ | ✔ | — |
| Richmond–Fredericksburg, VA | 3,896 | 828,972 | — | — | — | — | — | — | — | ✔ |
| Sacramento–Gold Rush Towns, CA | 6,009 | 1,125,000* | — | — | — | — | ✔ | — | — | — |
| St. Augustine–Northeast Coast, FL | 4,971 | 1,042,476 | ✔ | ✔ | ✔ | ✔ | — | — | — | ✔ |
| St. Louis–Mark Twain Country, MO–IL | 6,349 | 1,898,983 | — | — | — | — | ✔ | — | — | ✔ |
| Salt Lake City, UT | 6,447 | 1,192,521 | — | — | — | ✔ | ✔ | ✔ | — | ✔ |
| San Antonio, TX | 2,516 | 1,071,952 | ✔ | ✔ | — | — | — | — | — | — |
| San Diego, CA | 4,212 | 1,861,846 | ✔ | ✔ | ✔ | — | ✔ | — | — | — |
| San Francisco, CA | 2,482 | 3,250,605 | ✔ | — | ✔ | — | ✔ | — | — | ✔ |
| Santa Barbara–San Simeon, CA | 6,056 | 454,129 | — | ✔ | ✔ | — | ✔ | — | — | — |
| Savannah–Golden Isles, GA | 2,721 | 331,338 | — | ✔ | ✔ | — | — | — | — | ✔ |
| Seattle–Mount Rainier–North Cascades, WA | 10,366 | 2,455,324 | — | — | ✔ | ✔ | ✔ | ✔ | — | — |
| Spokane–Coeur d'Alene, WA–ID | 13,292 | 498,134 | — | — | — | ✔ | ✔ | ✔ | ✔ | — |
| Tampa Bay–Southwest Coast, FL | 3,868 | 1,964,317 | — | ✔ | ✔ | — | — | — | — | — |
| Traverse City–Petoskey, MI | 3,061 | 150,156 | — | — | — | ✔ | — | ✔ | — | — |
| Tucson, AZ | 10,425 | 551,902 | — | ✔ | — | — | ✔ | — | — | — |

| | Area (in square miles) | Population | Bright Lights | Warm Winters | Sea-coast | Lakes | Mountains | Plenty of Snow | Open Space | Special Attractions |
|---|---|---|---|---|---|---|---|---|---|---|
| Tulsa–Lake O' The Cherokees, OK | 11,186 | 967,302 | — | — | — | ✓ | — | — | — | — |
| Vicksburg–Natchez–Baton Rouge, MS–LA | 4,982 | 545,865 | — | — | — | — | — | — | — | ✓ |
| Washington, DC–MD–VA | 3,956 | 3,250,921 | ✓ | — | ✓ | — | — | — | — | ✓ |
| White Mountains, NH | 4,456 | 128,884 | — | — | — | ✓ | ✓ | ✓ | ✓ | — |
| Williamsburg–Colonial Triangle, VA | 2,317 | 1,187,960 | — | — | ✓ | — | — | — | — | ✓ |
| Wilmington–Cape Fear, NC | 1,046 | 139,248 | — | — | ✓ | — | — | — | — | — |
| Wine Country, CA | 7,122 | 501,984 | — | — | ✓ | ✓ | ✓ | — | — | ✓ |
| Wisconsin Dells, WI | 5,515 | 616,882 | — | — | — | ✓ | — | ✓ | — | ✓ |
| Yellowstone–Jackson–Tetons, WY–ID–MT | 13,716 | 64,184 | — | — | — | ✓ | ✓ | ✓ | ✓ | ✓ |
| Yosemite–Sequoia–Death Valley, CA | 19,956 | 74,000* | — | — | — | ✓ | ✓ | ✓ | ✓ | ✓ |
| Zion–Bryce Canyon, UT | 14,644 | 70,000* | — | — | — | — | ✓ | ✓ | ✓ | ✓ |

*Estimated.

# The Places We Rate
## 107 Vacation Places and Component Counties

**Adirondack Mountains, NY**
Clinton, Essex, Franklin, Fulton, Hamilton, Warren, and parts of Herkimer and St. Lawrence counties

**Albuquerque–Santa Fe–Taos, NM**
Bernalillo, Los Alamos, Santa Fe, Taos, and parts of Mora, Rio Arriba, Sandoval, and San Miguel counties

**Anchorage–Kenai Peninsula, AK**
Anchorage and Kenai boroughs

**Asheville–Smoky Mountains, NC**
Buncombe, Clay, Graham, Haywood, Jackson, Macon, and Swain counties

**Aspen–Vail, CO**
Eagle, Lake, Pitkin, and Summit counties

**Atlanta, GA**
Barrow, Bartow, Butts, Carroll, Cherokee, Clayton, Cobb, Coweta, Dawson, DeKalb, Douglas, Fayette, Floyd, Forsyth, Fulton, Gilmer, Gordon, Gwinnett, Hall, Haralson, Heard, Henry, Lumpkin, Meriwether, Murray, Newton, Paulding, Pickens, Polk, Rockdale, Spalding, Troup, and Walton counties

**Atlantic City, NJ**
Atlantic and Cape May counties

**Austin–Hill Country, TX**
Bastrop, Blanco, Burnet, Caldwell, Hays, Travis, and Williamson counties

**Baltimore–Chesapeake Bay, MD**
Baltimore city; Anne Arundel, Baltimore, Carroll, Harford, Howard, Kent, Queen Annes, and Talbot counties

**Bar Harbor–Acadia, ME**
Hancock, Knox, and Waldo counties

**Bend–Cascade Mountains, OR**
Crook, Deschutes, and Jefferson counties

**Berkshire Hills–Pioneer Valley, MA**
Berkshire and parts of Franklin, Hampden, and Hampshire counties

**Black Hills, SD**
Custer, Fall River, Lawrence, Pennington, Shannon, and part of Meade counties

**Blue Ridge Mountains, VA**
Charlottesville city; Albemarle, Augusta, Clarke, Fluvanna, Frederick, Greene, Madison, Page, Rappahannock, Rockingham, Shenandoah, and Warren counties

**Boise–Sun Valley, ID**
Ada, Boise, Camas, Canyon, Elmore, Gem, Gooding, Jerome, Lincoln, Payette, and part of Blaine counties

**Boone–High Country, NC**
Avery, Burke, Caldwell, McDowell, Watauga, and Wilkes counties

**Boston, MA**
Essex, Middlesex, Norfolk, Plymouth, and Suffolk counties

**Brownsville–Rio Grande Valley, TX**
Cameron, Hidalgo, and Willacy counties

**Cape Cod–The Islands, MA**
Barnstable, Dukes, and Nantucket counties

**Catskill Mountains, NY**
Albany, Columbia, Delaware, Dutchess, Greene, Orange, Schoharie, Sullivan, and Ulster counties

**Charleston, SC**
Berkeley, Charleston, and Dorchester counties

**Chattanooga–Huntsville, TN–AL–GA**
Franklin, Hamilton, Marion, and Sequatchie counties, TN; De Kalb, Jackson, Madison, and Marshall counties, AL; Catoosa, Dade, and Walker counties, GA

**Chicago, IL**
Cook, Du Page, Lake, and McHenry counties

**Cincinnati, OH–KY**
Clermont, Hamilton, Montgomery, and Warren counties, OH; Boone, Campbell, and Kenton counties, KY

**Colorado Springs, CO**
El Paso, Fremont, Pueblo, and Teller counties

**Coos Bay–South Coast, OR**
Coos, Curry, and part of Douglas counties

**Corpus Christi–Padre Island, TX**
Aransas, Kleberg, Nueces, Refugio, and San Patricio counties

**Crater Lake–Klamath Falls, OR**
Jackson, Klamath, and parts of Douglas and Josephine counties

**Dallas–Fort Worth, TX**
Collin, Dallas, Denton, Ellis, Johnson, Kaufman, Parker, Rockwall, and Tarrant counties

**Denver–Rocky Mountain National Park, CO**
Boulder, Denver, Douglas, Gilpin, Jefferson, and parts of Adams, Arapahoe, and Larimer counties

**Door County, WI**

**Eastern Shore, VA**
Accomack and Northampton counties

**Finger Lakes, NY**
Cayuga, Cortland, Livingston, Onondaga, Ontario, Schuyler, Seneca, Steuben, Tompkins, Wayne, and Yates counties

**Flaming Gorge, UT–WY–CO**
Daggett and part of Uintah counties, UT; part of Sweetwater county, WY; part of Moffat county, CO

**Glacier National Park–Flathead Lake, MT**
Flathead, Glacier, and Lake counties

**Grand Canyon Country, AZ**
Parts of Apache, Coconino, Mohave, and Navajo counties

**Green Mountains, VT**
Addison, Chittenden, Grand Isle, Lamoille, and Washington counties

**Hawaii**
Hawaii, Honolulu, Kalawao, Kauai, and Maui counties

**Hilton Head, SC**
Beaufort county

**Holland–Lake Michigan Shore, MI**
Allegan, Berrien, Cass, Muskegon, Ottawa, and Van Buren counties

**Houston–Galveston, TX**
Brazoria, Chambers, Fort Bend, Galveston, Harris, Jefferson, Liberty, Montgomery, and Waller counties

**Jersey Shore, NJ**
Monmouth and Ocean counties

**Knoxville–Smoky Mountains, TN**
Anderson, Blount, Cocke, Grainger, Greene, Jefferson, Knox, Loudon, Roane, Sevier, Union, and Washington counties

**Lake of the Ozarks, MO**
Benton, Camden, Henry, Hickory, Miller, Morgan, and St. Clair counties

**Lake Powell–Glen Canyon, AZ–UT**
Parts of Coconino and Navajo counties, AZ; San Juan, Wayne, and parts of Emery, Garfield, Grand, and Kane counties, UT

**Lake Tahoe–Reno, NV–CA**
Carson City; Douglas, Lyon, Storey, and part of Washoe counties, NV; Alpine and parts of El Dorado, Nevada, Placer, and Sierra counties, CA

**Las Vegas–Lake Mead, NV–AZ**
Clark county, NV; part of Mohave county, AZ

**Lexington–Bluegrass Country, KY**
Anderson, Bourbon, Boyle, Bullitt, Clark, Estill, Fayette, Franklin, Garrard, Jefferson, Jessamine, Madison, Mercer, Montgomery, Nelson, Powell, Scott, Shelby, Spencer, and Woodford counties

**Long Island, NY**
Nassau and Suffolk counties

**Los Angeles, CA**
Los Angeles, Orange, and Ventura counties

**Mackinac Island–Sault Ste. Marie, MI**
Cheboygan, Chippewa, and Mackinac counties

**Memphis, TN–AR–MS**
Shelby and Tipton counties, TN; Crittenden county, AR; De Soto county, MS

**Miami–Gold Coast–Keys, FL**
Broward, Dade, Monroe, and part of Palm Beach counties

**Minneapolis–St. Paul, MN–WI**
Anoka, Benton, Carver, Chisago, Dakota, Goodhue, Hennepin, Isanti, Ramsey, Rice, Scott, Sherburne, Washington, and Wright counties, MN; St. Croix county, WI

**Mobile Bay–Gulfport, AL–MS**
Baldwin and Mobile counties, AL; Hancock, Harrison, and Jackson counties, MS

**Monterey–Big Sur, CA**
Monterey, San Benito, Santa Clara, and Santa Cruz counties

**Myrtle Beach–Grand Strand, SC**
Georgetown and Horry counties

**Mystic Seaport–Connecticut Valley, CT**
Middlesex and New London counties

**Nashville, TN**
Cheatham, Davidson, Dickson, Robertson, Rutherford, Sumner, Williamson, and Wilson counties

**New Orleans, LA**
Jefferson, Lafourche, Orleans, Plaquemines, St. Bernard, St. Charles, St. John The Baptist, and St. Tammany parishes

**New York City, NY**
Bronx, Kings, New York, Queens, Richmond, Rockland, and Westchester counties

**Niagara Falls–Western New York, NY**
Cattaraugus, Chautauqua, Erie, and Niagara counties

**North Woods–Land O'Lakes, WI**
Forest, Iron, Oneida, and Vilas counties

**Oklahoma City–Cherokee Strip, OK**
Canadian, Cleveland, Lincoln, Logan, McClain, Noble, Oklahoma, Payne, and Pottawatomie counties

**Olympic Peninsula, WA**
Clallam, Grays Harbor, Jefferson, Mason, and Thurston counties

**Orlando–Space Coast, FL**
Brevard, Indian River, Orange, Osceola, Polk, and Seminole counties

**Outer Banks, NC**
Beaufort, Carteret, Craven, Dare, Hyde, and Pamlico counties

**Ozarks–Eureka Springs, AR–MO**
Baxter, Benton, Boone, Carroll, Madison, Marion, Newton, Searcy, and Washington counties, AR; Barry, Christian, Greene, Lawrence, McDonald, Newton, Ozark, Stone, and Taney counties, MO

**Palm Springs–Desert Playgrounds, CA**
Riverside and part of San Bernardino counties

**Panhandle, FL**
Bay, Escambia, Gulf, Okaloosa, Santa Rosa, and Walton counties

**Pennsylvania Dutch Country, PA**
Adams, Berks, Cumberland, Dauphin, Lancaster, Lebanon, Perry, and York counties

**Philadelphia, PA–DE–NJ**
Bucks, Chester, Delaware, Montgomery, and Philadelphia counties, PA; New Castle county, DE; Burlington, Camden, and Gloucester counties, NJ

**Phoenix–Valley of the Sun, AZ**
Maricopa and Pinal counties

**Pocono Mountains, PA**
Carbon, Columbia, Lackawanna, Lehigh, Luzerne, Monroe, Northampton, Pike, Schuylkill, and Wyoming counties

**Portland, ME**
Androscoggin, Cumberland, Kennebec, Lincoln, and Sagadahoc counties

**Portland–Columbia River, OR**
Clackamas, Clatsop, Columbia, Hood River, Marion, Multnomah, Polk, Tillamook, Washington, and Yamhill counties

**Portsmouth–Kennebunk, NH–ME**
Rockingham and Strafford counties, NH; York county, ME

**Providence–Newport, RI**
Bristol, Kent, Newport, Providence, and Washington counties

**Put-in-Bay–Lake Erie Shore, OH**
Erie, Fulton, Lucas, Ottawa, Sandusky, and Wood counties

**Rangeley Lakes, ME**
Parts of Franklin, Oxford, Piscataquis, and Somerset counties

**Redwoods–Shasta–Lassen, CA**
Del Norte, Humboldt, Shasta, Siskiyou, and Trinity counties

OLYMPIC PENINSULA

SEATTLE—
MOUNT RAINIER—
NORTH CASCADES

WA

PORTLAND—
COLUMBIA RIVER

SPOKANE—
COEUR D'ALENE

GLACIER NATIONAL PARK—
FLATHEAD LAKE

MT ND

MN

ID

OR

BEND—
CASCADE
MOUNTAINS

COOS BAY—
SOUTH COAST

CRATER LAKE—
KLAMATH FALLS

BOISE—
SUN VALLEY

SD

YELLOWSTONE—
JACKSON—
TETONS

WY

REDWOODS—
SHASTA—
LASSEN

CA NV

BLACK
HILLS

SACRAMENTO—
GOLD RUSH TOWNS

NE

IA

WINE COUNTRY

LAKE TAHOE—RENO

UT

SALT LAKE CITY

FLAMING GORGE

SAN FRANCISCO

DENVER—
ROCKY MOUNTAIN
NATIONAL PARK

CO

MONTEREY—
BIG SUR

YOSEMITE—
SEQUOIA—
DEATH VALLEY

ZION—BRYCE
CANYON

LAKE POWELL—
GLEN CANYON

ASPEN—
VAIL

KS

SANTA BARBARA—
SAN SIMEON

LAS VEGAS—
LAKE MEAD

COLORADO
SPRINGS

AZ NM

TULSA—
LAKE O' THE
CHEROKEES

LOS ANGELES

PALM SPRINGS—
DESERT PLAYGROUNDS

GRAND CANYON
COUNTRY

ALBUQUERQUE—
SANTA FE—
TAOS

OK

OKLAHOMA CITY—
CHEROKEE STRIP

SAN DIEGO

TX

PHOENIX—
VALLEY
OF THE SUN

TUCSON

DALLAS—FORT WORTH

AK

AUSTIN—HILL COUNTRY

SAN ANTONIO

ANCHORAGE—
KENAI PENINSULA

HI

CORPUS CHRISTI—
PADRE ISLAND

HAWAII

©1986 Rand McNally & Co.

BROWNSVILLE—RIO GRANDE VALLEY

# Vacation Places

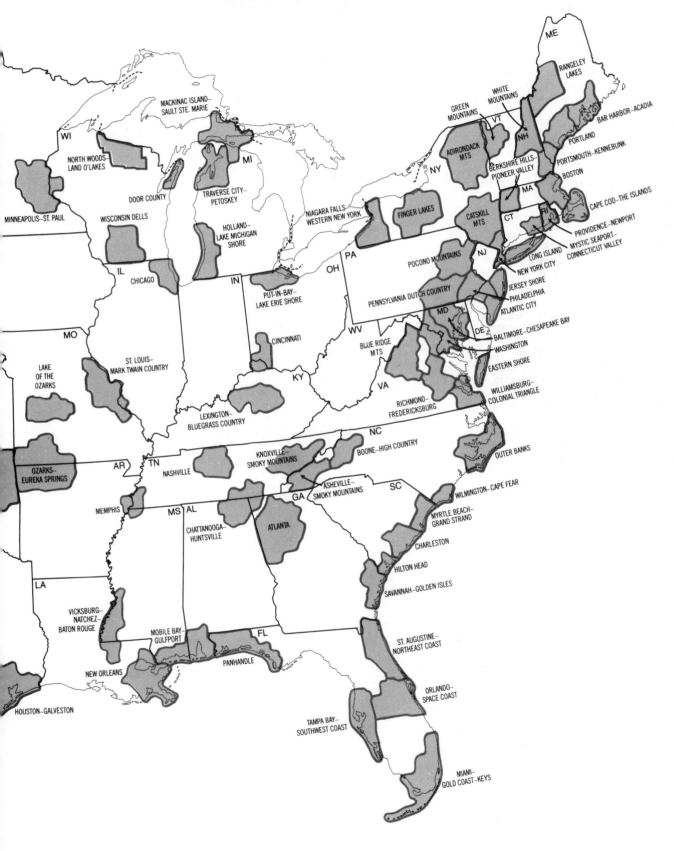

**Richmond–Fredericksburg, VA**
Colonial Heights, Fredericksburg, Hopewell, Petersburg, and Richmond cities; Caroline, Charles City, Chesterfield, Dinwiddie, Goochland, Hanover, Henrico, New Kent, Powhatan, Prince George, and Spotsylvania counties

**Sacramento–Gold Rush Towns, CA**
Amador, Sacramento, Sutter, Yuba, and parts of El Dorado, Nevada, Placer, and Sierra counties

**St. Augustine–Northeast Coast, FL**
Clay, Duval, Flagler, Nassau, Putnam, St. Johns, and Volusia counties

**St. Louis–Mark Twain Country, MO–IL**
St. Louis city; Franklin, Jefferson, Lincoln, Montgomery, Pike, Ralls, St. Charles, Ste. Genevieve, St. Louis, and Warren counties, MO; Monroe county, IL

**Salt Lake City, UT**
Cache, Davis, Morgan, Rich, Salt Lake, Utah, and Weber counties

**San Antonio, TX**
Bexar, Comal, and Guadalupe counties

**San Diego, CA**
San Diego county

**San Francisco, CA**
Alameda, Contra Costa, Marin, San Francisco, and San Mateo counties

**Santa Barbara–San Simeon, CA**
San Luis Obispo and Santa Barbara counties

**Savannah–Golden Isles, GA**
Bryan, Chatham, Effingham, Glynn, Liberty, and McIntosh counties

**Seattle–Mount Rainier–North Cascades, WA**
Island, King, Kitsap, Pierce, Skagit, Snohomish, and Whatcom counties

**Spokane–Coeur d'Alene, WA–ID**
Pend Oreille, Spokane, and Stevens counties, WA; Benewah, Bonner, Boundary, Kootenai, and Shoshone counties, ID

**Tampa Bay–Southwest Coast, FL**
Hernando, Hillsborough, Manatee, Pasco, Pinellas, and Sarasota counties

**Traverse City–Petoskey, MI**
Antrim, Benzie, Charlevoix, Emmet, Grand Traverse, Kalkaska, and Leelanau counties

**Tucson, AZ**
Pima and Santa Cruz counties

**Tulsa–Lake O' The Cherokees, OK**
Adair, Cherokee, Craig, Delaware, Haskell, Mayes, McIntosh, Muskogee, Nowata, Okmulgee, Washington, and part of Osage, Ottawa, Rogers, Sequoyah, Tulsa, Wagoner, Washington, Adams, counties

**Vicksburg–Natchez–Baton Rouge, MS–LA**
East Baton Rouge, East Feliciana, West Baton Rouge, and West Feliciana counties, LA; Adams, Claiborne, Franklin, Jefferson, Warren, and Wilkinson counties, MS

**Washington, DC–MD–VA**
District of Columbia; Calvert, Charles, Frederick, Montgomery, and Prince Georges counties, MD; Alexandria, Fairfax, Falls Church, Manassas, and Manassas Park cities; Arlington, Fairfax, Loudoun, Prince William, and Stafford counties, VA

**White Mountains, NH**
Carroll, Coos, and Grafton counties

**Williamsburg–Colonial Triangle, VA**
Chesapeake, Hampton, Newport News, Norfolk, Poquoson, Portsmouth, Suffolk, Virginia Beach, and Williamsburg cities; Gloucester, Isle of Wight, James City, Surry, and York counties

**Wilmington–Cape Fear, NC**
Brunswick and New Hanover counties

**Wine Country, CA**
Lake, Mendocino, Napa, and Sonoma counties

**Wisconsin Dells, WI**
Columbia, Dane, Green, Iowa, Lafayette, Rock, and Sauk counties

**Yellowstone–Jackson–Tetons, WY–ID–MT***
Park and Teton counties, WY; Fremont, Madison, and Teton counties, ID

**Yosemite–Sequoia–Death Valley, CA**
Inyo, Mono, and parts of Fresno, Madera, Mariposa, Tulare, and Tuolumne counties

**Zion–Bryce Canyon, UT**
Beaver, Iron, Piute, Sevier, Washington, and parts of Garfield and Kane counties

*Parts of Montana bordering on Yellowstone National Park have been included for sightseeing but not for statistical purposes.

# Blessings of Nature

Land, Lakes, and Forests

# INTRODUCTION: Blessings of Nature

"From sea to shining sea . . ."

Next to love, nothing has inspired so many poets to hunt for new ways to express their enthusiasm as has the beauty of nature. And few countries have such a varied supply of natural beauty and wonder as the United States. Mountains, lakes, canyons; rivers, caves, deserts; oceans, prairies, waterfalls; glaciers, volcanoes, forests—the United States has them in abundance. Colorful waterfowl crowd the marshlands. Reindeer cross the frozen tundra of the far north. Wildflowers of every hue hail the coming of spring.

Sometimes we want to take a vacation to commune with nature in as much isolation and stillness as we can find—we want to sit on an uninhabited lakeshore or hike through a deep forest. Sometimes we are so anxious to see one of the great natural wonders of the world—such as Old Faithful, Niagara Falls, or the Grand Canyon—that we drive hundreds of miles for the sight, even though we know we will be standing elbow to elbow with hundreds of other spectators at the viewpoint. Sometimes we want to put our own strength and stamina to the test against the challenges of nature by climbing a steep, rocky peak or maneuvering a canoe through white-water rapids.

Whatever our taste in leisure-time activity, most of us spend at least some of our vacation outdoors. Every vacation destination contains its share of the natural blessings that are found in an outdoor setting—and some have more than others.

This chapter counts and evaluates natural blessings —those unspoiled features of the landscape that set the stage for an outdoor vacation. The attributes of the natural environment as described in this chapter fall into several categories: Terrain, Open Space, Forests, Inland Water, Shoreline, Rivers, Nature-Preservation Areas, and Nature's Spectaculars. Of course, the landscape contains many other features, but when combined as they are here, these criteria describe the basic natural character of each Vacation Place. Climate is also important to vacation planning, and the chapter includes a general description of weather conditions for the Vacation Places. The total evaluation of the

**U.S. Terrain**

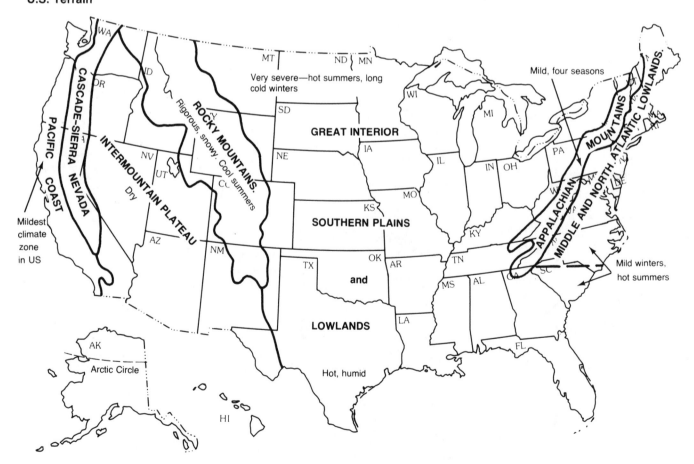

## Wildlife Watching in the Refuges

Uncertainty, and the thrill of discovery, is what makes watching wildlife so interesting. Conditions differ with the location and the season, and while the habits and migrations of birds and animals can be predicted in a general way, there's never a guarantee that you'll find what you are looking for. The officials of wildlife refuges are good sources of information for the happenings in a given place at a given time. To have the best possible chance of good sightings, make inquiries before planning a trip.

Some refuges are maintained primarily as wintering homes; others as migratory stops. Following is a general discussion of the annual activities of birds and other wildlife in the major refuges of the United States.

### Spring (March to May)

This is the season of northbound migrations of waterfowl, shorebirds, wading birds, and songbirds.

Most animals mate and nest in spring. Some of the most fascinating to watch are wood ducks, Canada geese, hawks, owls, egrets, herons, pelicans, roseate spoonbills, Florida sandhill cranes, red-cockaded woodpeckers, turkeys, and laughing gulls. Many of these birds nest on island sites. Mallards, pintails, and shoveler ducks nest in marshes. Sharp-tailed grouse return to dancing grounds to hoot and stamp in daybreak mate-calling rites. Prairie chickens and western grebes perform courtship antics.

April and May are generally the best months to listen for warblers and vireos and glimpse colorful tanagers, indigo buntings, orioles, grosbeaks, meadowlarks, song sparrows, robins, and phoebes.

Alligators come out of hibernation to sun themselves and mate. Prairie dogs emerge from burrows. Bison calves are born in April or May; elk calves in May or June.

Toward the end of the season, you may see broods of young wood ducks and goslings.

### Summer (June to August)

This is nesting time for skimmers, stilts, terns, oystercatchers, and other shorebirds. Large flocks of wading birds are seen along shores. Families of great blue herons, black-crowned night herons, avocets, godwits, willets, common terns, egrets, bitterns, cormorants, and gulls are active in wetland habitats. Pelican fledglings join parents in practicing aerial maneuvers. Rare trumpeter swans are seen at some northwestern refuges. Exotic Mexican birds migrate north to some southern refuges.

Baby alligators may be heard clucking to their mothers. Fox kits may be seen at dusk in some areas. Spotted fawns are seen feeding with does. Buck deer are showing their new, velvet-covered antlers.

Sounds include choruses of frogs and the songs of the whippoorwill and chuck-will's-widow.

Crabs are plentiful on many beaches. Coastal islands provide glimpses of sea lions and seals with pups.

### Fall (September to November)

The southbound migration of waterfowl brings huge concentrations of birds to some refuges: mallard, pintail, teal, gadwall, wigeon, black, scaup, scoter, shoveler, canvasback, redhead, goldeneye, and merganser ducks; Canada and snow geese; and whistling swans. Sandhill cranes on their way south sometimes bring a few rare whooping cranes along. In some places sightings are made of ring-billed and Franklin's gulls, common and least terns, double-crested cormorants, and white pelicans.

Monarch butterflies also migrate at this time of year.

This is the mating season of elk, and their bugling can be heard in the evenings in some areas.

Manatees concentrate in some Florida locations.

### Winter (December to February)

Sightings include golden and bald eagles, American kestrels, peregrine falcons, and other migrators. Birdwatchers look for juncos; "winter" sparrows; finches; and at dusk, barn owls.

Woodcocks begin display and mating activities. Peak concentrations of waterfowl and sandhill cranes move into some southern and coastal refuges for the winter.

Whales can be seen migrating off the coasts at this time of year.

---

natural environment and the climate helps vacationers compare many potential destinations to find the ideal natural setting for their vacation.

## TERRAIN

A Vermont farmer who was talking on the phone to a real-estate agent tried to convince the realtor that his farm was a choice piece of property. The realtor was interested in its value as a vacation home, while the owner had in mind only its potential as farmland.

"What can you see when you look out the window?" asked the agent, trying to determine whether a beautiful view was a selling point.

"Waal," said the farmer, "from the kitchen you can see the bah'n real good, but otherwise there's nothin' to look at but a whole passel of mountains."

It's all in your point of view.

Seeing different landforms is one of the experiences that makes travel so interesting. In many parts of the United States a drive of half a day will take you through several vastly different areas, with hills, plains, mountains, and plateaus arranged in an infinite number of combinations. The western half of the country has higher, more rugged mountains and deeper, wider canyons; but the hills, low forest-covered mountains, and gorges of the East offer plenty of natural beauty, too.

## OPEN SPACE

"In the United States there is more space where nobody is than where anybody is. That is what makes America what it is," wrote Gertrude Stein in 1936. The nation's population has just about doubled since then, but so far Stein's statements are still valid. Lack of crowds, solitude, open space—these are natural blessings truly appreciated by many vacationers.

It is national policy to preserve certain open spaces. In the Wilderness Act of 1964, Congress directed three federal agencies to study lands within their jurisdiction to determine the suitability of these lands for inclusion in a national wilderness-preservation system. Many units of the National Park System have been designated as wilderness areas by Congress since then. Their management should assure that they retain their primitive character without permanent improvements or human habitation, including commercial enterprise and permanent roads. Most importantly, there should be no use of motorized vehicles within these areas.

These wilderness areas are, of course, the real unspoiled open spaces left for our enjoyment. Although they allow hiking and, in some places, horseback riding and primitive camping, only the hardiest of outdoors lovers seek such remote and inaccessible places for vacations; most vacationers looking for open space are satisfied with areas where there are fewer people to brush against than there are back home.

## FORESTS

When Europeans first came to this continent, they found vast expanses covered with forests. Cutting the trees was a number-one priority: trees represented building material for cabins and ships—and troublesome growth that interfered with farming. Despite

---

### The National Park System

The National Park System is more than a century old; it was born when Congress established Yellowstone National Park, in 1872, "as a public park or pleasuring ground for the benefit and enjoyment of the people," to be preserved "under exclusive control of the Secretary of the Interior."

This action of our government was an event of extreme significance, not only for the United States, but for the entire world. Although parks had been around since ancient times, the concept of national parks was new. National parks caught on in other countries as well as in the United States, and today more than 100 nations have national parks and equivalent preserves.

It was not until 1916 that the National Park Service was established as an agency charged with administering the system, though a number of national parks and monuments had been set aside during the intervening years. The act setting up the agency states:

> The service thus established shall promote and regulate the use of the Federal areas known as national parks, monuments and reservations . . . by such means and measures as conform to the fundamental purpose of the said parks, monuments and reservations, which purpose is to conserve the scenery and the natural and historic objects and the wild life therein and to provide for the enjoyment of the same in such manner and by such means as will leave them unimpaired for the enjoyment of future generations.

Units of the National Park System have a variety of titles. The following paragraphs, quoted from the U.S. government publication entitled *Index 1982, National Park System and Related Areas*, define the different types of areas.

Generally, a *national park* covers a large area. It contains a variety of resources and encompasses sufficient land or water to ensure adequate protection of the resources.

A *national monument* is intended to preserve at least one nationally significant resource. It is usually smaller than a national park and lacks its diversity of attractions.

In 1974, Big Cypress [in Florida] and Big Thicket [in Texas] were authorized as the first *national preserves*. This category is established primarily for the protection of certain resources. Activities such as hunting and fishing or the extraction of minerals and fuels may be permitted if they do not jeopardize the natural values.

Preserving shoreline areas and off-shore islands, the *national lakeshores* and *national seashores* focus on the preservation of natural values while at the same time providing water-oriented recreation. Although national lakeshores can be established on any natural freshwater lake, the existing four are all located on the Great Lakes. The national seashores are on the Atlantic, Gulf, and Pacific coasts. . . .

Originally, *national recreation areas* in the Park System were units surrounding reservoirs impounded by dams built by other Federal agencies. The National Park Service manages many of these areas under cooperative agreements. The concept of recreational areas has grown to encompass other lands and waters set aside for recreational use by acts of Congress and now includes major areas in urban centers. There are also national recreation areas outside the National Park System that are administered by the Forest Service, U.S. Department of Agriculture.

*National parkways* encompass ribbons of land flanking roadways and offer an opportunity for leisurely driving through areas of scenic interest. They are not designed for high speed point-to-point travel. Besides the areas set aside as parkways, other units of the National Park System include parkways within their boundaries.

several centuries of cutting and a scarcity of remaining virgin forests, one-third of the United States is still forested.

Forests provide vacationers with much more than sheer beauty. Their canopies serve as a home and protection for wildlife, and their roots anchor the soil upon which plant life grows. But to millions of vacationers, forests are seen primarily as a huge national playground. Many different federal and state agencies protect forestland for recreation as well as for conservation.

Forests differ widely from one part of the country to another. Eastern forests are more varied than those in the West, with many more species of hardwoods. The most prevalent trees in eastern forests are pine, spruce, oak, elm, maple, and birch. The brilliance of autumn foliage and the variety of colors provided by the mixture of these hardwood and evergreen trees draw thousands of visitors to the woodlands of New England, Pennsylvania, the Great Smoky Mountains, and the northern regions of the Midwest during the month of October. In Colorado, less variety but equal brilliance is provided as millions of stately aspens turn from green to gold. Giants of the forest grow in the West—redwood, sequoia, Douglas fir, Sitka spruce. As one travels north, there is even less variety; in many parts of Alaska one can travel for many miles and see only one or two types of trees.

## INLAND WATER

Like a varied terrain, inland water affords scenic beauty and opportunities for outdoor activities. The waters themselves and the land surrounding them offer a wide range of recreational uses—camping, hiking, boating, swimming, fishing, and other water sports. But the sound and appearance of water impart a serenity not offered by scenic terrain. Few things are more soothing than the sound of water lapping gently against a shore. Even people who never put on a swimsuit or step into a boat are calmed by the mere sight of lovely lakes and reservoirs.

## SHORELINE

Twenty-three states have an ocean or a gulf coastline, and eight more border on one or more of the Great Lakes. These coastlines vary a great deal in type and appearance. The wide, smooth beaches of Florida appeal to sunbathers. Hawaii's magnificent waters call out to surfers. The rocky coast of Maine, pounded by crashing waves, attracts artists and photographers in droves. Huge rocks off the shores of California and Oregon are the homes of seals and sea lions; tourists line the highways, binoculars focused, watching the marine animals at play. Some devoted sports fishermen and women tell you the very best deep-sea fishing is found off the coast of North Carolina; others

### Coastlines of Ocean and Gulf States

| Atlantic Ocean | General Coastline (in miles) | Gulf of Mexico | General Coastline (in miles) |
|---|---|---|---|
| Delaware | 28 | Alabama | 53 |
| Florida | | Florida | |
| (Atlantic only) | 580 | (Gulf only) | 770 |
| Georgia | 100 | Louisiana | 397 |
| Maine | 228 | Mississippi | 44 |
| Maryland | 31 | Texas | 367 |
| Massachusetts | 192 | | |
| New Hampshire | 13 | Pacific Ocean | |
| New Jersey | 130 | Alaska | |
| New York | 127 | (Arctic and Pacific) | 6,640 |
| North Carolina | 301 | California | 840 |
| Rhode Island | 40 | Hawaii | 750 |
| South Carolina | 187 | Oregon | 296 |
| Virginia | 112 | Washington | 157 |

Source: U.S. Department of Commerce, National Oceanic and Atmospheric Administration, The Coastline of the United States.

Connecticut and Pennsylvania are not included because their coastlines are considered bay areas.

### U.S. Shorelines of the Great Lakes

| | Shoreline (in miles) |
|---|---|
| Erie | 470 |
| Huron | 840 |
| Michigan | 1,640 |
| Ontario | 330 |
| Superior | 1,250 |

Source: U.S. Department of Commerce, National Oceanic and Atmospheric Administration, The Coastline of the United States.

make the same claim for the Gulf waters off Mississippi. The mangrove swamps of southern Florida are ideal for bird-watching; whale watchers take excursions from Cape Cod in search of their (photographic) prey.

## RIVERS

A couple are sitting in old-fashioned, wire-backed chairs, tapping their feet to the strains of Dixieland jazz. Nearby, young people are boarding a steamboat as a calliope plays, and around the corner a group of children are listening to Mark Twain tell stories.

This is Memphis, Tennessee, at Mud Island's unique River Museum, where the many contributions of rivers in general and the Mississippi in particular are illustrated in lively hands-on exhibits.

The presence of an exceptionally scenic, large, or rapidly flowing river within a vacation destination is a plus that sets the destination apart from others. Riverfronts are major visitor attractions in many cities: San Antonio, Texas; Savannah, Georgia; and Wilmington, North Carolina, to name just a few. Landscaped walkways, outdoor cafés, strolling musicians, shops, and pleasure-boat rides are part of the scene. And in more rural settings, rivers are important for recreation and scenery. They are places in which to wade, swim, fish, canoe, boat, raft, tube—and they are places at which to just sit and watch the river flow by.

The total mileage of rivers and streams in the United States, not including Alaska and Hawaii, is estimated to be about 3.25 million. In the eastern half of the United States and in parts of the Pacific Coast, greater rainfall means more stream segments with a more consistent flow. In the drier West, fewer but longer rivers are present, often cutting across the land in a spectacular fashion.

In 1968 the U.S. Congress passed legislation estab-

lishing a system of wild and scenic rivers to preserve designated waterways for recreational uses that are compatible with conservation. Some 60 stretches have been selected by the Department of the Interior to be national rivers and wild and scenic riverways. They were chosen according to their natural qualities and the degree to which the area seen from the river is free from human encroachment. To qualify, a *wild river* must bear little evidence of human presence, must not have been dammed, and for the most part must be accessible only by trails. A *scenic river* must have undeveloped shorelines but may be accessible by roads. A *recreational river* may have been dammed and may be somewhat developed and accessible by road or railroad.

A recent nationwide inventory reveals that there are an additional 61,700 miles of river, involving 1,524 river segments, that have attributes necessary to qualify them as wild and scenic rivers, but this status is not yet official.

## Preserving Wildlife

The U.S. Fish and Wildlife Service, an agency of the Department of the Interior, is charged with administering a collection of lands and waters known as national wildlife refuges. There are more than 400 refuges nationwide, containing more than 88 million acres of land and water.

The first of these, Pelican Island National Wildlife Refuge in Florida, was established by then president Theodore Roosevelt in 1903. This refuge was set aside primarily for the protection of Florida's birds, particularly the herons and egrets that were being killed in large numbers at the turn of the century. Women's fashions of the day called for huge, fancy hats trimmed with plumes of these exotic birds. At the same time, drought and the drainage of wetlands threatened many other species of wildlife.

In the 80–plus years since that beginning, several other federal laws have been passed to protect endangered species of birds and animals.

Systematic management of the land for the benefit of the wildlife is carried out in many refuges. Conservation programs such as periodic thinning, planting, burning, or harvesting are implemented in forests and grasslands as needed. Systems of water control create and regulate the shallow marshes needed by waterfowl. Some of the refuges, on the other hand, are left in a completely wild and natural state.

Wildlife refuges are popular places for nature study, wildlife observation, and photography, as well as for hiking, boating, and fishing and hunting under carefully controlled conditions. About 27 million visitors visit the refuges each year. However, while most of them can be visited and many have visitor centers, the refuges do not exist primarily for people's enjoyment but for the sake of the wildlife.

Visitors are urged to make inquiries in advance of a planned trip in order to get specific directions for access and information about regulations.

For more information about wildlife refuges, write to the Department of the Interior, U.S. Fish and Wildlife Service, Washington, DC, 20240.

## NATURE-PRESERVATION AREAS

Adding to an area's natural attractiveness for vacationers is the amount of wild plant and animal life that it contains. Therefore, animals and birds, fish, wildflowers, and trees and grasses create more natural blessings. Throughout the United States, local, state, and national wildlife preserves and conservation districts attempt to promote and preserve the natural heritage and wildlife of the country.

Particularly relevant to the possibility of observing wildlife in a vacation destination is the presence of a unit of the National Park System, which supervises parks, monuments, preserves, recreation areas, riverways, parkways, lakeshores, and seashores. Areas in the National Park System contain at least one distinctive attribute, such as forest, grassland, tundra, desert, estuary, or river system. They may be "windows," giving a view of geological history; or they may be imposing landforms, such as mountains, mesas, thermal areas, or caverns. In each of these National Park System areas, scenery and natural historic phenomena are preserved, and the areas may also be habitats of abundant or rare wild plant and animal life. Thus, areas within the National Park System constitute one of our most important public assets for nature preservation. There are now nearly 333 National Park Service areas, comprising about 79 million acres, within the United States and its possessions.

Equally important to the preservation of nature are the 400 national wildlife refuges in the United States. Containing more than 88 million acres of land and water, national wildlife refuges are found almost everywhere—in the mountains and deserts, on seashores, and in forests and grasslands. A number of them are resting and feeding areas established along the major flyways of migrating birds. In some instances, plant and water controls regulate the environment; in others the refuge is left in a completely wild and natural state. Refuges attract some 27 million visitors a year and are popular places for studying nature, observing wildlife, and taking photographs as well as for hiking, boating, fishing, and hunting.

## NATURE'S SPECTACULARS

In hundreds of family photo albums there are faded snapshots of relatives posing in front of one of the great natural wonders of the United States—Old Faithful or the Grand Canyon for example. If you were to ask almost any group of people to list the most spectacular natural tourist attractions in the United States, these two would certainly appear on almost every list.

All around the world there are places like these that have a very special meaning to millions of people and importance to all humanity now and in the future. In November 1972, the Convention for the Protection of the World Cultural and Natural Heritage was adopted by the UNESCO General Conference, establishing a committee of member governments to decide on sites for inclusion on a World Heritage List. A booklet listing sites selected for inclusion on the list, *The World's Greatest Natural Areas*, was published by the International Union for Conservation of Nature and Natural Resources in 1982. Natural sites on the World Heritage List include "areas which are of superlative natural beauty, sites which illustrate significant geological processes, and natural habitats crucial to the survival of threatened plants and animals. These sites ensure the maintenance of the natural diversity upon which all mankind depends."

Included on the World Heritage List are 19 sites in the United States. Fourteen of them are found within the 107 selected Vacation Places. As internationally recognized places of unusual natural beauty, they are included in this chapter as Nature's Spectaculars.

---

### World Heritage Sites in the United States

The areas included on the World Heritage List were selected by an international committee as sites of exceptional beauty or special geological significance. Places that play a vital role in the preservation of flora and fauna are also included.

Acadia National Park, ME
Arctic National Wildlife Refuge, AK
Big Bend National Park, TX
Bryce Canyon National Park, UT
Death Valley National Monument, CA
Grand Canyon National Park, AZ
Great Smoky Mountains National Park, NC and TN
Joshua Tree National Monument, CA
Mammoth Cave National Park, KY
Mesa Verde National Park, CO
Olympic National Park, WA
Organ Pipe Cactus National Monument/Cabeza Prieta
    National Wildlife Refuge, AZ
Point Reyes National Seashore, CA
Redwood National Park, CA
Sequoia-Kings Canyon National Parks, CA
Virginia Coast Reserve, VA
Wrangell-St. Elias National Park, AK
Yellowstone National Park, WY
Yosemite National Park, CA

---

## CLIMATE

Few factors have had greater influence, historically, on choices of vacation destinations than has weather. The kings and queens of Spain and France had winter palaces and summer palaces in locations selected for the most favorable climate in each season. Even today, with ubiquitous air-conditioning in hot climates and efficient heating in cold ones, people do like to escape from their everyday environment and experience something different. In some cases it is a simple trade-off: people from the mountains of the middle South go to Florida in winter; Floridians travel north to the mountains in summer.

 **SCORING:** Blessings of Nature

The natural environment, which provides the setting for a Vacation Place, can be the primary focus of a vacation. Countless elements make up this environment, and their importance varies from individual to individual and vacation to vacation. To assess the potential of each Vacation Place to satisfy the vacationer's desire for unspoiled nature, the most visible features of the natural environment within each place were counted and evaluated. The chapter rates highest those natural elements whose presence offers the greatest opportunity for the vacationer to interact with the blessings of nature.

### Terrain

*Terrain* is defined as the character of the land. The percentage of the Vacation Place covered by six interesting and potentially scenic and spectacular terrain types was measured in relation to the total area of the Vacation Place. Points were given for the variety and expanse of the six terrain types within an area. Taken into consideration were the following:

1. *High mountains.* Includes high mountains, open high mountains, and plains with high mountains.
2. *Deep canyons.* Includes tablelands (plateaus) with very high relief and canyonlands.
3. *Low mountains.* Includes low mountains, open low mountains, and plains with low mountains.
4. *Moderate canyons.* Includes tablelands with high relief and canyonlands.
5. *Hills.* Includes high hills, hills, open high hills, and open hills.
6. *Hills and deep cuts.* Includes plains with high hills and tablelands with considerable relief.

Because plains and irregular plains (essentially flat areas) are not potentially scenic, they were not given points in the scoring of terrain. Scores range from 0 for those areas that are almost completely flat to 1,240 for the rugged area of southwestern Utah that includes Bryce Canyon and Zion national parks and Cedar Breaks National Monument.

#### Top Ten for Terrain

| | Points |
|---|---|
| 1. Zion–Bryce Canyon, UT | 1,240 |
| 2. Lake Powell–Glen Canyon, AZ–UT | 1,120 |
| 3. Albuquerque–Santa Fe–Taos, NM | 1,000 |
| 3. Yosemite–Sequoia–Death Valley, CA | 1,000 |
| 5. Redwoods–Shasta–Lassen, CA | 970 |
| 6. Anchorage–Kenai Peninsula, AK | 940 |
| 6. Lake Tahoe–Reno, NV–CA | 940 |
| 6. Phoenix–Valley of the Sun, AZ | 940 |
| 6. Salt Lake City, UT | 940 |
| 6. Yellowstone–Jackson–Tetons, WY–ID–MT | 940 |

### Open Space

It is difficult to enjoy the blessings of nature while fighting for elbowroom with thousands of other people. An uncrowded environment—the existence of some open space—is essential for an outdoor vacation. Scores for this factor are based on the approximate population-density average for the total Vacation Place area, with the premise that a low density is an asset and a high density a liability. Density figures are, of course, measures of the number of people living in the area, but they give a good idea of open space. It should be remembered that nearly every Vacation Place has some pockets of open space, some places were one can escape to solitude. On the other hand, some of the places with the highest overall score for open space may have some spots that are extremely popular—therefore crowded—at least during certain seasons.

Vacation Places with a population density between 250 and 500 people per square mile received a score of 0 for open space. Those with a higher density were given a negative score (–200 or –300), those with lower density were scored 200, 300, 700, or 1000.

#### Top Ten for Open Space

| | Population Density (per square mile) |
|---|---|
| 1. Lake Powell–Glen Canyon, AZ–UT | 1.8 |
| 2. Yosemite–Sequoia–Death Valley, CA | 3.7 |
| 3. Grand Canyon Country, AZ | 4.6 |
| 4. Yellowstone–Jackson–Tetons, WY–ID–MT | 4.7 |
| 5. Zion–Bryce Canyon, UT | 4.8 |
| 6. Rangeley Lakes, ME | 5.3 |
| 7. Flaming Gorge, UT–WY–CO | 5.8 |
| 8. Glacier National Park–Flathead Lake, MT | 8.5 |
| 9. Bend–Cascade Mountains, OR | 11.1 |
| 10. Anchorage–Kenai Peninsula, AK | 11.2 |

### Forests

Although the scoring for forests takes into account the character and the variety of each Vacation Place's forestland, the extent of forestland in each place establishes its rating. The greater the expanse of forestland in relation to the boundaries of the Vacation Place, the higher the rating.

The expanse within the boundaries of each Vacation Place covered by forests was estimated by using maps of forest cover of the United States. A small number of the Vacation Places had no forested areas of any measurable extent—less than 5 percent—and received a score of 0. The other Vacation Places fell into one of four categories and were scored as follows:

1. 5–29 percent of area in forests (100 points)
2. 30–49 percent of area in forests (400 points)
3. 50–74 percent of area in forests (600 points)
4. 75–100 percent of area in forests (800 points)

## Inland Water

The scoring of inland water was determined by measuring the surface area of natural lakes, man-made reservoirs, and coastal embayments. Because some of the largest bodies of water in this country today were created by the damming of rivers, man-made lakes were included along with natural lakes and embayments. Figures for the total area of inland water and for the combined land and water area for each Vacation Place were taken from 1980 U.S. census statistics. The percentage of inland water to the total land-water area of the place was used to assign scores ranging from a low of 0 to a high of 500. Bonus points (100) were given to the Vacation Places fronting on the Great Lakes.

## Shoreline

Considered for this factor were both the extent and character of frontage on either ocean waters or one or more of the Great Lakes. Unspoiled areas—such as sandy, pocket, or coral beaches; rocky shorelines; cliffs; or mangrove swamps—were deemed to be assets, while shorelines made up primarily of mud flats or commercial, industrial, or urban areas were not. From 200 to 1,000 points were scored for each Vacation Place with a shoreline, depending on its extent. Then the point value was decreased by the percentage of shoreline "spoiled" by mud flats or built-up areas (those areas that are heavily commercial or industrial, usually associated with large urban areas).

## Rivers

There were two ways to gain points in the scoring of this section. First, Vacation Places that had an exceptionally large river flowing through them gained points under the premises that these rivers afforded extraordinary scenery and their breadth and shoreline offered considerably greater opportunity for water activities than smaller streams. The Colorado, Columbia, Mississippi, Missouri, and Ohio rivers qualified as exceptionally large rivers. Second, those Vacation Places that contained rivers under the protection of the National Park Service as national or wild and scenic rivers also gained points. Two hundred points were

given for the presence of one such river, 100 more for a second, and 75 more for a third.

## Nature-Preservation Areas

Plants and animals in their wild, relatively untouched state deserve special recognition as blessings of nature enjoyed by vacationers. Responsibility for the preservation and conservation of the natural environment in the United States is shared by many local, state, and federal governmental agencies. Singling out only two of these agencies does not mean that the work of many others should not be recognized or applauded. It is simply that the National Park Service and the Fish and Wildlife Service, in most cases, manage the largest preserves and the most extensive conservation programs.

Scoring for this factor is as follows: from 100 to 700 points were given for the presence of a National Park Service unit, depending on the size and number of the units. One hundred points were given for the presence of one or more national wildlife refuges.

## Nature's Spectaculars

Those world-famous spectacles of nature that are major attractions for sightseers gained 500 points for one in an area, 700 points for two or more. These exceptional areas include sites found on the World's Heritage List, which designates places of great natural beauty, and other wonders of nature, such as Niagara Falls, selected by the author.

## Climate

Because of the different climatological requirements of vacationers, assigning ratings on the basis of climate has not been attempted. How does one apply a meaningful climatic rank that would take into account different vacation preferences? The climate that would rank Denver very high for a winter skier would be absurd to the sun, surf, and sand worshiper who prefers the heat of Hawaii. Likewise, summer finds some vacationers looking for cool breezes, some for hot sand.

Instead of climate ratings, climatic data are presented in the Places Profiles for those months that represent the various seasons.

# ❧ PLACE PROFILES: Blessings of Nature

In these pages, the 107 Vacation Places are described in terms of their natural geographic features and attractions—their blessings of nature. Each profile lists the major mountains, bodies of water, rivers, and other features. Areas managed primarily for the conservation of their natural features, wildlife, and "nature's spectaculars" are also listed.

All basic climatological data presented in the Place Profiles have been taken from official U.S. government publications—mostly those of the weather bureau under its various names. Current climatological "normals" have been used wherever possible. These normals are recent (1951 to 1980) 30-year averages. When normals are not available or for some reason are not strictly applicable, data have been taken from either more recent or somewhat earlier compilations—depending upon which is more useful in terms of length, consistency, and suitability.

Very little of this basic information is presented in the original form in which it was published by the government. Published weather information appears to be intended primarily for the use of agriculturists and aviators: it does not normally lend itself to the needs of vacationers. As a consequence, these raw data have been mathematically processed by computer programs to produce such useful concepts as chances of a sunny day, chances of a dry day, and mean relative humidity.

A few of the Vacation Places have never had any weather measurements taken within their boundaries, or have had very brief records, or records not representative of most of the area. In these cases, the compiler has interpolated and extrapolated from nearby and similar locations, using known climatological principles and relationships.

The *hours of sunshine* are averages over the entire month. These values are expressed in whole hours to the left of the colon and in minutes to the right of that dividing mark. Visitors should be encouraged to note that those days that are sunny are actually likely to have more sunshine than the amount shown. This is because the cloudy and overcast days have little or no sunshine, and the amount shown in the data is the average of all days in the month—whether the sun shines or not.

*Chances of a sunny day* are based on the number of days in which there are blue skies and sunshine for at least one-quarter of the daylight hours.

*Afternoon temperatures* reflect the monthly averages of the highest temperatures reached each day of the given month. These high temperatures normally occur during the middle of the afternoon and last for two or three hours—the duration depending upon the season. The daily high temperature hangs around longer during the summer than it does during the winter.

In most of the Place Profiles, the figures for *relative humidity* are the mean of the highest and lowest humidities of each day. Sometimes, however, the numbers are the average of all the daily readings for the month. As a general rule, you can consider conditions to be very humid if the mean-monthly relative humidity exceeds 75 percent and very dry if it is less than 40 percent. In between these two monthly values, daily humidities are usually some form of moderate.

*Chances of a dry day* reflect days in which no more than a tenth of an inch of precipitation of some kind falls. If this precipitation is in the form of sleet or hail or snow, then the liquid equivalent must be less than a tenth of an inch.

*Total precipitation* figures include both inches of rain and the liquid equivalent of any snow, sleet, and hail. You should be careful not to use these figures to predict how many hours (or a similar measure) of rain to expect in any given month. The thunderstorms of summer can bring more rain in an hour than falls on an entire day during the drizzle of cooler months.

*Snowfall* is also measured in inches and is shown to the nearest tenth of an inch. Because months with an average of less than an inch of snow are usually snowless in most years, data for those Vacation Places with an inch or more of snow during any given month have been listed in the Place Profiles, and data for those places with less than an inch of snow during any given month have been omitted.

Weather is notoriously changeable and is legally considered to be an act of God. The values shown in the profiles are long-term averages. Consequently, they do not necessarily predict future weather conditions at any particular spot on any particular day of the year. When in doubt, call just before you leave and ask what the weather is like. Even with the best possible preparation, you must still take your chances on the weather. Long-term forecasts are not much better than educated guesses.

A star (★) preceding a Vacation Place highlights that place as one of the top ten in this chapter.

# Adirondack Mountains, NY

## Natural Environment

Much of this Vacation Place is wilderness, with hills, mountains, lakes, streams, and forests. Lake Champlain runs along its eastern border. The terrain includes open low mountains and plains with high hills.

MAJOR GEOGRAPHIC FEATURES
   Terrain: Adirondack Mountains, Mount Marcy (5,344 ft.)
   Lakes and Reservoirs: Lake Champlain, Lake George
   Rivers: Black, Hudson

| Terrain | Open Space | Forests | Inland Water | Shore-line | Rivers | Nature Preser-vation | Nature's Spectac-ulars |
|---|---|---|---|---|---|---|---|
| 470 | 700 | 800 | 220 | — | — | — | — |

Places Rated Score: 2,190        Places Rated Rank: 34

## Climate

| ADIRONDACK MOUNTAINS, NY | January | April | July | October |
|---|---|---|---|---|
| Hours of Sunshine | 3:39 | 6:31 | 9:35 | 5:08 |
| Chances of a Sunny Day | 40% | 50% | 68% | 48% |
| Afternoon Temperatures | 25° | 50° | 76° | 56° |
| Relative Humidity | 71% | 67% | 70% | 73% |
| Chances of a Dry Day | 74% | 73% | 75% | 76% |
| Total Precipitation | 2.8" | 2.9" | 3.4" | 3.2" |
| Snowfall | 27.6" | 6.5" | — | 1.1" |

Comment: Skiers, snowmobilers, and winter campers should be prepared for occasional below-zero temperatures.

# Albuquerque–Santa Fe–Taos, NM

## Natural Environment

There is a great deal of variety in the landscape of this Vacation Place, from forests and mountains to the lush bottomlands of the Rio Grande valley. The terrain includes high mountains, low mountains, and tablelands with various degrees of relief.

MAJOR GEOGRAPHIC FEATURES
   Terrain: Jemez Mountains, Rocky Mountains, Sangre de Cristo Mountains, San Juan Mountains, Wheeler Peak (13,161 ft.)
   Rivers: Rio Grande

NATURE-PRESERVATION AREAS
   Las Vegas National Wildlife Refuge

| Terrain | Open Space | Forests | Inland Water | Shore-line | Rivers | Nature Preser-vation | Nature's Spectac-ulars |
|---|---|---|---|---|---|---|---|
| 1,000 | 700 | 600 | 20 | — | 200 | 100 | — |

Places Rated Score: 2,620        Places Rated Rank: 24

## Climate

| ALBUQUERQUE, NM | January | April | July | October |
|---|---|---|---|---|
| Hours of Sunshine | 7:16 | 10:04 | 10:51 | 9:04 |
| Chances of a Sunny Day | 68% | 73% | 84% | 81% |
| Afternoon Temperatures | 47° | 71° | 93° | 72° |
| Relative Humidity | 55% | 33% | 44% | 45% |
| Chances of a Dry Day | 97% | 96% | 90% | 92% |
| Total Precipitation | 0.4" | 0.4" | 1.3" | 0.9" |
| Snowfall | 2.5" | 0.5" | — | — |

Comment: Lots of blue skies and sunshine. Summer thunder showers raise the humidity without easing the heat.

| SANTA FE, NM | January | April | July | October |
|---|---|---|---|---|
| Hours of Sunshine | 7:14 | 9:33 | 9:53 | 9:03 |
| Chances of a Sunny Day | 84% | 83% | 87% | 87% |
| Afternoon Temperatures | 42° | 62° | 85° | 65° |
| Relative Humidity | 60% | 43% | 51% | 52% |
| Chances of a Dry Day | 94% | 93% | 81% | 90% |
| Total Precipitation | 0.6" | 0.7" | 2.5" | 1.1" |
| Snowfall | 6.5" | 2.2" | — | 0.3" |

Comment: Dry, sunny, and seasonal. One of the most delightful metropolitan climates of the Southwest.

| TAOS, NM | January | April | July | October |
|---|---|---|---|---|
| Hours of Sunshine | 7:18 | 9:26 | 10:09 | 8:53 |
| Chances of a Sunny Day | 84% | 82% | 87% | 87% |
| Afternoon Temperatures | 40° | 64° | 86° | 66° |
| Relative Humidity | 61% | 43% | 51% | 51% |
| Chances of a Dry Day | 90% | 90% | 84% | 90% |
| Total Precipitation | 0.8" | 1.0" | 1.8" | 1.1" |
| Snowfall | 9.1" | 2.9" | — | 0.1" |

Comment: A typical southwestern mountain climate: hot summers, cold winters, blue skies, and sunshine.

# ★Anchorage–Kenai Peninsula, AK

## Natural Environment

Anchorage, Alaska's largest city, sits at the tip of Cook Inlet. It experiences some of the greatest tidal variations (number of feet from high to low tide) in the world. High and low mountains, many with glaciers, characterize much of the area. The fjords of the Kenai Peninsula are especially scenic.

MAJOR GEOGRAPHIC FEATURES
   Terrain: Kenai Mountains, Moose Range
   Lakes and Reservoirs: Kenai Lake, Skilak Lake
   Rivers: Knik
   Shoreline: Cook Inlet, Gulf of Alaska, Kachemak Bay, Knik Arm, Turnagain Arm
   Other: Harding Icefield, Knik Glacier, Sargent Icefield

NATURE-PRESERVATION AREAS
   Kenai Fjords National Park
   Kenai National Wildlife Refuge

NATURE'S SPECTACULARS
   Kenai Fjords National Park

| Terrain | Open Space | Forests | Inland Water | Shore-line | Rivers | Nature Preser-vation | Nature's Spectac-ulars |
|---|---|---|---|---|---|---|---|
| 940 | 1,000 | 600 | 160 | 800 | — | 400 | 500 |

Places Rated Score: 4,400        Places Rated Rank: 2

## Climate

| ANCHORAGE–UPPER COOK INLET, AK | January | April | July | October |
|---|---|---|---|---|
| Hours of Sunshine | 2:37 | 7:38 | 8:05 | 3:45 |
| Chances of a Sunny Day | 42% | 40% | 29% | 32% |
| Afternoon Temperatures | 20° | 43° | 65° | 41° |
| Relative Humidity | 72% | 64% | 71% | 73% |
| Chances of a Dry Day | 91% | 93% | 80% | 85% |
| Total Precipitation | 0.8" | 0.7" | 2.0" | 1.7" |
| Snowfall | 10.0" | 5.3" | — | 7.5" |

Comment: Many residents recommend late spring and early summer as the best time for a visit.

**KENAI PENINSULA, AK**

| | January | April | July | October |
|---|---|---|---|---|
| Chances of a Sunny Day | 42% | 40% | 39% | 32% |
| Afternoon Temperatures | 19° | 42° | 62° | 42° |
| Relative Humidity | 77% | 76% | 82% | 80% |
| Chances of a Dry Day | 86% | 88% | 77% | 75% |
| Total Precipitation | 1.4" | 1.1" | 1.7" | 2.8" |
| Snowfall | 11.5" | 4.3" | — | 2.8" |

Comment: Conditions are generally wetter, cloudier, and cooler toward the mouth of the inlet.

**KENAI FJORDS NATIONAL PARK, AK**

| | January | April | July | October |
|---|---|---|---|---|
| Chances of a Sunny Day | 33% | 33% | 27% | 20% |
| Afternoon Temperatures | 29° | 44° | 63° | 45° |
| Relative Humidity | 79% | 79% | 87% | 85% |
| Chances of a Dry Day | 67% | 66% | 66% | 50% |
| Total Precipitation | 4.2" | 3.9" | 2.7" | 10.1" |
| Snowfall | 16.0" | 7.6" | — | 1.9" |

Comment: Data show sea-level conditions. The mountains are much colder, wetter, snowier, and cloudier.

# Asheville–Smoky Mountains, NC

## Natural Environment

Asheville, in the foothills of the Great Smoky Mountains, is surrounded by beautiful scenery. The low mountains of the area are usually covered by a haze that has given them their name. A great variety of vegetation adds to their attractiveness. Mountain lovers have been gravitating to this Vacation Place for many years and have established resort communities.

MAJOR GEOGRAPHIC FEATURES
Terrain: Appalachian Mountains, Clingmans Dome (6,643 ft.), Great Smoky Mountains
Lakes and Reservoirs: Fontana Lake
Rivers: Chattooga, Little Tennessee

NATURE-PRESERVATION AREAS
Blue Ridge Parkway
Great Smoky Mountains National Park

NATURE'S SPECTACULARS
Great Smoky Mountains National Park (World Heritage Site)

| Terrain | Open Space | Forests | Inland Water | Shore-line | Rivers | Nature Preser-vation | Nature's Spectac-ulars |
|---|---|---|---|---|---|---|---|
| 470 | 300 | 800 | 60 | — | 200 | 300 | 500 |

Places Rated Score: 2,630          Places Rated Rank: 23

## Climate

**ASHEVILLE, NC**

| | January | April | July | October |
|---|---|---|---|---|
| Hours of Sunshine | 5:32 | 8:38 | 8:27 | 6:54 |
| Chances of a Sunny Day | 58% | 66% | 69% | 71% |
| Afternoon Temperatures | 48° | 69° | 84° | 69° |
| Relative Humidity | 73% | 69% | 80% | 76% |
| Chances of a Dry Day | 77% | 74% | 68% | 82% |
| Total Precipitation | 3.5" | 3.8" | 4.4" | 3.3" |
| Snowfall | 5.2" | 0.3" | — | — |

Comment: Asheville's climate is characteristic of communities in the southeastern foothills of the Great Smokies.

**SMOKY MOUNTAINS, NC**

| | January | April | July | October |
|---|---|---|---|---|
| Hours of Sunshine | 4:44 | 8:19 | 8:40 | 6:54 |
| Chances of a Sunny Day | 47% | 60% | 61% | 65% |
| Afternoon Temperatures | 42° | 61° | 76° | 62° |
| Relative Humidity | 75% | 67% | 85% | 84% |
| Chances of a Dry Day | 73% | 73% | 69% | 82% |
| Total Precipitation | 3.9" | 4.4" | 4.8" | 3.6" |
| Snowfall | 8.2" | 1.2" | — | 0.3" |

Comment: These conditions are typical of the higher (over 3,000 feet) resort communities of the Great Smokies area.

# Aspen–Vail, CO

## Natural Environment

Aspen has an elevation of 7,900 feet, Vail's is 8,200, and Leadville is 10,200 feet above sea level. Glenwood Springs is considered low—at 5,750 feet. River valleys bordered with willows and aspens cut through the high peaks, some of which stand stark and bare above the timberline.

MAJOR GEOGRAPHIC FEATURES
Terrain: Mount Elbert (14,433 ft.), Rocky Mountains, Sawatch Range
Lakes and Reservoirs: Dillon Reservoir
Rivers: Colorado

| Terrain | Open Space | Forests | Inland Water | Shore-line | Rivers | Nature Preser-vation | Nature's Spectac-ulars |
|---|---|---|---|---|---|---|---|
| 760 | 1,000 | 800 | 30 | — | 200 | — | — |

Places Rated Score: 2,790          Places Rated Rank: 19

## Climate

**ASPEN, CO**

| | January | April | July | October |
|---|---|---|---|---|
| Hours of Sunshine | 6:22 | 8:00 | 10:59 | 8:14 |
| Chances of a Sunny Day | 57% | 60% | 82% | 74% |
| Afternoon Temperatures | 34° | 53° | 80° | 60° |
| Relative Humidity | 67% | 51% | 50% | 52% |
| Chances of a Dry Day | 81% | 83% | 84% | 87% |
| Total Precipitation | 2.0" | 1.7" | 1.5" | 1.5" |
| Snowfall | 25.8" | 12.1" | — | 6.1" |

Comment: The snow season is usually from late November through early April. Independence Pass (on Colorado 82) is closed by snow from late October through early June.

**VAIL, CO**

| | January | April | July | October |
|---|---|---|---|---|
| Hours of Sunshine | 6:15 | 9:00 | 11:11 | 8:14 |
| Chances of a Sunny Day | 55% | 60% | 83% | 74% |
| Afternoon Temperatures | 33° | 52° | 80° | 60° |
| Relative Humidity | 72% | 59% | 52% | 57% |
| Chances of a Dry Day | 90% | 87% | 84% | 91% |
| Total Precipitation | 1.0" | 1.1" | 1.4" | 0.8" |
| Snowfall | 18.6" | 13.8" | — | 5.7" |

Comment: Respect the intense mountain sunshine and take it easy until you get used to the 8,200-foot elevation.

# Atlanta, GA

## Natural Environment

Georgia's northern sector, with Atlanta as its hub city, is the southern end of the Appalachian range. These southern highlands consist of foothills and low mountains. Lake Sidney Lanier, created by the U.S. Army Corps of Engineers, is one of the most popular recreation areas of all federal lands. From Atlanta northward, the population density decreases considerably. Taken as a whole, this destination has both "bright lights" and "open spaces" in abundance.

MAJOR GEOGRAPHIC FEATURES
Terrain: Appalachian Mountains
Lakes and Reservoirs: Lake Sidney Lanier
Rivers: Chattahoochee

| Terrain | Open Space | Forests | Inland Water | Shore-line | Rivers | Nature Preser-vation | Nature's Spectac-ulars |
|---|---|---|---|---|---|---|---|
| 260 | 200 | 600 | 80 | — | — | — | — |

Places Rated Score: 1,140          Places Rated Rank: 85

## Climate

| ATLANTA, GA | January | April | July | October |
|---|---|---|---|---|
| Hours of Sunshine | 4:54 | 8:28 | 8:55 | 7:44 |
| Chances of a Sunny Day | 48% | 60% | 61% | 68% |
| Afternoon Temperatures | 51° | 73° | 88° | 73° |
| Relative Humidity | 69% | 65% | 75% | 69% |
| Chances of a Dry Day | 77% | 78% | 73% | 87% |
| Total Precipitation | 4.9" | 4.4" | 4.7" | 2.5" |

Comment: Long, hot summers, with thunderstorms common. Some early morning fog during the cooler months.

# Atlantic City, NJ

## Natural Environment

Excellent beaches are found on the stretch of islands from Atlantic City to Cape May. These barrier islands are part of the chain that guards the eastern coast of the United States between New York City and Miami. Vacationers like to gather "Cape May diamonds" (pure quartz stones made round and smooth by the ocean waves) on the shores of Delaware Bay.

MAJOR GEOGRAPHIC FEATURES
Shoreline: Atlantic Ocean, Cape May, Delaware Bay

NATURE-PRESERVATION AREAS
Brigantine National Wildlife Refuge

| Terrain | Open Space | Forests | Inland Water | Shore-line | Rivers | Nature Preser-vation | Nature's Spectac-ulars |
|---|---|---|---|---|---|---|---|
| — | — | 400 | 360 | 800 | — | 100 | — |

Places Rated Score: 1,660          Places Rated Rank: 64

## Climate

| ATLANTIC CITY, NJ | January | April | July | October |
|---|---|---|---|---|
| Hours of Sunshine | 4:55 | 7:40 | 9:30 | 6:07 |
| Chances of a Sunny Day | 52% | 57% | 58% | 61% |
| Afternoon Temperatures | 41° | 62° | 84° | 66° |
| Relative Humidity | 68% | 64% | 72% | 72% |
| Chances of a Dry Day | 78% | 77% | 83% | 85% |
| Total Precipitation | 3.5" | 3.2" | 4.0" | 3.1" |
| Snowfall | 5.0" | 0.3" | — | — |

Comment: In summer, sea breezes make afternoon beach locations cooler than shown in the data.

# Austin–Hill Country, TX

## Natural Environment

Austin is situated on the dividing line between the flat coastal plains of eastern Texas and the rolling land called the Texas Hill Country. A fault line known as the Balcones Escarpment cuts through the state from the Rio Grande to the Red River. The Edwards Plateau begins at the escarpment, and the line of demarcation is quite pronounced in

this part of the state. Lakes created by dams on the Colorado River, northwest of the city, are popular recreational areas.

MAJOR GEOGRAPHIC FEATURES
Lakes and Reservoirs: Lake Lyndon B. Johnson, Lake Travis
Rivers: Colorado, Pedernales

| Terrain | Open Space | Forests | Inland Water | Shore-line | Rivers | Nature Preser-vation | Nature's Spectac-ulars |
|---|---|---|---|---|---|---|---|
| 180 | 300 | 400 | 50 | — | — | — | — |

Places Rated Score: 930          Places Rated Rank: 90

## Climate

| AUSTIN–HILL COUNTRY, TX | January | April | July | October |
|---|---|---|---|---|
| Hours of Sunshine | 5:07 | 6:50 | 10:34 | 7:27 |
| Chances of a Sunny Day | 48% | 50% | 81% | 71% |
| Afternoon Temperatures | 59° | 79° | 95° | 81° |
| Relative Humidity | 68% | 69% | 67% | 69% |
| Chances of a Dry Day | 87% | 85% | 92% | 88% |
| Total Precipitation | 1.6" | 3.1" | 1.9" | 3.4" |

Comment: Winters are short and mild, but temperatures top 90 degrees Fahrenheit most afternoons from June through mid-September.

# Baltimore–Chesapeake Bay, MD

## Natural Environment

Chesapeake Bay contributes much to the Baltimore area and Maryland's Eastern Shore: it provides recreational opportunities and the seafood for which the region is justly famous. John Smith, observing the area in 1608, is said to have called it a "delightsome land." Fertile farmlands, small fishing villages, rivers and wetlands alive with waterfowl: these are the characteristics of rural Maryland.

MAJOR GEOGRAPHIC FEATURES
Lakes and Reservoirs: Liberty Lake, Loch Raven Reservoir, Prettyboy Reservoir
Rivers: Susquehanna
Shoreline: Chesapeake Bay

NATURE-PRESERVATION AREAS
Eastern Neck National Wildlife Refuge

| Terrain | Open Space | Forests | Inland Water | Shore-line | Rivers | Nature Preser-vation | Nature's Spectac-ulars |
|---|---|---|---|---|---|---|---|
| — | –200 | 400 | 320 | 800 | — | 100 | — |

Places Rated Score: 1,420          Places Rated Rank: 74

## Climate

| BALTIMORE–UPPER CHESAPEAKE BAY, MD | January | April | July | October |
|---|---|---|---|---|
| Hours of Sunshine | 4:59 | 7:24 | 9:31 | 6:30 |
| Chances of a Sunny Day | 52% | 57% | 68% | 65% |
| Afternoon Temperatures | 41° | 65° | 87° | 68° |
| Relative Humidity | 64% | 60% | 67% | 68% |
| Chances of a Dry Day | 79% | 76% | 80% | 85% |
| Total Precipitation | 3.0" | 3.4" | 3.9" | 3.1" |
| Snowfall | 5.4" | — | — | — |

Comment: Early-morning temperatures in the inner city are measurably warmer, both summer and winter, than those outside the city.

# ★Bar Harbor–Acadia, ME

## Natural Environment

Like most coastal areas, this part of Maine is fairly flat, with only a few low hills. Early fall is a particularly beautiful season; most visitors are gone almost as soon as the leaves have fallen.

MAJOR GEOGRAPHIC FEATURES
  Shoreline: Atlantic Ocean, Penobscot Bay
  Islands: Mount Desert

NATURE-PRESERVATION AREAS
  Acadia National Park
  Franklin Island National Wildlife Refuge

NATURE'S SPECTACULARS
  Acadia National Park (World Heritage Site)

| Terrain | Open Space | Forests | Inland Water | Shore-line | Rivers | Nature Preser-vation | Nature's Spectac-ulars |
|---|---|---|---|---|---|---|---|
| 120 | 700 | 800 | 500 | 800 | — | 400 | 500 |

Places Rated Score: 3,820          Places Rated Rank: 8

## Climate

| BAR HARBOR–ACADIA, ME | January | April | July | October |
|---|---|---|---|---|
| Hours of Sunshine | 4:35 | 7:05 | 8:59 | 5:52 |
| Chances of a Sunny Day | 53% | 52% | 63% | 56% |
| Afternoon Temperatures | 32° | 52° | 78° | 58° |
| Relative Humidity | 71% | 71% | 78% | 74% |
| Chances of a Dry Day | 74% | 75% | 81% | 79% |
| Total Precipitation | 4.8" | 4.1" | 3.0" | 4.8" |
| Snowfall | 16.1" | 2.6" | — | 0.3" |

Comment: Boaters not familiar with the local weather patterns should be alert for sudden changes in the weather.

# Bend–Cascade Mountains, OR

## Natural Environment

The Cascade Range is a chain of dormant volcanoes. The area consists of high mountains, tablelands with high relief, and plains with low mountains and high hills. The river valleys on the western slopes are green and fertile; to the east the piny country is drier and more open; along the ridge the wilderness is Alpine.

MAJOR GEOGRAPHIC FEATURES
  Terrain: Cascade Range, Mount Jefferson (10,497 ft.)
  Lakes and Reservoirs: Lake Chinook, Prineville Reservoir, Wickiup Reservoir
  Rivers: Crooked, Deschutes, Ochoco, Trout, Warm Springs

| Terrain | Open Space | Forests | Inland Water | Shore-line | Rivers | Nature Preser-vation | Nature's Spectac-ulars |
|---|---|---|---|---|---|---|---|
| 880 | 1,000 | 600 | 20 | — | — | — | — |

Places Rated Score: 2,500          Places Rated Rank: 25

## Climate

| BEND, OR | January | April | July | October |
|---|---|---|---|---|
| Hours of Sunshine | 3:02 | 7:32 | 12:15 | 5:45 |
| Chances of a Sunny Day | 58% | 70% | 94% | 74% |
| Afternoon Temperatures | 41° | 57° | 82° | 63° |
| Relative Humidity | 73% | 57% | 48% | 63% |
| Chances of a Dry Day | 84% | 93% | 95% | 94% |
| Total Precipitation | 2.0" | 0.5" | 0.3" | 0.7" |
| Snowfall | 11.5" | 1.1" | — | 0.4" |

Comment: A cool, dry climate with warm, sunny summers.

| NORTHERN CASCADE MOUNTAINS (EASTERN SLOPES), OR | January | April | July | October |
|---|---|---|---|---|
| Hours of Sunshine | 2:52 | 7:13 | 11:42 | 5:22 |
| Chances of a Sunny Day | 37% | 51% | 87% | 59% |
| Afternoon Temperatures | 33° | 47° | 74° | 53° |
| Relative Humidity | 78% | 73% | 60% | 66% |
| Chances of a Dry Day | 58% | 70% | 97% | 74% |
| Total Precipitation | 9.6" | 3.7" | 0.5" | 5.3" |
| Snowfall | 71.8" | 19.3" | — | 7.5" |

Comment: Data describe the 5,000-foot level. The western slopes are much cooler, cloudier, and wetter.

# Berkshire Hills–Pioneer Valley, MA

## Natural Environment

The pleasant terrain of western Massachusetts consists of open high hills and low mountains, brilliantly colored in autumn. Many small lakes, rivers, and streams help to keep the countryside green.

MAJOR GEOGRAPHIC FEATURES
  Terrain: Berkshire Hills, Mount Greylock (3,491 ft.)
  Rivers: Connecticut

| Terrain | Open Space | Forests | Inland Water | Shore-line | Rivers | Nature Preser-vation | Nature's Spectac-ulars |
|---|---|---|---|---|---|---|---|
| 710 | 200 | 800 | 100 | — | — | — | — |

Places Rated Score: 1,810          Places Rated Rank: 60

## Climate

| BERKSHIRE HILLS, MA | January | April | July | October |
|---|---|---|---|---|
| Hours of Sunshine | 4:48 | 7:22 | 9:29 | 6:02 |
| Chances of a Sunny Day | 39% | 43% | 61% | 58% |
| Afternoon Temperatures | 32° | 57° | 80° | 61° |
| Relative Humidity | 72% | 63% | 71% | 75% |
| Chances of a Dry Day | 78% | 74% | 77% | 81% |
| Total Precipitation | 3.2" | 3.9" | 3.9" | 3.4" |
| Snowfall | 16.9" | 3.3" | — | — |

Comment: Extremely changeable weather.

# Black Hills, SD

## Natural Environment

This is the land where the buffalo roam—America's largest herd lives in Custer State Park. The eroded landscape of the Badlands is wild and eerie; numerous fossils of prehistoric animals have been found in the soft rock. Jagged rocky peaks look like fairy towers and castles. Not far from the Badlands, grassy prairies are the home of pronghorn antelope, prairie dogs, and coyotes.

MAJOR GEOGRAPHIC FEATURES
  Terrain: Badlands, Black Hills, Harney Peak (7,242 ft.), Mount Rushmore (5,725 ft.)
  Lakes and Reservoirs: Angostura Reservoir, Pactola Reservoir
  Rivers: Belle Fourche, Cheyenne

NATURE-PRESERVATION AREAS
  Badlands National Park
  Jewel Cave National Monument
  Wind Cave National Park

| Terrain | Open Space | Forests | Inland Water | Shore-line | Rivers | Nature Preser-vation | Nature's Spectac-ulars |
|---|---|---|---|---|---|---|---|
| 290 | 1,000 | 400 | — | — | — | 400 | — |

Places Rated Score: 2,090          Places Rated Rank: 40

## Climate

| BLACK HILLS, SD | January | April | July | October |
|---|---|---|---|---|
| Hours of Sunshine | 5:08 | 7:55 | 10:52 | 7:11 |
| Chances of a Sunny Day | 51% | 50% | 83% | 66% |
| Afternoon Temperatures | 34° | 51° | 80° | 60° |
| Relative Humidity | 68% | 68% | 65% | 61% |
| Chances of a Dry Day | 90% | 80% | 82% | 89% |
| Total Precipitation | 0.7" | 2.4" | 2.7" | 1.0" |
| Snowfall | 10.1" | 11.8" | — | 4.0" |

Comment: Warm, dry chinook winds keep winter temperatures warmer in the Black Hills than in the rest of the state.

# Blue Ridge Mountains, VA

## Natural Environment

The terrain of the Blue Ridge includes plains with high hills and low mountains. The Skyline Drive along the Ridge tempts motorists to make frequent stops to view and photograph the pastoral vistas spread out in the valleys below.

MAJOR GEOGRAPHIC FEATURES
Terrain: Appalachian Mountains, Blue Ridge, Elliott Knob (4,463 ft.), Shenandoah Mountain, Shenandoah Valley
Rivers: Shenandoah

NATURE-PRESERVATION AREAS
Shenandoah National Park

NATURE'S SPECTACULARS
Shenandoah National Park

| Terrain | Open Space | Forests | Inland Water | Shore-line | Rivers | Nature Preser-vation | Nature's Spectac-ulars |
|---|---|---|---|---|---|---|---|
| 470 | 300 | 600 | — | — | — | 300 | 500 |

Places Rated Score: 2,170     Places Rated Rank: 35

## Climate

| CHARLOTTESVILLE, VA | January | April | July | October |
|---|---|---|---|---|
| Hours of Sunshine | 4:00 | 8:02 | 9:21 | 6:47 |
| Chances of a Sunny Day | 50% | 57% | 63% | 63% |
| Afternoon Temperatures | 44° | 68° | 87° | 69° |
| Relative Humidity | 63% | 59% | 72% | 69% |
| Chances of a Dry Day | 81% | 78% | 76% | 84% |
| Total Precipitation | 3.3" | 3.3" | 3.7" | 3.6" |
| Snowfall | 5.9" | 0.3" | — | — |

Comment: The Blue Ridge, west of the city, protects city dwellers from the worst of the winter storms.

| SHENANDOAH NATIONAL PARK, VA | January | April | July | October |
|---|---|---|---|---|
| Hours of Sunshine | 3:59 | 6:56 | 8:44 | 6:11 |
| Chances of a Sunny Day | 39% | 47% | 56% | 60% |
| Afternoon Temperatures | 36° | 57° | 75° | 58° |
| Relative Humidity | 66% | 62% | 78% | 78% |
| Chances of a Dry Day | 81% | 73% | 77% | 84% |
| Total Precipitation | 3.5" | 3.8" | 4.1" | 5.2" |
| Snowfall | 10.9" | 1.9" | — | 0.4 |

Comment: The haze that gives the Blue Ridge its name is least apparent in October: skies and colors are brilliant.

# Boise–Sun Valley, ID

## Natural Environment

The mountains of Idaho's Sawtooth Range are rocky pinnacles that do, indeed, look like the teeth of a saw. Sheep and cattle graze verdant pastures beneath beautiful peaks. Streams and rivers of the area teem with chinook and sockeye salmon and steelhead trout; the forests are alive with deer, elk, mountain goats, and other wildlife.

MAJOR GEOGRAPHIC FEATURES
Terrain: Hyndman Peak (12,009 ft.), Salmon River Mountains, Sawtooth Range
Lakes and Reservoirs: Cascade Reservoir, Magic Reservoir, Twin Lakes Reservoir
Rivers: Snake

NATURE-PRESERVATION AREAS
Deer Flat National Wildlife Refuge

| Terrain | Open Space | Forests | Inland Water | Shore-line | Rivers | Nature Preser-vation | Nature's Spectac-ulars |
|---|---|---|---|---|---|---|---|
| 710 | 700 | 600 | 40 | — | — | 100 | — |

Places Rated Score: 2,150     Places Rated Rank: 36

## Climate

| BOISE, ID | January | April | July | October |
|---|---|---|---|---|
| Hours of Sunshine | 3:39 | 8:59 | 13:16 | 7:31 |
| Chances of a Sunny Day | 29% | 50% | 90% | 65% |
| Afternoon Temperatures | 37° | 61° | 91° | 65° |
| Relative Humidity | 75% | 53% | 38% | 54% |
| Chances of a Dry Day | 81% | 89% | 99% | 90% |
| Total Precipitation | 1.6" | 1.2" | 0.3" | 0.8" |
| Snowfall | 7.3" | 0.7" | — | 0.1" |

Comment: Hot, sunny, dry summers and cold, cloudy, wet winters. A stimulating and varied climate.

| SUN VALLEY, ID | January | April | July | October |
|---|---|---|---|---|
| Hours of Sunshine | 3:33 | 8:52 | 12:54 | 7:38 |
| Chances of a Sunny Day | 29% | 48% | 89% | 66% |
| Afternoon Temperatures | 31° | 52° | 83° | 61° |
| Relative Humidity | 74% | 48% | 34% | 48% |
| Chances of a Dry Day | 81% | 90% | 94% | 90% |
| Total Precipitation | 2.6" | 1.0" | 0.7" | 0.9" |
| Snowfall | 33.4" | 4.2" | — | 1.8" |

Comment: Summer days are warm and nights are cool. Campers should be prepared for frosty mornings in every month of the year.

# Boone–High Country, NC

## Natural Environment

North Carolina's section of the Blue Ridge is known as the High Country. There are low mountains and plains with high hills. Spring and fall are especially pleasant here.

MAJOR GEOGRAPHIC FEATURES
Terrain: Appalachian Mountains, Blue Ridge, Grandfather Mountain (5,964 ft.), Hawksbill (4,050 ft.)
Lakes and Reservoirs: Lake James
Rivers: Catawba

NATURE-PRESERVATION AREAS
Blue Ridge Parkway

| Terrain | Open Space | Forests | Inland Water | Shore-line | Rivers | Nature Preser-vation | Nature's Spectac-ulars |
|---|---|---|---|---|---|---|---|
| 530 | 300 | 800 | 40 | — | 200 | — | — |

Places Rated Score: 1,870     Places Rated Rank: 56

## Climate

| BOONE-HIGH COUNTRY, NC | January | April | July | October |
|---|---|---|---|---|
| Hours of Sunshine | 5:00 | 8:05 | 8:46 | 7:05 |
| Chances of a Sunny Day | 47% | 57% | 60% | 68% |
| Afternoon Temperatures | 42° | 63° | 78° | 63° |
| Relative Humidity | 75% | 67% | 85% | 84% |
| Chances of a Dry Day | 72% | 73% | 65% | 81% |
| Total Precipitation | 4.1″ | 4.6″ | 4.7″ | 4.2″ |
| Snowfall | 8.2″ | 1.2″ | — | 0.3″ |

Comment: The climate and scenery of the Great Smokies, without the crowds.

# Boston, MA

## Natural Environment

The Boston area has a few small hills, but for the most part the terrain is insignificant. Its outstanding geographic attraction is the Atlantic Ocean. There are few open spaces in this heavily populated metropolitan area. Nevertheless, autumn is a gorgeous time of year, with every village green and small hillside saturated with color.

MAJOR GEOGRAPHIC FEATURES
Lakes and Reservoirs: Sudbury Reservoir, Whitehall Reservoir
Rivers: Charles, Merrimack
Shoreline: Atlantic Ocean, Boston Bay, Massachusetts Bay

NATURE-PRESERVATION AREAS
Great Meadows National Wildlife Refuge
Oxbow National Wildlife Refuge
Parker River National Wildlife Refuge

| Terrain | Open Space | Forests | Inland Water | Shore-line | Rivers | Nature Preser-vation | Nature's Spectac-ulars |
|---|---|---|---|---|---|---|---|
| — | −300 | 100 | 350 | 300 | — | 100 | — |

Places Rated Score: 550          Places Rated Rank: 100

## Climate

| BOSTON, MA | January | April | July | October |
|---|---|---|---|---|
| Hours of Sunshine | 5:07 | 7:37 | 9:52 | 6:40 |
| Chances of a Sunny Day | 52% | 53% | 61% | 61% |
| Afternoon Temperatures | 36° | 57° | 82° | 63° |
| Relative Humidity | 67% | 63% | 69% | 69% |
| Chances of a Dry Day | 76% | 75% | 82% | 82% |
| Total Precipitation | 4.0″ | 3.7″ | 2.7″ | 3.4″ |
| Snowfall | 12.4″ | 0.7″ | — | — |

Comment: Bay-shore areas are cooler in summer and a bit warmer in winter.

# Brownsville-Rio Grande Valley, TX

## Natural Environment

The Rio Grande is the natural boundary between Texas and Mexico; it has created a lush valley whose subtropical landscape includes palm trees and bougainvillea, citrus groves and vegetable gardens. South Padre Island, reached by causeway from the mainland, has deep sand topped with waving sea oats. Many species of fish live in both the shallow and deep waters of the Gulf.

MAJOR GEOGRAPHIC FEATURES
Rivers: Rio Grande
Shoreline: Gulf of Mexico
Islands: Padre

NATURE-PRESERVATION AREAS
Laguna Atascosa National Wildlife Refuge
Rio Grande Valley National Wildlife Refuge
Santa Ana National Wildlife Refuge

| Terrain | Open Space | Forests | Inland Water | Shore-line | Rivers | Nature Preser-vation | Nature's Spectac-ulars |
|---|---|---|---|---|---|---|---|
| — | 200 | 100 | 500 | 420 | — | 100 | — |

Places Rated Score: 1,320          Places Rated Rank: 80

## Climate

| BROWNSVILLE, TX | January | April | July | October |
|---|---|---|---|---|
| Hours of Sunshine | 4:30 | 7:17 | 10:52 | 7:31 |
| Chances of a Sunny Day | 42% | 53% | 84% | 77% |
| Afternoon Temperatures | 70° | 83° | 93° | 84° |
| Relative Humidity | 77% | 73% | 73% | 74% |
| Chances of a Dry Day | 92% | 93% | 92% | 88% |
| Total Precipitation | 1.3″ | 1.6″ | 1.5″ | 3.5″ |

# Cape Cod-The Islands, MA

## Natural Environment

Magnificent sand dunes, covered with a rich variety of vegetation, blanket much of Cape Cod. The terrain is quite flat, with inland lakes and ponds. Martha's Vineyard is different; it has rolling hills, farmlands, and some brilliantly colored cliffs at the edge of the ocean. From early spring through late fall, finback, humpback, and minke whales glide and splash in Cape Cod Bay.

MAJOR GEOGRAPHIC FEATURES
Shoreline: Atlantic Ocean, Cape Cod Bay, Nantucket Sound
Islands: Martha's Vineyard, Monomoy, Nantucket
Other: Cape Cod

NATURE-PRESERVATION AREAS
Cape Cod National Seashore
Monomoy National Wildlife Refuge
Nantucket National Wildlife Refuge

| Terrain | Open Space | Forests | Inland Water | Shore-line | Rivers | Nature Preser-vation | Nature's Spectac-ulars |
|---|---|---|---|---|---|---|---|
| — | — | 600 | 500 | 800 | — | 300 | — |

Places Rated Score: 2,200          Places Rated Rank: 32

## Climate

| CAPE COD-THE ISLANDS, MA | January | April | July | October |
|---|---|---|---|---|
| Hours of Sunshine | 4:12 | 7:04 | 8:47 | 6:17 |
| Chances of a Sunny Day | 55% | 63% | 69% | 66% |
| Afternoon Temperatures | 37° | 51° | 74° | 60° |
| Relative Humidity | 76% | 77% | 82% | 80% |
| Chances of a Dry Day | 75% | 74% | 84% | 81% |
| Total Precipitation | 4.3″ | 3.9″ | 2.9″ | 3.7″ |
| Snowfall | 6.4″ | — | — | — |

Comment: Ocean-side locations have cooler summers and warmer winters than bay-side communities.

# Catskill Mountains, NY

## Natural Environment

The Catskill Mountains are low in comparison with the ranges west of the Mississippi, but they are picturesque and popular. The air is clear and crisp; fertile farmlands dot the countryside; luxuriant vineyards line the shores of the Hudson River; clear, rushing streams and rivers teem with fish.

MAJOR GEOGRAPHIC FEATURES
Terrain: Catskill Mountains, Slide Mountain (4,190 ft.)
Lakes and Reservoirs: Ashokan Reservoir
Rivers: Delaware, Hudson

| Terrain | Open Space | Forests | Inland Water | Shore-line | Rivers | Nature Preser-vation | Nature's Spectac-ulars |
|---|---|---|---|---|---|---|---|
| 530 | 200 | 600 | 90 | — | 200 | — | — |

Places Rated Score: 1,620          Places Rated Rank: 66

### Climate

| CATSKILL MOUNTAINS, NY | January | April | July | October |
|---|---|---|---|---|
| Hours of Sunshine | 4:01 | 7:05 | 9:28 | 5:38 |
| Chances of a Sunny Day | 38% | 44% | 61% | 52% |
| Afternoon Temperatures | 30° | 54° | 78° | 59° |
| Relative Humidity | 76% | 67% | 74% | 77% |
| Chances of a Dry Day | 75% | 71% | 76% | 74% |
| Total Precipitation | 3.7″ | 4.5″ | 4.2″ | 3.9″ |
| Snowfall | 14.9″ | 3.8″ | — | 0.7″ |

Comment: A pleasant summer's relief from the heat of the city.

# Charleston, SC

## Natural Environment

Charleston is part of the flat, marshy land that South Carolinians call the Low Country. Of the two rivers on either side of the city, Charlestonians say, "This is where the Ashley and Cooper meet and form the Atlantic Ocean." Islands near the city are being developed as resort areas; trees and shrubs grow in a lush, junglelike atmosphere.

MAJOR GEOGRAPHIC FEATURES
Lakes and Reservoirs: Lake Moultrie
Rivers: Ashley, Cooper, Santee
Shoreline: Atlantic Ocean
Islands: Johns, Kiawah, Seabrook
NATURE-PRESERVATION AREAS
Cape Romain National Wildlife Refuge

| Terrain | Open Space | Forests | Inland Water | Shore-line | Rivers | Nature Preser-vation | Nature's Spectac-ulars |
|---|---|---|---|---|---|---|---|
| — | 200 | 400 | 380 | 600 | — | 100 | — |

Places Rated Score: 1,680          Places Rated Rank: 63

### Climate

| CHARLESTON, SC | January | April | July | October |
|---|---|---|---|---|
| Hours of Sunshine | 5:57 | 9:13 | 9:35 | 7:31 |
| Chances of a Sunny Day | 48% | 63% | 55% | 65% |
| Afternoon Temperatures | 59° | 76° | 89° | 77° |
| Relative Humidity | 69% | 67% | 77% | 72% |
| Chances of a Dry Day | 80% | 83% | 69% | 88% |
| Total Precipitation | 3.3″ | 2.6″ | 7.3″ | 2.9″ |

Comment: Summer afternoons are slightly cooler near the harbor, while winter mornings are significantly warmer.

# Chattanooga–Huntsville, TN–AL–GA

## Natural Environment

Chattanooga and Huntsville are surrounded by the hills, lakes, reservoirs, and rivers of the southern highlands. There are open low mountains and hills and tablelands with considerable relief. Spelunkers and casual sightseers enjoy the numerous caves tucked away under the mountains. Chattanooga is a very hilly city; some of the streets pass through tunnels in order to avoid climbing up and down the slopes. Driving conditions are sometimes hazardous in winter.

MAJOR GEOGRAPHIC FEATURES
Terrain: Appalachian Mountains, Cumberland Plateau
Lakes and Reservoirs: Chickamauga Lake, Nickajack Lake
Rivers: Tennessee
NATURE-PRESERVATION AREAS
Blowing Wind Cave National Wildlife Refuge

| Terrain | Open Space | Forests | Inland Water | Shore-line | Rivers | Nature Preser-vation | Nature's Spectac-ulars |
|---|---|---|---|---|---|---|---|
| 410 | 300 | 400 | 150 | — | — | 100 | — |

Places Rated Score: 1,360          Places Rated Rank: 78

### Climate

| CHATTANOOGA, TN | January | April | July | October |
|---|---|---|---|---|
| Hours of Sunshine | 4:15 | 7:50 | 8:42 | 7:08 |
| Chances of a Sunny Day | 45% | 57% | 65% | 68% |
| Afternoon Temperatures | 48° | 73° | 89° | 72° |
| Relative Humidity | 72% | 65% | 73% | 71% |
| Chances of a Dry Day | 74% | 75% | 75% | 85% |
| Total Precipitation | 5.2″ | 4.6″ | 4.6″ | 2.9″ |
| Snowfall | 1.7″ | — | — | — |

Comment: Snowfalls vary considerably from year to year; some winters are virtually snowless.

| HUNTSVILLE, AL | January | April | July | October |
|---|---|---|---|---|
| Hours of Sunshine | 4:15 | 7:50 | 8:41 | 7:09 |
| Chances of a Sunny Day | 42% | 53% | 68% | 65% |
| Afternoon Temperatures | 49° | 73° | 89° | 73° |
| Relative Humidity | 74% | 67% | 74% | 71% |
| Chances of a Dry Day | 74% | 77% | 77% | 87% |
| Total Precipitation | 5.2″ | 4.9″ | 5.1″ | 2.9″ |
| Snowfall | 1.4″ | — | — | — |

Comment: Long, warm, sunny summers and short, mild, cloudy winters. Always humid.

# Chicago, IL

## Natural Environment

Chicago is a flat city, built on the rich bottomland of Lake Michigan. The lake is its finest feature; parks and public beaches dot the shoreline from the Indiana border to Wisconsin. A few rolling hills can be found in the southern suburbs, and some small ravines give a bit of contrast to the North Shore. The cornfields and truck farms that once surrounded the city are constantly being wiped out by the spreading metropolis, but a green belt of forest preserves remains, providing cool shade and a bit of quiet countryside for hikers, horseback riders, cyclists, fishers, picnickers, and nature lovers.

MAJOR GEOGRAPHIC FEATURES
Rivers: Chicago, Illinois
Shoreline: Lake Michigan

| Terrain | Open Space | Forests | Inland Water | Shore-line | Rivers | Nature Preser-vation | Nature's Spectac-ulars |
|---|---|---|---|---|---|---|---|
| — | –300 | 100 | 150 | 160 | — | — | — |

Places Rated Score: 110          Places Rated Rank: 107

## Climate

| CHICAGO, IL | January | April | July | October |
|---|---|---|---|---|
| Hours of Sunshine | 4:12 | 7:12 | 10:26 | 6:47 |
| Chances of a Sunny Day | 42% | 47% | 71% | 61% |
| Afternoon Temperatures | 33° | 57° | 82° | 62° |
| Relative Humidity | 72% | 65% | 68% | 67% |
| Chances of a Dry Day | 86% | 80% | 82% | 85% |
| Total Precipitation | 1.9″ | 3.0″ | 3.1″ | 2.7″ |
| Snowfall | 10.5″ | 1.4″ | — | 0.3″ |

Comment: Lakeshore areas may receive heavier snowfalls, but they also get cool lake breezes in the summer.

# Cincinnati, OH–KY

## Natural Environment

Cincinnati is first and foremost a river city. Commerce and transportation grew from its location on the Ohio River. There is not a great deal of variety in the terrain of southwestern Ohio, except for a few hills and bluffs along the river.

MAJOR GEOGRAPHIC FEATURES
Rivers: Great Miami, Little Miami, Ohio

| Terrain | Open Space | Forests | Inland Water | Shore-line | Rivers | Nature Preser-vation | Nature's Spectac-ulars |
|---|---|---|---|---|---|---|---|
| 90 | −200 | 100 | 80 | — | 300 | — | — |

Places Rated Score: 370          Places Rated Rank: 104

## Climate

| CINCINNATI, OH–KY | January | April | July | October |
|---|---|---|---|---|
| Hours of Sunshine | 4:00 | 7:16 | 9:57 | 6:30 |
| Chances of a Sunny Day | 35% | 43% | 61% | 58% |
| Afternoon Temperatures | 38° | 65° | 86° | 67° |
| Relative Humidity | 74% | 65% | 71% | 69% |
| Chances of a Dry Day | 79% | 73% | 77% | 85% |
| Total Precipitation | 3.1″ | 3.7″ | 4.0″ | 2.5″ |
| Snowfall | 5.1″ | 0.5″ | — | 0.1″ |

Comment: An area with moderately hot summers, moderately cold winters, and moderate amounts of moisture.

# Colorado Springs, CO

## Natural Environment

Colorado Springs is in the midst of high mountains and tablelands with considerable relief. Some of the rock formations are particularly unusual and scenic; an example is the Garden of the Gods at the edge of the city. Royal Gorge is spanned by one of the world's highest suspension bridges (for the view from the bottom, take an incline railway ride down into the gorge). Caves and warm springs are additional natural attractions in the area.

MAJOR GEOGRAPHIC FEATURES
Terrain: Front Range, Pikes Peak (14,110 ft.), Rocky Mountains, Wet Mountains
Rivers: Arkansas

NATURE'S SPECTACULARS
Royal Gorge

| Terrain | Open Space | Forests | Inland Water | Shore-line | Rivers | Nature Preser-vation | Nature's Spectac-ulars |
|---|---|---|---|---|---|---|---|
| 650 | 700 | 100 | 20 | — | — | — | 500 |

Places Rated Score: 1,970          Places Rated Rank: 48

## Climate

| COLORADO SPRINGS, CO | January | April | July | October |
|---|---|---|---|---|
| Hours of Sunshine | 7:22 | 9:27 | 11:03 | 8:41 |
| Chances of a Sunny Day | 65% | 63% | 77% | 74% |
| Afternoon Temperatures | 41° | 60° | 85° | 65° |
| Relative Humidity | 50% | 47% | 52% | 45% |
| Chances of a Dry Day | 97% | 90% | 76% | 92% |
| Total Precipitation | 0.3″ | 1.4″ | 2.9″ | 0.8″ |
| Snowfall | 4.5″ | 6.8″ | — | 2.8″ |

Comment: The nearby Rocky Mountains are colder, wetter, and cloudier in almost all seasons.

# Coos Bay–South Coast, OR

## Natural Environment

Oregon's southern coast is marked by wide vistas of the Pacific Ocean. Cliffs and freestanding boulders guard part of the shoreline. In other places forested mountains slope to the sea, the hillsides cut here and there by wild and scenic rivers. Many freshwater lakes and secluded beaches add to the natural beauty and variety.

MAJOR GEOGRAPHIC FEATURES
Terrain: Coast Ranges
Rivers: Rogue, Umpqua
Shoreline: Coos Bay, Pacific Ocean
Other: Cape Blanco

| Terrain | Open Space | Forests | Inland Water | Shore-line | Rivers | Nature Preser-vation | Nature's Spectac-ulars |
|---|---|---|---|---|---|---|---|
| 620 | 700 | 800 | 50 | 600 | 200 | — | — |

Places Rated Score: 2,970          Places Rated Rank: 17

## Climate

| COOS BAY–SOUTH COAST, OR | January | April | July | October |
|---|---|---|---|---|
| Hours of Sunshine | 3:31 | 7:08 | 7:47 | 5:08 |
| Chances of a Sunny Day | 32% | 43% | 52% | 49% |
| Afternoon Temperatures | 51° | 53° | 58° | 58° |
| Relative Humidity | 85% | 81% | 83% | 86% |
| Chances of a Dry Day | 44% | 66% | 96% | 71% |
| Total Precipitation | 13.6″ | 5.3″ | 0.5″ | 5.5″ |

Comment: Heavy fogs roll in from the Pacific during the summer months but dissipate a few miles inland.

# Corpus Christi–Padre Island, TX

## Natural Environment

North Padre Island, separated from the mainland by Laguna Madre, has been set aside for conservation and public enjoyment as Padre Island National Seashore. Dozens of species of shorebirds live on the island or spend part of their migration here.

MAJOR GEOGRAPHIC FEATURES
Shoreline: Corpus Christi Bay, Gulf of Mexico, Laguna Madre
Islands: Mustang, Padre

NATURE-PRESERVATION AREAS
Aransas National Wildlife Refuge
Padre Island National Seashore

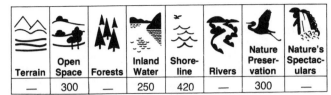

| Terrain | Open Space | Forests | Inland Water | Shore-line | Rivers | Nature Preser-vation | Nature's Spectac-ulars |
|---|---|---|---|---|---|---|---|
| — | 300 | — | 250 | 420 | — | 300 | — |

Places Rated Score: 1,270          Places Rated Rank: 81

## Climate

| CORPUS CHRISTI-NORTH PADRE ISLAND, TX | January | April | July | October |
|---|---|---|---|---|
| Hours of Sunshine | 4:53 | 7:19 | 11:15 | 7:57 |
| Chances of a Sunny Day | 45% | 50% | 81% | 74% |
| Afternoon Temperatures | 67° | 82° | 94° | 84° |
| Relative Humidity | 79% | 77% | 75% | 75% |
| Chances of a Dry Day | 89% | 91% | 91% | 87% |
| Total Precipitation | 1.6" | 2.0" | 2.0" | 3.2" |

Comment: Padre Island and other coastal areas are a bit cooler on summer afternoons and quite a bit warmer on winter mornings.

## ★Crater Lake-Klamath Falls, OR

### Natural Environment

Few areas have a richer mix of natural beauty than this section of Oregon. The mountains to the west of Klamath Falls are filled with lakes and streams; to the east is a semiarid desert. Public buildings in the town are heated by geothermal energy, coming from a subterranean reservoir of high-pressure steam. Crater Lake, cradled in the rim of an extinct volcano, is the deepest lake in the United States. Its color is an incredibly brilliant blue.

MAJOR GEOGRAPHIC FEATURES
   Terrain: Cascade Range, Mount McLoughlin (9,495 ft.)
   Lakes and Reservoirs: Crater Lake, Upper Klamath Lake
   Rivers: Rogue

NATURE-PRESERVATION AREAS
   Bear Valley National Wildlife Refuge
   Crater Lake National Park
   Klamath Forest National Wildlife Refuge
   Oregon Caves National Monument
   Upper Klamath National Wildlife Refuge

NATURE'S SPECTACULARS
   Crater Lake National Park

| Terrain | Open Space | Forests | Inland Water | Shore-line | Rivers | Nature Preser-vation | Nature's Spectac-ulars |
|---|---|---|---|---|---|---|---|
| 880 | 1,000 | 800 | 80 | — | — | 400 | 500 |

Places Rated Score: 3,860          Places Rated Rank: 6

## Climate

| CRATER LAKE, OR | January | April | July | October |
|---|---|---|---|---|
| Hours of Sunshine | 2:16 | 6:50 | 11:51 | 4:39 |
| Chances of a Sunny Day | 31% | 52% | 90% | 63% |
| Afternoon Temperatures | 33° | 42° | 69° | 52° |
| Relative Humidity | 89% | 83% | 74% | 86% |
| Chances of a Dry Day | 48% | 70% | 94% | 74% |
| Total Precipitation | 11.3" | 4.5" | 0.5" | 5.2" |
| Snowfall | 109.1" | 43.3" | — | 21.2" |

Comment: Snow usually closes the Rim Drive from early October until they get it dug out again sometime in July.

| KLAMATH FALLS, OR | January | April | July | October |
|---|---|---|---|---|
| Hours of Sunshine | 2:17 | 6:49 | 11:48 | 4:40 |
| Chances of a Sunny Day | 23% | 47% | 90% | 61% |
| Afternoon Temperatures | 39° | 58° | 85° | 64° |
| Relative Humidity | 75% | 56% | 51% | 61% |
| Chances of a Dry Day | 81% | 90% | 97% | 90% |
| Total Precipitation | 2.1" | 0.7" | 0.2" | 1.2" |
| Snowfall | 14.6" | 1.4" | — | 0.2" |

Comment: Warm, dry, sunny summers and cold, snowy winters offer many opportunities for the hardier vacationer.

## Dallas-Fort Worth, TX

### Natural Environment

This rapidly growing metropolitan area is set on the plains of central Texas. Several lakes north of the city are popular for water sports.

MAJOR GEOGRAPHIC FEATURES
   Lakes and Reservoirs: Eagle Mountain Lake, Lavon Lake, Lewisville Lake
   Rivers: Brazos, Trinity

| Terrain | Open Space | Forests | Inland Water | Shore-line | Rivers | Nature Preser-vation | Nature's Spectac-ulars |
|---|---|---|---|---|---|---|---|
| — | — | 100 | 130 | — | — | — | — |

Places Rated Score: 230          Places Rated Rank: 106

## Climate

| DALLAS-FORT WORTH, TX | January | April | July | October |
|---|---|---|---|---|
| Hours of Sunshine | 5:26 | 8:09 | 11:05 | 7:47 |
| Chances of a Sunny Day | 48% | 53% | 81% | 68% |
| Afternoon Temperatures | 54° | 77° | 98° | 80° |
| Relative Humidity | 69% | 69% | 62% | 69% |
| Chances of a Dry Day | 89% | 80% | 89% | 87% |
| Total Precipitation | 1.7" | 3.6" | 2.0" | 2.5" |
| Snowfall | 1.5" | — | — | — |

Comment: Rainfall is most common at night. Afternoon temperatures usually exceed 90 degrees Fahrenheit from early June through the middle of September.

## Denver-Rocky Mountain National Park, CO

### Natural Environment

Denver, the Mile High City, is at the western end of the high plains of eastern Colorado, with the Rockies rising sharply to the west. While the city itself has had problems with smog and pollution in recent years, the mountains still are havens of brisk, clear air. In Rocky Mountain National Park elevations range from 8,000 feet on the valley floors to 14,255 feet at the top of Longs Peak. There are 59 peaks in the park that top 12,000 feet, making this one of the highest regions in the country.

MAJOR GEOGRAPHIC FEATURES
   Terrain: Front Range, Longs Peak (14,255 ft.), Rocky Mountains
   Lakes and Reservoirs: Carter Lake Reservoir, Lake Granby
   Rivers: South Platte
   Other: Continental Divide

NATURE-PRESERVATION AREAS
   Rocky Mountain National Park

NATURE'S SPECTACULARS
   Rocky Mountain National Park

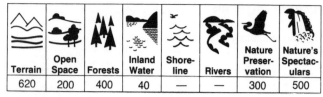

| Terrain | Open Space | Forests | Inland Water | Shore-line | Rivers | Nature Preser-vation | Nature's Spectac-ulars |
|---------|-----------|---------|--------------|-----------|--------|---------------------|----------------------|
| 620 | 200 | 400 | 40 | — | | 300 | 500 |

Places Rated Score: 2,060          Places Rated Rank: 42

## Climate

| DENVER, CO | January | April | July | October |
|------------|---------|-------|------|---------|
| Hours of Sunshine | 6:00 | 9:01 | 10:34 | 8:10 |
| Chances of a Sunny Day | 61% | 60% | 81% | 74% |
| Afternoon Temperatures | 43° | 61° | 88° | 67° |
| Relative Humidity | 55% | 51% | 51% | 50% |
| Chances of a Dry Day | 95% | 89% | 87% | 91% |
| Total Precipitation | 0.5″ | 1.8″ | 1.9″ | 1.0″ |
| Snowfall | 7.8″ | 9.2″ | — | 3.6″ |

Comment: Many Denver residents consider autumn to be the most pleasant time of the year.

| ROCKY MOUNTAIN NATIONAL PARK (EASTERN SLOPE), CO | January | April | July | October |
|------------|---------|-------|------|---------|
| Hours of Sunshine | 6:28 | 8:34 | 10:19 | 7:56 |
| Chances of a Sunny Day | 60% | 57% | 81% | 73% |
| Afternoon Temperatures | 38° | 53° | 79° | 60° |
| Relative Humidity | 51% | 48% | 45% | 44% |
| Chances of a Dry Day | 91% | 85% | 79% | 92% |
| Total Precipitation | 0.4″ | 1.3″ | 2.1″ | 0.8″ |
| Snowfall | 14.0″ | 23.2″ | — | 9.3″ |

Comment: The Hidden Valley area is open for winter sports from about late November to mid-April.

| ROCKY MOUNTAIN NATIONAL PARK (GRAND LAKE AREA), CO | January | April | July | October |
|------------|---------|-------|------|---------|
| Hours of Sunshine | 5:54 | 8:25 | 10:32 | 7:54 |
| Chances of a Sunny Day | 56% | 56% | 82% | 72% |
| Afternoon Temperatures | 30° | 48° | 75° | 57° |
| Relative Humidity | 63% | 58% | 56% | 58% |
| Chances of a Dry Day | 80% | 77% | 80% | 90% |
| Total Precipitation | 1.9″ | 1.8″ | 2.1″ | 1.1″ |
| Snowfall | 26.6″ | 18.8″ | — | 6.5″ |

Comment: The park service tries to get the Trail Ridge Road open each year by Memorial Day. They usually succeed.

## Door County, WI

### Natural Environment

Door Peninsula, reaching like a thumb into Lake Michigan, is a region of small villages, tiny resorts, and rural areas. Colorful spring blooms decorate the fruit orchards; lacy white birches turn a golden yellow in autumn. The blue lake waters are never more than three or four miles away. Native flowers include many species of wild orchids, also called lady's slippers.

MAJOR GEOGRAPHIC FEATURES
 Shoreline: Green Bay, Lake Michigan
 Islands: Chambers, Washington
 Other: Door Peninsula

| Terrain | Open Space | Forests | Inland Water | Shore-line | Rivers | Nature Preser-vation | Nature's Spectac-ulars |
|---------|-----------|---------|--------------|-----------|--------|---------------------|----------------------|
| — | 700 | 400 | 290 | 200 | | — | — |

Places Rated Score: 1,590          Places Rated Rank: 69

## Climate

| DOOR COUNTY, WI | January | April | July | October |
|-----------------|---------|-------|------|---------|
| Hours of Sunshine | 4:10 | 7:13 | 10:03 | 5:17 |
| Chances of a Sunny Day | 45% | 51% | 70% | 53% |
| Afternoon Temperatures | 25° | 52° | 79° | 58° |
| Relative Humidity | 73% | 69% | 71% | 74% |
| Chances of a Dry Day | 88% | 80% | 82% | 84% |
| Total Precipitation | 1.3″ | 2.9″ | 3.4″ | 2.3″ |
| Snowfall | 10.7″ | 2.3″ | — | 0.2″ |

Comment: Sturgeon Bay usually freezes over each winter, but the ice breaks up by late March or early April.

## Eastern Shore, VA

### Natural Environment

Virginia's Eastern Shore is a 70-mile-long peninsula across the Chesapeake Bay from the rest of the state. Along with a few secluded barrier islands, it is a haven for thousands of snow geese and herds of wild ponies. There are saltwater marshes, quiet coves and lagoons, and unspoiled beaches.

MAJOR GEOGRAPHIC FEATURES
 Shoreline: Atlantic Ocean, Chesapeake Bay
 Islands: Assateague, Chincoteague
 Other: Cape Charles

NATURE-PRESERVATION AREAS
 Assateague Island National Seashore
 Chincoteague National Wildlife Refuge

NATURE'S SPECTACULARS
 Virginia Coast Reserve (World Heritage Site)

| Terrain | Open Space | Forests | Inland Water | Shore-line | Rivers | Nature Preser-vation | Nature's Spectac-ulars |
|---------|-----------|---------|--------------|-----------|--------|---------------------|----------------------|
| — | 700 | 100 | 500 | 450 | — | 200 | 500 |

Places Rated Score: 2,450          Places Rated Rank: 27

## Climate

| EASTERN SHORE, VA | January | April | July | October |
|-------------------|---------|-------|------|---------|
| Hours of Sunshine | 5:24 | 8:33 | 9:33 | 6:49 |
| Chances of a Sunny Day | 50% | 58% | 63% | 61% |
| Afternoon Temperatures | 47° | 67° | 86° | 69° |
| Relative Humidity | 68% | 64% | 73% | 74% |
| Chances of a Dry Day | 81% | 80% | 79% | 87% |
| Total Precipitation | 3.4″ | 2.9″ | 4.1″ | 3.6″ |
| Snowfall | 3.6″ | — | — | — |

Comment: The weather is nicer and the crowds are thinner after Labor Day.

## Finger Lakes, NY

### Natural Environment

The 11 long, fingerlike lakes that give this region its identity were scraped into the landscape by glaciers. More than 100 waterfalls have been counted within the city of Ithaca. A few high hills, along with gorges, rapids, and glens, give additional variety to the countryside, a fertile area largely planted in vineyards.

MAJOR GEOGRAPHIC FEATURES
 Terrain: Allegheny Plateau, Appalachian Mountains
 Lakes and Reservoirs: Canandaigua Lake, Cayuga Lake, Owasco Lake, Seneca Lake, Skaneateles Lake
 Rivers: Chenango
 Shoreline: Lake Ontario

NATURE-PRESERVATION AREAS
Montezuma National Wildlife Refuge

| Terrain | Open Space | Forests | Inland Water | Shore-line | Rivers | Nature Preser-vation | Nature's Spectac-ulars |
|---|---|---|---|---|---|---|---|
| 260 | 200 | 400 | 260 | 200 | — | 100 | — |

Places Rated Score: 1,420          Places Rated Rank: 74

## Climate

| FINGER LAKES, NY | January | April | July | October |
|---|---|---|---|---|
| Hours of Sunshine | 3:07 | 6:33 | 9:27 | 4:53 |
| Chances of a Sunny Day | 29% | 43% | 65% | 46% |
| Afternoon Temperatures | 33° | 58° | 83° | 63° |
| Relative Humidity | 76% | 66% | 71% | 74% |
| Chances of a Dry Day | 80% | 73% | 77% | 79% |
| Total Precipitation | 1.8″ | 2.6″ | 2.9″ | 2.9″ |
| Snowfall | 14.8″ | 3.4″ | — | 0.4″ |

Comment: Short, warm summers and long, cold winters. Sunny days are treasured.

# Flaming Gorge, UT–WY–CO

## Natural Environment

Flaming Gorge National Recreation Area, in southwestern Wyoming and eastern Utah, was established in 1968 by Congress, under the management of the National Forest Service. The area consists of more than 100,000 acres of land surrounding (and including) Flaming Gorge Reservoir. This 90-mile-long reservoir is fed by the Green River and is set in scenic desert country, where multicolored mountains, rock formations, and canyons provide an ever-changing backdrop for the reservoir. This is a favorite recreation destination for residents of both Utah and Wyoming.

MAJOR GEOGRAPHIC FEATURES
Terrain: Marsh Peak (12,240 ft.), Rocky Mountains, Uinta Mountains
Lakes and Reservoirs: Flaming Gorge Reservoir
Rivers: Green

NATURE-PRESERVATION AREAS
Browns Park National Wildlife Refuge
Dinosaur National Monument
Flaming Gorge National Recreation Area

| Terrain | Open Space | Forests | Inland Water | Shore-line | Rivers | Nature Preser-vation | Nature's Spectac-ulars |
|---|---|---|---|---|---|---|---|
| 850 | 1,000 | 100 | 110 | — | — | 300 | — |

Places Rated Score: 2,360          Places Rated Rank: 29

## Climate

| FLAMING GORGE, UT–WY–CO | January | April | July | October |
|---|---|---|---|---|
| Hours of Sunshine | 5:19 | 8:55 | 11:52 | 7:55 |
| Chances of a Sunny Day | 48% | 53% | 84% | 69% |
| Afternoon Temperatures | 32° | 56° | 87° | 63° |
| Relative Humidity | 72% | 54% | 38% | 50% |
| Chances of a Dry Day | 95% | 90% | 94% | 94% |
| Total Precipitation | 0.4″ | 0.8″ | 0.6″ | 0.7″ |
| Snowfall | 5.2″ | 4.7″ | — | 2.8″ |

Comment: Short, hot, sunny, dry summers. Long, cold, dry winters. A demanding climate.

# Glacier National Park–Flathead Lake, MT

## Natural Environment

Glacier National Park is a portion of Waterton-Glacier International Peace Park, a huge piece of awe-inspiring landscape that covers more than a million acres in Montana and lies both east and west of the Continental Divide and both north and south of the U.S.–Canadian border. There are high mountains, tablelands with considerable relief, nearly 50 glaciers, and dozens of lakes and streams. Many species of wildlife can be found in abundance, as well as hundreds of types of trees, plants, and flowers. Flathead Lake is the largest natural freshwater lake west of the Mississippi River.

MAJOR GEOGRAPHIC FEATURES
Terrain: Lewis Range, Mount St. Nicholas (9,376 ft.), Rocky Mountains
Lakes and Reservoirs: Flathead Lake, Hungry Horse Reservoir
Other: Continental Divide

NATURE-PRESERVATION AREAS
Glacier National Park
National Bison Range

NATURE'S SPECTACULARS
Glacier National Park

| Terrain | Open Space | Forests | Inland Water | Shore-line | Rivers | Nature Preser-vation | Nature's Spectac-ulars |
|---|---|---|---|---|---|---|---|
| 850 | 1,000 | 600 | 170 | — | — | 400 | 500 |

Places Rated Score: 3,520          Places Rated Rank: 12

## Climate

| GLACIER NATIONAL PARK, MT | January | April | July | October |
|---|---|---|---|---|
| Hours of Sunshine | 2:28 | 7:48 | 12:04 | 5:26 |
| Chances of a Sunny Day | 19% | 33% | 77% | 42% |
| Afternoon Temperatures | 28° | 52° | 80° | 53° |
| Relative Humidity | 77% | 57% | 54% | 67% |
| Chances of a Dry Day | 71% | 80% | 87% | 77% |
| Total Precipitation | 3.6″ | 1.8″ | 1.6″ | 2.2″ |
| Snowfall | 35.4″ | 4.1″ | — | 2.6″ |

Comment: Data are for park headquarters at West Glacier. The eastern slopes of the park are much drier, while the higher elevations are much colder and very much snowier.

| FLATHEAD LAKE, MT | January | April | July | October |
|---|---|---|---|---|
| Hours of Sunshine | 2:35 | 7:30 | 12:10 | 5:36 |
| Chances of a Sunny Day | 21% | 33% | 81% | 44% |
| Afternoon Temperatures | 31° | 56° | 82° | 57° |
| Relative Humidity | 77% | 60% | 59% | 68% |
| Chances of a Dry Day | 87% | 87% | 92% | 87% |
| Total Precipitation | 1.3″ | 1.2″ | 1.1″ | 1.0″ |
| Snowfall | 11.2″ | 0.7″ | — | 0.7″ |

Comment: Flathead Lake occupies a curiously warm pocket in this otherwise quite cold section of the northern Rockies.

# Grand Canyon Country, AZ

## Natural Environment

"In form, size, glowing color, or geological significance, nothing approaches the Grand Canyon of the Colorado River," writes Michael Frome in the Rand McNally National Park Guide. Can there be anyone who has ever glimpsed this natural wonder who would dispute that statement? The abyss is more than a mile deep at its deepest point, more than 18 miles wide at its widest. The enormous variation in elevation causes an even more impressive variation in climate and temperatures, from summer readings as high as 110 degrees Fahrenheit on the floor of the inner canyon to subarctic weather on the North

Rim in winter. But magnificent as the Grand Canyon is, there are also many other natural attractions for visitors to this part of northern Arizona—the lush green, cool forests surrounding the city of Flagstaff, the brilliantly colored Oak Creek Canyon, the unique Painted Desert, and more.

MAJOR GEOGRAPHIC FEATURES
Terrain: Coconino Plateau, Grand Canyon, Humphreys Peak (12,633 ft.), Meteor Crater, Oak Creek Canyon, San Francisco Mountains, Sunset Crater
Lakes and Reservoirs: Lake Mead, Lake Powell
Rivers: Colorado
Other: Glen Canyon Dam, Painted Desert, Petrified Forest

NATURE-PRESERVATION AREAS
Grand Canyon National Park
Petrified Forest National Park
Sunset Crater National Monument

NATURE'S SPECTACULARS
Grand Canyon National Park (World Heritage Site)

| Terrain | Open Space | Forests | Inland Water | Shore-line | Rivers | Nature Preser-vation | Nature's Spectac-ulars |
|---|---|---|---|---|---|---|---|
| 910 | 1,000 | 400 | 40 | — | 200 | 600 | 500 |

Places Rated Score: 3,650          Places Rated Rank: 11

## Climate

**GRAND CANYON NATIONAL PARK (INNER CANYONS AND RIVER), AZ**

| | January | April | July | October |
|---|---|---|---|---|
| Hours of Sunshine | 3:42 | 5:15 | 5:36 | 4:38 |
| Chances of a Sunny Day | 59% | 71% | 82% | 81% |
| Afternoon Temperatures | 55° | 81° | 106° | 84° |
| Relative Humidity | 40% | 21% | 33% | 30% |
| Chances of a Dry Day | 87% | 90% | 87% | 94% |
| Total Precipitation | 0.8″ | 0.5″ | 0.9″ | 0.7″ |

Comment: Fewer hours of sunshine are caused by the shadowing of the canyon walls, not by cloud cover.

**GRAND CANYON NATIONAL PARK (NORTH RIM), AZ**

| | January | April | July | October |
|---|---|---|---|---|
| Hours of Sunshine | 7:04 | 10:06 | 10:21 | 9:06 |
| Chances of a Sunny Day | 56% | 67% | 78% | 77% |
| Afternoon Temperatures | 36° | 52° | 78° | 58° |
| Relative Humidity | 64% | 51% | 55% | 55% |
| Chances of a Dry Day | 74% | 83% | 81% | 87% |
| Total Precipitation | 3.2″ | 1.7″ | 1.8″ | 1.5″ |
| Snowfall | 31.0″ | 10.1″ | — | 4.1″ |

Comment: The only road access is closed by snow from about mid-November to about mid-May.

**GRAND CANYON NATIONAL PARK (SOUTH RIM), AZ**

| | January | April | July | October |
|---|---|---|---|---|
| Hours of Sunshine | 7:15 | 10:29 | 11:03 | 9:21 |
| Chances of a Sunny Day | 58% | 70% | 71% | 77% |
| Afternoon Temperatures | 41° | 60° | 84° | 65° |
| Relative Humidity | 63% | 49% | 52% | 53% |
| Chances of a Dry Day | 87% | 90% | 84% | 90% |
| Total Precipitation | 1.5″ | 0.9″ | 1.9″ | 1.2″ |
| Snowfall | 15.8″ | 3.2″ | — | 0.9″ |

Comment: Summer thundershowers over the canyon are spectacular, as are the snows of winter.

# Green Mountains, VT

## Natural Environment

Vermont's beauty is quiet and understated in comparison with the splashes of color and far-reaching vistas of the West. Except in autumn, that is, when the color of the foliage is as brilliant as any found anywhere. But there is a lovely landscape to be seen at any time of year from almost any window in the Green Mountains, consisting of varicolored forests; low, tree-covered mountains; granite cliffs; clear, rocky streams; and small, mirrorlike lakes. In winter the scene is a black-and-white photo. Snows come early and cover everything in sight for several months.

MAJOR GEOGRAPHIC FEATURES
Terrain: Green Mountains, Mount Mansfield (4,393 ft.)
Lakes and Reservoirs: Lake Champlain
Rivers: Winooski

NATURE-PRESERVATION AREAS
Missisquoi National Wildlife Refuge

| Terrain | Open Space | Forests | Inland Water | Shore-line | Rivers | Nature Preser-vation | Nature's Spectac-ulars |
|---|---|---|---|---|---|---|---|
| 470 | 300 | 600 | 390 | — | — | 100 | — |

Places Rated Score: 1,860          Places Rated Rank: 57

## Climate

**GREEN MOUNTAINS, VT**

| | January | April | July | October |
|---|---|---|---|---|
| Hours of Sunshine | 4:01 | 6:24 | 8:18 | 5:21 |
| Chances of a Sunny Day | 42% | 43% | 53% | 49% |
| Afternoon Temperatures | 27° | 48° | 75° | 56° |
| Relative Humidity | 68% | 66% | 70% | 76% |
| Chances of a Dry Day | 77% | 74% | 75% | 78% |
| Total Precipitation | 4.5″ | 4.6″ | 4.4″ | 4.2″ |
| Snowfall | 23.4″ | 9.6″ | — | 1.0″ |

Comment: Short, mild summers and long, cold winters. Some early morning fog in the valleys.

**BURLINGTON, VT**

| | January | April | July | October |
|---|---|---|---|---|
| Hours of Sunshine | 3:48 | 6:36 | 9:43 | 5:18 |
| Chances of a Sunny Day | 35% | 43% | 58% | 45% |
| Afternoon Temperatures | 25° | 53° | 81° | 57° |
| Relative Humidity | 67% | 64% | 68% | 72% |
| Chances of a Dry Day | 80% | 77% | 77% | 79% |
| Total Precipitation | 1.9″ | 2.8″ | 3.4″ | 2.8″ |
| Snowfall | 18.5″ | 4.0″ | — | 0.2″ |

Comment: Winter lakeshore temperatures are slightly warmer than those shown in the data. Delightfully cool summers.

# ★Hawaii

## Natural Environment

Hawaii's varied nature includes warm waters for surfing and swimming year-round, subtropical vegetation and rain forests, and even snow skiing on the slopes of its highest mountain in winter. Its beaches and volcanoes are without equal anywhere else in the United States, as are its constant warm weather and sunshine. Warm coats are needed for forays into the mountains, and rain gear for certain spots, but at the beaches it is never cold.

MAJOR GEOGRAPHIC FEATURES
Terrain: Diamond Head (760 ft.), Haleakala Crater (10,023 ft.), Kilauea Crater (4,090 ft.), Mauna Kea (13,796 ft.), Mauna Loa (13,679 ft.)
Shoreline: Kaneohe Bay, Mamala Bay, Pacific Ocean

NATURE-PRESERVATION AREAS
  Haleakala National Park
  Hanalei National Wildlife Refuge
  Hawaii Volcanoes National Park
  James C. Campbell National Wildlife Refuge
  Kakahaia National Wildlife Refuge
  Kilauea Point National Wildlife Refuge
  Pearl Harbor National Wildlife Refuge

NATURE'S SPECTACULARS
  Haleakala National Park
  Hawaii Volcanoes National Park

| Terrain | Open Space | Forests | Inland Water | Shore-line | Rivers | Nature Preser-vation | Nature's Spectac-ulars |
|---|---|---|---|---|---|---|---|
| 850 | 300 | 800 | 30 | 800 | — | 600 | 700 |

Places Rated Score: 4,080          Places Rated Rank: 5

## Climate

| HALEAKALA NATIONAL PARK (MAUI), HI | January | April | July | October |
|---|---|---|---|---|
| Hours of Sunshine | 7:17 | 8:05 | 9:41 | 8:11 |
| Chances of a Sunny Day | 74% | 63% | 84% | 77% |
| Afternoon Temperatures | 59° | 61° | 66° | 65° |
| Relative Humidity | 83% | 75% | 70% | 73% |
| Chances of a Dry Day | 77% | 77% | 84% | 84% |
| Total Precipitation | 10.2″ | 4.5″ | 2.1″ | 2.5″ |

Comment: Very rare snowfalls near the summit can leave up to a foot of snow.

| HILO (HAWAII), HI | January | April | July | October |
|---|---|---|---|---|
| Hours of Sunshine | 5:13 | 4:32 | 5:33 | 4:34 |
| Chances of a Sunny Day | 58% | 30% | 42% | 45% |
| Afternoon Temperatures | 80° | 80° | 83° | 83° |
| Relative Humidity | 75% | 79% | 78% | 78% |
| Chances of a Dry Day | 56% | 32% | 33% | 43% |
| Total Precipitation | 9.4″ | 13.1″ | 8.7″ | 10.0″ |

Comment: Hilo's climate is typical of the cloudier and rainier windward coasts of the Hawaiian islands.

| HONOLULU (OAHU), HI | January | April | July | October |
|---|---|---|---|---|
| Hours of Sunshine | 6:43 | 8:21 | 9:42 | 7:56 |
| Chances of a Sunny Day | 71% | 63% | 84% | 74% |
| Afternoon Temperatures | 80° | 83° | 87° | 87° |
| Relative Humidity | 73% | 66% | 62% | 64% |
| Chances of a Dry Day | 81% | 89% | 93% | 88% |
| Total Precipitation | 3.8″ | 1.5″ | 0.5″ | 1.9″ |

Comment: Honolulu's climate is typical of the sunnier and drier leeward coasts of the Hawaiian islands.

# Hilton Head, SC

## Natural Environment

Hilton Head Island, like Charleston, is in South Carolina's hot and humid Low Country. The developers of this resort community have been careful to conserve and improve on the native vegetation of the island; the landscaping is lush and plentiful.

MAJOR GEOGRAPHIC FEATURES
  Shoreline: Atlantic Ocean, Port Royal Sound, St. Helena Sound
  Islands: Hilton Head, Parris

NATURE-PRESERVATION AREAS
  Pinckney Island National Wildlife Refuge

| Terrain | Open Space | Forests | Inland Water | Shore-line | Rivers | Nature Preser-vation | Nature's Spectac-ulars |
|---|---|---|---|---|---|---|---|
| — | 300 | 100 | 500 | 600 | — | 100 | — |

Places Rated Score: 1,600          Places Rated Rank: 68

## Climate

| HILTON HEAD, SC | January | April | July | October |
|---|---|---|---|---|
| Hours of Sunshine | 5:45 | 9:07 | 8:55 | 7:22 |
| Chances of a Sunny Day | 48% | 63% | 57% | 65% |
| Afternoon Temperatures | 60° | 75° | 89° | 77° |
| Relative Humidity | 70% | 67% | 76% | 72% |
| Chances of a Dry Day | 82% | 83% | 68% | 88% |
| Total Precipitation | 2.3″ | 2.4″ | 6.1″ | 3.2″ |

Comment: Spring and fall are this popular resort area's most pleasant seasons.

# Holland–Lake Michigan Shore, MI

## Natural Environment

The waters of Lake Michigan and the high dunes along its shores have attracted vacationers from Detroit and Chicago for decades. The story is told that tourism started here when city people discovered that they could pick and buy berries and cherries from Michigan fruit farmers. They traveled here by train, then sought accommodations for over-night stays. Country lanes lead to pleasant farmlands and orchards; in autumn they are shaded with colorful foliage.

MAJOR GEOGRAPHIC FEATURES
  Shoreline: Lake Michigan

| Terrain | Open Space | Forests | Inland Water | Shore-line | Rivers | Nature Preser-vation | Nature's Spectac-ulars |
|---|---|---|---|---|---|---|---|
| — | 200 | 100 | 190 | 200 | — | — | — |

Places Rated Score: 690          Places Rated Rank: 95

## Climate

| HOLLAND–LAKE MICHIGAN SHORE, MI | January | April | July | October |
|---|---|---|---|---|
| Hours of Sunshine | 2:35 | 7:13 | 10:24 | 5:19 |
| Chances of a Sunny Day | 19% | 45% | 71% | 48% |
| Afternoon Temperatures | 31° | 57° | 82° | 62° |
| Relative Humidity | 78% | 67% | 72% | 74% |
| Chances of a Dry Day | 79% | 77% | 84% | 81% |
| Total Precipitation | 2.3″ | 3.6″ | 3.2″ | 3.1″ |
| Snowfall | 20.8″ | 1.3″ | — | 0.7″ |

Comment: Steady winds off of Lake Michigan delay spring and lengthen autumn. Late summer and early autumn are the best seasons.

# Houston–Galveston, TX

## Natural Environment

Vacationers looking for natural beauty and outdoor enjoyment head for Galveston Island and its 32 miles of clean sand beach. Many species of birds inhabit the salt marshes of the island. Torrential rainstorms and now and then a hurricane have created problems for both cities.

MAJOR GEOGRAPHIC FEATURES
  Lakes and Reservoirs: Lake Houston
  Rivers: Brazos
  Shoreline: Galveston Bay, Gulf of Mexico
  Islands: Galveston

NATURE-PRESERVATION AREAS
  Anahuac National Wildlife Refuge
  Attwater Prairie Chicken National Wildlife Refuge
  Brazoria National Wildlife Refuge
  McFaddin National Wildlife Refuge
  San Bernard National Wildlife Refuge
  Texas Point National Wildlife Refuge

| Terrain | Open Space | Forests | Inland Water | Shore-line | Rivers | Nature Preser-vation | Nature's Spectac-ulars |
|---------|-----------|---------|--------------|-----------|--------|---------------------|------------------------|
| — | — | 400 | 190 | 450 | — | 100 | — |

Places Rated Score: 1,140          Places Rated Rank: 85

## Climate

| HOUSTON–GALVESTON, TX | January | April | July | October |
|-----------------------|---------|-------|------|---------|
| Hours of Sunshine | 4:58 | 7:34 | 9:52 | 8:08 |
| Chances of a Sunny Day | 38% | 41% | 71% | 70% |
| Afternoon Temperatures | 62° | 79° | 94° | 82° |
| Relative Humidity | 79% | 78% | 76% | 73% |
| Chances of a Dry Day | 83% | 87% | 84% | 87% |
| Total Precipitation | 3.1″ | 3.4″ | 3.6″ | 3.1″ |

Comment: Coastal temperatures are slightly cooler on summer
  afternoons and warmer on winter mornings.

# Jersey Shore, NJ

## Natural Environment

Miles and miles and miles of beaches, invigorating surf, and pleasant
temperatures are the physical attractions of the Jersey Shore. At the
north end of the shore, Gateway National Recreation Area at Sandy
Hook is a barrier peninsula with popular beaches.

MAJOR GEOGRAPHIC FEATURES
  Shoreline: Atlantic Ocean, Barnegat Bay
  Other: Long Beach, Sandy Hook

NATURE-PRESERVATION AREAS
  Barnegat National Wildlife Refuge
  Gateway National Recreation Area

| Terrain | Open Space | Forests | Inland Water | Shore-line | Rivers | Nature Preser-vation | Nature's Spectac-ulars |
|---------|-----------|---------|--------------|-----------|--------|---------------------|------------------------|
| — | −200 | 400 | 480 | 720 | — | 100 | — |

Places Rated Score: 1,500          Places Rated Rank: 71

## Climate

| JERSEY SHORE, NJ | January | April | July | October |
|------------------|---------|-------|------|---------|
| Hours of Sunshine | 4:57 | 7:41 | 9:25 | 6:36 |
| Chances of a Sunny Day | 53% | 57% | 61% | 63% |
| Afternoon Temperatures | 40° | 56° | 83° | 65° |
| Relative Humidity | 70% | 67% | 74% | 71% |
| Chances of a Dry Day | 81% | 77% | 83% | 84% |
| Total Precipitation | 3.7″ | 3.8″ | 4.5″ | 3.7″ |
| Snowfall | 6.7″ | 0.6″ | — | — |

Comment: This seashore climate is at its very best in September.

# Knoxville–Smoky Mountains, TN

## Natural Environment

Knoxville sits in a valley between the Great Smoky Mountains and the
Cumberland Mountains. It is a gateway to the wonderful, vast wilderness areas of Great Smoky Mountains National Park. This area is
especially blessed with natural beauty and variety: there are lakes and
streams for swimming, rafting, and fishing; caves for exploring; hills,
cliffs, and mountains for climbing. It would be hard to choose among
the seasons for the best time to visit the Smokies. The colors of both
spring blooms and autumn leaves are outstanding.

MAJOR GEOGRAPHIC FEATURES
  Terrain: Appalachian Mountains, Clingmans Dome (6,643 ft.),
    Great Smoky Mountains
  Lakes and Reservoirs: Cherokee Lake, Douglas Lake, Norris
    Lake, Watts Bar Lake
  Rivers: Tennessee

NATURE-PRESERVATION AREAS
  Great Smoky Mountains National Park

NATURE'S SPECTACULARS
  Great Smoky Mountains National Park (World Heritage Site)

| Terrain | Open Space | Forests | Inland Water | Shore-line | Rivers | Nature Preser-vation | Nature's Spectac-ulars |
|---------|-----------|---------|--------------|-----------|--------|---------------------|------------------------|
| 500 | 200 | 400 | 50 | — | — | 300 | 500 |

Places Rated Score: 1,950          Places Rated Rank: 52

## Climate

| KNOXVILLE, TN | January | April | July | October |
|---------------|---------|-------|------|---------|
| Hours of Sunshine | 3:51 | 8:02 | 9:00 | 6:52 |
| Chances of a Sunny Day | 42% | 57% | 65% | 65% |
| Afternoon Temperatures | 47° | 71° | 87° | 71° |
| Relative Humidity | 72% | 66% | 76% | 73% |
| Chances of a Dry Day | 71% | 74% | 77% | 85% |
| Total Precipitation | 4.7″ | 3.9″ | 4.3″ | 2.7″ |
| Snowfall | 3.9″ | 0.2″ | — | — |

Comment: From late June through early September, thunderstorms
  can be heard about one day in three.

| SMOKY MOUNTAINS, TN | January | April | July | October |
|---------------------|---------|-------|------|---------|
| Hours of Sunshine | 4:44 | 8:19 | 8:40 | 6:54 |
| Chances of a Sunny Day | 47% | 60% | 61% | 65% |
| Afternoon Temperatures | 42° | 61° | 76° | 62° |
| Relative Humidity | 75% | 67% | 85% | 84% |
| Chances of a Dry Day | 73% | 73% | 69% | 82% |
| Total Precipitation | 3.9″ | 4.4″ | 4.8″ | 3.6″ |
| Snowfall | 8.2″ | 1.2″ | — | 0.3″ |

Comment: These conditions are typical of the higher (over 3,000
  feet) resort communities of the Great Smokies area.

# Lake of the Ozarks, MO

## Natural Environment

The landscape around the Lake of the Ozarks offers open hills, green
forests, and rolling farmland. This lake is the largest in the state, with
1,375 miles of shoreline. Some of the shore has been heavily
developed with resorts; part of it is nearly wilderness.

MAJOR GEOGRAPHIC FEATURES
  Terrain: Ozark Plateau
  Lakes and Reservoirs: Harry S. Truman Reservoir, Lake of the
    Ozarks, Pomme de Terre Reservoir
  Rivers: Osage

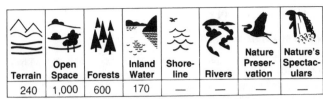

| Terrain | Open Space | Forests | Inland Water | Shore-line | Rivers | Nature Preser-vation | Nature's Spectac-ulars |
|---|---|---|---|---|---|---|---|
| 240 | 1,000 | 600 | 170 | — | — | — | — |

Places Rated Score: 2,010 — Places Rated Rank: 45

## Climate

| LAKE OF THE OZARKS, MO | January | April | July | October |
|---|---|---|---|---|
| Hours of Sunshine | 4:58 | 7:35 | 10:19 | 7:05 |
| Chances of a Sunny Day | 47% | 50% | 69% | 63% |
| Afternoon Temperatures | 42° | 71° | 92° | 73° |
| Relative Humidity | 70% | 66% | 70% | 69% |
| Chances of a Dry Day | 87% | 77% | 82% | 84% |
| Total Precipitation | 1.6″ | 3.9″ | 3.9″ | 3.6″ |
| Snowfall | 4.3″ | 0.3″ | — | 0.1″ |

Comment: A good climate for fishing in spring, water sports in summer, and sightseeing in autumn.

## Lake Powell–Glen Canyon, AZ–UT

### Natural Environment

Lake Powell is the second largest man-made reservoir in the United States. Its nearly 2,000 miles of shoreline is virtually undeveloped. There are 96 side canyons, plus uncounted rock formations, islands, inlets, caves, and coves. Plains with high mountains and tablelands with very high relief create awesome spectacles.

MAJOR GEOGRAPHIC FEATURES
    Terrain: Glen Canyon, Henry Mountains, Monument Valley, Mount Pennell (11,371 ft.), Rocky Mountains
    Lakes and Reservoirs: Lake Powell
    Rivers: Colorado

NATURE-PRESERVATION AREAS
    Arches National Park
    Canyonlands National Park
    Capitol Reef National Park
    Glen Canyon National Recreation Area
    Hovenweep National Monument
    Natural Bridges National Monument
    Rainbow Bridge National Monument

| Terrain | Open Space | Forests | Inland Water | Shore-line | Rivers | Nature Preser-vation | Nature's Spectac-ulars |
|---|---|---|---|---|---|---|---|
| 1,120 | 1,000 | 400 | 120 | — | 200 | 600 | — |

Places Rated Score: 3,440 — Places Rated Rank: 13

## Climate

| LAKE POWELL–GLEN CANYON, AZ–UT | January | April | July | October |
|---|---|---|---|---|
| Hours of Sunshine | 7:05 | 10:16 | 11:16 | 9:18 |
| Chances of a Sunny Day | 55% | 64% | 80% | 76% |
| Afternoon Temperatures | 47° | 74° | 100° | 77° |
| Relative Humidity | 48% | 26% | 21% | 31% |
| Chances of a Dry Day | 95% | 94% | 96% | 94% |
| Total Precipitation | 0.5″ | 0.4″ | 0.6″ | 0.6″ |
| Snowfall | 1.3″ | — | — | — |

Comment: Boaters should watch for very strong winds up the lake in late spring and early summer.

## Lake Tahoe–Reno, NV–CA

### Natural Environment

Lake Tahoe is the largest Alpine lake in North America and the second deepest. Mark Twain said of it, "it must surely be the fairest picture the whole earth affords." Situated at 6,000 feet above sea level, the deep-blue lake and the snow-tipped high Sierra reflected on its surface certainly tempt one to use such superlatives in describing it. The surrounding countryside consists of open high mountains and plains with vistas of low and high mountains.

MAJOR GEOGRAPHIC FEATURES
    Terrain: Freel Peak (10,881 ft.), Mount Grant (11,239 ft.), Sierra Nevada, Wassuk Range
    Lakes and Reservoirs: Lake Tahoe, Pyramid Lake

| Terrain | Open Space | Forests | Inland Water | Shore-line | Rivers | Nature Preser-vation | Nature's Spectac-ulars |
|---|---|---|---|---|---|---|---|
| 940 | 700 | 100 | 220 | — | — | — | — |

Places Rated Score: 1,960 — Places Rated Rank: 50

## Climate

| LAKE TAHOE, CA | January | April | July | October |
|---|---|---|---|---|
| Hours of Sunshine | 5:24 | 10:43 | 13:53 | 9:28 |
| Chances of a Sunny Day | 45% | 57% | 97% | 71% |
| Afternoon Temperatures | 38° | 52° | 79° | 59° |
| Relative Humidity | 77% | 58% | 41% | 55% |
| Chances of a Dry Day | 71% | 85% | 97% | 90% |
| Total Precipitation | 5.1″ | 1.8″ | 0.3″ | 1.3″ |
| Snowfall | 45.5″ | 16.0″ | — | 2.3″ |

Comment: The nearby Squaw Valley winter sports area gets about 270 inches of snow each year.

| RENO, NV | January | April | July | October |
|---|---|---|---|---|
| Hours of Sunshine | 6:26 | 10:43 | 13:38 | 9:24 |
| Chances of a Sunny Day | 52% | 63% | 94% | 74% |
| Afternoon Temperatures | 45° | 63° | 91° | 70° |
| Relative Humidity | 64% | 48% | 42% | 50% |
| Chances of a Dry Day | 89% | 96% | 97% | 96% |
| Total Precipitation | 1.2″ | 0.5″ | 0.3″ | 0.3″ |
| Snowfall | 6.1″ | 1.5″ | — | 0.3″ |

Comment: Reno's climate is a mountain one. Frosty mornings can be expected from late September through early May.

## Las Vegas–Lake Mead, NV–AZ

### Natural Environment

Some visitors to Las Vegas may never get beyond its casinos and theaters; if so, they will be missing some of the best scenery in the Southwest. The Valley of Fire, north of the city, has thousands of acres of huge shifting sand dunes, complemented by labyrinths of fire-red and gleaming-white sandstone sculptures. Three lakes in the area have been formed by dams on the Colorado River—Mead, Mohave, and Havasu. There are plains with high mountains and tablelands with very high relief. Bullhead City, Arizona, a few miles south of Lake Mohave, is often cited by newscasters for having the highest temperature reading in the country on a given day.

MAJOR GEOGRAPHIC FEATURES
    Terrain: Charleston Peak (11,918 ft.), Sheer Range, Spring Mountains
    Lakes and Reservoirs: Lake Havasu, Lake Mead, Lake Mohave
    Rivers: Colorado
    Other: Mohave Desert

NATURE-PRESERVATION AREAS
    Lake Mead National Recreation Area

| Terrain | Open Space | Forests | Inland Water | Shore-line | Rivers | Nature Preser-vation | Nature's Spectac-ulars |
|---|---|---|---|---|---|---|---|
| 680 | 700 | 100 | 150 | — | 200 | 100 | — |

Places Rated Score: 1,930          Places Rated Rank: 53

## Climate

| LAS VEGAS, NV | January | April | July | October |
|---|---|---|---|---|
| Hours of Sunshine | 7:37 | 11:16 | 12:30 | 9:50 |
| Chances of a Sunny Day | 65% | 80% | 90% | 87% |
| Afternoon Temperatures | 56° | 77° | 105° | 82° |
| Relative Humidity | 43% | 25% | 21% | 29% |
| Chances of a Dry Day | 97% | 97% | 97% | 97% |
| Total Precipitation | 0.5" | 0.2" | 0.5" | 0.3" |
| Snowfall | 1.3" | — | — | — |

Comment: Only about one winter in four brings any measurable snowfall.

| LAKE MEAD, NV–AZ | January | April | July | October |
|---|---|---|---|---|
| Hours of Sunshine | 7:37 | 11:16 | 12:29 | 9:50 |
| Chances of a Sunny Day | 65% | 80% | 90% | 87% |
| Afternoon Temperatures | 54° | 76° | 102° | 80° |
| Relative Humidity | 45% | 24% | 20% | 28% |
| Chances of a Dry Day | 94% | 97% | 96% | 97% |
| Total Precipitation | 0.6" | 0.4" | 0.5" | 0.4" |
| Snowfall | 1.6" | — | — | — |

Comment: With clear skies, low humidities, and reflections off of the lake, summer sunburns can develop in minutes.

# Lexington–Bluegrass Country, KY

## Natural Environment

Northern Kentucky has a rolling landscape, with open hills, farmlands and pastures, and small rivers and streams. The deep blue-green grass cultivated here covers lawns and pastures and gives the area its popular name. White fences outline fields in which Thoroughbred horses graze. Thick hardwood forests mark the western edge of the Cumberland Plateau.

MAJOR GEOGRAPHIC FEATURES
  Rivers: Kentucky, Ohio

| Terrain | Open Space | Forests | Inland Water | Shore-line | Rivers | Nature Preser-vation | Nature's Spectac-ulars |
|---|---|---|---|---|---|---|---|
| 180 | 200 | 100 | 20 | — | 200 | — | — |

Places Rated Score: 700          Places Rated Rank: 94

## Climate

| LEXINGTON–BLUEGRASS COUNTRY, KY | January | April | July | October |
|---|---|---|---|---|
| Hours of Sunshine | 3:33 | 6:59 | 9:18 | 6:31 |
| Chances of a Sunny Day | 39% | 50% | 65% | 65% |
| Afternoon Temperatures | 40° | 66° | 86° | 68° |
| Relative Humidity | 75% | 65% | 72% | 70% |
| Chances of a Dry Day | 77% | 73% | 74% | 85% |
| Total Precipitation | 3.6" | 4.0" | 5.0" | 2.3" |
| Snowfall | 6.1" | — | — | — |

Comment: Weather comes in spells lasting about three to five days. September and October are local favorites.

# Long Island, NY

## Natural Environment

Water is the main attraction here. The island is flat and heavily populated in most places.

MAJOR GEOGRAPHIC FEATURES
  Shoreline: Atlantic Ocean, Block Island Sound, Great Peconic Bay, Long Island Sound
  Islands: Fire, Long

NATURE-PRESERVATION AREAS
  Fire Island National Seashore
  Morton National Wildlife Refuge
  Oyster Bay National Wildlife Refuge
  Target Rock National Wildlife Refuge

| Terrain | Open Space | Forests | Inland Water | Shore-line | Rivers | Nature Preser-vation | Nature's Spectac-ulars |
|---|---|---|---|---|---|---|---|
| — | –300 | 600 | 500 | 800 | — | 200 | — |

Places Rated Score: 1,800          Places Rated Rank: 61

## Climate

| LONG ISLAND, NY | January | April | July | October |
|---|---|---|---|---|
| Hours of Sunshine | 4:42 | 7:40 | 9:32 | 6:48 |
| Chances of a Sunny Day | 54% | 56% | 61% | 63% |
| Afternoon Temperatures | 38° | 55° | 79° | 63° |
| Relative Humidity | 73% | 75% | 78% | 77% |
| Chances of a Dry Day | 77% | 77% | 84% | 84% |
| Total Precipitation | 4.2" | 3.7" | 2.8" | 3.7" |
| Snowfall | 8.1" | 0.3" | — | — |

Comment: This popular resort area has summers like Portland, Maine, and winters like Washington, DC.

# Los Angeles, CA

## Natural Environment

High and low mountains ring the Los Angeles basin. They are both an advantage and a curse, furnishing interest to the horizon, a welcome escape from the city's heat, a wide variety of recreational opportunities, and a barrier between the metropolitan area and the Mohave Desert. On the other hand, they form a trap for the city's infamous smog. Sun worshipers love Los Angeles and its environs: beaches are easily accessible, the subtropical vegetation is gorgeous, and it is never cold.

MAJOR GEOGRAPHIC FEATURES
  Terrain: Mount San Antonio (10,064 ft.), San Gabriel Mountains
  Shoreline: Pacific Ocean, San Pedro Bay, Santa Monica Bay
  Islands: Santa Catalina

NATURE-PRESERVATION AREAS
  Santa Monica Mountains National Recreation Area

| Terrain | Open Space | Forests | Inland Water | Shore-line | Rivers | Nature Preser-vation | Nature's Spectac-ulars |
|---|---|---|---|---|---|---|---|
| 710 | –300 | 400 | 40 | 510 | — | 100 | — |

Places Rated Score: 1,460          Places Rated Rank: 72

## Climate

| LOS ANGELES, CA | January | April | July | October |
|---|---|---|---|---|
| Hours of Sunshine | 7:01 | 9:07 | 11:38 | 8:18 |
| Chances of a Sunny Day | 71% | 73% | 97% | 81% |
| Afternoon Temperatures | 67° | 71° | 84° | 79° |
| Relative Humidity | 56% | 64% | 67% | 62% |
| Chances of a Dry Day | 84% | 92% | 99% | 98% |
| Total Precipitation | 3.7" | 1.2" | — | 0.2" |

Comment: Everybody's idea of the ideal southern California climate.

# Mackinac Island–Sault Ste. Marie, MI

## Natural Environment

The short drive from St. Ignace to Sault Ste. Marie offers views of three of the Great Lakes—Superior, the largest single body of fresh water in the world; Huron, with shores that in places resemble the rock-bound coast of Maine; and Michigan, graced by long stretches of sandy beach and high dunes. Mackinac Island is unspoiled by the fumes of gasoline—no automobiles are permitted on the island. This part of the state is heavily forested, with pine, oak, sumac, and birch.

MAJOR GEOGRAPHIC FEATURES
Lakes and Reservoirs: Burt Lake, Mullet Lake
Shoreline: Lake Huron, Lake Michigan, Lake Superior, Straits of Mackinac

| Terrain | Open Space | Forests | Inland Water | Shore-line | Rivers | Nature Preser-vation | Nature's Spectac-ulars |
|---|---|---|---|---|---|---|---|
| — | 1,000 | 600 | 500 | 600 | — | — | — |

Places Rated Score: 2,700       Places Rated Rank: 22

## Climate

| MACKINAC ISLAND–SAULT STE. MARIE, MI | January | April | July | October |
|---|---|---|---|---|
| Hours of Sunshine | 3:10 | 7:27 | 9:43 | 4:23 |
| Chances of a Sunny Day | 32% | 47% | 61% | 39% |
| Afternoon Temperatures | 21° | 47° | 75° | 54° |
| Relative Humidity | 78% | 71% | 76% | 78% |
| Chances of a Dry Day | 82% | 81% | 84% | 79% |
| Total Precipitation | 2.2" | 2.4" | 3.0" | 2.9" |
| Snowfall | 28.0" | 5.4" | — | 2.3" |

Comment: Mackinac Island's climate is a bit less harsh than shown in the data.

# Memphis, TN–AR–MS

## Natural Environment

Memphis is another river city: everything relates to the Mississippi. Residents are fond of claiming that "the Mississippi Delta begins in the lobby of the Peabody Hotel." A short distance away from the hustle and bustle of this, one of the largest cities in the Southeast, are quiet woods and rural areas of Tennessee, Arkansas, and Mississippi. The scenery is serene rather than spectacular.

MAJOR GEOGRAPHIC FEATURES
Lakes and Reservoirs: Arkabutla Lake
Rivers: Mississippi

NATURE-PRESERVATION AREAS
Wapanocca National Wildlife Refuge

| Terrain | Open Space | Forests | Inland Water | Shore-line | Rivers | Nature Preser-vation | Nature's Spectac-ulars |
|---|---|---|---|---|---|---|---|
| — | — | 100 | 160 | — | 200 | 100 | — |

Places Rated Score: 560       Places Rated Rank: 99

## Climate

| MEMPHIS, TN | January | April | July | October |
|---|---|---|---|---|
| Hours of Sunshine | 5:03 | 8:22 | 10:34 | 8:03 |
| Chances of a Sunny Day | 45% | 53% | 71% | 71% |
| Afternoon Temperatures | 48° | 73° | 92° | 75° |
| Relative Humidity | 71% | 66% | 71% | 67% |
| Chances of a Dry Day | 77% | 75% | 81% | 87% |
| Total Precipitation | 4.6" | 5.8" | 4.0" | 2.4" |
| Snowfall | 2.3" | — | — | — |

Comment: The climate of Memphis, with its long hot summers and short mild winters, is much more southern than midwestern.

# Miami–Gold Coast–Keys, FL

## Natural Environment

Florida's southeast coast and the Keys have been so attractive to so many vacationers during this century that environmentalists are forced to wage a constant battle to preserve the very elements that originally brought people in—the fish-filled waters, the wetlands where food for the fish is grown, and the untamed subtropical vegetation. Year-round warm weather, the ocean, the Gulf, the Everglades, the birds, the coral reefs—there's no place else quite like this.

MAJOR GEOGRAPHIC FEATURES
Shoreline: Atlantic Ocean, Biscayne Bay, Florida Bay, Gulf of Mexico, Straits of Florida
Islands: Florida Keys
Other: Cape Sable, Everglades

NATURE-PRESERVATION AREAS
Biscayne National Park
Everglades National Park
Great White Heron National Wildlife Refuge
Key West National Wildlife Refuge
Loxahatchee National Wildlife Refuge
National Key Deer Refuge

| Terrain | Open Space | Forests | Inland Water | Shore-line | Rivers | Nature Preser-vation | Nature's Spectac-ulars |
|---|---|---|---|---|---|---|---|
| — | −200 | 100 | 430 | 1,000 | — | 500 | — |

Places Rated Score: 1,830       Places Rated Rank: 58

## Climate

| MIAMI–GOLD COAST, FL | January | April | July | October |
|---|---|---|---|---|
| Hours of Sunshine | 7:06 | 9:27 | 9:05 | 7:20 |
| Chances of a Sunny Day | 71% | 77% | 65% | 65% |
| Afternoon Temperatures | 75° | 82° | 89° | 84° |
| Relative Humidity | 72% | 67% | 74% | 76% |
| Chances of a Dry Day | 89% | 86% | 66% | 69% |
| Total Precipitation | 2.1" | 3.1" | 6.0" | 7.1" |

Comment: Hurricanes are rare—about one year in seven—and are most likely in September and October.

## KEYS, FL

| | January | April | July | October |
|---|---|---|---|---|
| Hours of Sunshine | 7:53 | 10:42 | 10:24 | 8:07 |
| Chances of a Sunny Day | 71% | 83% | 68% | 68% |
| Afternoon Temperatures | 72° | 82° | 89° | 84° |
| Relative Humidity | 76% | 71% | 72% | 76% |
| Chances of a Dry Day | 86% | 86% | 79% | 72% |
| Total Precipitation | 1.7″ | 1.5″ | 3.7″ | 4.8″ |

Comment: There is no record of Key West ever having had frost, snow, sleet, or freezing rain. A true subtropical climate.

# Minneapolis–St. Paul, MN–WI

## Natural Environment

Despite its severe winter weather, the Minneapolis–St. Paul area is one of the country's most attractive metro areas. The terrain features a few green, low hills. Land of 10,000 Lakes, the state boasts; recent counts have upped the figure to nearly 12,000. The large lakes lie to the north of the Twin Cities, but scores of small ones are situated within and all around the cities.

MAJOR GEOGRAPHIC FEATURES
Lakes and Reservoirs: Lake Minnetonka
Rivers: Mississippi, St. Croix

NATURE-PRESERVATION AREAS
Lower St. Croix National Scenic River
Minnesota Valley National Wildlife Refuge
Sherburne National Wildlife Refuge

| Terrain | Open Space | Forests | Inland Water | Shore-line | Rivers | Nature Preser-vation | Nature's Spectac-ulars |
|---|---|---|---|---|---|---|---|
| 90 | — | 100 | 210 | — | 300 | 100 | — |

Places Rated Score: 800          Places Rated Rank: 92

## Climate

### MINNEAPOLIS–ST. PAUL, MN

| | January | April | July | October |
|---|---|---|---|---|
| Hours of Sunshine | 4:48 | 7:33 | 10:49 | 6:10 |
| Chances of a Sunny Day | 52% | 50% | 71% | 58% |
| Afternoon Temperatures | 20° | 56° | 83° | 60° |
| Relative Humidity | 69% | 64% | 67% | 70% |
| Chances of a Dry Day | 92% | 82% | 79% | 84% |
| Total Precipitation | 0.8″ | 2.1″ | 3.5″ | 1.9″ |
| Snowfall | 9.9″ | 3.1″ | — | 0.4″ |

Comment: A changeable and invigorating climate. Short, warm summers and long, very cold winters.

# Mobile Bay–Gulfport, AL–MS

## Natural Environment

Springtime colors along the Gulf Coast of Alabama and Mississippi are white, aqua, flame-bright pink and coral—the white of the soft powdery sand beaches, the light blue-green of the Gulf waters, and the brilliant colors of the azaleas that bloom in nearly every yard. The scenery of the area is soft and pleasant, except when Gulf hurricanes churn up the usually calm waters.

MAJOR GEOGRAPHIC FEATURES
Shoreline: Gulf of Mexico, Mississippi Sound, Mobile Bay
Islands: Dauphin

NATURE-PRESERVATION AREAS
Gulf Islands National Seashore
Mississippi Sandhill Crane National Wildlife Refuge

| Terrain | Open Space | Forests | Inland Water | Shore-line | Rivers | Nature Preser-vation | Nature's Spectac-ulars |
|---|---|---|---|---|---|---|---|
| — | 200 | 600 | 180 | 600 | — | 300 | — |

Places Rated Score: 1,880          Places Rated Rank: 55

## Climate

### MOBILE–MOBILE BAY, AL

| | January | April | July | October |
|---|---|---|---|---|
| Hours of Sunshine | 5:25 | 8:55 | 8:21 | 8:01 |
| Chances of a Sunny Day | 45% | 60% | 61% | 74% |
| Afternoon Temperatures | 61° | 78° | 91° | 79° |
| Relative Humidity | 71% | 70% | 74% | 69% |
| Chances of a Dry Day | 79% | 83% | 68% | 90% |
| Total Precipitation | 4.6″ | 5.4″ | 7.7″ | 2.6″ |

Comment: The bay shores are a bit cooler in summer and a bit warmer in winter.

### GULFPORT–BILOXI, MS

| | January | April | July | October |
|---|---|---|---|---|
| Hours of Sunshine | 5:16 | 8:31 | 8:12 | 8:01 |
| Chances of a Sunny Day | 45% | 62% | 63% | 74% |
| Afternoon Temperatures | 61° | 77° | 90° | 80° |
| Relative Humidity | 76% | 74% | 77% | 72% |
| Chances of a Dry Day | 79% | 82% | 71% | 88% |
| Total Precipitation | 5.1″ | 5.0″ | 6.4″ | 3.0″ |

Comment: October and November are this resort area's most delightful months.

# Monterey–Big Sur, CA

## Natural Environment

The 17-mile drive through Del Monte Forest, on Monterey Peninsula, has often been called the prettiest stretch of road anywhere. The unique, wind-twisted Monterey cypress trees grow only here and on Point Lobos, a few miles south. Two huge offshore rocks, named Bird Rock and Seal Rock, provide home and playground for hundreds of shorebirds and sea lions. The ocean-side drive from Monterey and Point Lobos south to Big Sur is another one that calls for grandiose descriptions. The road has been chiseled out of cliffs overhanging the Pacific (which is often anything but pacific here); it crosses river canyons and sweeps along at the foot of forested mountains and past fields of wildflowers.

MAJOR GEOGRAPHIC FEATURES
Terrain: Coast Ranges, Junipero Serra Peak (5,862 ft.), Santa Lucia Range
Lakes and Reservoirs: Lake San Antonio
Shoreline: Monterey Bay, Pacific Ocean
Other: Point Sur

NATURE-PRESERVATION AREAS
Pinnacles National Monument
Salinas Lagoon National Wildlife Refuge

| Terrain | Open Space | Forests | Inland Water | Shore-line | Rivers | Nature Preser-vation | Nature's Spectac-ulars |
|---|---|---|---|---|---|---|---|
| 710 | — | 600 | 30 | 600 | — | 200 | — |

Places Rated Score: 2,140          Places Rated Rank: 37

## Climate

| MONTEREY, CA | January | April | July | October |
|---|---|---|---|---|
| Hours of Sunshine | 5:29 | 9:28 | 9:56 | 8:03 |
| Chances of a Sunny Day | 68% | 83% | 94% | 87% |
| Afternoon Temperatures | 60° | 65° | 71° | 72° |
| Relative Humidity | 78% | 76% | 81% | 76% |
| Chances of a Dry Day | 76% | 87% | 99% | 94% |
| Total Precipitation | 5.3" | 2.1" | 0.1" | 1.0" |

Comment: A sunny seaside climate with mild dry summers and mild wet winters.

| BIG SUR, CA | January | April | July | October |
|---|---|---|---|---|
| Hours of Sunshine | 5:19 | 8:47 | 10:45 | 8:22 |
| Chances of a Sunny Day | 57% | 71% | 92% | 82% |
| Afternoon Temperatures | 58° | 57° | 61° | 62° |
| Relative Humidity | 86% | 81% | 87% | 81% |
| Chances of a Dry Day | 85% | 93% | 99% | 97% |
| Total Precipitation | 7.0" | 2.7" | — | 1.3" |

Comment: Morning and late afternoon fogs are common along this coast.

# Myrtle Beach–Grand Strand, SC

## Natural Environment

The Grand Strand, a 55-mile-long beach, is a comparative newcomer to the Atlantic beach-resort family, having been developed only during the past three or four decades. Most of the strip along the fine beach is built up with resorts and business for tourists, but there are creeks and marshlands here and there, and a 9,000-acre wildlife preserve and garden, Brookgreen Gardens.

MAJOR GEOGRAPHIC FEATURES
Rivers: Great Pee Dee
Shoreline: Atlantic Ocean, Long Bay

| Terrain | Open Space | Forests | Inland Water | Shore-line | Rivers | Nature Preservation | Nature's Spectaculars |
|---|---|---|---|---|---|---|---|
| — | 700 | 600 | 130 | 600 | — | — | — |

Places Rated Score: 2,030          Places Rated Rank: 44

## Climate

| MYRTLE BEACH– GRAND STRAND, SC | January | April | July | October |
|---|---|---|---|---|
| Hours of Sunshine | 5:52 | 9:11 | 9:16 | 7:23 |
| Chances of a Sunny Day | 50% | 63% | 56% | 65% |
| Afternoon Temperatures | 57° | 73° | 88° | 75° |
| Relative Humidity | 76% | 74% | 82% | 77% |
| Chances of a Dry Day | 78% | 83% | 70% | 87% |
| Total Precipitation | 3.4" | 2.8" | 6.7" | 2.9" |

Comment: Water temperatures top 70 degrees Fahrenheit from about mid-May through mid-October. Many residents feel that September and October are the nicest months of the year.

# Mystic Seaport–Connecticut Valley, CT

## Natural Environment

The part of the state of Connecticut that lies close to Long Island Sound is mostly flat, but as one travels north a few hills appear. There are numerous picturesque bluffs along the Connecticut River. Many small lakes and streams keep the countryside green and fertile.

MAJOR GEOGRAPHIC FEATURES
Rivers: Connecticut, Thames
Shoreline: Fishers Island Sound, Long Island Sound

NATURE-PRESERVATION AREAS
Salt Meadow National Wildlife Refuge

| Terrain | Open Space | Forests | Inland Water | Shore-line | Rivers | Nature Preservation | Nature's Spectaculars |
|---|---|---|---|---|---|---|---|
| 210 | — | 600 | 220 | 200 | — | 100 | — |

Places Rated Score: 1,330          Places Rated Rank: 79

## Climate

| MYSTIC SEAPORT, CT | January | April | July | October |
|---|---|---|---|---|
| Hours of Sunshine | 4:32 | 7:33 | 9:24 | 6:43 |
| Chances of a Sunny Day | 54% | 56% | 60% | 61% |
| Afternoon Temperatures | 38° | 59° | 82° | 65° |
| Relative Humidity | 66% | 62% | 71% | 70% |
| Chances of a Dry Day | 78% | 73% | 81% | 84% |
| Total Precipitation | 3.9" | 4.1" | 3.5" | 3.5" |
| Snowfall | 7.5" | 0.4" | — | 0.1" |

Comment: Warm summer days and nights just cool enough for comfortable snoozing. A pleasant summer vacation climate.

# Nashville, TN

## Natural Environment

Nashville sits on the banks of the Cumberland River, smack in the middle of Tennessee. A few open hills give some variety to the landscape; the land is green and fertile.

MAJOR GEOGRAPHIC FEATURES
Lakes and Reservoirs: Old Hickory Lake, J. Percy Priest Lake
Rivers: Cumberland

| Terrain | Open Space | Forests | Inland Water | Shore-line | Rivers | Nature Preservation | Nature's Spectaculars |
|---|---|---|---|---|---|---|---|
| 240 | 200 | 100 | 90 | — | — | — | — |

Places Rated Score: 630          Places Rated Rank: 97

## Climate

| NASHVILLE, TN | January | April | July | October |
|---|---|---|---|---|
| Hours of Sunshine | 4:06 | 7:44 | 9:11 | 7:07 |
| Chances of a Sunny Day | 39% | 57% | 68% | 68% |
| Afternoon Temperatures | 46° | 71° | 90° | 72° |
| Relative Humidity | 72% | 66% | 74% | 70% |
| Chances of a Dry Day | 74% | 75% | 78% | 85% |
| Total Precipitation | 4.5" | 4.5" | 3.8" | 2.6" |
| Snowfall | 4.1" | 0.1" | — | — |

Comment: A pleasant but undistinguished climate. Midsummer thunderstorms bring welcome relief from the heat.

# New Orleans, LA

## Natural Environment

Hot, humid, subject to floods—New Orleans manages to be an above-average vacation destination in spite of its weather, not because of it! Spring is a good time to visit here, before the mosquitoes have had a chance to take over the bayous. The land is unusual and well worth seeing—misty, lazy streams; wetlands alive with birds; huge, moss-draped live oaks; the mighty Mississippi; and Lake Pontchartrain.

MAJOR GEOGRAPHIC FEATURES
  Lakes and Reservoirs: Lac des Allemands, Lake Pontchartrain
  Rivers: Mississippi
  Shoreline: Chandeleur Sound, Gulf of Mexico
  Other: Mississippi Delta

| Terrain | Open Space | Forests | Inland Water | Shore-line | Rivers | Nature Preser-vation | Nature's Spectac-ulars |
|---|---|---|---|---|---|---|---|
| — | — | 100 | 500 | 200 | 200 | — | — |

Places Rated Score: 1,000          Places Rated Rank: 89

## Climate

| NEW ORLEANS, LA | January | April | July | October |
|---|---|---|---|---|
| Hours of Sunshine | 5:07 | 7:57 | 8:06 | 7:00 |
| Chances of a Sunny Day | 45% | 63% | 65% | 74% |
| Afternoon Temperatures | 62° | 78° | 91° | 80° |
| Relative Humidity | 76% | 74% | 79% | 73% |
| Chances of a Dry Day | 80% | 85% | 68% | 89% |
| Total Precipitation | 4.9" | 4.7" | 7.2" | 2.5" |

Comment: October is New Orleans's very best month.

# New York City, NY

## Natural Environment

Just about the only seminatural area left on Manhattan Island is Central Park, where one can get a small idea of the hills and cliffs that were here before New York was paved over. Much of Westchester County is rolling and wooded, however, and the more open areas of the Catskills, the Poconos, and New England are not too far away.

MAJOR GEOGRAPHIC FEATURES
  Rivers: Hudson River
  Shoreline: Atlantic Ocean, Jamaica Bay, Long Island Sound, Lower New York Bay, Upper New York Bay

NATURE-PRESERVATION AREAS
  Gateway National Recreation Area

| Terrain | Open Space | Forests | Inland Water | Shore-line | Rivers | Nature Preser-vation | Nature's Spectac-ulars |
|---|---|---|---|---|---|---|---|
| 150 | -300 | 100 | 500 | 120 | — | — | — |

Places Rated Score: 570          Places Rated Rank: 98

## Climate

| NEW YORK CITY, NY | January | April | July | October |
|---|---|---|---|---|
| Hours of Sunshine | 4:49 | 7:51 | 9:37 | 6:48 |
| Chances of a Sunny Day | 55% | 60% | 68% | 71% |
| Afternoon Temperatures | 38° | 61° | 85° | 66° |
| Relative Humidity | 64% | 59% | 65% | 66% |
| Chances of a Dry Day | 78% | 78% | 78% | 82% |
| Total Precipitation | 3.2" | 3.8" | 3.8" | 3.4" |
| Snowfall | 7.6" | 1.0" | — | — |

Comment: Data are for Central Park. The suburbs are a bit cooler in all seasons and snowier in winter.

# Niagara Falls–Western New York, NY

## Natural Environment

Western New York fronts on two Great Lakes—Ontario and Erie—and in between the lakes the Niagara River drops 325 feet. More than half that drop takes place at the spectacular, world-famous Niagara Falls. There are open high hills in western New York, small lakes in addition

to the Great ones, lots of rivers, and vineyards. Allegany State Park is a 65,000-acre nature preserve.

MAJOR GEOGRAPHIC FEATURES
  Rivers: Niagara
  Shoreline: Lake Erie, Lake Ontario
  Other: Niagara Gorge

NATURE'S SPECTACULARS
  Niagara Falls

| Terrain | Open Space | Forests | Inland Water | Shore-line | Rivers | Nature Preser-vation | Nature's Spectac-ulars |
|---|---|---|---|---|---|---|---|
| 180 | — | 400 | 170 | 200 | — | — | 500 |

Places Rated Score: 1,450          Places Rated Rank: 73

## Climate

| NIAGARA FALLS–WESTERN NEW YORK, NY | January | April | July | October |
|---|---|---|---|---|
| Hours of Sunshine | 3:01 | 6:58 | 10:13 | 5:39 |
| Chances of a Sunny Day | 26% | 43% | 65% | 48% |
| Afternoon Temperatures | 33° | 57° | 83° | 63° |
| Relative Humidity | 76% | 67% | 68% | 71% |
| Chances of a Dry Day | 77% | 75% | 83% | 79% |
| Total Precipitation | 2.0" | 2.7" | 2.5" | 2.2" |
| Snowfall | 13.0" | 1.4" | — | — |

Comment: Very pleasant during the summer, and with half of Buffalo's snow during the winter.

# North Woods–Land O'Lakes, WI

## Natural Environment

The map of northern Wisconsin looks rain-spattered—dozens of small lakes take up much of the space in Vilas and Oneida counties. If they were all strung together, undoubtedly they could connect Lakes Superior and Michigan. This is a popular destination for people who enjoy flatland winter sports—Rhinelander calls itself the "snowmobile capital of the world."

MAJOR GEOGRAPHIC FEATURES
  Terrain: Timms Hill (1,951 ft.)
  Rivers: Wisconsin
  Shoreline: Lake Superior

| Terrain | Open Space | Forests | Inland Water | Shore-line | Rivers | Nature Preser-vation | Nature's Spectac-ulars |
|---|---|---|---|---|---|---|---|
| — | 1,000 | 800 | 400 | — | — | — | — |

Places Rated Score: 2,200          Places Rated Rank: 32

## Climate

| NORTH WOODS–LAND O'LAKES, WI | January | April | July | October |
|---|---|---|---|---|
| Hours of Sunshine | 4:06 | 7:31 | 10:03 | 5:13 |
| Chances of a Sunny Day | 45% | 52% | 69% | 50% |
| Afternoon Temperatures | 21° | 53° | 79° | 56° |
| Relative Humidity | 73% | 69% | 73% | 74% |
| Chances of a Dry Day | 86% | 81% | 78% | 83% |
| Total Precipitation | 1.2" | 2.6" | 3.8" | 2.3" |
| Snowfall | 14.9" | 6.3" | — | 2.0" |

Comment: The month of October offers uncrowded lakes, colorful foliage, and invigorating weather.

# Oklahoma City–Cherokee Strip, OK

## Natural Environment

Oklahoma claims to have more man-made lakes than any other state, and a few of the smaller ones are close to Oklahoma City. Chickasaw National Recreation Area, about an hour's drive south of the capital city, is a woodland area containing low mountains; streams; freshwater and cold mineral springs; waterfalls; and the clear, deep Lake of the Arbuckles. The Arbuckle Mountains, marked by outcroppings, gorges, and fossil-bearing sites, are interesting and geologically unusual.

MAJOR GEOGRAPHIC FEATURES
  Terrain: Arbuckle Mountains
  Lakes and Reservoirs: Lake McMurtry, Lake of the Arbuckles, Lake Thunderbird
  Rivers: Canadian, Cimarron

NATURE-PRESERVATION AREAS
  Chickasaw National Recreation Area

| Terrain | Open Space | Forests | Inland Water | Shore-line | Rivers | Nature Preser-vation | Nature's Spectac-ulars |
|---|---|---|---|---|---|---|---|
| — | 300 | 100 | 50 | — | — | 100 | — |

Places Rated Score: 550          Places Rated Rank: 100

## Climate

| OKLAHOMA CITY–CHEROKEE STRIP, OK | January | April | July | October |
|---|---|---|---|---|
| Hours of Sunshine | 5:50 | 8:30 | 11:09 | 7:42 |
| Chances of a Sunny Day | 52% | 57% | 77% | 71% |
| Afternoon Temperatures | 47° | 72° | 94° | 74° |
| Relative Humidity | 69% | 63% | 63% | 65% |
| Chances of a Dry Day | 92% | 84% | 87% | 87% |
| Total Precipitation | 1.0″ | 2.9″ | 3.0″ | 2.7″ |
| Snowfall | 2.8″ | — | — | — |

Comment: Oklahoma City is virtually smog free—a rarity for a major American city.

# ★ Olympic Peninsula, WA

## Natural Environment

The mountains of the Olympic Peninsula are a vast collection of open peaks—high mountains, low mountains, and high hills. In addition, there are rain forests of huge, ancient trees; some 60 glaciers (6 on Mount Olympus alone); Alpine meadows; and an unbelievable abundance of plants and wildflowers. Olympic National Park is the home of several thousand Olympic elk, along with more than 50 different other species of mammals. And all of this is a short distance from the shorelines of the Pacific Ocean and Puget Sound.

MAJOR GEOGRAPHIC FEATURES
  Terrain: Mount Olympus (7,965 ft.), Olympic Mountains
  Lakes and Reservoirs: Ozette Lake
  Shoreline: Grays Harbor, Hood Canal, Pacific Ocean, Puget Sound, Strait of Juan de Fuca
  Other: Cape Flattery

NATURE-PRESERVATION AREAS
  Dungeness National Wildlife Refuge
  Olympic National Park

NATURE'S SPECTACULARS
  Olympic National Park (World Heritage Site)

| Terrain | Open Space | Forests | Inland Water | Shore-line | Rivers | Nature Preser-vation | Nature's Spectac-ulars |
|---|---|---|---|---|---|---|---|
| 740 | 700 | 800 | 170 | 800 | — | 400 | 500 |

Places Rated Score: 4,110          Places Rated Rank: 3

## Climate

| OLYMPIC NATIONAL PARK (PACIFIC COASTAL STRIP), WA | January | April | July | October |
|---|---|---|---|---|
| Hours of Sunshine | 2:12 | 5:49 | 7:14 | 4:08 |
| Chances of a Sunny Day | 24% | 38% | 45% | 39% |
| Afternoon Temperatures | 45° | 55° | 69° | 59° |
| Relative Humidity | 88% | 80% | 80% | 84% |
| Chances of a Dry Day | 39% | 55% | 85% | 55% |
| Total Precipitation | 15.1″ | 7.1″ | 2.3″ | 10.5″ |
| Snowfall | 6.4″ | 0.2″ | — | — |

Comment: Mornings can be quite foggy in summer and early autumn, but the fog usually lifts by noon.

| OLYMPIA, WA | January | April | July | October |
|---|---|---|---|---|
| Hours of Sunshine | 1:48 | 6:40 | 9:27 | 3:23 |
| Chances of a Sunny Day | 19% | 37% | 65% | 35% |
| Afternoon Temperatures | 44° | 59° | 77° | 61° |
| Relative Humidity | 86% | 74% | 71% | 81% |
| Chances of a Dry Day | 55% | 73% | 93% | 69% |
| Total Precipitation | 8.5″ | 3.1″ | 0.8″ | 4.7″ |
| Snowfall | 8.5″ | 0.1″ | — | — |

Comment: Summer is far and away Olympia's most pleasant season, and it is very pleasant indeed!

# Orlando–Space Coast, FL

## Natural Environment

Orlando is the hub city of a fertile part of Florida that was devoted to growing oranges and raising cattle before Disney World was built. The city has 54 lakes, and there are more in surrounding communities. Situated in the middle of the state, the beaches of the Atlantic Coast are only about an hour away, and those of the Gulf not much farther. The Merritt Island National Wildlife Refuge, which surrounds the John F. Kennedy Space Center, is a favorite spot for bird-watchers. Close by is Canaveral National Seashore, one of the few remaining wild areas along the coast of Florida. Fourteen miles of the seashore is protected from vehicle traffic.

MAJOR GEOGRAPHIC FEATURES
  Lakes and Reservoirs: Blue Cypress Lake, East Lake Tohopekaliga, Lake Apopka, Lake Hatchineha, Lake Kissimmee, Lake Tohopekaliga, Lake Weohyakapka
  Rivers: Indian
  Shoreline: Atlantic Ocean
  Islands: Merritt
  Other: Canaveral Peninsula, Cape Canaveral

NATURE-PRESERVATION AREAS
  Canaveral National Seashore
  Merritt Island National Wildlife Refuge
  Pelican Island National Wildlife Refuge

| Terrain | Open Space | Forests | Inland Water | Shore-line | Rivers | Nature Preser-vation | Nature's Spectac-ulars |
|---|---|---|---|---|---|---|---|
| — | 200 | 400 | 500 | 600 | — | 300 | — |

Places Rated Score: 2,000          Places Rated Rank: 46

## Climate

| ORLANDO, FL | January | April | July | October |
|---|---|---|---|---|
| Hours of Sunshine | 6:33 | 9:30 | 8:24 | 7:29 |
| Chances of a Sunny Day | 65% | 73% | 65% | 68% |
| Afternoon Temperatures | 72° | 84° | 92° | 84° |
| Relative Humidity | 71% | 67% | 75% | 72% |
| Chances of a Dry Day | 87% | 87% | 60% | 82% |
| Total Precipitation | 2.1" | 2.2" | 7.8" | 2.8" |

Comment: April and November offer the most pleasant weather for general sightseeing.

| SPACE COAST, FL | January | April | July | October |
|---|---|---|---|---|
| Hours of Sunshine | 6:14 | 9:19 | 8:36 | 6:20 |
| Chances of a Sunny Day | 63% | 72% | 63% | 66% |
| Afternoon Temperatures | 72° | 83° | 92° | 83° |
| Relative Humidity | 72% | 68% | 76% | 74% |
| Chances of a Dry Day | 86% | 87% | 67% | 73% |
| Total Precipitation | 2.2" | 2.2" | 8.4" | 5.5" |

Comment: November through May is the drier time of year, and the time with the best weather.

# Outer Banks, NC

## Natural Environment

The Outer Banks of North Carolina are a part of the chain of barrier islands all along the eastern seaboard of the United States. These reach out into the ocean at a greater distance from the mainland than most of the others; thus they are a bit less accessible than many beach-resort areas. Cape Hatteras National Seashore and Cape Lookout National Seashore together protect narrow strips of land (most of it less than 1½ miles wide) for about 128 miles. Several small resort towns lie north and south of the two seashores. Sand dunes and wildlife—birds and sea creatures—are the principal natural attractions of the Outer Banks.

MAJOR GEOGRAPHIC FEATURES
  Shoreline: Albemarle Sound, Atlantic Ocean, Pamlico Sound
  Islands: Hatteras
  Other: Core Banks

NATURE-PRESERVATION AREAS
  Cape Hatteras National Seashore
  Cape Lookout National Seashore
  Cedar Island National Wildlife Refuge
  Mackay Island National Wildlife Refuge
  Mattamuskeet National Wildlife Refuge
  Pea Island National Wildlife Refuge
  Swanquarter National Wildlife Refuge

| Terrain | Open Space | Forests | Inland Water | Shore-line | Rivers | Nature Preser-vation | Nature's Spectac-ulars |
|---|---|---|---|---|---|---|---|
| — | 700 | 600 | 500 | 1,000 | — | 300 | — |

Places Rated Score: 3,100          Places Rated Rank: 14

## Climate

| OUTER BANKS, NC | January | April | July | October |
|---|---|---|---|---|
| Hours of Sunshine | 4:56 | 8:38 | 8:51 | 6:41 |
| Chances of a Sunny Day | 52% | 63% | 52% | 58% |
| Afternoon Temperatures | 53° | 67° | 84° | 72° |
| Relative Humidity | 74% | 70% | 80% | 74% |
| Chances of a Dry Day | 79% | 81% | 73% | 83% |
| Total Precipitation | 4.7" | 3.2" | 5.4" | 4.8" |

Comment: Quite pleasant beach climate in spring and summer but absolutely delightful in September and early October.

# Ozarks–Eureka Springs, AR–MO

## Natural Environment

The high hills and low mountains of Missouri's and Arkansas's Ozark region have much to offer in addition to the pleasant slopes—there are deep woods, lakes, rushing rivers, bubbling natural springs, and a delightful climate for much of the year. Eureka Springs was discovered more than a century ago by visitors who believed in the healing power of its mineral waters—they also got a great deal of healthful exercise climbing up its steep streets. More recently, vacationers have enjoyed the therapeutic effect of spending lazy days on the huge man-made lakes in the area.

MAJOR GEOGRAPHIC FEATURES
  Terrain: Boston Mountains, Ozark Plateau
  Lakes and Reservoirs: Beaver Lake, Bull Shoals Lake, Table Rock Lake
  Rivers: Buffalo, White

| Terrain | Open Space | Forests | Inland Water | Shore-line | Rivers | Nature Preser-vation | Nature's Spectac-ulars |
|---|---|---|---|---|---|---|---|
| 440 | 700 | 600 | 120 | — | 200 | — | — |

Places Rated Score: 2,060          Places Rated Rank: 42

## Climate

| SPRINGFIELD–WESTERN OZARKS, MO | January | April | July | October |
|---|---|---|---|---|
| Hours of Sunshine | 4:58 | 7:53 | 10:24 | 7:26 |
| Chances of a Sunny Day | 48% | 53% | 71% | 65% |
| Afternoon Temperatures | 42° | 68° | 90° | 71° |
| Relative Humidity | 69% | 66% | 71% | 67% |
| Chances of a Dry Day | 88% | 76% | 83% | 84% |
| Total Precipitation | 1.6" | 4.0" | 3.6" | 3.2" |
| Snowfall | 4.2" | 0.5" | | |

Comment: Springfield's location atop the Ozark Plateau makes it virtually smog free.

| EUREKA SPRINGS, AR | January | April | July | October |
|---|---|---|---|---|
| Hours of Sunshine | 5:02 | 7:41 | 10:21 | 7:22 |
| Chances of a Sunny Day | 50% | 55% | 72% | 67% |
| Afternoon Temperatures | 47° | 72° | 91° | 73° |
| Relative Humidity | 69% | 65% | 69% | 67% |
| Chances of a Dry Day | 87% | 77% | 84% | 84% |
| Total Precipitation | 1.9" | 4.2" | 4.1" | 3.3" |
| Snowfall | 3.1" | 0.3" | — | 0.1" |

Comment: One of the most underrated vacation climates in the country—especially in the spring and autumn.

# Palm Springs–Desert Playgrounds, CA

## Natural Environment

Love of desert country is an acquired taste, but for many people it doesn't take long to acquire it. The strange vegetation, the arid mountains that change color as the sun strikes them from different angles, the dry gulches that can become rushing torrents after a rain in the mountains—all this is a very different kind of beauty from that in greener landscapes. Yet there is much to observe and learn in the desert—it is far from lifeless. Plenty of flora and fauna flourish here; they are simply unfamiliar to first-time visitors and are often small and subtle in appearance. Palm Springs and the other towns of the area sit on a flat plain surrounded by mountains. Nearby is the wonderful—and again, strange—Joshua Tree National Monument. The tree for which the monument is named grows only in dry sections of California, western Arizona, Nevada, and southern Utah.

MAJOR GEOGRAPHIC FEATURES
  Terrain: San Bernardino Mountains, San Jacinto Mountains, San Jacinto Peak (10,804 ft.)
  Rivers: Colorado
  Other: Mohave Desert, Salton Sea

NATURE-PRESERVATION AREAS
  Joshua Tree National Monument

NATURE'S SPECTACULARS
  Joshua Tree National Monument (World Heritage Site)

| Terrain | Open Space | Forests | Inland Water | Shore-line | Rivers | Nature Preser-vation | Nature's Spectac-ulars |
|---|---|---|---|---|---|---|---|
| 710 | 300 | 100 | 50 | — | — | 300 | 500 |

Places Rated Score: 1,960          Places Rated Rank: 50

## Climate

| PALM SPRINGS–DESERT PLAYGROUNDS, CA | January | April | July | October |
|---|---|---|---|---|
| Hours of Sunshine | 7:45 | 10:42 | 12:12 | 9:24 |
| Chances of a Sunny Day | 71% | 80% | 94% | 85% |
| Afternoon Temperatures | 69° | 86° | 109° | 92° |
| Relative Humidity | 55% | 38% | 29% | 36% |
| Chances of a Dry Day | 91% | 98% | 98% | 96% |
| Total Precipitation | 1.3" | 0.2" | 0.2" | 0.2" |

Comment: Most winters are sunny, dry, and totally without any measurable snowfall.

# Panhandle, FL

## Natural Environment

Most habitual Florida vacationers have their favorite area, one they think has better beaches, better weather, and better fishing than the rest. The Panhandle is no exception. Its boosters will tell you the sand here is different—it's sugary white, and the beaches stretch unbroken for 100 miles along the aquamarine Gulf. Santa Rosa Island, part of Gulf Islands National Seashore, is accessible by highway from Navarre. Sea oats grow where the salt level is high; their root systems reach deep into the sand and help keep the dunes from blowing away. Behind the dunes are freshwater marshes and small trees.

MAJOR GEOGRAPHIC FEATURES
  Shoreline: Choctawhatchee Bay, Gulf of Mexico, Pensacola Bay
  Islands: Santa Rosa
  Other: Cape San Blas

NATURE-PRESERVATION AREAS
  Gulf Islands National Seashore
  St. Vincent National Wildlife Refuge

| Terrain | Open Space | Forests | Inland Water | Shore-line | Rivers | Nature Preser-vation | Nature's Spectac-ulars |
|---|---|---|---|---|---|---|---|
| — | 300 | 600 | 430 | 600 | — | 200 | — |

Places Rated Score: 2,130          Places Rated Rank: 39

## Climate

| PANHANDLE, FL | January | April | July | October |
|---|---|---|---|---|
| Hours of Sunshine | 5:54 | 9:17 | 8:57 | 8:29 |
| Chances of a Sunny Day | 66% | 65% | 66% | 76% |
| Afternoon Temperatures | 64° | 78° | 90° | 81° |
| Relative Humidity | 74% | 73% | 78% | 72% |
| Chances of a Dry Day | 83% | 85% | 69% | 90% |
| Total Precipitation | 3.9" | 4.0" | 7.8" | 3.4" |

Comment: Sea breezes keep the beach areas a bit cooler in summer and a bit warmer in winter. May is a very nice month in the Florida Panhandle.

# Pennsylvania Dutch Country, PA

## Natural Environment

Pennsylvania's mountains are open, low, and flattopped. They're also beautifully decorated twice a year, first with delicate spring blooms and later on with showy autumn foliage. Every area where the leaves turn in autumn is considered most beautiful in the world by its residents. In Pennsylvania Dutch Country they will tell you this area is best because they have an incomparable mixture of northern trees that don't grow south of here and southern trees that aren't hardy enough to survive the winters to the north.

MAJOR GEOGRAPHIC FEATURES
  Terrain: Appalachian Mountains, Blue Mountain, South Mountain
  Rivers: Susquehanna

| Terrain | Open Space | Forests | Inland Water | Shore-line | Rivers | Nature Preser-vation | Nature's Spectac-ulars |
|---|---|---|---|---|---|---|---|
| 210 | — | 400 | 70 | — | — | — | — |

Places Rated Score: 680          Places Rated Rank: 96

## Climate

| HARRISBURG–PENNSYLVANIA DUTCH COUNTRY, PA | January | April | July | October |
|---|---|---|---|---|
| Hours of Sunshine | 4:44 | 7:50 | 10:10 | 6:29 |
| Chances of a Sunny Day | 45% | 50% | 61% | 58% |
| Afternoon Temperatures | 37° | 63° | 86° | 65° |
| Relative Humidity | 65% | 60% | 66% | 68% |
| Chances of a Dry Day | 81% | 76% | 80% | 85% |
| Total Precipitation | 3.0" | 3.2" | 3.3" | 2.7" |
| Snowfall | 9.5" | 0.5" | — | 0.1" |

Comment: Long, warm, sunny, lazy summer days for the tourists mean more time for work for the local farmers.

# Philadelphia, PA–DE–NJ

## Natural Environment

The city of Philadelphia was built around the confluence of the Schuylkill and Delaware rivers. The surrounding areas have a few hills, and the mountains of Pennsylvania and Virginia are only an hour or two away. In addition, the Atlantic Ocean can be reached in an hour's drive across New Jersey.

MAJOR GEOGRAPHIC FEATURES
  Rivers: Delaware, Schuylkill
  Other: Pine Barrens

NATURE-PRESERVATION AREAS
  Tinicum National Environmental Center

| Terrain | Open Space | Forests | Inland Water | Shore-line | Rivers | Nature Preser-vation | Nature's Spectac-ulars |
|---|---|---|---|---|---|---|---|
| 90 | –300 | 100 | 70 | — | 200 | 100 | — |

Places Rated Score: 260          Places Rated Rank: 105

## Climate

| PHILADELPHIA, PA | January | April | July | October |
|---|---|---|---|---|
| Hours of Sunshine | 4:51 | 7:33 | 9:07 | 6:36 |
| Chances of a Sunny Day | 48% | 53% | 61% | 61% |
| Afternoon Temperatures | 39° | 63° | 86° | 67° |
| Relative Humidity | 66% | 59% | 68% | 68% |
| Chances of a Dry Day | 80% | 76% | 80% | 87% |
| Total Precipitation | 3.2″ | 3.5″ | 3.9″ | 2.8″ |
| Snowfall | 6.3″ | 0.3″ | — | 0.1″ |

Comment: Inner-city areas are slightly warmer in the morning than outlying areas.

# Phoenix–Valley of the Sun, AZ

## Natural Environment

Phoenix was a sleepy little frontier town not many decades ago; by the end of 1983, according to the latest population estimates, it had climbed to tenth place among U.S. cities. Sunshine, more than any other single factor, has brought the new residents here. Several mountain peaks are found within the city limits. Their desert coloration, changing from hour to hour, is fascinating. Unfortunately this place is not exempt from the smog problems that beset so many large metropolises; thus the beautiful mountains are often obscured from view.

MAJOR GEOGRAPHIC FEATURES
  Terrain: Four Peaks (7,657 ft.), Gila Bend Mountains, Mazatzal Mountains, Table Top (4,373 ft.)
  Rivers: Gila, Salt, Verde

| Terrain | Open Space | Forests | Inland Water | Shore-line | Rivers | Nature Preser-vation | Nature's Spectac-ulars |
|---|---|---|---|---|---|---|---|
| 940 | 300 | 100 | 40 | — | — | — | — |

Places Rated Score: 1,380    Places Rated Rank: 76

## Climate

| PHOENIX–VALLEY OF THE SUN, AZ | January | April | July | October |
|---|---|---|---|---|
| Hours of Sunshine | 7:52 | 11:27 | 12:01 | 10:01 |
| Chances of a Sunny Day | 65% | 80% | 87% | 87% |
| Afternoon Temperatures | 65° | 83° | 105° | 88° |
| Relative Humidity | 50% | 30% | 33% | 37% |
| Chances of a Dry Day | 92% | 97% | 93% | 95% |
| Total Precipitation | 0.7″ | 0.3″ | 0.7″ | 0.6″ |

Comment: Phoenix is the sunniest major city in the United States, with the sun shining 86 percent of the daylight hours.

# Pocono Mountains, PA

## Natural Environment

Lakes, rivers, streams, and forests—the Poconos have them all. The Pocono Mountains themselves have a rounded look, as if nature had rubbed off the sharp peaks characteristic of many other ranges. Glacial action created the Delaware Water Gap, a gorge where the Delaware River cuts through the mountains.

MAJOR GEOGRAPHIC FEATURES
  Terrain: Appalachian Mountains, Hardwood Ridge (2,229 ft.), Pocono Mountains
  Lakes and Reservoirs: Lake Wallenpaupack
  Rivers: Delaware
  Other: Delaware Water Gap

| Terrain | Open Space | Forests | Inland Water | Shore-line | Rivers | Nature Preser-vation | Nature's Spectac-ulars |
|---|---|---|---|---|---|---|---|
| 530 | — | 600 | 50 | — | 200 | — | — |

Places Rated Score: 1,380    Places Rated Rank: 76

## Climate

| POCONO MOUNTAINS, PA | January | April | July | October |
|---|---|---|---|---|
| Hours of Sunshine | 4:07 | 7:11 | 9:12 | 5:41 |
| Chances of a Sunny Day | 39% | 47% | 61% | 55% |
| Afternoon Temperatures | 32° | 54° | 77° | 60° |
| Relative Humidity | 75% | 71% | 84% | 83% |
| Chances of a Dry Day | 77% | 73% | 74% | 81% |
| Total Precipitation | 3.4″ | 4.2″ | 5.2″ | 4.6″ |
| Snowfall | 13.6″ | 3.3″ | | |

Comment: Summer brings a cool retreat from the city's heat, while winter offers excellent ski touring.

# Portland, ME

## Natural Environment

Portland's moist and salty air leaves no room for doubt that this is a city originally built by and for seafarers. The Atlantic Ocean is Portland's premier geographic feature; its influence is everywhere. Within the Portland vacation area there are lakes, rivers, and hills, as well as the picturesque rocky coast.

MAJOR GEOGRAPHIC FEATURES
  Lakes and Reservoirs: Sebago Lake
  Rivers: Androscoggin, Kennebec
  Shoreline: Atlantic Ocean, Casco Bay

| Terrain | Open Space | Forests | Inland Water | Shore-line | Rivers | Nature Preser-vation | Nature's Spectac-ulars |
|---|---|---|---|---|---|---|---|
| 120 | 200 | 600 | 500 | 800 | — | — | — |

Places Rated Score: 2,220    Places Rated Rank: 31

## Climate

| PORTLAND, ME | January | April | July | October |
|---|---|---|---|---|
| Hours of Sunshine | 5:14 | 7:23 | 9:39 | 6:25 |
| Chances of a Sunny Day | 55% | 50% | 61% | 58% |
| Afternoon Temperatures | 31° | 53° | 79° | 59° |
| Relative Humidity | 69% | 67% | 74% | 72% |
| Chances of a Dry Day | 76% | 76% | 80% | 81% |
| Total Precipitation | 3.8″ | 3.9″ | 2.8″ | 3.8″ |
| Snowfall | 19.0″ | 3.1″ | — | 0.3″ |

Comment: Very pleasant in the summer and early autumn.

# Portland–Columbia River, OR

## Natural Environment

The "other Portland," the one on the Pacific Coast, is a major center for many kinds of water sports. The Columbia River, in Portland's front yard, is almost as popular as the ocean, a few miles away. Mount Hood, snowcapped all year round, stands like a giant guard over the city. Also visible from the city, a few miles to the north, the topless Mount St. Helens is a reminder that the Cascade Range consists of volcanic mountains that could be active at any time. Portland, with its mild temperatures, abundant rainfall, and magnificent scenery, is one of the country's most attractive cities.

MAJOR GEOGRAPHIC FEATURES
  Terrain: Cascade Range, Coast Ranges, Mount Hood (11,239 ft.), Trask Mountain (3,424 ft.), Willamette Valley
  Rivers: Columbia, Willamette
  Shoreline: Pacific Ocean, Tillamook Bay
  Other: Columbia River Gorge

NATURE-PRESERVATION AREAS
  Ankeny National Wildlife Refuge
  Baskett Slough National Wildlife Refuge
  Cape Meares National Wildlife Refuge
  Lewis and Clark National Wildlife Refuge

NATURE'S SPECTACULARS
  Mount St. Helens

| Terrain | Open Space | Forests | Inland Water | Shore-line | Rivers | Nature Preser-vation | Nature's Spectac-ulars |
|---|---|---|---|---|---|---|---|
| 790 | 200 | 600 | 110 | 600 | 200 | 100 | 500 |

Places Rated Score: 3,100          Places Rated Rank: 14

## Climate

| PORTLAND–LOWER WILLAMETTE RIVER VALLEY, OR | January | April | July | October |
|---|---|---|---|---|
| Hours of Sunshine | 2:23 | 7:10 | 10:33 | 4:43 |
| Chances of a Sunny Day | 19% | 33% | 71% | 39% |
| Afternoon Temperatures | 44° | 60° | 80° | 64° |
| Relative Humidity | 81% | 71% | 64% | 77% |
| Chances of a Dry Day | 56% | 78% | 97% | 72% |
| Total Precipitation | 6.2" | 2.3" | 0.5" | 3.1" |
| Snowfall | 4.0" | — | — | — |

Comment: Summer and winter are both mild. July, August, and September are the most pleasant months for a visit.

| MOUNT HOOD, OR | January | April | July | October |
|---|---|---|---|---|
| Hours of Sunshine | 2:18 | 7:01 | 10:23 | 4:37 |
| Chances of a Sunny Day | 18% | 30% | 68% | 37% |
| Afternoon Temperatures | 36° | 46° | 69° | 55° |
| Relative Humidity | 91% | 83% | 73% | 81% |
| Chances of a Dry Day | 42% | 60% | 94% | 65% |
| Total Precipitation | 13.1" | 7.2" | 0.7" | 7.9" |
| Snowfall | 62.2" | 28.3" | — | 6.7" |

Comment: July, August, and early September are the best times to visit the Mount Hood area—unless you are a skier, of course!

## Portsmouth–Kennebunk, NH–ME

### Natural Environment

The seacoast region of New Hampshire and Maine has been a popular resort area for generations. New Hampshire's short coastline has some fine white beaches; Maine's varies between sand and craggy rocks. Twice a day the views of the coast and the size of the beach change with the ebb and flow of the tides. Tidal pools are interesting to look at and to photograph.

MAJOR GEOGRAPHIC FEATURES
  Rivers: Piscatauqua
  Shoreline: Atlantic Ocean, Great Bay

NATURE-PRESERVATION AREAS
  Rachel Carson National Wildlife Refuge

| Terrain | Open Space | Forests | Inland Water | Shore-line | Rivers | Nature Preser-vation | Nature's Spectac-ulars |
|---|---|---|---|---|---|---|---|
| — | 200 | 800 | 130 | 600 | — | 100 | — |

Places Rated Score: 1,830          Places Rated Rank: 58

## Climate

| PORTSMOUTH–KENNEBUNK, NH–ME | January | April | July | October |
|---|---|---|---|---|
| Hours of Sunshine | 5:05 | 7:14 | 9:32 | 6:12 |
| Chances of a Sunny Day | 55% | 50% | 63% | 58% |
| Afternoon Temperatures | 32° | 54° | 79° | 61° |
| Relative Humidity | 67% | 65% | 73% | 71% |
| Chances of a Dry Day | 78% | 75% | 79% | 81% |
| Total Precipitation | 3.9" | 3.9" | 3.3" | 3.9" |
| Snowfall | 16.3" | 2.0" | — | 0.1" |

Comment: This area's weather is highly variable from one year to another as well as from day to day.

## Providence–Newport, RI

### Natural Environment

The entire state of Rhode Island is contained in only slightly more than 1,000 square miles, but its seacoast, wandering back and forth along countless bays and inlets, is 400 miles long. From its southwestern corner, at Watch Hill Point, out to Block Island and up through Narragansett Bay, this is a superb water playground. Freshwater lakes abound as well; small ones are scattered all over the state.

MAJOR GEOGRAPHIC FEATURES
  Rivers: Pawtuxet, Seekonk
  Shoreline: Atlantic Ocean, Narragansett Bay, Newport Bay, Rhode Island Sound
  Islands: Block
  Other: Point Judith

NATURE-PRESERVATION AREAS
  Ninigret National Wildlife Refuge
  Sachuest Point National Wildlife Refuge
  Trustom Pond National Wildlife Refuge

| Terrain | Open Space | Forests | Inland Water | Shore-line | Rivers | Nature Preser-vation | Nature's Spectac-ulars |
|---|---|---|---|---|---|---|---|
| — | -200 | 600 | 500 | 540 | — | 100 | — |

Places Rated Score: 1,540          Places Rated Rank: 70

## Climate

| PROVIDENCE–NEWPORT, RI | January | April | July | October |
|---|---|---|---|---|
| Hours of Sunshine | 5:26 | 7:28 | 9:23 | 6:40 |
| Chances of a Sunny Day | 55% | 53% | 61% | 61% |
| Afternoon Temperatures | 36° | 58° | 82° | 63° |
| Relative Humidity | 63% | 58% | 68% | 67% |
| Chances of a Dry Day | 78% | 77% | 84% | 84% |
| Total Precipitation | 4.1" | 4.0" | 3.0" | 3.8" |
| Snowfall | 9.6" | 0.8" | — | 0.2" |

Comment: The proximity of Narragansett Bay and Rhode Island Sound keep summer temperatures pleasant and also keep winters warmer than at locations farther inland.

## Put-in-Bay–Lake Erie Shore, OH

### Natural Environment

Lake Erie is Ohio's "north coast," and its islands are a favorite playground. Both the islands and the northern mainland areas are heavily planted in vineyards. From the top of Perry's Monument, on South Bass Island, views of the lake and the rich farmlands of southern Ontario are superb.

MAJOR GEOGRAPHIC FEATURES
Rivers: Maumee
Shoreline: Lake Erie, Maumee Bay, Sandusky Bay
Islands: Kelleys

NATURE-PRESERVATION AREAS
Ottawa National Wildlife Refuge

| Terrain | Open Space | Forests | Inland Water | Shore-line | Rivers | Nature Preser-vation | Nature's Spectac-ulars |
|---|---|---|---|---|---|---|---|
| — | — | 100 | 260 | 600 | — | 100 | — |

Places Rated Score: 1,060          Places Rated Rank: 88

## Climate

**PUT-IN-BAY–LAKE ERIE SHORE, OH**

| | January | April | July | October |
|---|---|---|---|---|
| Hours of Sunshine | 3:21 | 6:56 | 10:34 | 6:07 |
| Chances of a Sunny Day | 42% | 53% | 81% | 61% |
| Afternoon Temperatures | 32° | 57° | 83° | 64° |
| Relative Humidity | 75% | 67% | 64% | 68% |
| Chances of a Dry Day | 84% | 77% | 84% | 87% |
| Total Precipitation | 2.0″ | 3.1″ | 3.1″ | 2.0″ |
| Snowfall | 6.0″ | 0.7″ | — | — |

Comment: These peninsulas and islands possess a very pleasant summer climate. Snowfalls are much heavier on the mainland.

# Rangeley Lakes, ME

## Natural Environment

The Rangeley Lakes region of Maine is one of America's few remaining vacation spots where one can truly escape most of the disadvantages of civilization. There are a half-dozen major lakes and several dozen ponds within ten miles of Rangeley, all surrounded by deep forests and open high hills and low mountains. The area is halfway between the North Pole and the equator.

MAJOR GEOGRAPHIC FEATURES
Terrain: Appalachian Mountains, Blue Mountains, Sugarloaf Mountain (4,250 ft.)
Lakes and Reservoirs: Aziscohos Lake, Brassua Lake, Canada Falls Lake, Flagstaff Lake, Moosehead Lake, Mooselookmeguntic Lake, Rangeley Lake, Richardson Lakes, Umbagog Lake

| Terrain | Open Space | Forests | Inland Water | Shore-line | Rivers | Nature Preser-vation | Nature's Spectac-ulars |
|---|---|---|---|---|---|---|---|
| 530 | 1,000 | 800 | 500 | — | — | — | — |

Places Rated Score: 2,830          Places Rated Rank: 18

## Climate

**RANGELEY LAKES–SUGARLOAF MOUNTAIN, ME**

| | January | April | July | October |
|---|---|---|---|---|
| Hours of Sunshine | 3:58 | 6:49 | 9:04 | 5:24 |
| Chances of a Sunny Day | 34% | 38% | 42% | 42% |
| Afternoon Temperatures | 21° | 45° | 74° | 53° |
| Relative Humidity | 72% | 69% | 73% | 76% |
| Chances of a Dry Day | 76% | 74% | 74% | 75% |
| Total Precipitation | 2.6″ | 2.7″ | 3.8″ | 3.0″ |
| Snowfall | 26.9″ | 10.6″ | — | 2.6″ |

Comment: The mountain ski resorts of the area receive much heavier snowfalls, of course.

# ★Redwoods–Shasta–Lassen, CA

## Natural Environment

This vast area offers several different kinds of vacation opportunities. Even though the total territory is large, distances are not too great to sample the seacoast on one day, the interior mountains on the next.

MAJOR GEOGRAPHIC FEATURES
Terrain: Boulder Peak (8,299 ft.), Cascade Range, Coast Ranges, Klamath Mountains, Lassen Peak (10,457 ft.), Mount Shasta (14,162 ft.)
Lakes and Reservoirs: Shasta Lake
Rivers: Sacramento
Shoreline: Humboldt Bay, Pacific Ocean

NATURE-PRESERVATION AREAS
Humboldt Bay National Wildlife Refuge
Lassen Volcanic National Park
Lava Beds National Monument
Redwood National Park
Whiskeytown-Shasta-Trinity National Recreation Area

NATURE'S SPECTACULARS
Redwood National Park (World Heritage Site)

| Terrain | Open Space | Forests | Inland Water | Shore-line | Rivers | Nature Preser-vation | Nature's Spectac-ulars |
|---|---|---|---|---|---|---|---|
| 970 | 1,000 | 800 | 60 | 600 | 375 | 700 | 500 |

Places Rated Score: 5,005          Places Rated Rank: 1

## Climate

**REDWOOD NATIONAL PARK, CA**

| | January | April | July | October |
|---|---|---|---|---|
| Hours of Sunshine | 4:00 | 7:28 | 7:53 | 5:27 |
| Chances of a Sunny Day | 39% | 50% | 55% | 55% |
| Afternoon Temperatures | 54° | 61° | 69° | 66° |
| Relative Humidity | 82% | 84% | 88% | 86% |
| Chances of a Dry Day | 50% | 73% | 97% | 74% |
| Total Precipitation | 11.9″ | 4.6″ | 0.3″ | 5.1″ |

Comment: Redwoods thrive on fog, which is especially common in autumn and early winter.

**WHISKEYTOWN–SHASTA–TRINITY NATIONAL RECREATION AREA, CA**

| | January | April | July | October |
|---|---|---|---|---|
| Hours of Sunshine | 5:12 | 10:38 | 14:12 | 9:02 |
| Chances of a Sunny Day | 48% | 67% | 94% | 71% |
| Afternoon Temperatures | 42° | 58° | 85° | 65° |
| Relative Humidity | 71% | 58% | 48% | 59% |
| Chances of a Dry Day | 66% | 82% | 99% | 89% |
| Total Precipitation | 7.2″ | 2.8″ | 0.3″ | 2.0″ |
| Snowfall | 30.6″ | 9.2″ | — | 0.4″ |

Comment: A distinctly mountain climate, but a rather mild one. Tremendous summers.

**LASSEN VOLCANIC NATIONAL PARK, CA**

| | January | April | July | October |
|---|---|---|---|---|
| Hours of Sunshine | 5:13 | 10:37 | 14:10 | 9:03 |
| Chances of a Sunny Day | 42% | 60% | 97% | 74% |
| Afternoon Temperatures | 40° | 50° | 79° | 60° |
| Relative Humidity | 60% | 60% | 40% | 48% |
| Chances of a Dry Day | 60% | 72% | 98% | 84% |
| Total Precipitation | 6.9″ | 3.6″ | 0.4″ | 3.0″ |
| Snowfall | 48.2″ | 19.8″ | — | 3.3″ |

Comment: Heavy snows keep all of the park's roads closed from late October to early June.

# Richmond–Fredericksburg, VA

## Natural Environment

The Virginia corridor encompassing three of the state's most historically interesting cities (Richmond, Fredericksburg, and Petersburg) lies along the edge of the Piedmont, just west of the area known as Tidewater Virginia. Here the flat lands of the coastal plain give way to a wedge-shaped plateau that gradually slopes upward toward the mountains of western Virginia. Richmond was settled at the falls of the James River. Small farms and orchards make up the rural scenes outside the cities.

MAJOR GEOGRAPHIC FEATURES
  Lakes and Reservoirs: Lake Anna
  Rivers: James

NATURE-PRESERVATION AREAS
  Presquile National Wildlife Refuge

| Terrain | Open Space | Forests | Inland Water | Shore-line | Rivers | Nature Preser-vation | Nature's Spectac-ulars |
|---|---|---|---|---|---|---|---|
| — | 200 | 800 | 90 | — | — | 100 | — |

Places Rated Score: 1,190        Places Rated Rank: 83

## Climate

| RICHMOND–WASHINGTON CORRIDOR, VA | January | April | July | October |
|---|---|---|---|---|
| Hours of Sunshine | 5:15 | 8:25 | 9:42 | 6:52 |
| Chances of a Sunny Day | 48% | 57% | 61% | 61% |
| Afternoon Temperatures | 47° | 71° | 88° | 71° |
| Relative Humidity | 69% | 61% | 73% | 71% |
| Chances of a Dry Day | 80% | 79% | 76% | 86% |
| Total Precipitation | 3.2″ | 2.9″ | 5.1″ | 3.7″ |
| Snowfall | 5.1″ | 0.1″ | — | — |

Comment: A typical southern tidewater climate: long, warm, humid summers and short, mild winters. Both spring and autumn are enjoyable seasons.

# Sacramento–Gold Rush Towns, CA

## Natural Environment

The forty-niners chugged up the Sacramento River to this, the Mother Lode country, in the foothills of the Sierra Nevada. Today's vacationers can still enjoy panning for gold, but many of them prefer taking pictures of the hillsides, bright with wildflowers in the spring and with shiny foliage in the fall. This is one of the few western spots where autumn foliage is truly spectacular, because some of the easterners who came in search of wealth brought with them seedlings of several varieties of trees not native to California. They have flourished and today add a great bonus to sightseeing here.

MAJOR GEOGRAPHIC FEATURES
  Terrain: Sacramento Valley, Sierra Nevada
  Lakes and Reservoirs: Folsom Lake
  Rivers: Sacramento

NATURE-PRESERVATION AREAS
  Sutter National Wildlife Refuge

| Terrain | Open Space | Forests | Inland Water | Shore-line | Rivers | Nature Preser-vation | Nature's Spectac-ulars |
|---|---|---|---|---|---|---|---|
| 560 | 200 | 800 | 50 | — | — | 100 | — |

Places Rated Score: 1,710        Places Rated Rank: 62

## Climate

| SACRAMENTO, CA | January | April | July | October |
|---|---|---|---|---|
| Hours of Sunshine | 4:19 | 10:42 | 14:08 | 9:33 |
| Chances of a Sunny Day | 39% | 73% | 97% | 81% |
| Afternoon Temperatures | 53° | 71° | 93° | 78° |
| Relative Humidity | 81% | 63% | 52% | 60% |
| Chances of a Dry Day | 76% | 89% | 99% | 94% |
| Total Precipitation | 4.0″ | 1.3″ | 0.1″ | 0.9″ |

Comment: Summers are very hot, sunny, and dry. Low humidities, however, make these high temperatures much more bearable than similar temperatures in the more humid East.

| GOLD RUSH TOWNS, CA | January | April | July | October |
|---|---|---|---|---|
| Hours of Sunshine | 5:25 | 10:42 | 13:51 | 9:29 |
| Chances of a Sunny Day | 46% | 68% | 95% | 77% |
| Afternoon Temperatures | 51° | 65° | 92° | 73° |
| Relative Humidity | 86% | 58% | 48% | 57% |
| Chances of a Dry Day | 71% | 82% | 99% | 91% |
| Total Precipitation | 7.9″ | 3.5″ | 0.2″ | 1.9″ |
| Snowfall | 2.6″ | 0.3″ | — | — |

Comment: This climate is typical of the Sierra foothills of California.

# St. Augustine–Northeast Coast, FL

## Natural Environment

Northeastern Florida has a slightly more rugged look and a more varied climate than the coastal areas farther south. Low sand dunes on the barrier islands are topped with sea oats. The blue of the ocean is a cooler hue than it is around Miami.

MAJOR GEOGRAPHIC FEATURES
  Lakes and Reservoirs: Lake George
  Rivers: St. Johns
  Shoreline: Atlantic Ocean
  Islands: Amelia, Anastasia

NATURE-PRESERVATION AREAS
  Lake Woodruff National Wildlife Refuge

| Terrain | Open Space | Forests | Inland Water | Shore-line | Rivers | Nature Preser-vation | Nature's Spectac-ulars |
|---|---|---|---|---|---|---|---|
| — | 200 | 600 | 400 | 600 | — | 100 | — |

Places Rated Score: 1,900        Places Rated Rank: 54

## Climate

| ST. AUGUSTINE–NORTHEAST COAST, FL | January | April | July | October |
|---|---|---|---|---|
| Hours of Sunshine | 6:04 | 9:17 | 8:28 | 6:32 |
| Chances of a Sunny Day | 58% | 68% | 61% | 63% |
| Afternoon Temperatures | 68° | 78° | 90° | 81° |
| Relative Humidity | 73% | 70% | 77% | 77% |
| Chances of a Dry Day | 84% | 86% | 71% | 77% |
| Total Precipitation | 2.5″ | 2.9″ | 5.8″ | 5.5″ |

Comment: Most warm days have a pleasant and vigorous sea breeze. Hurricanes brush this part of Florida only about one year in forty.

# St. Louis–Mark Twain Country, MO–IL

## Natural Environment

The Mississippi and Missouri rivers are the dominant features of this area. Numerous smaller streams contribute to this great river system. There are a few hills, as well as bluffs along the rivers.

MAJOR GEOGRAPHIC FEATURES
Lakes and Reservoirs: Mark Twain Lake
Rivers: Mississippi, Missouri

NATURE-PRESERVATION AREAS
Clarence Cannon National Wildlife Refuge

| Terrain | Open Space | Forests | Inland Water | Shore-line | Rivers | Nature Preser-vation | Nature's Spectac-ulars |
|---|---|---|---|---|---|---|---|
| 270 | — | 400 | 90 | — | 300 | 100 | |

Places Rated Score: 1,160          Places Rated Rank: 84

## Climate

| ST. LOUIS–MARK TWAIN COUNTRY, MO–IL | January | April | July | October |
|---|---|---|---|---|
| Hours of Sunshine | 4:49 | 7:43 | 10:28 | 7:11 |
| Chances of a Sunny Day | 45% | 50% | 68% | 68% |
| Afternoon Temperatures | 38° | 67° | 89° | 69° |
| Relative Humidity | 75% | 67% | 71% | 71% |
| Chances of a Dry Day | 86% | 76% | 83% | 82% |
| Total Precipitation | 1.7″ | 3.6″ | 3.6″ | 2.3″ |
| Snowfall | 5.4″ | 0.4″ | — | — |

Comment: Typical midwestern climate, with four distinct seasons.

# Salt Lake City, UT

## Natural Environment

Northern Utah has an abundance of high mountains, blanketed with several feet of snow in winter. There are numerous lakes in the area; Bear Lake is especially scenic. Canyons and waterfalls, fertile valleys, and the unique Great Salt Lake add to the area's sightseeing interest.

MAJOR GEOGRAPHIC FEATURES
Terrain: Spanish Fork Peak (10,192 ft.), Wasatch Range
Lakes and Reservoirs: Bear Lake, Great Salt Lake, Utah Lake

NATURE-PRESERVATION AREAS
Bear River Migratory Bird Refuge
Timpanogos Cave National Monument

NATURE'S SPECTACULARS
Great Salt Lake

| Terrain | Open Space | Forests | Inland Water | Shore-line | Rivers | Nature Preser-vation | Nature's Spectac-ulars |
|---|---|---|---|---|---|---|---|
| 940 | 200 | 600 | 450 | — | — | 100 | 500 |

Places Rated Score: 2,790          Places Rated Rank: 19

## Climate

| SALT LAKE CITY, UT | January | April | July | October |
|---|---|---|---|---|
| Hours of Sunshine | 4:26 | 8:54 | 12:25 | 8:02 |
| Chances of a Sunny Day | 39% | 53% | 87% | 71% |
| Afternoon Temperatures | 37° | 61° | 93° | 67° |
| Relative Humidity | 73% | 53% | 36% | 55% |
| Chances of a Dry Day | 87% | 82% | 95% | 88% |
| Total Precipitation | 1.4″ | 2.2″ | 0.7″ | 1.1″ |
| Snowfall | 13.3″ | 5.0″ | — | 1.0″ |

Comment: Salt Lake City lies on the flanks of the Wasatch Mountains. The higher neighborhoods are a bit cooler and wetter.

| WASATCH RANGE AREA, UT | January | April | July | October |
|---|---|---|---|---|
| Hours of Sunshine | 4:26 | 8:54 | 12:24 | 8:02 |
| Chances of a Sunny Day | 35% | 50% | 84% | 68% |
| Afternoon Temperatures | 31° | 44° | 73° | 52° |
| Relative Humidity | 78% | 67% | 51% | 69% |
| Chances of a Dry Day | 65% | 67% | 87% | 81% |
| Total Precipitation | 5.6″ | 4.4″ | 1.3″ | 2.9″ |
| Snowfall | 65.1″ | 45.9″ | — | 19.1″ |

Comment: A hiker's paradise during the brief summer, and a powder-snow skier's paradise during the rest of the year.

# San Antonio, TX

## Natural Environment

Like Austin, San Antonio is situated on the edge of the Balcones Escarpment; west of the city the terrain begins to rise into open high hills. The city has made the most of one of its natural attractions; the walkways along the San Antonio River are beautifully landscaped. Natural Bridge Cavern, near New Braunfels, and Aquarena Springs, in San Marcos, are two other attractions nature has provided for the area.

MAJOR GEOGRAPHIC FEATURES
Terrain: Balcones Escarpment
Lakes and Reservoirs: Canyon Lake

| Terrain | Open Space | Forests | Inland Water | Shore-line | Rivers | Nature Preser-vation | Nature's Spectac-ulars |
|---|---|---|---|---|---|---|---|
| 90 | — | 400 | 60 | — | — | — | — |

Places Rated Score: 550          Places Rated Rank: 100

## Climate

| SAN ANTONIO, TX | January | April | July | October |
|---|---|---|---|---|
| Hours of Sunshine | 5:02 | 7:05 | 10:14 | 7:21 |
| Chances of a Sunny Day | 48% | 50% | 77% | 71% |
| Afternoon Temperatures | 62° | 80° | 95° | 82° |
| Relative Humidity | 69% | 67% | 66% | 69% |
| Chances of a Dry Day | 90% | 87% | 92% | 86% |
| Total Precipitation | 1.6″ | 2.7″ | 1.9″ | 2.9″ |

Comment: Summers are long and hot. Seven out of eight winters have no measurable snowfall.

# San Diego, CA

## Natural Environment

San Diego has a particularly fortunate location, with the Pacific Ocean on one side and grassy hills on the other. As you travel east, the hills turn into mountains, then into desert. Cleveland National Forest has stands of coniferous trees and strange-looking hills strewn with boulders.

MAJOR GEOGRAPHIC FEATURES
Terrain: Cuyamaca Peak (6,512 ft.), Laguna Mountains
Shoreline: Mission Bay, Pacific Ocean, San Diego Bay

| Terrain | Open Space | Forests | Inland Water | Shore-line | Rivers | Nature Preser-vation | Nature's Spectac-ulars |
|---|---|---|---|---|---|---|---|
| 560 | — | 400 | 60 | 600 | — | — | — |

Places Rated Score: 1,620          Places Rated Rank: 66

## Climate

| SAN DIEGO, CA | January | April | July | October |
|---|---|---|---|---|
| Hours of Sunshine | 7:18 | 8:34 | 9:34 | 7:45 |
| Chances of a Sunny Day | 65% | 67% | 84% | 77% |
| Afternoon Temperatures | 65° | 68° | 76° | 75° |
| Relative Humidity | 63% | 66% | 73% | 68% |
| Chances of a Dry Day | 85% | 93% | 98% | 95% |
| Total Precipitation | 2.1" | 0.8" | — | 0.3" |

Comment: San Diego has the least stressful climate of any major city in the United States.

# San Francisco, CA

## Natural Environment

This hilly city has one great view after another—of the ocean, the bay, and the mountains. Even though the air is frequently fog filled and winds can make the evenings uncomfortably chilly, most people enjoy San Francisco's weather—or at least enjoy the city enough that the weather doesn't seem very important. Watching the sun set over the Golden Gate is an unforgettable experience. A short distance north of the city is the beautiful coastal wilderness of Point Reyes National Seashore, an area of long beaches, sand dunes, steep cliffs, and wooded ridges.

MAJOR GEOGRAPHIC FEATURES
  Terrain: Coast Ranges, Mount Tamalpais (2,571 ft.), Santa Cruz
    Mountains
  Shoreline: Pacific Ocean, San Francisco Bay

NATURE-PRESERVATION AREAS
  Antioch Dunes National Wildlife Refuge
  Golden Gate National Recreation Area
  Muir Woods National Monument
  Point Reyes National Seashore
  San Francisco Bay National Wildlife Refuge

NATURE'S SPECTACULARS
  Point Reyes National Seashore (World Heritage Site)

| Terrain | Open Space | Forests | Inland Water | Shore-line | Rivers | Nature Preser-vation | Nature's Spectac-ulars |
|---|---|---|---|---|---|---|---|
| 440 | −300 | 400 | 500 | 300 | — | 300 | 500 |

Places Rated Score: 2,140          Places Rated Rank: 37

## Climate

| SAN FRANCISCO, CA | January | April | July | October |
|---|---|---|---|---|
| Hours of Sunshine | 5:32 | 9:37 | 9:34 | 7:53 |
| Chances of a Sunny Day | 52% | 70% | 90% | 81% |
| Afternoon Temperatures | 56° | 61° | 64° | 68° |
| Relative Humidity | 77% | 71% | 74% | 70% |
| Chances of a Dry Day | 77% | 89% | 99% | 94% |
| Total Precipitation | 4.5" | 1.5" | — | 1.1" |

Comment: Never really cold and never really hot. Jackets and light coats make comfortable evening wear in all seasons.

# Santa Barbara–San Simeon, CA

## Natural Environment

Palm trees, date gardens, and citrus groves; white beaches and blue sea; wild wooded foothills—all these combine to make the portion of California's coast from Santa Barbara to San Simeon idyllically beautiful. Vineyards flourish in the valleys east of San Luis Obispo.

MAJOR GEOGRAPHIC FEATURES
  Terrain: San Rafael Mountains, Timber Mountain (4,764 ft.)
  Lakes and Reservoirs: Lake Cachuma, Nacimiento Reservoir,
    Santa Margarita Lake, Twitchell Reservoir
  Rivers: Santa Ynez
  Shoreline: Pacific Ocean, Santa Barbara Channel
  Islands: Channel

| Terrain | Open Space | Forests | Inland Water | Shore-line | Rivers | Nature Preser-vation | Nature's Spectac-ulars |
|---|---|---|---|---|---|---|---|
| 650 | 300 | 400 | 20 | 600 | — | — | — |

Places Rated Score: 1,970          Places Rated Rank: 48

## Climate

| SANTA BARBARA, CA | January | April | July | October |
|---|---|---|---|---|
| Hours of Sunshine | 6:25 | 8:59 | 11:18 | 8:20 |
| Chances of a Sunny Day | 65% | 75% | 94% | 81% |
| Afternoon Temperatures | 63° | 67° | 74° | 73° |
| Relative Humidity | 69% | 77% | 82% | 77% |
| Chances of a Dry Day | 82% | 90% | 99% | 97% |
| Total Precipitation | 3.8" | 1.4" | — | 0.4" |

Comment: One of the most pleasant of the California coastal climates.

| SAN SIMEON, CA | January | April | July | October |
|---|---|---|---|---|
| Hours of Sunshine | 5:19 | 8:47 | 10:45 | 8:22 |
| Chances of a Sunny Day | 57% | 71% | 92% | 82% |
| Afternoon Temperatures | 58° | 57° | 61° | 62° |
| Relative Humidity | 86% | 81% | 87% | 81% |
| Chances of a Dry Day | 85% | 93% | 99% | 97% |
| Total Precipitation | 7.0" | 2.7" | — | 1.3" |

Comment: Morning and late afternoon fogs are common along this coast.

# Savannah–Golden Isles, GA

## Natural Environment

Golden beaches, forests draped in Spanish moss, and marshes teeming with wild turkeys and other birds give Georgia's short and lovely coastal area a magic appeal. Glynn County, which is a part of this Vacation Place, is the area about which Sidney Lanier wrote his poem "The Marshes of Glynn." The Golden Isles are a group of barrier islands; a few are populated, several others have few or no inhabitants.

MAJOR GEOGRAPHIC FEATURES
  Rivers: Savannah
  Shoreline: Atlantic Ocean

NATURE-PRESERVATION AREAS
  Blackbeard Island National Wildlife Refuge
  Cumberland Island National Seashore
  Harris Neck National Wildlife Refuge
  Tybee National Wildlife Refuge
  Wassaw National Wildlife Refuge
  Wolf Island National Wildlife Refuge

| Terrain | Open Space | Forests | Inland Water | Shore-line | Rivers | Nature Preser-vation | Nature's Spectac-ulars |
|---|---|---|---|---|---|---|---|
| — | 300 | 600 | 310 | 750 | — | 300 | — |

Places Rated Score: 2,260          Places Rated Rank: 30

## Climate

| SAVANNAH, GA | January | April | July | October |
|---|---|---|---|---|
| Hours of Sunshine | 5:41 | 9:04 | 8:42 | 7:18 |
| Chances of a Sunny Day | 48% | 63% | 58% | 65% |
| Afternoon Temperatures | 60° | 78° | 91° | 78° |
| Relative Humidity | 68% | 65% | 74% | 70% |
| Chances of a Dry Day | 81% | 82% | 67% | 87% |
| Total Precipitation | 3.1" | 3.2" | 7.4" | 2.3" |

Comment: Most winters are without any measurable snowfall.

| GOLDEN ISLES, GA | January | April | July | October |
|---|---|---|---|---|
| Hours of Sunshine | 5:54 | 9:12 | 8:34 | 6:51 |
| Chances of a Sunny Day | 52% | 65% | 60% | 63% |
| Afternoon Temperatures | 61° | 76° | 90° | 77° |
| Relative Humidity | 70% | 66% | 73% | 73% |
| Chances of a Dry Day | 84% | 87% | 69% | 84% |
| Total Precipitation | 3.1″ | 2.8″ | 6.2″ | 3.3″ |

Comment: These relatively little-known islands have a magnificent resort climate virtually all year long.

# ★Seattle–Mount Rainier–North Cascades, WA

## Natural Environment

Mount Rainier, towering more than two-and-one-half miles above sea level, is Seattle's, and the state of Washington's, trademark. It is the tallest volcanic peak in the North Cascades, and it is frosted with 41 glaciers. The Cascades are rugged, sharply peaked mountains. The heavy moisture that flows off the mountains makes the lower elevations extremely luxuriant with vegetation. Seattle gives the impression of being a glossy-green city because of its abundance of trees and plants. No less important, for both scenery and recreation, is the shoreline on Puget Sound.

MAJOR GEOGRAPHIC FEATURES
  Mountains: Cascade Range, Mount Baker (10,778 ft.), Mount Rainier (14,410 ft.)
  Lakes and Reservoirs: Lake Washington
  Shoreline: Puget Sound

NATURE-PRESERVATION AREAS
  Lake Chelan National Recreation Area
  Mount Rainier National Park
  Nisqually National Wildlife Refuge
  North Cascades National Park
  Ross Lake National Recreation Area
  San Juan Islands National Wildlife Refuge

NATURE'S SPECTACULARS
  Mount Rainier National Park

| Terrain | Open Space | Forests | Inland Water | Shore-line | Rivers | Nature Preser-vation | Nature's Spectac-ulars |
|---|---|---|---|---|---|---|---|
| 740 | 200 | 800 | 170 | 800 | 200 | 700 | 500 |

Places Rated Score: 4,110          Places Rated Rank: 3

## Climate

| SEATTLE, WA | January | April | July | October |
|---|---|---|---|---|
| Hours of Sunshine | 2:30 | 6:24 | 9:48 | 4:02 |
| Chances of a Sunny Day | 26% | 47% | 71% | 42% |
| Afternoon Temperatures | 45° | 58° | 75° | 60° |
| Relative Humidity | 77% | 70% | 66% | 77% |
| Chances of a Dry Day | 60% | 75% | 93% | 72% |
| Total Precipitation | 5.9″ | 2.5″ | 0.9″ | 3.4″ |
| Snowfall | 3.7″ | — | — | — |

Comment: Genial, fairly dry summers with mild, cloudy, and wet winters.

| MOUNT RAINIER, WA | January | April | July | October |
|---|---|---|---|---|
| Hours of Sunshine | 1:48 | 6:39 | 9:26 | 3:23 |
| Chances of a Sunny Day | 16% | 27% | 65% | 35% |
| Afternoon Temperatures | 31° | 41° | 62° | 48° |
| Relative Humidity | 91% | 84% | 76% | 82% |
| Chances of a Dry Day | 39% | 60% | 87% | 61% |
| Total Precipitation | 18.4″ | 7.6″ | 1.7″ | 9.7″ |
| Snowfall | 122.1″ | 52.6″ | 0.3″ | 21.7″ |

Comment: These data are for Paradise ranger station, at 5,550 feet above sea level. Attractions at lower elevations are warmer, with less snow. Higher elevations are inaccessible by road in the winter months.

| MOUNT BAKER, WA | January | April | July | October |
|---|---|---|---|---|
| Hours of Sunshine | 2:22 | 6:18 | 9:45 | 3:54 |
| Chances of a Sunny Day | 13% | 23% | 61% | 32% |
| Afternoon Temperatures | 33° | 43° | 64° | 50° |
| Relative Humidity | 91% | 83% | 73% | 81% |
| Chances of a Dry Day | 52% | 60% | 81% | 61% |
| Total Precipitation | 11.9″ | 8.5″ | 3.3″ | 11.3″ |
| Snowfall | 88.0″ | 50.2″ | — | 14.7″ |

Comment: These data are typical of the 4,000- to 5,000-foot levels of the western slopes of the northern Cascade Range.

# Spokane–Coeur d'Alene, WA–ID

## Natural Environment

Spokane, the major city in eastern Washington, is in a bowl surrounded by hills and mountains. A few miles to the east is Coeur d'Alene, Idaho. The panhandle of northern Idaho is covered with forests and dotted with lakes and rivers. The largest stand of white pine in the country is in St. Joe National Forest.

MAJOR GEOGRAPHIC FEATURES
  Terrain: Coeur d'Alene Mountains, Grizzly Mountain (5,950 ft.), Rocky Mountains, Selkirk Mountains
  Lakes and Reservoirs: Coeur d'Alene Lake, Lake Pend Oreille, Priest Lake
  Rivers: Pend Oreille

NATURE-PRESERVATION AREAS
  Kootenai National Wildlife Refuge
  Turnbull National Wildlife Refuge

| Terrain | Open Space | Forests | Inland Water | Shore-line | Rivers | Nature Preser-vation | Nature's Spectac-ulars |
|---|---|---|---|---|---|---|---|
| 850 | 700 | 800 | 130 | — | 200 | 100 | — |

Places Rated Score: 2,780          Places Rated Rank: 21

## Climate

| SPOKANE, WA | January | April | July | October |
|---|---|---|---|---|
| Hours of Sunshine | 2:19 | 8:10 | 12:27 | 5:47 |
| Chances of a Sunny Day | 23% | 43% | 81% | 48% |
| Afternoon Temperatures | 31° | 57° | 84° | 58° |
| Relative Humidity | 81% | 60% | 45% | 64% |
| Chances of a Dry Day | 75% | 85% | 94% | 82% |
| Total Precipitation | 2.5″ | 1.1″ | 0.5″ | 1.1″ |
| Snowfall | 17.6″ | 0.7″ | — | 0.5″ |

Comment: Summers are warm, sunny, and fairly dry. Winters are cold, cloudy, and wet.

# Tampa Bay–Southwest Coast, FL

## Natural Environment

The usually serene Gulf of Mexico occasionally kicks up a humdinger of a hurricane in this part of Florida. Usually, however, the subtropical climate is intoxicatingly pleasant. Several spots in this part of Florida are quite unusual and well worth noting. The beaches of Sanibel and Captiva islands are the best shell-collecting areas in the Western Hemisphere. Safety Harbor, just north of Clearwater, has mineral springs that have been known and appreciated since Native Americans discovered them. Northwest of Naples is a rich and wonderful wetlands preserve, the Audubon Society's Corkscrew Swamp Sanctuary.

MAJOR GEOGRAPHIC FEATURES
  Shoreline: Gulf of Mexico, Tampa Bay
  Islands: Longboat Key, Mullet Key, Sand Key

NATURE-PRESERVATION AREAS
  Caloosahatchee National Wildlife Refuge
  Egmont Key National Wildlife Refuge
  Island Bay National Wildlife Refuge
  J.N. "Ding" Darling National Wildlife Refuge
  Matlacha Pass National Wildlife Refuge
  Passage Key National Wildlife Refuge
  Pine Island National Wildlife Refuge
  Pinellas National Wildlife Refuge

| Terrain | Open Space | Forests | Inland Water | Shore-line | Rivers | Nature Preser-vation | Nature's Spectac-ulars |
|---|---|---|---|---|---|---|---|
| — | –200 | — | 280 | 750 | — | 100 | — |

Places Rated Score: 930        Places Rated Rank: 90

## Climate

| TAMPA BAY, FL | January | April | July | October |
|---|---|---|---|---|
| Hours of Sunshine | 6:53 | 9:37 | 8:31 | 7:22 |
| Chances of a Sunny Day | 65% | 73% | 58% | 71% |
| Afternoon Temperatures | 70° | 82° | 90° | 84° |
| Relative Humidity | 73% | 69% | 76% | 73% |
| Chances of a Dry Day | 86% | 88% | 63% | 85% |
| Total Precipitation | 2.2" | 1.8" | 7.4" | 2.3" |

Comment: April, May, October, and November are the most pleasant months in this very popular visitor center.

| FORT MYERS–SOUTHWEST COAST, FL | January | April | July | October |
|---|---|---|---|---|
| Hours of Sunshine | 7:23 | 10:10 | 9:28 | 7:45 |
| Chances of a Sunny Day | 74% | 80% | 65% | 74% |
| Afternoon Temperatures | 74° | 85° | 91° | 85° |
| Relative Humidity | 73% | 69% | 74% | 73% |
| Chances of a Dry Day | 90% | 88% | 60% | 82% |
| Total Precipitation | 1.9" | 1.5" | 8.6" | 3.9" |

Comment: A subtropical climate, with afternoon and evening thunderstorms common during the long summers.

# Traverse City–Petoskey, MI

## Natural Environment

Wooded hills—particularly colorful in autumn—inland lakes, calm bays, beaches, and magnificent sand dunes are the attractions of Grand Traverse Bay and the Leelanau Peninsula. Rockhounds walk the shores of Lake Michigan looking for the unusual Petoskey stones found only here.

MAJOR GEOGRAPHIC FEATURES
  Lakes and Reservoirs: Elk Lake, Glen Lake, Lake Charlevoix, Lake Leelanau, Torch Lake
  Shoreline: Grand Traverse Bay, Lake Michigan
NATURE-PRESERVATION AREAS
  Sleeping Bear Dunes National Lakeshore

| Terrain | Open Space | Forests | Inland Water | Shore-line | Rivers | Nature Preser-vation | Nature's Spectac-ulars |
|---|---|---|---|---|---|---|---|
| — | 700 | 600 | 370 | 600 | — | 200 | — |

Places Rated Score: 2,470        Places Rated Rank: 26

## Climate

| TRAVERSE CITY–PETOSKEY, MI | January | April | July | October |
|---|---|---|---|---|
| Hours of Sunshine | 3:38 | 7:25 | 10:08 | 5:04 |
| Chances of a Sunny Day | 38% | 50% | 70% | 47% |
| Afternoon Temperatures | 26° | 53° | 81° | 59° |
| Relative Humidity | 80% | 69% | 71% | 75% |
| Chances of a Dry Day | 82% | 80% | 82% | 79% |
| Total Precipitation | 1.9" | 2.5" | 2.9" | 2.6" |
| Snowfall | 20.7" | 2.9" | — | 0.7" |

Comment: Lake Michigan, Grand Traverse and Little Traverse bays, and dozens of inland lakes keep this popular Vacation Place wonderfully cool during the summer.

# Tucson, AZ

## Natural Environment

Southern Arizona is desert land, but this doesn't mean that it is in any way lacking in life or natural interest. There are stark mountains, tablelands with high relief, rocky canyons, and dry gulches; there are also many species of cactus, as well as desert bighorn sheep, pronghorn, coyote, a wide variety of birds, and somewhat less friendly animals such as rattlesnakes and Gila monsters.

MAJOR GEOGRAPHIC FEATURES
  Terrain: Baboquivari Peak (7,734 ft.), Growler Mountains
  Rivers: Santa Cruz
NATURE-PRESERVATION AREAS
  Chiricahua National Monument
  Organ Pipe Cactus National Monument/Cabeza Prieta National Wildlife Refuge
  Saguaro National Monument
NATURE'S SPECTACULARS
  Organ Pipe Cactus National Monument/Cabeza Prieta National Wildlife Refuge (World Heritage Site)

| Terrain | Open Space | Forests | Inland Water | Shore-line | Rivers | Nature Preser-vation | Nature's Spectac-ulars |
|---|---|---|---|---|---|---|---|
| 850 | 700 | 100 | — | — | — | 300 | 500 |

Places Rated Score: 2,450        Places Rated Rank: 27

## Climate

| TUCSON, AZ | January | April | July | October |
|---|---|---|---|---|
| Hours of Sunshine | 8:15 | 11:56 | 10:57 | 10:09 |
| Chances of a Sunny Day | 68% | 83% | 71% | 84% |
| Afternoon Temperatures | 64° | 80° | 99° | 84° |
| Relative Humidity | 48% | 29% | 43% | 39% |
| Chances of a Dry Day | 91% | 95% | 81% | 94% |
| Total Precipitation | 0.8" | 0.3" | 2.4" | 0.9" |

Comment: About half of the winters have no measurable snowfall at all.

# Tulsa–Lake O' The Cherokees, OK

## Natural Environment

Sparkling streams, wooded hills, an abundance of man-made lakes, and lush greenery are the natural assets of northeastern Oklahoma. The Illinois River is clear and scenic. Sequoyah State Park, on Fort Gibson Reservoir, is the site of a state waterfowl refuge and is near the rugged foothills of the Boston Mountains.

MAJOR GEOGRAPHIC FEATURES
  Lakes and Reservoirs: Eufaula Lake, Keystone Lake, Lake O' The Cherokees, Oolagah Reservoir, Robert S. Kerr Reservoir, Tenkiller Reservoir
  Rivers: Arkansas, Illinois

NATURE-PRESERVATION AREAS
Sequoyah National Wildlife Refuge

| Terrain | Open Space | Forests | Inland Water | Shore-line | Rivers | Nature Preser-vation | Nature's Spectac-ulars |
|---|---|---|---|---|---|---|---|
| 90 | 300 | 400 | 220 | — | | 100 | — |

Places Rated Score: 1,110          Places Rated Rank: 87

## Climate

| TULSA–LAKE O' THE CHEROKEES, OK | January | April | July | October |
|---|---|---|---|---|
| Hours of Sunshine | 5:13 | 7:28 | 10:20 | 7:14 |
| Chances of a Sunny Day | 52% | 57% | 74% | 68% |
| Afternoon Temperatures | 46° | 72° | 94° | 75° |
| Relative Humidity | 69% | 64% | 66% | 67% |
| Chances of a Dry Day | 88% | 78% | 87% | 87% |
| Total Precipitation | 1.4″ | 4.2″ | 3.5″ | 3.4″ |
| Snowfall | 3.2″ | — | — | — |

Comment: Long hot summers, short mild winters, and pretty steady winds characterize this city.

# Vicksburg–Natchez–Baton Rouge, MS–LA

## Natural Environment

In the days when sugarcane was a major source of wealth, and large plantations, with an economy based on slavery, held the resources necessary to make fortunes from sugar, more millionaires lived in the lower Mississippi Valley than in any other part of the United States. Spanish moss draped over huge old trees and a few lazy streams characterize the area.

MAJOR GEOGRAPHIC FEATURES
Rivers: Mississippi

| Terrain | Open Space | Forests | Inland Water | Shore-line | Rivers | Nature Preser-vation | Nature's Spectac-ulars |
|---|---|---|---|---|---|---|---|
| — | 300 | 600 | 100 | — | 200 | — | — |

Places Rated Score: 1,200          Places Rated Rank: 82

## Climate

| VICKSBURG–NATCHEZ–BATON ROUGE, MS–LA | January | April | July | October |
|---|---|---|---|---|
| Hours of Sunshine | 4:43 | 8:15 | 9:10 | 8:05 |
| Chances of a Sunny Day | 48% | 60% | 69% | 76% |
| Afternoon Temperatures | 59° | 78° | 92° | 80° |
| Relative Humidity | 75% | 72% | 77% | 72% |
| Chances of a Dry Day | 78% | 81% | 75% | 89% |
| Total Precipitation | 5.6″ | 6.0″ | 4.4″ | 2.7″ |

Comment: Long, hot, humid summers in which to drift lazily down the river.

# Washington, DC–MD–VA

## Natural Environment

The city of Washington is low-lying, hot and humid in summer, and altogether an unfortunate choice, as far as weather is concerned, for a national capital. But the Blue Ridge is not far away, Chesapeake Bay is even closer, and within the city a great deal of landscaping talent has created many places of beauty. Washington is at its most beautiful when the hundreds of cherry trees are in bloom (which is during an unpredictable few days, usually in early April).

MAJOR GEOGRAPHIC FEATURES
Terrain: Appalachian Mountains, Blue Ridge
Rivers: Potomac
Shoreline: Chesapeake Bay

NATURE-PRESERVATION AREAS
Mason Neck National Wildlife Refuge
Prince William Forest Park
Rock Creek Park
Theodore Roosevelt Island

| Terrain | Open Space | Forests | Inland Water | Shore-line | Rivers | Nature Preser-vation | Nature's Spectac-ulars |
|---|---|---|---|---|---|---|---|
| — | −200 | 400 | 140 | — | — | 100 | — |

Places Rated Score: 440          Places Rated Rank: 103

## Climate

| WASHINGTON, DC–MD–VA | January | April | July | October |
|---|---|---|---|---|
| Hours of Sunshine | 4:42 | 7:40 | 9:21 | 6:37 |
| Chances of a Sunny Day | 48% | 53% | 65% | 61% |
| Afternoon Temperatures | 43° | 67° | 88° | 69° |
| Relative Humidity | 61% | 58% | 65% | 65% |
| Chances of a Dry Day | 80% | 77% | 79% | 86% |
| Total Precipitation | 2.8″ | 2.9″ | 3.9″ | 2.9″ |
| Snowfall | 5.1″ | — | — | — |

Comment: The weather tends to be most comfortable for sightseeing in either spring or fall.

# White Mountains, NH

## Natural Environment

New Hampshire's mountains are low in comparison with the Rockies and other western ranges, but they are rocky, craggy, and impressive. Rocky rivers and streams tumble down the hillsides. In autumn the highways are choked with visitors who have come to enjoy the beauties of scarlet maples, bright-yellow birches, golden elms, and a dozen other varieties of hardwood trees. New Hampshire's best-known landmark is a natural one: the Great Stone Face, also known as the Old Man of the Mountains.

MAJOR GEOGRAPHIC FEATURES
Terrain: Mount Washington (6,288 ft.), White Mountains
Lakes and Reservoirs: Lake Winnipesaukee, Squam Lake, Umbagog Lake
Rivers: Merrimack

| Terrain | Open Space | Forests | Inland Water | Shore-line | Rivers | Nature Preser-vation | Nature's Spectac-ulars |
|---|---|---|---|---|---|---|---|
| 470 | 700 | 800 | 120 | — | — | — | — |

Places Rated Score: 2,090          Places Rated Rank: 40

## Climate

| WHITE MOUNTAINS, NH | January | April | July | October |
|---|---|---|---|---|
| Hours of Sunshine | 3:00 | 6:14 | 8:02 | 5:20 |
| Chances of a Sunny Day | 44% | 42% | 47% | 48% |
| Afternoon Temperatures | 26° | 47° | 73° | 54° |
| Relative Humidity | 82% | 75% | 74% | 81% |
| Chances of a Dry Day | 77% | 72% | 74% | 76% |
| Total Precipitation | 4.4″ | 4.4″ | 4.6″ | 5.2″ |
| Snowfall | 35.4″ | 19.5″ | — | 5.6″ |

Comment: The weather station at the summit of Mount Washington recorded the highest wind speed ever measured in North America: 231 miles per hour in April, 1934.

# Williamsburg–Colonial Triangle, VA

## Natural Environment

Tidewater Virginia is a region of harbor towns and beach resorts even better known for its historical significance than for its natural beauty and climate—both of which are truly outstanding. If you are looking for a tan, sand, and salt water, come to Virginia Beach in the summertime, as vacationers have been doing since the earliest days of this country's history. Ducks, swans, and egrets flock to the marshes of Back Bay National Wildlife Refuge. In Seashore State Park statuesque cypress trees, dripping with Spanish moss, stand in black mirrorlike water.

MAJOR GEOGRAPHIC FEATURES
 Rivers: James, York
 Shoreline: Atlantic Ocean, Chesapeake Bay
 Other: Great Dismal Swamp

NATURE-PRESERVATION AREAS
 Back Bay National Wildlife Refuge
 Great Dismal Swamp National Wildlife Refuge

| Terrain | Open Space | Forests | Inland Water | Shore-line | Rivers | Nature Preser-vation | Nature's Spectac-ulars |
|---|---|---|---|---|---|---|---|
| — | –200 | 600 | 500 | 640 | — | 100 | — |

Places Rated Score: 1,640    Places Rated Rank: 65

## Climate

| WILLIAMSBURG–COLONIAL TRIANGLE, VA | January | April | July | October |
|---|---|---|---|---|
| Hours of Sunshine | 5:25 | 8:33 | 9:32 | 6:49 |
| Chances of a Sunny Day | 50% | 58% | 63% | 61% |
| Afternoon Temperatures | 49° | 71° | 88° | 71° |
| Relative Humidity | 68% | 61% | 72% | 71% |
| Chances of a Dry Day | 78% | 80% | 76% | 85% |
| Total Precipitation | 3.7" | 3.0" | 5.2" | 3.6" |
| Snowfall | 3.8" | — | — | — |

Comment: Try a visit in October: chances of a dry day are at their best, the month is fairly sunny, and temperatures are just right for strolling about.

# Wilmington–Cape Fear, NC

## Natural Environment

The land of Cape Fear, southeastern North Carolina, is an extension of the same sort of wild, lovely, coastal land as that of the Outer Banks. Swamps and marshlands lie to the west and south of Wilmington, providing homeland and feeding areas for thousands of waterfowl. The sea is all-important here: sailing, fishing, and the study of maritime history and marine life are important activities for visitors as well as residents.

MAJOR GEOGRAPHIC FEATURES
 Rivers: Cape Fear
 Shoreline: Atlantic Ocean, Long Bay, Onslow Bay
 Other: Cape Fear, Green Swamp

| Terrain | Open Space | Forests | Inland Water | Shore-line | Rivers | Nature Preser-vation | Nature's Spectac-ulars |
|---|---|---|---|---|---|---|---|
| — | 300 | 800 | 290 | 600 | — | — | — |

Places Rated Score: 1,990    Places Rated Rank: 47

## Climate

| CAPE FEAR, NC | January | April | July | October |
|---|---|---|---|---|
| Hours of Sunshine | 5:48 | 9:07 | 8:56 | 7:16 |
| Chances of a Sunny Day | 52% | 63% | 58% | 65% |
| Afternoon Temperatures | 56° | 72° | 87° | 75° |
| Relative Humidity | 69% | 64% | 76% | 73% |
| Chances of a Dry Day | 77% | 83% | 71% | 84% |
| Total Precipitation | 4.3" | 2.7" | 6.3" | 3.5" |

Comment: Generally speaking, measurable snowfall can be expected in only about one year out of two—and then the snow never amounts to much or stays for any time.

# Wine Country, CA

## Natural Environment

California's Wine Country is usually considered to be concentrated in Napa and Sonoma counties, but wine grapes are actually grown pretty much throughout the state. The area called Wine Country consists of much more than vineyards, though these alone are colorful and enjoyable enough to bring visitors. High and low mountains of the Coast Ranges add variety to the landscape, and the Pacific coast forms the region's western border.

MAJOR GEOGRAPHIC FEATURES
 Terrain: Coast Ranges, Napa Valley
 Lakes and Reservoirs: Clear Lake
 Rivers: Russian

NATURE-PRESERVATION AREAS
 San Pablo Bay National Wildlife Refuge

| Terrain | Open Space | Forests | Inland Water | Shore-line | Rivers | Nature Preser-vation | Nature's Spectac-ulars |
|---|---|---|---|---|---|---|---|
| 770 | 700 | 800 | 90 | 600 | — | 100 | — |

Places Rated Score: 3,060    Places Rated Rank: 16

## Climate

| WINE COUNTRY, CA | January | April | July | October |
|---|---|---|---|---|
| Hours of Sunshine | 4:56 | 10:08 | 11:47 | 8:40 |
| Chances of a Sunny Day | 47% | 71% | 93% | 81% |
| Afternoon Temperatures | 57° | 70° | 84° | 78° |
| Relative Humidity | 85% | 69% | 71% | 74% |
| Chances of a Dry Day | 70% | 86% | 99% | 91% |
| Total Precipitation | 7.0" | 2.3" | 0.1" | 1.9" |

Comment: Try to plan your visit for late summer, when the vines are lush with ripe bunches of grapes.

# Wisconsin Dells, WI

## Natural Environment

Native Americans were familiar with the picturesque 7-mile stretch of the Wisconsin River where glacial action has created sculptured cliffs as high as 100 feet above the river. There are a few low hills in the vicinity, and many small lakes.

MAJOR GEOGRAPHIC FEATURES
 Terrain: Baraboo Range, Wisconsin Dells
 Lakes and Reservoirs: Devil's Lake, Lake Koshkonong, Lake Mendota, Lake Wisconsin
 Rivers: Wisconsin

| Terrain | Open Space | Forests | Inland Water | Shore-line | Rivers | Nature Preser-vation | Nature's Spectac-ulars |
|---|---|---|---|---|---|---|---|
| 180 | 300 | 200 | 70 | — | — | — | — |

Places Rated Score: 750          Places Rated Rank: 93

## Climate

| WISCONSIN DELLS, WI | January | April | July | October |
|---|---|---|---|---|
| Hours of Sunshine | 4:30 | 7:19 | 10:38 | 6:02 |
| Chances of a Sunny Day | 45% | 47% | 68% | 56% |
| Afternoon Temperatures | 24° | 57° | 82° | 61° |
| Relative Humidity | 75% | 70% | 72% | 74% |
| Chances of a Dry Day | 89% | 81% | 80% | 86% |
| Total Precipitation | 1.1″ | 3.4″ | 4.0″ | 2.3″ |
| Snowfall | 10.3″ | 1.4″ | — | 0.1″ |

Comment: A popular place to escape the summer heat of the Midwest's cities. Very colorful in the autumn.

# ★Yellowstone–Jackson–Tetons, WY–ID–MT

## Natural Environment

Yellowstone National Park's unique natural phenomena are the dozens of hot springs and geysers. There are few places in the world with anything that remotely compares to this, and no others in North America. In addition to the geysers, Yellowstone and the Tetons have high and low mountains, hills, canyons, rock formations, and lakes. The Tetons have a rugged Alpine look that differs markedly from other parts of the Rocky Mountain chain. The parks are heavily wooded, mostly with pine trees, and wildlife is abundant.

MAJOR GEOGRAPHIC FEATURES
  Terrain: Absaroka Range, Colter Peak (10,683 ft.), Grand Teton (13,770 ft.), Rocky Mountains, Teton Range
  Lakes and Reservoirs: Jackson Lake, Shoshone Lake, Yellowstone Lake
  Rivers: Yellowstone

NATURE-PRESERVATION AREAS
  Grand Teton National Park
  John D. Rockefeller, Jr., Memorial Parkway
  National Elk Refuge
  Red Rock Lakes National Wildlife Refuge
  Yellowstone National Park

NATURE'S SPECTACULARS
  Yellowstone National Park (World Heritage Site)

| Terrain | Open Space | Forests | Inland Water | Shore-line | Rivers | Nature Preser-vation | Nature's Spectac-ulars |
|---|---|---|---|---|---|---|---|
| 940 | 1,000 | 600 | 100 | — | — | 600 | 500 |

Places Rated Score: 3,740          Places Rated Rank: 10

## Climate

| YELLOWSTONE NATIONAL PARK, WY–ID–MT | January | April | July | October |
|---|---|---|---|---|
| Hours of Sunshine | 3:37 | 7:40 | 11:05 | 6:17 |
| Chances of a Sunny Day | 48% | 60% | 84% | 65% |
| Afternoon Temperatures | 28° | 49° | 81° | 56° |
| Relative Humidity | 75% | 57% | 48% | 54% |
| Chances of a Dry Day | 86% | 85% | 87% | 89% |
| Total Precipitation | 1.3″ | 1.2″ | 1.2″ | 0.9″ |
| Snowfall | 18.0″ | 7.5″ | 0.1″ | 5.5″ |

Comment: Data are for the Mammoth Hot Springs area. Most of the park is several degrees cooler and significantly wetter and snowier. Be prepared for frosty mornings even during the middle of summer.

| JACKSON HOLE, WY | January | April | July | October |
|---|---|---|---|---|
| Hours of Sunshine | 4:47 | 8:51 | 11:59 | 7:45 |
| Chances of a Sunny Day | 44% | 50% | 84% | 68% |
| Afternoon Temperatures | 27° | 51° | 82° | 59° |
| Relative Humidity | 85% | 56% | 47% | 54% |
| Chances of a Dry Day | 81% | 87% | 90% | 87% |
| Total Precipitation | 1.6″ | 1.1″ | 0.8″ | 1.1″ |
| Snowfall | 18.8″ | 6.0″ | — | 2.4″ |

Comment: Snowfall is much heavier up on the ski runs.

| GRAND TETON NATIONAL PARK, WY | January | April | July | October |
|---|---|---|---|---|
| Hours of Sunshine | 4:33 | 8:14 | 11:28 | 7:00 |
| Chances of a Sunny Day | 65% | 67% | 87% | 71% |
| Afternoon Temperatures | 25° | 46° | 77° | 54° |
| Relative Humidity | 86% | 57% | 48% | 55% |
| Chances of a Dry Day | 77% | 80% | 90% | 84% |
| Total Precipitation | 3.4″ | 1.8″ | 1.0″ | 1.4″ |
| Snowfall | 32.4″ | 10.8″ | 0.1″ | 6.3″ |

Comment: Try a visit after Labor Day for clear, crisp vistas and uncrowded facilities.

# ★Yosemite–Sequoia–Death Valley, CA

## Natural Environment

These three huge National Park Service areas are large enough and varied enough that one could spend a dozen month-long vacations here and still have new sights to see. The landforms run the gamut from high mountains, plains with high mountains, and towering cliffs, to deep canyons and desert. There are valleys and high meadows, waterfalls, rivers and streams, mountain lakes, forests of sequoia trees, and countless species of plants, birds, and animals. Even in arid Death Valley there are more than 600 species of plants. In the high meadows of Yosemite, even in midsummer, there is apt to be enough snow for a friendly snowball fight.

MAJOR GEOGRAPHIC FEATURES
  Terrain: Death Valley (282 ft. below sea level), Kings Canyon, Mount Whitney (14,494 ft.), Sierra Nevada
  Lakes and Reservoirs: Mono Lake

NATURE-PRESERVATION AREAS
  Death Valley National Monument
  Devils Postpile National Monument
  Sequoia-Kings Canyon National Parks
  Yosemite National Park

NATURE'S SPECTACULARS
  Death Valley National Monument (World Heritage Site)
  Sequoia-Kings Canyon National Parks (World Heritage Site)
  Yosemite National Park (World Heritage Site)

| Terrain | Open Space | Forests | Inland Water | Shore-line | Rivers | Nature Preser-vation | Nature's Spectac-ulars |
|---|---|---|---|---|---|---|---|
| 1,000 | 1,000 | 400 | 50 | — | — | 700 | 700 |

Places Rated Score: 3,850          Places Rated Rank: 7

---

## Climate

**YOSEMITE NATIONAL PARK (THE VALLEY), CA**

| | January | April | July | October |
|---|---|---|---|---|
| Hours of Sunshine | 3:57 | 7:38 | 9:34 | 6:45 |
| Chances of a Sunny Day | 39% | 70% | 97% | 81% |
| Afternoon Temperatures | 48° | 66° | 90° | 75° |
| Relative Humidity | 86% | 69% | 50% | 64% |
| Chances of a Dry Day | 74% | 80% | 97% | 94% |
| Total Precipitation | 6.8" | 3.3" | 0.4" | 1.5" |
| Snowfall | 25.4" | 4.5" | — | 0.2" |

Comment: High-country conditions are significantly cooler and much snowier during the winter months.

**SEQUOIA–KINGS CANYON NATIONAL PARKS, CA**

| | January | April | July | October |
|---|---|---|---|---|
| Hours of Sunshine | 3:53 | 8:56 | 11:06 | 7:54 |
| Chances of a Sunny Day | 39% | 73% | 97% | 84% |
| Afternoon Temperatures | 43° | 49° | 75° | 60° |
| Relative Humidity | 88% | 63% | 41% | 65% |
| Chances of a Dry Day | 77% | 80% | 99% | 94% |
| Total Precipitation | 8.7" | 4.3" | 0.1" | 1.4" |
| Snowfall | 35.3" | 30.9" | — | 2.0" |

Comment: During the snow season, check in advance on the road conditions. Many roads within the parks are closed by the heavy snows from late October to late May.

**DEATH VALLEY NATIONAL MONUMENT, CA**

| | January | April | July | October |
|---|---|---|---|---|
| Hours of Sunshine | 7:37 | 11:17 | 12:34 | 9:49 |
| Chances of a Sunny Day | 63% | 78% | 92% | 86% |
| Afternoon Temperatures | 65° | 90° | 115° | 93° |
| Relative Humidity | 46% | 29% | 31% | 25% |
| Chances of a Dry Day | 97% | 99% | 99% | 99% |
| Total Precipitation | 0.3" | 0.1" | 0.2" | 0.1" |

Comment: Death Valley holds the record for the highest shade temperature ever recorded in North America: 134 degrees Fahrenheit at Greenland Ranch on July 10, 1913.

# ★Zion–Bryce Canyon, UT

## Natural Environment

Southwestern Utah has some of the most dramatic variations in elevation and terrain on the continent. There are high mountains, deep canyons, plains with high mountains rising from them, plateaus, mesas, and tablelands with very high relief. The shapes and colors of the rock formations are equally impressive—the hues range from red and orange through purple, pink, and yellow to white. During spring and summer the cliffs in Zion are covered with wildflowers; thick green forests grow along the river bottoms.

MAJOR GEOGRAPHIC FEATURES
Terrain: Bryce Canyon, Delano Peak (12,169 ft.), Markagunt Plateau, Pahvant Range, Rocky Mountains
Other: Escalante Desert

NATURE-PRESERVATION AREAS
Bryce Canyon National Park
Cedar Breaks National Monument
Zion National Park

NATURE'S SPECTACULARS
Bryce Canyon National Park (World Heritage Site)

| Terrain | Open Space | Forests | Inland Water | Shore-line | Rivers | Nature Preser-vation | Nature's Spectac-ulars |
|---|---|---|---|---|---|---|---|
| 1,240 | 1,000 | 400 | 10 | — | — | 600 | 500 |

Places Rated Score: 3,750     Places Rated Rank: 9

## Climate

**ZION NATIONAL PARK, UT**

| | January | April | July | October |
|---|---|---|---|---|
| Hours of Sunshine | 6:54 | 9:42 | 11:20 | 9:14 |
| Chances of a Sunny Day | 69% | 78% | 88% | 85% |
| Afternoon Temperatures | 51° | 72° | 100° | 79° |
| Relative Humidity | 66% | 44% | 37% | 44% |
| Chances of a Dry Day | 87% | 90% | 94% | 90% |
| Total Precipitation | 1.8" | 1.1" | 1.0" | 0.9" |
| Snowfall | 4.1" | 0.7" | — | 0.3" |

Comment: During the heat of the summer, cool-air drainage down the canyons from the higher elevations drops the nighttime temperatures to comfortable levels.

**BRYCE CANYON NATIONAL PARK, UT**

| | January | April | July | October |
|---|---|---|---|---|
| Hours of Sunshine | 6:38 | 9:05 | 10:52 | 9:00 |
| Chances of a Sunny Day | 71% | 77% | 87% | 84% |
| Afternoon Temperatures | 36° | 53° | 81° | 60° |
| Relative Humidity | 72% | 54% | 51% | 56% |
| Chances of a Dry Day | 87% | 90% | 87% | 90% |
| Total Precipitation | 1.3" | 1.0" | 1.2" | 1.2" |
| Snowfall | 19.7" | 9.0" | — | 3.7" |

Comment: Before you hike down into the canyons, remember that you are at 8,000 feet above sea level. If you forget, coming back up will remind you!

# ✿ RANKINGS: Blessings of Nature

Eight criteria were used to determine the scores in this chapter: (1) terrain—its kind, coverage, variety, and expanse; (2) open space—that is, low population density; (3) forests—proportion of total area covered by forests; (4) inland water—proportion of total area covered by lakes, reservoirs, and embayments; (5) shoreline—miles of unspoiled shoreline along the ocean or Great Lakes; (6) prominent, scenic, and wild rivers; (7) plant and animal wildlife preservation; (8) "nature's spectaculars"—those unusually scenic features widely recognized as popular natural attractions.

Vacation Places that receive tie scores are given the same rank and are listed in alphabetic order.

## Vacation Places from First to Last

| Places Rated Rank | Places Rated Score | Places Rated Rank | Places Rated Score | Places Rated Rank | Places Rated Score |
|---|---|---|---|---|---|
| 1. Redwoods–Shasta–Lassen, CA | 5,005 | 32. Cape Cod–The Islands, MA | 2,200 | 64. Atlantic City, NJ | 1,660 |
| 2. Anchorage–Kenai Peninsula, AK | 4,400 | 32. North Woods–Land O'Lakes, WI | 2,200 | 65. Williamsburg–Colonial Triangle, VA | 1,640 |
| 3. Olympic Peninsula, WA | 4,110 | 34. Adirondack Mountains, NY | 2,190 | 66. Catskill Mountains, NY | 1,620 |
| 3. Seattle–Mount Rainier–North Cascades, WA | 4,110 | 35. Blue Ridge Mountains, VA | 2,170 | 66. San Diego, CA | 1,620 |
| 5. Hawaii | 4,080 | 36. Boise–Sun Valley, ID | 2,150 | 68. Hilton Head, SC | 1,600 |
| 6. Crater Lake–Klamath Falls, OR | 3,860 | 37. Monterey–Big Sur, CA | 2,140 | 69. Door County, WI | 1,590 |
| 7. Yosemite–Sequoia–Death Valley, CA | 3,850 | 37. San Francisco, CA | 2,140 | 70. Providence–Newport, RI | 1,540 |
| 8. Bar Harbor–Acadia, ME | 3,820 | 39. Panhandle, FL | 2,130 | 71. Jersey Shore, NJ | 1,500 |
| 9. Zion–Bryce Canyon, UT | 3,750 | 40. Black Hills, SD | 2,090 | 72. Los Angeles, CA | 1,460 |
| 10. Yellowstone–Jackson–Tetons, WY–ID–MT | 3,740 | 40. White Mountains, NH | 2,090 | 73. Niagara Falls–Western New York, NY | 1,450 |
| 11. Grand Canyon Country, AZ | 3,650 | 42. Denver–Rocky Mountain National Park, CO | 2,060 | 74. Baltimore–Chesapeake Bay, MD | 1,420 |
| 12. Glacier National Park–Flathead Lake, MT | 3,520 | 42. Ozarks–Eureka Springs, AR–MO | 2,060 | 74. Finger Lakes, NY | 1,420 |
| 13. Lake Powell–Glen Canyon, AZ–UT | 3,440 | 44. Myrtle Beach–Grand Strand, SC | 2,030 | 76. Phoenix–Valley of the Sun, AZ | 1,380 |
| 14. Outer Banks, NC | 3,100 | 45. Lake of the Ozarks, MO | 2,010 | 76. Pocono Mountains, PA | 1,380 |
| 14. Portland–Columbia River, OR | 3,100 | 46. Orlando–Space Coast, FL | 2,000 | 78. Chattanooga–Huntsville, TN–AL–GA | 1,360 |
| 16. Wine Country, CA | 3,060 | 47. Wilmington–Cape Fear, NC | 1,990 | 79. Mystic Seaport–Connecticut Valley, CT | 1,330 |
| 17. Coos Bay–South Coast, OR | 2,970 | 48. Colorado Springs, CO | 1,970 | 80. Brownsville–Rio Grande Valley, TX | 1,320 |
| 18. Rangeley Lakes, ME | 2,830 | 48. Santa Barbara–San Simeon, CA | 1,970 | 81. Corpus Christi–Padre Island, TX | 1,270 |
| 19. Aspen–Vail, CO | 2,790 | 50. Lake Tahoe–Reno, NV–CA | 1,960 | 82. Vicksburg–Natchez–Baton Rouge, MS–LA | 1,200 |
| 19. Salt Lake City, UT | 2,790 | 50. Palm Springs–Desert Playgrounds, CA | 1,960 | 83. Richmond–Fredericksburg, VA | 1,190 |
| 21. Spokane–Coeur d'Alene, WA–ID | 2,780 | 52. Knoxville–Smoky Mountains, TN | 1,950 | 84. St. Louis–Mark Twain Country, MO–IL | 1,160 |
| 22. Mackinac Island–Sault Ste. Marie, MI | 2,700 | 53. Las Vegas–Lake Mead, NV–AZ | 1,930 | 85. Atlanta, GA | 1,140 |
| 23. Asheville–Smoky Mountains, NC | 2,630 | 54. St. Augustine–Northeast Coast, FL | 1,900 | 85. Houston–Galveston, TX | 1,140 |
| 24. Albuquerque–Santa Fe–Taos, NM | 2,620 | 55. Mobile Bay–Gulfport, AL–MS | 1,880 | 87. Tulsa–Lake O' The Cherokees, OK | 1,110 |
| 25. Bend–Cascade Mountains, OR | 2,500 | 56. Boone–High Country, NC | 1,870 | 88. Put-in-Bay–Lake Erie Shore, OH | 1,060 |
| 26. Traverse City–Petoskey, MI | 2,470 | 57. Green Mountains, VT | 1,860 | 89. New Orleans, LA | 1,000 |
| 27. Eastern Shore, VA | 2,450 | 58. Miami–Gold Coast–Keys, FL | 1,830 | 90. Austin–Hill Country, TX | 930 |
| 27. Tucson, AZ | 2,450 | 58. Portsmouth–Kennebunk, NH–ME | 1,830 | 90. Tampa Bay–Southwest Coast, FL | 930 |
| 29. Flaming Gorge, UT–WY–CO | 2,360 | 60. Berkshire Hills–Pioneer Valley, MA | 1,810 | 92. Minneapolis–St. Paul, MN–WI | 800 |
| 30. Savannah–Golden Isles, GA | 2,260 | 61. Long Island, NY | 1,800 | | |
| 31. Portland, ME | 2,220 | 62. Sacramento–Gold Rush Towns, CA | 1,710 | | |
| | | 63. Charleston, SC | 1,680 | | |

| Places Rated Rank | Places Rated Score | Places Rated Rank | Places Rated Score | Places Rated Rank | Places Rated Score |
|---|---|---|---|---|---|
| 93. Wisconsin Dells, WI | 750 | 97. Nashville, TN | 630 | 103. Washington, DC–MD–VA | 440 |
| 94. Lexington–Bluegrass Country, KY | 700 | 98. New York City, NY | 570 | 104. Cincinnati, OH–KY | 370 |
| 95. Holland–Lake Michigan Shore, MI | 690 | 99. Memphis, TN–AR–MS | 560 | 105. Philadelphia, PA–DE–NJ | 260 |
| | | 100. Boston, MA | 550 | | |
| 96. Pennsylvania Dutch Country, PA | 680 | 100. Oklahoma City–Cherokee Strip, OK | 550 | 106. Dallas–Fort Worth, TX | 230 |
| | | 100. San Antonio, TX | 550 | 107. Chicago, IL | 110 |

## Vacation Places Listed Alphabetically

| Vacation Place | Places Rated Rank | Vacation Place | Places Rated Rank | Vacation Place | Places Rated Rank |
|---|---|---|---|---|---|
| Adirondack Mountains, NY | 34 | Green Mountains, VT | 57 | Phoenix–Valley of the Sun, AZ | 76 |
| Albuquerque–Santa Fe–Taos, NM | 24 | Hawaii | 5 | Pocono Mountains, PA | 76 |
| Anchorage–Kenai Peninsula, AK | 2 | Hilton Head, SC | 68 | Portland, ME | 31 |
| Asheville–Smoky Mountains, NC | 23 | Holland–Lake Michigan Shore, MI | 95 | | |
| Aspen–Vail, CO | 19 | | | Portland–Columbia River, OR | 14 |
| | | Houston–Galveston, TX | 85 | Portsmouth–Kennebunk, NH–ME | 58 |
| Atlanta, GA | 85 | Jersey Shore, NJ | 71 | Providence–Newport, RI | 70 |
| Atlantic City, NJ | 64 | Knoxville–Smoky Mountains, TN | 52 | Put-in-Bay–Lake Erie Shore, OH | 88 |
| Austin–Hill Country, TX | 90 | Lake of the Ozarks, MO | 45 | Rangeley Lakes, ME | 18 |
| Baltimore–Chesapeake Bay, MD | 74 | Lake Powell–Glen Canyon, AZ–UT | 13 | | |
| Bar Harbor–Acadia, ME | 8 | | | Redwoods–Shasta–Lassen, CA | 1 |
| | | Lake Tahoe–Reno, NV–CA | 50 | Richmond–Fredericksburg, VA | 83 |
| Bend–Cascade Mountains, OR | 25 | Las Vegas–Lake Mead, NV–AZ | 53 | Sacramento–Gold Rush Towns, CA | 62 |
| Berkshire Hills–Pioneer Valley, MA | 60 | Lexington–Bluegrass Country, KY | 94 | St. Augustine–Northeast Coast, FL | 54 |
| Black Hills, SD | 40 | Long Island, NY | 61 | St. Louis–Mark Twain Country, MO–IL | 84 |
| Blue Ridge Mountains, VA | 35 | Los Angeles, CA | 72 | | |
| Boise–Sun Valley, ID | 36 | | | Salt Lake City, UT | 19 |
| | | Mackinac Island–Sault Ste. Marie, MI | 22 | San Antonio, TX | 100 |
| Boone–High Country, NC | 56 | Memphis, TN–AR–MS | 99 | San Diego, CA | 66 |
| Boston, MA | 100 | Miami–Gold Coast–Keys, FL | 58 | San Francisco, CA | 37 |
| Brownsville–Rio Grande Valley, TX | 80 | Minneapolis–St. Paul, MN–WI | 92 | Santa Barbara–San Simeon, CA | 48 |
| Cape Cod–The Islands, MA | 32 | Mobile Bay–Gulfport, AL–MS | 55 | | |
| Catskill Mountains, NY | 66 | | | Savannah–Golden Isles, GA | 30 |
| | | Monterey–Big Sur, CA | 37 | Seattle–Mount Rainier–North Cascades, WA | 3 |
| Charleston, SC | 63 | Myrtle Beach–Grand Strand, SC | 44 | Spokane–Coeur d'Alene, WA–ID | 21 |
| Chattanooga–Huntsville, TN–AL–GA | 78 | Mystic Seaport–Connecticut Valley, CT | 79 | Tampa Bay–Southwest Coast, FL | 90 |
| Chicago, IL | 107 | Nashville, TN | 97 | Traverse City–Petoskey, MI | 26 |
| Cincinnati, OH–KY | 104 | New Orleans, LA | 89 | | |
| Colorado Springs, CO | 48 | | | Tucson, AZ | 27 |
| | | New York City, NY | 98 | Tulsa–Lake O' The Cherokees, OK | 87 |
| Coos Bay–South Coast, OR | 17 | Niagara Falls–Western New York, NY | 73 | Vicksburg–Natchez–Baton Rouge, MS–LA | 82 |
| Corpus Christi–Padre Island, TX | 81 | North Woods–Land O'Lakes, WI | 32 | Washington, DC–MD–VA | 103 |
| Crater Lake–Klamath Falls, OR | 6 | Oklahoma City–Cherokee Strip, OK | 100 | White Mountains, NH | 40 |
| Dallas–Fort Worth, TX | 106 | Olympic Peninsula, WA | 3 | | |
| Denver–Rocky Mountain National Park, CO | 42 | | | Williamsburg–Colonial Triangle, VA | 65 |
| | | Orlando–Space Coast, FL | 46 | Wilmington–Cape Fear, NC | 47 |
| Door County, WI | 69 | Outer Banks, NC | 14 | Wine Country, CA | 16 |
| Eastern Shore, VA | 27 | Ozarks–Eureka Springs, AR–MO | 42 | Wisconsin Dells, WI | 93 |
| Finger Lakes, NY | 74 | Palm Springs–Desert Playgrounds, CA | 50 | Yellowstone–Jackson–Tetons, WY–ID–MT | 10 |
| Flaming Gorge, UT–WY–CO | 29 | Panhandle, FL | 39 | | |
| Glacier National Park–Flathead Lake, MT | 12 | | | Yosemite–Sequoia–Death Valley, CA | 7 |
| | | Pennsylvania Dutch Country, PA | 96 | Zion–Bryce Canyon, UT | 9 |
| Grand Canyon Country, AZ | 11 | Philadelphia, PA–DE–NJ | 105 | | |

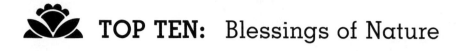

# TOP TEN: Blessings of Nature

| | Terrain | Open Space | Forests | Inland Water | Shore-line | Rivers | Nature Preser-vation | Nature's Spectac-ulars | Places Rated Score |
|---|---|---|---|---|---|---|---|---|---|
| 1. Redwoods–Shasta–Lassen, CA | 970 | 1,000 | 800 | 60 | 600 | 375 | 700 | 500 | 5,005 |
| 2. Anchorage–Kenai Peninsula, AK | 940 | 1,000 | 600 | 160 | 800 | — | 400 | 500 | 4,400 |
| 3. Olympic Peninsula, WA | 740 | 700 | 800 | 170 | 800 | — | 400 | 500 | 4,110 |
| 3. Seattle–Mount Rainier–North Cascades, WA | 740 | 200 | 800 | 170 | 800 | 200 | 700 | 500 | 4,110 |
| 5. Hawaii | 850 | 300 | 800 | 30 | 800 | — | 600 | 700 | 4,080 |
| 6. Crater Lake–Klamath Falls, OR | 880 | 1,000 | 800 | 80 | — | 200 | 400 | 500 | 3,860 |
| 7. Yosemite–Sequoia–Death Valley, CA | 1,000 | 1,000 | 400 | 50 | — | — | 700 | 700 | 3,850 |
| 8. Bar Harbor–Acadia, ME | 120 | 700 | 800 | 500 | 800 | — | 400 | 500 | 3,820 |
| 9. Zion–Bryce Canyon, UT | 1,240 | 1,000 | 400 | 10 | — | — | 600 | 500 | 3,750 |
| 10. Yellowstone–Jackson–Tetons, WY–ID–MT | 940 | 1,000 | 600 | 100 | — | — | 600 | 500 | 3,740 |

According to the measurements, nature has blessed the northwestern portion of the United States more than other portions. Of the ten Vacation Places with the highest score for the Blessings of Nature, six are in the Northwest (Redwoods, Anchorage, Olympic Peninsula, Seattle, Crater Lake, and Yellowstone). Three others are western (Hawaii, Yosemite, and Zion), and only one (Bar Harbor) is in the East.

All of the top ten have mountains; six have ocean frontage as well. Since a major purpose of the National Park Service is to "conserve the scenery and the natural and historic objects and the wild life therein . . ." it is not surprising that all of the top ten contain major national park units.

The top ten have mountains, water, wilderness, forests, and spectacular scenery in common, but more importantly, each has special qualities that make it unique.

## 1. Redwoods–Shasta–Lassen, CA

Coastal redwood forests and thick groves of huge and ancient trees create an ethereal atmosphere of sun filtered through leaves and fog. The world's tallest trees live here along a 40-mile strip of the Pacific shoreline.

Inland is Whiskeytown–Shasta–Trinity National Recreation Area, a large and mountainous backcountry area with a large reservoir.

Farther east is Lassen Volcanic National Park. Here are volcanic peaks, evergreen forests, blue lakes, hot springs, fumaroles, and mud pots. Lassen Peak, one of the volcanic mountains in the Cascades, erupted as recently as 1921.

## 2. Anchorage–Kenai Peninsula, AK

You cannot appreciate the scenic beauty of Alaska if you are unwilling to travel in small planes. The only way to get a panoramic view of the glaciers, fjords, and mountainous coastline of the area at the northern end of the Gulf of Alaska is from the sky. If you've never flown over a chain of glaciers, you have something unforgettable to look forward to when you visit south-central Alaska.

Planes are also the major means of transportation over Alaska's vastness. Anchorage has the largest seaplane airport in the world. These planes land on inland waters in summer; in winter the pontoons come off and are replaced with skis to make it possible to land on ice and snow.

Snow-covered mountains are visible from every spot in this Vacation Place. Moose and other wildlife can often be seen wandering through backyards in small towns.

From Homer, on the Kenai Peninsula, fishing and sightseeing boats take off into Kachemak Bay. Hundreds of gulls, Arctic terns, sandpipers, loons, cormorants, and puffins inhabit a natural rookery in the bay.

In Kenai Fjords National Park are deep, icy inlets not unlike the fjords of Norway. Sea lions, sea otters, seals, dolphins, whales, and more than 100,000 nesting birds make their permanent or temporary homes within the waters of the park, and mountain goats roam among the forests of Sitka spruce and hemlock.

## 3. Olympic Peninsula, WA

Fifty miles of the Pacific shoreline of the state of Washington is preserved in its wild and natural state as a portion of Olympic National Park. Small offshore islands are home for thousands of water birds and marine mammals.

Glacier-topped mountains, rain forests, and high

meadows are found inland. Huge trees cover the land in this northwestern wilderness.

The beautiful, long, uncrowded beaches of the Olympic Peninsula are only a part of the Vacation Place's aquatic advantages—lakes, rivers, streams, and Alpine pools add sparkle to the land.

## 3. Seattle–Mount Rainier–North Cascades, WA

Next door to the Olympic Peninsula, and tied with it for third place in the score for the Blessings of Nature, is the part of Washington containing the city of Seattle and two national parks—Mount Rainier and North Cascades.

Of all the major cities in the United States, Seattle is probably the most richly endowed with easily accessible scenic wonders and outdoor advantages. Mount Rainier stands sentinel over the area, visible for hundreds of miles when skies are clear. To the south march several other Titans of the Cascades chain. There are more glaciers atop Rainier than on any other U.S. mountain classified as a *single peak* outside the state of Alaska.

Rocky granite peaks surround wilderness valleys dotted with lakes in North Cascades National Park. Mountain goats, black and grizzly bears, deer, moose, and many smaller animals populate the wilderness areas.

## 5. Hawaii

Our Pacific island state is a marvelous tropical contrast to the rugged, ice-topped wilderness areas of the Northwest. Incomparable surf and romantic, always warm beaches are a part of the story, but only a part.

Volcanoes on Maui and Hawaii, the Big Island, are of great interest to residents and visitors alike. Mauna Loa and Kilauea erupt quite frequently, but the lava flow is gentle and slow enough that sightseers have plenty of time to get out of its way. When an eruption occurs, people rush toward the mountains, not away from them, in order to witness the show, as if it were an extravagant ground-level fireworks display.

Haleakala, on Maui, is a huge crater with a multitude of rare flowering plants and ferns growing among the cinders and ash of the venerable volcano. Unusual birds live here as well, including the Hawaiian goose, or nene (a word very familiar to crossword-puzzle addicts).

Humpback whales can be seen in winter and early spring in the waters along the islands' shores.

## 6. Crater Lake–Klamath Falls, OR

A view of sapphire-blue Crater Lake, sitting within a ring of sharp lava cliffs that are often dusted with snow, is a picture almost too perfect to be real.

The Rogue River changes its face and mood from a tumbling mountain stream to a vigorous white-water channel to a deep and quietly flowing river on its way

---

### Author's Favorites

**Caves**
Mammoth Cave, KY
Lost Sea, TN

**Islands**
St. Simons, GA

**Lakes**
Tahoe, CA–NV
Winnipesaukee, NH

**Mountains**
Mount Hood, OR
Mount Mansfield, VT
Mount Rainier, WA

**Rivers**
Mississippi

**Scenic Drives**
Through the Adirondacks, from Albany, NY, to Canada, via I-87
Along the Big Sur, from San Simeon to Monterey, CA via CA 1
Along the Connecticut River, VT, via U.S. 5
From Durango to Ouray, CO, via the Million Dollar Highway (U.S. 550)
Through the Florida Keys, via U.S. 1
Along the coast of Oregon, via U.S. 101
From Phoenix to Flagstaff, AZ, via I-17
Through Shenandoah National Park, VA, via the Skyline Drive
Along the Snake River, from Blackfoot, ID, to Jackson, WY, via U.S. 26
Through the White Mountains, from Franconia to Conway, NH, via NH 18 and 112

**Views**
Atlantic Ocean from Acadia National Park, ME
Atlantic Ocean from the beach at Kill Devil Hills, NC
El Capitan, Yosemite National Park, CA
Chicago (IL) skyline from Lake Michigan
Columbia River Gorge, OR
Fall foliage, anywhere in Vermont
Glaciers from a plane, Juneau to Skagway AK
Grand Canyon (AZ) from any viewpoint
Lake Michigan from Lake Shore Drive, Chicago, IL
Sunset from Lumahai Beach, Kauai, HI

**Waterfalls**
Moltnomah Falls, OR

---

from the snowy Cascades to the sea. Lacy white and pink blooms on pear, peach, and apple trees decorate the orchards of Applegate Valley each spring. A huge cavern known as the Oregon Caves is a beauty spot near the California border.

## 7. Yosemite–Sequoia–Death Valley, CA

It would be difficult to imagine a single area with as many delights for a photographer—or sightseer—as Yosemite National Park. And when combined as a Vacation Place with the twin parks of Sequoia-Kings Canyon and Death Valley National Monument, the blessings of nature are almost mind-boggling.

Some of the world's largest and oldest trees are found in these parks, as are some of the highest waterfalls, lowest and driest points, sheerest granite cliffs, and rarest types of invertebrate animals.

## 8. Bar Harbor–Acadia, ME

Maine's rocky coast is sometimes a scene of gray and black shadows—foreboding skies and crashing waves. At other times the sun rising over the Atlantic Ocean turns everything to gold. In spring wildflowers in delicate pastels climb over rocks and hills. Summer colors are the blue of the sea and the green of the forests. And the autumn rusts and bronzes of marsh grasses rival the brilliant reds of the maples and wines of the oaks.

The rise and fall of the tides leave pools alive with tiny creatures, and mixed into the sand of the beaches are broken bits of shells.

Winters are rugged in Maine, but storms often leave behind a coating of ice that dresses every bush in diamonds and sequins; it's well worth battling the cold and the winds to see the sight.

## 9. Zion–Bryce Canyon, UT

Brilliant colors scream from the huge sandstone walls of southwestern Utah. The yellows and golds and sunset reds of the rock formations are as intense as the hues of New England forests in October. Photographers, professional and amateur alike, bring home slides that months later fill them with awe and disbelief.

The scenery in these national parks is very different from that in more northern areas. At first look it seems barren and lifeless, but closer acquaintance brings recognition of hundreds of types of birds, many small animals, and a host of wildflowers carpeting the cliffs.

Rocks and cliffs have been formed over millions of years into castles, towers, arches, and giant figures. A major pastime for visitors is making up names for the strange shapes.

## 10. Yellowstone–Jackson–Tetons, WY–ID–MT

More than 10,000 hot springs and geysers within the boundaries of America's oldest national park would be enough to bring millions of gazing visitors, but Yellowstone and Grand Teton, its neighboring park, have many other blessings of nature.

The sharply peaked Tetons rise up abruptly from plains, without any lower hills to interrupt the spectacle. Large herds of elk roam the mountainsides, along with antelope, deer, and bison.

West of the Tetons the Snake River winds its serpentine way through Idaho to Wyoming. Views of this river from the highway are superb.

Yellowstone is famous for its bears, and visitors are often foolishly friendly with them. Many of the roads in the park are left unplowed in winter, but visitors can enjoy the pristine winter landscape on skis or snowshoes. Even before the snow has melted, early spring brings wildflowers to the areas close to hot bubbling waters.

# Fun in the Great Outdoors

Sports and Recreation

# INTRODUCTION: Fun in the Great Outdoors

The Decade of Fitness—that's the label historians may pin on the 1980s. More adults are running, biking, lifting weights, going to aerobics classes, and working out in gymnasiums and health clubs or at home than at any previous time. As more and more people move to cities and work at indoor jobs, the lure of the outdoors increases.

Each year athletes invent new sports or new methods of practicing old ones, and each year sports-equipment manufacturers develop new gear to make outdoor recreation more appealing, more glamorous, and more varied. Thus any list of types of outdoor recreation becomes incomplete almost as soon as it is compiled. Such sports as waterskiing, surfing, and snorkeling—commonplace today—were virtually unknown a few decades ago, and the future is sure to see many new recreational activities become popular.

Outdoor recreation encompasses a wide range of effort; it can be as sedentary as lying on a beach or as challenging as rappelling down a sheer, perpendicular cliff. Some vacationers want to be outdoors but are interested in rest and relaxation where balmy breezes blow and nature is kind; others welcome the adventure of climbing mountains, crossing glaciers, skydiving, or canoeing down white-water streams.

In this chapter, the 107 Vacation Places are judged according to the opportunities they afford for active, participatory outdoor sports and recreation. The Place Profiles describe, briefly, some of the most popular of these activities in each area. Certain sports are limited because of climate or terrain—snow skiing and mountain climbing, for example; others—such as swimming —are available virtually everywhere.

## SPORTS AT VACATION RESORTS

The word *resort* has several meanings. A resort can range all the way from a simple lodge catering to people interested in a single sport, as a fishing resort, to a community or area frequented by vacationers. In *Vacation Places Rated*, the word *resort* refers to a modern

### Public Golf Courses in the U.S.

| | Municipal 9-hole | Municipal 18-hole | Daily Fee 9-hole | Daily Fee 18-hole | | Municipal 9-hole | Municipal 18-hole | Daily Fee 9-hole | Daily Fee 18-hole |
|---|---|---|---|---|---|---|---|---|---|
| Alabama | 10 | 20 | 16 | 18 | Missouri | 24 | 15 | 59 | 29 |
| Alaska | — | — | 4 | 1 | Montana | 14 | 6 | 21 | 4 |
| Arizona | 8 | 16 | 18 | 41 | Nebraska | 19 | 10 | 40 | 9 |
| Arkansas | 5 | 7 | 19 | 14 | Nevada | 6 | 7 | 2 | 13 |
| California | 21 | 101 | 77 | 152 | New Hampshire | — | 3 | 37 | 23 |
| Colorado | 19 | 33 | 20 | 15 | New Jersey | 6 | 34 | 18 | 51 |
| Connecticut | 6 | 26 | 24 | 24 | New Mexico | 10 | 11 | 11 | 10 |
| Delaware | — | 2 | — | 4 | New York | 21 | 77 | 167 | 152 |
| District of Columbia | 2 | 2 | — | — | North Carolina | 6 | 17 | 48 | 125 |
| Florida | 11 | 44 | 44 | 230 | North Dakota | 33 | 4 | 25 | 1 |
| Georgia | 16 | 22 | 35 | 26 | Ohio | 18 | 52 | 129 | 227 |
| Hawaii | 1 | 6 | 8 | 24 | Oklahoma | 22 | 25 | 34 | 14 |
| Idaho | 10 | 10 | 22 | 9 | Oregon | 6 | 5 | 39 | 34 |
| Illinois | 29 | 79 | 99 | 103 | Pennsylvania | 7 | 27 | 103 | 186 |
| Indiana | 14 | 39 | 63 | 92 | Rhode Island | 1 | 2 | 12 | 12 |
| Iowa | 22 | 26 | 92 | 13 | South Carolina | 1 | 4 | 27 | 85 |
| Kansas | 24 | 19 | 49 | 9 | South Dakota | 17 | 6 | 30 | — |
| Kentucky | 14 | 17 | 35 | 18 | Tennessee | 11 | 29 | 43 | 27 |
| Louisiana | 9 | 16 | 16 | 6 | Texas | 57 | 73 | 81 | 56 |
| Maine | 4 | 2 | 64 | 19 | Utah | 22 | 15 | 11 | 5 |
| Maryland | 6 | 18 | 4 | 12 | Vermont | — | — | 22 | 17 |
| Massachusetts | 11 | 23 | 78 | 62 | Virginia | 6 | 14 | 24 | 51 |
| Michigan | 30 | 40 | 182 | 235 | Washington | 10 | 23 | 42 | 48 |
| Minnesota | 23 | 36 | 101 | 44 | West Virginia | 6 | 6 | 30 | 20 |
| Mississippi | 5 | 5 | 8 | 12 | Wisconsin | 17 | 31 | 123 | 92 |
| | | | | | Wyoming | 9 | 6 | 16 | 3 |

Source: National Golf Foundation, *Statistical Profile of Golf in the United States*, 1983 Annual Review.

vacation complex centered around a luxury hotel with a wide variety of recreational offerings, such as swimming pools or beaches, tennis courts, golf courses, health clubs, and perhaps winter sports.

## Golf

Just as the presence of mineral springs provided an impetus for the development of vacation resorts in earlier days, the game of golf became a major factor in attracting vacationers at the turn of the century. Golf historians report that the first formally organized golf club in the United States was established in Yonkers, New York, in the 1880s. By 1900, summer-resort operators at Poland Spring, Maine, Saratoga and Lake Placid, New York, and Manchester, Vermont, had built golf courses. Soon golf was being played year-round in Florida, at Palm Beach, Ormond Beach, Tampa, and Belleair.

Nearly 18 million Americans now play golf, according to the National Golf Foundation. In 1983, the foundation reported that about 434 million rounds of golf were played. There are more than 13,000 courses in the United States, and the number increases each year.

The number of public facilities has exceeded the number of private clubs since 1962. In 1983, 61 percent of all golf facilities in the United States were open to the public, a marked contrast to the situation 30 years earlier when only 41 percent were open for public play.

A *frequent golfer* is defined by the National Golf Foundation as a person who plays 15 or more rounds a year; in 1983 more than 14 million players were in this category. An average golfer spends about $900 a year on this sport for golf equipment, clothing, and shoes; golf-cart rentals; and greens fees and dues. By age category, the foundation estimates that 73 percent of all rounds of golf are played by golfers in the 19–64 group, 7 percent by people 18 and under, and 20 percent by people 65 and over.

A close look at golf-related statistics reveals several leaders in several different categories. A number of Chicagoans were early promoters of the game, and it may come as a surprise to some that of all 107 Vacation Places, Chicago leads in number of public courses. Florida has recently been leading all the states in the development of new courses, with Texas, Arizona, and California not far behind. The East North Central states (Ohio, Michigan, Indiana, Illinois, and Wisconsin) led in the number of rounds played in 1983 (103 million); the South Atlantic states (Maryland, Delaware, West Virginia, Virginia, North Carolina, South Carolina, Georgia, and Florida) were second with 93 million rounds.

## Tennis

As in the case of golf, tennis continues to grow in popularity, and new resorts spring up yearly. Tennis courts can be found in almost every part of the country, in city parks, school yards, and indoor facilities.

Avid tennis enthusiasts, especially those who enjoy spending a lot of vacation time playing and improving their game, often seek resorts that cater to their special interest.

The 1985 yearbook issue of *Tennis* magazine reported that many exceptional new tennis facilities opened in 1984, with more planned for 1985. The competition among these resorts is keen. "Since one tennis court is pretty much like another," wrote contributing editor Roger Cox, "resorts are focusing not so much on the tennis facilities themselves as on services, programs—and mystique—to lure racquet-toting vacationers."

Major tennis stars are wooed with excellent contracts to serve as resident professionals at many resorts. Exhibition tournaments are sought to give resorts additional prestige. Frequent clinics are offered, with big-name players starring as instructors. Resorts that have not had them previously are adding indoor courts to permit year-round playing. Only three resorts, according to the yearbook, offer all three types of court surfaces: grass, clay, and hard surface. These three are Port Royal Resort, Hilton Head, South Carolina; La Quinta Resort, La Quinta, California; and Sandestin Beach Resort, Destin, Florida.

And tennis resorts, like other vacation playgrounds, make the most of their physical setting and the natural appeal of their surroundings. At the Nauna Lani Bay Hotel, on Hawaii's Big Island, a 10-court tennis "garden" is set off by beautiful tropical landscaping.

## Winter Sports

In Woodstock, Vermont, a historical marker reads as follows:

> In January, 1934, on this pasture
> hill of Clinton Gilbert's farm
> an endless-rope tow, powered by
> a Model 'T' Ford engine, hauled
> skiers uphill for the first time.

This ingenious contraption launched a new era in winter sports.

Skiing, both Alpine (downhill) and Nordic (cross-country or ski touring), has been popular in Europe for generations, but its widespread appeal in the United States dates only from the 1930s.

Skiing can be done on any slope with a good snow cover, but ski resorts offer a variety of ways to get up the slopes—rope tows, chair lifts, and gondolas, for example—along with snow-making machinery to make up for the times when nature doesn't provide enough of the natural stuff, pro shops for the sale and rental of equipment, instructional classes and clinics, gourmet dining rooms, and après-ski entertainment.

Ski resorts are concentrated in the mountains of the Northeast and the Far West, but a number of flatland resorts attract midwesterners to the gentler slopes found in Michigan, Wisconsin, and Minnesota.

Ski resorts were first built where weather conditions and terrain were ideal for downhill skiing. As resorts expanded and competition among them increased, facilities for other winter sports were added—ice-skating rinks, toboggan slides, and, on less moun-

---

# Top U.S. Ski Resorts

Skiers looking for new areas to try out are interested in several things: the length of the runs, the amount of skiable land that is supplied with snow-making equipment, the number of people that can be moved up the slopes per hour, the proximity of the accommodations to the slopes, the number of runs that are easily accessible from the hotel, and the price and flexibility of the lift tickets (for example, you buy a three-day ticket, but you want to ski other areas on alternate days—can you then use the ticket on Monday, Wednesday, and Friday?).

The perpendicular distance from the base to the highest skiable point on a hill or mountain is the *vertical rise*. The distance of any one continuous trail is the *run*.

| The Nine Greatest Vertical Rises | Height (in feet) | The Nine Longest Ski Runs | Length (in miles) |
|---|---|---|---|
| 1. Jackson Hole, WY | 4,139 | 1. Killington, VT | 10.2 |
| 2. Aspen Highlands, CO | 3,800 | 2. Jackson Hole, WY | 7.0 |
| 3. High Wallowas, OR | 3,700 | 3. Heavenly Valley, CA | 5.5 |
| 4. Heavenly Valley, CA | 3,600 | 3. Taos Ski Valley, NM | 5.5 |
| 4. Snowmass, CO | 3,600 | 5. Mission Ridge, WA | 5.0 |
| 4. Steamboat, CO | 3,600 | 6. Okemo Mountain, VT | 4.5 |
| 7. Timberline, OR | 3,500 | 6. Stowe, VT | 4.5 |
| 8. Sun Valley, ID | 3,400 | 6. Vail, CO | 4.5 |
| 9. Beaver Creek, CO | 3,340 | 9. Stratton, VT | 4.0 |

*Source:* Inter-Ski Services, *The White Book of Ski Areas,* 1983.

One measure of the capacity of any ski resort is *vertical transportation feet* (VTF) *per hour.* This is the total number of lifts multiplied by the distance they can cover each hour. These lifts may include simple rope tows on the beginner slopes; chair lifts; and large gondolas that take many skiers to the top of the mountain in the morning, bring them back in late afternoon, and are not heavily used during the middle of the day (see below left).

Fourteen of the most popular ski resorts in the United States, as measured by the number of skier visits, are in only three states: California, Colorado, and Utah (see below right).

| The Twenty Greatest Lift Capacities | VTF per Hour | The Twenty Most Popular Ski Resorts | Skier Visits |
|---|---|---|---|
| 1. Mammoth Mountain, CA | 32,451,400 | 1. Vail, CO | 1,255,626 |
| 2. Vail, CO | 25,597,440 | 2. Mammoth Mountain, CA | 1,200,000 |
| 3. Heavenly Valley, CA | 23,388,000 | 3. Heavenly Valley, CA | 781,000 |
| 4. Killington, VT | 22,795,800 | 4. Winter Park, CO | 757,647 |
| 5. Sun Valley, ID | 22,204,000 | 5. Steamboat, CO | 745,104 |
| 6. Squaw Valley USA, CA | 21,637,230 | 6. Keystone, CO | 732,164 |
| 7. Steamboat, CO | 19,072,000 | 7. Killington, VT | 694,384 |
| 8. Snowmass, CO | 18,294,900 | 8. Snowmass, CO | 679,849 |
| 9. Park City, UT | 17,163,550 | 9. Breckenridge, CO | 673,129 |
| 10. Sugarbush Valley, VT | 15,539,000 | 10. Squaw Valley USA, CA | 653,192 |
| 11. Winter Park, CO | 15,108,300 | 11. Copper Mountain, CO | 641,771 |
| 12. Breckenridge, CO | 15,024,441 | 12. Mount Bachelor, OR | 505,000 |
| 13. Copper Mountain, CO | 14,580,400 | 13. Alta, UT | 480,139 |
| 14. Hunter Mountain, NY | 14,000,000 | 14. Park City, UT | 476,000 |
| 15. Mount Snow, VT | 13,606,800 | 15. Sun Valley, ID | 450,000 |
| 16. Crested Butte, CO | 13,306,860 | 16. Sugarbush Valley, VT | 425,000 |
| 17. Keystone, CO | 13,234,000 | 17. Snowbird, UT | 360,000 |
| 18. Beaver Creek, CO | 13,067,592 | 18. Northstar-at-Tahoe, CA | 340,179 |
| 19. Mount Bachelor, OR | 12,690,445 | 19. Snoqualmie Summit/Ski Acres, WA | 331,000 |
| 20. Snoqualmie Summit/Ski Acres, WA | 11,543,500 | 20. Mount Hood Meadows, OR | 316,265 |

*Source:* Business Research Division, University of Colorado.

Figures reflect 1982–83 data.

tainous land, trails for cross-country skiing. Gentle slopes are used for ski instruction, usually available for all levels of expertise. "Bring the whole family," the advertisements proclaim.

If you don't have your own skis, boots, snowshoes, skates, or toboggans, you can usually rent them at or near a winter resort. Snowmobiles, on the other hand, are not commonly rented. In many places you must own your own snowmobile and belong to a club in order to use certain trails.

## WILDERNESS SPORTS

Wilderness areas have a definite fascination for most people. The call of the wild makes both beginners and seasoned outdoors lovers want to go camping, hiking, mountain climbing, and fishing. *Wilderness*, strictly defined, is an area that has been preserved in a completely natural state—a virgin forest, for example. More commonly, the word is used to refer to any stretch of forest, desert, or prairie that is relatively free of buildings, roads, and habitation.

Some campers hike into the wilderness with only a backpack as luggage. They traverse long stretches of the Appalachian Trail and other marked pathways, climb mountains, and fish for their dinners. They join such organizations as the Sierra Club, Wilderness Society, and local hiking and mountaineering clubs in order to be with other people whose interests are similar to theirs.

Some hikers stick to the comparatively easy and well-marked trails; others are interested in scaling steep mountains. Why? "Because it's there," is the familiar response.

Rock-climbing and rappelling (descending from a mountainside or cliff with the assistance of a double rope passed under one thigh and over the opposite shoulder) are specialized skills.

As you drive through mountainous areas, you may run across a pocket of sightseers gazing at something high above. Expecting to catch a glimpse of rare mountain goats or other wildlife, you stop and reach for your binoculars—and discover that it is a group of climbers that has everyone spellbound.

Age, sex, occupation, and economic status are factors that have little or no bearing on a person's enjoyment of vigorous wilderness activities. Teenagers and octogenarians share trails in harmony. Whole families hike together, and it's not unusual to see a dog, carrying a custom-fitted backpack, hiking along with a group.

Whatever your level of skill, however, never venture off on a hike or wilderness camping trip alone. The most experienced person can sprain an ankle or run into other difficulties. And if you are a beginner, take plenty of time to learn about the area, plan your trip carefully, and be prepared. Try easy jaunts on

well-traveled trails first, preferably with other people who know more than you do about how to get the most out of a vacation in the great outdoors.

## ON THE GO

Bike touring and trail riding are two other methods of exploring the countryside. One can cover more territory on a bicycle or horse than on foot, and the exercise can be just as vigorous. Both trail riding and bike touring usually involve groups of riders.

### Trail Riding

Trail riding is done in backcountry, and caravans are ordinarily led by professional guides or outfitters. Additional horses, burros, or mules are brought along with the riding horses to carry food, tents, sleeping equipment, and other necessities. Most commonly the outfitters furnish everything except your sleeping bag; some may even provide that.

Vacationers have the rare experience of riding deep into canyons or forests, eating food seasoned with the pure air of the wilderness, and enjoying the pleasant, old-fashioned camaraderie of telling stories and singing songs around an evening campfire.

If you are interested in going on a trail ride, get in touch with one of the outfitters who specialize in this activity. Both the Wilderness Society and the Sierra Club conduct trail-riding trips, and state departments of tourism can provide lists of outfitters in their areas.

A few dude ranches still provide for horseback riding. Unfortunately, it is becoming harder to find any that do, because the cost of liability insurance has increased astronomically. One of the few resorts east of the Mississippi that organizes trail rides is the Cataloochee Ranch, bordering on Great Smoky Mountains National Park outside Maggie Valley, North Carolina. Riders spend several days exploring the wilderness areas of the park.

### Bicycle Touring

Bicycle touring is a sport with a long history. In 1880 a group of bicycle enthusiasts organized the League of American Wheelmen, a nonprofit association that drew people together to pursue their mutual interest and to lobby for legislation to make the roads safe for cyclists. At first the bikers were fighting for the right to share the roads with horse-drawn vehicles; today Bicycle USA, as the league is now called, still works for legislation that will benefit bikers.

There are nearly 500 local clubs affiliated with Bicycle USA. They conduct biking classes and organize both short and long-distance rides. An organized bike tour might take you on a 5-day tour of the historic villages on Maryland's Eastern Shore, a trip along the Blue Ridge Parkway of North Carolina with overnight accommodations in lodge-camps, or a ride through

Vermont's Green Mountains with stops at night in cozy country inns. (Vermont Bicycle Touring claims to have conducted tours for 30,000 cyclists from all 50 states and 18 countries since 1972.)

And if you want to steep yourself in bicycle lore to an even greater extent, attend one of the several huge rallies, lasting four days or longer, that Bicycle USA holds each year.

Bike tours do not necessitate quite as much formal organization as trail rides do; families or groups of friends can get together and plan their own trip. They can eat in restaurants and stay at motels or hostels along the way if they wish. But bicycle accidents are a serious danger, and extreme care should be given to choosing the route. Some states—Wisconsin, for one —publish maps of marked bike trails. County highway departments are usually able to provide detailed information about lightly used roads. In some areas old towpaths along canals or no longer used railroad beds have been set aside for bike paths. And in many large cities there are miles and miles of trails through forest preserves.

### Recreational Vehicles

A woman was sitting outside a recreational vehicle in a Colorado state park, working with some gemstones. Handcrafted Jewelry for Sale said a sign on the RV. "This truck camper is my shop, and that van over there is our home," she was saying. "My husband and I travel all over the country, staying in state and national parks, and sell my jewelry. We've made lots of friends among other retirees who live most of the year in their campers, traveling north for the summer and south for the winter. We have year-round vacations."

Thousands of vacationers love to travel and enjoy spending time in the woods but are not interested in roughing it. These are the people who have made the recreational-vehicle industry so important.

Life in a recreational vehicle can be as comfortable as it is at home. The vehicles can be equipped with every convenience, from showers to televisions and microwave ovens. A purist camper may not call RV travel "camping," but it is certainly vacationing. With RV ownership come all the advantages of owning a vacation cottage plus the added asset of mobility. Campsites for RVs range from remote, secluded national-forest campgrounds to luxurious parks that offer hot showers, coin laundries, grocery stores, swimming pools, restaurants, and recreation halls.

And you don't have to own your own— recreational vehicles are available for rent in most major urban areas.

### WATER SPORTS

Virtually every vacation area offers some kind of water for recreational purposes, even if it is only a swimming pool. If the water comes in the form of a lake, river, or ocean, the list of potential recreational activities is almost endless.

Vacationers swim in the water, sunbathe beside it, ride over it, dive under it, and paint and photograph it. They gather shells and driftwood on seashores and lakeshores. They use boats as towing craft for waterskiing.

One person views the water as a huge store of fish, waiting to be caught. Another is more interested in watching the migration of whales, the cavorting of seals, the activities of water birds and shorebirds.

For some, a major allure is the world under the sea. John Pennekamp Coral Reef State Park, off Key Largo, Florida, is one of the many areas where scuba divers and snorkelers explore wrecks of long-submerged ships and examine brilliantly colored plant-and-animal life below the surface of the ocean. Some divers are also photographers, making use of underwater camera equipment.

Surfing can be done in several ways. Riding the ocean waves, with or without a surfboard, is popular in areas where the water and wind conditions are right, such as Hawaii, California, and Florida. Wind surfing—riding a board with an attached sail—is done on the ocean, in bays, on lakes, and even on rivers.

### Fishing

Fishing, like swimming, is a sport enjoyed nearly everywhere—in man-made lakes and reservoirs, natural lakes and ponds, rivers, streams, and oceans. Recreational freshwater fishing is most commonly done with hooks and lines; nets, spears, and bows and arrows are also used by hundreds of thousands of fishers. First-time fishers should be sure to check local fishing laws and regulations, which differ from state to state.

Some 42 million Americans aged 16 and over went fishing during 1980, according to a survey published in 1982 by the Fish and Wildlife Service of the U.S. Department of the Interior. About 36.4 million of these adults fished in fresh water, 12.3 million in salt water (and some in both, obviously). Thirty-six percent of adult American men and 15 percent of women participated in this activity. All income groups were represented, and every section of the country.

The survey reported that nearly 2 million people went ice fishing, using a hook and line through holes in the ice. Saltwater fishing was divided into three major categories; 55 percent of saltwater anglers fished from the surf or shore; 43 percent in saltwater sounds, bays, and tidal inlets and streams; and 37 percent in deep water.

Vacationers will find fishing-boat operators ready to accommodate their needs along the coast wherever the fishing is good. Groups, usually of four, six, or more, can charter a boat for a half-day, full day, or longer. In certain areas—on the coast of North Caroli-

## Vacation Places with the Best Bass Fishing

Black bass are found in lakes and rivers in every state except Alaska. *Field and Stream* recently named the 50 best bass-fishing spots in the United States and Canada—22 are within or very near the 107 Vacation Places. Here's where to find them.

**Adirondack Mountains, NY**
LAKE GEORGE, at the southern edge of the Adirondack region, is known for an abundance of trout, salmon, and smallmouth and largemouth bass.

**Asheville–Smoky Mountains, NC**
FONTANA LAKE, at the western end of North Carolina, is a good location for smallmouth bass, but it also has largemouths, white bass, trout, and walleyes.

**Atlanta, GA**
LAKE SIDNEY LANIER, 35 miles north of Atlanta, draws anglers to try for largemouth, striped, and white bass.

**Chattanooga–Huntsville, TN–AL–GA**
GUNTERSVILLE LAKE, in northeastern Alabama, is known even more for crappie than for bass, but it is an excellent place to fish for largemouths, also.

**Green Mountains, VT**
Smallmouth bass are plentiful in all the waters of LAKE CHAMPLAIN, especially in the northern part. Other fish found in abundance here are largemouths, walleyes, trout, salmon, and perch.

**Lake of the Ozarks, MO**
LAKE OF THE OZARKS is one of the finest bass-fishing areas in Missouri.

**Lake Powell–Glen Canyon, AZ–UT**
LAKE POWELL is known as the Bass Capital of the West. It is an especially pleasant place to fish because of the gorgeous scenery surrounding it.

**Las Vegas–Lake Mead, NV–AZ**
Two scenic lakes prized for bass fishing lie within this Vacation Place—LAKE MEAD and LAKE MOHAVE. Trout are caught at the north end of Mohave, where the water is colder.

**Minneapolis–St. Paul, MN–WI**
The MISSISSIPPI RIVER from St. Cloud to Elk River, northwest of Minneapolis, offers good smallmouth angling.

*Source: Rand McNally, Field & Stream 50 Great Bass Fishing Areas, 1985.*

**Orlando–Space Coast, FL**
The shallow, grassy lakes of the KISSIMMEE RIVER chain are good to excellent for largemouth bass. Lake Tohopekaliga, one of the chain, is rated one of the best places for trophy bass. Another spot nearby where trophy-sized fish are caught is in the FLORIDA PHOSPHATE PITS, near Lakeland and Winter Haven.

**Outer Banks, NC**
Fishers ordinarily seek out this part of the country for ocean fishing, but the brackish water of CURRITUCK SOUND provides a good environment for fly-fishing and angling for largemouths.

**Ozarks–Eureka Springs, AR–MO**
Both TABLE ROCK LAKE and BULL SHOALS LAKE—in the scenic Ozarks on both sides of the Arkansas–Missouri line—are renowned for trout, crappie, and largemouth, smallmouth, and white bass.

**Pennsylvania Dutch Country, PA**
Many sections of the SUSQUEHANNA RIVER, both north and south of Harrisburg, have good bass fishing.

**Put-in-Bay–Lake Erie Shore, OH**
Three islands in LAKE ERIE north of Port Clinton are named North Bass, Middle Bass, and South Bass for good reason.

**St. Augustine–Northeast Coast, FL**
Fishing for largemouth bass is good in many parts of the ST. JOHNS RIVER, especially between Palatka and Astor.

**San Diego, CA**
More than 15 lakes of the SAN DIEGO COUNTY LAKES system are open to the public for fishing, and they have some of the best catch rates in the state.

**White Mountains, NH**
SQUAM LAKE, site of the movie *On Golden Pond*, and its neighbor LAKE WINNIPESAUKEE, are both noted for lake trout, landlocked salmon, and smallmouth and largemouth bass.

na, for example—"head boats" are available: boat owners charge so much a head, so individuals can hop on board without being obliged to organize their own group in order to charter the entire boat. Inland, outfitters take fishers into remote wilderness areas; they furnish the craft, food supplies, and equipment—even fishing gear if the client has not brought any. State tourism offices can furnish lists of outfitters in specific areas.

### Riding the Currents and Waves

What's your pleasure in boating?

Strong swimmers may like to paddle canoes or kayaks down white-water rivers; the less daring (or proficient) vacationer may prefer a rowboat or a sightseeing cruiser.

Windjamming along the coast of Maine appeals to people who like to spend their vacations barefoot and in jeans, eating freshly caught lobster and acting as part-time crew of the sailboat. You can write to the Maine Windjammer Association, Box 317B, Rockport, Maine, 04856, for information about this type of vacationing; there are many sailboat owners in the area. Windjammer operators can be found in various other Atlantic coast areas also.

River rafting is popular in many parts of the country, especially in several national parks. Park superintendents can provide lists of licensed operators who take groups on trips of several days, traveling in large rubber rafts. Riding a raft on the Colorado River through the Grand Canyon, where the sheer rock walls stretch upward for more than a mile in some spots, is an unforgettable experience.

And for those who want to be on the water but look forward to vacations as a time to take it easy, there are houseboats and river cruises. Completely provisioned houseboats can be rented in many areas. A variation on this theme is the Camp-A-Float: a barge-type cruiser is used to carry a recreational vehicle. You can either rent the barge and have your own RV fastened to it or use one with an RV already attached. For information, write to CAF Industries, 101 South 30th Street, Phoenix, Arizona, 85034.

The Delta Queen Steamboat Company (511 Main Street, Cincinnati, Ohio, 45202) has two paddle-wheel steamboats that ply the Ohio and Mississippi rivers and offer cruises lasting from three to seven days. On the Pacific coast, Exploration Cruise Lines (1500 Metropolitan Park Building, Olive Way at Boren Street, Seattle, Washington, 98101) conducts cruises on the Columbia River and other locations.

## AIR SPORTS

An extremely common dream, according to psychiatrists, involves flying—on one's own power, that is. It's usually a very pleasant and exhilarating dream. Perhaps the increasing interest in air sports—hang gliding, skydiving, and hot-air ballooning—stems at least partly from these dreams.

Near Kitty Hawk, North Carolina, where the Wright brothers first took off in a flying machine, is a school for would-be hang gliders. At the opposite end of the state, on Grandfather Mountain, an annual Masters of Hang Gliding Championship contest is held for nine days each August. Similar contests and exhibitions take place in other localities.

Balloonists offer rides in their wicker baskets to paying customers. Some furnish such extra touches as French pastries and champagne in an attempt to create the Victorian-era atmosphere of *Around the World in 80 Days*. Church Street Station, in Orlando, Florida, features balloon rides among its various attractions.

Hot-air balloon rallies and races are annual events in several places. Two of the best known are in Wisconsin Dells, Wisconsin, and Phoenix, Arizona. These shows attract the hobbyists who fly the balloons as well as large crowds who enjoy the spectacle of large, brightly colored orbs drifting silently in the sky.

## FEDERAL RECREATION LANDS

Publicly owned recreational lands are bonanzas of opportunity for outdoor vacations. Fees for use range from reasonable to nonexistent, and government lands are often the most scenic and well-cared-for preserves in any given area.

The most abundant source of open space in the world for outdoor sports and recreation is the 740 million acres of land under the management of the U.S. government. Of course not all the lands are open to the public for recreation, but large tracts are, in every section of the country.

Several agencies are involved in the administration of public lands; the majority of them are under the Department of the Interior. Seventy percent of the federal lands are under the jurisdiction of that department's National Park Service, Bureau of Land Management, Bureau of Reclamation, Fish and Wildlife Service, and Bureau of Indian Affairs.

Other recreational lands are managed by the Department of Agriculture's National Forest Service, the Tennessee Valley Authority, and the Department of Defense.

Many of the units owned or controlled by these agencies contain campgrounds, marked hiking trails, ski runs, and other recreational facilities. Most national parks and some other National Park Service units have educational programs that include audiovisual presentations, small nature museums, guided nature walks, and campfire talks.

The Golden Eagle Passport is a great bargain for anyone planning several trips, or one trip involving

---

### For More Information . . .

The federal agencies mentioned in this chapter have published informational materials about the recreational areas under their jurisdiction—maps, listings, descriptive brochures, etc. These are available either free of charge or for a small fee.

To date, the federal government has not published a complete directory of all federally managed recreational lands. Therefore, for further information, send your specific requests to the following agencies. Tell them what part of the country you are interested in visiting and what kind of information you need. In some cases you may be referred to a district office in your area.

Department of Defense
U.S. Army Corps of Engineers
Information Office
Washington, DC 20301

Department of the Interior
Bureau of Land Management
Information Office
Washington, DC 20240

Department of the Interior
Bureau of Reclamation
Information Office
Washington, DC 20240

Department of the Interior
National Park Service
Information Office
Washington, DC 20240

Tennessee Valley Authority
Information Office
Knoxville, TN 37902

more than one federal area. It costs $10, can be purchased at any federal recreation area, and admits any driver plus passengers to all federal recreational areas without further admission fees. Camping fees are additional; however, not all federal camping areas charge a fee. The passport is valid for a year.

Senior citizens and disabled persons are given further privileges in federal recreation areas. Persons 65 and over can obtain a free lifetime Golden Age Passport, which entitles the holder to a 50 percent reduction in camping fees as well as free admissions. The Golden Access Passport gives the same privileges to U.S. residents who are permanently disabled, blind, or otherwise eligible for federal disability benefits.

The government is eliminating all barriers to handicapped persons in federal areas. If you are handicapped or plan to travel with someone who is, you should obtain the booklet, *Access National Parks: A Guide for Handicapped Visitors.* It costs $6.50 and can be ordered from the Superintendent of Documents, U.S. Government Printing Office, Washington, DC, 20402.

## Department of the Interior

*National Park Service.* The National Park Service administers recreational lands in national parks, monuments, lakeshores, seashores, rivers and riverways, recreation areas, and trails. See the previous chapter for definitions of these different units. For further information about specific recreational facilities and services in individual park units, read Michael Frome's *National Park Guide,* published by Rand McNally and Company.

*Fish and Wildlife Service.* The 400 national wildlife refuges are maintained primarily for the conservation of the environment on which the fish, animals, and birds who live there depend. However, many of them also have designated areas for certain kinds of recreation, such as hiking, biking, boating, swimming, fishing, camping, and observing wildlife.

*Bureau of Land Management.* Its functions are not nearly as familiar to most vacationers as are those of the National Park Service and the National Forest Service, but the Bureau of Land Management actually has jurisdiction over 43 percent of the entire expanse of federal lands. Much of the land is used for grazing and mining, some of it for timber.

More than 200 recreational areas in the western states (including Alaska) are administered by this bureau. Most have campgrounds and picnic facilities; some provide opportunities for hiking, fishing, hunting, boating, canoeing, and rafting. Rock collecting, nature study, and cave exploring are often available as well, and the use of snowmobiles and other off-road vehicles is allowed in some areas.

Some of the campsites are primitive and natural; others are developed with such amenities as drinking water, fireplaces, picnic tables, and boat ramps.

Most Bureau of Land Management campsites do not require advance reservations; some charge fees for overnight camping.

*Bureau of Reclamation.* The Reclamation Act of 1902 gave the U.S. Geological Survey (USGS) responsibility for reclaiming arid and semiarid lands through the development and management of water resources. The agency became independent of the USGS in 1907 and in 1923 was named the Bureau of Reclamation. Its many duties and functions are carried out in 17 western states.

This is the agency that built and still operates some of the largest and most powerful dams in the country. It provides water for public use and for irrigation, hydroelectric power, flood control, research, and related services. In addition, it operates 281 recreation areas situated on lands adjacent to man-made lakes. Most of these areas have campsites, boat ramps, drinking water, restrooms, and picnic areas; some also offer swimming, fishing, hunting, marked trails, winter-sports areas, and proximity to hotels or motels, grocery stores, and restaurants.

## National Forests

The National Forest Service manages 25 percent of U.S. public lands, in accordance with a philosophy of multiple use. Timber harvesting, livestock grazing, and other commercial pursuits are carried out along with conservation programs and recreation.

Campgrounds within national forests are very often much less crowded, and the campsites more spacious, than those in nearby national parks and monuments. A good way to enjoy the splendors of some of the national parks and escape the crowds, at least at night, is to find a campsite in an adjacent national forest and commute to the park by day.

Types of forests vary from groves of cypress and sand pines in the South to Alpine meadows and tall firs in the Rockies and giant sequoias in California. Some forests are dense and humid; some are open timberlands.

The Forest Service also manages desert ranges, grasslands, and the National Bison Range in Montana. Flaming Gorge National Recreation Area, on the border of Utah and Wyoming, is also managed by Forest Service, though most national recreation areas are under the National Park Service.

Some national-forest recreation sites have visitor centers and naturalists on duty; others are remote, secluded, and wild. Some 400 resorts are found on national-forest lands, most of them owned—and all of them operated—by private concessionaires.

The 2,000-mile Appalachian Trail, beloved by hikers, winds through 8 national forests on its path from Maine to Georgia. Shelters and lean-tos are found at intervals along the trail. In the West, the Pacific Crest Trail System, stretching for 2,500 miles from Canada to Mexico, runs through 25 national forests for two-thirds

## The Most Popular National Park Service Areas

National Parks and other recreational areas administered by the National Park Service are among the most popular vacation spots in the nation. Records kept by the agency reflect of the number of people who visit the parks and other areas for daytime recreational purposes and for overnight stays. These four tables give the number of daytime visits to the most popular parks, daytime visits to the other National Park Service areas that are most popular, overnight stays in the most popular parks and other areas, and the top 20 states in number of daytime recreational visits to National Park Service areas.

### Top States in Daytime Visits to Park Service Areas

| | Daytime Recreational Visits |
|---|---|
| 1. California | 30,919 |
| 2. Virginia | 22,833 |
| 3. District of Columbia | 19,329 |
| 4. North Carolina | 15,986 |
| 5. New York | 11,830 |
| 6. Mississippi | 11,706 |
| 7. Pennsylvania | 10,757 |
| 8. Maryland | 10,113 |
| 9. Massachusetts | 8,823 |
| 10. Tennessee | 7,443 |
| 11. Florida | 6,566 |
| 12. Arizona | 6,107 |
| 13. Nevada | 5,944 |
| 14. Washington | 5,564 |
| 15. Colorado | 5,389 |
| 16. Utah | 5,003 |
| 17. Texas | 4,665 |
| 18. Hawaii | 4,546 |
| 19. Missouri | 4,529 |
| 20. New Jersey | 4,364 |

Source: National Park Service, *National Park Statistical Abstract, 1983,* as published in *Tourism's Top Twenty,* 1984.

### Daytime Visits to National Recreation Areas, Seashores, Lakeshores, Riverways, and Monuments

| | Daytime Recreational Visits |
|---|---|
| 1. Golden Gate National Recreation Area, CA | 16,731,706 |
| 2. Gateway National Recreation Area, NJ–NY | 7,881,106 |
| 3. Lake Mead National Recreation Area, AZ–NV | 6,276,562 |
| 4. Gulf Islands National Seashore, FL–MS | 5,803,384 |
| 5. Cape Cod National Seashore, MA | 4,560,713 |
| 6. Point Reyes National Seashore, CA | 2,032,238 |
| 7. Chickasaw National Recreation Area, OK | 2,026,727 |
| 8. Lake Meredith Recreation Area, TX | 1,944,648 |
| 9. Glen Canyon National Recreation Area, AZ–UT | 1,813,415 |
| 10. Delaware Water Gap National Recreation Area, NJ–PA | 1,621,909 |
| 11. Indiana Dunes National Lakeshore, IN | 1,560,324 |
| 12. Ozark National Scenic Riverways, MO | 1,429,268 |
| 13. Cape Hatteras National Seashore, NC | 1,396,076 |
| 14. Whiskeytown-Shasta-Trinity National Recreation Area, CA | 1,299,089 |
| 15. Muir Woods National Monument, CA | 1,220,310 |
| 16. Canaveral National Seashore, FL | 1,181,302 |
| 17. Amistad National Recreation Area, TX | 1,164,338 |
| 18. Assateague Island National Seashore, MD–VA | 1,093,240 |
| 19. Cuyahoga Valley National Recreation Area, OH | 1,018,828 |

Source: National Park Service Statistical Office, Denver, CO, 1984.

### Daytime Visits to National Parks

| | Daytime Recreational Visits |
|---|---|
| 1. Great Smoky Mountains, NC–TN | 8,508,390 |
| 2. Acadia, ME | 3,734,763 |
| 3. Olympic, WA | 2,759,011 |
| 4. Yosemite, CA | 2,738,467 |
| 5. Rocky Mountain, CO | 2,231,448 |
| 6. Yellowstone, ID–MT–WY | 2,222,027 |
| 7. Grand Canyon, AZ | 2,173,584 |
| 8. Hawaii Volcanoes, HI | 2,008,608 |
| 9. Glacier, MT | 1,946,703 |
| 10. Shenandoah, VA | 1,869,307 |
| 11. Mammoth Cave, KY | 1,501,450 |
| 12. Zion, UT | 1,377,254 |
| 13. Grand Teton, WY | 1,360,898 |
| 14. Mount Rainier, WA | 1,152,411 |
| 15. Badlands, SD | 1,113,675 |
| 16. Hot Springs, AR | 1,071,853 |
| 17. Haleakala, HI | 1,003,821 |

Source: National Park Service Statistical Office, Denver, CO, 1984.

### Overnight Stays in Park Service Areas

| | Overnight Stays |
|---|---|
| 1. Yosemite National Park, CA | 2,210,915 |
| 2. Glen Canyon National Recreation Area, AZ–UT | 1,473,495 |
| 3. Lake Mead National Recreation Area, AZ–NV | 1,388,840 |
| 4. Yellowstone National Park, ID–MT–WY | 1,284,974 |
| 5. Grand Canyon National Park, AZ | 779,489 |
| 6. Grand Teton National Park, WY | 462,257 |
| 7. Great Smoky Mountains National Park, NC–TN | 455,592 |
| 8. Sequoia National Park, CA | 440,931 |
| 9. Shenandoah National Park, VA | 414,499 |
| 10. Olympic National Park, WA | 335,710 |
| 11. Death Valley National Monument, CA–NV | 332,862 |
| 12. Glacier National Park, MT | 326,084 |
| 13. Kings Canyon National Park, CA | 272,376 |
| 14. Zion National Park, UT | 252,516 |
| 15. Cape Hatteras National Seashore, NC | 247,627 |
| 16. Ozark National Scenic Riverways, MO | 235,799 |
| 17. Big Bend National Park, TX | 228,195 |
| 18. Lake Meredith National Recreation Area, TX | 223,926 |
| 19. Virgin Islands National Park, St. John, VI | 214,595 |

Source: National Park Service Statistical Office, Denver, CO, 1984.

of its length. Thousands of lesser-known trails criss-cross other sections of the National Forest System. The trails themselves are maintained as units of the National Park Service.

Planned for eventual development are several cross-country trails, including one that will follow the 3,700-mile route of the Lewis and Clark Expedition from Illinois to Oregon.

### Tennessee Valley Authority

The Tennessee Valley Authority's lakes in the states of Alabama, Georgia, Kentucky, Mississippi, North Carolina, and Tennessee encompass more than 1,000 square miles of water surface and 11,000 miles of shoreline. While the Tennessee Valley Authority lakes were created first and foremost for the purposes of flood control, generation of electricity, navigation, and the reforestation of surrounding lands, recreational services and facilities have become an important by-product of the work of the authority. Each year, many thousands of visitors enjoy swimming, boating, and fishing in the lakes and camping, hiking, and picnicking along the shores.

There is not much wilderness left in the eastern United States, but a few Tennessee Valley Authority "small wild areas" have been established to preserve interesting and unique natural features.

A favorite Tennessee Valley Authority area is a 170,000-acre peninsula between Kentucky Lake and Lake Barkley in western Kentucky and Tennessee known as the Land Between the Lakes. There are extensive facilities for recreation: a 5,000-acre environmental-education area near Kentucky Lake has an interpretive center, trails, a living-history farm, a contemporary farm, an overlook with a panoramic view of the lake, and an outdoor school. A herd of buffalo lives on a nearby range.

### U.S. Army Corps of Engineers

The U.S. Army Corps of Engineers has existed since the early days of the Continental Army. Since 1802, when Congress established the U.S. Military Academy at West Point, New York, the army has been training engineers to serve the country in a variety of ways.

The corps takes its place alongside the Bureau of Reclamation and the Tennessee Valley Authority as a builder of dams for a number of purposes, one of which is recreation.

Some of the recreation areas situated on lands managed by the Corps of Engineers are operated by state and local governments. For example, one of the most popular public recreation areas in the country is the Corps of Engineers Lake Sidney Lanier, north of Atlanta, Georgia, operated as a public park by the state of Georgia. One island is reserved for group outings and entertainment; a second has a swimming beach, a water slide, docks, rental boats, stables, tennis courts, and rental cottages. A third island is reserved for campers and offers about 350 campsites, tennis, a swimming pool, boat ramps, and a recreation center. On the fourth island is a complete resort hotel and championship golf course.

### STATE PARKS AND BEACHES

State parks and beaches are as full of resources for outdoor vacationers as federal recreation lands. The facilities in many states are at least equal in quality to

## State Parks and Recreation Areas

| The Most Land | Acres (in thousands) | The Most Popular | Visitors (in thousands) |
|---|---|---|---|
| 1. Alaska | 2,973 | 1. California | 63,051 |
| 2. California | 1,058 | 2. Ohio | 55,860 |
| 3. Illinois | 338 | 3. New York | 49,075 |
| 4. Ohio | 305 | 4. Washington | 40,626 |
| 5. New Jersey | 279 | 5. Oregon | 32,215 |
| 6. Pennsylvania | 269 | 6. Pennsylvania | 31,129 |
| 7. Massachusetts | 261 | 7. Illinois | 30,972 |
| 8. New York | 256 | 8. Kentucky | 25,117 |
| 9. Florida | 250 | 9. Michigan | 20,812 |
| 10. Michigan | 248 | 10. Tennessee | 19,066 |
| 11. Washington | 219 | 11. Hawaii | 18,111 |
| 12. Minnesota | 217 | 12. Oklahoma | 16,770 |
| 13. Maryland | 212 | 13. Texas | 16,747 |
| 14. Connecticut | 202 | 14. Iowa | 14,000 |
| 15. Texas | 189 | 15. South Carolina | 13,045 |
| 16. Colorado | 160 | 16. Florida | 12,967 |
| 17. Vermont | 157 | 17. Massachusetts | 10,423 |
| 18. Nevada | 153 | 18. Georgia | 10,277 |
| 19. West Virginia | 150 | 19. Missouri | 9,656 |
| 20. Nebraska | 137 | 20. Wisconsin | 8,523 |

*Source:* National Association of State Park Directors, *Annual Information Exchange*, as published in *Tourism's Top Twenty*, 1984.

Figures reflect 1982 data.

those on federal lands, the fees are often as reasonable, and in many areas state lands are even more popular.

State beaches are particularly important along the Pacific coastlines of California, Oregon, Washington, and Hawaii, where many miles of beach and scenic shores have been protected from private development. Most of the public beaches are open only for day use, but some also have camping facilities.

State parks range from simple day-use parks in wooded areas or on lakeshores, offering not much more than picnic tables and playfields, to full-scale resorts complete with first-class lodges or hotels, golf courses, swimming pools, tennis courts, museums, and recreational directors.

An outstanding example of a state-resort park is Fall Creek Falls Park, about 60 miles north of Chattanooga, Tennessee. Within the preserve's 16,000 acres are chasms, gorges, forests, and majestic cascades. The falls for which the park is named plunge downward for 265 feet into a shaded pool. The facilities here are as extensive as at any privately run luxury resort. They include an inn, a restaurant, cabins, camping and picnic areas, an 18-hole golf course and pro shop, snack bars, a general store and other shops, a nature center and trails, playfields and playgrounds, an Olympic-sized swimming pool, an amphitheater, convention facilities, and a recreation lodge. And despite all the amenities, there is plenty of space in which to enjoy the outdoors.

# SCORING: Fun in the Great Outdoors

Many outdoor sports can be enjoyed nearly everywhere: walking, swimming, and biking, for example. But when you are deciding where to go on vacation, the availability of space and facilities for your favorite outdoor activity can be an important factor in your choice.

The scoring in this chapter was based on the availability of areas and facilities for selected outdoor activities, under the assumption that the more opportunities there were within a Vacation Place for outdoor sports and recreation, the more desirable the place was to the traveler looking to pursue his or her favorite outdoor activity. The superior quality of a golf course or a body of water over another was not considered in the scoring, mainly because quality judgments of this sort were not available. Certain experts do, from time to time, come up with lists of "bests"—best ski runs, best beaches, or best fishing areas, for example—but most such lists are limited in scope and entirely subjective. As of yet, no one has made a quality judgment of all of the available facilities of a variety of recreational activities.

Golf, tennis, and skiing were chosen as representative of the sports that influence many vacationers' choices of where to go. Availability of facilities for these activities were three of the factors used in calculating an overall score for Fun in the Great Outdoors.

Since most of the wilderness or near-wilderness land open to the public for recreational purposes is owned or managed by agencies of the state and federal governments, the number of these areas in each Vacation Place was another factor used in scoring.

Finally, a score was added for the general availability of bodies of water for swimming, fishing, boating, and other water sports.

In this chapter and in later ones, certain outstanding points of interest—nearby but not strictly within the area defined as the Vacation Place—are listed in the Place Profiles in italics. These listings were included because they were considered easily accessible and important or interesting enough to be worth a short side trip; they were given one-half the point score of similar places within the Vacation Place boundaries.

## Golf

Private courses, such as most country-club courses, were not included in the scoring because their use was generally limited to members: thus they were not considered a major resource for vacationers.

The National Golf Foundation classifies a public course as *municipal* if it is owned and administered by any tax-supported agency such as a city, county, school, or park district; a course is classified as *daily fee* if it is privately owned but accessible to the public for a fee. Courses at vacation resorts generally fall into the latter category.

A Vacation Place received 20 points for each 18-hole course and 10 points for each 9-hole course. Chicago, Illinois, with 91 18-hole courses and 49 9-hole courses, earned 2,310 points for golf, giving it first place in this category. Following is a list of the top 11 Vacation Places for the availability of public golf courses (Finger Lakes, New York, and Seattle, Washington, are tied for tenth place). Large cities are well represented, and 7 of the 11 are in northern areas where the game can be played only part of the year.

### Top Eleven for Golf

|  | | Points |
|---|---|---|
| 1. | Chicago, IL | 2,310 |
| 2. | Miami–Gold Coast–Keys, FL | 2,190 |
| 3. | Los Angeles, CA | 2,110 |
| 4. | Tampa Bay–Southwest Coast, FL | 1,840 |
| 5. | Philadelphia, PA–DE–NJ | 1,560 |
| 6. | Minneapolis–St. Paul, MN–WI | 1,550 |
| 7. | Boston, MA | 1,270 |
| 8. | Orlando–Space Coast, FL | 1,150 |
| 9. | Catskill Mountains, NY | 1,080 |
| 10. | Finger Lakes, NY | 1,070 |
| 10. | Seattle–Mount Rainier–North Cascades, WA | 1,070 |

## Tennis

Tennis resorts only were included in the scoring of tennis. Of course tennis courts are available nearly everywhere, but for vacationers, the availability of resorts that place a major emphasis on tennis was considered the important factor.

Each tennis resort within a Vacation Place earned 100 points, with 1 point added for each resort court. For example, Hilton Head, South Carolina, had 12 such resorts with a total of 275 courts; therefore its score for tennis was 1,475.

Only one Vacation Place among the top ten—Green Mountains, Vermont—is outside the warm climes where the game can be played year-round.

### Top Ten for Tennis

|  | | Points |
|---|---|---|
| 1. | Miami–Gold Coast–Keys, FL | 3,239 |
| 2. | Hawaii | 2,587 |
| 3. | Tampa Bay–Southwest Coast, FL | 2,367 |
| 4. | Phoenix–Valley of the Sun, AZ | 2,085 |
| 5. | Palm Springs–Desert Playgrounds, CA | 1,705 |
| 6. | Orlando–Space Coast, FL | 1,656 |
| 7. | Hilton Head, SC | 1,475 |
| 8. | St. Augustine–Northeast Coast, FL | 887 |
| 9. | Green Mountains, VT | 881 |
| 10. | Las Vegas–Lake Mead, NV–AZ | 741 |

## Skiing

New ski areas are constantly being developed, and there is stiff competition among such popular areas as Colorado's Rockies, Utah's Wasatch Range, and several sections of California, not to mention the well-established ski centers of New Hampshire and Vermont.

The 107 Vacation Places were rated according to the availability of skiing, with each developed ski area given 100 points. Added to that was a score for lift capacity, based on the total hourly capacity for all ski areas combined, divided by 100.

According to this method of scoring, the Lake Tahoe Vacation Place came in first, with its 19 ski areas and a combined lift capacity of 156,485 per hour. Half the top ten Vacation Places were in the East, one in the Midwest. Of the four western places, one may come as a surprise—Palm Springs. While much of the Palm Springs area is low-lying, flat, desert land, some of it is in the high San Bernardino and San Jacinto mountains —popular spots for skiers.

### Top Ten for Skiing

|  | Points |
| --- | --- |
| 1. Lake Tahoe–Reno, NV–CA | 3,465 |
| 2. White Mountains, NH | 2,253 |
| 3. Aspen–Vail, CO | 2,182 |
| 4. Green Mountains, VT | 1,812 |
| 5. Pocono Mountains, PA | 1,791 |
| 6. Salt Lake City, UT | 1,781 |
| 7. Traverse City–Petoskey, MI | 1,619 |
| 8. Catskill Mountains, NY | 1,609 |
| 9. Berkshire Hills–Pioneer Valley, MA | 1,576 |
| 10. Palm Springs–Desert Playgrounds, CA | 1,402 |

## Water Sports

Nearly every vacation destination in the United States has something to offer people interested in water sports—at least a fishing stream, a pond, or a swimming pool. Measurements based on the size of these water facilities are impossible to come by and would have little meaning for the average vacationer. In many vacation spots, however, the accessibility of water for swimming, boating, canoeing, fishing, and other sports is a prime attraction, while in others water is fairly scarce and visitors come to enjoy other facilities and activities.

Some credit for the availability of water sports was already implicit in the scoring for public recreational lands, since most of them include lakes, beachfronts, or streams. One hundred points were given to each Vacation Place with significant frontage on salt water or fresh water; 200 points were given if the area had both fresh and salt water. In addition, these places with significant water frontage were given 50 bonus points if they had relatively mild year-round temperatures. To qualify for the 50-point temperature bonus, the average afternoon temperature in January, as listed in the climate data in the previous chapter, must have been at least 55 degrees Fahrenheit.

## Federal Recreation Lands

In general, national parks, national forests, and national recreation areas are more extensive in area and in recreational opportunity than other federal lands. Therefore, the presence of each of these federal lands earned 500 points for the Vacation Place. Other units of the National Park Service (such as monuments and seashores) earned 200 points each for the place. All other federal recreation areas (those managed by the Bureau of Land Management, Tennessee Valley Authority, and other agencies) were given 100 points each. Albuquerque–Santa Fe–Taos, New Mexico, earned 2,700 points in this recreational category, with three national forests (1,500 points), a national monument (200 points), and ten other federal areas (1,000 points).

All of the top 11 in this category (Albuquerque–Santa Fe–Taos, New Mexico, and Denver–Rocky Mountain National Park, Colorado, tied for tenth place) are in the western part of the United States.

### Top Eleven for Federal Recreation Lands

|  | Points |
| --- | --- |
| 1. Crater Lake–Klamath Falls, OR | 4,800 |
| 2. Yellowstone–Jackson–Tetons, WY–ID–MT | 4,600 |
| 3. Lake Powell–Glen Canyon, AZ–UT | 4,400 |
| 3. Redwoods–Shasta–Lassen, CA | 4,400 |
| 5. Grand Canyon Country, AZ | 3,700 |
| 6. Yosemite–Sequoia–Death Valley, CA | 3,500 |
| 7. Seattle–Mount Rainier–North Cascades, WA | 3,250 |
| 8. Salt Lake City, UT | 3,100 |
| 9. Lake Tahoe–Reno, NV–CA | 2,900 |
| 10. Albuquerque–Santa Fe–Taos, NM | 2,700 |
| 10. Denver–Rocky Mountain National Park, CO | 2,700 |

## State Parks and Beaches

Only state parks that offered camping facilities were counted in the scoring of outdoor recreation, as these were the ones considered to be important to vacationers. All state-owned beaches within each Vacation Place were counted. Each beach and each qualifying park received 100 points.

The states along the Pacific Coast have preserved many stretches as state beaches; some are available for camping as well as for day use. Eight of the top eleven Vacation Places for numbers of state parks and beaches are in the Pacific states of California, Oregon, Washington, and Hawaii.

### Top Eleven for State Parks and Beaches

|  | Points |
| --- | --- |
| 1. Portland–Columbia River, OR | 3,900 |
| 2. Monterey–Big Sur, CA | 3,000 |
| 3. Hawaii | 2,500 |
| 4. Olympic Peninsula, WA | 2,200 |
| 5. Tulsa–Lake O' The Cherokees, OK | 2,000 |
| 6. Coos Bay–South Coast, OR | 1,900 |
| 7. Wine Country, CA | 1,800 |
| 8. Green Mountains, VT | 1,500 |
| 8. Los Angeles, CA | 1,500 |
| 10. Providence–Newport, RI | 1,300 |
| 10. Seattle–Mount Rainier–North Cascades, WA | 1,300 |

**PLACE PROFILES:** Fun in the Great Outdoors

In these pages, the availability of facilities for outdoor sports and recreation is enumerated and scored. The number of public golf courses, tennis resorts, developed ski areas, federal recreation lands, and state parks and beaches are given, along with an indication of the availability of freshwater and saltwater sports.

Only units of the National Park Service and the National Forest Service are listed by name. Areas outside the boundaries of Vacation Places but near enough and important enough to be worth a special trip are printed in italics and count for half the score given to comparable places within the boundaries.

A star (★) preceding a Vacation Place highlights that place as one of the top ten in this chapter.

### Adirondack Mountains, NY
**Golf Facilities:** 44 daily fee; 7 municipal
  23 eighteen-hole courses
  31 nine-hole courses
**Skiing:** 10 areas; total lift capacity 28,540/hr
**Water Sports:** Fresh water
**State Parks and Beaches:** 8
**Comment:** The vast Adirondack Park covers most of the area included in this destination; about one-third is a protected wilderness. Activities include fishing, swimming, waterskiing, sailing, canoeing; winter sports and summer ice-skating at the Lake Placid Olympic facilities.
**Places Rated Score:** 2,955
**Places Rated Rank:** 40

### Albuquerque–Santa Fe–Taos, NM
**Golf Facilities:** 5 daily fee; 7 municipal
  8 eighteen-hole courses
  6 nine-hole courses
**Tennis:** 2 resorts (12 courts)
**Skiing:** 7 areas; total lift capacity 34,090/hr
**Federal Recreation Lands:**
  Bandelier National Monument
  Carson National Forest
  Cibola National Forest
  Santa Fe National Forest
  8 Bureau of Land Management areas
  1 Bureau of Reclamation area
  1 Corps of Engineers area
**State Parks and Beaches:** 10
**Comment:** Area features diverse terrain plus an abundance of trout, bass, and waterfowl. White-water boating is available on the Rio Grande.
**Places Rated Score:** 5,173
**Places Rated Rank:** 14

### Anchorage–Kenai Peninsula, AK
**Golf Facilities:** 6 daily fee; 1 municipal
  2 eighteen-hole courses
  5 nine-hole courses
**Skiing:** 2 areas; total lift capacity 8,200/hr
**Water Sports:** Salt water
**Federal Recreation Lands:**
  Chugach National Forest
  *Denali National Park*
  Kenai Fjords National Park
**State Parks and Beaches:** 6
**Comment:** Much of the Kenai Peninsula is still wilderness; recreational opportunities include excellent salmon fishing, beachcombing, canoeing, boating, hiking, and camping.
**Places Rated Score:** 2,322
**Places Rated Rank:** 53

### Asheville–Smoky Mountains, NC
**Golf Facilities:** 12 daily fee; 4 municipal
  10 eighteen-hole courses
  6 nine-hole courses
**Tennis:** 3 resorts (18 courts)
**Skiing:** 2 areas; total lift capacity 6,210/hr
**Water Sports:** Fresh water
**Federal Recreation Lands:**
  Great Smoky Mountains National Park
  Nantahala National Forest
  Pisgah National Forest
  1 Tennessee Valley Authority area
**State Parks and Beaches:** 1
**Comment:** Mountain climbing, fishing, trail riding, rockhounding, and hiking are popular activities.
**Places Rated Score:** 2,640
**Places Rated Rank:** 46

### Aspen–Vail, CO
**Golf Facilities:** 4 daily fee; 4 municipal
  6 eighteen-hole courses
  2 nine-hole courses
**Tennis:** 6 resorts (55 courts)
**Skiing:** 10 areas; total lift capacity 118,172/hr
**Federal Recreation Lands:**
  White River National Forest
  1 Bureau of Land Management area
  4 Bureau of Reclamation areas
**Comment:** Best known for Alpine skiing and other winter sports, this area also offers mountain climbing, spelunking, and backpacking.
**Places Rated Score:** 3,977
**Places Rated Rank:** 24

### Atlanta, GA
**Golf Facilities:** 27 daily fee; 16 municipal
  25 eighteen-hole courses
  19 nine-hole courses
**Tennis:** 6 resorts (57 courts)
**Water Sports:** Fresh water
**Federal Recreation Lands:**
  Chattahoochee National Forest
  Chattahoochee River National Recreation Area
  3 Corps of Engineers areas
**State Parks and Beaches:** 8
**Comment:** The recreational areas on several lakes created by the Corps of Engineers in northern Georgia are among the most popular federal lands in the country for fishing, boating, and swimming.
**Places Rated Score:** 3,547
**Places Rated Rank:** 30

### Atlantic City, NJ
**Golf Facilities:** 3 daily fee; 1 municipal
  8 eighteen-hole courses
  4 nine-hole courses
**Water Sports:** Salt water
**State Parks and Beaches:** 2
**Comment:** Thousands of acres of wetlands make bird-watching a special treat here.
**Places Rated Score:** 500
**Places Rated Rank:** 104

### Austin–Hill Country, TX
**Golf Facilities:** 8 daily fee; 6 municipal
  8 eighteen-hole courses
  8 nine-hole courses
**Tennis:** 2 resorts (68 courts)
**Water Sports:** Fresh water, year-round
**Federal Recreation Lands:**
  3 Corps of Engineers areas
**State Parks:** 7
**Comment:** The Highland Lakes stretch northwest from Austin. They form the state's largest inland-water recreation region, well used for swimming, sailing, motorboating, and waterskiing.
**Places Rated Score:** 1,658
**Places Rated Rank:** 72

### Baltimore–Chesapeake Bay, MD
**Golf Facilities:** 9 daily fee; 11 municipal
  13 eighteen-hole courses
  7 nine-hole courses
**Skiing:** 1 area; total lift capacity 1,500/hr
**Water Sports:** Salt water
**Federal Recreation Lands:**
  1 Corps of Engineers area
**State Parks and Beaches:** 2
**Comment:** Throughout the huge "inland sea" that is Chesapeake Bay, widely practiced summer activities include fishing, crabbing, clamming, oyster digging, swimming, boating, and sailing.
**Places Rated Score:** 845
**Places Rated Rank:** 95

### Bar Harbor–Acadia, ME
**Golf Facilities:** 16 daily fee; 1 municipal
  4 eighteen-hole courses
  13 nine-hole courses

Skiing: 1 area; total lift capacity 2,000/hr
Water Sports: Salt water
Federal Recreation Lands:
  Acadia National Park
State Parks: 4
Comment: Visitors to Acadia enjoy fishing, walking, and bird-watching in summer; cross-country skiing and snowshoeing in winter.
Places Rated Score: 1,330
Places Rated Rank: 83

## Bend–Cascade Mountains, OR

Golf Facilities: 9 daily fee; no municipal
  6 eighteen-hole courses
  5 nine-hole courses
Skiing: 2 areas; total lift capacity 18,660/hr
Federal Recreation Lands:
  Deschutes National Forest
  Ochoco National Forest
  Willamette National Forest
  5 Bureau of Reclamation areas
State Parks: 5
Comment: Scores of lakes and reservoirs are well used for fishing, boating, and waterskiing. Many resorts have horse stables; rockhounding is also popular here.
Places Rated Score: 3,057
Places Rated Rank: 38

## Berkshire Hills–Pioneer Valley, MA

Golf Facilities: 40 daily fee; 5 municipal
  24 eighteen-hole courses
  21 nine-hole courses
Tennis: 1 resort (2 courts)
Skiing: 10 areas; total lift capacity 57,570/hr
Water Sports: Fresh water
Federal Recreation Lands:
  2 Corps of Engineers areas
State Parks: 1
Comment: The Appalachian Trail, well known to hikers for generations, passes through the Berkshires. There are streams and lakes for canoeing and fishing; trails for biking and horseback riding.
Places Rated Score: 2,768
Places Rated Rank: 44

## Black Hills, SD

Golf Facilities: 6 daily fee; 3 municipal
  1 eighteen-hole course
  8 nine-hole courses
Skiing: 2 areas; total lift capacity 7,800/hr
Federal Recreation Lands:
  Badlands National Park
  Black Hills National Forest
  Buffalo Gap National Grassland
  Jewel Cave National Monument
  Wind Cave National Park
  4 Bureau of Reclamation areas
  2 Corps of Engineers areas
State Parks: 2
Comment: Camping and hiking, trout fishing, exceptionally productive rockhounding, and spelunking are among the many outdoor activities in the Black Hills.
Places Rated Score: 3,078
Places Rated Rank: 37

## Blue Ridge Mountains, VA

Golf Facilities: 9 daily fee; 5 municipal
  8 eighteen-hole courses
  6 nine-hole courses

Tennis: 2 resorts (26 courts)
Skiing: 3 areas; total lift capacity 13,900/hr
Federal Recreation Lands:
  Blue Ridge Parkway
  George Washington National Forest
  Shenandoah National Park
Comment: The spectacular scenery of this area is the backdrop for hiking, riding, boating and fishing, and winter sports.
Places Rated Score: 2,085
Places Rated Rank: 59

## Boise–Sun Valley, ID

Golf Facilities: 11 daily fee; 7 municipal
  6 eighteen-hole courses
  12 nine-hole courses
Tennis: 2 resorts (36 courts)
Skiing: 4 areas; total lift capacity 9,350/hr
Federal Recreation Lands:
  Boise National Forest
  Payette National Forest
  Sawtooth National Forest
  1 Bureau of Land Management area
  5 Bureau of Reclamation areas
  1 Corps of Engineers area
State Parks: 2
Comment: Dozens of licensed outfitters and guides take adventurous vacationers on wilderness expeditions in this part of the country—for backpacking, mountaineering, kayaking, river running, trail riding, fishing, hunting, and much more. Sun Valley is also a premiere winter-sports resort area.
Places Rated Score: 3,370
Places Rated Rank: 33

## Boone–High Country, NC

Golf Facilities: 9 daily fee; no municipal
  8 eighteen-hole courses
  1 nine-hole course
Skiing: 6 areas; total lift capacity 23,100/hr
Water Sports: Fresh water
Federal Recreation Lands:
  Pisgah National Forest
State Parks: 3
Comment: White-water rafting and canoeing, hiking and mountain climbing, skiing, and hang gliding are popular in this part of the Appalachians.
Places Rated Score: 1,901
Places Rated Rank: 64

## Boston, MA

Golf Facilities: 59 daily fee; 19 municipal
  47 eighteen-hole courses
  33 nine-hole courses
Skiing: 8 areas; total lift capacity 23,600/hr
Water Sports: Salt water, fresh water
State Parks: 1
Comment: This area is almost entirely urban, but Walden Pond, close to the city, still has much of the quiet charm beloved by Henry David Thoreau. Whale-watching expeditions take off from here; Boston Harbor Islands State Park is an "escape hatch" from the city, with secluded islands and beaches. There are several ski resorts in the metropolitan area with facilities for a variety of winter sports.
Places Rated Score: 2,606
Places Rated Rank: 47

## Brownsville–Rio Grande Valley, TX

Golf Facilities: 6 daily fee; 5 municipal
  7 eighteen-hole courses
  7 nine-hole courses
Water Sports: Salt water, year-round
Federal Recreation Lands:
  Padre Island National Seashore
State Parks: 1
Comment: Brownsville offers access to South Padre Island and the secluded, unspoiled beaches of Brazos Island State Park, where visitors enjoy surfing and other water sports.
Places Rated Score: 660
Places Rated Rank: 101

## Cape Cod–The Islands, MA

Golf Facilities: 22 daily fee; 5 municipal
  14 eighteen-hole courses
  13 nine-hole courses
Tennis: 3 resorts (25 courts)
Water Sports: Salt water, fresh water
Federal Recreation Lands:
  Cape Cod National Seashore
  1 Corps of Engineers area
State Parks: 2
Comment: Both deep-sea and inland fishing, sailing, biking, horseback riding, and cross-country skiing are favorite activities here. Golf and tennis are also popular, as are bird-watching and whale watching.
Places Rated Score: 1,435
Places Rated Rank: 80

## Catskill Mountains, NY

Golf Facilities: 62 daily fee; 9 municipal
  30 eighteen-hole courses
  48 nine-hole courses
Tennis: 4 resorts (89 courts)
Skiing: 11 areas; total lift capacity 50,900/hr
Water Sports: Fresh water
State Parks: 7
Comment: Such adventurous sports as hang gliding and ballooning, rock climbing and rappelling, and spelunking and tubing are enjoyed in the Catskills—as well as the more usual sports of golf, tennis, and fishing.
Places Rated Score: 3,978
Places Rated Rank: 23

## Charleston, SC

Golf Facilities: 8 daily fee; 1 municipal
  5 eighteen-hole courses
  4 nine-hole courses
Tennis: 4 resorts (69 courts)
Water Sports: Salt water, year-round
Federal Recreation Lands:
  Francis Marion National Forest
State Parks and Beaches: 3
Comment: Visitors to Charleston and the recently developed "resort islands" nearby come mainly for golf, tennis, and the beaches.
Places Rated Score: 1,559
Places Rated Rank: 76

## Chattanooga–Huntsville, TN–AL–GA

Golf Facilities: 20 daily fee; 6 municipal
  15 eighteen-hole courses
  11 nine-hole courses
Skiing: 1 area; total lift capacity 1,500/hr
Water Sports: Fresh water

Federal Recreation Lands:
  Russell Cave National Monument
  11 Tennessee Valley Authority areas
State Parks and Beaches: 5
Comment: The Tennessee Valley Authority contributed outstanding facilities for water recreation to this area. In addition to lakeside parks, navigable streams, and wooded hills, there are numerous nearby caves to be enjoyed.
Places Rated Score: 2,425
Places Rated Rank: 49

## Chicago, IL

Golf Facilities: 62 daily fee; 55 municipal
  91 eighteen-hole courses
  49 nine-hole courses
Skiing: 4 areas; total lift capacity 11,000/hr
Water Sports: Fresh water
State Parks: 1
Comment: Chicago is justifiably proud of its beautiful frontage on Lake Michigan and of its parks and forest preserves. The beaches are good, and there is plenty of space for sailing and motorboating. Also, the Chicago area boasts more municipal and daily-fee golf courses than any other destination area covered in this book.
Places Rated Score: 3,020
Places Rated Rank: 39

## Cincinnati, OH–KY

Golf Facilities: 19 daily fee; 24 municipal
  34 eighteen-hole courses
  17 nine-hole courses
Skiing: 2 areas; total lift capacity 7,400/hr
Federal Recreation Lands:
  1 Corps of Engineers area
State Parks and Beaches: 3
Comment: Cincinnati is first and foremost a river town, and the principal outdoor activities are boating, fishing, and waterskiing on the Ohio River.
Places Rated Score: 1,524
Places Rated Rank: 77

## Colorado Springs, CO

Golf Facilities: 5 daily fee; 4 municipal
  5 eighteen-hole courses
  6 nine-hole courses
Tennis: 1 resort (16 courts)
Skiing: 2 areas; total lift capacity 1,600/hr
Federal Recreation Lands:
  Florissant Fossil Beds National Monument
  *Great Sand Dunes National Monument*
  Pike National Forest
  San Isabel National Forest
  1 Bureau of Land Management area
  1 Bureau of Reclamation area
Comments: Kayaking on the Arkansas River, trout fishing in the mountain streams, mountain climbing, backpacking, and trail riding are just a few of the things outdoors lovers find to do in beautiful Colorado.
Places Rated Score: 1,992
Places Rated Rank: 61

## Coos Bay–South Coast, OR

Golf Facilities: 6 daily fee; 1 municipal
  2 eighteen-hole courses
  5 nine-hole courses
Water Sports: Salt water, fresh water

Federal Recreation Lands:
  Siskiyou National Forest
  1 Bureau of Land Management area
State Parks and Beaches: 19
Comment: State parks and beaches make almost every inch of Oregon's South Coast accessible to sun worshipers, beachcombers, surfers, and fishers. Other amusements include flying kites and driving dune buggies over the sands.
Places Rated Score: 2,790
Places Rated Rank: 43

## Corpus Christi–Padre Island, TX

Golf Facilities: 2 daily fee; 3 municipal
  5 eighteen-hole courses
  1 nine-hole course
Water Sports: Salt water, year-round
Federal Recreation Lands:
  Padre Island National Seashore
State Parks and Beaches: 3
Comment: Padre Island, a 113-mile-long barrier island protected by the National Park Service, is a delight for bird-watchers. Many species of marine birds and shorebirds live or vacation here. Swimming, surf fishing, and shelling are popular year-round.
Places Rated Score: 760
Places Rated Rank: 98

## ★ Crater Lake–Klamath Falls, OR

Golf Facilities: 9 daily fee; 2 municipal
  2 eighteen-hole courses
  9 nine-hole courses
Skiing: 1 area; total lift capacity 3,500/hr
Water Sports: Fresh water
Federal Recreation Lands:
  Crater Lake National Park
  Oregon Caves National Monument
  Rogue River National Forest
  Umpqua National Forest
  Winema National Forest
  12 Bureau of Land Management areas
  7 Bureau of Reclamation areas
  7 Corps of Engineers areas
State Parks and Beaches: 6
Comment: Hiking trails in Crater Lake National Park vary from easy and leisurely to strenuous and challenging. Fishing in the national park does not require a license. Cross-country skiers and snowmobilers enjoy the park in winter.
Places Rated Score: 5,765
Places Rated Rank: 10

## Dallas–Fort Worth, TX

Golf Facilities: 10 daily fee; 22 municipal
  27 eighteen-hole courses
  11 nine-hole courses
Tennis: 1 resort (12 courts)
Water Sports: Fresh water
Federal Recreation Lands:
  Lyndon B. Johnson National Grassland
  4 Corps of Engineers areas
State Parks: 1
Comment: These two major cities have a mild climate and a good supply of green parks and lakes, offering water sports and other outdoor activities pretty much year-round.
Places Rated Score: 1,562
Places Rated Rank: 75

## Denver–Rocky Mountain National Park, CO

Golf Facilities: 14 daily fee; 22 municipal
  26 eighteen-hole courses
  15 nine-hole courses
Skiing: 4 areas; total lift capacity 8,800/hr
Federal Recreation Lands:
  Arapaho National Recreation Area
  Rocky Mountain National Park
  Roosevelt National Forest
  10 Bureau of Reclamation areas
  2 Corps of Engineers areas
State Parks: 5
Comment: The Rocky Mountains bring to mind almost every possible kind of rugged outdoor activity—hiking, backpacking, mountaineering, glacier exploring, trail riding, fishing, bird-watching, and ski touring.
Places Rated Score: 4,358
Places Rated Rank: 19

## Door County, WI

Golf Facilities: 6 daily fee; 1 municipal
  5 eighteen-hole courses
  3 nine-hole courses
Water Sports: Fresh water
Federal Recreation Lands:
  1 Corps of Engineers area
State Parks: 4
Comment: Water is the major attraction of this slim peninsula extending into Lake Michigan—boating, sailing, swimming, wind surfing, and fishing are popular, as well as scuba diving among the hundreds of shipwrecks lying at the bottom of Death's Door Straits.
Places Rated Score: 730
Places Rated Rank: 99

## Eastern Shore, VA

Water Sports: Salt water
Federal Recreation Lands:
  Assateague Island National Seashore
Comment: A 70-mile-long peninsula with secluded barrier islands, the Eastern Shore is famous for its wild ponies, birds, seafood, and beaches. Water sports, observing wildlife, and lazing in the sun are the major vacation pursuits.
Places Rated Score: 300
Places Rated Rank: 107

## Finger Lakes, NY

Golf Facilities: 67 daily fee; 4 municipal
  34 eighteen-hole courses
  39 nine-hole courses
Skiing: 8 areas; total lift capacity 31,400/hr
Water Sports: Fresh water
Federal Recreation Lands:
  1 Corps of Engineers area
State Parks: 9
Comment: Cool, clear lakes formed by glaciers provide beautiful water playgrounds for New York State. Wind surfing, boating, waterskiing, and sailing are among the many sports enjoyed on these 11 long lakes.
Places Rated Score: 3,284
Places Rated Rank: 34

## Flaming Gorge, UT–WY–CO

Golf Facilities: 1 daily fee; 3 municipal
  1 eighteen-hole course
  3 nine-hole courses

Skiing: 1 area; total lift capacity not available
Water Sports: Fresh water
Federal Recreation Lands:
Ashley National Forest
Dinosaur National Monument
Flaming Gorge National Recreation Area
1 Bureau of Reclamation area
State Parks: 1
Comment: The Flaming Gorge National Recreation Area, administered by the National Forest Service, is one of the most popular leisure spots in both Wyoming and Utah. Floating and trout fishing on the Green River, as well as ice fishing in winter, are popular water sports here.
Places Rated Score: 1,650
Places Rated Rank: 73

**Glacier National Park–Flathead Lake, MT**
Golf Facilities: 5 daily fee; 2 municipal
3 eighteen-hole courses
6 nine-hole courses
Skiing: 1 area; total lift capacity 7,496/hr
Water Sports: Fresh water
Federal Recreation Lands:
Flathead National Forest
Glacier National Park
1 Bureau of Reclamation area
1 Corps of Engineers area
State Parks: 8
Comment: In Glacier National Park, visitors take launch trips, trail rides, and fishing expeditions; they also hike, camp, and bird-watch. Hiking and horseback-riding trails lead to many vistas of spectacular scenery.
Places Rated Score: 2,395
Places Rated Rank: 50

**Grand Canyon Country, AZ**
Golf Facilities: 13 daily fee; 4 municipal
10 eighteen-hole courses
9 nine-hole courses
Skiing: 2 areas; total lift capacity 4,340/hr
Federal Recreation Lands:
Apache National Forest
Coconino National Forest
Grand Canyon National Park
Kaibab National Forest
Petrified Forest National Park
Sitgreaves National Forest
Sunset Crater National Monument
Walnut Canyon National Monument
Wupatki National Monument
1 Bureau of Land Management area
State Parks: 1
Comment: Unique recreational pursuits in Grand Canyon National Park include backpack hikes and guided mule-back trips into the canyon and float trips down the river. A huge proportion of this part of Arizona is federally owned, with large backcountry areas that invite exploration.
Places Rated Score: 4,333
Places Rated Rank: 20

**Green Mountains, VT**
Golf Facilities: 15 daily fee; no municipal
6 eighteen-hole courses
9 nine-hole courses
Tennis: 8 resorts (81 courts)

Skiing: 11 areas; total lift capacity 71,200/hr
Water Sports: Fresh water
Federal Recreation Lands:
Green Mountains National Forest
2 Corps of Engineers areas
State Parks: 15
Comment: All the usual wilderness activities are readily available in this sparsely settled, heavily wooded area: water sports on Lake Champlain, hiking the Long Trail, boating on the many mountain lakes, fishing in the streams, and above all, skiing (both Alpine and cross-country), sledding, skating, and snowshoeing in winter.
Places Rated Score: 5,203
Places Rated Rank: 12

**★ Hawaii**
Golf Facilities: 37 daily fee; 7 municipal
37 eighteen-hole courses
12 nine-hole courses
Tennis: 24 resorts (187 courts)
Water Sports: Salt water, year-round
Federal Recreation Lands:
Haleakala National Park
Hawaii Volcanoes National Park
State Parks and Beaches: 25
Comment: Hawaii's year-round mild temperatures and abundance of natural resources keep visitors engaged in outdoor activities most of the time. Golf and tennis are available everywhere; water and wind sports include swimming, sailing, waterskiing, canoeing, white-water rafting, surfing, wind surfing, parasailing, hang gliding, snorkeling, and scuba diving. There is even snow skiing in winter, on the slopes of Mauna Kea.
Places Rated Score: 7,097
Places Rated Rank: 3

**Hilton Head, SC**
Golf Facilities: 10 daily fee; no municipal
11 eighteen-hole courses
1 nine-hole course
Tennis: 12 resorts (275 courts)
Water Sports: Salt water, year-round
State Parks and Beaches: 1
Comment: Golf, tennis, and sunbathing are the favorite outdoor activities in this modern, highly developed resort area.
Places Rated Score: 1,955
Places Rated Rank: 63

**Holland–Lake Michigan Shore, MI**
Golf Facilities: 50 daily fee; 3 municipal
32 eighteen-hole courses
26 nine-hole courses
Skiing: 2 areas; total lift capacity 15,000/hr
Water Sports: Fresh water
Federal Recreation Lands:
Indiana Dunes National Lakeshore
State Parks and Beaches: 6
Comment: The sandy beaches and dunes of Lake Michigan are this area's first attraction; the waters are used for swimming, sailing, motorboating, and fishing. Hang gliding off the dunes and scuba diving are also popular.
Places Rated Score: 2,050
Places Rated Rank: 60

**Houston–Galveston, TX**
Golf Facilities: 17 daily fee; 15 municipal
24 eighteen-hole courses
10 nine-hole courses
Tennis: 2 resorts (44 courts)
Water Sports: Salt water, year-round
Federal Recreation Lands:
2 Corps of Engineers areas
State Parks: 4
Comment: Galveston Island is edged by 32 miles of sandy beach, well used for water sports and sunbathing. There is a large yacht harbor. Bird-watching is excellent along the estuarine bayous of the Texas coast.
Places Rated Score: 1,574
Places Rated Rank: 74

**Jersey Shore, NJ**
Golf Facilities: 13 daily fee; 6 municipal
15 eighteen-hole courses
5 nine-hole courses
Water Sports: Salt water
Federal Recreation Lands:
Gateway National Recreation Area
State Parks and Beaches: 3
Comment: This is one of the oldest ocean-resort areas in the nation, with some 60 beach-resort towns along its 127-mile beach. All of the traditional activities are abundant—golf, tennis, swimming, sailing, fishing, and shelling—and all are available within a few miles of the largest cities in the Northeast.
Places Rated Score: 1,250
Places Rated Rank: 86

**Knoxville–Smoky Mountains, TN**
Golf Facilities: 24 daily fee; 4 municipal
18 eighteen-hole courses
11 nine-hole courses
Tennis: 1 resort (4 courts)
Skiing: 1 area; total lift capacity 6,000/hr
Water Sports: Fresh water
Federal Recreation Lands:
Cherokee National Forest
Great Smoky Mountains National Park
6 Tennessee Valley Authority areas
State Parks: 4
Comment: The mountains and lakes of eastern Tennessee, including the Great Smoky Mountains National Park, offer a wide variety of activities for outdoor enthusiasts. A few of these: white-water canoeing and rafting, diving and underwater photography in the depths of the Tennessee Valley Authority lakes, rockhounding, mountain climbing, hang gliding, houseboating, cave exploring, and snow skiing.
Places Rated Score: 2,834
Places Rated Rank: 41

**Lake of the Ozarks, MO**
Golf Facilities: 5 daily fee; no municipal
3 eighteen-hole courses
3 nine-hole courses
Tennis: 2 resorts (12 courts)
Water Sports: Fresh water
Federal Recreation Lands:
1 Corps of Engineers area
State Parks: 5
Comment: This, the largest of Missouri's lakes, is nestled in the Ozark hills, and has 1,375 miles of shoreline. Some of this shore is highly developed, with all

the amenities of fine resorts; some is still nearly wilderness. Hiking and water sports, along with golf and tennis, are the most common activities.
Places Rated Score: 1,002
Places Rated Rank: 90

## Lake Powell–Glen Canyon, AZ–UT
Golf Facilities: 1 daily fee; 2 municipal
  3 nine-hole courses
Water Sports: Fresh water
Federal Recreation Lands:
  Arches National Park
  Canyonlands National Park
  Capitol Reef National Park
  Dixie National Forest
  Glen Canyon National Recreation Area
  Hovenweep National Monument
  Manti-La Sal National Forest
  Navajo National Monument
  Rainbow Bridge National Monument
  8 Bureau of Land Management areas
State Parks: 2
Comment: Glen Canyon National Recreation Area includes Lake Powell, formed by a 710-foot-high dam built by the Bureau of Reclamation. Boating, camping, swimming, and fishing on this lake are popular activities. The several other spectacularly scenic national parks and monuments in the area are explored on foot, on horseback, by boat, and in four-wheel-drive vehicles.
Places Rated Score: 4,730
Places Rated Rank: 17

## ★ Lake Tahoe–Reno, NV–CA
Golf Facilities: 13 daily fee; 6 municipal
  11 eighteen-hole courses
  8 nine-hole courses
Tennis: 4 resorts (32 courts)
Skiing: 19 areas; total lift capacity 156,485/hr
Water Sports: Fresh water
Federal Recreation Lands:
  Eldorado National Forest
  Stanislaus National Forest
  Tahoe National Forest
  Toiyabe National Forest
  3 Bureau of Land Management areas
  5 Bureau of Reclamation areas
  1 Corps of Engineers area
State Parks: 8
Comment: America's largest concentration of ski areas surrounds beautiful Lake Tahoe. The snowpack averages 20 feet and the annual snowfall 40 feet. While the indoor activities at the casinos of Reno may be more widely known, this area also boasts fine opportunities for hiking, horseback riding, boating, sailing, and hunting.
Places Rated Score: 7,997
Places Rated Rank: 1

## Las Vegas–Lake Mead, NV–AZ
Golf Facilities: 11 daily fee; 5 municipal
  13 eighteen-hole courses
  4 nine-hole courses
Tennis: 7 resorts (41 courts)
Skiing: 1 area; total lift capacity 3,000/hr
Water Sports: Fresh water
Federal Recreation Lands:
  Lake Mead National Recreation Area
  3 Bureau of Land Management areas
  2 Bureau of Reclamation areas

State Parks: 2
Comment: Like the Lake Tahoe–Reno area, this is a glitzy city of bright lights, gambling tables, and big-name entertainment surrounded by lots of wide open spaces to appeal to water lovers and other outdoors people. Lake Mead National Recreation Area is a stretch of more than 2,000 square miles along the dammed Colorado River. What was once empty desert now offers swimming, boating, fishing, and camping in abundance.
Places Rated Score: 2,471
Places Rated Rank: 48

## Lexington–Bluegrass Country, KY
Golf Facilities: 20 daily fee; 12 municipal
  16 eighteen-hole courses
  17 nine-hole courses
Federal Recreation Lands:
  Daniel Boone National Forest
  2 Corps of Engineers areas
State Parks: 5
Comment: Kentucky has a fine system of state parks and a great many private campgrounds. Houseboating is popular, as are fishing, hiking, and biking.
Places Rated Score: 1,690
Places Rated Rank: 70

## Long Island, NY
Golf Facilities: 22 daily fee; 26 municipal
  37 eighteen-hole courses
  23 nine-hole courses
Water Sports: Salt water
Federal Recreation Lands:
  Fire Island National Seashore
State Parks: 1
Comment: Surrounded by white sandy beaches and the blue Atlantic Ocean, Long Island, though heavily populated, remains a major playland. Fishing, sailing, camping, and whale watching are a few of the outdoor activities.
Places Rated Score: 1,370
Places Rated Rank: 82

## ★ Los Angeles, CA
Golf Facilities: 60 daily fee; 56 municipal
  81 eighteen-hole courses
  49 nine-hole courses
Tennis: 3 resorts (52 courts)
Skiing: 3 areas; total lift capacity 9,100/hr
Water Sports: Salt water, year-round
Federal Recreation Lands:
  Angeles National Forest
  Los Padres National Forest
  Santa Monica Mountains National Recreation Area
  1 Bureau of Reclamation area
  7 Corps of Engineers areas
State Parks and Beaches: 15
Comment: Los Angeles and the surrounding areas have all the warm-weather activities to be expected in a locale with a mild climate. In addition, the nearby Santa Monica Mountains offer skiing and rugged backcountry sports. Beachcombing, surfing, and scuba diving are complemented by horseback riding, river running, backpacking, and rock climbing.
Places Rated Score: 6,803
Places Rated Rank: 5

## Mackinac Island–Sault Ste. Marie, MI
Golf Facilities: 7 daily fee; 4 municipal
  1 eighteen-hole course
  10 nine-hole courses
Water Sports: Fresh water
Federal Recreation Lands:
  Hiawatha National Forest
State Parks: 10
Comment: This area commands frontage on three of the Great Lakes: Michigan, Huron, and Superior. Naturally, water sports are the main outdoor activities. Bicycles are ridden not only for sport on Mackinac Island, they are the principal means of transportation.
Places Rated Score: 1,720
Places Rated Rank: 68

## Memphis, TN–AR–MS
Golf Facilities: 2 daily fee; 10 municipal
  10 eighteen-hole courses
  2 nine-hole courses
State Parks: 2
Comment: Near this large city are several wooded state parks, in both Tennessee and Arkansas, with facilities for hiking, camping, swimming, fishing, and other outdoor activities.
Places Rated Score: 420
Places Rated Rank: 105

## ★ Miami–Gold Coast–Keys, FL
Golf Facilities: 73 daily fee; 26 municipal
  94 eighteen-hole courses
  31 nine-hole courses
Tennis: 27 resorts (539 courts)
Water Sports: Salt water, year-round
Federal Recreation Lands:
  Biscayne National Park
  Everglades National Park
State Parks and Beaches: 9
Comment: The Gold Coast of Florida is a mecca for golfers, tennis players, and sun worshipers. John Pennekamp Coral Reef State Park, the first underwater park in the nation, attracts scuba divers and snorkelers. All kinds of craft ply the waters, and bird-watching here is superb.
Places Rated Score: 7,479
Places Rated Rank: 2

## Minneapolis–St. Paul, MN–WI
Golf Facilities: 66 daily fee; 31 municipal
  45 eighteen-hole courses
  65 nine-hole courses
Skiing: 6 areas; total lift capacity 44,900/hr
Water Sports: Fresh water
Federal Recreation Lands:
  Lower St. Croix National Scenic Riverway
State Parks: 6
Comment: The Lower St. Croix National Scenic Riverway, within an hour's drive of the Twin Cities, is an unspoiled recreational river—one of the few accessible to inhabitants of a major metro area. Boating, fishing, and camping are available in a setting not unlike the original midwestern prairie. To the north of these cities are countless lakes and streams beloved by canoeists and other active people.
Places Rated Score: 3,499
Places Rated Rank: 31

## Mobile Bay–Gulfport, AL–MS
Golf Facilities: 15 daily fee; 5 municipal
  15 eighteen-hole courses
  8 nine-hole courses
Tennis: 3 resorts (22 courts)
Water Sports: Salt water, year-round
Federal Recreation Lands:
  Gulf Islands National Seashore
State Parks and Beaches: 2
Comment: Thirty miles of sugary
  white-sand beach in Alabama and 26
  more on the Mississippi coast make this
  an attractive area for sun worshipers.
Places Rated Score: 1,252
Places Rated Rank: 85

## Monterey–Big Sur, CA
Golf Facilities: 31 daily fee; 13 municipal
  32 eighteen-hole courses
  17 nine-hole courses
Tennis: 3 resorts (34 courts)
Water Sports: Salt water, year-round
Federal Recreation Lands:
  Los Padres National Forest
  Pinnacles National Monument
State Parks and Beaches: 30
Comment: The mountains almost fall into
  the sea in this part of California, making
  a great variety of outdoor activities
  possible. Golfing at world-famous
  Pebble Beach and watching sea lions,
  otters, and seals play on rocks near the
  shore are favorite pursuits.
Places Rated Score: 4,994
Places Rated Rank: 15

## Myrtle Beach–Grand Strand, SC
Golf Facilities: 31 daily fee; no municipal
  32 eighteen-hole courses
  7 nine-hole courses
Tennis: 2 resorts (17 courts)
Water Sports: Salt water, year-round
State Parks and Beaches: 2
Comment: These are highly developed
  family resorts, with 55 miles of beach on
  an oceanfront where the waters are
  warmed by the Gulf Stream. More than
  a million rounds of golf are played here
  each year.
Places Rated Score: 1,277
Places Rated Rank: 84

## Mystic Seaport–Connecticut Valley, CT
Golf Facilities: 11 daily fee; 2 municipal
  9 eighteen-hole courses
  4 nine-hole courses
Water Sports: Salt water, fresh water
Federal Recreation Lands:
  1 Corps of Engineers area
State Parks and Beaches: 4
Comment: Sailing is the major recreational
  interest along the Connecticut shore.
  Young people are taught the skills of
  sailing and rowing at Mystic Seaport.
  Wooded areas farther inland offer
  fishing, hiking, and camping.
Places Rated Score: 920
Places Rated Rank: 93

## Nashville, TN
Golf Facilities: 5 daily fee; 11 municipal
  11 eighteen-hole courses
  6 nine-hole courses
Water Sports: Fresh water
Federal Recreation Lands:
  3 Corps of Engineers areas

State Parks: 3
Comment: Canoeing on the Cumberland
  River is especially popular here, as are
  swimming, boating, and fishing on
  Percy Priest Lake.
Places Rated Score: 980
Places Rated Rank: 91

## New Orleans, LA
Golf Facilities: 6 daily fee; 3 municipal
  10 eighteen-hole courses
  3 nine-hole courses
Tennis: 1 resort (11 courts)
Water Sports: Salt water, fresh water,
  year-round
State Parks and Beaches: 2
Comment: Fishing and shrimping are a
  way of life for residents of the bayou
  country of southern Louisiana.
  Vacationers enjoy fishing for fun and
  exploring these lazy streams by boat.
  Fontainebleau State Park is a huge
  (2,700-acre) recreational area on the
  north shore of Lake Ponchartrain that
  offers facilities for camping, fishing, and
  boating.
Places Rated Score: 791
Places Rated Rank: 97

## New York City, NY
Golf Facilities: 4 daily fee; 22 municipal
  26 eighteen-hole courses
  2 nine-hole courses
Skiing: 6 areas; total lift capacity 15,000/hr
Water Sports: Salt water
Federal Recreation Lands:
  Gateway National Recreation Area
Comment: Jogging, biking, and playing
  tennis are popular activities within the
  city. The Gateway National Recreation
  Area, 26,000 acres surrounding New
  York Harbor, has beaches with good
  conditions for swimming, surfing, and
  surf fishing in the Sandy Hook section
  and a marvelous wildlife refuge in the
  Jamaica Bay unit.
Places Rated Score: 1,890
Places Rated Rank: 65

## Niagara Falls–Western New York, NY
Golf Facilities: 43 daily fee; 14 municipal
  32 eighteen-hole courses
  29 nine-hole courses
Skiing: 5 areas; total lift capacity 27,800/hr
Water Sports: Fresh water
State Parks: 4
Comment: Fronting on two Great Lakes,
  Ontario and Erie, this area offers all the
  usual water sports. Allegany State Park
  has 75 miles of hiking trails, as well as
  hills, streams, and small lakes. It is
  open year-round; winter activities
  include snowmobiling, tobogganing,
  and cross-country skiing.
Places Rated Score: 2,208
Places Rated Rank: 54

## North Woods–Land O'Lakes, WI
Golf Facilities: 6 daily fee; 1 municipal
  3 eighteen-hole courses
  8 nine-hole courses
Skiing: 1 area; total lift capacity 9,400/hr
Water Sports: Fresh water
Federal Recreation Lands:
  Chequamegon National Forest

Comment: Swimming, fishing, and just
  plain loafing in summer, and
  snowmobiling in winter, are the things
  most vacationers do in northern
  Wisconsin.
Places Rated Score: 934
Places Rated Rank: 92

## Oklahoma City–Cherokee Strip, OK
Golf Facilities: 11 daily fee; 14 municipal
  18 eighteen-hole courses
  11 nine-hole courses
Water Sports: Fresh water
Federal Recreation Lands:
  Chickasaw National Recreation Area
  2 Bureau of Reclamation areas
State Parks: 4
Comment: The Chickasaw National
  Recreation Area, in the Arbuckle
  Mountains south of Oklahoma City, has
  cold mineral springs, woods, and
  waterfalls. Vacationers go swimming,
  boating, and fishing in the Arbuckle
  Reservoir.
Places Rated Score: 1,670
Places Rated Rank: 71

## Olympic Peninsula, WA
Golf Facilities: 18 daily fee; no municipal
  10 eighteen-hole courses
  4 nine-hole courses
Skiing: 1 area; total lift capacity 800/hr
Water Sports: Salt water, fresh water
Federal Recreation Lands:
  Olympic National Forest
  Olympic National Park
  1 Corps of Engineers area
State Parks and Beaches: 22
Comment: Fishing is more than a pastime
  in the Northwest—for many folks it's a
  passion. No license is required within
  Olympic National Park. The flora and
  fauna in this very lush territory make
  bird-watching and nature walks very
  special delights.
Places Rated Score: 3,848
Places Rated Rank: 26

## Orlando–Space Coast, FL
Golf Facilities: 48 daily fee; 10 municipal
  50 eighteen-hole courses
  15 nine-hole courses
Tennis: 15 resorts (156 courts)
Water Sports: Salt water, fresh water,
  year-round
State Parks and Beaches: 4
Comment: Fun in the sun: golf, tennis, and
  water sports are Florida's greatest
  attractions.
Places Rated Score: 3,456
Places Rated Rank: 32

## Outer Banks, NC
Golf Facilities: 7 daily fee; no municipal
  7 eighteen-hole courses
  1 nine-hole course
Water Sports: Salt water
Federal Recreation Lands:
  Cape Hatteras National Seashore
  Cape Lookout National Seashore
  Croatan National Forest
State Parks and Beaches: 3
Comment: They claim that the temperature
  of the waters off the Outer Banks, where
  the warm Gulf Stream collides with the
  cold Labrador Current, makes for some

of the best deep-sea and bottom fishing on the Atlantic Coast. Two national seashores protect large portions of these unique barrier islands.
Places Rated Score: 1,450
Places Rated Rank: 79

## Ozarks–Eureka Springs, AR–MO
Golf Facilities: 19 daily fee; 6 municipal
  11 eighteen-hole courses
  15 nine-hole courses
Water Sports: Fresh water
Federal Recreation Lands:
  Buffalo National River
  Mark Twain National Forest
  4 Corps of Engineers areas
State Parks: 4
Comment: There are four great streams for floating and fishing in the Ozark Mountains: Buffalo National River (the first to be named as a national river; thus protected as a free-flowing stream), Crooked Creek, White River, and North Fork. In addition, there are lakes both large and small, and horseback riding, hiking, and backpacking are available.
Places Rated Score: 1,970
Places Rated Rank: 62

## Palm Springs–Desert Playgrounds, CA
Golf Facilities: 38 daily fee; 8 municipal
  35 eighteen-hole courses
  18 nine-hole courses
Tennis: 15 resorts (205 courts)
Skiing: 7 areas; total lift capacity 70,160/hr
Federal Recreation Lands:
  Joshua Tree National Monument
  San Bernardino National Forest
  1 Bureau of Reclamation area
State Parks: 4
Comment: Without a doubt, the resort pursuits of golf and tennis reign supreme here, but there are also ski resorts in the mountains and the unique ecosystems of the deserts to be explored.
Places Rated Score: 5,187
Places Rated Rank: 13

## Panhandle, FL
Golf Facilities: 18 daily fee; 2 municipal
  15 eighteen-hole courses
  7 nine-hole courses
Tennis: 6 resorts (55 courts)
Water Sports: Salt water, year-round
Federal Recreation Lands:
  Gulf Islands National Seashore
State Parks and Beaches: 8
Comment: Superb beaches command the most attention here. More than 250 species of birds have been identified on the Gulf Islands National Seashore.
Places Rated Score: 2,175
Places Rated Rank: 56

## Pennsylvania Dutch Country, PA
Golf Facilities: 52 daily fee; 2 municipal
  45 eighteen-hole courses
  14 nine-hole courses
Tennis: 1 resort (12 courts)
Skiing: 1 area; total lift capacity 6,800/hr
State Parks: 4

Comment: Travelers to the Pennsylvania Dutch Country are most likely to spend their time either sightseeing or golfing.
Places Rated Score: 1,720
Places Rated Rank: 68

## Philadelphia, PA–DE–NJ
Golf Facilities: 61 daily fee; 17 municipal
  68 eighteen-hole courses
  20 nine-hole courses
Skiing: 4 areas; total lift capacity 14,100/hr
State Parks: 1
Comment: Several state parks within the Philadelphia metropolitan area have facilities for swimming, boating (rentals are available), hiking, biking, sledding, iceboating, ice fishing, and ice-skating.
Places Rated Score: 2,201
Places Rated Rank: 55

## Phoenix–Valley of the Sun, AZ
Golf Facilities: 44 daily fee; 10 municipal
  35 eighteen-hole courses
  25 nine-hole courses
Tennis: 19 resorts (185 courts)
Federal Recreation Lands:
  Tonto National Forest
  7 Bureau of Reclamation areas
  1 Corps of Engineers area
State Parks: 3
Comment: This valley has one of the heaviest concentrations of first-class resorts in the country; they all offer fine facilities for golf, tennis, and swimming.
Places Rated Score: 4,635
Places Rated Rank: 18

## Pocono Mountains, PA
Golf Facilities: 58 daily fee; 4 municipal
  32 eighteen-hole courses
  34 nine-hole courses
Tennis: 3 resorts (42 courts)
Skiing: 13 areas; total lift capacity 49,120/hr
Water Sports: Fresh water
Federal Recreation Lands:
  4 Corps of Engineers areas
State Parks: 6
Comment: The Poconos are not just for honeymooners; active sports-minded vacationers will find many great spots for camping, hiking, white-water rafting and canoeing, skiing, and snowmobiling.
Places Rated Score: 4,213
Places Rated Rank: 22

## Portland, ME
Golf Facilities: 30 daily fee; 4 municipal
  12 eighteen-hole courses
  23 nine-hole courses
Skiing: 1 area; total lift capacity 3,300/hr
Water Sports: Salt water, fresh water
State Parks and Beaches: 6
Comment: The major outdoor interest in the Portland area is sailing—windjamming up and down the coast. Many charter boats are available for deep-sea fishing. Nearby Sebago Lake is popular for freshwater sports in summer, and there are good winter-sports facilities in the area as well.
Places Rated Score: 1,403
Places Rated Rank: 81

## ★ Portland–Columbia River, OR
Golf Facilities: 34 daily fee; 6 municipal
  26 eighteen-hole courses
  28 nine-hole courses
Skiing: 4 areas; total lift capacity 18,190/hr
Water Sports: Salt water, fresh water
Federal Recreation Lands:
  Mount Hood National Forest
  Siuslaw National Forest
  2 Bureau of Reclamation areas
  2 Corps of Engineers areas
State Parks and Beaches: 39
Comment: The Columbia River is often used for water sports right in downtown Portland; wind surfers consider this an ideal place to pursue their hobby. Mountain climbing, salmon fishing, skiing, golfing—almost any outdoor sport, from the pleasantly invigorating to the most challenging, is available in northwestern Oregon. The lovely scenery of Mount Hood and the Columbia River Gorge beckon both visitors and residents.
Places Rated Score: 6,882
Places Rated Rank: 4

## Portsmouth–Kennebunk, NH–ME
Golf Facilities: 20 daily fee; no municipal
  6 eighteen-hole courses
  14 nine-hole courses
Skiing: 2 areas; total lift capacity 2,800/hr
Water Sports: Salt water, fresh water
State Parks and Beaches: 8
Comment: Sailing and swimming in the chilly waters of the Atlantic appeal to hardy vacationers in these popular portions of the New England coast.
Places Rated Score: 1,488
Places Rated Rank: 78

## Providence–Newport, RI
Golf Facilities: 28 daily fee; 3 municipal
  16 eighteen-hole courses
  15 nine-hole courses
Skiing: 3 areas; total lift capacity 6,600/hr
Water Sports: Salt water, fresh water
State Parks and Beaches: 13
Comment: Yachting gets the most press, but many other water sports are also enjoyed in this tiny state with the long, long coastline.
Places Rated Score: 2,336
Places Rated Rank: 52

## Put-in-Bay–Lake Erie Shore, OH
Golf Facilities: 31 daily fee; 6 municipal
  23 eighteen-hole courses
  16 nine-hole courses
Water Sports: Fresh water
State Parks: 4
Comment: As the name implies, Put-in-Bay is a haven for sailors and boaters.
Places Rated Score: 1,120
Places Rated Rank: 89

## Rangeley Lakes, ME
Golf Facilities: 17 daily fee; 1 municipal
  1 eighteen-hole course
  17 nine-hole courses
Water Sports: Fresh water
State Parks: 3
Comment: This is a getaway area for northeasterners who want to leave the

bright lights far behind. Swimming, fishing, and hiking are popular.
Places Rated Score: 590
Places Rated Rank: 102

### ★ Redwoods–Shasta–Lassen, CA
Golf Facilities: 16 daily fee; no municipal
   3 eighteen-hole courses
   14 nine-hole courses
Skiing: 1 area; total lift capacity 2,800/hr
Water Sports: Salt water, fresh water
Federal Recreation Lands:
   Klamath National Forest
   Lassen National Forest
   Lassen Volcanic National Park
   Shasta National Forest
   Six Rivers National Forest
   Trinity National Forest
   Whiskeytown-Shasta-Trinity
      National Recreation Area
   4 Bureau of Land Management areas
   5 Bureau of Reclamation areas
State Parks and Beaches: 12
Comment: Hiking, mountain climbing, skiing; exploring glaciers, dormant volcanoes, and caves; fishing and boating: these are only a few of the dozens of ways to enjoy a vacation in this area, where so much of the territory has been set aside for nature lovers.
Places Rated Score: 6,128
Places Rated Rank: 9

### Richmond–Fredericksburg, VA
Golf Facilities: 20 daily fee; 2 municipal
   18 eighteen-hole courses
   4 nine-hole courses
Tennis: 1 resort (3 courts)
State Parks and Beaches: 2
Comment: Bear Creek Lake, west of Richmond, has a swimming beach, facilities for boating and fishing, a campground, and hiking trails. Richmond lies halfway between the beach resorts of the Chesapeake Bay and the wild areas of the Blue Ridge Mountains; both are easily accessible.
Places Rated Score: 703
Places Rated Rank: 100

### Sacramento–Gold Rush Towns, CA
Golf Facilities: 29 daily fee; 5 municipal
   15 eighteen-hole courses
   15 nine-hole courses
Federal Recreation Lands:
   Eldorado National Forest
   Tahoe National Forest
   1 Bureau of Land Management area
   3 Bureau of Reclamation areas
   1 Corps of Engineers area
State Parks: 4
Comment: Several outfitters based in Sacramento conduct white-water river-running trips through the foothills of the Sierras. In this area you can hike through ghost towns dating from gold-rush days.
Places Rated Score: 2,350
Places Rated Rank: 51

### St. Augustine–Northeast Coast, FL
Golf Facilities: 26 daily fee; 5 municipal
   28 eighteen-hole courses
   7 nine-hole courses
Tennis: 8 resorts (87 courts)
Water Sports: Salt water, fresh water, year-round
State Parks and Beaches: 9

Comment: While the beaches certainly get the most attention, northern Florida also has a number of inland state parks where one can go boating, hiking, and fishing.
Places Rated Score: 2,667
Places Rated Rank: 45

### St. Louis–Mark Twain Country, MO–IL
Golf Facilities: 30 daily fee; 3 municipal
   13 eighteen-hole courses
   22 nine-hole courses
State Parks: 7
Comment: This is the confluence of two great rivers intimately connected with the history of this country. Mark Twain publicized the Mississippi to the whole world; Lewis and Clark told us about the Missouri. The rivers still offer recreational enjoyment, and the caves near Hannibal (explored by Twain's Tom Sawyer) are interesting.
Places Rated Score: 1,180
Places Rated Rank: 88

### ★ Salt Lake City, UT
Golf Facilities: 15 daily fee; 17 municipal
   14 eighteen-hole courses
   20 nine-hole courses
Skiing: 11 areas; total lift capacity 68,050/hr
Water Sports: Salt water, fresh water
Federal Recreation Lands:
   Cache National Forest
   Timpanogos Cave National Monument
   Uinta National Forest
   Wasatch National Forest
   2 Bureau of Land Management areas
   12 Bureau of Reclamation areas
State Parks: 9
Comment: A surprisingly varied list of outdoor activities makes this area attractive—from swimming (or rather floating) on the unique Great Salt Lake to skiing and mountaineering, from hiking into canyons to walking through caves.
Places Rated Score: 6,461
Places Rated Rank: 7

### San Antonio, TX
Golf Facilities: 6 daily fee; 7 municipal
   10 eighteen-hole courses
   5 nine-hole courses
State Parks: 1
Comment: San Antonio's subtropical climate makes it possible to enjoy swimming, golf, tennis, and other outdoor activities year-round. There are more than 60 parks and plazas in this beautiful city.
Places Rated Score: 350
Places Rated Rank: 106

### San Diego, CA
Golf Facilities: 38 daily fee; 5 municipal
   42 eighteen-hole courses
   12 nine-hole courses
Tennis: 6 resorts (83 courts)
Water Sports: Salt water, year-round
Federal Recreation Lands:
   Cleveland National Forest
   2 Bureau of Land Management areas
State Parks and Beaches: 12
Comment: San Diego has the well-deserved reputation of having one of

the best climates in the country. Its coastline is crowded with state beaches; rolling hills, lakes, and a large desert lie to the east.
Places Rated Score: 3,693
Places Rated Rank: 29

### San Francisco, CA
Golf Facilities: 28 daily fee; 19 municipal
   31 eighteen-hole courses
   21 nine-hole courses
Tennis: 2 resorts (16 courts)
Water Sports: Salt water, year-round
Federal Recreation Lands:
   Golden Gate National Recreation Area
   Point Reyes National Seashore
   1 Bureau of Reclamation area
State Parks and Beaches: 8
Comment: San Francisco's enviable location on the bay, near the sea, makes water sports more accessible than they are in many cities of comparable size.
Places Rated Score: 2,796
Places Rated Rank: 42

### Santa Barbara–San Simeon, CA
Golf Facilities: 10 daily fee; 3 municipal
   8 eighteen-hole courses
   5 nine-hole courses
Water Sports: Salt water, year-round
Federal Recreation Lands:
   Los Padres National Forest
   1 Bureau of Reclamation area
State Parks and Beaches: 12
Comment: With plenty of ocean beaches, and nearby mountains and forests, Santa Barbara's coast shares the natural bounty that blesses the entire length of California.
Places Rated Score: 2,160
Places Rated Rank: 58

### Savannah–Golden Isles, GA
Golf Facilities: 6 daily fee; 2 municipal
   9 eighteen-hole courses
   4 nine-hole courses
Tennis: 3 resorts (35 courts)
Water Sports: Salt water, year-round
Federal Recreation Lands:
   Cumberland Island National Seashore
State Parks and Beaches: 3
Comment: Golfing, swimming, boating, sailing, beachcombing, bird-watching along the marshes, and exploring almost entirely uninhabited offshore islands are a few of the activities available along the coast of Georgia.
Places Rated Score: 1,205
Places Rated Rank: 87

### ★ Seattle–Mount Rainier–North Cascades, WA
Golf Facilities: 44 daily fee; 20 municipal
   40 eighteen-hole courses
   27 nine-hole courses
Skiing: 4 areas; total lift capacity 38,344/hr
Water Sports: Salt water, fresh water
Federal Recreation Lands:
   *Lake Chelan National Recreation Area*
   Mount Baker National Forest
   Mount Rainier National Park
   North Cascades National Park
   Ross Lake National Recreational Area
   Snoqualmie National Forest
   3 Bureau of Reclamation areas
   2 Corps of Engineers areas

State Parks and Beaches: 13
Comment: People who live here spend most of their leisure time outdoors; visitors find an almost unequaled wealth of national parks, forests, and recreation areas in which to pursue their favorite recreational pastimes. Name your sport; you're almost certain to find a chance to practice it here.
Places Rated Score: 6,603
Places Rated Rank: 6

## Spokane–Coeur d'Alene, WA–ID
Golf Facilities: 18 daily fee; 6 municipal
  10 eighteen-hole courses
  14 nine-hole courses
Skiing: 5 areas; total lift capacity 19,125/hr
Water Sports: Fresh water
Federal Recreation Lands:
  Coeur d'Alene National Forest
  Colville National Forest
  Kaniksu National Forest
  4 Bureau of Land Management areas
  1 Bureau of Reclamation area
State Parks: 6
Comment: Several large lakes and reservoirs are used for sailing, waterskiing, swimming, and fishing. Hiking, mountain climbing, and skiing add to the area's charms.
Places Rated Score: 3,731
Places Rated Rank: 28

## Tampa Bay–Southwest Coast, FL
Golf Facilities: 78 daily fee; 10 municipal
  85 eighteen-hole courses
  14 nine-hole courses
Tennis: 21 resorts (267 courts)
Water Sports: Salt water, year-round
Federal Recreation Lands:
  Big Cypress National Preserve
  Everglades National Park
State Parks and Beaches: 7
Comment: In addition to southwestern Florida's great wealth of seashore activities and resort facilities, Big Cypress National Preserve and Everglades National Park offer unequaled opportunities for observing, on foot or by boat, an unusual type of natural terrain and the wildlife that inhabits it.
Places Rated Score: 5,757
Places Rated Rank: 11

## Traverse City–Petoskey, MI
Golf Facilities: 28 daily fee; 1 municipal
  15 eighteen-hole courses
  18 nine-hole courses
Tennis: 2 resorts (21 courts)
Skiing: 9 areas; total lift capacity 71,900/hr
Water Sports: Fresh water
Federal Recreation Lands:
  Sleeping Bear Dunes National Lakeshore
State Parks and Beaches: 6
Comment: The mountains aren't high, but Alpine skiing is popular nonetheless in this part of the Midwest. In summer people sail, swim, and explore the dunes along the shore of Lake Michigan.
Places Rated Score: 3,220
Places Rated Rank: 36

## Tucson, AZ
Golf Facilities: 16 daily fee; 5 municipal
  18 eighteen-hole courses
  5 nine-hole courses
Tennis: 6 resorts (58 courts)
Federal Recreation Lands:
  Coronado National Forest
  Organ Pipe Cactus National Monument
  Saguaro National Monument
State Parks: 2
Comment: Nature watching in the desert is an experience quite unlike other types of backcountry exploration. Tucson is a popular winter resort for sun lovers; there are plenty of golf courses and tennis courts, as well as more rugged territory.
Places Rated Score: 2,168
Places Rated Rank: 57

## Tulsa–Lake O' The Cherokees, OK
Golf Facilities: 7 daily fee; 9 municipal
  12 eighteen-hole courses
  6 nine-hole courses
Water Sports: Fresh water
Federal Recreation Lands:
  14 Corps of Engineers areas
State Parks: 20
Comment: This area is well known for its concentration of man-made lakes, which are well used for recreation—boating, fishing, swimming, and camping.
Places Rated Score: 3,800
Places Rated Rank: 27

## Vicksburg–Natchez–Baton Rouge, MS–LA
Golf Facilities: 1 daily fee; 6 municipal
  3 eighteen-hole courses
  4 nine-hole courses
Federal Recreation Lands:
  Homochitto National Forest
State Parks: 2
Comment: Fishing, boating, and canoeing are popular activities here. Several streams and rivers flowing into the Mississippi are navigable for long distances, among them are Bayou Pierre, Big Black, and Buffalo. This is also an excellent area for bike touring—routes range from scenic and easy to difficult and challenging.
Places Rated Score: 800
Places Rated Rank: 96

## Washington, DC–MD–VA
Golf Facilities: 12 daily fee; 25 municipal
  31 eighteen-hole courses
  12 nine-hole courses
Water Sports: Salt water
Federal Recreation Lands:
  Kenilworth Aquatic Gardens
  Rock Creek Park
  Theodore Roosevelt Island
State Parks: 3
Comment: Washington's Rock Creek Park is a popular recreational area. Its more than 1,700 acres include a golf course, tennis courts, playfields, stables, bridle paths and biking trails, an exercise course, and self-guided nature trails. The beaches of the Chesapeake Bay and the mountains of northern Virginia are only a short drive from the city.
Places Rated Score: 1,740
Places Rated Rank: 67

## White Mountains, NH
Golf Facilities: 27 daily fee; 1 municipal
  10 eighteen-hole courses
  18 nine-hole courses
Tennis: 3 resorts (36 courts)
Skiing: 16 areas; total lift capacity 65,324/hr
Water Sports: Fresh water
Federal Recreation Lands:
  White Mountain National Forest
State Parks and Beaches: 7
Comment: Serious hikers and backpackers discovered the White Mountains at least as long ago as 1876, when the Appalachian Mountain Club was organized. A series of huts and lean-tos have been built along the Appalachian Trail for overnight shelter. More recently, skiers have been coming in droves each winter, as soon as the first snow cover is ready.
Places Rated Score: 4,269
Places Rated Rank: 21

## Williamsburg–Colonial Triangle, VA
Golf Facilities: 11 daily fee; 8 municipal
  17 eighteen-hole courses
  5 nine-hole courses
Tennis: 2 resorts (10 courts)
Water Sports: Salt water
Federal Recreation Lands:
  1 Corps of Engineers area
State Parks: 1
Comment: Golden sand covers 28 miles of ocean beach in this part of Virginia. All the ocean sports are popular, including simply sunbathing.
Places Rated Score: 900
Places Rated Rank: 94

## Wilmington–Cape Fear, NC
Golf Facilities: 8 daily fee; 1 municipal
  9 eighteen-hole courses
Water Sports: Salt water, year-round
Federal Recreation Lands:
  1 Corps of Engineers area
State Parks: 1
Comment: Both deep-sea and bottom ocean fishing are superior in the waters off North Carolina. The warm, northbound Gulf Stream mixes here with the cold, southbound Labrador Current to create an environment particularly suited to producing a great variety and quantity of fish. The season for enjoying the beaches is quite long.
Places Rated Score: 530
Places Rated Rank: 103

## Wine Country, CA
Golf Facilities: 20 daily fee; 6 municipal
  10 eighteen-hole courses
  18 nine-hole courses
Tennis: 1 resort (20 courts)
Water Sports: Salt water, fresh water, year-round
Federal Recreation Lands:
  Mendocino National Forest
  5 Bureau of Land Management areas
  2 Bureau of Reclamation areas
  1 Corps of Engineers area
State Parks and Beaches: 18
Comment: Eighteen state parks, most of them close to the coast, offer facilities

for camping, riding, hiking, swimming, rockhounding, and many other pursuits.
Places Rated Score: 3,850
Places Rated Rank: 25

### Wisconsin Dells, WI
Golf Facilities: 26 daily fee; 7 municipal
14 eighteen-hole courses
23 nine-hole courses
Skiing: 2 areas; total lift capacity 14,700/hr
Water Sports: Fresh water
State Parks: 9
Comment: Boating along the river, between the huge rock formations known as the Dells, and hot-air ballooning are two of the favorite activities here.
Places Rated Score: 1,857
Places Rated Rank: 66

### ★ Yellowstone–Jackson–Tetons, WY–ID–MT
Golf Facilities: 6 daily fee; 3 municipal
4 eighteen-hole courses
5 nine-hole courses
Skiing: 10 areas; total lift capacity 30,000/hr
Water Sports: Fresh water
Federal Recreation Lands:
Bridger National Forest
Gallatin National Forest
Grand Teton National Park
National Elk Refuge
Shoshone National Forest
Targhee National Forest
Teton National Forest
Yellowstone National Park
9 Bureau of Reclamation areas
State Parks: 1
Comment: Whether one vacations at one of Wyoming's many dude ranches or in Yellowstone National Park, the wide open spaces are the primary appeal. Trail riding, backpacking, floating, canoeing, mountain climbing, skiing, and big-game watching—all the more challenging sports of the backcountry are here.
Places Rated Score: 6,230
Places Rated Rank: 8

### Yosemite–Sequoia–Death Valley, CA
Golf Facilities: 25 daily fee; 5 municipal
16 eighteen-hole courses
15 nine-hole courses
Skiing: 4 areas; total lift capacity 46,100/hr
Water Sports: Fresh water
Federal Recreation Lands:
Death Valley National Monument
Devils Postpile National Monument
Inyo National Forest
Kings Canyon National Park
Sequoia National Park
Sierra National Forest
Yosemite National Park
5 Bureau of Land Management areas
1 Corps of Engineers area

Comment: Lazy walks through woods and high prairies or vigorous hikes and mountain climbing; mule-back riding on six-day guided trips through the high country; boating and fishing; or just watching the natural scene—a Yosemite vacation can be as relaxed or active as you choose. Sequoia and Death Valley lend additional variety.
Places Rated Score: 4,931
Places Rated Rank: 16

### Zion–Bryce Canyon, UT
Golf Facilities: 3 daily fee; 6 municipal
2 eighteen-hole courses
7 nine-hole courses
Skiing: 2 areas; total lift capacity 6,800/hr
Federal Recreation Lands:
Bryce Canyon National Park
Cedar Breaks National Monument
Dixie National Forest
Fishlake National Forest
Zion National Park
4 Bureau of Land Management areas
State Parks: 3
Comment: This is rough country; the timid can look at it from the windows of a bus or walk one of the easy self-guided nature trails. For the experienced outdoors person, there are backcountry trails and guided horseback trips.
Places Rated Score: 3,278
Places Rated Rank: 35

**RANKINGS:** Fun in the Great Outdoors

Six criteria were used to determine the scores in this chapter: (1) golf—the number of public (municipal and daily-fee) golf courses; (2) tennis—the number of resorts catering specifically (though not exclusively) to tennis buffs and the total number of courts available at those resorts; (3) skiing—the number of ski areas and their total lift capacity; (4) fresh or salt water and whether or not the weather permits its enjoyment year-round; (5) numbers and kinds of federal lands set aside for public use; (6) numbers of state parks and beaches. Places that receive tie scores are given the same rank and are listed in alphabetic order.

## Vacation Places from First to Last

| Places Rated Rank | Places Rated Score |
|---|---|
| 1. Lake Tahoe–Reno, NV–CA | 7,997 |
| 2. Miami–Gold Coast–Keys, FL | 7,479 |
| 3. Hawaii | 7,097 |
| 4. Portland–Columbia River, OR | 6,882 |
| 5. Los Angeles, CA | 6,803 |
| 6. Seattle–Mount Rainier–North Cascades, WA | 6,603 |
| 7. Salt Lake City, UT | 6,461 |
| 8. Yellowstone–Jackson–Tetons, WY–ID–MT | 6,230 |
| 9. Redwoods–Shasta–Lassen, CA | 6,128 |
| 10. Crater Lake–Klamath Falls, OR | 5,765 |
| 11. Tampa Bay–Southwest Coast, FL | 5,757 |
| 12. Green Mountains, VT | 5,203 |
| 13. Palm Springs–Desert Playgrounds, CA | 5,187 |
| 14. Albuquerque–Santa Fe–Taos, NM | 5,173 |
| 15. Monterey–Big Sur, CA | 4,994 |
| 16. Yosemite–Sequoia–Death Valley, CA | 4,931 |
| 17. Lake Powell–Glen Canyon, AZ–UT | 4,730 |
| 18. Phoenix–Valley of the Sun, AZ | 4,635 |
| 19. Denver–Rocky Mountain National Park, CO | 4,358 |
| 20. Grand Canyon Country, AZ | 4,333 |
| 21. White Mountains, NH | 4,269 |
| 22. Pocono Mountains, PA | 4,213 |
| 23. Catskill Mountains, NY | 3,978 |
| 24. Aspen–Vail, CO | 3,977 |
| 25. Wine Country, CA | 3,850 |
| 26. Olympic Peninsula, WA | 3,848 |
| 27. Tulsa–Lake O' The Cherokees, OK | 3,800 |
| 28. Spokane–Coeur d'Alene, WA–ID | 3,731 |
| 29. San Diego, CA | 3,693 |
| 30. Atlanta, GA | 3,547 |
| 31. Minneapolis–St. Paul, MN–WI | 3,499 |
| 32. Orlando–Space Coast, FL | 3,456 |

| Places Rated Rank | Places Rated Score |
|---|---|
| 33. Boise–Sun Valley, ID | 3,370 |
| 34. Finger Lakes, NY | 3,284 |
| 35. Zion–Bryce Canyon, UT | 3,278 |
| 36. Traverse City–Petoskey, MI | 3,220 |
| 37. Black Hills, SD | 3,078 |
| 38. Bend–Cascade Mountains, OR | 3,057 |
| 39. Chicago, IL | 3,020 |
| 40. Adirondack Mountains, NY | 2,955 |
| 41. Knoxville–Smoky Mountains, TN | 2,834 |
| 42. San Francisco, CA | 2,796 |
| 43. Coos Bay–South Coast, OR | 2,790 |
| 44. Berkshire Hills–Pioneer Valley, MA | 2,768 |
| 45. St. Augustine–Northeast Coast, FL | 2,667 |
| 46. Asheville–Smoky Mountains, NC | 2,640 |
| 47. Boston, MA | 2,606 |
| 48. Las Vegas–Lake Mead, NV–AZ | 2,471 |
| 49. Chattanooga–Huntsville, TN–AL–GA | 2,425 |
| 50. Glacier National Park–Flathead Lake, MT | 2,395 |
| 51. Sacramento–Gold Rush Towns, CA | 2,350 |
| 52. Providence–Newport, RI | 2,336 |
| 53. Anchorage–Kenai Peninsula, AK | 2,322 |
| 54. Niagara Falls–Western New York, NY | 2,208 |
| 55. Philadelphia, PA–DE–NJ | 2,201 |
| 56. Panhandle, FL | 2,175 |
| 57. Tucson, AZ | 2,168 |
| 58. Santa Barbara–San Simeon, CA | 2,160 |
| 59. Blue Ridge Mountains, VA | 2,085 |
| 60. Holland–Lake Michigan Shore, MI | 2,050 |
| 61. Colorado Springs, CO | 1,992 |
| 62. Ozarks–Eureka Springs, AR–MO | 1,970 |
| 63. Hilton Head, SC | 1,955 |
| 64. Boone–High Country, NC | 1,901 |

| Places Rated Rank | Places Rated Score |
|---|---|
| 65. New York City, NY | 1,890 |
| 66. Wisconsin Dells, WI | 1,857 |
| 67. Washington, DC–MD–VA | 1,740 |
| 68. Mackinac Island–Sault Ste. Marie, MI | 1,720 |
| 68. Pennsylvania Dutch Country, PA | 1,720 |
| 70. Lexington–Bluegrass Country, KY | 1,690 |
| 71. Oklahoma City–Cherokee Strip, OK | 1,670 |
| 72. Austin–Hill Country, TX | 1,658 |
| 73. Flaming Gorge, UT–WY–CO | 1,650 |
| 74. Houston–Galveston, TX | 1,574 |
| 75. Dallas–Fort Worth, TX | 1,562 |
| 76. Charleston, SC | 1,559 |
| 77. Cincinnati, OH–KY | 1,524 |
| 78. Portsmouth–Kennebunk, NH–ME | 1,488 |
| 79. Outer Banks, NC | 1,450 |
| 80. Cape Cod–The Islands, MA | 1,435 |
| 81. Portland, ME | 1,403 |
| 82. Long Island, NY | 1,370 |
| 83. Bar Harbor–Acadia, ME | 1,330 |
| 84. Myrtle Beach–Grand Strand, SC | 1,277 |
| 85. Mobile Bay–Gulfport, AL–MS | 1,252 |
| 86. Jersey Shore, NJ | 1,250 |
| 87. Savannah–Golden Isles, GA | 1,205 |
| 88. St. Louis–Mark Twain Country, MO–IL | 1,180 |
| 89. Put-in-Bay–Lake Erie Shore, OH | 1,120 |
| 90. Lake of the Ozarks, MO | 1,002 |
| 91. Nashville, TN | 980 |
| 92. North Woods–Land O'Lakes, WI | 934 |
| 93. Mystic Seaport–Connecticut Valley, CT | 920 |
| 94. Williamsburg–Colonial Triangle, VA | 900 |
| 95. Baltimore–Chesapeake Bay, MD | 845 |

| Places Rated Rank | Places Rated Score | Places Rated Rank | Places Rated Score | Places Rated Rank | Places Rated Score |
|---|---|---|---|---|---|
| 96. Vicksburg–Natchez–Baton Rouge, MS–LA | 800 | 100. Richmond–Fredericksburg, VA | 703 | 104. Atlantic City, NJ | 500 |
| 97. New Orleans, LA | 791 | 101. Brownsville–Rio Grande Valley, TX | 660 | 105. Memphis, TN–AR–MS | 420 |
| 98. Corpus Christi–Padre Island, TX | 760 | 102. Rangeley Lakes, ME | 590 | 106. San Antonio, TX | 350 |
| 99. Door County, WI | 730 | 103. Wilmington–Cape Fear, NC | 530 | 107. Eastern Shore, VA | 300 |

## Vacation Places Listed Alphabetically

| Vacation Place | Places Rated Rank | Vacation Place | Places Rated Rank | Vacation Place | Places Rated Rank |
|---|---|---|---|---|---|
| Adirondack Mountains, NY | 40 | Hawaii | 3 | Phoenix–Valley of the Sun, AZ | 18 |
| Albuquerque–Santa Fe–Taos, NM | 14 | Hilton Head, SC | 63 | Pocono Mountains, PA | 22 |
| Anchorage–Kenai Peninsula, AK | 53 | Holland–Lake Michigan Shore, MI | 60 | Portland, ME | 81 |
| Asheville–Smoky Mountains, NC | 46 | | | | |
| Aspen–Vail, CO | 24 | Houston–Galveston, TX | 74 | Portland–Columbia River, OR | 4 |
| | | Jersey Shore, NJ | 86 | Portsmouth–Kennebunk, NH–ME | 78 |
| Atlanta, GA | 30 | Knoxville–Smoky Mountains, TN | 41 | Providence–Newport, RI | 52 |
| Atlantic City, NJ | 104 | Lake of the Ozarks, MO | 90 | Put-in-Bay–Lake Erie Shore, OH | 89 |
| Austin–Hill Country, TX | 72 | Lake Powell–Glen Canyon, AZ–UT | 17 | Rangeley Lakes, ME | 102 |
| Baltimore–Chesapeake Bay, MD | 95 | | | | |
| Bar Harbor–Acadia, ME | 83 | Lake Tahoe–Reno, NV–CA | 1 | Redwoods–Shasta–Lassen, CA | 9 |
| | | Las Vegas–Lake Mead, NV–AZ | 48 | Richmond–Fredericksburg, VA | 100 |
| Bend–Cascade Mountains, OR | 38 | Lexington–Bluegrass Country, KY | 70 | Sacramento–Gold Rush Towns, CA | 51 |
| Berkshire Hills–Pioneer Valley, MA | 44 | Long Island, NY | 82 | St. Augustine–Northeast Coast, FL | 45 |
| Black Hills, SD | 37 | Los Angeles, CA | 5 | St. Louis–Mark Twain Country, MO–IL | 88 |
| Blue Ridge Mountains, Va | 59 | | | | |
| Boise–Sun Valley, ID | 33 | Mackinac Island–Sault Ste. Marie, MI | 68 | Salt Lake City, UT | 7 |
| Boone–High Country, NC | 64 | Memphis, TN–AR–MS | 105 | San Antonio, TX | 106 |
| Boston, MA | 47 | Miami–Gold Coast–Keys, FL | 2 | San Diego, CA | 29 |
| Brownsville–Rio Grande Valley, TX | 101 | Minneapolis–St. Paul, MN–WI | 31 | San Francisco, CA | 42 |
| Cape Cod–The Islands, MA | 80 | Mobile Bay–Gulfport, AL–MS | 85 | Santa Barbara–San Simeon, CA | 58 |
| Catskill Mountains, NY | 23 | | | | |
| | | Monterey–Big Sur, CA | 15 | Savannah–Golden Isles, GA | 87 |
| Charleston, SC | 76 | Myrtle Beach–Grand Strand, SC | 84 | Seattle–Mount Rainier–North Cascades, WA | 6 |
| Chattanooga–Huntsville, TN–AL–GA | 49 | Mystic Seaport–Connecticut Valley, CT | 93 | Spokane–Coeur d'Alene, WA–ID | 28 |
| Chicago, IL | 39 | Nashville, TN | 91 | Tampa Bay–Southwest Coast, FL | 11 |
| Cincinnati, OH–KY | 77 | New Orleans, LA | 97 | Traverse City–Petoskey, MI | 36 |
| Colorado Springs, CO | 61 | | | | |
| | | New York City, NY | 65 | Tucson, AZ | 57 |
| Coos Bay–South Coast, OR | 43 | Niagara Falls–Western New York, NY | 54 | Tulsa–Lake O' The Cherokees, OK | 27 |
| Corpus Christi–Padre Island, TX | 98 | North Woods–Land O'Lakes, WI | 92 | Vicksburg–Natchez–Baton Rouge, MS–LA | 96 |
| Crater Lake–Klamath Falls, OR | 10 | Oklahoma City–Cherokee Strip, OK | 71 | Washington, DC–MD–VA | 67 |
| Dallas–Fort Worth, TX | 75 | Olympic Peninsula, WA | 26 | White Mountains, NH | 21 |
| Denver–Rocky Mountain National Park, CO | 19 | | | | |
| | | Orlando–Space Coast, FL | 32 | Williamsburg–Colonial Triangle, VA | 94 |
| Door County, WI | 99 | Outer Banks, NC | 79 | Wilmington–Cape Fear, NC | 103 |
| Eastern Shore, VA | 107 | Ozarks–Eureka Springs, AR–MO | 62 | Wine Country, CA | 25 |
| Finger Lakes, NY | 34 | Palm Springs–Desert Playgrounds, CA | 13 | Wisconsin Dells, WI | 66 |
| Flaming Gorge, UT–WY–CO | 73 | Panhandle, FL | 56 | Yellowstone–Jackson–Tetons, WY–ID–MT | 8 |
| Glacier National Park–Flathead Lake, MT | 50 | | | | |
| | | Pennsylvania Dutch Country, PA | 68 | Yosemite–Sequoia–Death Valley, CA | 16 |
| Grand Canyon Country, AZ | 20 | Philadelphia, PA–DE–NJ | 55 | Zion–Bryce Canyon, UT | 35 |
| Green Mountains, VT | 12 | | | | |

# TOP TEN: Fun in the Great Outdoors

Western states dominate the first ten Vacation Places ranked for Fun in the Great Outdoors. Only numbers two and three—Miami–Gold Coast–Keys, Florida, and Hawaii—are not in the West. The presence of vast tracts of publicly owned land in the West has attracted lovers of the outdoors and provided limitless recreational resources for them.

| | Places Rated Score |
|---|---|
| 1. Lake Tahoe–Reno, NV–CA | 7,997 |
| 2. Miami–Gold Coast–Keys, FL | 7,479 |
| 3. Hawaii | 7,097 |
| 4. Portland–Columbia River, OR | 6,882 |
| 5. Los Angeles, CA | 6,803 |
| 6. Seattle–Mount Rainier–North Cascades, WA | 6,603 |
| 7. Salt Lake City, UT | 6,461 |
| 8. Yellowstone–Jackson–Tetons, WY–ID–MT | 6,230 |
| 9. Redwoods–Shasta–Lassen, CA | 6,128 |
| 10. Crater Lake–Klamath Falls, OR | 5,765 |

## 1. Lake Tahoe–Reno, NV–CA

A premiere skiing region, boasting 19 ski areas within the ring of mountain peaks that surround beautiful Lake Tahoe, this Vacation Place is also a year-round playground. Four of the busiest ski resorts in the country are here, according to various studies conducted by the University of Colorado. These are Alpine Meadows, Heavenly Valley, Northstar-at-Tahoe, and Squaw Valley USA.

Emerald Bay State Park, in California, is one of several California and Nevada parks along the border that offer a variety of activities. There are nature walks and boat trips in summer, and there is guided cross-country skiing in winter. Hundreds of water-skiers cut frothy strips of white across the delft blue of Lake Tahoe on sunny summer days.

In Washoe Lake State Park, about 20 miles south of Reno, visitors enjoy horseback riding in the dunes and fishing and sailboating on the lake.

With four national forests, nine other federal recreation areas, and eight state parks, the possibilities for outdoor activities here are nearly unlimited.

## 2. Miami–Gold Coast–Keys, FL

Perhaps Florida's Gold Coast conjures up images of huge hotels, brightly lit nightclubs, and crowded beaches. These are still there, but they are only small parts of the whole. First among the Vacation Places in tennis resorts, second in number of public golf courses available, and with balmy weather year-round, two national parks, and nine state parks and beaches—southeastern Florida has enormous resources for outdoor enjoyment.

Water sports are the most popular activities in the Keys: swimming and scuba diving, sailing, motorboating, and fishing. The Everglades are unmatched for bird-watching, alligator watching, and other nature study.

Several state parks have marine facilities for boat campers. Rental boats and bikes, and deep-sea fishing charter boats, are widely available.

## 3. Hawaii

America's tropical islands rank second among Vacation Places in availability of tennis resorts, third in the number of state parks and beaches. Nature lovers are entranced by the numbers and varieties of plants and birds found here. Year-round warm weather (except on mountaintops) is a definite asset.

Sun, surf, and sand are the major attractions, with virtually every sort of water sport available. Some mainlanders love to get an introduction to body-surfing, board surfing, and wind surfing. Sailing around the islands, in catamarans, trimarans, ketches, yachts, sloops, or other craft, is a special treat. Narrated sightseeing cruises often provide stopovers for swimming, diving, fishing, or whale watching.

Tent camping is permitted in numerous state recreation areas. Reservations are required; camping permits, for a maximum of five nights, are available free from the Hawaii Department of Land and Natural Resources. Applications must be received at least seven days prior to the date of use.

Hawaii also has a good supply of rain forests to explore, mountains to climb, and volcanoes to study.

## 4. Portland–Columbia River, OR

Gigantic Mount Hood, snowcapped all year, watches over the Portland area and advertises to all onlookers that this is an area for winter sports, mountain climbing, and wilderness exploration.

It's also an area for all kinds of water sports, whose enthusiasts have a choice of lakes, the ocean, or the magnificent Columbia River. Along the Pacific Coast there are many freshwater lakes found only a few steps away from the salt water. Lovely sand dunes separate the two. Hang gliders soar from the tops of the dunes to the beaches below. Dune buggies and other off-road vehicles are permitted in certain posted areas. Hikers enjoy tramping through dense coastal rain forests near Cape Lookout.

There are 39 state parks and beaches in this Vacation Place, more than any other of the 107.

## Author's Favorites

**Beaches for Shelling**
Sanibel Island, FL

**Beaches for Sunbathing and Swimming**
Marco Island, FL

**Golf Resorts**
Hound Ears, Blowing Rock, NC

**National Forests**
Carson, NM

**National Parks**
Yosemite, CA

**Rivers for Rafting**
Colorado River, AZ

**Ski Areas**
Stowe, VT

**Wildlife-Watching Areas**
Everglades National Park, FL
Kachemak Bay, AK
Sea Lion Caves, Florence, OR

## 5. Los Angeles, CA

The Los Angeles area ranks third among the 107 Vacation Places in number of public golf courses, eighth in number of state parks and beaches.

A teeming, sprawling metropolitan area, Los Angeles has appealed to many people who have moved there at least partially because of the proximity of the ocean and the mountains. One can swim in the surf and lie on the hot sand in the morning—and go skiing in the afternoon.

Southern Californians have the reputation of being sun worshipers who spend most of their time out-of-doors. This is probably an exaggeration, but the eternal sunshine, beautiful surf, and a relaxed life-style is a powerful attraction for vacationers.

## 6. Seattle–Mount Rainier–North Cascades, WA

Cooler than Hawaii, Miami, and Los Angeles, wetter than many other Vacation Places, Seattle's climate is regarded as perfect by most of its residents. Actually, despite its frequent rains, the chances of a dry day are above 80 percent from May through September.

The Seattle Vacation Place ranks tenth for golf, tenth for number of state parks, and seventh for federal recreation areas.

Hiking and fishing, along with other water sports, are the principal outdoor activities.

Mount Rainier National Park has more than 300 miles of hiking trails across mountaintops, past lakes, and beside rivers. All waters in the park, except where otherwise posted, are open for fishing without a license.

Horse trails lead through all units of North Cascades National Park. Boaters and canoeists are enthusiastic about Ross Lake, a large body of water ringed with steep canyonlike walls, in Ross Lake National Recreation Area.

## 7. Salt Lake City, UT

This part of northern Utah ranks sixth among Vacation Places for skiing, eighth for federal recreation areas.

Bear Lake, on the Idaho border, is popular for boating, waterskiing, swimming, sailing, and skin diving, plus fishing in summer and ice fishing in winter. Deer Creek Lake, southwest of Heber City, is a favorite among wind surfers.

Hikers can descend into canyons and climb high peaks in Wasatch National Forest. Wasatch Mountain State Park offers cross-country skiing and snowmobiling, with complete rental service for both activities available on-site.

## 8. Yellowstone–Jackson–Tetons, WY–ID–MT

This Vacation Place ranks second in federal recreation areas. Yellowstone and Grand Teton national parks lead the list; there are also five national forests, the National Elk Refuge, and nine Bureau of Reclamation areas.

Long visited by millions of vacationers during summer months, Yellowstone National Park has more recently gained recognition as an excellent place for winter activities. Many roads in the park are closed in winter, but the northeast entrance, near Mammoth Hot Springs, is open all year.

Park rangers lead hikes in some of the geyser areas as well as cross-country ski and snowshoe trips on unplowed roads and trails. Private snowmobiles are permitted on pathways only.

The magnificent scenery of Grand Teton National Park is a special treat for hikers in summer and skiers in winter.

## 9. Redwoods–Shasta–Lassen, CA

Since this Vacation Place ranked first in the Blessings of Nature chapter, it is not surprising to find it among the top ten in Fun in the Great Outdoors. It is third in the score for federal recreation lands, with five national forests, a national park, a national recreation area, four Bureau of Land Management areas, and five under the jurisdiction of the Bureau of Reclamation.

This is a huge area, with a long coastline on the Pacific for the enjoyment of water sports as well as large stretches of mountainous backcountry.

Whiskeytown Lake has five miles of open water, good for swimming, boating, waterskiing, scuba diving, and fishing.

## 10. Crater Lake–Klamath Falls, OR

This Vacation Place ranks first among the 107 in the availability of federal recreation lands; it has a national park, a national monument, 3 national forests, 12 Bureau of Land Management areas, 7 Bureau of Reclamation areas, and 7 Corps of Engineers areas.

Backpacking, camping, fishing, swimming, river running, and mountain climbing are available around every beautiful bend in the road.

# Basic Necessities

## Lodging, Food, and Transportation

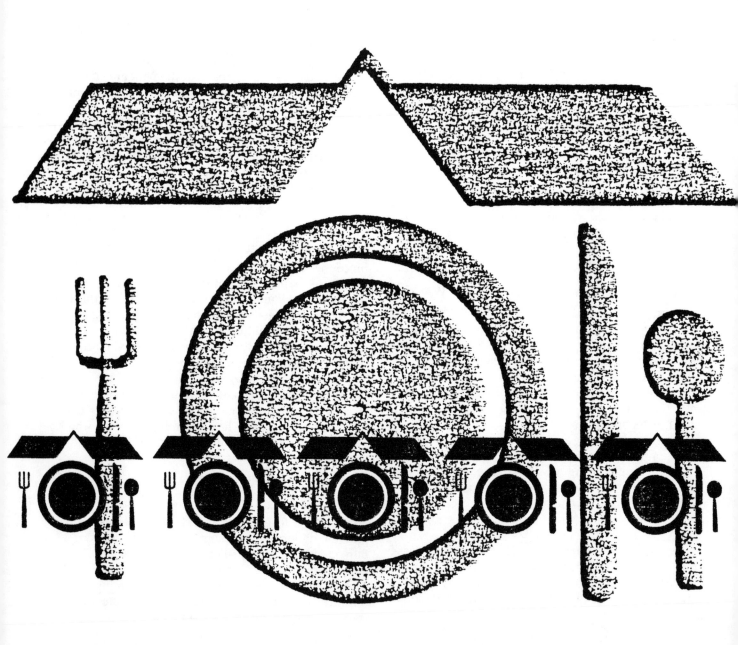

**INTRODUCTION:** Basic Necessities

"Give me the luxuries of life, and I will willingly do without the necessities," the noted architect Frank Lloyd Wright is said to have quipped.

Many vacationers are looking for both—necessities *and* luxuries. And what one person thinks of as a luxury is often considered absolutely necessary by someone else.

This chapter examines three things that are essential to a vacation no matter what sort of activities are planned: places to sleep, places to eat, and means of getting to a chosen destination.

## WHERE TO STAY

"There is nothing which has yet been contrived by man, by which so much happiness is produced as by a good tavern or inn," observed Samuel Johnson. The enormous number of hotels, motels, inns, restaurants, and all other establishments for the care and feeding of people away from home is proof that millions of people are willing to pay for a slice of that happiness.

From an apartment or a suite at today's newest and fanciest full-service resorts to the lightweight tent a hiker carries in a backpack, variations of overnight facilities for vacationers are without limit. There are hotels, motels, inns, and guest houses, or bed-and-breakfast stopovers. In addition, there are lodges, cabins, hostels, dude ranches, fishing camps, rental cottages, and rental vacation apartments. For those who want to be on the go while vacationing, there are houseboats and recreational vehicles—either of which can be rented by people who don't own their own. And then there are cruises and long train rides.

Owners and developers may call establishments whatever they choose, and a prospective guest can't tell from the name of a place just what it has to offer. But in general terms, accommodations fall into the following categories: resorts, hotels, motels and motor hotels, inns, and bed-and-breakfast accommodations. Some well-known national chains that call themselves inns are actually indistinguishable from motels; in certain areas the word *resort* is used for anything from a group of individual cottages or modest housekeeping apartments to the big complexes that command top dollar for their luxurious facilities. If you are making reservations at a place you have not seen before, find out as much as possible about it in advance to avoid being misled by a fancy but meaningless name.

### Resorts

A modern full-scale resort is a thing of wonder—a large and diversified business operation that has within it many kinds of facilities for recreation and service. The sports buff can find golf courses, pro shops, tennis courts, and instruction areas. Other active vacationers can enjoy jogging tracks; bike rentals and trails; horses, riding trails, and instruction; and boat rentals. In addition to one or more pools and often a beachfront, these resorts usually have a health club with sauna, whirlpool, exercise equipment, and massage service. Social directors organize parties, outings, and other events, and children and teens benefit from supervised recreational programs and game rooms. Several dining facilities of different types and levels of formality are often available along with a nightclub and dinner theater. A shopping mall, beauty and barber shops, laundry, cleaning service, and limousines to carry guests to and from airports and points of interest round out the services. Rooms and suites are luxurious; grounds are spacious and landscaped with gardens, flowering shrubs, and shade trees.

Such resorts are the ultimate in luxury for today's vacationer who is willing to pay top dollar in return for top-of-the-line facilities. Security and exclusivity are selling points—many places of this type are carefully guarded from intrusion by any outsiders.

Mountain resorts have been around for generations, but many of them used to be open only in warm seasons. In the past few decades, the increased interest in winter sports has made it feasible for mountain resorts in snowy regions to stay open year-round. As with resorts catering to golfers and tennis players, ski resorts also have pro shops, equipment for rent, and instruction. Some ski resorts start teaching children as young as three years of age to ski.

Professional instruction for all sports at the best resorts includes the latest in technology, such as videotaping so that novices can see exactly what their form looks like.

Some resorts are entirely or partially condominium owned: rooms, suites, and apartments are reserved for the owner-investors whenever they wish to occupy them and available for rental to guests during the rest of the year. In addition, the resort company may be engaged in real-estate development, offering homes for sale within the complex. In some cases the transactions are straightforward house sales; in others the buyers of the new homes become members of a home-owners club that gives them access to the facilities of the resort. If they wish, they may also avail themselves of certain amenities, such as security service and lawn and garden care. These resorts are new communities in the making.

Other variations offered by quite a few resort developers are time-sharing and interval ownership.

These are similar but technically and legally somewhat different. In both cases a part of a resort—a suite, an apartment, or a cottage—is offered for sale for a specified time each year: two weeks in July, for example. During that period the unit belongs to the buyer, who can stay in it, rent it, or let a friend use it. Some time-share plans include the privilege of swapping your right to a certain resort for a similar stay elsewhere.

## Hotels

The usual concept of a hotel is a multistory building with elevators, porter service for luggage, and switchboard telephone service. Today's standards in the United States call for color television sets, private bathrooms, and telephones. In-room movies are becoming more common; many hotels now offer concierge service and other amenities. Some of the fanciest hotels have some of the amenities of a resort, such as a swimming pool, a health club, and a shopping mall. One feature recently introduced will undoubtedly be a standard of the future: in a new hotel in Atlanta guests can turn to one channel on the television and get an up-to-the-moment tally of their bill.

## Motels or Motor Hotels

The idea of a low-rise building with parking at the door, a minimum of frills and extra services, and somewhat more reasonable prices than those charged in city hotels became very popular in the decades immediately after World War II. Both business travelers and families with children liked the convenience of easy unloading and reloading without going through a lobby.

Twenty years later, the pendulum began to swing back, and the difference between a motel and a hotel became less and less distinct. More floors were added, making elevators necessary. Since it is not possible to park at the door of your room in a high-rise building, bellhops once again became necessary. Restaurants and nightclubs, swimming pools, and direct-dial phones—most of the extras offered by hotels began to be commonplace in motels as well.

Rising prices that accompanied the increase in services and facilities gave impetus to new chains of budget-priced motels, some of which once again pared away the luxuries and offered bargain prices for minimum service.

## Inns

Inns have existed in the United States since colonial days and for centuries longer abroad. An inn, says one dictionary, is a small hotel, and that's how most people define the word. But there is a mystique today about an inn—the word conjures up images of rooms charmingly furnished with antiques, knickknacks, lace or ruffled curtains, and a handmade quilt or crocheted bedspread on a four-poster bed. A friendly couple run the place and are always around to give directions or just to chat. There are fireplaces in nearly every room; the smell of burning wood and the sound of crackling flames fill the air. Fresh flowers are everywhere; shelves are filled with books, and magazines lie on tables.

Actually, there are many inns that fit that description, and they are very popular with vacationers. Some of the most highly acclaimed have on staff—or are owned by—chefs whose gourmet meals have earned them international reputations.

Keep in mind, though, that some inns are nothing more than small, old hotels, with leaky faucets, shabby furniture, and indifferent service. And for the most part, even the most highly acclaimed inns do not offer some of the amenities taken for granted in hotels and motels, such as television sets and phones in each room, showers in addition to tubs, and room service. But these shortcomings are often considered unimportant when balanced against the other attractions of a well-run inn.

---

### Top U.S. Hotel/Motel Chains

A great many of the large hotel properties in the United States are owned or managed by a few nationwide or worldwide chains. Many customers prefer to stick with a familiar chain on whose standards they can depend.

#### Number of Rooms

| | |
|---|---|
| 1. Holiday Inns | 312,426 |
| 2. Sheraton Corp. | 118,584 |
| 3. Ramada Inns | 95,198 |
| 4. Hilton Hotels Corp. | 85,392 |
| 5. Howard Johnson Co. | 60,390 |
| 6. Quality International | 53,437 |
| 7. Marriott Corp. | 48,408 |
| 8. Days Inns of America | 45,530 |
| 9. Intercontinental Hotels | 39,533 |
| 10. Motel 6 | 37,683 |
| 11. Hyatt Hotels Corp. | 37,000 |
| 12. Hilton International | 33,034 |

Source: Hotels and Restaurants International, as published in Tourism's Top Twenty, 1984.

Figures reflect 1983 data.

#### Number of Properties

| | |
|---|---|
| 1. Holiday Inns | 1,740 |
| 2. Ramada Inns | 613 |
| 3. Howard Johnson Co. | 515 |
| 4. Sheraton Corp. | 447 |
| 5. Quality International | 446 |
| 6. Motel 6 | 344 |
| 7. Days Inns of America | 322 |
| 8. Hilton Hotels Corp. | 240 |
| 9. Econo-Travel Motor Hotel Corp. | 171 |
| 10. Rodeway Inns International | 152 |
| 11. La Quinta Motor Inns | 129 |
| 12. Marriott Corp. | 115 |

Source: Hotels and Restaurants International, as published in Tourism's Top Twenty, 1984.

Figures reflect 1982 data.

## Old and Elegant Hotels

Do you want to live like the Ewings of "Dallas" or the Carringtons of "Dynasty?" Stay in a grand old hotel and indulge your fantasies.

Glittering crystal chandeliers, marble fireplaces, carved mahogany doors, paintings by the Old Masters, and stained-glass ceilings designed by Tiffany—these were the marks of elegant hotels built at the turn of the century. The Plaza in New York City, the Ambassador East in Chicago, Hotel Utah in Salt Lake City, and the Beverly Wilshire in Beverly Hills are a few of these grand old hotels. They were built to cater to the rich and famous, to matinee idols and business tycoons, and to kings and queens of far-off countries.

Many of these fine hotels have retained their original glory; others have been rediscovered, restored, and modernized by new investors after many years of neglect. The old paintings have been cleaned, original moldings released from behind false walls, antique bars and breakfronts rescued from storage and put back to use. Modern conveniences have been added —but unobtrusively—so that they don't depart from the traditional elegance. Many of the furnishings are prohibitively expensive to reproduce today; some could not be duplicated at any price. At the Netherland Plaza in Cincinnati, for example, an entire ballroom is walled with mirrors that are backed with gold leaf!

Elegant old hotels offer luxurious service to match the decor. These are the places to go if you really want to be pampered.

Here are a few of these wonderful old hotels and resorts:

Ambassador East, Chicago, IL
Arizona Biltmore, Phoenix, AZ
The Balsams, Dixville Notch, NH
Belleview Biltmore, Clearwater, FL
Beverly Hills Hotel, Beverly Hills, CA
Beverly Wilshire, Beverly Hills, CA
Boca Raton Hotel, Boca Raton, FL
The Breakers, Palm Beach, FL
Broadmoor, Colorado Springs, CO
Cloister, Sea Island, GA
The Greenbrier, White Sulphur Springs, WV
The Homestead, Hot Springs, VA
Hotel Utah, Salt Lake City, UT
Netherland Plaza, Cincinnati, OH
The Peabody, Memphis, TN
St. Anthony Intercontinental, San Antonio, TX
The Westin Benson, Portland, OR
The Westin St. Francis, San Francisco, CA
The Wigwam, Litchfield Park, AZ
Williamsburg Inn, Williamsburg, VA

---

An inn is often an excellent choice for a Christmas vacation. In many inns the seasonal decorations are beautiful, the Christmas dinner is sumptuous, there are special events to which you will be invited, and in general you will be treated like an honored member of the family.

Most state tourism departments can send you a list of country inns, but neither the department nor the list can help you decide which inn will appeal to you. There are several guidebooks on the subject that are quite good; you can also read the travel sections of local newspapers, make inquiries of a travel agent, and listen to the advice of experienced people. It's not as easy to make a good choice in this category as in the others, but a little research will pay off.

### Bed-and-Breakfast Accommodations

A new-old concept in accommodations for travelers is the private home offering a bed and a breakfast. When automobile travel was in its first flush of popularity, many private-home owners hung out signs that expressed offers to take in tourists overnight. These places were known then as tourist homes. Later on, as motels became more numerous, tourist homes almost disappeared from the landscape.

Recently—largely within the past decade—the tourist home has reappeared with a new name and a somewhat different approach. The older tourist home was usually simple and inexpensive, offering no more than a bedroom and shared bathroom for overnight guests. Today's B and Bs, as they are popularly called, offer an alternative type of guest housing that is more intimate and friendly than the typical hotel or motel. The concept has been imported from Europe. Americans who have stayed in bed-and-breakfast accommodations in foreign countries have enjoyed meeting their hosts and getting acquainted with another way of life, and enterprising hosts in several parts of this country have begun to try out the idea here.

There are several different approaches to the bed-and-breakfast concept, and prices vary widely. In Savannah, Georgia, and along the Mississippi River in Louisiana and Mississippi, bed-and-breakfast accommodations are available in lavishly restored old mansions and antebellum plantation houses. Guests are greeted with champagne, put up in rooms furnished with antiques, and given breakfasts with as many courses—and calories—as you'd expect to consume at a fancy banquet. The charge for a stay at one of these places is about the same as that for a stay at a fine hotel.

In some other areas, bed-and-breakfast homes are real bargains. For a cost lower than the average hotel or motel rate, vacationers are treated as guests, not merely customers. They often spend the evenings with their hosts, swapping stories and building friendships.

The accommodations are comfortable and spotless but no more spacious or luxurious than those that most people have at home.

Since these accommodations are in private homes, hosts make the rules. It is not at all uncommon for bed-and-breakfast hosts to limit their clientele to adults or nonsmokers. Some also specify that no alcohol is to be brought into their homes. It is a good idea to check ahead of time with your host about the rules of the house to avoid unexpected and unnecessary unpleasantnesses.

Because hosts are small entrepreneurs, most cannot afford to advertise widely. If you want to find out about bed-and-breakfast homes in a particular area, send an inquiry to the department of tourism for that state or purchase a bed-and-breakfast guidebook—there are several good ones on the market.

## Other Accommodations

Many national and state parks offer accommodations in lodges and cabins that are somewhat rustic but comfortable. The settings usually more than make up for any slight loss of modernity.

Hundreds of resort areas, especially along the Atlantic coast and in many inland lakeside communities, are filled with rental cottages and apartments. To find out about availability of this kind of vacation home, send your inquiries to a local visitors bureau, chamber of commerce, or real-estate office.

If you are the type of traveler who wants to be sure of what you are going to find ahead of time, you may prefer to make your reservations at a well-known chain hotel or resort. They offer a standard of service that you can depend on, you can make reservations by calling toll-free central reservation services, and if you are already familiar with the chain you choose, you

will usually get what you expect. Any hotel can have its bad days, however. Let the manager know if things have gone wrong; he'll bend over backward to make up for any inconveniences you've encountered.

## WHO SHOULD STAY WHERE

How do you choose among the types of accommodations available? Two factors are of prime importance—budget and preference in vacation activities. Full-scale resorts are most expensive, but for people of all ages who don't want to travel around much while on vacation, aren't interested in sightseeing, and enjoy having a large variety of activities available on the premises, resorts are ideal. City visitors find the downtown hotels most convenient to the places they want to visit and the things they want to do. Vacationers on a budget or those who don't really care what their lodging offers beyond a clean room and a comfortable bed are perfectly happy at a low-cost motel. These people may want to spend all day sailing or swimming or exploring the area, returning at night just to sleep. People who want to get close to nature—but not in a tent—are very happy with a rustic cabin or lodge in a state or national park.

Families on a tight budget save money by finding accommodations that include cooking facilities. Three meals a day in restaurants for several people can eat a huge hole in the vacation wallet.

Be sure to check ahead if you have special needs, such as wheelchair access. In some states hotels are required by law to make a certain proportion of their rooms accessible to wheelchairs. Travelers with animals should find out in advance whether or not their pets can be accommodated.

Prices for hotel rooms are highest in major cities, especially in the Northeast. The range from high to low is greatest in such crowded resort areas as much of Florida. Bargains can be found in these areas if you look for them, as the presence of intense competition for the tourist dollar works to the advantage of the consumer, especially in the off-season. For example, some of the Myrtle Beach, South Carolina, hotels say that you can stay in that area in the winter for less than an average electricity bill in New York City.

If you are vacationing near the ocean, remember that prices go up as you get closer to the seashore. The same holds true for proximity to major attractions, physical or man-made. And major events, such as Mardi Gras in New Orleans, the Kentucky Derby, or popular football bowl games, all drive prices up for the duration of the event.

## WHERE TO EAT

The meals you eat on vacation should be a part of your total adventure. Plan for them, as you do for other

---

## Hostels—For the Young at Heart

Adventurers—of all ages from five up—who are interested in seeing the country as inexpensively as possible should join American Youth Hostels, an organization affiliated with the International Youth Hostel Federation. Low-cost overnight sleeping quarters are available to members, usually in dormitory-type rooms furnished with bunk beds.

However, providing sleeping facilities is only one of the services to vacationers offered by American Youth Hostels: the organization also sponsors a number of active adventure tours involving biking, hiking, canoeing, sailing, and photography safaris. Some of these treks include tent camping.

For a membership application, write to American Youth Hostels, 1332 I Street NW, Washington, DC, 20005, or telephone (202)783-6161.

## Is Pizza the All-American Food?

The hamburger may be the most-ordered food in U.S. restaurants, but hamburger restaurants are not the most numerous type of food outlet. There are many more pizza restaurants than hamburger establishments in the country, according to the National Restaurant Association, and the gap is widening.

Since 1982 the association has been gathering statistics on the types and distribution of the more than 300,000 restaurants in the United States. That year showed pizza establishments ahead of hamburger outlets by only 0.1 percent; in 1984 pizza's share of the total number of restaurant businesses had grown to 10.3 percent, while hamburger's had shrunk to 8.8 percent. Other gainers over the two-year period were Oriental restaurants and family-style eateries providing a full menu.

Different types of restaurants are not equally distributed in different sections of the United States: there are far more outlets for pizza than for hamburgers in the New England, Middle Atlantic, and East North Central states; in other sections the balance is reversed. The percentage of total restaurants serving primarily chicken is greatest in the East South Central states; steak houses as well as fish and other seafood restaurants are most numerous in the South Atlantic region.

More than half the nation's Mexican restaurants are in the West South Central and Pacific regions; the largest concentrations of Oriental eateries are in the Middle Atlantic and Pacific states.

### The Top 20 Types of Restaurants

| | Units | Percentage of Total |
|---|---|---|
| 1. Pizza | 31,053 | 10.3 |
| 2. Hamburger | 26,585 | 8.8 |
| 3. Ice cream | 18,014 | 6.0 |
| 4. Oriental | 12,487 | 4.1 |
| 5. Family style/full menu | 12,324 | 4.1 |
| 6. Mexican | 11,851 | 3.9 |
| 7. Café | 11,284 | 3.7 |
| 8. Chicken | 10,879 | 3.6 |
| 9. Fish/seafood | 8,531 | 2.8 |
| 10. Steak (all types) | 7,751 | 2.6 |
| 11. Barbecue | 5,228 | 1.7 |
| 12. Doughnut | 4,771 | 1.6 |
| 13. Italian | 4,096 | 1.4 |
| 14. Delicatessen/bagel | 4,076 | 1.3 |
| 15. Other sandwich | 3,983 | 1.3 |
| 16. Submarine sandwich | 3,766 | 1.2 |
| 17. Coffee shop | 3,584 | 1.2 |
| 18. Refreshment/snack | 3,210 | 1.1 |
| 19. Cafeteria | 2,624 | 0.9 |
| 20. Grill | 2,388 | 0.8 |

*Source:* National Restaurant Association.

Figures reflect 1984 data.

tioners are regional specialties. Lobster really tastes better when eaten in Maine, a few minutes away from its saltwater home. So do freshly caught salmon in Seattle, fried Mississippi catfish in Memphis, Creole and Cajun foods in Louisiana, biscuits and "sawmill" (sausage) gravy in Chattanooga, baked beans and codfish cakes in Boston, barbecued beef in Texas, just-squeezed orange juice in Florida, date desserts in Palm Springs, venison steak in Wisconsin, vegetables purchased at truck-farm roadside stands in California, tree-ripened pears in Oregon, pecans and peaches in Georgia, and fried country-ham sandwiches in Kentucky.

Major cities—and many smaller ones—in the United States offer a great variety of ethnic restaurants. Maybe you don't ever expect to travel to India or Thailand, but you can get a taste of many foreign cultures—both literally and figuratively—by visiting ethnic restaurants. Look in the phone book for restaurant types not available where you live. You can take home memories of locales more exotic and distant than the area you visited.

In a typical restaurant, breakfast is the biggest bargain meal of the day. Of course there are restau-

### Tips for the Single Traveler

Several factors make it difficult for people to travel alone, not the least of which is cost. Traveling alone ordinarily imposes much more than half the expense that a couple traveling together can expect. This is especially true for the price of a single hotel room or stateroom on a cruise ship.

If you don't mind sharing a room but haven't been able to find a friend who wants to go where you want to, investigate packaged-tour operators. Some of them offer guaranteed share plans, meaning they either assign a roommate (of the same sex) to you or give you a single room without charging you more than you would pay for sharing a double.

You can increase your chances of getting a roommate with whom you have something in common if you take one of the many special-interest tours on the market. You can go on an archeological dig in Arizona, attend a baseball camp in Vermont and get some coaching from retired big-league players, steep yourself in classical music at a summer music festival in Michigan, study the geology of the Rocky Mountains in Colorado, or go to a tennis clinic at a resort in Texas. Universities and museums are usually good sources of information about special-interest tours.

There are some advantages to traveling alone, too. You can spend all your time doing exactly what you enjoy most without compromising to keep the peace. And last-minute cancellations for plane, tour, theater, or concert tickets are often available for one, not two.

aspects; investigate the local cuisine; go to the colorful restaurants you've heard about; enjoy the pleasures of fine food.

Some of the greatest gastronomic delights for vaca-

## Busiest U.S. Ports of Entry

Eighteen of the 20 ports of entry most used by visitors to the United States are within the 107 Vacation Places covered in this book; the other 2 are in off-shore U.S. possessions. The following list shows the number of foreign-visitor air arrivals in 1982.

| | Airport Arrivals |
|---|---|
| 1. New York, NY | 3,234,222 |
| 2. Miami, FL | 2,442,102 |
| 3. Los Angeles, CA | 1,138,498 |
| 4. Honolulu, HI | 1,058,252 |
| 5. San Francisco, CA | 423,126 |
| 6. Chicago, IL | 349,083 |
| 7. Houston, TX | 299,590 |
| 8. Agana, Guam | 291,756 |
| 9. San Juan, Puerto Rico | 271,560 |
| 10. Boston, MA | 211,580 |
| 11. Seattle, WA | 179,893 |
| 12. Atlanta, GA | 164,025 |
| 13. Dallas, TX | 123,202 |
| 14. Washington, DC | 83,305 |
| 15. New Orleans, LA | 79,100 |
| 16. San Antonio, TX | 58,537 |
| 17. Anchorage, AK | 55,399 |
| 18. Baltimore, MD | 41,191 |
| 19. Fort Lauderdale, FL | 38,381 |
| 20. Bangor, ME | 35,104 |

*Source:* Transportation Systems Center, U.S. Department of Transportation, *U.S. International Air Travel Statistics*, 1982.

Air travel is expensive these days, except for the many supersaver and other special fares available, but the tremendous savings in travel time often makes it worth the cost. To purchase air travel at the lowest possible cost, follow these tips:

- **Plan ahead.** Substantial savings are often available when tickets are purchased in advance. Be aware of restrictions, requirements in length of stay, certain blacked-out periods, a limited number of seats, and penalties for changes or cancellations.
- **Pay for your tickets immediately.** Try to pay on the day you make your reservation. If fares go up, you will not be charged extra; if, on the other hand, fares decrease you are entitled to a refund of the difference.
- **Shop around.** Your travel or ticket agent may not be quoting you the best price. Consult more than one source.
- **Ask about fare differences.** Many airlines offer different prices at different times of the day. Certain routes have red-eye specials (flights in the middle of the night) at greatly reduced rates.
- **Be flexible.** If your schedule permits you to make last-minute decisions, you may be able to pick up a seat on a charter that would otherwise go unsold. Tell your travel agent that you would be interested in hearing of such opportunities.

rants that charge as much for breakfast as for any other meal, but in many eateries you can really get a good start for the day with a big breakfast at a reasonable price. Vacationers on tight budgets do well nutrionally and save time and money if they eat breakfast in a restaurant and go on picnics or cook the other two meals in the motel kitchenette.

## HOW TO GET THERE

By far the largest proportion of pleasure travel in the United States is done by private auto, truck, or recreational vehicle. According to the U.S. Travel Data Center's 1984 *National Travel Survey*, 77 percent of all vacation trips and 86 percent of weekend pleasure trips were made using these means of transportation.

The interstate highway system has made long-distance driving much simpler and easier than it once was. Of course every traveler knows that long drives over superhighways are also more boring and sleep inducing than drives on other roads. The best way to handle vacation driving is to use the interstates for quick and easy access to distant places and break the monotony with frequent scenic shunpiking in selected spots.

### Busiest U.S. Airports

| | Passengers per year (in thousands) |
|---|---|
| 1. Chicago-O'Hare International | 42,874 |
| 2. William B. Hartsfield Atlanta International | 37,920 |
| 3. Los Angeles International | 33,427 |
| 4. John F. Kennedy International (Jamaica, NY) | 27,904 |
| 5. Dallas–Fort Worth International | 26,786 |
| 6. Stapleton International (Denver, CO) | 25,247 |
| 7. San Francisco International | 23,167 |
| 8. Miami International | 19,322 |
| 9. La Guardia (Flushing, NY) | 18,813 |
| 10. Gen. Edward L. Logan International (Boston, MA) | 17,849 |
| 11. Newark International | 17,411 |
| 12. Lambert-St. Louis International | 16,241 |
| 13. Honolulu International | 15,262 |
| 14. Washington National (Washington, DC) | 14,166 |
| 15. Houston Intercontinental | 12,985 |
| 16. Greater Pittsburgh International | 11,832 |
| 17. Seattle-Tacoma International | 10,142 |
| 18. McCarran International (Las Vegas, NV) | 10,057 |
| 19. Detroit Metropolitan Wayne County | 9,606 |
| 20. Philadelphia International | 9,498 |

*Source:* Airport Operators Council International, *Worldwide Airport Traffic Report, 1983,* as published in *Tourism's Top Twenty,* 1984.

Figures reflect 1983 data.

# Interstate Highways

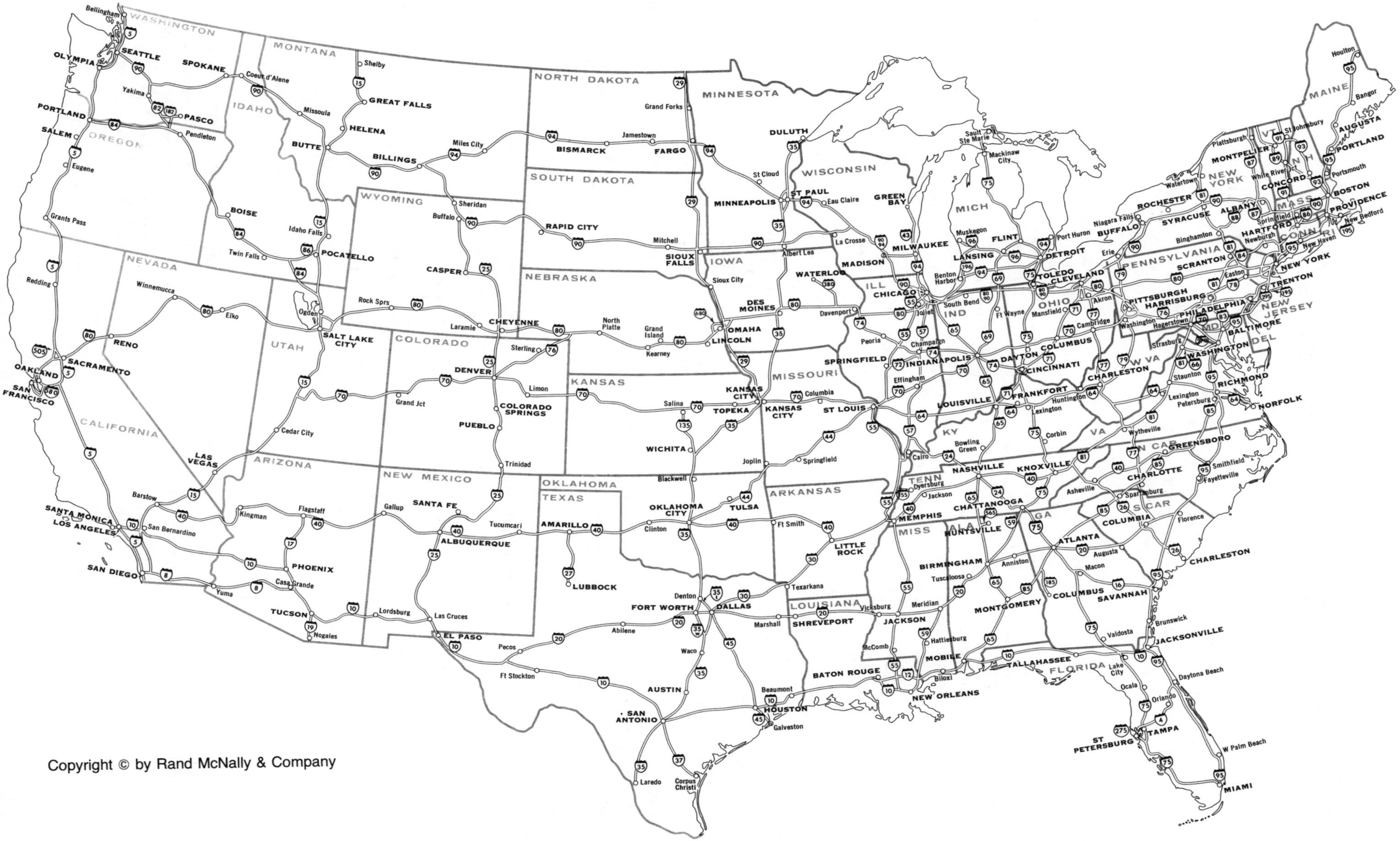

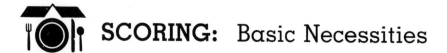

# SCORING: Basic Necessities

Scores in this chapter were based on the availability of hotels, motels, and resorts; campgrounds; and establishments designated by the U.S. Bureau of the Census as eating and drinking places. Bonus points were added for the outstanding quality of certain hotels and restaurants.

Availability of places to stay and to eat is a basic necessity for vacationers. The beauty of the scenery you have traveled thousands of miles to view, tickets to the latest popular Broadway show, the excitement of watching Mardi Gras parades—all these things lose their appeal if you don't have a bed to sleep in or if you're ravenously hungry and discover that the nearest restaurant is two hours away by car.

To arrive at a score for the average availability of hotels and motels, campgrounds, and restaurants in each Vacation Place, a ratio was calculated to reflect the total number of establishments per 1,000 square miles, and points were assigned accordingly. It was assumed that most vacationers would be able to use nearly any place within an area of that size as a base without being too far away from other points they might wish to visit. To visualize how much space 1,000 square miles covers, think of a circle with a radius of slightly less than 18 miles.

## Hotels and Motels

In the Place Profiles, the number of hotels and motels indicated for each Vacation Place includes all establishments counted by the U.S. Bureau of the Census as "hotels, motor hotels, and motels." Their figures include all such firms subject to federal income tax.

Availability of hotels and motels was scored as follows: the number of establishments per 1,000 square miles was determined, and each establishment was given 1 point, up to a maximum of 200 points. It was decided that 200 hotels per 1,000 square miles represented a very high average availability and that any higher point value for this segment would distort the total picture of basic necessities.

To use Jersey Shore, New Jersey, as an example: the total number of hotels and motels (216), was divided by the total number of square miles in the Vacation Place area (1,113). This figure of 0.194 was then multiplied by 1,000 to yield a point score of 194, equal to its availability ratio of 194 hotels and motels per 1,000 square miles.

The top five Vacation Places for availability of hotels received the maximum score of 200 points. Four of the top ten were major cities: New York, Chicago, Los Angeles, and San Francisco; the other six were resort areas along the Atlantic Coast.

### Top Ten for Hotels and Motels

| | Availability Ratio |
|---|---|
| 1. Atlantic City, NJ | 650 |
| 2. Cape Cod–The Islands, MA | 616 |
| 3. New York City, NY | 558 |
| 4. San Francisco, CA | 222 |
| 5. Chicago, IL | 202 |
| 6. Los Angeles, CA | 197 |
| 6. Miami–Gold Coast–Keys, FL | 197 |
| 8. Jersey Shore, NJ | 194 |
| 9. Long Island, NY | 186 |
| 10. Myrtle Beach–Grand Strand, SC | 176 |

## Campgrounds

Availability of campgrounds was scored in the same manner as hotels—the number of campgrounds per 1,000 square miles was calculated and this number became the score. No maximum was set for this element of the scoring.

Eastern resort areas again were the top scorers in availability of campgrounds, holding eight of the top ten places. While there are many, many camping areas in the wide open spaces of the West, distances between them are also far greater than in the East.

Atlantic City, New Jersey, in first place for this segment, had 57 campgrounds within its 831-square-mile area, or an availability ratio of 68.6 per 1,000 square miles. Its point score for campgrounds was rounded off to 69.

### Top Ten for Campgrounds

| | Availability Ratio |
|---|---|
| 1. Atlantic City, NJ | 69 |
| 2. Cape Cod–The Islands, MA | 44 |
| 3. Portsmouth–Kennebunk, NH–ME | 41 |
| 4. Tampa Bay–Southwest Coast, FL | 35 |
| 5. Mystic Seaport–Connecticut Valley, CT | 34 |
| 6. Green Mountains, VT | 29 |
| 7. Providence–Newport, RI | 28 |
| 8. Aspen–Vail, CO | 27 |
| 9. Door County, WI | 26 |
| 9. Portland, ME | 26 |

## Eating and Drinking Places

The count of eating and drinking places made by the U.S. Bureau of the Census included all such establishments that provided food and drink for consumption on the premises or to carry out for immediate consumption.

Again, the base of 1,000 square miles was used for scoring; this time the maximum allowable score was fixed at 2,000. It was assumed that a vacationer ordinarily uses only one motel or hotel in a given area but might wish to patronize several different eating places during the stay.

Five Vacation Places had more than 2,000 eating

and drinking places per 1,000 square miles and thus received the maximum score. Not surprisingly, all the top scorers for availability of eating and drinking places were heavily populated areas.

### Top Ten for Eating and Drinking Places

| | | Availability Ratio |
|---|---|---|
| 1. | New York City, NY | 12,383 |
| 2. | Chicago, IL | 3,682 |
| 3. | Long Island, NY | 3,259 |
| 4. | San Francisco, CA | 2,368 |
| 5. | Boston, MA | 2,179 |
| 6. | Philadelphia, PA–DE–NJ | 1,709 |
| 7. | Los Angeles, CA | 1,673 |
| 8. | Providence–Newport, RI | 1,491 |
| 9. | Cincinnati, OH–KY | 1,263 |
| 10. | Jersey Shore, NJ | 1,203 |

### Award-winning Hotels and Restaurants

Bonus points were awarded to Vacation Places with significant numbers of hotels and restaurants that have been designated outstanding by nationally recognized organizations. For award-winning hotels, the publications of these organizations were studied: *Mobil Travel Guide, AAA TourBook,* and *Meetings and Conventions* magazine.

All hotels and motels listed in *Mobil Travel Guide* and *AAA TourBook* are inspected annually by trained and experienced personnel, who call on establishments without warning. The Gold Key awards given annually by *Meetings and Conventions* are determined by vote of the readers of the magazine—most of whom are official meeting planners.

Four points were given for each four-star rating by *Mobil Travel Guide* and for each four-diamond rating by *AAA TourBook* awarded to a hotel, motel, or resort within the boundaries of each Vacation Place; 5 points for each five-star and for each five-diamond rating. Five points were also given for each Gold Key award given by *Meetings and Conventions.* Thus a single hotel was eligible for up to 15 points, which signified it received the five-star, the five-diamond, and the Gold Key awards.

### Top Ten for Award-winning Hotels

| | | Award-winning Hotels |
|---|---|---|
| 1. | Dallas–Fort Worth, TX | 36 |
| 2. | San Francisco, CA | 31 |
| 3. | Los Angeles, CA | 28 |
| 4. | Seattle–Mount Rainier–North Cascades, WA | 27 |
| 5. | Houston–Galveston, TX | 25 |
| 6. | Chicago, IL | 23 |
| 6. | Miami–Gold Coast–Keys, FL | 23 |
| 8. | Atlanta, GA | 22 |
| 9. | Hawaii | 21 |
| 9. | New York City, NY | 21 |

The country's largest metropolitan areas were the big winners in this category, with the exception of the Seattle area, which ranked fourth, and Hawaii, in ninth place.

For restaurant recognition, the authorities consulted were *Mobil Travel Guide* and the annual award issue of *Travel-Holiday* magazine. Five points were given for all four- and five-star ratings in *Mobil Travel Guide* and all winners of the *Travel-Holiday* award. A restaurant receiving both awards was given ten points.

The top ten Vacation Places in number of award-winning restaurants were the same as those with award-winning hotels (though not in the same order), with two exceptions. New Orleans, Louisiana, and Washington, DC, appeared on the restaurant list but not on the hotel list.

### Top Ten for Award-winning Restaurants

| | | Award-winning Restaurants |
|---|---|---|
| 1. | New York City, NY | 68 |
| 2. | Los Angeles, CA | 59 |
| 3. | San Francisco, CA | 56 |
| 4. | Chicago, IL | 43 |
| 5. | New Orleans, LA | 22 |
| 6. | Miami–Gold Coast–Keys, FL | 18 |
| 7. | Hawaii | 17 |
| 8. | Washington, DC–MD–VA | 16 |
| 9. | Dallas–Fort Worth, TX | 14 |
| 10. | Houston–Galveston, TX | 13 |

### Transportation and Accessibility

Information about access to the Vacation Places by air and by interstate highway was included in the Place Profiles for this chapter, but these data were not used as criteria for scoring. All destinations included in *Vacation Places Rated* are easily accessible, though many of the larger and less congested places also include some extremely remote areas within the designated boundaries. All have some air service nearby, and all have good access by automobile, even if not via an interstate highway.

For many vacationers remoteness is an asset, not a liability. Therefore, it was decided not to reward or penalize any Vacation Place on the basis of ease of access.

PLACE PROFILES: Basic Necessities

In these pages, the elements used for scoring in this chapter are listed. The scoring categories are as follows: Accommodations (Hotels, Motels, and Campgrounds), Eating and Drinking Places, and Award Winners (Hotels and Restaurants). The numbers that follow these categories are the actual number of establishments found within the boundaries of the Vacation Place.

Also listed in these Place Profiles are several other categories not included in the scoring. These elements pertain to the accessibility of the Vacation Places and are not scored because all the Vacation Places are easily accessible. In addition, it is often the remoteness of a destination—not the accessibility—that proves to be an asset to many vacationers.

The *square miles* figure was used to determine the availability ratio for the different scoring categories (see the individual categories in the scoring section).

*Interstate highways,* *airport locations,* and *number of carriers* indicate ease of access to the Vacation Place.

Air service to and from a Vacation Place is further indicated by a *hub rating.* This is a designation determined by the Federal Aviation Administration and given to U.S. metropolitan areas defined by an agency of the federal government. These metropolitan areas do not necessarily duplicate the boundaries of the Vacation Places. However, the hub ratings were included in the Place Profiles to help vacationers determine the sizes of the airports within the major cities of the Vacation Places.

Hub ratings are indicated in the Place Profiles in the following manner:

| If the number of passengers leaving its airport(s) totaled: | The metro area within a Vacation Place was a: | The Vacation Place then received a hub rating of: |
|---|---|---|
| 1% or more | large hub | *** |
| 0.25% to 0.99% | medium hub | ** |
| 0.05% to 0.24% | small hub | * |
| less than 0.05% of all U.S. airline passengers in a year | nonhub | no hub rating |

A star (★) preceding a Vacation Place highlights that place as one of the top ten in this chapter.

| Vacation Place (Square Miles) | Interstate Highways | Airport Locations (Number of Carriers) | Hub Ratings | Accommodations | Eating and Drinking Places | Award Winners | Places Rated Score | Places Rated Rank |
|---|---|---|---|---|---|---|---|---|
| Adirondack Mountains, NY (10,119) | I-87 | Plattsburgh (1) Saranac Lake (1) | | Hotels, Motels: 351 Campgrounds: 147 | 785 | Hotels: 7 Restaurants: — | 155 | 76 |
| Albuquerque–Santa Fe–Taos, NM (11,728) | I-25 I-40 | Albuquerque (19) Los Alamos (1) Santa Fe (1) | ** | Hotels, Motels: 181 Campgrounds: 73 | 895 | Hotels: 10 Restaurants: 2 | 148 | 81 |
| Anchorage–Kenai Peninsula, AK (17,788) | — | Anchorage (23) Homer (3) Kenai (4) | ** | Hotels, Motels: 60 Campgrounds: 69 | 376 | Hotels: 2 Restaurants: 3 | 51 | 102 |
| Asheville–Smoky Mountains, NC (3,250) | I-26 I-40 | Asheville (6) | * | Hotels, Motels: 182 Campgrounds: 74 | 398 | Hotels: 2 Restaurants: — | 209 | 70 |
| Aspen–Vail, CO (3,644) | I-70 | Aspen (3) Crested Butte (1) Vail (1) | | Hotels, Motels: 115 Campgrounds: 98 | 263 | Hotels: 12 Restaurants: 1 | 194 | 71 |
| Atlanta, GA (10,667) | I-20 I-75 I-85 | Atlanta (27) | *** | Hotels, Motels: 302 Campgrounds: 70 | 3,355 | Hotels: 22 Restaurants: 9 | 499 | 34 |
| Atlantic City, NJ (831) | — | Atlantic City (6) Cape May (1) | | Hotels, Motels: 540 Campgrounds: 57 | 823 | Hotels: 6 Restaurants: 1 | 1,296 | 13 |
| Austin–Hill Country, TX (5,953) | I-35 | Austin (15) Killeen (1) | | Hotels, Motels: 112 Campgrounds: 35 | 1,115 | Hotels: 6 Restaurants: 1 | 245 | 62 |
| Baltimore–Chesapeake Bay, MD (3,156) | I-70 I-83 I-95 | Baltimore (33) | ** | Hotels, Motels: 159 Campgrounds: 8 | 2,957 | Hotels: 6 Restaurants: 3 | 1,029 | 16 |
| Bar Harbor–Acadia, ME (2,637) | — | Bar Harbor (1) Rockland (1) | | Hotels, Motels: 122 Campgrounds: 37 | 175 | Hotels: — Restaurants: — | 127 | 87 |
| Bend–Cascade Mountains, OR (7,798) | — | Redmond (2) | | Hotels, Motels: 42 Campgrounds: 97 | 164 | Hotels: 5 Restaurants: — | 63 | 98 |
| Berkshire Hills–Pioneer Valley, MA (1,853) | I-91 | Pittsfield (1) | | Hotels, Motels: 118 Campgrounds: 37 | 795 | Hotels: 4 Restaurants: 1 | 534 | 33 |
| Black Hills, SD (10,716) | I-90 | Rapid City (5) | | Hotels, Motels: 131 Campgrounds: 94 | 260 | Hotels: 2 Restaurants: — | 53 | 101 |

| Vacation Place (Square Miles) | Interstate Highways | Airport Locations (Number of Carriers) | Hub Ratings | Accommodations | Eating and Drinking Places | Award Winners | Places Rated Score | Places Rated Rank |
|---|---|---|---|---|---|---|---|---|
| **Blue Ridge Mountains, VA** (5,260) | I-81 | Charlottesville (5) Staunton (1) | | Hotels, Motels: 73 Campgrounds: 42 | 342 | Hotels: 1 Restaurants: — | 91 | 94 |
| **Boise–Sun Valley, ID** (12,932) | I-84 | Boise (11) Twin Falls (2) Sun Valley (1) | | Hotels, Motels: 70 Campgrounds: 85 | 579 | Hotels: 5 Restaurants: — | 81 | 96 |
| **Boone–High Country, NC** (2,726) | — | — | | Hotels, Motels: 65 Campgrounds: 29 | 282 | Hotels: 1 Restaurants: — | 146 | 82 |
| ★ **Boston, MA** (2,429) | I-90 I-93 I-95 | Bedford (3) Boston (53) Lawrence (1) | *** | Hotels, Motels: 315 Campgrounds: 18 | 5,292 | Hotels: 18 Restaurants: 9 | 2,262 | 5 |
| **Brownsville–Rio Grande Valley, TX** (3,063) | — | Brownsville (4) Harlingen (4) McAllen (3) | | Hotels, Motels: 112 Campgrounds: 73 | 639 | Hotels: 5 Restaurants: — | 289 | 55 |
| ★ **Cape Cod–The Islands, MA** (549) | — | Hyannis (6) Nantucket (11) Provincetown (1) Vineyard Haven (7) | | Hotels, Motels: 338 Campgrounds: 24 | 629 | Hotels: 7 Restaurants: 3 | 1,432 | 9 |
| **Catskill Mountains, NY** (7,611) | I-84 I-87 | Albany (13) Monticello (1) Newburgh (3) Oneonta (1) Poughkeepsie (5) Sidney (1) | ** | Hotels, Motels: 462 Campgrounds: 116 | 2,013 | Hotels: 2 Restaurants: 6 | 378 | 43 |
| **Charleston, SC** (2,621) | I-26 | Charleston (6) | * | Hotels, Motels: 68 Campgrounds: 9 | 454 | Hotels: 6 Restaurants: 1 | 241 | 64 |
| **Chattanooga–Huntsville, TN–AL–GA** (5,865) | I-24 I-59 I-75 | Chattanooga (8) Huntsville, AL (6) | * * | Hotels, Motels: 114 Campgrounds: 26 | 846 | Hotels: 2 Restaurants: — | 184 | 72 |
| ★ **Chicago, IL** (2,356) | I-55 I-57 I-80 I-90 I-94 | Chicago (61) | *** | Hotels, Motels: 477 Campgrounds: 10 | 8,676 | Hotels: 23 Restaurants: 43 | 2,562 | 3 |
| ★ **Cincinnati, OH–KY** (2,290) | I-71 I-74 I-75 | Cincinnati (16) Dayton (12) | ** ** | Hotels, Motels: 174 Campgrounds: 24 | 2,893 | Hotels: 9 Restaurants: 9 | 1,431 | 10 |
| **Colorado Springs, CO** (6,603) | I-25 | Colorado Springs (7) Pueblo (3) | * | Hotels, Motels: 136 Campgrounds: 79 | 812 | Hotels: 3 Restaurants: — | 179 | 73 |
| **Coos Bay–South Coast, OR** (3,285) | — | North Bend (1) | | Hotels, Motels: 58 Campgrounds: 36 | 190 | Hotels: 1 Restaurants: — | 95 | 93 |
| **Corpus Christi–Padre Island, TX** (3,444) | — | Corpus Christi (6) | * | Hotels, Motels: 99 Campgrounds: 35 | 602 | Hotels: 3 Restaurants: — | 226 | 66 |
| **Crater Lake–Klamath Falls, OR** (12,083) | I-5 | Eugene (4) Klamath Falls (2) Medford (3) | | Hotels, Motels: 129 Campgrounds: 121 | 566 | Hotels: 7 Restaurants: 2 | 110 | 89 |
| **Dallas–Fort Worth, TX** (6,998) | I-20 I-30 I-35 I-45 | Dallas (45) | *** | Hotels, Motels: 318 Campgrounds: 66 | 4,273 | Hotels: 36 Restaurants: 14 | 922 | 17 |
| **Denver–Rocky Mountain National Park, CO** (4,931) | I-25 I-70 I-76 | Denver (33) | *** | Hotels, Motels: 314 Campgrounds: 93 | 2,752 | Hotels: 16 Restaurants: 9 | 768 | 21 |
| **Door County, WI** (492) | — | — | | Hotels, Motels: 66 Campgrounds: 13 | 79 | Hotels: — Restaurants: — | 321 | 50 |
| **Eastern Shore, VA** (702) | — | — | | Hotels, Motels: 29 Campgrounds: 12 | 51 | Hotels: — Restaurants: 1 | 136 | 84 |
| **Finger Lakes, NY** (6,730) | I-81 I-90 | Ithaca (3) Syracuse (17) | ** | Hotels, Motels: 164 Campgrounds: 81 | 1,744 | Hotels: 4 Restaurants: 3 | 331 | 48 |
| **Flaming Gorge, UT–WY–CO** (7,967) | I-80 | Vernal, UT (3) Rock Springs, WY (3) | | Hotels, Motels: 45 Campgrounds: 39 | 100 | Hotels: 2 Restaurants: — | 31 | 104 |
| **Glacier National Park–Flathead Lake, MT** (9,552) | — | Kalispell (3) | | Hotels, Motels: 71 Campgrounds: 77 | 211 | Hotels: 4 Restaurants: — | 54 | 100 |
| **Grand Canyon Country, AZ** (24,607) | I-17 I-40 | Flagstaff (2) Grand Canyon (8) Sedona (2) Winslow (1) | | Hotels, Motels: 133 Campgrounds: 61 | 360 | Hotels: 3 Restaurants: — | 39 | 103 |
| **Green Mountains, VT** (2,553) | I-89 | Burlington (9) Montpelier (1) Morrisville (1) Rutland (1) | | Hotels, Motels: 143 Campgrounds: 73 | 368 | Hotels : 14 Restaurants : — | 293 | 52 |

| Vacation Place (Square Miles) | Interstate Highways | Airport Locations (Number of Carriers) | Hub Ratings | Accommodations | Eating and Drinking Places | Award Winners | Places Rated Score | Places Rated Rank |
|---|---|---|---|---|---|---|---|---|
| Hawaii (6,427) | — | Hana (1)<br>Hilo (7)<br>Honolulu (28)<br>Koanapali (1)<br>Kahului (9)<br>Kailua Kona (6)<br>Kalaupapa (2)<br>Kamuela (2)<br>Kaunakakai (4)<br>Lanai City (3)<br>Lihue (5)<br>Princeville (1)<br>Upolu Point (1) | ***<br> | Hotels, Motels: 209<br>Campgrounds: 43 | 1,741 | Hotels: 21<br>Restaurants: 17 | 488 | 36 |
| Hilton Head, SC (579) | I-95 | Beaufort (1)<br>Hilton Head (5) | | Hotels, Motels: 23<br>Campgrounds: 8 | 111 | Hotels: 5<br>Restaurants: — | 278 | 57 |
| Holland–Lake Michigan Shore, MI (3,590) | I-94<br>I-96<br>I-196 | Benton Harbor (1)<br>Grand Rapids (11)<br>Kalamazoo (2)<br>Muskegon (4) | *<br>* | Hotels, Motels: 88<br>Campgrounds: 33 | 868 | Hotels: 3<br>Restaurants: 1 | 292 | 53 |
| Houston–Galveston, TX (8,704) | I-10<br>I-45 | Clear Lake City (1)<br>Lake Jackson (1)<br>Houston (42) | ***<br> | Hotels, Motels: 388<br>Campgrounds: 31 | 4,523 | Hotels: 25<br>Restaurants: 13 | 738 | 22 |
| Jersey Shore, NJ (1,113) | — | Asbury Park (1) | | Hotels, Motels: 216<br>Campgrounds: 16 | 1,339 | Hotels: —<br>Restaurants: — | 1,411 | 11 |
| Knoxville–Smoky Mountains, TN (4,719) | I-40<br>I-75<br>I-81 | Knoxville (10) | * | Hotels, Motels: 315<br>Campgrounds: 71 | 951 | Hotels: 5<br>Restaurants: 2 | 313 | 51 |
| Lake of the Ozarks, MO (4,363) | I-44 | Lake Ozark (2) | | Hotels, Motels: 76<br>Campgrounds: 46 | 213 | Hotels: 2<br>Restaurants: 1 | 99 | 92 |
| Lake Powell–Glen Canyon, AZ–UT (22,494) | I-70 | Page, AZ (1)<br>Blanding, UT (1)<br>Moab, UT (1)<br>Monticello, UT (1) | | Hotels, Motels: 49<br>Campgrounds: 50 | 54 | Hotels: —<br>Restaurants: — | 7 | 107 |
| Lake Tahoe–Reno, NV-CA (8,867) | I-80 | Reno, NV (16)<br>South Lake Tahoe, CA (2) | ** | Hotels, Motels: 307<br>Campgrounds: 93 | 804 | Hotels: 11<br>Restaurants: 5 | 228 | 65 |
| Las Vegas-Lake Mead, NV-AZ (12,309) | I-15 | Bullhead City, AZ (1)<br>Kingman, AZ (1)<br>Lake Havasu City, AZ (1)<br>Las Vegas, NV (29) | ***<br> | Hotels, Motels: 229<br>Campgrounds: 56 | 782 | Hotels: 7<br>Restaurants: 4 | 153 | 79 |
| Lexington–Bluegrass Country, KY (5,330) | I-64<br>I-65<br>I-71<br>I-75 | Lexington (9)<br>Louisville (14) | *<br>** | Hotels, Motels: 164<br>Campgrounds: 20 | 1,638 | Hotels: 9<br>Restaurants: 6 | 436 | 39 |
| ★ Long Island, NY (1,199) | — | East Hampton (1)<br>Farmingdale (2)<br>Garden City (1)<br>Islip (7) | | Hotels, Motels: 223<br>Campgrounds: 4 | 3,908 | Hotels: 3<br>Restaurants: 1 | 2,206 | 6 |
| ★ Los Angeles, CA (6,730) | I-5<br>I-10<br>I-15 | Burbank (10)<br>Catalina (2)<br>Fullerton (1)<br>Long Beach (7)<br>Los Angeles (65)<br>Oxnard (1)<br>Palmdale (1)<br>Santa Ana (10) | ***<br> | Hotels, Motels: 1,323<br>Campgrounds: 116 | 11,259 | Hotels: 28<br>Restaurants: 59 | 2,357 | 4 |
| Mackinac Island–Sault Ste. Marie, MI (3,335) | I-75 | Mackinac Island (1)<br>Sault Ste. Marie (1) | | Hotels, Motels: 176<br>Campgrounds: 39 | 205 | Hotels: 2<br>Restaurants: — | 138 | 83 |
| Memphis, TN–AR–MS (2,308) | I-40 | Memphis (20) | ** | Hotels, Motels: 110<br>Campgrounds: 8 | 939 | Hotels: 3<br>Restaurants: 1 | 479 | 37 |
| Miami-Gold Coast-Keys, FL (5,197) | I-75<br>I-95 | Fort Lauderdale (27)<br>Homestead (1)<br>Key West (5)<br>Marathon (2)<br>Miami (82)<br>West Palm Beach (20) | ***<br>** | Hotels, Motels: 1,024<br>Campgrounds: 61 | 4,803 | Hotels: 23<br>Restaurants: 18 | 1,370 | 12 |
| Minneapolis–St. Paul, MN–WI (7,157) | I-35<br>I-94 | Mankato (1)<br>Minneapolis (26) | *** | Hotels, Motels: 240<br>Campgrounds: 43 | 2,968 | Hotels: 17<br>Restaurants: 5 | 551 | 32 |
| Mobile Bay–Gulfport, AL–MS (4,617) | I-10<br>I-65 | Gulfport, MS (1)<br>Mobile, AL (7) | * | Hotels, Motels: 138<br>Campgrounds: 24 | 862 | Hotels: 3<br>Restaurants: 1 | 251 | 60 |

| Vacation Place (Square Miles) | Interstate Highways | Airport Locations (Number of Carriers) | Hub Ratings | Accommodations | Eating and Drinking Places | Award Winners | Places Rated Score | Places Rated Rank |
|---|---|---|---|---|---|---|---|---|
| Monterey–Big Sur, CA (6,430) | — | Monterey (5) San Jose (14) | * | Hotels, Motels: 410 Campgrounds: 38 | 2,774 | Hotels: 12 Restaurants: 11 | 612 | 26 |
| Myrtle Beach–Grand Strand, SC (1,965) | — | Myrtle Beach (4) | | Hotels, Motels: 345 Campgrounds: 12 | 380 | Hotels: 12 Restaurants: — | 431 | 40 |
| Mystic Seaport–Connecticut Valley, CT (1,042) | I-95 | Hartford (30) New London (3) | ** | Hotels, Motels: 69 Campgrounds: 35 | 590 | Hotels: 1 Restaurants: — | 670 | 24 |
| Nashville, TN (4,060) | I-24 I-40 I-65 | Nashville (16) | ** | Hotels, Motels: 145 Campgrounds: 27 | 1,009 | Hotels: 7 Restaurants: 4 | 360 | 45 |
| New Orleans, LA (4,580) | I-10 I-55 | New Orleans (26) | *** | Hotels, Motels: 193 Campgrounds: 10 | 1,783 | Hotels: 11 Restaurants: 22 | 610 | 27 |
| ★ New York City, NY (914) | I-78 I-80 I-87 | New York City (100) White Plains (7) | *** | Hotels, Motels: 510 Campgrounds: 1 | 11,318 | Hotels: 21 Restaurants: 68 | 2,663 | 1 |
| Niagara Falls–Western New York, NY (3,942) | I-90 | Buffalo (16) Jamestown (1) Niagara Falls (2) | ** | Hotels, Motels: 179 Campgrounds: 71 | 2,570 | Hotels: 2 Restaurants: — | 723 | 23 |
| North Woods–Land O'Lakes, WI (3,749) | — | Rhinelander (1) | | Hotels, Motels: 113 Campgrounds: 68 | 224 | Hotels: — Restaurants: — | 108 | 90 |
| Oklahoma City–Cherokee Strip, OK (6,642) | I-35 I-40 | Oklahoma City (18) Enid (1) Ponca City (1) Stillwater (1) | ** | Hotels, Motels: 135 Campgrounds: 15 | 1,545 | Hotels: 4 Restaurants: — | 275 | 58 |
| Olympic Peninsula, WA (7,164) | — | Port Angeles (1) | | Hotels, Motels: 103 Campgrounds: 136 | 506 | Hotels: 5 Restaurants: 1 | 129 | 86 |
| Orlando–Space Coast, FL (5,873) | I-4 | Melbourne (4) Orlando (24) Vero Beach (1) | * ** | Hotels, Motels: 389 Campgrounds: 87 | 1,642 | Hotels: 6 Restaurants: 5 | 419 | 41 |
| Outer Banks, NC (3,409) | — | New Bern (1) | | Hotels, Motels: 150 Campgrounds: 29 | 267 | Hotels: — Restaurants: — | 131 | 85 |
| Ozarks–Eureka Springs, AR–MO (12,061) | I-44 | Fayetteville, AR (3) Harrison, AR (1) Mountain Home, AR (1) Springdale, AR (1) Joplin, MO (3) Springfield, MO (6) | * | Hotels, Motels: 214 Campgrounds: 127 | 938 | Hotels: 5 Restaurants: — | 126 | 88 |
| Palm Springs–Desert Playgrounds, CA (12,230) | I-10 | Blythe (1) Palm Springs (5) Riverside (1) | | Hotels, Motels: 315 Campgrounds: 55 | 1,791 | Hotels : 11 Restaurants: 1 | 248 | 61 |
| Panhandle, FL (5,004) | I-10 | Fort Walton Beach (4) Panama City (4) Pensacola (6) | * | Hotels, Motels: 211 Campgrounds: 43 | 780 | Hotels: 1 Restaurants: — | 215 | 67 |
| Pennsylvania Dutch Country, PA (5,236) | I-81 I-83 | Blue Bell (1) Harrisburg (7) Lancaster (1) Reading (2) | * | Hotels, Motels: 257 Campgrounds: 71 | 2,254 | Hotels: 5 Restaurants: 6 | 556 | 30 |
| ★ Philadelphia, PA–DE–NJ (3,928) | I-76 I-95 | Philadelphia (39) Wilmington, DE (2) | *** | Hotels, Motels: 439 Campgrounds: 23 | 6,712 | Hotels: 9 Restaurants: 11 | 1,922 | 7 |
| Phoenix–Valley of the Sun, AZ (14,470) | I-10 | Phoenix (30) | *** | Hotels, Motels: 275 Campgrounds: 84 | 2,349 | Hotels: 15 Restaurants: 2 | 335 | 47 |
| Pocono Mountains, PA (5,287) | I-80 I-81 I-84 | Allentown (7) Wilkes–Barre (4) | * * | Hotels, Motels: 247 Campgrounds: 68 | 2,027 | Hotels: 10 Restaurants: 2 | 497 | 35 |
| Portland, ME (2,944) | I-95 | Augusta (2) Lewiston (1) Portland (7) | * | Hotels, Motels: 226 Campgrounds: 76 | 702 | Hotels: 4 Restaurants: — | 357 | 46 |
| Portland–Columbia River, OR (8,744) | I-5 I-84 | Portland (24) Salem (1) | ** | Hotels, Motels: 249 Campgrounds: 173 | 2,499 | Hotels: 9 Restaurants: 4 | 404 | 42 |
| Portsmouth–Kennebunk, NH–ME (2,077) | I-93 I-95 | Manchester (8) | | Hotels, Motels: 310 Campgrounds: 85 | 692 | Hotels: 7 Restaurants: 1 | 556 | 30 |
| ★ Providence–Newport, RI (1,054) | I-95 | Providence (14) Westerly (1) | * | Hotels, Motels: 107 Campgrounds: 29 | 1,571 | Hotels: 1 Restaurants: — | 1,624 | 8 |
| Put-in-Bay–Lake Erie Shore, OH (2,293) | I-75 I-80 I-90 | Toledo (12) | * | Hotels, Motels: 133 Campgrounds: 28 | 1,336 | Hotels: — Restaurants: — | 653 | 25 |

| Vacation Place (Square Miles) | Interstate Highways | Airport Locations (Number of Carriers) | Hub Ratings | Accommodations | Eating and Drinking Places | Award Winners | Places Rated Score | Places Rated Rank |
|---|---|---|---|---|---|---|---|---|
| Rangeley Lakes, ME (4,496) | — | — | | Hotels, Motels: 32 Campgrounds: 14 | 73 | Hotels: — Restaurants: — | 26 | 105 |
| Redwoods–Shasta–Lassen, CA (17,843) | I-5 | Crescent City (1) Eureka (4) Redding (5) | | Hotels, Motels: 172 Campgrounds: 205 | 618 | Hotels: 3 Restaurants: — | 68 | 97 |
| Richmond–Fredericksburg, VA (3,896) | I-64 I-85 I-95 | Richmond (17) | * | Hotels, Motels: 127 Campgrounds: 17 | 652 | Hotels: 2 Restaurants: — | 212 | 69 |
| Sacramento–Gold Rush Towns, CA (6,009) | I-5 I-80 | Marysville (1) Sacramento (16) | * | Hotels, Motels: 232 Campgrounds: 78 | 1,718 | Hotels: 7 Restaurants: — | 366 | 44 |
| St. Augustine–Northeast Coast, FL (4,971) | I-10 I-95 | Daytona Beach (5) Jacksonville (15) St. Augustine (1) | * ** | Hotels, Motels: 425 Campgrounds: 44 | 1,541 | Hotels: 8 Restaurants: — | 448 | 38 |
| St. Louis–Mark Twain Country, MO–IL (6,349) | I-44 I-55 I-64 | St. Louis (31) | *** | Hotels, Motels: 200 Campgrounds: 26 | 2,606 | Hotels: 13 Restaurants: 12 | 574 | 29 |
| Salt Lake City, UT (6,447) | I-15 I-80 I-84 | Logan (1) Mount Pleasant (1) Provo (1) Salt Lake City (17) | ** | Hotels, Motels: 152 Campgrounds: 121 | 1,276 | Hotels: 15 Restaurants: 3 | 325 | 49 |
| San Antonio, TX (2,516) | I-10 I-35 I-37 | San Antonio (19) | ** | Hotels, Motels: 139 Campgrounds: 31 | 1,612 | Hotels: 10 Restaurants: 3 | 771 | 20 |
| San Diego, CA (4,212) | I-5 I-8 I-15 | Borrego Springs (1) Carlsbad (1) San Diego (23) | ** | Hotels, Motels: 402 Campgrounds: 70 | 2,855 | Hotels: 13 Restaurants: 6 | 881 | 18 |
| ★ San Francisco, CA (2,482) | I-80 | Oakland (15) San Francisco (40) | *** | Hotels, Motels: 551 Campgrounds: 20 | 5,878 | Hotels: 31 Restaurants: 56 | 2,651 | 2 |
| Santa Barbara–San Simeon, CA (6,056) | — | Santa Barbara (8) San Luis Obispo (2) Santa Maria (1) | | Hotels, Motels: 230 Campgrounds: 52 | 849 | Hotels: 12 Restaurants: 3 | 254 | 59 |
| Savannah–Golden Isles, GA (2,721) | I-95 | Brunswick (1) Savannah (9) | * | Hotels, Motels: 93 Campgrounds: 10 | 446 | Hotels: 5 Restaurants: 1 | 242 | 63 |
| Seattle–Mount Rainier–North Cascades, WA (10,366) | I-5 I-90 | Bellingham (1) Blakely Island (1) Friday Harbor (1) Mount Vernon (1) Oak Harbor (1) Seattle (35) | *** | Hotels, Motels: 363 Campgrounds: 168 | 3,812 | Hotels: 27 Restaurants: 11 | 594 | 28 |
| Spokane–Coeur d'Alene, WA–ID (13,292) | I-90 | Spokane (12) | ** | Hotels, Motels: 113 Campgrounds: 115 | 799 | Hotels: 5 Restaurants: — | 101 | 91 |
| Tampa Bay–Southwest Coast, FL (3,868) | I-4 I-75 | Fort Myers (12) Marco (1) Naples (3) Punta Gorda (1) Sarasota (14) Tampa (26) | * * *** | Hotels, Motels: 584 Campgrounds: 134 | 2,856 | Hotels: 16 Restaurants: 7 | 1,071 | 15 |
| Traverse City–Petoskey, MI (3,061) | — | Traverse City (3) | | Hotels, Motels: 106 Campgrounds: 53 | 299 | Hotels: 3 Restaurants: — | 166 | 75 |
| Tucson, AZ (10,425) | I-10 I-19 | Bisbee (1) Douglas (1) Tucson (18) | ** | Hotels, Motels: 119 Campgrounds: 79 | 865 | Hotels: 7 Restaurants: 3 | 149 | 80 |
| Tulsa–Lake O' The Cherokees, OK (11,186) | I-44 | Tulsa (18) | ** | Hotels, Motels: 144 Campgrounds: 106 | 1,322 | Hotels: 5 Restaurants: — | 177 | 74 |
| Vicksburg–Natchez–Baton Rouge, MS–LA (4,982) | I-10 I-12 I-20 | Baton Rouge, LA (6) Jackson, MS (7) Natchez (1) | * * | Hotels, Motels: 78 Campgrounds: 10 | 636 | Hotels: 1 Restaurants: 1 | 154 | 77 |
| Washington, DC–MD–VA (3,956) | I-66 I-95 | Washington (51) Manassas, VA (1) | *** | Hotels, Motels: 323 Campgrounds: 15 | 3,770 | Hotels: 20 Restaurants: 16 | 1,237 | 14 |
| White Mountains, NH (4,456) | I-93 | Berlin (1) | | Hotels, Motels: 223 Campgrounds: 99 | 277 | Hotels: 5 Restaurants: — | 154 | 77 |
| Williamsburg–Colonial Triangle, VA (2,317) | I-64 | Newport News (2) Norfolk (18) | ** | Hotels, Motels: 293 Campgrounds: 25 | 1,527 | Hotels: 3 Restaurants: 2 | 823 | 19 |
| Wilmington–Cape Fear, NC (1,046) | — | Wilmington (4) | | Hotels, Motels: 56 Campgrounds: 5 | 235 | Hotel: — Restaurants: — | 283 | 56 |
| Wine Country, CA (7,122) | — | Santa Rosa (2) | | Hotels, Motels: 206 Campgrounds: 76 | 911 | Hotels: 3 Restaurants: 5 | 214 | 68 |

| Vacation Place (Square Miles) | Interstate Highways | Airport Locations (Number of Carriers) | Hub Ratings | Accommodations | Eating and Drinking Places | Award Winners | Places Rated Score | Places Rated Rank |
|---|---|---|---|---|---|---|---|---|
| **Wisconsin Dells, WI** (5,515) | I-90 I-94 | Beloit (2) Madison (9) | * | Hotels, Motels: 187 Campgrounds: 81 | 1,289 | Hotels: 2 Restaurants: — | **290** | **54** |
| **Yellowstone–Jackson–Tetons, WY–ID–MT** (13,716) | — | Idaho Falls, ID (3) West Yellowstone, MT (2) Cody, WY (1) Jackson, WY (2) | | Hotels, Motels: 136 Campgrounds: 156 | 142 | Hotels: 10 Restaurants: 2 | **82** | **95** |
| **Yosemite–Sequoia–Death Valley, CA** (19,956) | — | Bishop (1) Death Valley (1) Mammoth Lakes (2) | | Hotels, Motels: 151 Campgrounds: 239 | 640 | Hotels: 1 Restaurants: — | **56** | **99** |
| **Zion–Bryce Canyon, UT** (14,644) | I-15 | Cedar City (1) Kanab (1) Panguitch (1) St. George (1) | | Hotels, Motels: 92 Campgrounds: 63 | 113 | Hotels: 1 Restaurants: — | **22** | **106** |

# RANKINGS: Basic Necessities

Five criteria were used to determine the scores for this chapter: (1) the number of hotels and motels and resorts per 1,000 square miles; (2) the number of campgrounds per 1,000 square miles; (3) the number of eating and drinking places per 1,000 square miles; (4) awards given for quality to certain hotels, motels, and resorts; (5) awards given for quality to certain restaurants.

Vacation Places that receive tie scores are given the same rank and are listed in alphabetic order.

## Vacation Places from First to Last

| Places Rated Rank | Places Rated Score | Places Rated Rank | Places Rated Score | Places Rated Rank | Places Rated Score |
|---|---|---|---|---|---|
| 1. New York City, NY | 2,663 | 38. St. Augustine–Northeast Coast, FL | 448 | 73. Colorado Springs, CO | 179 |
| 2. San Francisco, CA | 2,651 | 39. Lexington–Bluegrass Country, KY | 436 | 74. Tulsa–Lake O' The Cherokees, OK | 177 |
| 3. Chicago, IL | 2,562 | 40. Myrtle Beach–Grand Strand, SC | 431 | 75. Traverse City–Petoskey, MI | 166 |
| 4. Los Angeles, CA | 2,357 | 41. Orlando–Space Coast, FL | 419 | 76. Adirondack Mountains, NY | 155 |
| 5. Boston, MA | 2,262 | 42. Portland–Columbia River, OR | 404 | 77. Vicksburg–Natchez–Baton Rouge, MS–LA | 154 |
| 6. Long Island, NY | 2,206 | 43. Catskill Mountains, NY | 378 | 77. White Mountains, NH | 154 |
| 7. Philadelphia, PA–DE–NJ | 1,922 | 44. Sacramento–Gold Rush Towns, CA | 366 | 79. Las Vegas–Lake Mead, NV–AZ | 153 |
| 8. Providence–Newport, RI | 1,624 | 45. Nashville, TN | 360 | 80. Tucson, AZ | 149 |
| 9. Cape Cod–The Islands, MA | 1,432 | 46. Portland, ME | 357 | 81. Albuquerque–Santa Fe–Taos, NM | 148 |
| 10. Cincinnati, OH–KY | 1,431 | 47. Phoenix–Valley of the Sun, AZ | 335 | 82. Boone–High Country, NC | 146 |
| 11. Jersey Shore, NJ | 1,411 | 48. Finger Lakes, NY | 331 | 83. Mackinac Island–Sault Ste. Marie, MI | 138 |
| 12. Miami–Gold Coast–Keys, FL | 1,370 | 49. Salt Lake City, UT | 325 | 84. Eastern Shore, VA | 136 |
| 13. Atlantic City, NJ | 1,296 | 50. Door County, WI | 321 | 85. Outer Banks, NC | 131 |
| 14. Washington, DC–MD–VA | 1,237 | 51. Knoxville–Smoky Mountains, TN | 313 | 86. Olympic Peninsula, WA | 129 |
| 15. Tampa Bay–Southwest Coast, FL | 1,071 | 52. Green Mountains, VT | 293 | 87. Bar Harbor–Acadia, ME | 127 |
| 16. Baltimore–Chesapeake Bay, MD | 1,029 | 53. Holland–Lake Michigan Shore, MI | 292 | 88. Ozarks–Eureka Springs, AR–MO | 126 |
| 17. Dallas–Fort Worth, TX | 922 | 54. Wisconsin Dells, WI | 290 | 89. Crater Lake–Klamath Falls, OR | 110 |
| 18. San Diego, CA | 881 | 55. Brownsville–Rio Grande Valley, TX | 289 | 90. North Woods–Land O'Lakes, WI | 108 |
| 19. Williamsburg–Colonial Triangle, VA | 823 | 56. Wilmington–Cape Fear, NC | 283 | 91. Spokane–Coeur d'Alene, WA–ID | 101 |
| 20. San Antonio, TX | 771 | 57. Hilton Head, SC | 278 | 92. Lake of the Ozarks, MO | 99 |
| 21. Denver–Rocky Mountain National Park, CO | 768 | 58. Oklahoma City–Cherokee Strip, OK | 275 | 93. Coos Bay–South Coast, OR | 95 |
| 22. Houston–Galveston, TX | 738 | 59. Santa Barbara–San Simeon, CA | 254 | 94. Blue Ridge Mountains, VA | 91 |
| 23. Niagara Falls–Western New York, NY | 723 | 60. Mobile Bay–Gulfport, AL–MS | 251 | 95. Yellowstone–Jackson–Tetons, WY–ID–MT | 82 |
| 24. Mystic Seaport–Connecticut Valley, CT | 670 | 61. Palm Springs–Desert Playgrounds, CA | 248 | 96. Boise–Sun Valley, ID | 81 |
| 25. Put-in-Bay–Lake Erie Shore, OH | 653 | 62. Austin–Hill Country, TX | 245 | 97. Redwoods–Shasta–Lassen, CA | 68 |
| 26. Monterey–Big Sur, CA | 612 | 63. Savannah–Golden Isles, GA | 242 | 98. Bend–Cascade Mountains, OR | 63 |
| 27. New Orleans, LA | 610 | 64. Charleston, SC | 241 | 99. Yosemite–Sequoia–Death Valley, CA | 56 |
| 28. Seattle–Mount Rainier–North Cascades, WA | 594 | 65. Lake Tahoe–Reno, NV–CA | 228 | 100. Glacier National Park–Flathead Lake, MT | 54 |
| 29. St. Louis–Mark Twain Country, MO–IL | 574 | 66. Corpus Christi–Padre Island, TX | 226 | 101. Black Hills, SD | 53 |
| 30. Pennsylvania Dutch Country, PA | 556 | 67. Panhandle, FL | 215 | 102. Anchorage–Kenai Peninsula, AK | 51 |
| 30. Portsmouth–Kennebunk, NH–ME | 556 | 68. Wine Country, CA | 214 | 103. Grand Canyon Country, AZ | 39 |
| 32. Minneapolis–St. Paul, MN–WI | 551 | 69. Richmond—Fredericksburg, VA | 212 | 104. Flaming Gorge, UT–WY–CO | 31 |
| 33. Berkshire Hills–Pioneer Valley, MA | 534 | 70. Asheville–Smoky Mountains, NC | 209 | 105. Rangeley Lakes, ME | 26 |
| 34. Atlanta, GA | 499 | 71. Aspen–Vail, CO | 194 | 106. Zion–Bryce Canyon, UT | 22 |
| 35. Pocono Mountains, PA | 497 | 72. Chattanooga–Huntsville, TN–AL–GA | 184 | 107. Lake Powell–Glen Canyon, AZ–UT | 7 |
| 36. Hawaii | 488 | | | | |
| 37. Memphis, TN–AR–MS | 479 | | | | |

## Vacation Places Listed Alphabetically

| Vacation Place | Places Rated Rank | Vacation Place | Places Rated Rank | Vacation Place | Places Rated Rank |
|---|---|---|---|---|---|
| Adirondack Mountains, NY | 76 | Hilton Head, SC | 57 | Portland, ME | 46 |
| Albuquerque–Santa Fe–Taos, NM | 81 | Holland–Lake Michigan Shore, MI | 53 | | |
| Anchorage–Kenai Peninsula, AK | 102 | | | Portland–Columbia River, OR | 42 |
| Asheville–Smoky Mountains, NC | 70 | Houston–Galveston, TX | 22 | Portsmouth–Kennebunk, NH–ME | 30 |
| Aspen–Vail, CO | 71 | Jersey Shore, NJ | 11 | Providence–Newport, RI | 8 |
| | | Knoxville–Smoky Mountains, TN | 51 | Put-in-Bay–Lake Erie Shore, OH | 25 |
| Atlanta, GA | 34 | Lake of the Ozarks, MO | 92 | Rangeley Lakes, ME | 105 |
| Atlantic City, NJ | 13 | Lake Powell–Glen Canyon, AZ–UT | 107 | | |
| Austin–Hill Country, TX | 62 | | | Redwoods–Shasta–Lassen, CA | 97 |
| Baltimore–Chesapeake Bay, MD | 16 | Lake Tahoe–Reno, NV–CA | 65 | Richmond–Fredericksburg, VA | 69 |
| Bar Harbor–Acadia, ME | 87 | Las Vegas–Lake Mead, NV–AZ | 79 | Sacramento–Gold Rush Towns, CA | 44 |
| | | Lexington–Bluegrass Country, KY | 39 | St. Augustine–Northeast Coast, FL | 38 |
| Bend–Cascade Mountains, OR | 98 | Long Island, NY | 6 | St. Louis–Mark Twain Country, MO–IL | 29 |
| Berkshire Hills–Pioneer Valley, MA | 33 | Los Angeles, CA | 4 | | |
| Black Hills, SD | 101 | | | Salt Lake City, UT | 49 |
| Blue Ridge Mountains, VA | 94 | Mackinac Island–Sault Ste. Marie, MI | 83 | San Antonio, TX | 20 |
| Boise–Sun Valley, ID | 96 | Memphis, TN–AR–MS | 37 | San Diego, CA | 18 |
| | | Miami–Gold Coast–Keys, FL | 12 | San Francisco, CA | 2 |
| Boone–High Country, NC | 82 | Minneapolis–St. Paul, MN–WI | 32 | Santa Barbara–San Simeon, CA | 59 |
| Boston, MA | 5 | Mobile Bay–Gulfport, AL–MS | 60 | | |
| Brownsville–Rio Grande Valley, TX | 55 | | | Savannah–Golden Isles, GA | 63 |
| Cape Cod–The Islands, MA | 9 | Monterey–Big Sur, CA | 26 | Seattle–Mount Rainier–North Cascades, WA | 28 |
| Catskill Mountains, NY | 43 | Myrtle Beach–Grand Strand, SC | 40 | Spokane–Coeur d'Alene, WA–ID | 91 |
| | | Mystic Seaport–Connecticut Valley, CT | 24 | Tampa Bay–Southwest Coast, FL | 15 |
| Charleston, SC | 64 | Nashville, TN | 45 | Traverse City–Petoskey, MI | 75 |
| Chattanooga–Huntsville, TN–AL–GA | 72 | New Orleans, LA | 27 | | |
| Chicago, IL | 3 | | | Tucson, AZ | 80 |
| Cincinnati, OH–KY | 10 | New York City, NY | 1 | Tulsa–Lake O' The Cherokees, OK | 74 |
| Colorado Springs, CO | 73 | Niagara Falls–Western New York, NY | 23 | Vicksburg–Natchez–Baton Rouge, MS–LA | 77 |
| | | North Woods–Land O'Lakes, WI | 90 | Washington, DC–MD–VA | 14 |
| Coos Bay–South Coast, OR | 93 | Oklahoma City–Cherokee Strip, OK | 58 | White Mountains, NH | 77 |
| Corpus Christi–Padre Island, TX | 66 | Olympic Peninsula, WA | 86 | | |
| Crater Lake–Klamath Falls, OR | 89 | | | Williamsburg–Colonial Triangle, VA | 19 |
| Dallas–Fort Worth, TX | 17 | Orlando–Space Coast, FL | 41 | Wilmington–Cape Fear, NC | 56 |
| Denver–Rocky Mountain National Park, CO | 21 | Outer Banks, NC | 85 | Wine Country, CA | 68 |
| | | Ozarks–Eureka Springs, AR–MO | 88 | Wisconsin Dells, WI | 54 |
| Door County, WI | 50 | Palm Springs–Desert Playgrounds, CA | 61 | Yellowstone–Jackson–Tetons, WY–ID–MT | 95 |
| Eastern Shore, VA | 84 | Panhandle, FL | 67 | | |
| Finger Lakes, NY | 48 | | | Yosemite–Sequoia–Death Valley, CA | 99 |
| Flaming Gorge, UT–WY–CO | 104 | Pennsylvania Dutch Country, PA | 30 | Zion–Bryce Canyon, UT | 106 |
| Glacier National Park–Flathead Lake, MT | 100 | Philadelphia, PA–DE–NJ | 7 | | |
| | | Phoenix–Valley of the Sun, AZ | 47 | | |
| Grand Canyon Country, AZ | 103 | Pocono Mountains, PA | 35 | | |
| Green Mountains, VT | 52 | | | | |
| Hawaii | 36 | | | | |

# TOP TEN: Basic Necessities

It is not surprising to see that the major cities and heavily populated areas earn the most points in Basic Necessities. Sheer numbers of people congregating in and passing through these major metropolitan areas create a constant demand for sleeping and eating accommodations.

New York, Chicago, Los Angeles, and Philadelphia, ranking first, third, fourth, and seventh, respectively, are four of the five largest cities in the United States. Such cities as Houston, Dallas, San Diego, San Antonio, and Phoenix, all of which are now among the largest in the country, have not yet caught up with the older metro areas in availability of accommodations. They are certainly working on catching up, however, with new places springing up every few weeks.

Unfortunately, the latest figures available from U.S. Bureau of the Census publications concerning total numbers of these business establishments are already several years old. No doubt the next census will show tremendous increases in this category in the Sun Belt cities that have recently climbed toward the top in population.

At the same time, however, such cities as New York and Boston have been, and still are, experiencing a healthy growth in new construction of hotels and related businesses.

| | Places Rated Score |
|---|---|
| 1. New York City, NY | 2,663 |
| 2. San Francisco, CA | 2,651 |
| 3. Chicago, IL | 2,562 |
| 4. Los Angeles, CA | 2,357 |
| 5. Boston, MA | 2,262 |
| 6. Long Island, NY | 2,206 |
| 7. Philadelphia, PA–DE–NJ | 1,922 |
| 8. Providence–Newport, RI | 1,624 |
| 9. Cape Cod–The Islands, MA | 1,432 |
| 10. Cincinnati, OH–KY | 1,431 |

## 1. New York City, NY

Campgrounds are scarce in and around the Big Apple, but New York City ranks third among all Vacation Places in the number of hotels and motels per square mile. Despite this, rooms are often in short supply here, and travelers should make advance reservations to be sure of having a bed. Several of the city's award-winning hotels have been famous for many years: the Waldorf-Astoria, Ritz-Carlton, St. Regis, and Plaza to name a few.

New York placed first in the number of award-winning restaurants. As an entry point for generations of newcomers from all over the world, New York has ethnic neighborhoods that represent all continents and nearly every nation. This ethnic diversity is reflected in the number and variety of restaurants, offering foods originating from not just dozens of countries but also from scores of regions within those countries. Whether your taste runs to Greek, Chinese, or French—or more unusual types such as Brazilian, Korean, or Armenian —a quick browse through the phone book leads you to just about any kind of food you can think of. And New York delicatessens are in a class by themselves—they are imitated widely but not really duplicated anywhere.

## 2. San Francisco, CA

The City by the Bay has an enviable (and deserved) reputation as a place to visit. The hospitality industry, responding to the city's popularity, has provided both quantity and quality in hotels and restaurants. It ranks fourth among Vacation Places in availability of hotels and motels, fourth in availability of eating and drinking places, second in number of award-winning hotels, and third in award-winning restaurants. Like New York, San Francisco is a cosmopolitan city with many cultures represented among its residents— especially Oriental cultures. San Francisco's Chinatown has several top-notch Oriental spots.

## 3. Chicago, IL

Chicago has enjoyed a hotel-building boom in recent years, and at the same time a number of well-known older hotels have been rejuvenated. For example, the old Conrad Hilton, built in 1927 and at one time billed as the largest hotel in the world, was reopened as the Chicago Hilton and Towers in late 1985 after a nine-month, $150-million reconstruction project. Chicago ranks fifth among Vacation Places in availability of hotels, second in availability of eating and drinking places, sixth in award-winning hotels, and fourth in award-winning restaurants.

## 4. Los Angeles, CA

Los Angeles placed sixth in availability of hotels and motels, seventh in availability of eating and drinking places, third in the number of award-winning hotels, and second in award-winning restaurants. Several major chains have award-winning hotels in Los Angeles. Award winners in Beverly Hills include two old and elegant hotels along with a couple of newer ones. Anaheim, Long Beach, and a few other suburbs also contributed to the high score of this Vacation Place.

## 5. Boston, MA

Boston ranks fifth among Vacation Places for availability of restaurants. Seafood is a specialty here near the source of all kinds of saltwater bounties. While it did not place among the top ten in any other single category for this chapter, Boston's list of four-star and four-diamond hotels and restaurants is quite long, and several of its hotels—such as the Copley Plaza, the Parker House, and the Ritz-Carlton—have a long and fascinating history. Two excellent restaurants that should not be missed are Anthony's Pier Four and the Cafe Budapest. Also, any visitor to Boston should be sure to investigate the various eating places in historic Faneuil Hall and Quincy Market.

## 6. Long Island, NY

More than 7 million people live on this 120-mile island, yet its beaches and resort areas make it a fine vacation destination. It has an excellent supply of sleeping and eating accommodations: it ranks ninth among the Vacation Places for availability of hotels and third for availability of eating and drinking places. As one travels east from New York City, city becomes suburbia and then gives way to smaller villages and finally to seaside resort communities.

## 7. Philadelphia, PA–DE–NJ

Philadelphia placed sixth for the availability of eating and drinking places. Le Bec Fin, a very expensive French-style restaurant, is considered to be one of the finest in the nation, and Bookbinder's, established in 1865, is a tourist attraction for its historic atmosphere and a few of its world-famous dishes.

## 8. Providence–Newport, RI

This Vacation Place, which actually takes in the entire tiny state of Rhode Island, ranks seventh in availability of campgrounds and eighth in availability of restaurants. Italians and Portuguese were major settlers in Providence, and excellent restaurants reflect these influences. Newport's waterfront has a row of fine seafood restaurants. Visitors to this city should visit the White Horse Tavern, claimed to be the oldest operating tavern in America. The building, originally constructed as a residence, dates from the 17th century.

## 9. Cape Cod–The Islands, MA

Cape Cod and the islands of Nantucket and Martha's Vineyard, some of the oldest popular vacationing areas in the United States, rank second in availability of hotels and motels and second in campgrounds. There are a number of historic and charming country inns in the area: one is the Jared Coffin House on Nantucket, a restored mansion built in 1845; another is the Daniel Webster Inn in Sandwich—not old but very nice.

## 10. Cincinnati, OH–KY

Cincinnati ranks ninth in availability of restaurants, and while it did not place in the top ten for number of award winners, the Queen City, as it has been popularly called since the poet Longfellow coined the nickname, has enjoyed a reputation for some time of having some of the best restaurants between New York and Chicago. Among them are Maisonette, Pigall's French Restaurant, La Normandie Taverne and Chop House, the Gourmet Room at the Terrace Hilton, and Robert's at the Carrousel Inn. Visitors to this city should make a point of taking a look at the Netherland Plaza, a beautifully restored hotel built more than 50 years ago.

---

### Author's Favorites

**Cities for Eating Out**
Chicago, IL
Cincinnati, OH
New Orleans, LA
San Francisco, CA
Savannah, GA

**City Hotels**
Hyatt Regency, Long Beach, CA
L'Ermitage, Beverly Hills, CA
Mayfair Regent, Chicago, IL
Netherland Plaza, Cincinnati, OH
Peabody Hotel, Memphis, TN
Regency, New York, NY

**Resort Hotels**
Amelia Island Plantation, Amelia Island, FL
Boca Raton Hotel and Club, Boca Raton, FL
Cloister, Sea Island, GA
Mauna Kea Beach Hotel, Waimea, HI
Topnotch at Stowe, Stowe, VT

**Restaurants**
Cafe Chauveron, Miami, FL
Harralds, Fishkill, NY
Kennebunk Inn, Kennebunk, ME
Maisonette, Cincinnati, OH
Rancho del Rio Tack Room, Tucson, AZ
Tony's, St. Louis, MO
Yoshi's Cafe, Chicago, IL

# Discovering Our Heritage

## Historical Landmarks and Museums

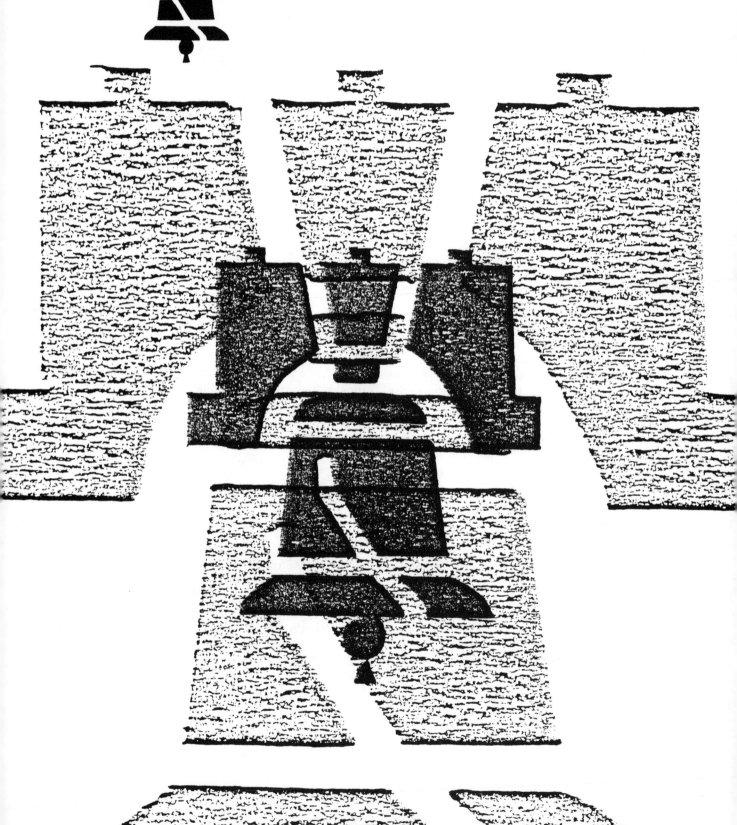

# INTRODUCTION: Discovering Our Heritage

"What is the main thing that brings people here?" a reporter asked the director of one of the country's best-known living history museums.

"Guilt!" he replied. "That's what brings parents here with their children. They feel guilty about taking their kids on a vacation that doesn't include something a little bit educational.

"As for the adults who come without children, the operative word is *nostalgia*. People are very sentimental about bygone days. There's a widespread notion that people who lived in earlier periods had a simpler —and happier—life."

Pride in our heritage and curiosity about our ancestors are two of humankind's most universal traits. What did our ancestors eat, wear, read, and do for fun? What were their homes like? How did they survive without supermarkets and shopping malls?

This curiosity, this fascination with the past, accounts for the high ratings of historic television dramas, keeps writers of historic novels—such as James Michener—producing best-sellers, and explains the proliferation of history museums and history publications. More than half of the 6,000-plus museums listed in *The Official Museum Directory*, published annually by the American Association of Museums, are history museums or include historic collections among their displays. According to the *Standard Periodical Directory*, more than 800 periodicals devoted to history and archeology are published in the United States and Canada.

## HISTORIC SIGHTSEEING

Long lines of travelers visit the famous historic landmarks of the United States nearly every day of the year. One does not have to be a student of history to enjoy the beauty of the nation's Capitol, in Washington, DC; to appreciate the genius of Thomas Jefferson, illustrated by the many practical inventions on display at his home, Monticello, near Charlottesville, Virginia; or to be thrilled by the sight of the rock onto which the Pilgrims first stepped, on display at Plymouth, Massachusetts. Many people who actually hated history as a school subject get turned on to the past by traveling to such fascinating national shrines as the Liberty Bell Pavillion, in Philadelphia, or the Museum of Westward Expansion housed at the base of the Gateway Arch in St. Louis. Nearly 6 million visits were made to Philadelphia's Independence National Historic Park in 1983; just under 3 million to the Jefferson National Expansion Memorial in St. Louis.

These are only some of the most obvious examples of the historic sightseeing opportunities available in the United States. Each state has its own treasure trove of local history in its capital city and other locations. In any state capital, especially during the spring months, throngs of schoolchildren crowd into the balconies of legislative chambers to watch government in action, finger the exhibits in museums of state history, climb over the statues of state heroes, and snap pictures of each other shaking hands with governors and state senators. Even greater hordes—honeymooners, packaged-tour customers, school and club groups, and families—descend on Washington, DC, each year.

Some of the more than 3,000 historic museums and other historic buildings and sites in every section of this country are so extensive and elaborate that one could spend weeks just scratching the surface of what they offer; others can be toured in less than an hour.

A little-known local museum or site can be as interesting for a short visit as some of those with an international reputation. A one-room schoolhouse where a visitor might read the century-old minutes of a board-of-education session and perhaps follow a debate over the salary and duties of a new schoolmarm or schoolmaster; a railroad station where a child can click out a message in Morse code on an ancient Western Union transmitter; or a log cabin in Texas chinked with stones that were made to be removed on hot summer days to provide a little natural air-conditioning—local sites such as these can be as enlightening as more famous national attractions.

## Events and Activities

In Manteo, North Carolina, near the site where Sir Walter Raleigh's expedition first came ashore in 1585, a historic drama called *The Lost Colony* that portrays the story of that ill-fated early settlement has been performed for nearly 50 years. This successful and popular production, originally staged in 1937, was the first of dozens of outdoor dramas that have been presented in various amphitheaters ever since. Some have achieved an enviable longevity; others have endured for only a few seasons.

The historic drama or pageant is one way people celebrate the past; there are many others. An increasingly popular one is the *reenactment*. Revolutionary and Civil War battles and other historic events are reenacted, some of them annually, on the exact spot and anniversary of the original happening. Participants research the event as thoroughly as possible, select roles of people who actually took part in the experience, create or procure authentic costumes, and convene at the appointed time and place to play out the piece of history.

One of the more elaborate reenactments is the

*Overmountain Victory Trail.* Each year marchers start from various points in Virginia, North Carolina, and Tennessee; convene at Sycamore Shoals, Tennessee; and on September 26 begin a ten-day trek following a trail over the mountains of North Carolina and Tennessee to Kings Mountain National Military Park in South Carolina. The battle of Kings Mountain, on October 7, 1780, is credited with turning the tide of the Revolution.

Anniversaries of historic events are celebrated with parades, fairs, reunions, and special projects. Towns and cities often mark a centennial, sesquicentennial, bicentennial, or tricentennial with a homecoming, encouraging all past residents and descendants of residents to convene and have a good time.

## Preservation and Restoration

Anniversaries often provide an impetus for residents of an area to establish something that commemorates the past more permanently than does a celebration. Public parks, monuments, fountains, and museums are built; preservation and restoration projects are undertaken. Hundreds of continuing projects have resulted from the nationwide celebration of the American Revolution Bicentennial in 1976.

The Mount Vernon Ladies' Association, founded in 1853 and still going strong, is considered to be the first major force to have accomplished the restoration and preservation of an important historic site. A woman named Ann Pamela Cunningham is known as the founder of this preservation movement. She prodded a small group of women to do something about the rapidly deteriorating condition of Mount Vernon, George Washington's estate. Their efforts resulted in nationwide publicity and interest, and they raised enough money to repair and restore the mansion and grounds. Original furnishings were recovered and returned to the mansion, and the house and grounds were opened to the public as a national shrine. Mount Vernon continues to be maintained and managed by the association today.

A few other voluntary organizations followed the example of the Mount Vernon Ladies' Association and successfully initiated local preservation projects over

## Colonial Williamsburg

The two men primarily responsible for arousing the interest of 20th-century Americans in the preservation and restoration of important historic landmarks in the United States were the Reverend W. A. R. Goodwin, at one time the rector of a church in Williamsburg, Virginia, and philanthropist John D. Rockefeller, Jr.

Goodwin had the dream, and he persuaded Rockefeller to provide the initial capital. The first steps were taken in 1926, when the Colonial Williamsburg Foundation was established.

Williamsburg's historic importance as the colonial capital of Virginia is unique. It was here that a young man named Thomas Jefferson came to study law and later to take a seat in the colonial legislature. It was in Williamsburg that George Washington, Patrick Henry, George Mason, Peyton Randolph, Richard Henry Lee, and other prominent Virginians helped develop the concepts of self-government and individual liberty that led to the American Revolution and the subsequent establishment of a new nation.

In addition to historic significance, as the site of world-changing events, Williamsburg was almost without equal as a gem of 18th-century architecture. It had some of the most striking public buildings that existed in all of the English colonies. When restoration was begun, the original colonial town plan was still relatively undisturbed, and many of the original buildings still stood.

The first restoration project, the Wren Building at the College of William and Mary, was finished in 1931. Today Colonial Williamsburg consists of about 150 restored and reconstructed buildings—shops, taverns, houses, and public buildings. Nearly 50 are open to visitors. Many of the private houses are rented to members of the Colonial Williamsburg staff, so the lovely old village is a lively, lived-in place. Everything on display under the auspices of the Colonial Williamsburg Foundation is authentic to the period; nothing is allowed that would not have been used before 1800.

More than 100 employees of the foundation are master craftspeople, journeymen, and apprentices who demonstrate the skills and crafts of colonial days; they work with the same tools in use in the 18th century. Interpreters in colonial dress are on hand in all buildings open to the public, ready to answer questions and offer information. The scene includes horse-drawn carriages and carts, fruit trees, vegetable gardens, and a herdsman with his sheep, all of which illustrate the rural nature of colonial towns—even those that were important capital cities. Food prepared from colonial recipes is served in the restaurants; special celebrations for such holidays as Christmas and Independence Day reflect the customs of two centuries ago.

Servants' quarters are furnished with appropriately humble furniture; the former homes of people of high standing display the finest of antique furniture, china, glass, and fabrics.

Without a doubt, Colonial Williamsburg has inspired the residents of many other towns and historic districts to take steps to preserve their community's uniqueness: excellent preservation and restoration work has been done in countless other places. But none has yet equaled Williamsburg in sheer size and effort. This is not a place for a casual afternoon's visit; it charms most visitors into staying longer and coming back more often than they had originally planned.

## Outstanding Historical Sites

### Outstanding Living History Museums, Archeological Sites and Museums, and Presidential Sites

Listed below are the special sites that are designated with two flags (◄ ◄) in the Place Profiles. The two-flag symbol means that an attraction, because of its extensive exhibits and importance, was judged to be worth a visit of at least a day.

**Living History Museums**
Colonial Williamsburg, Williamsburg, VA
Greenfield Village, Dearborn, MI
Meadow Farm Museum, Richmond, VA
Mystic Seaport, Mystic, CT
Old Sturbridge Village, Sturbridge, MA
Plimoth Plantation, Plymouth, MA

**Archeological Sites and Museums**
Bandelier National Monument, Los Alamos, NM
Casa Grande Ruins, near Coolidge, AZ
Chaco Culture National Historical Park, Bloomfield, NM
Montezuma Castle National Monument, Cottonwood, AZ
Pecos National Monument, Santa Fe, NM
Salinas National Monument, Mountainair, NM
Serpent Mound State Memorial, Locust Grove, OH
Tonto National Monument, Globe, AZ
Tuzigoot National Monument, Clarkdale, AZ
Walnut Canyon, Flagstaff, AZ
Wupatki National Monument, Flagstaff, AZ

**Presidential Sites**
Home of Franklin D. Roosevelt National Historic Site, Hyde Park, NY
Monticello, Charlottesville, VA
Sagamore Hill National Historic Site, Oyster Bay, NY
Truman Home, Library, and Museum, Independence, MO

## History and Tourism

In a questionnaire circulated by Editorial/Research Service in 1984, state tourism directors were asked what they considered to be the major attractions that brought visitors to their respective states. Answers were usually based on surveys the states had conducted at welcome centers. Nearly half mentioned history or something similar, such as western heritage.

A town, city, or region that preserves and celebrates its past discovers some important side benefits, not the least of which is the increased civic pride that results from their "clean-up, fix-up" campaigns. A snowball effect starts to work: parks are beautified; hotels are refurbished and new ones are built; store owners give their properties a face-lift; and contemporary uses are found for sound old buildings—such as factories—no longer in service for their original purpose.

## HISTORIC SITES AND MUSEUMS

Historic Marker Ahead proclaims a roadside sign, and many a driver slows down and pulls off the highway to read the sign and find out just what significant event occurred on this spot.

Historic sites come in all shapes and sizes. Some are as simple as the roadside marker, some are entire towns, and some are battlefields and cemeteries covering thousands of acres.

This chapter looks at several kinds of historic sites and museums, which have been divided into the following categories: Living History Museums, History Museums, Archeological Sites and Museums, Presidential Sites, House Museums and Historic Buildings, Military Landmarks, Historic Districts, and Special Attractions.

### Living History Museums—Where the Past Is Relived

Swinging a pail in time to her long stride, a young woman in a long muslin gown, white apron, and sunbonnet sets off across the fields toward a barn. She stops at a pump to draw a drink of water—and discovers that her pail is leaking.

She is one of the interpreters at Old Sturbridge Village, a living history museum in Massachusetts. Her job is to milk the cows and discuss the life-style of the 1830s in New England with onlookers.

You might expect that at this point she would go to a "prop room" and get another pail, but not so. The rules of her employment are such that she must react to the situation as a milkmaid of the period would have—so she goes to the village smithy and says, "Please, kind Sir, can you repair my bucket for me right away? The cows are waiting, and I haven't another bucket."

The best living history museums go to great lengths

the next 73 years, but the next huge push toward arousing public interest in restoration was the establishment of the Colonial Williamsburg Foundation in 1926. Since then, local history associations, preservation societies, and architectural organizations have had great success in saving historic houses and neighborhoods in many towns and cities.

Some areas have always had a tradition of preservation. Looking at old houses in New England villages might make you think that these thrifty Yankees never threw anything away. Many of the venerable mansions in Charleston, South Carolina, and some of the James River plantations in Virginia are still owned and kept up by descendants of the families who originally built them. And in Lexington, Kentucky, your tour guide will tell you proudly, "We haven't needed a restoration project here; we've *preserved* our heritage."

for authenticity in order to give visitors as realistic a view as possible of everyday life during a particular period in history.

Living history museums typically consist of several buildings representing an entire plantation, settlement, or village of a given time. Authentic buildings, standing on their original site or moved from a nearby location, are a part of the scene. Occasionally a reproduction of an important structure is added to round out the picture. The buildings are filled with furniture, personal possessions, tools, and other artifacts of the period portrayed. As far as possible the setting includes nothing that could not have been in existence at that place and at that given time. Costumed guides and interpreters play the parts of farmers, shopkeepers, bankers, housewives, ministers, dressmakers, teachers, and craftspeople; all demonstrate and explain their respective occupations.

Living history museums give visitors a unique opportunity to experience life at a particular time in the past—to travel figuratively through time. You can smell the smells of open-hearth cooking and freshly sawed lumber; sit on the hard bench of an early Puritan church and sense the rigor of listening attentively to two-hour sermons; feel the strain of carrying every drop of water needed for drinking, cooking, and washing from a well situated several hundred feet away from the kitchen; and imagine the pain of trying to sleep in subfreezing weather in drafty attic rooms with no source of heat.

In some cases it is hard to draw a line separating a living history museum from other types. Craft demonstrations and other types of historic interpretations are offered in some museums—either during the peak tourist season or all year-round. The National Park Service produces special interpretive programs at scheduled times at a number of their units, while at other times the buildings may simply be open for viewing, without any guide service.

*Village Museums.* Living history museums are usually also *village museums*. That is, they are housed in a group of varied structures originally built for other uses, not as display buildings. Not all village museums fit the definition of *living history museums*, however, because they do not have craft demonstrations and costumed interpreters acting out roles.

Two of the most interesting village museums in this country are the Shelburne Museum in Shelburne, Vermont, and the Museum of Appalachia in Norris, Tennessee.

Electra Havemeyer Webb created the Shelburne Museum. She came from a wealthy family and had been taught to appreciate fine art. Her family considered her interest in handmade, primitive objects and such mundane items as buggies to be eccentric, if not downright crazy. Museum experts call the Shelburne Museum a "collection of collections." It doesn't represent any one historic period but is rather an eclectic hodgepodge of Americana. There are farmhouses and barns; a sawmill, church, general store, and lighthouse; and a couple of dozen other buildings containing old quilts, hooked rugs, hatboxes, dolls, ships' figureheads, cigar-store Indians, and many other items. There's even a steamboat that once cruised the waters of Lake Champlain.

The Museum of Appalachia, in Norris, Tennessee, is an impressive collection of 30 buildings from nearby mountain settlements that contain literally hundreds of thousands of implements, tools, and gadgets used by the people of the area. This museum is also the work of one individual, John Rice Irwin, who has meticulously documented and labeled nearly every item on display.

## History Museums

On the main street of the tiny (population 274) village of Andersonville, Georgia, a single room houses The Drummer Boy Civil War Exposition, a history museum containing a million-dollar collection of flags, uniforms, weapons, documents, and other period pieces. This collection, gathered over a lifetime by another single collector (Gerald Lamby), is excellently displayed and documented.

Museums of this modest size exist in hundreds of U.S. towns. Not all are of this quality, but every one represents the efforts of individuals and local groups to preserve bits of the past for the enjoyment and education of future generations.

At the other end of the scale in size is the Smithsonian Institution, or "Uncle Sam's attic," in Washington, DC. Established in 1846 by Congress with funds bequeathed to the United States by James Smithson, an Englishman who had never even visited the United States, the institution is involved in many educational and research activities and administers nearly a dozen museums. The National Museum of American History is one of the Smithsonian branches. Its exhibits include collections of decorative arts, coins, stamps, gowns worn by each of the first ladies, ship models, and dozens of other displays.

Major history museums exist in nearly all state capitals and large cities. Some cover a wide span of history; some are limited to a certain period, a specific region, or a particular subject. In San Antonio, Texas, the Institute of Texan Cultures examines the contributions made to the state by 26 different ethnic groups who have migrated there. A fine small museum in Cherokee, North Carolina, traces the history of a single Native American tribe—the Cherokee. People especially interested in the history of Native Americans also enjoy the Sioux Indian Museum in Rapid City, South Dakota, and the Museum of Native American Culture in Spokane, Washington.

The past of Key West, Florida, is commemorated in the East Martello Gallery and Museum, housed in an old fort. Exhibits range from pieces of "gingerbread" railings from the Bahamian-style houses typical of the town to personal possessions of the late Ernest Hemingway, whose home was here. The museum's curator actually followed a truck and rescued some of the items now on display as they were being carted off to the town dump.

If you are particularly fond of the vacation destination you have chosen to visit, your appreciation of it will be even deeper if you find out a bit about its past by visiting the local museum. All but 10 of the 107 Vacation Places in this book have history museums, and their variety is enormous.

## Archeological Sites and Museums

Imagine what it would be like to live in a home built of tree branches or animal skins or carved out of a cliff; to make every item needed for clothing, for preparing and storing food, and for fishing and hunting; to have no stores, no schools, and no transportation other than horses. Archeology is the discipline that has grown out of humankind's curiosity about the life-styles of people who lived in the distant past. Archeological sites and museums are places any of us can visit to satisfy some of that curiosity pleasantly and painlessly.

Thanks to the efforts of archeologists encouraged and assisted by universities and such government agencies as the National Park Service, National Forest Service, and Bureau of Land Management, recreations of ancient homes and villages have been built to give vacationers exceptional opportunities to glimpse life as it was lived by Native Americans who lived many hundreds of years ago.

Most of the archeological sites and museums listed in the Place Profiles for this chapter are concerned with the life of prehistoric Native Americans, but a few relate to the dinosaur age and some contain relics of colonial settlements. Of the approximately 50 sites listed, half are in the southwestern United States: Arizona, Colorado, Nevada, New Mexico, Utah and southern California. There is a good reason for this: the study of archeology is a much simpler and more successful undertaking in places where the climate is hot and dry. Ancient artifacts, well preserved in desertlike areas, rot and crumble in soils that are subjected to dampness and severe changes in temperature. Nevertheless, some important finds have also been made in the Mississippi River valley and in Florida and Georgia.

The most famous and important archeological site in this country—Mesa Verde National Park in southwestern Colorado—is not within one of the 107 Vacation Places, but it is well worth a side trip for anyone who can fit it into the vacation itinerary. Not as elaborate as Mesa Verde and representing a slightly later period (15th century)—but equally fascinating—is Bandelier National Monument near Los Alamos, New Mexico. This is a preserve of more than 36,000 acres, of which two-thirds is wilderness—an ideal spot

for combining archeology with camping and hiking.

True archeology buffs can find enough sites in northern Arizona and New Mexico to keep them busy for several vacations.

Three interesting archeological sites and museums are in the Southeast. The Chucalissa Indian Village and Museum, in Memphis, Tennessee, is a reconstructed settlement with very informative exhibits about the inhabitants of the ancient Mississippi Valley. Temple Mound Museum, Fort Walton Beach, Florida, is built atop an Indian mound right in the middle of the city; its exhibits illustrate 10,000 years of life in Florida's Panhandle. The museum at Etowah Mounds Archaeological Area, Cartersville, Georgia, near Atlanta, has two remarkable figurines; they are two feet tall, carved of marble, and in excellent condition. These and other grave goods found at this site illustrate a wealthy and sophisticated society that was once established here.

## Presidential Sites

As you board the tour bus in Johnson City, Texas, a voice on the loudspeaker says, "This is my country, the hill country of Texas where I'd always return," and if you're old enough, you recognize the tones and accent of Lyndon B. Johnson himself.

A battered felt hat hangs on the hook by the back door of a modest home in Independence, Missouri. It's the same one seen in so many news photos snapped of the late Harry S Truman as he set out on his morning constitutionals.

A shiny (though slightly dented) Ford V-8 is displayed in a glass cage in Warm Springs, Georgia. The hand controls are a reminder that, even though he couldn't walk, Franklin D. Roosevelt drove himself over the hills and back roads surrounding his retreat, the little cabin in the woods, as he called it.

A huge living room in Oyster Bay, New York, is decorated with the mounted heads of big game and furnished with heavy, massive chairs and couches. It looks so appropriate for his bombastic personality, you almost expect to see Teddy Roosevelt stride in.

Among the most popular historic attractions in the United States are the homes in which presidents have lived. Some, such as Washington's Mount Vernon and Jackson's Hermitage in Nashville, Tennessee, reflect a degree of opulent living to be admired, maybe even envied; while others, like Lincoln's quite ordinary house in Springfield, Illinois, and Hoover's in West Branch, Iowa, are surprising in their modesty.

Perhaps the aspect of presidents' homes that makes each of them so fascinating, in addition to what they tell us about the men themselves, is that the homes reflect with great authenticity the American way of life at very specific moments in time. We can look at the buggies in which earlier presidents made the long trip to Washington and marvel at the men's stamina; admire the fashionable furnishings of the period in the

## Old Mills, New Uses

Factories—are they the lifeblood of the economy or eyesores on the landscape? Sources of jobs or well-springs of water and air pollution? Crumbling old buildings to be torn down or gems of architecture to be preserved for imaginative new uses?

The northeastern part of the United States, from Philadelphia to Chicago and (mostly) northward, was once looked upon as the industrial underpinning of the country. The area is now called—sadly or derisively, depending on your point of view—the Rust Belt.

But here and there old factories have had a rebirth. Abandoned structures, rotting and falling down, have been discovered by imaginative developers and preservationists and given new life. Some of them are used as homes for new industry; many others are being cleaned up, repaired, and converted into space for a variety of new uses.

In Winooski, Vermont, a handsome four-story brick building stands on a river bank; outside the front entrance is a tidy, circular lawn surrounded by a brick walk and flanked by resting and strolling areas. The old Champlain Mill is now a shopping mall, complete with boutiques, restaurants, and coffee shops. Many other small New England factories have been given similar treatment.

In Columbus, Georgia, the city's convention center is a huge building with vast, imposing exhibit and dining areas; it is a former textile factory. Parts of old machinery are displayed on the walls as modern art and incorporated into pieces of furniture.

One of the most extensive storehouses of structurally sound, architecturally attractive factory buildings is in Lowell, Massachusetts—a city that claims to be the birthplace of the Industrial Revolution. Lowell was the first planned industrial city in the United States, where the mass production of textiles originated. New England farm girls were recruited to run the new power looms and were given housing in local boarding houses.

The National Park Service, the state of Massachusetts, and various local groups are cooperating to restore, little by little, the many blocks of old factories, boarding houses, and other historic buildings—many of which still stand idle. Some have been converted into housing units, both low-rent apartments for senior citizens and low-income families, and condominiums for sale to more affluent Lowell residents. Some areas are in use as museum rooms and interpretive centers by the federal and state park services; some have become shopping and eating spaces; some are occupied once again by industrial firms.

The conversion of old industrial buildings for new uses is an economic advantage—the conversions ordinarily take much less time and cost far less than the construction of new facilities. The bonus for the sightseer is that these places open a window on America's industrial past and offer a new appreciation of a part of America's heritage.

home given to General Ulysses S. Grant by the grateful townspeople of Galena, Illinois, when he returned from the Civil War; peek at the bedroom in which Calvin Coolidge was sworn in as president by lantern light and contrast the world of national office with that of his boyhood in a tiny Vermont hamlet.

## House Museums and Historic Buildings

The most numerous history museums are individual buildings—houses, log cabins, and mansions; forts, lighthouses, and railroad stations; theaters and opera houses, schools, and mills. Some are important because of their connection with famous people or significant events, some because they are particularly representative of a certain period of history, some primarily because of their interesting architectural style or the beauty and value of their furnishings—and some simply because they are unusual or curious.

In many cases wealthy owners have attempted to make sure of their place in history by willing their estates—for use as museums—to a city, county, state, or institution. Those who really wanted to ensure their own immortality created nonprofit foundations to take care of the upkeep.

Two of the grandest house museums in the country are Biltmore House and Gardens, which includes a mansion of more than 200 rooms on several thousand acres in Asheville, North Carolina, and La Casa Grande, the castle built by William Randolph Hearst in San Simeon, California. Biltmore was the home of George W. Vanderbilt, grandson of "Commodore" Cornelius Vanderbilt, who made a huge fortune based on steamships and railroads. Hearst, the newspaper magnate, was a voracious art collector who gathered—in addition to paintings, sculpture, and priceless antiques—parts of old European castles, monasteries, and other buildings. He engaged an architect to design his 100-room castle to incorporate and show off his treasures. Formal gardens surround the mansion, which sits on top of a hill overlooking the Pacific Ocean.

## Military Landmarks

In Harlingen, Texas, a World War II bomber zooms overhead as a fighter plane zips up and down and around it. No, these are not the maneuvers or war games of a nearby armed-services base. This is the Confederate Air Force.

The Confederate Air Force Museum displays an impressive collection of aircraft used during World War II. A group of volunteers have been working on this project for some time; they find and acquire the old planes and restore them to flying condition. A one-day flying demonstration is held each spring and a four-day air show in October. This is one of the more unusual memorials to military history in this country.

For a peace-loving nation, the United States has been remarkably diligent about preserving reminders of the nation's wars. There are museums and forts, preserved ships and submarines, and monuments and shrines. Americans commemorate the places where battles were planned or fought and others where peace agreements were signed. The United States has honored many who fought in wars by burying them in national cemeteries. Each branch of the armed services has at least one special museum, as do most military installations. Some military museums honor an individual war hero: the Admiral Nimitz State Historic Park in Fredericksburg, Texas, and the George C. Marshall Museum in Lexington, Virginia, for example.

There are reminders of the Revolution, the French and Indian Wars, the Mexican War, the Civil War, the Spanish-American War, World Wars I and II, and there is one large museum called the War Memorial Museum of Virginia, in Newport News, where mementos of every major U.S. military involvement are

displayed. The collections include more than 30,000 items, including recruiting posters, medals, uniforms, weapons, and so on.

Veterans of the most recent conflict have been honored with a moving and unusual monument in Washington, DC—the Vietnam Veterans Memorial. It is reported that despite an early controversy over its design, this V-shaped wall, engraved with the names of 58,000 persons who died or are still missing, attracts more visitors than any other landmark in the capital city.

## Historic Districts

A tour guide in Savannah, Georgia, observed, "This city was rich enough during the 19th century to have acquired a personality of its own—and poor enough in the first part of the 20th that its citizens couldn't afford to destroy it."

One important contribution to the preservation of some historically important landmarks and lovely historic districts has been, ironically, poverty. When a city falls on hard times, developers are not interested in clearing away blocks of buildings in order to put up bigger and better shopping centers, apartment com-

---

### If the Ramparts Could Talk

The variety among the structures, locations, and histories of fortified outposts in the United States is impressive, from the massive walls of Castillo de San Marcos in St. Augustine, Florida, the oldest masonry fort in the United States—to the log structure in Astoria, Oregon—where explorers Lewis and Clark and their group spent the winter of 1805–06 after making the journey from St. Louis. Forts comprise a vital component of U.S. history and thus have many stories to tell.

Not all forts were places where shots were fired in anger against an enemy, but the inhabitants of all forts pitted their strength and will against often unknown and presumed hostile outsiders. After all, that is what a fort is—a wall built to protect those inside from anyone on the outside. All represent a harsh and difficult way of life. Here is a brief sampling of the forts that can be visited and the places they hold in history.

Fort Matanzas, near St. Augustine, recalls the days of Spanish and French conflicts over the territory that is now Florida. The preserved and restored structure was built in 1740, but it was named *matanzas*, Spanish for "slaughter," in remembrance of an earlier (1565) battle near this site in which Spanish soldiers killed 245 Frenchmen.

Fort Frederica, on St. Simons Island, Georgia, guarded the town established here more than 200 years ago by the idealistic and farsighted General James Oglethorpe. Oglethorpe founded Savannah, often called America's first planned city.

The star-shaped Fort McHenry, in Baltimore, Mary-

land, is remembered best as the site of the battle that inspired Francis Scott Key to write "The Star Spangled Banner." Fort Ticonderoga, New York, overlooking Lake Champlain, was originally a French fort. It was later taken by the British, who lost it and then regained it during the American Revolution.

Fort Harrod, in Harrodsburg, Kentucky, was reconstructed from the stockade built in the 1770s, when pioneers started to push the frontier westward.

Fort Meigs, Toledo, Ohio, was built under the supervision of William Henry Harrison for use during the War of 1812.

Fort Union, on the border of North Dakota and Montana, and Fort Vancouver, Washington, were established as fur-trading centers in the early 1800s.

During the 19th century, strongholds such as Fort Smith, Arkansas; Fort Scott, Kansas; Fort Davis, Texas; Bent's Old Fort near La Junta, Colorado; Fort Union, New Mexico; and Fort Laramie, Wyoming, were constructed along trails to guard the wagon trains and stages of westward-bound settlers and traders and to establish military outposts in the frontier. All of these sites are maintained by the National Park Service.

Two forts commemorating one of the saddest chapters in American history are Fort Sumter, in Charleston, South Carolina, where the first shots of the Civil War were fired, and Fort Jefferson, on an island 70 miles west of Key West, Florida, which served as a federal military prison during the same war.

plexes, and parking garages. Thus economic depressions are sometimes good friends of preservation. Landmarks and fine buildings may be neglected and suffer some deterioration, but at least they are not torn down.

Savannah is a city that illustrates this point. It is claimed to be America's first planned city, laid out in neat squares with numerous small parks by its founder, James Oglethorpe, more than two centuries ago. The basic city plan survives to this day. In the 1800s cotton warehousing and shipping provided great wealth for the city, and lovely Georgian townhouses and English Regency mansions lined the streets. So beautiful was 19th-century Savannah that General William Sherman spared it from the holocaust of his march to the sea. Instead, he captured it and "presented" it to President Lincoln as a Christmas gift in 1864.

When cotton no longer created fortunes for the businesses of Savannah, the city became stagnant, and many of its citizens overlooked the beauty and value of the formerly impressive neighborhoods. A turnaround began in the 1950s, and today homes and other buildings have been restored to their former elegance.

Historic districts are restored or preserved areas of architectural or historic significance, where visitors can take guided or self-guided walking tours. Most of the buildings are private homes that are not open to the public, except in some cases on special occasions. Many, but not necessarily all, of the districts are listed on the National Register of Historic Places.

## Special Attractions

Some Vacation Places have points of historic interest and importance that are unique or so unusual that they defy classification. Examples are the pueblos in the Albuquerque, New Mexico, area and the site of the first permanent European settlement in what is now the United States, in St. Augustine, Florida.

## Antiquity

Many places are more interesting than others from a historic point of view simply because of their age, regardless of any specific museums, sites, or landmarks they may possess. History buffs like to visit these places and see what they can discover for themselves about their past.

---

### Ethnic Sightseeing

Overseas travel is a dream that many people share—and that many people realize. But few people who really love to travel ever have the opportunity to spend as much time exploring foreign countries as they would like.

A good substitute for foreign travel is to find and enjoy the many pockets of foreign culture here in the United States. There are neighborhoods that look as if they had been imported intact from other countries; museums devoted to the history of certain ethnic groups both abroad and since their immigration to the United States; villages originally settled almost entirely by people from one part of the world, where evidence of the particular heritage has been carefully preserved; and of course, hundreds of ethnic restaurants and dozens of ethnic festivals.

Your own exploration can lead you to discover far more than the few we can mention here, but these are some of the outstanding places for ethnic sightseeing.

**Chicago, IL**
Balzekas Museum of Lithuanian Culture, Chicago
Du Sable Museum of Afro-American History, Chicago
Oriental Institute Museum, Chicago
Polish Museum of America, Chicago

**Hawaii**
Polynesian Cultural Center, Laie, Oahu

**Miami-Gold Coast-Keys, FL**
Little Havana, Miami (Cuban culture)

**New York City, NY**
Chinese Museum, Manhattan
El Museo del Barrio, Manhattan (Latin American culture)
Hispanic Society of America, Manhattan
The Jewish Museum, Manhattan
Ukrainian Museum, Manhattan

**San Antonio, TX**
La Villita, San Antonio (Old Mexican culture)
Institute of Texan Cultures, San Antonio

**San Francisco, CA**
Chinese Culture Center, San Francisco
Japan Center, San Francisco

**Tampa Bay—Southwest Coast, FL**
Ybor City, Tampa (Cuban culture)

**Washington, DC—MD—VA**
Anacostia Neighborhood Museum, Washington (black culture)

**Wisconsin Dells, WI**
Little Norway, near Madison
Pendarvis, Mineral Point (Cornish culture)
Swiss Historical Village, New Glarus

**SCORING:** Discovering Our Heritage

In this chapter, historic points of interest were evaluated for each of the 107 Vacation Places. The museums and other attractions were selected and scored on the basis of their appeal to large numbers of people. All historic sites and buildings that could be entered or toured and were available to the public at least five days a week during the peak tourist season for that area were included. Certain outstanding historic districts were also rated, though many of these consisted primarily of private dwellings. Many districts were considered important principally because of their well-preserved architectural styles, typical of a certain period; others had a significance beyond their architectural interest because of famous people or events connected with the area.

Subjective judgment entered into the scoring in this chapter; the author asked herself certain questions as she read about or visited each site, then used the answers to the following questions as a basis for scoring:

1. How important to an average traveler (not necessarily to a history scholar) was the historic person, event, or period commemorated at this site?
2. How well did the exhibits, demonstrations, and illustrative talks presented at this site illuminate that event or period in history?
3. How extensive were the collections and exhibits?
4. When compared with other historic sites, how much time would the average traveler enjoy spending here?

The subjectivity of this approach obviously invites argument, but the rationale is that any method of scoring based on acreage, square feet, or number of items in a collection would be far less useful to the traveler. Popular appeal is the yardstick, although it may or may not be the measure that would be used by a serious history researcher.

A flag (◄) to the left of a listing in the Place Profiles indicates the author's opinion that this is an attraction that definitely should not be missed. Two flags (◄◄) mean a recommendation that you plan at least one entire day for a visit. These flags do not necessarily reflect the scoring, but they can be used to plan the amount of time you might want to spend at the attraction.

As in other chapters, certain sites that are nearby but not precisely within the area defined as the Vacation Place are printed in italics in the Place Profiles. These were included because they were considered easily accessible and important or interesting enough

to be worth a short side trip; they were given one-half the point score of listings within the Vacation Place boundaries.

## Living History Museums

Living history museums were given from 400 to 700 points, depending on size, number of buildings, and elaborateness of interpretive programs. Small complexes (fewer than six structures) were given 400 points; more than six structures, 500. Larger complexes, such as extensive plantations or entire villages, received 600 or 700 points.

About 30 living history museums were rated in this chapter; six were marked with two flags. Four of the Vacation Places earned a score of 1,000 or more points.

### Top Four for Living History Museums

|  | Living History Museums | Points |
|---|---|---|
| 1. Washington, DC–MD–VA | 4 | 2,300 |
| 2. Boston, MA | 3 | 1,450 |
| 3. Hawaii | 2 | 1,100 |
| 4. Pennsylvania Dutch Country, PA | 2 | 1,000 |

## History Museums

History museums were given from 100 to 600 points. Small museums of primarily local interest, housed in ordinary buildings, were given a score of 100. Those of local interest, but containing larger and more varied collections, earned 200 points. Museums with collections of at least statewide interest received 400 points; unusually large museums and those of national significance received 600 points.

Listed in the table are the ten Vacation Places with the highest scores in this category (1,400 or more points). The Southwest, Northeast, and Midwest are all represented among the top ten.

### Top Ten for History Museums

|  | History Museums | Points |
|---|---|---|
| 1. Oklahoma City–Cherokee Strip, OK | 12 | 2,950 |
| 2. New York City, NY | 12 | 2,300 |
| 3. Washington, DC–MD–VA | 6 | 2,100 |
| 4. Boston, MA | 10 | 1,900 |
| 5. New Orleans, LA | 5 | 1,700 |
| 5. Phoenix–Valley of the Sun, AZ | 7 | 1,700 |
| 7. Chicago, IL | 8 | 1,600 |
| 8. Adirondack Mountains, NY | 10 | 1,550 |
| 9. Baltimore–Chesapeake Bay, MD | 3 | 1,400 |
| 9. Cape Cod–The Islands, MA | 10 | 1,400 |

## Archeological Sites and Museums

Archeological sites received from 200 to 500 points. Sites only, interesting of themselves but without any accompanying museum or interpretive program, were given 200 points; museums only, not part of a site, 300 points; site and museum, both small, 400 points; major site, (usually) with museum, 500 points.

Of the 32 Vacation Places with archeological sites or museums, 7 received 500 or more points. The top 5 are all in the southwestern United States. An especially rewarding trip for vacationers with strong interest in exploring the evidence of prehistoric life-styles in North America is a loop that includes northern New Mexico, northern Arizona, southern Utah, and southern Colorado.

### Top Seven for Archeological Sites and Museums

| | Archeological Sites and Museums | Points |
|---|---|---|
| 1. Albuquerque–Santa Fe–Taos, NM | 8 | 2,450 |
| 2. Grand Canyon Country, AZ | 5 | 2,300 |
| 3. Phoenix–Valley of the Sun, AZ | 3 | 1,400 |
| 4. Lake Powell–Glen Canyon, AZ–UT | 2 | 800 |
| 5. Los Angeles, CA | 2 | 600 |
| 5. Memphis, TN–AR–MS | 2 | 600 |
| 7. Olympic Peninsula, WA | 2 | 500 |

## Presidential Sites

Presidential sites (primarily homes, libraries, and museums) were given from 200 to 700 points. A presidential home or birthplace, small, not fully developed, or open only part-time, received 200 points; a single building connected with the life of a president, or a small museum of memorabilia related to a president, 300 points; a complex of buildings, worth at least a half-day's visit, 500 points; home plus presidential library or major museum, 700 points.

Twenty-three Vacation Places contained at least one presidential site; five had at least two and earned a score of 1,500 or more.

### Top Five for Presidential Sites

| | Presidential Sites | Points |
|---|---|---|
| 1. Washington, DC–MD–VA | 6 | 1,800 |
| 2. Richmond–Fredericksburg, VA | 4 | 1,750 |
| 3. Blue Ridge Mountains, VA | 4 | 1,700 |
| 3. Boston, MA | 4 | 1,700 |
| 5. Austin–Hill Country, TX | 2 | 1,500 |

## House Museums and Historic Buildings

Entries in this category received from 100 to 600 points, based on the amount of time the average sightseer would spend for a visit. Those of casual interest that could be toured in an hour or so gained 100 points; a somewhat larger structure, containing an unusually interesting collection or connected with a famous person or event, 200 points; a place of national significance, or one that an average traveler would linger in for more than an hour, 300 points; a major building or mansion, worth more than a half-day's visit, 500 points; an especially interesting complex of several buildings, 600 points.

All but 10 of the 107 Vacation Places had at least one historic building that was scored and listed in the

Place Profiles. Eleven earned more than 4,000 points for house museums and historic buildings (Houston–Galveston, Texas, tied with New York City, New York, for tenth place). The winner in this category was Boston, with 60 house museums and historic buildings.

### Top Eleven for House Museums and Historic Buildings

| | Listings* | Points |
|---|---|---|
| 1. Boston, MA | 60 | 12,700 |
| 2. Washington, DC–MD–VA | 34 | 8,900 |
| 3. Providence–Newport, RI | 29 | 7,300 |
| 4. Vicksburg–Natchez–Baton Rouge, MS–LA | 31 | 6,800 |
| 5. Philadelphia, PA–DE–NJ | 26 | 6,600 |
| 6. Catskill Mountains, NY | 24 | 6,000 |
| 7. Pennsylvania Dutch Country, PA | 22 | 5,400 |
| 8. Lexington–Bluegrass Country, KY | 21 | 4,750 |
| 9. Berkshire Hills–Pioneer Valley, MA | 15 | 4,600 |
| 10. Houston–Galveston, TX | 22 | 4,200 |
| 10. New York City, NY | 16 | 4,200 |

*Some listings consist of more than one building.

## Military Landmarks

Nearly 190 military landmarks, found in 70 of the 107 Vacation Places, were scored and listed in the Place Profiles. Landmarks received from 200 to 500 points. National military cemeteries, battlefields, submarines and ships, and small forts (either original or reconstructed) received 200 points; major forts or special military museums, 400; groups of buildings, military installations (either active or commemorative) offering public tours, historic military sites with museums or interpretive programs, 500; military academies, all of which have museums and offer tours, 500.

Ten Vacation Places earned 1,800 or more points for their military landmarks. Williamsburg–Colonial Triangle, Virginia, heads the list with nine sites and 3,400 points.

### Top Ten for Military Landmarks

| | Military Landmarks | Points |
|---|---|---|
| 1. Williamsburg–Colonial Triangle, VA | 9 | 3,400 |
| 2. Washington, DC–MD–VA | 8 | 2,450 |
| 3. Charleston, SC | 5 | 2,300 |
| 4. Catskill Mountains, NY | 6 | 2,200 |
| 5. Panhandle, FL | 6 | 2,000 |
| 5. Richmond–Fredericksburg, VA | 9 | 2,000 |
| 7. Chicago, IL | 4 | 1,900 |
| 7. Mobile Bay–Gulfport, AL–MS | 6 | 1,900 |
| 9. Lexington–Bluegrass Country, KY | 5 | 1,800 |
| 9. Philadelphia, PA–DE–NJ | 4 | 1,800 |

## Historic Districts

Historic districts received from 300 to 700 points: 300 for a district one block long or less, 400 for several blocks. Districts that have a historic significance beyond their architectural interest gained 600 points; major areas that have enough to interest visitors for more than half a day, 700.

About half the Vacation Places have one or more historic districts listed in the Place Profiles.

## Top Ten for Historic Districts

| | Historic Districts | Points |
|---|---|---|
| 1. Washington, DC–MD–VA | 8 | 4,200 |
| 2. Boston, MA | 6 | 2,700 |
| 3. Savannah–Golden Isles, GA | 5 | 2,400 |
| 4. Philadelphia, PA–DE–NJ | 4 | 1,700 |
| 5. Lexington–Bluegrass Country, KY | 7 | 1,500 |
| 6. Williamsburg–Colonial Triangle, VA | 2 | 1,400 |
| 7. Baltimore–Chesapeake Bay, MD | 3 | 1,300 |
| 7. Catskill Mountains, NY | 4 | 1,300 |
| 7. Charleston, SC | 3 | 1,300 |
| 10. St. Louis–Mark Twain Country, MO–IL | 2 | 1,200 |

## Special Attractions

Scoring for this category was determined as follows: 500 points for a state capital and its complex of historic buildings; 500 points for a regularly scheduled historic drama; 500, 700, or 1,000 points, depending on importance, for other truly unique historic points of interest.

## Antiquity Score

The antiquity score for each Vacation Place represents the age as of 1986 of the oldest important city or town in the area, measured by European settlement.

Listed here are the 10 oldest and the 7 newest (all of which are less than 100 years old) of the 107 Vacation Places.

### The Oldest Vacation Places

| | Antiquity Score |
|---|---|
| 1. St. Augustine–Northeast Coast, FL | 421 |
| 2. Williamsburg–Colonial Triangle, VA | 379 |
| 3. Albuquerque–Santa Fe–Taos, NM | 376 |
| 4. New York City, NY | 371 |
| 5. Cape Cod–The Islands, MA | 366 |
| 6. Boston, MA | 356 |
| 6. Portsmouth–Kennebunk, NH–ME | 356 |
| 8. Portland, ME | 355 |
| 9. Providence–Newport, RI | 350 |
| 10. Long Island, NY | 338 |

### The Newest Vacation Places

| | Antiquity Score |
|---|---|
| 1. Lake of the Ozarks, MO | 55 |
| 2. Anchorage–Kenai Peninsula, AK | 72 |
| 3. Lake Powell–Glen Canyon, AZ–UT | 81 |
| 4. Crater Lake–Klamath Falls, OR | 84 |
| 5. Bend–Cascade Mountains, OR | 86 |
| 6. Glacier National Park–Flathead Lake, MT | 95 |
| 7. Yosemite–Sequoia–Death Valley, CA | 96 |
| 8. Oklahoma City–Cherokee Strip, OK | 97 |

**PLACE PROFILES:** Discovering Our Heritage

In these pages, points of interest for historic sightseeing are listed for the 107 Vacation Places. The listings include living history museums, history museums, archeological sites and museums, presidential sites, house museums and historic buildings, military landmarks, historic districts, and special attractions. The antiquity score, described in the scoring section, is also given.

A flag (◄) to the left of a listing in the Place Profiles indicates that, in the author's opinion, this is an attraction that definitely should not be missed. Two flags (◄◄) mean a recommendation that you plan at least one entire day for a visit.

Points of interest are listed in alphabetic order first by town, then within the town.

As in other chapters, certain listings nearby but not precisely within the area defined as the Vacation Place are printed in italics. These were included because they were considered easily accessible and important or interesting enough to be worth a short side trip; they were given one-half the point score of listings within the Vacation Place boundaries.

The abbreviations that appear in the Place Profiles are as follows:

A.F.B. Air Force Base
N.B.P. National Battlefield Park
N.B.S. National Battlefield Site
N.H.D. National Historic District
N.H.P. National Historical Park

N.H.S. National Historic Site
N.M.P. National Military Park
S.H.P. State Historic Park
S.H.S. State Historic Site
U.S.S. United States Ship

A star (★) preceding a Vacation Place highlights that place as one of the top ten in this chapter.

### Adirondack Mountains, NY
History Museums (1,550)
◄◄ Adirondack Museum (Blue Mountain Lake)
Penfield Homestead Museum (Crown Point)
The Chapman History Museum (Glens Falls)
Fulton County Museum (Gloversville)
Lake Placid Historical Society Museum (Lake Placid)
Franklin County Historical Society (Malone)
*Historical Society of Saratoga Springs (Saratoga Springs)*
Heritage Museum (Ticonderoga)
*Oneida Historical Society (Utica)*
Warrensburg Museum of Local History (Warrensburg)
Archeological Sites and Museums (300)
Six Nations Indian Museum (Saranac Lake)
Presidential Sites (100)
*Grant Cottage S.H.S. (Saratoga Springs)*
House Museums and Historic Buildings (2,000)
Constable Hall (Boonville)
Gristmill (Glens Falls)
◄◄ Tupper's Early American and Farm Museum (Glens Falls)
John Brown Farm Historical Site (Lake Placid)
Ballard Mill (Malone)
Alice T. Miner Colonial Collection (Plattsburgh)
Kent-Delord House Museum (Plattsburgh)
Robert Louis Stevenson Memorial Cottage (Saranac Lake)
*General Philip Schuyler House (Saratoga N.H.P.)*
*John Neilson House (Saratoga N.H.P.)*
*Munson-Williams-Proctor Institute (Utica)*
Military Landmarks (1,300)
Crown Point S.H.S. (Crown Point)
Fort William Henry Museum (Lake George)
Fort Lennox (Rouses Point)
Fort Mound Hope (Ticonderoga)
◄ Fort Ticonderoga (Ticonderoga)
Antiquity Score: 222 (Ticonderoga founded 1764)
Places Rated Score: 5,472     Places Rated Rank: 31

### Albuquerque–Santa Fe–Taos, NM
History Museums (800)
Albuquerque Museum (Albuquerque)
County Historical Museum (Los Alamos)
Billy the Kid Museum (Santa Rosa)
Kit Carson Home and Museum (Taos)

Archeological Sites and Museums (2,450)
◄ Coronado State Monument (Albuquerque)
Indian Petroglyph State Park (Albuquerque)
◄◄ *Chaco Culture N.H.P. (Bloomfield)*
◄◄ Bandelier National Monument (Los Alamos)
Jemez State Monument (Los Alamos)
◄◄ *Salinas National Monument (Mountainair)*
*Folsom Museum (Raton)*
◄◄ Pecos National Monument (Santa Fe)
House Museums and Historic Buildings (1,400)
Old Aztec Mill Museum (Cimarron)
Oldest House (Santa Fe)
Palace of the Governors (Santa Fe)
San Miguel Mission (Santa Fe)
Ernest L. Blumenschein Home (Taos)
Governor Bent House Museum (Taos)
La Hacienda de Don Antonio Severino Martinez (Taos)
Ranchos de Taos (Taos)
Military Landmarks (700)
◄◄ Fort Union National Monument (Las Vegas)
◄◄ Fort Sumner State Monument (Santa Rosa)
Historic Districts (800)
Old Town (Albuquerque)
The Plaza (Santa Fe)
Special Attractions (1,000)
State capital buildings (Santa Fe)
Unique pueblos of Acoma, Isleta, Laguna, San Ildefonso, Taos, Zuni
Antiquity Score: 376 (Santa Fe founded 1610)
Places Rated Score: 7,526     Places Rated Rank: 14

### Anchorage–Kenai Peninsula, AK
History Museums (900)
◄ Anchorage History Museum (Anchorage)
Cordova Museum (Cordova)
◄ Pratt Museum (Homer)
House Museums and Historic Buildings (200)
Oscar Anderson House (Anchorage)
Crow Creek Mine (Girdwood)
Military Landmarks (200)
Fort Kenai Museum (Kenai)
Antiquity Score: 72 (Anchorage founded 1914)
Places Rated Score: 1,372     Places Rated Rank: 84

## Asheville–Smoky Mountains, NC
History Museums (400)
◀ Museum of the Cherokee Indian (Cherokee)
House Museums and Historic Buildings (2,200)
◀◀ Biltmore House and Gardens (Asheville)
Thomas Wolfe Memorial (Asheville)
Zebulon B. Vance S.H.S. (Asheville)
◀◀ Oconaluftee Indian Village (Cherokee)
Carl Sandburg Home (Hendersonville)
Special Attractions (500)
Historical drama *Unto These Hills* (Cherokee)
Antiquity Score: 192 (Asheville settled 1794)
Places Rated Score: 3,292        Places Rated Rank: 59

## Aspen–Vail, CO
History Museums (200)
Aspen Historical Society Museum (Aspen)
Heritage Museum (Leadville)
House Museums and Historic Buildings (1,400)
◀◀ South Park City Museum (Fairplay)
Healy House–Dexter Cabin (Leadville)
Historic Home of H. A. W. Tabor (Leadville)
House with the Eye (Leadville)
Matchless Mine (Leadville)
Tabor Opera House (Leadville)
Antiquity Score: 107 (Aspen settled 1879)
Places Rated Score: 1,707        Places Rated Rank: 80

## Atlanta, GA
History Museums (900)
◀ Georgia Department of Archives and History (Atlanta)
McElreath Hall (Atlanta)
Dahlonega Courthouse Gold Museum (Dahlonega)
Green Street Station (Gainesville)
Museum of the Hills (Helen)
Chieftains Museum (Rome)
Archeological Sites and Museums (400)
◀ Etowah Indian Mounds (Cartersville)
Presidential Sites (300)
F.D.R.'s Little White House (Warm Springs)
House Museums and Historic Buildings (2,000)
Fox Theatre (Atlanta)
◀◀ Stone Mountain Park (Atlanta)
Tullie Smith House (Atlanta)
Wren's Nest (Atlanta)
◀ New Echota Historic Site (Calhoun)
Vann House (Chatsworth)
Uncle Remus Museum (Eatonton)
Traveler's Rest (Toccoa)
Military Landmarks (400)
Big Shanty Museum (Marietta)
Kennesaw Mountain N.B.P. (Marietta)
Historic Districts (700)
Martin Luther King N.H.D. (Atlanta)
Green Street Historic District (Gainesville)
Special Attractions (500)
State capital buildings (Atlanta)
Antiquity Score: 149 (Atlanta founded 1837)
Places Rated Score: 5,349        Places Rated Rank: 32

## Atlantic City, NJ
History Museums (300)
Cape May County Historical Museum (Cape May
Court House)
Ocean City Historical Museum (Ocean City)
House Museums and Historic Buildings (300)
◀◀ *Batsto S.H.S. (Batsto)*
Historic Districts (1,000)
Historic Gardner's Basin (Atlantic City)
Historic Towne of Smithville (Atlantic City)
Victorian homes (Cape May Court House)
Antiquity Score: 134 (Atlantic City settled 1852)
Places Rated Score: 1,734        Places Rated Rank: 79

## Austin–Hill Country, TX
History Museums (850)
Daughters of the Republic of Texas Museum
(Austin)
Texas Confederate Museum (Austin)
◀ Texas Memorial Museum (Austin)
*Fayette Heritage Museum (La Grange)*
Presidential Sites (1,500)
Johnson Presidential Library and Museum (Austin)
Johnson N.H.P., 4 separate sites (Johnson City)
House Museums and Historic Buildings (750)
Neill-Cochran House (Austin)
O. Henry Museum (Austin)
Old French Legation (Austin)
Pioneer Museum (Fredericksburg)
*Faison Home and Museum (La Grange)*
Military Landmarks (1,100)
◀ Fort Croghan Museum (Burnet)
Admiral Nimitz S.H.P. (Fredericksburg)
◀◀ Fort Hood (Killeen)
Historic Districts (300)
Fredericksburg
Special Attractions (500)
State capital buildings (Austin)
Antiquity Score: 147 (Austin founded 1839)
Places Rated Score: 5,147        Places Rated Rank: 35

## Baltimore–Chesapeake Bay, MD
Living History Museums (600)
◀ Carroll County Farm Museum (Westminster)
History Museums (1,400)
◀◀ Darnall Young People's Museum of Maryland History
(Baltimore)
◀◀ Maryland Historical Society (Baltimore)
Peale Museum (Baltimore)
House Museums and Historic Buildings (2,900)
Chase-Lloyd House (Annapolis)
Hammond-Harwood House (Annapolis)
McDowell Hall (Annapolis)
William Paca House (Annapolis)
Babe Ruth Birthplace (Baltimore)
Carroll Mansion (Baltimore)
Edgar Allan Poe House (Baltimore)
Mount Clare Museum (Baltimore)
Star-Spangled Banner Flag House and 1812 War
Museum (Baltimore)
◀ Hampton N.H.S. (Towson)
Union Mills Homestead (Westminster)
Military Landmarks (1,300)
◀ Naval Academy Museum (Annapolis)
◀◀ U.S. Naval Academy (Annapolis)
◀ Fort McHenry National Monument (Baltimore)
Historic Districts (1,300)
◀ Historic Annapolis
Chesapeake & Ohio Canal N.H.P.
St. Mary's Square (St. Michaels)
Special Attractions (500)
State capital buildings (Annapolis)
Antiquity Score: 337 (Annapolis founded 1649)
Places Rated Score: 8,337        Places Rated Rank: 13

## Bar Harbor–Acadia, ME
History Museums (150)
*Bangor Historical Museum (Bangor)*
Islesford Historical Museum (Cranberry Isles)
Archeological Sites and Museums (300)
Abbe Museum of Archaeology (Bar Harbor)
House Museums and Historic Buildings (1,150)
Holt House (Blue Hill)
Parson Fisher House (Blue Hill)
Jed Prouty Tavern (Bucksport)
Wilson Museum (Bucksport)
*Ruggles House (Cherryfield)*
John Black Mansion (Ellsworth)
Tisdale House (Ellsworth)
Montpelier (Thomaston)
Antiquity Score: 217 (Belfast settled 1769)
Places Rated Score: 1,817        Places Rated Rank: 76

## Bend–Cascade Mountains, OR
History Museums (100)
   Oregon High Desert Museum (Bend)
Antiquity Score: 86 (Bend settled 1900)
Places Rated Score: 186          Places Rated Rank: 107

## Berkshire Hills–Pioneer Valley, MA
History Museums (400)
   Hadley Farm Museum (Amherst)
   Memorial Hall Museum (Deerfield)
   Mission House (Springfield)
   Edwin Smith Historical Museum (Westfield)
Archeological Sites and Museums (400)
◄ Granby Dinosaur Museum (Holyoke)
Presidential Sites (200)
   Calvin Coolidge Memorial Room (Northampton)
House Museums and Historic Buildings (4,600)
   Dickinson Homestead (Amherst)
◄◄ Historic Deerfield, 12 homes (Deerfield)
   Indian House Memorial (Deerfield)
   Colonel Ashley House (Great Barrington)
   Tanglewood (Lenox)
   Arrowhead (Pittsfield)
◄◄ Hancock Shaker Village (Pittsfield)
◄ Springfield Armory N.H.S. (Springfield)
◄◄ Storrowton Village (Springfield)
   Chesterwood (Stockbridge)
   Col. John Ashley House (Stockbridge)
   Merwin House (Stockbridge)
   Naumkeag (Stockbridge)
   Norman Rockwell Museum and Corner House
      (Stockbridge)
   William Cullen Bryant Homestead (Williamsburg)
Antiquity Score: 236 (Lenox settled 1750)
Places Rated Score: 5,836          Places Rated Rank: 27

## Black Hills, SD
History Museums (900)
   Tri-State Museum (Belle Fourche)
   Custer County Museum (Custer)
   Adams Memorial Museum (Deadwood)
   Dianne's Hillyo Museum (Hill City)
   *Buechel Memorial Lakota Museum (Mission)*
   *Robinson Museum (Pierre)*
   Minnilusa Pioneer Museum (Rapid City)
   Sioux Indian Museum (Rapid City)
House Museums and Historic Buildings (300)
◄◄ *Pioneer Auto Museum and Antique Town (Murdo)*
Military Landmarks (200)
   Old Fort Meade Cavalry Museum (Sturgis)
Special Attractions (250)
   *State capital buildings (Pierre)*
Antiquity Score: 110 (Rapid City founded 1876)
Places Rated Score: 1,760          Places Rated Rank: 78

## Blue Ridge Mountains, VA
History Museums (300)
   Western Virginia Visitors Center (Charlottesville)
   Harrisonburg-Rockingham Historical Society
      (Harrisonburg)
Presidential Sites (1,700)
◄ Ash Lawn (Charlottesville)
◄◄ Monticello (Charlottesville)
   Woodrow Wilson Birthplace (Staunton)
   Washington's Office Museum (Winchester)
House Museums and Historic Buildings (2,200)
   Humpback Rocks Visitor Center (Blue Ridge
      Parkway)
   Castle Hill (Charlottesville)
◄ Historic Michie Tavern (Charlottesville)
   Stonewall Jackson House (Lexington)
◄◄ Tuttle & Spice 1886 General Store (New Market)
   Abram's Delight and Log Cabin (Winchester)
   Stonewall Jackson's Headquarters (Winchester)

Military Landmarks (600)
◄ George C. Marshall Museum (Lexington)
   New Market Battlefield Park (New Market)
Historic Districts (300)
   University of Virginia Campus (Charlottesville)
Antiquity Score: 224 (Charlottesville founded 1762)
Places Rated Score: 5,324          Places Rated Rank: 33

## Boise–Sun Valley, ID
History Museums (850)
◄ Idaho State Historical Society Museum (Boise)
   *Cassia County Historical Museum (Burley)*
   Elmore Historical Foundation Museum (Mountain
      Home)
   Twin Falls Historical Society Museum (Twin Falls)
   Intermountain Cultural Center and Museum
      (Weiser)
House Museums and Historic Buildings (100)
   Old Idaho Penitentiary (Boise)
Military Landmarks (400)
◄ Mountain Home A.F.B. (Mountain Home)
Special Attractions (500)
   State capital buildings (Boise)
Antiquity Score: 134 (Boise settled 1852)
Places Rated Score: 1,984          Places Rated Rank: 73

## Boone–High Country, NC
Special Attractions (500)
   Outdoor historical drama *Horn in the West* (Boone)
Antiquity Score: 214 (Boone settled 1772)
Places Rated Score: 714          Places Rated Rank: 97

## ★ Boston, MA
Living History Museums (1,450)
   Drumlin Farm Education Center (Concord)
◄◄ Plimoth Plantation (Plymouth)
◄◄ *Old Sturbridge Village (Sturbridge)*
History Museums (1,900)
   Cape Ann Historical Association (Gloucester)
◄◄ Haverhill Historical Society (Haverhill)
   Museum of Our National Heritage (Lexington)
   Lowell Museum (Lowell)
   Lynn Historical Society Museum (Lynn)
   Quincy Historical Society (Quincy)
   Sandy Bay Historical Society (Rockport)
   Peabody Museum (Salem)
   Salem Seaport Museum (Salem)
   Salem Witch Museum (Salem)
Presidential Sites (1,700)
   John F. Kennedy Library and Museum (Boston)
   John F. Kennedy N.H.S. (Boston)
   Abigail Adams House (Braintree)
   Adams N.H.S.; 4 buildings (Quincy)
House Museums and Historic Buildings (12,700)
   Amos Blanchard House and Barn Museum
      (Andover)
   Balch House (Beverly)
   Cabot House (Beverly)
   Hale House (Beverly)
   Faneuil Hall (Boston)
   Harrison Gray Otis House (Boston)
   Nichols House Museum (Boston)
   Old Corner Book Store Building (Boston)
   Old North Church (Boston)
   Old South Meeting House (Boston)
   Old State House (Boston)
   Paul Revere House (Boston)
   Royall House (Boston)
   General Sylvanus Thayer Birthplace (Braintree)
   Blacksmith House (Cambridge)
◄ Longfellow N.H.S. (Cambridge)
   Codman House (Concord)
   Concord Antiquarian Museum (Concord)
◄◄ Fruitlands Museum (Concord)
   The Old Manse (Concord)
   Orchard House (Concord)
   Ralph Waldo Emerson House (Concord)

Thoreau Lyceum (Concord)
The Wayside (Concord)
Glen Magna (Danvers)
Rebecca Nurse Homestead (Danvers)
Fairbanks House (Dedham)
Beauport (Gloucester)
Hammond Castle Museum (Gloucester)
Sargent House Museum (Gloucester)
John Greenleaf Whittier Birthplace (Haverhill)
Jacobs Farm (Hingham)
The Old Ordinary (Hingham)
John Heard House (Ipswich)
John Whipple House (Ipswich)
Lexington Historical Society (Lexington)
Whistler House (Lowell)
Mary Baker Eddy Historical Home (Lynn)
Jeremiah Lee Mansion (Marblehead)
King Hooper Mansion (Marblehead)
Coffin House (Newburyport)
Cushing House Museum (Newburyport)
Jackson Homestead (Newton)
Harlow Old Fort House (Plymouth)
Howland House (Plymouth)
Jenney Grist Mill Village (Plymouth)
Major John Bradford House (Plymouth)
Mayflower Society House (Plymouth)
Pilgrim Hall Museum (Plymouth)
Richard Sparrow House (Plymouth)
Spooner House (Plymouth)
Josiah Quincy House (Quincy)
Quincy Homestead (Quincy)
James Babson Museum (Rockport)
Old Castle (Rockport)
House of Seven Gables (Salem)
Pioneer Village (Salem)
Stephen Phillips Memorial Trust House (Salem)
◄ Saugus Iron Works N.H.S. (Saugus)
Longfellow's Wayside Inn (Sudbury Center)
**Military Landmarks (1,300)**
Bunker Hill Monument (Charlestown)
U.S.S. *Constitution* (Charlestown)
◄◄ Minute Man N.H.P. (Concord)
Battle Green (Lexington)
Grand Army of the Republic Museum (Lynn)
**Historic Districts (2,700)**
◄◄ Freedom Trail (Boston)
Louisburg Square (Boston)
Lowell N.H.P. (Lowell)
◄ Essex Institute Museum (Salem)
Pickering Wharf (Salem)
Salem Maritime N.H.S. (Salem)
**Special Attractions (500)**
State capital buildings (Boston)
Antiquity Score: 356 (Boston founded 1630)
Places Rated Score: 22,606    Places Rated Rank: 2

### Brownsville–Rio Grande Valley, TX
**History Museums (200)**
Hidalgo County Historical Museum (Edinburg)
McAllen Hudson Museum (McAllen)
**House Museums and Historic Buildings (200)**
La Lomita Chapel (Mission)
Port Isabel Lighthouse S.H.S. (Port Isabel)
**Military Landmarks (400)**
◄ Confederate Air Force Museum (Harlingen)
Antiquity Score: 138 (Brownsville founded 1848)
Places Rated Score: 938    Places Rated Rank: 94

### Cape Cod–The Islands, MA
**History Museums (1,400)**
Donald G. Trayser Memorial Museum (Barnstable)
Drummer Boy Museum (Brewster)
New England Fire and History Museum (Brewster)
Centerville Historical Society Museum (Centerville)
◄ Falmouth Historical Society Museum (Falmouth)

Dukes County Historical Society (Martha's Vineyard)
Truro Historical Society Museum (North Truro)
Osterville Historical Society Museum (Osterville)
Historical Museum at Pilgrim Monument (Provincetown)
Provincetown Heritage Museum (Provincetown)
**House Museums and Historic Buildings (800)**
Old Grist Windmill (Eastham)
Seth Nickerson House (Provincetown)
Dexter Gristmill (Sandwich)
Hoxie House (Sandwich)
Historical Society Museum (Wellfleet)
Captain Bangs Hallet House (Yarmouth)
**Historic Districts (1,000)**
Aptucxet Trading Post (Bourne)
◄◄ Main Street (Nantucket)
Antiquity Score: 366 (Cape Cod settled 1620)
Places Rated Score: 3,566    Places Rated Rank: 56

### ★ Catskill Mountains, NY
**Living History Museums (300)**
◄ *Farmers' Museum and Village Crossroads (Cooperstown)*
**History Museums (500)**
*Fenimore House (Cooperstown)*
Clinton House S.H.S. (Poughkeepsie)
Schenectady County Historical Society (Schenectady)
Cherry Valley Museum (Sharon Springs)
Yorktown Museum (Yorktown)
**Presidential Sites (900)**
Martin Van Buren N.H.S. (Hudson)
◄◄ Home of Franklin D. Roosevelt N.H.S. (Hyde Park)
**House Museums and Historic Buildings (6,000)**
Arbour Hill (Albany)
Fort Crailo (Albany)
Historic Cherry Hill (Albany)
Schuyler Mansion (Albany)
Zane Grey Museum (Barryville)
◄ Frisbee House Museum (Delhi)
Madam Brett Homestead (Fishkill)
Mount Gulian (Fishkill)
Van Wyck Homestead Museum (Fishkill)
Old Stone Fort Museum Complex (Howes Cave)
Clermont S.H.P. (Hudson)
House of History (Hudson)
Luykas Van Alen House (Hudson)
Olana S.H.S. (Hudson)
◄◄ Shaker Museum (Hudson)
Mills Mansion (Hyde Park)
Vanderbilt Mansion N.H.S. (Hyde Park)
Hurley Patentee Manor (Kingston)
Senate House (Kingston)
Crawford House (Newburgh)
Locust Lawn (New Paltz)
Snyder Estate (New Paltz)
Locust Grove (Poughkeepsie)
Lansing Manor (Stamford)
**Military Landmarks (2,200)**
◄◄ Fort Delaware Museum of Colonial History (Narrowsburg)
Knox's Headquarters (Newburgh)
◄ New Windsor Cantonment (Newburgh)
◄ Washington's Headquarters S.H.S. (Newburgh)
Fort Putnam (West Point)
◄◄ U.S. Military Academy (West Point)
**Historic Districts (1,300)**
Rensselaerville (Albany)
Newburgh
New Paltz
Historic Stockade Area (Schenectady)
**Special Attractions (500)**
State capital buildings (Albany)
Antiquity Score: 308 (New Paltz founded 1678)
Places Rated Score: 12,008    Places Rated Rank: 4

## Charleston, SC
History Museums (300)
  Charleston Museum (Charleston)
  Old Slave Mart Museum (Charleston)
House Museums and Historic Buildings (3,200)
  Boone Hall Plantation (Charleston)
  Calhoun Mansion (Charleston)
  Dock Street Theater (Charleston)
  Drayton Hall (Charleston)
  Edmondston-Alston House (Charleston)
  Heyward-Washington House (Charleston)
  Joseph Manigault House (Charleston)
◄◄ Magnolia Plantation (Charleston)
◄◄ Middleton Place (Charleston)
  Nathaniel Russell House (Charleston)
  Old Exchange and Provost Dungeon (Charleston)
  Thomas Elfe Workshop (Charleston)
Military Landmarks (2,300)
◄◄ Aircraft Carrier Yorktown–Patriots Point, Naval and Maritime
    Museum, and other vessels (Charleston)
◄ The Citadel Archives-Museum (Charleston)
◄◄ Fort Moultrie (Charleston)
◄◄ Fort Sumter (Charleston)
◄ The Powder Magazine (Charleston)
Historic Districts (1,300)
◄◄ Charleston
  Charles Towne Landing
  Walterboro
Antiquity Score: 316 (Charleston founded 1670)
Places Rated Score: 7,416     Places Rated Rank: 16

## Chattanooga–Huntsville, TN–AL–GA
House Museums and Historic Buildings (850)
  Confederama (Chattanooga, TN)
  Cravens House (Chattanooga)
  Joe Wheeler Plantation (Decatur, AL)
  Fort Payne Opera House (Fort Payne, AL)
  Huntsville Depot (Huntsville, AL)
  Hundred Oaks Castle (Winchester, TN)
Military Landmarks (300)
  Lookout Mountain, Point Park (Chattanooga)
  Chickamauga & Chattanooga N.M.P. (sites in both
    Tennessee and Georgia)
Historic Districts (750)
  Mooresville (Decatur)
  Old Decatur (Decatur)
  Twickenham Historic District (Huntsville)
Antiquity Score: 151 (Chattanooga settled 1835)
Places Rated Score: 2,051     Places Rated Rank: 72

## Chicago, IL
Living History Museums (600)
◄ Blackberry Historical Farm Village (Aurora)
History Museums (1,600)
  Aurora Historical Museum (Aurora)
  Balzekas Museum of Lithuanian Culture (Chicago)
◄◄ Chicago Historical Society (Chicago)
  Du Sable Museum of Afro-American History
    (Chicago)
◄ Oriental Institute Museum (Chicago)
  Polish Museum of America (Chicago)
  Elmhurst Historical Museum (Elmhurst)
  Highland Park Historical Society (Highland Park)
House Museums and Historic Buildings (3,800)
◄◄ Naper Settlement (Aurora)
  Glessner House (Chicago)
  Jane Addams' Hull House (Chicago)
  Robie House (Chicago)
  Dawes House (Evanston)
  Frances Willard Home (Evanston)
  Grosse Point Lighthouse (Evanston)
  Francis Stupey Log Cabin (Highland Park)
  Rialto Square Theatre (Joliet)
  Victorian Manor (Joliet)
◄◄ Illinois & Michigan Canal Museum (Lockport)
  Old Graue Mill and Museum (Oak Brook)

  Frank Lloyd Wright Home and Studio (Oak Park)
  Cantigny (Wheaton)
Military Landmarks (1,900)
◄◄ Great Lakes Naval and Maritime Museum (Chicago)
◄◄ Fort Sheridan (Highwood)
◄◄ Great Lakes Naval Training Center (Waukegan)
◄ Robert R. McCormick Museum (Wheaton)
Historic Districts (400)
  Prairie Avenue Historic District (Chicago)
Antiquity Score: 183 (Chicago settled 1803)
Places Rated Score: 8,483     Places Rated Rank: 12

## Cincinnati, OH–KY
History Museums (300)
  Behringer-Crawford Museum (Covington, KY)
  Warren County Historical Society Museum
    (Lebanon, OH)
Archeological Sites and Museums (250)
◄◄ Serpent Mound State Memorial (Locust Grove, OH)
Presidential Sites (300)
  William Howard Taft N.H.S. (Cincinnati, OH)
House Museums and Historic Buildings (1,700)
  Harriet Beecher Stowe Memorial (Cincinnati)
  John Hauck House Museum (Cincinnati)
  Loveland Castle (Cincinnati)
◄◄ Sharon Woods Village (Cincinnati)
  Union Terminal (Cincinnati)
  Glendower State Memorial (Lebanon)
Antiquity Score: 208 (Cincinnati settled in 1778)
Places Rated Score: 2,758     Places Rated Rank: 62

## Colorado Springs, CO
History Museums (400)
  Canon City Municipal Museum (Canon City)
  Pioneers Museum (Colorado Springs)
  Cripple Creek District Museum (Cripple Creek)
Archeological Sites and Museums (300)
  Manitou Cliff Dwellings Museum (Manitou Springs)
House Museums and Historic Buildings (1,200)
  El Pomar Carriage House Museum (Colorado
    Springs)
◄◄ Flying W Ranch (Colorado Springs)
  McAllister House Museum (Colorado Springs)
  Old Homestead (Cripple Creek)
  Pueblo Metropolitan Museum (Manitou Springs)
Military Landmarks (1,000)
◄◄ U.S. Air Force Academy (Colorado Springs)
◄◄ Pueblo Depot (Pueblo)
Antiquity Score: 115 (Colorado Springs founded
  1871)
Places Rated Score: 3,015     Places Rated Rank: 60

## Coos Bay–South Coast, OR
History Museums (400)
  Bandon Historical Society (Bandon)
  Native American Museum (Coos Bay)
  Coos County Historical Society Museum (North
    Bend)
House Museums and Historic Buildings (150)
  Heceta Head Lighthouse (Florence)
  Umpqua Lighthouse (Winchester Bay)
Antiquity Score: 132 (Coos Bay founded 1854)
Places Rated Score: 682     Places Rated Rank: 98

## Corpus Christi–Padre Island, TX
History Museums (300)
  Museum of Oriental Culture (Corpus Christi)
  John E. Conner Museum (Kingsville)
House Museums and Historic Buildings (300)
  Mission Espiritu Santo de Zuniga (Goliad)
  Presidio La Bahia (Goliad)
  Fulton Mansion (Rockport)
Military Landmarks (500)
◄◄ U.S. Naval Air Station (Corpus Christi)
Antiquity Score: 147 (Corpus Christi founded 1839)
Places Rated Score: 1,247     Places Rated Rank: 88

## Crater Lake–Klamath Falls, OR
History Museums (500)
   Cottage Grove Historical Museum (Cottage Grove)
   Lane County Museum (Eugene)
   Klamath County Museum (Klamath Falls)
   Douglas County Museum (Roseburg)
House Museums and Historic Buildings (1,550)
◄ *Kerbyville Museum (Cave Junction)*
◄◄ Jacksonville Museum (Jacksonville)
◄◄ Pioneer Village (Jacksonville)
   Klamath County Baldwin Hotel Museum (Klamath
   Falls)
Antiquity Score: 84 (Crater Falls Park established
   1902)
Places Rated Score: 2,134        Places Rated Rank: 69

## Dallas–Fort Worth, TX
Living History Museums (600)
◄ Old City Park (Dallas)
History Museums (650)
   *Limestone County Historical Museum (Groesbeck)*
   *Historical Museum (Jefferson)*
   *Caddo Indian Museum (Longview)*
   Sherman Historical Museum (Sherman)
◄ *Governor Hogg S.H.P. (Sulphur Springs)*
   *Texas Ranger Museum (Waco)*
Presidential Sites (150)
   *Eisenhower Birthplace S.H.S. (Denison)*
House Museums and Historic Buildings (2,250)
◄◄ *Sam Rayburn House and Library (Bonham)*
◄◄ Pioneer Village (Corsicana)
◄◄ Log Cabin Village (Fort Worth)
   Thistle Hill (Fort Worth)
   *Excelsior House (Jefferson)*
   *Freeman Plantation (Jefferson)*
   *House of the Seasons (Jefferson)*
   *Maxey House (Paris)*
   *Goodman Museum (Tyler)*
   *Highlands Museum (Waco)*
Military Landmarks (200)
   *Fort Inghlish (Bonham)*
   *Old Fort Parker S.H.S. (Groesbeck)*
Historic Districts (200)
   *Waco*
Antiquity Score: 145 (Dallas founded 1841)
Places Rated Score: 4,195        Places Rated Rank: 48

## Denver–Rocky Mountain National Park, CO
History Museums (1,100)
   Boulder Historical Society (Boulder)
   Gilpin County Historical Society Museum (Central
   City)
◄ Colorado Heritage Center (Denver)
   Fort Collins Museum (Fort Collins)
   D.A.R. Pioneer Museum (Golden)
   Municipal Museum (Greeley)
   Longmont Pioneer Museum (Longmont)
House Museums and Historic Buildings (1,600)
   Comanche Crossing Museum (Denver)
   Molly Brown House (Denver)
   Hiwan Homestead Museum (Evergreen)
   Hamill House Museum (Georgetown)
   Hotel de Paris Museum (Georgetown)
   Astor House Hotel Museum (Golden)
   Centennial Village (Greeley)
   Meeker Home (Greeley)
Military Landmarks (200)
   Fort Vasquez (Greeley)
Historic Districts (900)
   Larimer Square (Denver)
   Georgetown Loop Historical Area (Georgetown)
   Heritage Square (Golden)
Special Attractions (500)
   State capital buildings (Denver)
Antiquity Score: 128 (Denver settled 1858)
Places Rated Score: 4,428        Places Rated Rank: 42

## Door County, WI
History Museums (100)
   Door County Historical Museum (Sturgeon Bay)
Archeological Sites and Museums (200)
   Chief Oshkosh Indian Museum (Egg Harbor)
House Museums and Historic Buildings (300)
   Bjorklunden (Baileys Harbor)
   Eagle Bluff Lighthouse Museum (Ephraim)
   Pioneer Schoolhouse Museum (Ephraim)
Antiquity Score: 116 (Sturgeon Bay settled 1870)
Places Rated Score: 716        Places Rated Rank: 96

## Eastern Shore, VA
Special Attractions (500)
   Although Tangier Island, part of the Eastern Shore
   region, has no museums or sites of outstanding
   historic significance, the appearance of the
   entire island is that of another period. There are
   almost no automobiles on the island, and
   streets are only eight to ten feet wide. The
   island was discovered in 1608 by Capt. John
   Smith.
Antiquity Score: 300 (Tangier Island settled 1686)
Places Rated Score: 800        Places Rated Rank: 95

## Finger Lakes, NY
History Museums (1,350)
   Cayuga Museum of History (Auburn)
   *Canastota Canal Town Museum (Canastota)*
   Suggett House Museum (Cortland)
   *Chemung County Historical Society (Elmira)*
   Livingston County Historical Museum (Geneseo)
   Geneva Historical Society Museum (Geneva)
   Glenn H. Curtiss Museum (Hammondsport)
   DeWitt Historical Society (Ithaca)
   *Oswego County Historical Society (Oswego)*
   Seneca Falls Historical Society Museum (Seneca
   Falls)
   Onondaga Historical Association (Syracuse)
   Waterloo Memorial Day Museum (Waterloo)
Archeological Sites and Museums (400)
◄ Owasco Stockaded Indian Village (Auburn)
House Museums and Historic Buildings (2,100)
   Harriet Tubman Home (Auburn)
   Seward House (Auburn)
   Granger Homestead (Canandaigua)
   Benjamin Patterson Inn (Corning)
   1890 House Museum (Cortland)
   Rose Hill Mansion (Geneva)
   E. B. Grandin Print Shop (Palmyra)
   Joseph Smith Home (Palmyra)
   Oliver House Museum (Penn Yan)
   Peter Whitmer Farm (Waterloo)
Military Landmarks (300)
   *Newtown Battlefield Reservation (Elmira)*
◄ Fort Ontario S.H.S. (Oswego)
Antiquity Score: 197 (Syracuse settled 1789)
Places Rated Score: 4,347        Places Rated Rank: 43

## Flaming Gorge, UT–WY–CO
History Museums (400)
◄ *Fort Bridger State Museum (Evanston, WY)*
   Sweetwater County Historical Museum (Green
   River, WY)
   Daughters of Utah Pioneers Museum (Vernal, UT)
Antiquity Score: 124 (Green River settled 1862)
Places Rated Score: 524        Places Rated Rank: 102

## Glacier National Park–Flathead Lake, MT
History Museums (100)
   Polson-Flathead Historical Museum (Polson)
House Museums and Historic Buildings (100)
   Conrad Mansion (Kalispell)
Antiquity Score: 95 (Kalispell founded 1891)
Places Rated Score: 295        Places Rated Rank: 106

## Grand Canyon Country, AZ
History Museums (400)
  Northern Arizona Pioneers Historical Museum
    (Flagstaff)
  Jerome S.H.P. (Jerome)
Archeological Sites and Museums (2,300)
◄◄ Tuzigoot National Monument (Clarkdale)
◄◄ Montezuma Castle National Monument (Cottonwood)
  Museum of Northern Arizona (Flagstaff)
◄◄ Walnut Canyon (Flagstaff)
◄◄ Wupatki National Monument (Flagstaff)
Military Landmarks (400)
◄ Fort Verde S.H.P. (Camp Verde)
Historic Districts (300)
◄ *Sharlot Hall Museum (Prescott)*
Antiquity Score: 110 (Flagstaff settled 1876)
Places Rated Score: 3,510        Places Rated Rank: 58

## Green Mountains, VT
History Museums (1,250)
◄ *Bennington Museum (Bennington)*
◄ Sheldon Museum (Middlebury)
◄ Vermont Historical Museum (Montpelier)
  Franklin County Museum (St. Albans)
  *Fairbanks Museum (St. Johnsbury)*
  Woodstock Historical Society (Woodstock)
Presidential Sites (700)
  Chester A. Arthur Birthplace (Fairfield)
◄ Calvin Coolidge Homestead (Plymouth)
House Museums and Historic Buildings (2,500)
  *Park-McCullough House (Bennington)*
  *Peter Matteson Tavern Museum (Bennington)*
  *The Old Tavern (Grafton)*
  *Historic Hildene (Manchester)*
  Kent Tavern Museum (Montpelier)
  Norman Rockwell Museum (Rutland)
  Wilson Castle (Rutland)
◄◄ Shelburne Museum (Shelburne)
  Bloody Brook School House (Stowe)
  Chimney Point Tavern (Vergennes)
  John Strong Mansion (Vergennes)
  *Farrar-Mansur House Museum (Weston)*
  *Constitution House (Windsor)*
Military Landmarks (200)
  Hubbardton Battlefield and Museum (Rutland)
Historic Districts (200)
  *Old Bennington (Bennington)*
Special Attractions (500)
  State capital buildings (Montpelier)
Antiquity Score: 216 (First settlements before 1770)
Places Rated Score: 5,566        Places Rated Rank: 30

## Hawaii
Living History Museums (1,100)
  Pu'uhonua O Honaunau N.H.P. (Honaunau,
    Hawaii)
◄ Polynesian Cultural Center (Laie, Oahu)
History Museums (1,200)
◄◄ Bishop Museum (Honolulu, Oahu)
  Kauai Museum (Lihue, Kauai)
◄ Kamuela Museum (Waimea, Hawaii)
  Parker Ranch Visitor Center Museum (Waimea)
House Museums and Historic Buildings (2,000)
  Waioli Mission House (Hanalei, Kauai)
  Lyman Mission House and Museum (Hilo, Hawaii)
  Queen Emma Summer Palace (Honolulu)
  Hulihee Palace (Kailua-Kona, Hawaii)
  Mokuaikaua Church (Kailua-Kona)
  Byodo-in Temple (Kaneohe, Oahu)
  Lapakahi S.H.P. (Kawaihae, Hawaii)
  Puukohola Heiau N.H.S. (Kawaihae)
  *Carthaginian II* Floating Museum (Lahaina, Maui)
Military Landmarks (1,100)
◄◄ U.S. Army Museum of Hawaii (Honolulu)
  Pacific Submarine Museum (Pearl Harbor, Oahu)
  U.S.S. *Arizona* National Memorial (Pearl Harbor)
  U.S.S. *Bowfin* (Pearl Harbor)

Historic Districts (400)
  Kalaupapa N.H.P. (Kalaupapa, Molokai)
Special Attractions (500)
  State capital buildings (Honolulu)
Antiquity Score: 208 (Hawaii reached by Europeans
  1778)
Places Rated Score: 6,508        Places Rated Rank: 20

## Hilton Head, SC
History Museums (100)
  Beaufort Museum (Beaufort)
House Museums and Historic Buildings (200)
  George P. Elliott House (Beaufort)
  John Mark Verdier House (Beaufort)
Military Landmarks (1,000)
  Marine Corps Air Station (Beaufort)
  Parris Island (Beaufort)
Antiquity Score: 276 (Beaufort settled 1710)
Places Rated Score: 1,576        Places Rated Rank: 82

## Holland–Lake Michigan Shore, MI
History Museums (400)
  Grand Rapids Public Museum (Grand Rapids)
  Netherlands Museum (Holland)
  Saugatuck Marine Museum (Saugatuck)
Presidential Sites (300)
  Gerald R. Ford Museum (Grand Rapids)
House Museums and Historic Buildings (500)
  Hackley House (Muskegon)
  Hume House (Muskegon)
  Liberty Hyde Bailey Memorial Museum (South
    Haven)
Antiquity Score: 139 (Holland founded 1847)
Places Rated Score: 1,339        Places Rated Rank: 85

## Houston–Galveston, TX
History Museums (250)
  Spindletop Museum (Beaumont)
  *Star of the Republic Museum (Brenham)*
  *Brazos Valley Museum (Bryan)*
  *Lufkin Historical Center (Lufkin)*
Archeological Sites and Museums (100)
  *Indian Mound (Nacogdoches)*
House Museums and Historic Buildings (4,200)
◄◄ Gladys City–Spindletop Boomtown (Beaumont)
  John Jay French House Museum (Beaumont)
  *Anson Jones House (Brenham)*
  *Independence Hall (Brenham)*
  *Mission Tejas (Crockett)*
  *Monroe Crook House (Crockett)*
  Ashton Villa (Galveston)
  Bishop's Place (Galveston)
  Elissa Pier 21 (Galveston)
  Sydnor-Powhatan House (Galveston)
  Bayou Bend Collection (Houston)
◄◄ Sam Houston Park (Houston)
  *Sam Houston Residence (Huntsville)*
  *Steamboat House (Huntsville)*
◄ *Millard's Crossing (Nacogdoches)*
  *The Stark House (Orange)*
  La Maison des Acadian Museum (Port Arthur)
  Nederland Windmill Museum (Port Arthur)
  Pompeiian Villa (Port Arthur)
  Rose Hill Manor (Port Arthur)
  *Allan Shivers Museum (Woodville)*
◄◄ *Heritage Garden Village (Woodville)*
Military Landmarks (1,300)
  Seawolf Park; 2 vessels, museum (Galveston)
  Battleship *Texas* (Houston)
  San Jacinto Battleground and Museum (Houston)
  *Old Stone Fort Museum (Nacogdoches)*
Historic Districts (400)
  Strand District (Galveston)
Antiquity Score: 150 (Houston founded 1836)
Places Rated Score: 6,400        Places Rated Rank: 22

## Jersey Shore, NJ
History Museums (200)
  Long Branch Historical Museum (Asbury Park)
House Museums and Historic Buildings (100)
  Barnegat Lighthouse (Long Beach Island)
Antiquity Score: 307 (Trenton settled 1679)
Places Rated Score: 607        Places Rated Rank: 99

## Knoxville–Smoky Mountains, TN
Living History Museums (200)
  Tipton-Haynes Living History Farm (Johnson City)
History Museums (1,300)
◄ ◄ *Abraham Lincoln Museum (Harrogate)*
  Overmountain Museum (Johnson City)
  Jonesboro History Museum (Jonesboro)
  Confederate Memorial Hall (Knoxville)
◄ Museum of Appalachia (Norris)
  The Old Mill (Pigeon Forge)
Presidential Sites (500)
◄ Andrew Johnson N.H.S. (Greeneville)
House Museums and Historic Buildings (3,300)
◄ ◄ Sycamore Shoals State Historic Area (Elizabethton)
  Davy Crockett Birthplace (Greeneville)
  Glenmore (Jefferson)
◄ ◄ Rocky Mount Historic Site (Johnson City)
  Chester Inn (Jonesboro)
  Armstrong-Lockett House (Knoxville)
  Blount Mansion (Knoxville)
◄ ◄ Marble Springs (Knoxville)
  Ramsey House (Knoxville)
  Sam Houston Schoolhouse (Maryville)
  Davy Crockett Tavern-Museum (Morristown)
Military Landmarks (700)
◄ ◄ James White's Fort (Knoxville)
  Fort Loudon (Vonore)
Historic Districts (400)
  Jonesborough Historic District (Jonesborough)
Antiquity Score: 199 (Knoxville settled 1787)
Places Rated Score: 6,599      Places Rated Rank: 19

## Lake of the Ozarks, MO
History Museums (250)
  Cole County Historical Society Museum (Jefferson
  City)
◄ Missouri State Museum (Jefferson City)
Archeological Sites and Museums (300)
  Indian Burial Ground and Museum (Osage Beach)
Presidential Sites (500)
  *Truman Courtroom and Office (Independence)*
◄ ◄ *Truman Home, Library, and Museum (Independence)*
House Museums and Historic Buildings (1,900)
◄ ◄ *Arrow Rock S.H.S. (Arrow Rock)*
◄ ◄ Kumberland Gap Pioneer Settlement (Clinton)
  *Bingham-Waggoner Estate (Independence)*
  *1859 Marshal's Home and Museum (Independence)*
  *Log Courthouse (Independence)*
  *Pioneer Spring Cabin (Independence)*
  *John Wornall House Museum (Kansas City)*
  *Sexton's Cottage (Kansas City)*
◄ ◄ Old Frontier Town Museum (Osage Beach)
Military Landmarks (500)
◄ ◄ *Fort Osage (Independence)*
◄ *Liberty Memorial and Museum (Kansas City)*
  *Union Cemetery (Kansas City)*
Historic Districts (150)
  *Jefferson Landing (Jefferson City)*
Special Attractions (250)
  *State capital buildings (Jefferson City)*
Antiquity Score: 55 (Lake of the Ozarks, an artificial
  lake, completed 1931)
Places Rated Score: 3,905      Places Rated Rank: 52

## Lake Powell–Glen Canyon, AZ–UT
History Museums (200)
  Moab Museum (Moab, UT)
  John Wesley Powell Museum (Page, AZ)

Archeological Sites and Museums (800)
◄ Edges of the Cedars Historic Memorial (Blanding, UT)
◄ Hovenweep National Monument (Blanding)
Antiquity Score: 81 (Blanding settled 1905)
Places Rated Score: 1,081      Places Rated Rank: 92

## Lake Tahoe–Reno, NV–CA
History Museums (600)
◄ Nevada State Museum (Carson City, NV)
  Nevada Historical Society Museum (Reno, NV)
House Museums and Historic Buildings (400)
  Bowers Mansion (Carson City)
  The Castle (Virginia City, NV)
Military Landmarks (200)
  Fort Churchill State Monument (Yerington, NV)
Special Attractions (500)
  State capital buildings (Carson City)
Antiquity Score: 118 (Reno founded 1868)
Places Rated Score: 1,818      Places Rated Rank: 75

## Las Vegas–Lake Mead, NV–AZ
History Museums (700)
  Clark County Southern Nevada Museum
  (Henderson, NV)
◄ Mohave Museum of History and Art (Kingman, AZ)
  Colorado River Indian Museum (Parker, AZ)
Archeological Sites and Museums (400)
◄ Lost City Museum of Archeology (Overton, NV)
Antiquity Score: 131 (Las Vegas, NV, settled 1855)
Places Rated Score: 1,231      Places Rated Rank: 89

## ★ Lexington–Bluegrass Country, KY
History Museums (400)
  Appalachian Museum (Berea)
  Museum of History and Science (Louisville)
Archeological Sites and Museums (300)
  Anthropology Museum (Lexington)
Presidential Sites (150)
  *A. Lincoln Birthplace Site (Elizabethtown)*
House Museums and Historic Buildings (4,750)
  Wickland (Bardstown)
  McDowell House and Apothecary (Danville)
  *Brown-Pusey House (Elizabethtown)*
  *Lincoln Heritage House (Elizabethtown)*
  Liberty Hall (Frankfort)
  Orlando Brown House (Frankfort)
  Ward Hall (Georgetown)
◄ ◄ Shakertown at Pleasant Hill (Harrodsburg)
  Ashland (Lexington)
  Hopemont (Lexington)
  Mary Todd Lincoln House (Lexington)
  Opera House (Lexington)
  Parker Place (Lexington)
◄ ◄ Waveland State Shrine (Lexington)
  Col. Harland Sanders Museum (Louisville)
  Farmington (Louisville)
◄ Locust Grove (Louisville)
  Thomas Edison House (Louisville)
  *William Whitley House (Mount Vernon)*
  Duncan Tavern Historic Shrine (Paris)
  Lincoln Homestead State Park (Springfield)
Military Landmarks (1,800)
◄ *Patton Museum of Cavalry and Armor (Fort Knox)*
◄ Kentucky Military History Museum (Frankfort)
◄ ◄ Old Fort Harrod State Park (Harrodsburg)
  Perryville Battlefield State Shrine (Perryville)
◄ ◄ Fort Boonesborough State Park (Winchester)
Historic Districts (1,500)
  Constitution Square (Danville)
  Morgan Row (Harrodsburg)
  Gratz Park (Lexington)
  Butchertown (Louisville)
  Cherokee Triangle (Louisville)
  Old Louisville (Louisville)
  Phoenix Hill (Louisville)

Special Attractions (500)
  State capital buildings (Frankfort)
Antiquity Score: 207 (Lexington founded 1779)
Places Rated Score: 9,607          Places Rated Rank: 7

## Long Island, NY
History Museums (500)
  Lauder Museum (Amityville)
  Black History Museum (Hempstead)
  Wightman House (Oyster Bay)
  Suffolk County Historical Society (Riverhead)
  Southampton Historical Museum (Southampton)
Archeological Sites and Museums (300)
  Archaeological Museum (Southold)
Presidential Sites (700)
◄◄ Sagamore Hill N.H.S. (Oyster Bay)
House Museums and Historic Buildings (2,800)
  Sagtikos Manor (Bay Shore)
  "Home, Sweet Home" House (East Hampton)
  Hook Mill (East Hampton)
  Saddle Rock Grist Mill (Great Neck)
  David Conklin Farmhouse (Huntington)
  Huntington Trade School (Huntington)
  Joseph Lloyd Manor House (Huntington)
  Powell-Jarvis House (Huntington)
  Walt Whitman Birthplace (Huntington)
  Raynham Hall Museum (Oyster Bay)
  Thompson House (Port Jefferson)
  Rock Hall (Rockville Centre)
  Old House (Southhold)
  Village Green Complex (Southold)
  Museums at Stony Brook (Stony Brook)
Military Landmarks (500)
◄◄ U.S. Merchant Marine Academy (Great Neck)
Antiquity Score: 338 (East Hampton settled 1648)
Places Rated Score: 5,138          Places Rated Rank: 36

## Los Angeles, CA
History Museums (1,300)
  Catalina Museum (Avalon)
  Long Beach Heritage Museum (Long Beach)
◄ Southwest Museum (Los Angeles)
  Wells Fargo History Museum (Los Angeles)
  Ojai Valley Historical Society and Museum (Ojai)
  Pasadena Historical Museum (Pasadena)
  Heritage Square Museum (Santa Monica)
  Ventura County Historical Society Museum
    (Ventura)
Archeological Sites and Museums (600)
  George C. Page La Brea Discoveries Museum
    (Los Angeles)
  Albinger Archeology Museum (Ventura)
House Museums and Historic Buildings (2,900)
  Rancho Los Alamitos (Long Beach)
  Rancho Los Cerritos (Long Beach)
  Los Encinos S.H.P. (Los Angeles)
  Lummis Home (Los Angeles)
  Will Rogers S.H.P. (Los Angeles)
  J. Paul Getty Museum (Malibu)
  Gamble House (Pasadena)
  Adobe de Palomares (Pomona)
  Mission San Fernandino (San Fernando)
  Mission San Gabriel Arcangel (San Gabriel)
  Old Mission San Juan Capistrano (San Juan
    Capistrano)
  O'Neil Museum (San Juan Capistrano)
  El Molino Viejo (San Marino)
  Stagecoach Inn Museum Complex (Thousand
    Oaks)
  Olivas Adobe (Ventura)
  Oretega Adobe (Ventura)
  San Buenaventura Mission (Ventura)
Military Landmarks (800)
◄ Museum of World Wars (Buena Park)
◄ CEC/Seabee Museum (Oxnard)

Historic Districts (600)
  El Pueblo de Los Angeles (Los Angeles)
  Old adobe houses (San Juan Capistrano)
Antiquity Score: 205 (Los Angeles founded 1781)
Places Rated Score: 6,405          Places Rated Rank: 21

## Mackinac Island–Sault Ste. Marie, MI
House Museums and Historic Buildings (600)
  Agency House (Mackinac Island)
  American Fur Company Trading Post (Mackinac
    Island)
  Mackinac Island State Park Complex (Mackinac
    Island)
Military Landmarks (500)
◄◄ Old Fort Mackinac (Mackinac Island)
Antiquity Score: 305 (Mackinaw City settled 1681)
Places Rated Score: 1,405          Places Rated Rank: 83

## Memphis, TN–AR–MS
History Museums (200)
  Pink Palace Museum (Memphis, TN)
Archeological Sites and Museums (600)
◄ Pinson Mounds State Archaeological Park (Jackson, TN)
◄ Chucalissa Indian Village and Museum (Memphis)
House Museums and Historic Buildings (1,050)
  Casey Jones Home and Museum (Jackson)
  Fontaine House (Memphis)
  Graceland (Memphis)
  Magevney House (Memphis)
  Mallory-Neely House (Memphis)
Military Landmarks (100)
  Shiloh N.M.P. (Savannah, TN)
Historic Districts (300)
  Victorian Village (Memphis)
Antiquity Score: 167 (Memphis settled 1819)
Places Rated Score: 2,417          Places Rated Rank: 64

## Miami–Gold Coast–Keys, FL
History Museums (500)
  Florida Pioneer Museum (Florida City)
  East Martello Gallery and Museum (Key West)
  Historical Museum of Southern Florida (Miami)
House Museums and Historic Buildings (1,100)
  Audubon House (Key West)
  Ernest Hemingway Home (Key West)
  Oldest House Museum (Key West)
  Vizcaya (Miami)
  Henry Morrison Flagler Museum (Palm Beach)
Military Landmarks (600)
◄ Lighthouse Tower and Military Museum (Key West)
◄ Fort Jefferson National Monument (islands west of Key West)
Historic Districts (300)
  Art Deco District (Miami Beach)
Antiquity Score: 116 (Miami settled 1870)
Places Rated Score: 2,616          Places Rated Rank: 63

## Minneapolis–St. Paul, MN–WI
Living History Museums (400)
  Oliver H. Kelley Farm and Interpretive Center (Elk
    River)
History Museums (1,300)
◄ Kensington Runestone Museum (Alexandria)
  Crow Wing County Historical Museum (Brainerd)
  Charles A. Weyerhaeuser Memorial Museum (Little
    Falls)
  Blue Earth County Historical Society Museum
    (Mankato)
  Hennepin County Historical Society Museum
    (Minneapolis)
  Brown County Historical Museum (New Ulm)
  Mille Lacs Indian Museum (Onamia)
  Goodhue County Historical Museum (Red Wing)
  Lower Sioux Agency (Redwood Falls)
  Olmsted County Historical Museum (Rochester)
  Minnesota Historical Society (St. Paul)

Washington County Historical Museum (Stillwater)
*Winona County Historical Society Museum*
*(Winona)*
Archeological Sites and Museums (200)
Indian Mounds Park (St. Paul)
House Museums and Historic Buildings (2,300)
Alexander Faribault House (Faribault)
LeDuc Mansion (Hastings)
W. W. Mayo House (Le Sueur)
◄ *Meeker County Historical Society Museum (Litchfield)*
*Charles A. Lindbergh House (Little Falls)*
◄◄ Village of Yesteryear (Owatonna)
*Mayowood (Rochester)*
Sibley House Museum (St. Paul)
*Sinclair Lewis Boyhood Home (Sauk Centre)*
W. H. C. Folsom House (Taylors Falls)
*Arches Branch Museum (Winona)*
*Bunnell House (Winona)*
Military Landmarks (500)
◄◄ Fort Snelling (St. Paul)
Historic Districts (600)
Historic Corner, Scandia (Stillwater)
Angel Hill Historic District (Taylors Falls)
Special Attractions (500)
State capital buildings (St. Paul)
Antiquity Score: 146 (St. Paul settled 1840)
Places Rated Score: 5,946    Places Rated Rank: 24

**Mobile Bay–Gulfport, AL–MS**
House Museums and Historic Buildings (1,100)
Beauvoir (Biloxi, MS)
Biloxi Lighthouse (Biloxi)
Magnolia Hotel and Museum (Biloxi)
Carlin House Museum (Mobile, AL)
Conde-Charlotte House (Mobile)
Oakleigh (Mobile)
Richards-D.A.R. House (Mobile)
Military Landmarks (1,900)
Fort Massachusetts (Biloxi)
◄ Fort Gaines (Dauphin Island, AL)
◄ Fort Morgan (Gulf Shores, AL)
Fort Morgan Museum (Gulf Shores)
U.S.S. *Alabama* (Mobile)
◄◄ Old Spanish Fort (Pascagoula, MS)
Historic Districts (300)
Fort Conde and Village (Mobile)
Antiquity Score: 275 (Mobile founded 1711)
Places Rated Score: 3,575    Places Rated Rank: 55

**Monterey–Big Sur, CA**
History Museums (500)
Los Gatos Museum (Los Gatos)
Colton Hall Museum (Monterey)
Santa Cruz City Museum (Santa Cruz)
Historical Museum (Saratoga)
House Museums and Historic Buildings (2,200)
Mission San Carlos Borromeo del Rio Carmelo
(Carmel)
Mission San Antonio de Padua (King City)
Monterey S.H.P. (Monterey)
Point Pinos Light Station (Pacific Grove)
◄◄ Historic San Jose (San Jose)
◄ San Juan Bautista S.H.P. (San Juan Bautista)
Military Landmarks (400)
◄ Fort Ord Museum (Monterey)
Historic Districts (600)
Historic Homes Walk (Monterey)
Presidio of Monterey (Monterey)
Antiquity Score: 216 (Monterey founded 1770)
Places Rated Score: 3,916    Places Rated Rank: 51

**Myrtle Beach–Grand Strand, SC**
House Museums and Historic Buildings (300)
Harold Kaminski House (Georgetown)
Hopsewee Plantation (Georgetown)
Antiquity Score: 257 (Georgetown founded 1729)
Places Rated Score: 557    Places Rated Rank: 101

**Mystic Seaport–Connecticut Valley, CT**
Living History Museums (700)
◄◄ Mystic Seaport (Mystic)
Archeological Sites and Museums (300)
Tantaquidgeon Indian Museum (Norwich)
House Museums and Historic Buildings (2,300)
Amasa Day House (East Haddam)
Gillette Castle State Park (East Haddam)
Goodspeed Opera House (East Haddam)
Nathan Hale Schoolhouse (East Haddam)
Denison Homestead (Mystic)
Deshon-Allyn House (New London)
Joshua Hempsted House (New London)
Monte Cristo Cottage (New London)
Old Town Mill (New London)
Shaw Mansion (New London)
Leffingwell Inn (Norwich)
Old Lighthouse Museum (Stonington)
Whitehall (Stonington)
Jillson House Museum (Willimantic)
Military Landmarks (1,600)
◄◄ Naval Submarine Base (Groton)
Submarine Memorial U.S.S. *Croaker* (Groton)
◄◄ U.S. Coast Guard Academy (New London)
◄ World War II Victory Museum (Willimantic)
Special Attractions (500)
State capital buildings (Hartford)
Antiquity Score: 332 (Mystic settled 1654)
Places Rated Score: 5,732    Places Rated Rank: 28

**Nashville, TN**
History Museums (400)
◄ Tennessee State Museum (Nashville)
Presidential Sites (650)
*Ancestral Home, James K. Polk (Columbia)*
◄ The Hermitage (Nashville)
House Museums and Historic Buildings (2,550)
*The Athenaeum (Columbia)*
Carnton Mansion (Franklin)
Cragfont (Gallatin)
Wynnewood (Gallatin)
◄◄ Cannonsburgh Pioneer Village (Murfreesboro)
Oaklands (Murfreesboro)
Belle Meade (Nashville)
Sam Davis Home (Nashville)
Traveller's Rest (Nashville)
Military Landmarks (1,000)
Stones River National Battlefield (Murfreesboro)
◄ Fort Nashborough (Nashville)
◄ Military Museum (Nashville)
Special Attractions (500)
State capital buildings (Nashville)
Antiquity Score: 207 (Nashville settled 1779)
Places Rated Score: 5,307    Places Rated Rank: 34

**New Orleans, LA**
History Museums (1,700)
The Cabildo (New Orleans)
◄ Confederate Museum (New Orleans)
Historic New Orleans Collection (New Orleans)
Madame John's Legacy (New Orleans)
The Presbytere (New Orleans)
House Museums and Historic Buildings (3,000)
Southdown Plantation (Houma)
Beauregard-Keyes House (New Orleans)
Destrehan Plantation (New Orleans)
The 1850 House (New Orleans)
Gallier House (New Orleans)
Hermann-Grima House (New Orleans)
Longue Vue House (New Orleans)
The Old Absinthe House (New Orleans)
Pharmacy Museum (New Orleans)
St. Louis Cathedral (New Orleans)
San Francisco Plantation (New Orleans)
U.S. Custom House (New Orleans)
Edward Douglas White Museum (Thibodaux)
◄ Madewood Plantation House (Thibodaux)
Oak Valley Plantation (Thibodaux)

Military Landmarks (200)
  Chalmette (New Orleans)
Historic Districts (1,100)
  The Garden District (New Orleans)
◄ ◄ Vieux Carré (New Orleans)
Special Attractions (700)
  Jean Lafitte N.H.P.; several areas and walking
    tours (New Orleans)
Antiquity Score: 268 (New Orleans founded 1718)
Places Rated Score: 6,968    Places Rated Rank: 17

★ **New York City, NY**
Living History Museums (400)
  Richmondtown Restoration (Staten Island)
History Museums (2,300)
  Museum of Bronx History (Bronx)
  *Boxwood Hall (Elizabeth, NJ)*
  Von Steuben House (Hackensack, NJ)
  Chinese Museum (Manhattan)
  El Museo del Barrio (Manhattan)
  Hispanic Society of America (Manhattan)
  The Jewish Museum (Manhattan)
  Museum of the American Indian (Manhattan)
◄ Museum of the City of New York (Manhattan)
◄ ◄ The New York Historical Society (Manhattan)
  The Ukrainian Museum (Manhattan)
  Huguenot–Thomas Paine Historical Association
    (New Rochelle)
Presidential Sites (300)
  Theodore Roosevelt Birthplace N.H.S. (Manhattan)
House Museums and Historic Buildings (4,200)
  Bartow-Pell Mansion Museum (Bronx)
  Edgar Allan Poe Cottage (Bronx)
  Van Cortlandt Mansion Museum (Bronx)
◄ ◄ Castle Clinton National Monument (Manhattan)
  Dyckman House (Manhattan)
  Federal Hall National Museum (Manhattan)
  Fraunces Tavern Museum (Manhattan)
  Morris-Jumel Mansion (Manhattan)
  Statue of Liberty National Monument (Manhattan)
◄ ◄ United Nations Complex (Manhattan)
  Thomas Paine Cottage (New Rochelle)
  Bowne House (Queens)
  Conference House (Staten Island)
  Phillipse Manor Hall S.H.S. (White Plains)
  Washington's Headquarters (White Plains)
  Sherwood House (Yonkers)
Military Landmarks (900)
◄ ◄ Fort Lee Historic Park (Fort Lee, NJ)
  U.S.S. *Ling* Submarine (Hackensack, NJ)
  Miller Hill Restoration (White Plains)
Historic Districts (1,100)
◄ ◄ South Street Seaport (Manhattan)
  Richmondtown Restoration (Staten Island)
Antiquity Score: 371 (Manhattan Island settled 1615)
Places Rated Score: 9,571    Places Rated Rank: 8

**Niagara Falls–Western New York, NY**
History Museums (350)
  *Holland Land Office Museum (Batavia)*
  Buffalo and Erie County Historical Society (Buffalo)
  Chautauqua County Historical Society
    (Chautauqua)
Archeological Sites and Museums (300)
  Seneca-Iroquois National Museum (Salamanca)
Presidential Landmarks (800)
◄ Theodore Roosevelt Inaugural N.H.S. (Buffalo)
  Millard Fillmore Museum (East Aurora)
Historic Districts (700)
  Allentown (Buffalo)
  The Chautauqua Institution (Chautauqua)
Antiquity Score: 180 (Niagara Falls settled 1806)
Places Rated Score: 2,330    Places Rated Rank: 66

**North Woods–Land O'Lakes, WI**
History Museums (200)
  Old Town Hall Museum (Park Falls)
  Rhinelander Logging Museum (Rhinelander)
Antiquity Score: 106 (Rhinelander settled 1880)
Places Rated Score: 306    Places Rated Rank: 105

**Oklahoma City–Cherokee Strip, OK**
History Museums (2,950)
  *Southern Plains Indian Museum (Anadarko)*
  Canadian County Historical Society Museum (El
    Reno)
  Museum of the Cherokee Strip (Enid)
◄ Oklahoma Territorial Museum (Guthrie)
◄ ◄ *Museum of the Great Plains (Lawton)*
◄ ◄ State Museum of Oklahoma (Oklahoma City)
  Washita Valley Museum (Pauls Valley)
  Cherokee Strip Museum (Perry)
  Cultural Center Museums (Ponca City)
  Pioneer Woman Museum (Ponca City)
  Seminole National Museum (Shawnee)
  *Chisholm Trail Historical Museum (Waurika)*
House Museums and Historic Buildings (1,300)
◄ ◄ *Indian City–USA (Anadarko)*
  Homesteader's Sod House (Enid)
◄ ◄ *The Old Post N.H.L. (Lawton)*
  Harn Museum (Oklahoma City)
  Murray-Lindsay Mansion (Pauls Valley)
  Marland Mansion (Ponca City)
Military Landmarks (850)
  Fort Reno (El Reno)
◄ ◄ *Fort Sill Military Reservation (Lawton)*
◄ Forty-fifth Infantry Division Museum (Oklahoma City)
Special Attractions (500)
  State capital buildings (Oklahoma City)
Antiquity Score: 97 (Oklahoma City founded 1889)
Places Rated Score: 5,697    Places Rated Rank: 29

**Olympic Peninsula, WA**
History Museums (400)
◄ State Capitol Museum (Olympia)
Archeological Sites and Museums (500)
  Makah Cultural and Research Center (Neah Bay)
  Manis Mastodon Site (Sequim)
House Museums and Historic Buildings (400)
  Hoquiam's "Castle" (Hoquiam)
  Polson Park and Museum (Hoquiam)
  Rothschild House (Port Townsend)
Military Landmarks (400)
  Borst Blockhouse and Farmhouse (Centralia)
  Fort Lewis (Olympia)
Special Attractions (500)
  State capital buildings (Olympia)
Antiquity Score: 136 (Olympia founded 1850)
Places Rated Score: 2,336    Places Rated Rank: 65

**Orlando–Space Coast, FL**
History Museums (900)
◄ ◄ Visitors Center (Kennedy Space Center)
  Orange County Historical Museum (Orlando)
  McLarty Visitor Center (Vero Beach)
House Museums and Historic Buildings (100)
  Gilbert's Bar House of Refuge (Stuart)
Antiquity Score: 149 (Orlando settled 1837)
Places Rated Score: 1,149    Places Rated Rank: 91

**Outer Banks, NC**
History Museums (100)
  *Museum of the Albemarle (Elizabeth City)*
House Museums and Historic Buildings (2,800)
◄ ◄ Beaufort Historical Association (Beaufort)
  Bodie Lighthouse (Cape Hatteras National
    Seashore)
  Cape Hatteras Lighthouse (Cape Hatteras
    National Seashore)
  *Newbold-White House (Edenton)*

◄◄ *Somerset Place S.H.S. (Edenton)*
◄ Wright Brothers National Memorial (Kill Devil Hills)
*Elizabeth II S.H.S. (Manteo)*
◄◄ Tryon Palace and Gardens (New Bern)
Hope Plantation (Williamston)
Historic Districts (1,000)
◄ *Historic Edenton (Edenton)*
◄◄ Fort Raleigh N.H.S. (Manteo)
Special Attractions (500)
Historical drama *The Lost Colony* (Manteo)
Antiquity Score: 321 (Outer Banks first settled about 1665)
Places Rated Score: 4,721     Places Rated Rank: 39

### Ozarks–Eureka Springs, AR–MO
Living History Museums (300)
◄ *Ozark Folk Center (Mountain View, AR)*
History Museums (1,100)
Carroll County Heritage Center (Berryville, AR)
Ralph Foster Museum (Branson, MO)
Eureka Springs Historical Museum (Eureka Springs, AR)
Dorothea B. Hoover Historical Museum (Joplin, MO)
◄ Shiloh Museum (Rogers, AR)
Laura Ingalls Wilder–Rose Wilder Lane Home and Museum (Springfield, MO)
House Museums and Historic Buildings (2,000)
◄ George Washington Carver National Monument (Diamond, MO)
The Castle at Inspiration Point (Eureka Springs)
The Rosalie House (Eureka Springs)
Headquarters House (Fayetteville, AR)
Robinson Farm Museum (Harrison, AR)
Wolf House (Mountain Home, AR)
Hawkins House and Museum (Rogers)
Museum of the Ozarks (Springfield)
Shepherd of the Hills Farm (Table Rock Area, MO)
Military Landmarks (500)
Prairie Grove Battlefield (Fayetteville)
Pea Ridge N.M.P. (Rogers)
Springfield National Cemetery (Springfield)
Historic Districts (300)
Shiloh Historic District (Springdale, AR)
Antiquity Score: 107 (Eureka Springs founded 1879)
Places Rated Score: 4,307     Places Rated Rank: 46

### Palm Springs–Desert Playgrounds, CA
History Museums (250)
*Mojave River Valley Museum (Barstow)*
Riverside Municipal Museum (Riverside)
Sherman Indian Museum (Riverside)
Archeological Sites and Museums (100)
*Calico Early Man Site (Barstow)*
House Museums and Historic Buildings (850)
◄◄ *Calico Ghost Town Park (Barstow)*
McCallum Adobe (Palm Springs)
Miss Cornelia's "Little House" (Palm Springs)
Asistencia Mission de San Gabriel (Redlands)
Mission Inn (Riverside)
*Roy Rogers–Dale Evans Museum (Victorville)*
Antiquity Score: 110 (Palm Springs founded 1876)
Places Rated Score: 1,310     Places Rated Rank: 87

### Panhandle, FL
History Museums (1,100)
John Gorrie State Museum (Apalachicola)
Junior Museum of Bay County (Panama City)
Pensacola Historical Museum (Pensacola)
Wentworth Museum (Pensacola)
West Florida Museum of History (Pensacola)
Constitution Convention State Museum (Port St. Joe)
◄ *Museum of Florida History (Tallahassee)*
◄ *San Marcos de Apalache State Museum (Tallahassee)*

Archeological Sites and Museums (400)
◄ Temple Mound Museum and Park (Fort Walton Beach)
House Museums and Historic Buildings (450)
Charles Lavalle House (Pensacola)
Dorr House (Pensacola)
Piney Woods Sawmill (Pensacola)
Quina House (Pensacola)
*The Columns (Tallahassee)*
Military Landmarks (2,000)
◄◄ Eglin A.F.B. (Fort Walton Beach)
Fort Barrancas (Pensacola)
Fort Pickens (Pensacola)
◄◄ Naval Air Station (Pensacola)
◄ Naval Aviation Museum (Pensacola)
U.S.S. *Lexington* (Pensacola)
Historic Districts (400)
Seville Square (Pensacola)
Special Attractions (250)
*State capital buildings (Tallahassee)*
Antiquity Score: 263 (Pensacola settled 1723)
Places Rated Score: 4,863     Places Rated Rank: 38

### ★ Pennsylvania Dutch Country, PA
Living History Museums (1,000)
Mill Bridge Village (Lancaster)
◄ Pennsylvania Farm Museum of Landis County (Lancaster)
History Museums (300)
Hershey Museum of American Life (Hershey)
Lebanon County Historical Society (Lebanon)
Historical Society of Berks County (Reading)
Presidential Sites (500)
Lincoln Room Museum (Gettysburg)
Wheatland (Lancaster)
House Museums and Historic Buildings (5,400)
Amish Village (Bird-in-Hand)
Cornwall Iron Furnace (Cornwall)
◄◄ Historic Schaefferstown (Cornwall)
◄◄ Ephrata Cloister (Ephrata)
Abraham Lincoln's Place Theatre (Gettysburg)
The Conflict (Gettysburg)
General Lee's Headquarters (Gettysburg)
Gettysburg Battle Theater (Gettysburg)
Fort Hunter Mansion (Harrisburg)
John Harris Mansion (Harrisburg)
Amish Farm and House (Lancaster)
Amish Homestead (Lancaster)
Fulton Opera House (Lancaster)
Hans Herr House (Lancaster)
Conrad Weiser Homestead (Reading)
◄◄ Daniel Boone Homestead (Reading)
Donegal Mills Plantation (Wrightsville)
Bobb Log House (York)
Bonham House (York)
General Gates' House (York)
Golden Plough Tavern (York)
Little Red Schoolhouse Museum (York)
Military Landmarks (1,300)
◄ Carlisle Barracks (Carlisle)
Gettysburg N.M.P. (Gettysburg)
◄ Soldier's National Museum (Gettysburg)
Special Attractions (500)
State capital buildings (Harrisburg)
Antiquity Score: 265 (Lancaster settled 1721)
Places Rated Score: 9,265     Places Rated Rank: 9

### ★ Philadelphia, PA–DE–NJ
Living History Museums (600)
◄ Hopewell Village N.H.S. (Hopewell Village, PA)
History Museums (800)
◄◄ Balch Institute (Philadelphia, PA)
Mennonite Heritage Center (Quakertown, PA)
House Museums and Historic Buildings (6,600)
Historic Falsington (Bristol, PA)
Pennsbury Manor (Bristol)
◄◄ Burlington County Historical Society (Burlington, NJ)
Landingford Plantation (Chester, PA)
Morton Homestead (Chester)

Historic Yellow Springs (Downingtown, PA)
Mercer Mile (Doylestown, PA)
Pearl Buck's House (Doylestown)
Hope Lodge (Fort Washington, PA)
Harriton House (King of Prussia, PA)
Morgan Log House (Kulpsville, PA)
Colonial Pennsylvania Plantation (Media, PA)
Newlin Grist Mill (Media)
Ferry House (Washington Crossing S.H.P., New Hope)
Parry Mansion (New Hope, PA)
Peter Wentz Farmstead (Norristown, PA)
"A Man Full of Trouble" Tavern (Philadelphia)
Betsy Ross House (Philadelphia)
Cliveden (Philadelphia)
Edgar Allan Poe N.H.P. (Philadelphia)
Hill-Physick-Keith House (Philadelphia)
Powel House (Philadelphia)
Stenton (Philadelphia)
Walnut Street Theatre (Philadelphia)
William Trent House (Trenton, NJ)
◄ Winterthur Museum (Winterthur, DE)
**Military Landmarks (1,800)**
◄◄ Naval Air Station (Horsham, PA)
◄◄ Valley Forge N.H.P. (King of Prussia)
◄ Washington Crossing S.H.P. (New Hope)
◄ Old Barracks Museum (Trenton)
**Historic Districts (1,700)**
The Bourse (Philadelphia)
Elfreth's Alley (Philadelphia)
◄◄ Independence N.H.P. (Philadelphia)
Society Hill (Philadelphia)
**Special Attractions (500)**
State capital buildings (Trenton)
Antiquity Score: 304 (Philadelphia founded 1682)
**Places Rated Score: 12,304        Places Rated Rank: 3**

## Phoenix–Valley of the Sun, AZ
**History Museums (1,700)**
Pinal County Historical Society Museum (Florence)
Clara T. Woody Museum (Globe)
Mesa Museum (Mesa)
◄ Arizona Museum (Phoenix)
◄ Central Arizona Museum of History (Phoenix)
◄ Tempe Historical Museum (Tempe)
Desert Caballeros Western Museum (Wickenburg)
**Archeological Sites and Museums (1,400)**
◄◄ Casa Grande Ruins (near Coolidge)
◄◄ Tonto National Monument (Globe)
◄ Pueblo Grande Museum (Phoenix)
**House Museums and Historic Buildings (400)**
Taliesin West (Scottsdale)
Niels Petersen House (Tempe)
**Military Landmarks (400)**
◄ Champlin Fighter Museum (Mesa)
**Historic Districts (600)**
◄ Heritage Square (Phoenix)
**Special Attractions (500)**
State capital buildings (Phoenix)
Antiquity Score: 122 (Phoenix settled 1864)
**Places Rated Score: 5,122        Places Rated Rank: 37**

## Pocono Mountains, PA
**Living History Museums (800)**
Kempton Farm Museum (Hamburg)
Quiet Valley Living Historical Farm (Stroudsburg)
**History Museums (400)**
Lehigh County Museum (Allentown)
Catlin House (Scranton)
Stroud Mansion (Stroudsburg)
Wyoming Historical Museum (Stroudsburg)
**Archeological Sites and Museums (300)**
Pocono Indian Museum (Bushkill)
**House Museums and Historic Buildings (2,300)**
Liberty Bell Shrine (Allentown)
Trout Hall (Allentown)

◄ Historic Bethlehem (Bethlehem)
Moravian Museum of Bethlehem (Bethlehem)
Sun Inn (Bethlehem)
◄ Pennsylvania Dutch Folk Culture Center (Hamburg)
Eckley Miners' Village (Hazleton)
Asa Packer Mansion (Jim Thorpe)
Swetland Homestead (Wilkes-Barre)
Antiquity Score: 215 (Scranton settled 1771)
**Places Rated Score: 4,015        Places Rated Rank: 49**

## Portland, ME
**History Museums (950)**
Androscoggin Historical Society Museum (Auburn)
*Moses Mason House (Bethel)*
Boothbay Region Historical Society Museum (Boothbay Harbor)
Pejepscot Historical Society Museum (Brunswick)
◄ Maine Historical Society (Portland)
Redington Museum (Waterville)
Yarmouth Historical Society Museum (Yarmouth)
**Archeological Sites and Museums (400)**
◄ Colonial Pemaquid State Memorial (Damariscotta)
**House Museums and Historic Buildings (2,700)**
Blaine House (Augusta)
Maine Maritime Museum (Bath)
Stowe House (Brunswick)
Chapman-Hall House (Damariscotta)
Pemaquid Point Light (Damariscotta)
◄◄ Shaker Museum (Poland Spring)
Portland Headlight (Portland)
Tate House (Portland)
Victoria Mansion (Portland)
Wadsworth-Longfellow House (Portland)
Marret House and Garden (Sebago Lake)
Castle Tucker (Wiscasset)
Nikhels-Sortwell House (Wiscasset)
Pownalborough Court House and Museum (Wiscasset)
Old Ledge School (Yarmouth)
**Military Landmarks (1,000)**
Fort Western Museum (Augusta)
Fort Popham Memorial (Bath)
Fort William Henry State Memorial (Damariscotta)
Old Fort Halifax (Waterville)
Fort Edgecomb State Memorial (Wiscasset)
**Historic Districts (400)**
Old Port Exchange (Portland)
**Special Attractions (500)**
State capital buildings (Augusta)
Antiquity Score: 355 (Portland settled 1631)
**Places Rated Score: 6,305        Places Rated Rank: 23**

## Portland–Columbia River, OR
**History Museums (900)**
Clatsop County Historical Museum (Astoria)
Hood River County Museum (Hood River)
*Lincoln County Historical Society (Newport)*
Clackamas County Historical Society (Oregon City)
Oregon History Center (Portland)
County Museum (Silverton)
Fort Dalles Museum (The Dalles)
Tillamook County Pioneer Museum (Tillamook)
**House Museums and Historic Buildings (2,100)**
Hoover-Minthorn House (Newberg)
◄ McLaughlin House (Oregon City)
Ox Barn Museum (Oregon City)
Pittock Mansion (Portland)
Bush House (Salem)
Deepwood (Salem)
Mission Mill Museum (Salem)
**Special Attractions (500)**
State capital buildings (Salem)
Antiquity Score: 144 (Portland settled 1842)
**Places Rated Score: 3,644        Places Rated Rank: 54**

## Portsmouth–Kennebunk, NH–ME
**History Museums (700)**
New Hampshire Historical Society (Concord, NH)
Tuck Memorial Museum (Hampton Beach, NH)
Kittery Historical and Naval Museum (Kittery, ME)
Manchester Historic Association (Manchester, NH)
Dyer-York Library and Museum (Saco, ME)
**Presidential Sites (300)**
Pierce Manse (Concord)
**House Museums and Historic Buildings (3,800)**
◄◄ Canterbury Shaker Village (Concord)
Brick Store Museum (Kennebunk, ME)
Taylor-Barry House (Kennebunk)
Town House School (Kennebunkport, ME)
Sayward-Wheeler House (Kittery)
◄◄ Amoskeag Mills Complex (Manchester)
Governor John Langdon House (Portsmouth, NH)
John Paul Jones House (Portsmouth)
Moffatt-Ladd House (Portsmouth)
Rundlet-May House (Portsmouth)
Warner House (Portsmouth)
Wentworth-Coolidge Mansion (Portsmouth)
Wentworth Gardner House (Portsmouth)
Clark House (Wolfeboro, NH)
◄◄ York Village (York, ME)
**Military Landmarks (600)**
Fort McClary Memorial (Kittery)
◄ Fort Constitution Site (New Castle, NH)
**Historic Districts (600)**
◄ Strawbery Banke (Portsmouth)
**Special Attractions (500)**
State capital buildings (Concord)
Antiquity Score: 356 (Portsmouth settled 1630)
Places Rated Score: 6,856        Places Rated Rank: 18

## ★ Providence–Newport, RI
**History Museums (900)**
◄ *Fall River Historical Society (Fall River, MA)*
Newport Historical Society Museum (Newport)
South County Museum (North Kingstown)
Museum of Rhode Island History at Aldrich House
(Providence)
Warwick Historical Society (Warwick)
**House Museums and Historic Buildings (7,300)**
Fayerweather House (Kingston)
Astor's Beechwood (Newport)
Bellcourt Castle (Newport)
The Breakers (Newport)
Chateau-sur-Mer (Newport)
The Elms (Newport)
Hammersmith Farm (Newport)
Hunter House (Newport)
Kingscote (Newport)
Marble House (Newport)
Old Colony House (Newport)
Old Stone Mill (Newport)
Rosecliff (Newport)
Samuel Whitehorne House (Newport)
Touro Synagogue (Newport)
Wanton-Lyman-Hazard House (Newport)
Whitehall Museum House (Newport)
Gilbert Stuart Birthplace (North Kingstown)
Smith's Castle (North Kingstown)
Green Animals (Portsmouth)
Prescott Farm and Windmill House (Portsmouth)
Arcade (Providence)
First Baptist Church in America (Providence)
Governor Stephen Hopkins House (Providence)
John Brown House (Providence)
Roger Williams National Memorial (Providence)
Sprague Mansion (Providence)
Wilbor House and Barn (Tiverton)
Babcock-Smith House (Westerly)
**Military Landmarks (1,000)**
*Battleship Cover (Fall River, MA)*
◄ Artillery Company of Newport Museum (Newport)
Fort Barton (Tiverton)

**Historic Districts (400)**
Main Street, Wickford Village (North Kingstown)
**Special Attractions (500)**
State capital buildings (Providence)
Antiquity Score: 350 (Providence settled 1636)
Places Rated Score: 10,450        Places Rated Rank: 5

## Put-in-Bay–Lake Erie Shore, OH
**Living History Museums (350)**
◄◄ *Greenfield Village (Dearborn, MI)*
**History Museums (800)**
*Western Reserve Historical Society Museum
(Cleveland)*
◄◄ *Henry Ford Museum (Dearborn, MI)*
Milan Historical Museum (Milan)
Ottawa County Historical Museum (Port Clinton)
Great Lakes Historical Society Museum (Vermilion)
**Presidential Sites (500)**
◄ Hayes Presidential Center (Fremont)
**House Museums and Historic Buildings (1,750)**
◄◄ Historic Lyme Village (Bellevue)
*The Educational Memorabilia Center (Bowling
Green)*
*Cleveland Arcade (Cleveland)*
*Dunham Tavern Museum (Cleveland)*
*Oldest Stone House (Cleveland)*
Thomas A. Edison Birthplace (Milan)
◄ Wolcott House Museum Complex (Toledo)
**Military Landmarks (900)**
Fort Stephenson Park (Fremont)
Perry's Victory Memorial (Put-in-Bay)
◄◄ Fort Meigs State Memorial (Toledo)
Antiquity Score: 175 (Put-in-Bay settled 1811)
Places Rated Score: 4,475        Places Rated Rank: 41

## Rangeley Lakes, ME
**House Museums and Historic Buildings (150)**
*Little Red Schoolhouse Museum (Farmington)*
*Nordica Homestead Museum (Farmington)*
*History House (Skowhegan)*
Antiquity Score: 161 (Rangeley settled 1825)
Places Rated Score: 311        Places Rated Rank: 104

## Redwoods–Shasta–Lassen, CA
**History Museums (200)**
Del Norte City Historical Society Museum
(Crescent City)
J. J. Jackson Memorial Museum (Weaverville)
**House Museums and Historic Buildings (300)**
Battery Point Lighthouse (Crescent City)
Weaverville Joss House S.H.P. (Weaverville)
**Military Landmarks (300)**
Fort Humboldt S.H.P. (Eureka)
*Roop Fort and William Pratt Museum (Susanville)*
**Historic Districts (700)**
Old Town (Eureka)
Shasta S.H.P. (Redding)
Antiquity Score: 136 (Eureka founded 1850)
Places Rated Score: 1,636        Places Rated Rank: 81

## ★ Richmond–Fredericksburg, VA
**Living History Museums (700)**
◄◄ Meadow Farm Museum (Richmond)
**History Museums (600)**
◄◄ Museum of the Confederacy (Richmond)
**Presidential Sites (1,750)**
Berkeley Plantation (Charles City)
Sherwood Forest (Charles City)
◄ James Monroe Museum and Library (Fredericksburg)
◄ *George Washington Birthplace, "Wakefield" (near
Fredericksburg)*
**House Museums and Historic Buildings (3,500)**
Edgewood Plantation (Charles City)
Shirley Plantation (Charles City)
Belmont (Fredericksburg)
Chatham Manor (Fredericksburg)

Fredericksburg Masonic Lodge #4
(Fredericksburg)
Hugh Mercer Apothecary Shop (Fredericksburg)
Kenmore (Fredericksburg)
Mary Washington House (Fredericksburg)
Old Stone Warehouse (Fredericksburg)
Rising Sun Tavern (Fredericksburg)
Stonewall Jackson Memorial Shrine
(Fredericksburg)
Merchants Hope Church (Hopewell)
Centre Hill Mansion (Petersburg)
Siege Museum (Petersburg)
Agecroft Hall (Richmond)
Edgar Allan Poe Museum (Richmond)
John Marshall House (Richmond)
St. John's Episcopal Church (Richmond)
Virginia House (Richmond)
Wilton (Richmond)
**Military Landmarks (2,000)**
◄◄ *Appomattox Court House N.H.P.
and Confederate Cemetery (Appomattox)*
Confederate Cemetery (Fredericksburg)
Fredericksburg & Spotsylvania N.M.P.
(Fredericksburg)
Fredericksburg National Cemetery
(Fredericksburg)
◄ Shannon Air Museum (Fredericksburg)
◄ Fort Lee Quartermaster Museum (Petersburg)
Petersburg National Battlefield (Petersburg)
Poplar Grove National Cemetery (Petersburg)
Richmond N.B.P. (Richmond)
**Historic Districts (600)**
◄ Church Hill Restored Area (Richmond)
**Special Attractions (500)**
State capital buildings (Richmond)
**Antiquity Score:** 249 (Richmond founded 1737)
**Places Rated Score:** 9,899    **Places Rated Rank:** 6

## Sacramento–Gold Rush Towns, CA

**History Museums (600)**
Placer County Museum (Auburn)
Empire Mine S.H.P. (Grass Valley)
Amador County Museum (Jackson)
State Indian Museum (Sacramento)
Sutter's Fort S.H.P. (Sacramento)
**Archeological Sites and Museums (200)**
Indian Grinding Rock S.H.P. (Jackson)
**House Museums and Historic Buildings (1,500)**
Bernhard Museum Complex (Auburn)
*Bidwell Mansion (Chico)*
American Victorian Museum (Nevada City)
National Hotel (Nevada City)
Chinese Temple (Oroville)
Historic Judge C. F. Lott Home (Oroville)
Marshall Gold Discovery S.H.P. (Placerville)
Governor's Mansion (Sacramento)
**Historic Districts (600)**
The Old Town (Auburn)
Old Sacramento Historic District (Sacramento)
**Special Attractions (500)**
State capital buildings (Sacramento)
**Antiquity Score:** 147 (Sacramento settled 1839)
**Places Rated Score:** 3,547    **Places Rated Rank:** 57

## St. Augustine–Northeast Coast, FL

**History Museums (300)**
De Land Museum (De Land)
◄ *Florida State Museum (Gainesville)*
**House Museums and Historic Buildings (1,900)**
*Marjorie Kinnan Rawlings Home (Cross Creek)*
Sugar Mill Gardens (Daytona Beach)
Delius House (Jacksonville)
Kingsley Plantation (Mayport)
Bulow Plantation (Ormond Beach)
Casa del Hidalgo (St. Augustine)

Dr. Peck House (St. Augustine)
Mission of Nombre de Dios (St. Augustine)
Oldest House (St. Augustine)
Oldest Store Museum (St. Augustine)
Old Wooden Schoolhouse (St. Augustine)
Sanchez House (St. Augustine)
Ximenez-Fatio House (St. Augustine)
Zorayda Castle (St. Augustine)
**Military Landmarks (1,600)**
Fort Matanzas National Monument (Anastasia
Island)
Fort Clinch State Park (Fernandina Beach)
Fort Caroline National Monument (Jacksonville)
◄◄ U.S. Naval Station (Mayport)
◄◄ Castillo de San Marcos National Monument (St.
Augustine)
**Historic Districts (700)**
◄◄ San Agustin Antiguo (St. Augustine)
**Special Attractions (1,000)**
Historical drama *Cross and Sword* (St. Augustine)
First permanent European settlement in what is
now U.S.
**Antiquity Score:** 421 (St. Augustine founded 1565)
**Places Rated Score:** 5,921    **Places Rated Rank:** 25

## St. Louis–Mark Twain Country, MO–IL

**History Museums (1,200)**
Historic Hermann Museum (Hermann, MO)
Ste. Genevieve Museum (Ste. Genevieve, MO)
◄ Missouri Historical Society, Jefferson Memorial (St.
Louis, MO)
◄◄ Museum of Westward Expansion (St. Louis)
**House Museums and Historic Buildings (3,700)**
Becky Thatcher House (Hannibal, MO)
Garth Woodside Mansion (Hannibal)
John Clemens Law Office (Hannibal)
Mark Twain Museum and Home (Hannibal)
Molly Brown House (Hannibal)
Pilaster House (Hannibal)
Rockcliffe Mansion (Hannibal)
Stonecroft Manor (Hannibal)
Mark Twain Birthplace (Monroe City, MO)
First Missouri Capitol (St. Charles, MO)
Marten-Becker House (St. Charles)
Newbill-McElhiney House Museum (St. Charles)
Amoureaux House (Ste. Genevieve)
Bolduc House (Ste. Genevieve)
Felix Valle Home (Ste. Genevieve)
Green Tree Inn (Ste. Genevieve)
Gulbourd-Valle House (Ste. Genevieve)
Campbell House Museum (St. Louis)
Chatillon-De Menil House (St. Louis)
Eugene Field House (St. Louis)
Gen. Daniel Bissell House (St. Louis)
Grant's Farm (St. Louis)
John B. Myers House and Barn (St. Louis)
Powell Symphony Hall (St. Louis)
Daniel Boone Home (Wentzville, MO)
**Military Landmarks (1,100)**
Civil War Fort (Hannibal)
◄◄ Jefferson Barracks Historic Park (St. Louis)
◄ Soldiers' Memorial Military Museum (St. Louis)
**Historic Districts (1,200)**
◄ Hermann
◄ St. Charles
**Antiquity Score:** 222 (St. Louis settled 1764)
**Places Rated Score:** 7,422    **Places Rated Rank:** 15

## Salt Lake City, UT

**Living History Museums (400)**
Old Deseret Pioneer Village (Salt Lake City)
**History Museums (1,300)**
Brigham City Museum (Brigham City)
◄ Golden Spike N.H.S. (Brigham City)
Daughters of the Utah Pioneers Museum (Logan)
Daughters of Utah Pioneers Visitor Center (Ogden)
◄ Camp Floyd and Stagecoach Inn Historic Monument (Provo)

Pioneer Museum (Provo)
Pioneer Memorial Museum (Salt Lake City)
**House Museums and Historic Buildings (900)**
Egyptian Theatre (Park City)
Beehive House (Salt Lake City)
Council Hall (Salt Lake City)
Lion House (Salt Lake City)
**Military Landmarks (200)**
Fort Buenaventura State Historic Monument
(Ogden)
**Historic Districts (300)**
Temple Square (Salt Lake City)
**Special Attractions (500)**
State capitol buildings (Salt Lake City)
Antiquity Score: 139 (Salt Lake City founded 1847)
Places Rated Score: 3,739      Places Rated Rank: 53

## San Antonio, TX
**History Museums (550)**
*Gonzales Memorial Museum (Gonzales)*
◄ Institute of Texan Cultures (San Antonio)
Texas Ranger Museum (San Antonio)
**House Museums and Historic Buildings (2,500)**
*Eggleston House (Gonzales)*
Lindheimer Home (New Braunfels)
The Alamo (San Antonio)
Jose Antonio Navarro S.H.S. (San Antonio)
Menger Hotel (San Antonio)
San Antonio Missions (4 missions, administered by
the National Park Service)
Spanish Governor's Palace (San Antonio)
Steves Homestead (San Antonio)
Yturri-Edmunds Home and Mill (San Antonio)
Garner Memorial Museum (Uvalde)
**Historic Districts (600)**
◄ La Villita (San Antonio)
Antiquity Score: 268 (San Antonio founded 1718)
Places Rated Score: 3,918      Places Rated Rank: 50

## San Diego, CA
**History Museums (100)**
Old Town San Diego S.H.P. (San Diego)
**House Museums and Historic Buildings (900)**
Mission San Luis Rey de Francia (Oceanside)
◄ Cabrillo National Monument (San Diego)
Derby-Pendleton House (San Diego)
Mission Basilica San Diego (San Diego)
Villa Montezuma (San Diego)
**Military Landmarks (500)**
◄◄ Naval Training Center (San Diego)
**Historic Districts (400)**
Old Town (San Diego)
Antiquity Score: 217 (San Diego founded 1769)
Places Rated Score: 2,117      Places Rated Rank: 70

## San Francisco, CA
**History Museums (1,300)**
East Bay Negro Historical Society (Oakland)
◄ Oakland Museum (Oakland)
California Historical Society Whittier Mansion
(San Francisco)
Society of California Pioneers Museum (San
Francisco)
Wells Fargo Bank Historical Room (San Francisco)
County Historical Association (San Mateo)
*Haggin Museum (Stockton)*
Sunnyvale Historical Museum (Sunnyvale)
**House Museums and Historic Buildings (1,000)**
Mission San Jose (Fremont)
John Muir N.H.S. (Martinez)
Dunsmuir House and Garden (Oakland)
Paramount Theatre (Oakland)
Hoover Tower (Palo Alto)
Mission Dolores (San Francisco)
Woodside Store (San Mateo)
Mission San Rafael Arcangel (San Rafael)

**Historic Districts (300)**
Jack London Square (Oakland)
Antiquity Score: 210 (San Francisco founded 1776)
Places Rated Score: 2,810      Places Rated Rank: 61

## Santa Barbara–San Simeon, CA
**History Museums (200)**
San Luis Obispo County Historical Museum (San
Luis Obispo)
Santa Maria Historical Museum (Santa Maria)
**House Museums and Historic Buildings (1,400)**
Mission La Purisma S.H.P. (Lompoc)
Mission San Miguel Arcangel (Paso Robles)
Mission San Luis Obispo de Tolosa (San Luis
Obispo)
◄◄ Hearst–San Simeon State Historical Monument (San
Simeon)
Fernald House (Santa Barbara)
Mission Santa Barbara (Santa Barbara)
Santa Barbara Historical Society Museum (Santa
Barbara)
Trussell-Winchester Adobe (Santa Barbara)
Old Mission Santa Ines (Solvang)
Antiquity Score: 204 (Santa Barbara founded 1782)
Places Rated Score: 1,804      Places Rated Rank: 77

## Savannah–Golden Isles, GA
**History Museums (600)**
Midway Museum (Midway)
Museum of Coastal History (St. Simons)
◄ Tybee Museum (Tybee Island)
**House Museums and Historic Buildings (1,000)**
Hofwyl-Broadfield Plantation (Darien)
St. Simons Lighthouse (St. Simons)
Andrew Low House (Savannah)
Davenport House (Savannah)
Juliette Gordon Low Birthplace (Savannah)
Owens-Thomas House (Savannah)
William Scarbrough House (Savannah)
**Military Landmarks (1,600)**
◄ Fort King George (Darien)
◄ Fort McAllister Historical Park (near Richmond Hill)
◄ Fort Frederica National Monument (St. Simons)
◄ Fort Pulaski National Monument (near Savannah)
**Historic Districts (2,400)**
Jekyll Club Village (Jekyll Island)
Factors Walk (Savannah)
Historic Savannah Waterfront Area (Savannah)
◄◄ Savannah Historic District (Savannah)
◄◄ Savannah Victorian Historic District (Savannah)
Antiquity Score: 253 (Savannah founded 1733)
Places Rated Score: 5,853      Places Rated Rank: 26

## Seattle–Mount Rainier–North Cascades, WA
**History Museums (1,200)**
Anacortes Museum (Anacortes)
Whatcom Museum (Bellingham)
Kitsap County Historical Society Museum
(Bremerton)
Island County Historical Museum (Coupeville)
Snoqualmie Valley Historical Museum (North Bend)
Port Gamble Historical Museum (Port Gamble)
Frontier Museum (Puyallup)
◄ Museum of History and Industry (Seattle)
State Historical Society Museum (Tacoma)
**House Museums and Historic Buildings (1,200)**
Ezra Meeker Mansion (Puyallup)
◄ Klondike Gold Rush N.H.P.; one unit of Alaska park (Seattle)
Camp Six–Western Washington Forest Industries
Museum (Tacoma)
Pioneer Farm (Tacoma)
**Military Landmarks (1,000)**
◄ Naval Shipyard Museum (Bremerton)
U.S.S. *Missouri* (Bremerton)
Alexander Blockhouse (Coupeville)
Fort Nisqually (Tacoma)

Historic Districts (300)
  Pioneer Square (Seattle)
Special Attractions (500)
  San Juan Island N.H.S. (San Juan Islands)
Antiquity Score: 134 (Seattle founded 1852)
Places Rated Score: 4,334     Places Rated Rank: 44

### Spokane–Coeur d'Alene, WA–ID
History Museums (100)
  Bonner County Historical Society Museum
    (Sandpoint, ID)
Archeological Sites and Museums (400)
  ◄ Museum of Native American Culture (Spokane, WA)
House Museums and Historic Buildings (500)
  Keller Historical Park (Colville, WA)
  Old Mission State Park (Kellogg, ID)
Military Landmarks (200)
  Fort Sherman (Coeur d'Alene, ID)
Antiquity Score: 115 (Spokane settled 1871)
Places Rated Score: 1,315     Places Rated Rank: 86

### Tampa Bay–Southwest Coast, FL
History Museums (1,300)
◄ ◄ De Soto National Memorial (Bradenton)
  South Florida Museum (Bradenton)
  Pioneer Florida Museum (Dade City)
  St. Petersburg Historical Museum
    (St. Petersburg)
  Hillsborough County Historical Museum (Tampa)
  Ybor City State Museum (Tampa)
Archeological Sites and Museums (300)
  *Crystal River State Archaeological Site (Crystal
    River)*
  Collier County Museum (Naples)
House Museums and Historic Buildings (1,450)
  Gamble Plantation (Bradenton)
  Thomas A. Edison Home (Fort Myers)
  *Yulee Sugar Mill S.H.S. (Homosassa Springs)*
  Grace S. Turner House (St. Petersburg)
  Haas Museum (St. Petersburg)
  Lowe House (St. Petersburg)
  Ringling Residence (Sarasota)
  Old Tampa Bay Hotel (Tampa)
Military Landmarks (500)
  *Dade Battlefield N.H.S. (Bushnell)*
  Fort De Soto Park (St. Petersburg)
  U.S.S. *Requin* (Tampa)
Historic Districts (600)
  ◄ Ybor City (Tampa)
Antiquity Score: 163 (Tampa settled 1823)
Places Rated Score: 4,313     Places Rated Rank: 45

### Traverse City–Petoskey, MI
History Museums (200)
  Benzie Area Historical Museum (Beulah)
  Chief Andrew J. Blackbird Museum (Harbor
    Springs)
Antiquity Score: 139 (Traverse City settled 1847)
Places Rated Score: 339     Places Rated Rank: 103

### Tucson, AZ
History Museums (1,000)
  Pimeria Alta Historical Society Museum (Nogales)
  ◄ Arizona State Museum (Sierra Vista)
  ◄ Arizona Heritage Center (Tucson)
House Museums and Historic Buildings (500)
  Tumacacori National Monument (near Nogales)
  John C. Fremont House (Tucson)
Military Landmarks (400)
  Fort Huachuca (Sierra Vista)
  Fort Lowell Museum (Tucson)
Antiquity Score: 211 (Tucson founded 1775)
Places Rated Score: 2,111     Places Rated Rank: 71

### Tulsa–Lake O' The Cherokees, OK
Living History Museums (600)
  ◄ Cherokee Heritage Center (Talequah)

History Museums (1,000)
  Creek Council House Museum (Okmulgee)
  Osage County Historical Society Museum
    (Pawhuska)
  Coo-Y-Yah Museum (Pryor)
  ◄ Thomas Gilcrease Institute of American History and
    Art (Tulsa)
House Museums and Historic Buildings (2,000)
  Frank Phillips Home (Bartlesville)
  Lynn Riggs Memorial (Claremore)
  Will Rogers Birthplace (Claremore)
  Will Rogers Memorial (Claremore)
◄ ◄ Har-Ber Village (Grand Lake)
  Thomas-Foreman Home (Muskogee)
  Sequoyah's Home (Sallisaw)
  Murrell Home (Talequah)
Military Landmarks (600)
  ◄ Fort Gibson Stockade (Muskogee)
  U.S.S. *Batfish* (Muskogee)
Antiquity Score: 107 (Tulsa founded 1879)
Places Rated Score: 4,307     Places Rated Rank: 46

### Vicksburg–Natchez–Baton Rouge, MS–LA
History Museums (200)
  ◄ *State Historical Museum (Jackson, MS)*
Archeological Sites and Museums (400)
  ◄ Grand Village of Natchez Indians (Natchez, MS)
House Museums and Historic Buildings (6,800)
  Heritage Museum and Village (Baker, LA)
  Ashland-Belle Helene Plantation (Baton Rouge,
    LA)
  Houmas House (Baton Rouge)
  Magnolia Mound (Baton Rouge)
  Mount Hope (Baton Rouge)
  Nottaway Plantation (Baton Rouge)
  Old Governor's Mansion (Baton Rouge)
  Parlange Plantation (Baton Rouge)
◄ ◄ Rural Life Museum (Baton Rouge)
  Asphodel (Jackson, LA)
  Glencoe (Jackson, LA)
  *Manship House (Jackson, MS)*
  *The Oaks (Jackson, MS)*
  Connelly's Tavern (Natchez)
  Dunleith (Natchez)
  Historic Jefferson College (Natchez)
  Historic Springfield Plantation (Natchez)
  Longwood (Natchez)
  Monmouth (Natchez)
  Rosalie (Natchez)
  Stanton Hall (Natchez)
  Oak Square (Port Gibson, MS)
  Catalpa (St. Francisville, LA)
  Cottage (St. Francisville)
  The Myrtles (St. Francisville)
  Oakley (St. Francisville)
  Biedenham Candy Company and Coca-Cola
    Museum (Vicksburg, MS)
  Cedar Grove (Vicksburg)
  McRaven Home (Vicksburg)
  Old Court House Museum (Vicksburg)
  Rosemont Plantation (Woodville, MS)
Military Landmarks (500)
  Grand Gulf Military Park (Port Gibson)
  Vicksburg N.M.P. and Cemetery
    (Vicksburg)
Special Attractions (750)
  State capital buildings (*Jackson, MS*, and Baton
    Rouge)
Antiquity Score: 270 (Natchez settled 1716)
Places Rated Score: 8,920     Places Rated Rank: 11

### ★ Washington, DC–MD–VA
Living History Museums (2,300)
  Rose Hill Manor Children's Museum (Frederick,
    MD)
  ◄ Turkey Run Farm (McLean, VA)
  ◄ National Colonial Farm (Washington)
  ◄ Oxon Hill Farm (Washington)

History Museums (2,100)
    Historical Society of Frederick City Museum
        (Frederick)
    Loudon Museum (Leesburg, VA)
    *Historical Society Museum (Leonardtown, MD)*
◄ Anacostia Neighborhood Museum (Washington)
◄◄ D.A.R. Buildings (Washington)
◄◄ National Museum of American History (Washington)
Presidential Sites (1,800)
◄ George Washington Home (Mount Vernon, VA)
    Ford's Theater (Washington)
    House Where Lincoln Died (Washington)
    Jefferson Memorial (Washington)
    Lincoln Memorial (Washington)
    Woodrow Wilson House (Washington)
House Museums and Historic Buildings (8,900)
    Carlyle House (Alexandria, VA)
    Gadsby's Tavern Museum (Alexandria)
    George Washington Masonic National Memorial
        (Alexandria)
    Gunston Hall (Alexandria)
    Lee-Fendall House (Alexandria)
    Lyceum (Alexandria)
    Ramsay House (Alexandria)
    Robert E. Lee Boyhood Home (Alexandria)
    Stabler-Leadbeater Apothecary (Alexandria)
    Arlington House (Arlington, VA)
    Sully Plantation (Fairfax, VA)
    The Falls Church (Falls Church, VA)
    Barbara Fritchie House (Frederick)
    Schifferstadt (Frederick)
    *Jonathan Hager House and Museum (Hagerstown,
        MD)*
    *Miller House (Hagerstown)*
    Montpelier Mansion (Laurel, MD)
    Oatlands (Leesburg)
    *Sotterley (Leonardtown)*
    Grist Mill Historical State Park (Mount Vernon)
    Woodlawn Plantation (Mount Vernon)
    Beall-Dawson House (Rockville, MD)
◄ The Capitol (Washington)
    Clara Barton Home (Washington)
    Decatur House (Washington)
    Frederick Douglass Memorial Home (Washington)
    Hillwood Museum (Washington)
    J. Edgar Hoover Building (Washington)
    Library of Congress (Washington)
    National Archives (Washington)
    The Octagon (Washington)
    Sewall-Belmont House (Washington)
    Supreme Court Building (Washington)
◄ The White House (Washington)
Military Landmarks (2,450)
◄ Fort Ward Museum (Alexandria)
    Arlington National Cemetery (Arlington)
    Monocacy Battlefield (Frederick)
◄◄ *Fort Frederick (Hagerstown)*
◄ National Battlefield Park and Museum (Manassas, VA)
    *Antietam National Battlefield Site and Cemetery
        (Sharpsburg, MD)*
◄ Marine Corps Aviation Museum (Triangle, VA)
◄ U.S. Navy Memorial Museum (Washington)
    Vietnam Veterans Memorial
Historic Districts (4,200)
◄◄ Alexandria Historic District (Alexandria)
    Frederick Historic District (Frederick)
    Waterford Quaker Village (Leesburg)
◄ *St. Maries Citty (St. Mary's City, MD)*
◄◄ Capitol Hill Historic District (Washington)
◄◄ Georgetown Historic District (Washington)
◄◄ Lafayette Square Historic District (Washington)
    Massachusetts Avenue Historic District (Washington)
Special Attractions (1,000)
    As the U.S. capital, Washington is a unique city of
        national historical interest.
Antiquity Score: 196 (Washington founded 1790)
Places Rated Score: 22,946        Places Rated Rank: 1

## White Mountains, NH
House Museums and Historic Buildings (350)
    Frost Place (Franconia)
    *Webster Cottage (Hanover)*
Antiquity Score: 222 (North Conway settled 1764)
Places Rated Score: 572        Places Rated Rank: 100

## ★ Williamsburg–Colonial Triangle, VA
Living History Museums (700)
◄◄ Colonial Williamsburg (Williamsburg)
House Museums and Historic Buildings (2,100)
    Cape Henry Lighthouse (Cape Henry)
    Colonial N.H.P. (Jamestown)
    Myers House (Norfolk)
    Willoughby-Baylor House (Norfolk)
    Chippokes Plantation (Surry)
    Adam Thoroughgood House (Virginia Beach)
    Lynnhaven House (Virginia Beach)
    Carter's Grove Plantation (Williamsburg)
    Nelson House (Yorktown)
Military Landmarks (3,400)
◄ Army Transportation Museum (Newport News)
◄ Fort Eustis (Newport News)
◄ War Memorial Museum of Virginia (Newport News)
◄◄ Norfolk Naval Air Station (Norfolk)
◄◄ Norfolk Naval Station (Norfolk)
◄ Portsmouth Lightship Museum (Portsmouth)
◄ Portsmouth Naval Shipyard Museum (Portsmouth)
    Yorktown Battlefield (Yorktown)
    Yorktown National Civil War Cemetery (Yorktown)
Historic Districts (1,400)
◄◄ Portsmouth
◄◄ Williamsburg
Special Attractions (1,000)
    Colonial Williamsburg was the first major effort
        in this country to restore and reconstruct an
        entire historic town. Nearly $100 million has
        been spent on more than 130 houses and
        public buildings.
Antiquity Score: 379 (Jamestown settled 1607)
Places Rated Score: 8,979        Places Rated Rank: 10

## Wilmington–Cape Fear, NC
History Museums (200)
    New Hanover County Museum (Wilmington)
House Museums and Historic Buildings (600)
    Burgwin-Wright House (Wilmington)
    Poplar Grove Plantation (Wilmington)
Military Landmarks (1,200)
◄ Brunswick Town–Fort Anderson (Southport)
◄ Fort Fisher S.H.S. (Southport)
    Moores Creek National Battlefield (Wilmington)
    U.S.S. *North Carolina* Battleship (Wilmington)
Antiquity Score: 254 (Wilmington settled 1732)
Places Rated Score: 2,254        Places Rated Rank: 67

## Wine Country, CA
History Museums (500)
    Sharpsteen Museum and Sam Brannan Cottage
        (Calistoga)
    Kelly House Museum (Mendocino)
    Silverado Museum (St. Helena)
    Vallejo Naval and Historical Museum (Vallejo)
    Mendocino County Museum (Willits)
House Museums and Historic Buildings (900)
    Petaluma Adobe S.H.P. (Petaluma)
    Bale Grist Mill S.H.P. (St. Helena)
    Luther Burbank Home (Santa Rosa)
    Jack London S.H.P. (Sonoma)
    Sonoma Depot Museum (Sonoma)
    Sonoma S.H.P. (Sonoma)
    Benicia Capitol S.H.P. (Vallejo)
Military Landmarks (400)
◄ Fort Ross S.H.P. (Jenner)
Antiquity Score: 157 (Santa Rosa settled 1829)
Places Rated Score: 1,957        Places Rated Rank: 74

## Wisconsin Dells, WI
Living History Museums (400)
  Shake Rag Alley (Mineral Point)
History Museums (950)
  Sauk County Historical Museum (Baraboo)
  Dodge County Historical Museum (Beaver Dam)
◄ Bartlett Memorial Historical Museum (Beloit)
  *Ann and Wilson Cunningham Museum (Platteville)*
  Winnebago Public Indian Museum (Wisconsin
    Dells)
House Museums and Historic Buildings (2,350)
  Rasey House (Beloit)
  Little Norway (near Madison)
  Gundry House (Mineral Point)
  The Looms (Mineral Point)
◄ Swiss Historical Village (New Glarus)
  *Mitchell-Rountree Stone Cottage (Platteville)*
  House on the Rock (Spring Green)
  The Spring Green (Spring Green)
  Taliesin Fellowship Buildings (Spring Green)
  Octagon House (Watertown)
Historic Districts (300)
  Pendarvis, Cornish Restoration (Mineral Point)
Special Attractions (500)
  State capital buildings (Madison)
Antiquity Score: 128 (Wisconsin Dells settled 1858)
Places Rated Score: 4,628      Places Rated Rank: 40

## Yellowstone–Jackson–Tetons, WY–ID–MT
History Museums (450)
  *Bingham City Historical Museum (Blackfoot, ID)*
  Jackson Hole Museum (Jackson, WY)
  *Lava Hot Springs Museum (Lava Hot Springs, ID)*
  *Park County Museum (Livingston, MT)*
  Bannock City Historical Museum (Pocatello, ID)
  *Hot Springs County Museum (Thermopolis, WY)*
  *Thompson-Hickman Memorial Museum (Virginia
    City, MT)*
  *Virginia City–Madison County Museum (Virginia
    City)*
House Museums and Historic Buildings (400)
  *Copper King Mansion (Butte, MT)*

  *Bale of Hay Saloon (Virginia City)*
  *Nevada City (Virginia City)*
Military Landmarks (100)
  *Old Fort Hall Replica (Pocatello)*
Historic Districts (150)
  *Restored buildings (Virginia City)*
Antiquity Score: 114 (Yellowstone National Park
  established 1872)
Places Rated Score: 1,214      Places Rated Rank: 90

## Yosemite–Sequoia–Death Valley, CA
History Museums (300)
  Mono County Historical Museum (Bridgeport)
  The Indian Cultural Museum (Yosemite National
    Park)
House Museums and Historic Buildings (1,800)
◄◄ Laws Railroad Museum and Historical Site (Bishop)
  Bodie S.H.P. (Bridgeport)
  Scotty's Castle (Death Valley)
  The Commander's House (Lone Pine)
◄◄ *Tulare County Museum (Visalia)*
  Pioneer Yosemite Historical Center (Yosemite
    National Park)
Antiquity Score: 96 (Yosemite National Park
  established 1890)
Places Rated Score: 2,196      Places Rated Rank: 68

## Zion–Bryce Canyon, UT
History Museums (200)
  *Territorial Statehouse State Historical Museum
    (Fillmore)*
  Daughters of Utah Pioneers College (St. George)
Archeological Sites and Museums (400)
  Robinson's Tours–Indian ruins (Kanab)
  Anasazi Indian Village State Historical Museum
    (Panguitch)
House Museums and Historic Buildings (300)
  Brigham Young Winter Home (Panguitch)
  Jacob Hamblin Home (St. George)
Antiquity Score: 125 (St. George founded 1861)
Places Rated Score: 1,025      Places Rated Rank: 93

**RANKINGS:** Discovering Our Heritage

Nine criteria were used to determine the scores in this chapter: (1) living history museums, (2) history museums, (3) archeological sites and museums, (4) presidential sites, (5) house museums and historic build- ings, (6) military landmarks, (7) historic districts, (8) special attractions, and (9) antiquity score.

Places that receive tie scores are given the same rank and are listed in alphabetic order.

## Vacation Places from First to Last

| Places Rated Rank | Places Rated Score |
|---|---|
| 1. Washington, DC–MD–VA | 22,946 |
| 2. Boston, MA | 22,606 |
| 3. Philadelphia, PA–DE–NJ | 12,304 |
| 4. Catskill Mountains, NY | 12,008 |
| 5. Providence–Newport, RI | 10,450 |
| 6. Richmond–Fredericksburg, VA | 9,899 |
| 7. Lexington–Bluegrass Country, KY | 9,607 |
| 8. New York City, NY | 9,571 |
| 9. Pennsylvania Dutch Country, PA | 9,265 |
| 10. Williamsburg–Colonial Triangle, VA | 8,979 |
| 11. Vicksburg–Natchez–Baton Rouge, MS–LA | 8,920 |
| 12. Chicago, IL | 8,483 |
| 13. Baltimore–Chesapeake Bay, MD | 8,337 |
| 14. Albuquerque–Santa Fe–Taos, NM | 7,526 |
| 15. St. Louis–Mark Twain Country, MO–IL | 7,422 |
| 16. Charleston, SC | 7,416 |
| 17. New Orleans, LA | 6,968 |
| 18. Portsmouth–Kennebunk, NH–ME | 6,856 |
| 19. Knoxville–Smoky Mountains, TN | 6,599 |
| 20. Hawaii | 6,508 |
| 21. Los Angeles, CA | 6,405 |
| 22. Houston–Galveston, TX | 6,400 |
| 23. Portland, ME | 6,305 |
| 24. Minneapolis–St. Paul, MN–WI | 5,946 |
| 25. St. Augustine–Northeast Coast, FL | 5,921 |
| 26. Savannah–Golden Isles, GA | 5,853 |
| 27. Berkshire Hills–Pioneer Valley, MA | 5,836 |
| 28. Mystic Seaport–Connecticut Valley, CT | 5,732 |
| 29. Oklahoma City–Cherokee Strip, OK | 5,697 |
| 30. Green Mountains, VT | 5,566 |
| 31. Adirondack Mountains, NY | 5,472 |
| 32. Atlanta, GA | 5,349 |
| 33. Blue Ridge Mountains, VA | 5,324 |
| 34. Nashville, TN | 5,307 |
| 35. Austin–Hill Country, TX | 5,147 |
| 36. Long Island, NY | 5,138 |

| Places Rated Rank | Places Rated Score |
|---|---|
| 37. Phoenix–Valley of the Sun, AZ | 5,122 |
| 38. Panhandle, FL | 4,863 |
| 39. Outer Banks, NC | 4,721 |
| 40. Wisconsin Dells, WI | 4,628 |
| 41. Put-in-Bay–Lake Erie Shore, OH | 4,475 |
| 42. Denver–Rocky Mountain National Park, CO | 4,428 |
| 43. Finger Lakes, NY | 4,347 |
| 44. Seattle–Mount Rainier–North Cascades, WA | 4,334 |
| 45. Tampa Bay–Southwest Coast, FL | 4,313 |
| 46. Ozarks–Eureka Springs, AR–MO | 4,307 |
| 46. Tulsa–Lake O' The Cherokees, OK | 4,307 |
| 48. Dallas–Fort Worth, TX | 4,195 |
| 49. Pocono Mountains, PA | 4,015 |
| 50. San Antonio, TX | 3,918 |
| 51. Monterey–Big Sur, CA | 3,916 |
| 52. Lake of the Ozarks, MO | 3,905 |
| 53. Salt Lake City, UT | 3,739 |
| 54. Portland–Columbia River, OR | 3,644 |
| 55. Mobile Bay–Gulfport, AL–MS | 3,575 |
| 56. Cape Cod–The Islands, MA | 3,566 |
| 57. Sacramento–Gold Rush Towns, CA | 3,547 |
| 58. Grand Canyon Country, AZ | 3,510 |
| 59. Asheville–Smoky Mountains, NC | 3,292 |
| 60. Colorado Springs, CO | 3,015 |
| 61. San Francisco, CA | 2,810 |
| 62. Cincinnati, OH–KY | 2,758 |
| 63. Miami–Gold Coast–Keys, FL | 2,616 |
| 64. Memphis, TN–AR–MS | 2,417 |
| 65. Olympic Peninsula, WA | 2,336 |
| 66. Niagara Falls–Western New York, NY | 2,330 |
| 67. Wilmington–Cape Fear, NC | 2,254 |
| 68. Yosemite–Sequoia–Death Valley, CA | 2,196 |
| 69. Crater Lake–Klamath Falls, OR | 2,134 |
| 70. San Diego, CA | 2,117 |
| 71. Tucson, AZ | 2,111 |
| 72. Chattanooga–Huntsville, TN–AL–GA | 2,051 |

| Places Rated Rank | Places Rated Score |
|---|---|
| 73. Boise–Sun Valley, ID | 1,984 |
| 74. Wine Country, CA | 1,957 |
| 75. Lake Tahoe–Reno, NV–CA | 1,818 |
| 76. Bar Harbor–Acadia, ME | 1,817 |
| 77. Santa Barbara–San Simeon, CA | 1,804 |
| 78. Black Hills, SD | 1,760 |
| 79. Atlantic City, NJ | 1,734 |
| 80. Aspen–Vail, CO | 1,707 |
| 81. Redwoods–Shasta–Lassen, CA | 1,636 |
| 82. Hilton Head, SC | 1,576 |
| 83. Mackinac Island–Sault Ste. Marie, MI | 1,405 |
| 84. Anchorage–Kenai Peninsula, AK | 1,372 |
| 85. Holland–Lake Michigan Shore, MI | 1,339 |
| 86. Spokane–Coeur d'Alene, WA–ID | 1,315 |
| 87. Palm Springs–Desert Playgrounds, CA | 1,310 |
| 88. Corpus Christi–Padre Island, TX | 1,247 |
| 89. Las Vegas–Lake Mead, NV–AZ | 1,231 |
| 90. Yellowstone–Jackson–Tetons, WY–ID–MT | 1,214 |
| 91. Orlando–Space Coast, FL | 1,149 |
| 92. Lake Powell–Glen Canyon, AZ–UT | 1,081 |
| 93. Zion–Bryce Canyon, UT | 1,025 |
| 94. Brownsville–Rio Grande Valley, TX | 938 |
| 95. Eastern Shore, VA | 800 |
| 96. Door County, WI | 716 |
| 97. Boone–High Country, NC | 714 |
| 98. Coos Bay–South Coast, OR | 682 |
| 99. Jersey Shore, NJ | 607 |
| 100. White Mountains, NH | 572 |
| 101. Myrtle Beach–Grand Strand, SC | 557 |
| 102. Flaming Gorge, UT–WY–CO | 524 |
| 103. Traverse City–Petoskey, MI | 339 |
| 104. Rangeley Lakes, ME | 311 |
| 105. North Woods–Land O'Lakes, WI | 306 |
| 106. Glacier National Park–Flathead Lake, MT | 295 |
| 107. Bend–Cascade Mountains, OR | 186 |

## Vacation Places Listed Alphabetically

| Vacation Place | Places Rated Rank | Vacation Place | Places Rated Rank | Vacation Place | Places Rated Rank |
|---|---|---|---|---|---|
| Adirondack Mountains, NY | 31 | Green Mountains, VT | 30 | Phoenix–Valley of the Sun, AZ | 37 |
| Albuquerque–Santa Fe–Taos, NM | 14 | Hawaii | 20 | Pocono Mountains, PA | 49 |
| Anchorage–Kenai Peninsula, AK | 84 | Hilton Head, SC | 82 | Portland, ME | 23 |
| Asheville–Smoky Mountains, NC | 59 | Holland–Lake Michigan Shore, MI | 85 | | |
| Aspen–Vail, CO | 80 | | | Portland–Columbia River, OR | 54 |
| | | Houston–Galveston, TX | 22 | Portsmouth–Kennebunk, NH–ME | 18 |
| Atlanta, GA | 32 | Jersey Shore, NJ | 99 | Providence–Newport, RI | 5 |
| Atlantic City, NJ | 79 | Knoxville–Smoky Mountains, TN | 19 | Put-in-Bay–Lake Erie Shore, OH | 41 |
| Austin–Hill Country, TX | 35 | Lake of the Ozarks, MO | 52 | Rangeley Lakes, ME | 104 |
| Baltimore–Chesapeake Bay, MD | 13 | Lake Powell–Glen Canyon, AZ–UT | 92 | | |
| Bar Harbor–Acadia, ME | 76 | | | Redwoods–Shasta–Lassen, CA | 81 |
| | | Lake Tahoe–Reno, NV–CA | 75 | Richmond–Fredericksburg, VA | 6 |
| Bend–Cascade Mountains, OR | 107 | Las Vegas–Lake Mead, NV–AZ | 89 | Sacramento–Gold Rush Towns, CA | 57 |
| Berkshire Hills–Pioneer Valley, MA | 27 | Lexington–Bluegrass Country, KY | 7 | St. Augustine–Northeast Coast, FL | 25 |
| Black Hills, SD | 78 | Long Island, NY | 36 | St. Louis–Mark Twain Country, MO–IL | 15 |
| Blue Ridge Mountains, VA | 33 | Los Angeles, CA | 21 | | |
| Boise–Sun Valley, ID | 73 | | | Salt Lake City, UT | 53 |
| | | Mackinac Island–Sault Ste. Marie, MI | 83 | San Antonio, TX | 50 |
| Boone–High Country, NC | 97 | Memphis, TN–AR–MS | 64 | San Diego, CA | 70 |
| Boston, MA | 2 | Miami–Gold Coast–Keys, FL | 63 | San Francisco, CA | 61 |
| Brownsville–Rio Grande Valley, TX | 94 | Minneapolis–St. Paul, MN–WI | 24 | Santa Barbara–San Simeon, CA | 77 |
| Cape Cod–The Islands, MA | 56 | Mobile Bay–Gulfport, AL–MS | 55 | | |
| Catskill Mountains, NY | 4 | | | Savannah–Golden Isles, GA | 26 |
| | | Monterey–Big Sur, CA | 51 | Seattle–Mount Rainier–North Cascades, WA | 44 |
| Charleston, SC | 16 | Myrtle Beach–Grand Strand, SC | 101 | Spokane–Coeur d'Alene, WA–ID | 86 |
| Chattanooga–Huntsville, TN–AL–GA | 72 | Mystic Seaport–Connecticut Valley, CT | 28 | Tampa Bay–Southwest Coast, FL | 45 |
| Chicago, IL | 12 | Nashville, TN | 34 | Traverse City–Petoskey, MI | 103 |
| Cincinnati, OH–KY | 62 | New Orleans, LA | 17 | | |
| Colorado Springs, CO | 60 | | | Tucson, AZ | 71 |
| | | New York City, NY | 8 | Tulsa–Lake O' The Cherokees, OK | 46 |
| Coos Bay–South Coast, OR | 98 | Niagara Falls–Western New York, NY | 66 | Vicksburg–Natchez–Baton Rouge, MS–LA | 11 |
| Corpus Christi–Padre Island, TX | 88 | North Woods–Land O'Lakes, WI | 105 | Washington, DC–MD–VA | 1 |
| Crater Lake–Klamath Falls, OR | 69 | Oklahoma City–Cherokee Strip, OK | 29 | White Mountains, NH | 100 |
| Dallas–Fort Worth, TX | 48 | Olympic Peninsula, WA | 65 | | |
| Denver–Rocky Mountain National Park, CO | 42 | | | Williamsburg–Colonial Triangle, VA | 10 |
| | | Orlando–Space Coast, FL | 91 | Wilmington–Cape Fear, NC | 67 |
| Door County, WI | 96 | Outer Banks, NC | 39 | Wine Country, CA | 74 |
| Eastern Shore, VA | 95 | Ozarks–Eureka Springs, AR–MO | 46 | Wisconsin Dells, WI | 40 |
| Finger Lakes, NY | 43 | Palm Springs–Desert Playgrounds, CA | 87 | Yellowstone–Jackson–Tetons, WY–ID–MT | 90 |
| Flaming Gorge, UT–WY–CO | 102 | Panhandle, FL | 38 | | |
| Glacier National Park–Flathead Lake, MT | 106 | | | Yosemite–Sequoia–Death Valley, CA | 68 |
| | | Pennsylvania Dutch Country, PA | 9 | Zion–Bryce Canyon, UT | 93 |
| Grand Canyon Country, AZ | 58 | Philadelphia, PA–DE–NJ | 3 | | |

# TOP TEN: Discovering Our Heritage

The ten top-scoring Vacation Places for historic sightseeing are all on or very close to the Atlantic coast, and all but one—Lexington–Bluegrass Country, Kentucky —are in one of the 13 original states. In these places the first colonies were settled; this is where the nation was conceived and born. Historic landmarks are most numerous in the eastern part of the country; easterners had a two-century head start on the rest of the country in which to collect, document, preserve, and restore their treasures.

|   | | Places Rated Score |
|---|---|---|
| 1. | Washington, DC–MD–VA | 22,946 |
| 2. | Boston, MA | 22,606 |
| 3. | Philadelphia, PA–DE–NJ | 12,304 |
| 4. | Catskill Mountains, NY | 12,008 |
| 5. | Providence–Newport, RI | 10,450 |
| 6. | Richmond–Fredericksburg, VA | 9,899 |
| 7. | Lexington–Bluegrass Country, KY | 9,607 |
| 8. | New York City, NY | 9,571 |
| 9. | Pennsylvania Dutch Country, PA | 9,265 |
| 10. | Williamsburg–Colonial Triangle, VA | 8,979 |

## 1. Washington, DC–MD–VA

Washington, as capital city, quite naturally ranks first among Vacation Places for historic sightseeing. The golden-domed Capitol, the White House, the monuments, memorials, museums, and historic mansions all work together to make the city itself a symbol of the nation's history. It ranks first for living history museums, presidential sites, and historic districts; second for house museums and military landmarks, and third for history museums.

There are reminders of historic figures and events in almost every park and public building in the city. The area has had a connection with every president; all except George Washington lived in the White House (it wasn't completed until after he left office), and Mount Vernon, Washington's estate, is only a few miles away.

First-time visitors will certainly want to visit the Capitol, Lincoln Memorial, Washington Memorial, and Jefferson Memorial. Next priority, for most people, is the White House if the visit is at a time when tours are being conducted (there are many occasions on which the house is not open to visitors because important affairs are going on inside). After that the choices are almost endless. Do be sure to spend some time walking slowly through a few lovely neighborhoods—especially Lafayette Square, Capitol Hill, and Georgetown. And don't forget that Alexandria, Virginia, with its many examples of colonial architecture, is just across the Potomac River.

## 2. Boston, MA

The streets of Boston and surrounding towns and cities fairly shout with history. More than 350 years of important events are commemorated here. You can visit the recreation of Plymouth Colony, hear the story of the hysteria over witchcraft in Salem, visit the waterfronts of Boston and other coastal towns, and imagine the harbors filled with sailing ships. You can walk through Paul Revere's home and follow the route of his famous ride to Lexington. You can climb Bunker Hill and walk the decks of *Old Ironsides*.

You can visit the homes of presidents John Adams, John Quincy Adams, and John F. Kennedy; of writers Ralph Waldo Emerson, Henry David Thoreau, Henry

---

### Author's Favorites

**Archeological Sites and Museums**
Bandelier National Monument, Los Alamos, NM
Effigy Mounds National Monument, Marquette, IA
Mesa Verde National Park, CO

**Cities for Exploring Historic Neighborhoods**
Boston, MA
Savannah, GA
Washington, DC

**History Museums**
National Museum of American History, Washington, DC

**House Museums**
Biltmore House and Gardens, Asheville, NC
Hearst–San Simeon State Historical Monument,
  San Simeon, CA
Ringling Residence, Sarasota, FL
Tryon Palace and Gardens, New Bern, NC

**Living History Museums**
Colonial Williamsburg, Williamsburg, VA
Greenfield Village, Dearborn, MI
Lincoln's New Salem State Park, Petersburg, IL
Old Sturbridge Village, Sturbridge, MA
Plimoth Plantation, Plymouth, MA

**Military Landmarks**
Valley Forge National Historic Park, King of Prussia, PA
Vicksburg National Military Park and Cemetery,
  Vicksburg, MS

**Presidential Sites**
Calvin Coolidge Homestead, Plymouth, VT
George Washington Home, Mount Vernon, VA
Herbert Hoover National Historic Site, West Branch, IA
The Hermitage, Nashville, TN
Home of Franklin D. Roosevelt National Historic
  Site, Hyde Park, NY
Johnson Presidential Library and Museum, Austin, TX
Monticello, Charlottesville, VA
Ulysses S. Grant Home State Historic Site,
  Galena, IL

Wadsworth Longfellow, John Greenleaf Whittier, Nathaniel Hawthorne, Louisa May Alcott, and Mary Baker Eddy.

Stop first at the information center on Boston Common and pick up maps anad walking guides. The Freedom Trail is designated by markers; it passes 16 important historic points of interest, many of which charge no admission fee.

### 3. Philadelphia, PA–DE–NJ

William Penn, a Quaker, founded the City of Brotherly Love, and nearly a century later Philadelphia was the site of important events that led to the establishment of a new nation. The First and Second Continental Congresses met here, the headquarters of the American Revolution was here and, except for a brief priod, the city was the capital of the new nation from the end of the conflict until 1800.

Philadelphia was given a major face-lift in honor of the Bicentennial celebration in 1976. Its historic landmarks were spruced up, and many of its deteriorated areas were transformed with bright new buildings. Independence Hall is now the focal point of a dramatic historic park.

In nearby towns are memorials to several early groups who settled Pennsylvania—Moravians, Mennonites, and Pennsylvania Dutch.

### 4. Catskill Mountains, NY

The Catskills and nearby Hudson River valley have several towns dating from colonial days. Six stone houses in the town of New Paltz, built by some of the French Huguenot settlers who founded the town in 1678, are furnished with original furnishings and are open to the public during the summer.

Two presidential homes can be visited in this area—Franklin D. Roosevelt's in Hyde Park and Martin Van Buren's in Hudson. Near Roosevelt's home is the lavish home of Cornelius Vanderbilt; a combination ticket is sold that admits the visitor to both estates.

The U.S. Military Academy at West Point is a special attraction; another special place is the Fort Delaware Museum of Colonial History in Narrowsburg.

### 5. Providence–Newport, RI

The two major cities of Rhode Island have a history that started in 1636, when Roger Williams left the restrictive Massachusetts Bay Colony to establish a settlement where people of all religious faiths could be free to follow their consciences. He helped to found the first Baptist congregation in America in 1638. The First Baptist Church, built in 1775, is well worth visiting for its beauty as well as its historic interest. Another beautiful and historically important house of worship is in Newport: the Touro Synagogue, dating from 1763, is the oldest synagogue building in America.

House museums are numerous in Newport; this was the country's leading summer resort for wealthy vacationers in the last part of the 19th century. In addition to several mansions from that period that are now open as house museums, there are two fine restorations of pre-Revolutionary dwellings—the Wanton-Lyman-Hazard House and the Hunter House.

### 6. Richmond–Fredericksburg, VA

The Richmond area echoes with the footsteps of some of the continent's early colonists as well as with the sad sounds of civil war. Three plantations on the James River—Berkeley, Shirley, and Sherwood Forest—were started by 1730, in a time when a plantation was essentially a self-sufficient village. They are all open to the public. Richmond and Fredericksburg were founded at about the same time. Many of the buildings in Fredericksburg are beautifully preserved pre-Revolutionary structures. Friends and relatives of George Washington lived here; James Monroe, later the fifth president of the United States, practiced law here.

St. John's Episcopal Church in Richmond was the site of Patrick Henry's inspirational speech advocating independence for the colonies with the words "Give me liberty or give me death." Other important historic sites include the Museum of the Confederacy, the largest collection in the nation of documents, art, and items related to the years of the Confederacy. Several Civil War battlefields and cemeteries are nearby.

### 7. Lexington–Bluegrass Country, KY

Lexington and the surrounding areas of northern Kentucky were being explored at the time of the American Revolution. The city was given its name in honor of the Battle of Lexington, in Massachusetts.

Lexington prides itself on the fact that its historic areas are not restored or reconstructed; for the most part they have been preserved. Several stately mansions date from the early 19th century; among them are Henry Clay's home and the girlhood home of Mary Todd Lincoln (this one has been restored).

In Harrodsburg, the state's oldest town, is a reproduction of a complete stockaded village as it existed 200 years ago. Shakertown at Pleasant Hill, northeast of Harrodsburg, preserves the way of life of a religious sect who lived here for nearly a century.

### 8. New York City, NY

New York is certainly much more a city of tomorrow than of yesterday. Real estate is so valuable in the heart of Manhattan for use by high-rise office buildings, hotels, and apartment complexes, it is remarkable that anything old is ever preserved.

But this was also one of the first spots on the Atlantic Coast to be settled by Europeans, and its roots do reach back more than 350 years.

It was also the first destination of many waves of

later immigrants, who established new homes here and built a fabulous metropolis consisting of countless colorful ethnic neighborhoods. Architecture reflects this diversity, as do churches, museums, and ethnic clubs.

It is probably safe to say that most vacationers who choose New York City as their primary destination are not looking for historic sightseeing as their first choice of activity; the plays, the shopping, and the glitter of the country's largest city are greater draws. But the Statue of Liberty, the United Nations complex, a few 18th-century structures such as the Morris-Jumel Mansion, and many fine ethnic museums give visitors lots of opportunities to take a look at the city's and the nation's past.

## 9. Pennsylvania Dutch Country, PA

The term *Pennsylvania Dutch* refers to the descendants of German immigrants who were the principal settlers of southeastern Pennsylvania. Some of the earliest were Mennonites, members of a religious sect that is still strong in the area. The Amish, or Plain People, are a branch of the Mennonites. Most of them are farmers who as a matter of principle choose not to use modern technology. They wear plain clothing, drive about the countryside in black buggies, and plow their fertile fields with the assistance of teams of horses. Travelers in Amish territory can observe a life-style that has not changed in generations.

Other Pennsylvania Dutch paint colorful hex signs on their barns, run restaurants where gargantuan meals of country-style foods are served, and manage gift shops offering a multitude of local crafts and souvenirs.

The most famous historic site in this part of Pennsylvania is Gettysburg National Military Park, commemorating the great Civil War battle and Abraham Lincoln's famous speech that followed it.

Lancaster was the capital of the United States for one day—September 27, 1777. The city has many charming Georgian townhouses. Wheatland, a Greek Revival mansion that was the home of President James Buchanan, is here.

## 10. Williamsburg–Colonial Triangle, VA

Williamsburg is unique—an entire city of more than 150 buildings restored and reconstructed to recreate a village that was at one time the seat of government for Britain's largest colony in America. During the years that led to the overthrow of British rule it was the political headquarters for Virginia's patriots. After the Declaration of Independence was proclaimed, Williamsburg was the wartime capital of the colony.

Colonial Williamsburg is worth a visit of several days, but vacationers should not overlook the two other places that, along with Williamsburg, make up what is known as the Colonial Triangle: Jamestown, site of the first settlement in Virginia, begun in 1607, and Yorktown, where the final battle of the Revolution was fought.

# Feeding the Mind and Spirit

Museums and Special Attractions

**INTRODUCTION:** Feeding the Mind and Spirit

When your daily routine gets the best of you, and you think your next vacation period is never going to come, give some thought to the many things there are to see and do close to home. With a little planning, you can give yourself a minivacation every couple of weeks.

Many of us never really explore the possibilities in our own backyards. Most Americans live within a hundred miles or so of medium-sized or large metropolitan areas with dozens of great sightseeing opportunities—botanic gardens, zoos, planetariums, and a great variety of museums. Sightseeing trips by bus, buggy, boat, or other means of transportation are a routine part of many vacations—have you ever taken a sightseeing tour in your own town or in the nearby city where you go to shop?

Watching monkeys or dolphins at play, wandering through acres of lush ground planted with brilliant flowers, watching the movements of the planets, studying the works of Old Masters and innovative contemporary artists—these are activities that can take you as far away from the everyday world as a trip to distant lands.

The previous chapter dealt with museums and special sites concerned with history. This one looks at other types of man-made sightseeing attractions, many of which are included in the broad definition of *museums*. The American Association of Museums publishes *The Official Museum Directory;* some of the major classifications of museums listed are art, children's and junior museums, science, history, and specialized. Botanical gardens, planetariums, zoos, and wildlife refuges are subcategories of science museums. More than 30 types of specialized museums are identified in the directory; the list starts with agriculture and ends with wood carving.

Museums of all types are places for study and research as well as for the enjoyment of people who come just to see what's there. Botanic gardens are laboratories of experimentation with plants, astronomers use planetariums to find out more about outer space, zoos are breeding places for rare and endangered species, and so on. Even some commercial tourist attractions generally identified as family theme parks, such as Florida Cypress Gardens and Sea World, in San Diego, California, carry on a great deal of serious scientific work behind the scenes.

## BOTANIC GARDENS

A few miles north of Charleston, South Carolina, is a large plantation surrounded by terraces, lakes, walkways topped with canopies of flowering trees and shrubs, and some of the oldest trees in the Southeast. Middleton Place was the home of Henry Middleton, a president of the First Continental Congress, and later of his son Arthur, one of the signers of the Declaration of Independence. The gardens, laid out in 1741, are considered to be the oldest formally landscaped gar-

---

### Where to Find Your Favorite Blooms

Different parts of the country are famous for certain varieties of plants, shrubs, and trees that create special effects during their peak seasons. Here are a few hints as to where to find the most spectacular shows of certain specific blooms.

**Camellias** bloom in winter in most southern gardens. The Alfred B. Maclay State Gardens in Tallahassee, Florida, has an outstanding collection.

**Azaleas** begin to bloom in late February in Florida and other southern states. Ravine State Gardens, Palatka, Florida, and Bellingrath Gardens, Theodore, Alabama, have extensive acreage planted in azaleas.

**Cherry blossoms** are the trademark of spring in Washington, DC. They are in their glory in late March or early April.

**Dogwood** casts an ethereal rosy glow over hundreds of yards in the residential sections of Atlanta in April.

**Rhododendrons** are at their peak in Oregon in May and in the southern Appalachians in June and July. Roan Mountain, on the border of Tennessee and North Carolina (near Boone, North Carolina), is virtually covered with these snowy blooms in their season.

**Roses** bloom all summer and most of the fall in two outstanding rose gardens on opposite sides of the United States—Hershey Rose Gardens and Arboretum in Hershey, Pennsylvania, and the International Rose Test Garden in Portland, Oregon. Hershey Gardens has a 23-acre display of 1,200 varieties of roses; the Portland garden has 8,000 rose bushes.

**Orchids** bring fanatic fanciers to the Big Island of Hawaii to see acres of their favorite blooms growing in commercial gardens. A little more accessible to many vacationers is Orchid Jungle, Homestead, Florida (south of Miami). There are many species of orchids, and some of them are in bloom every season of the year.

Several family entertainment parks are renowned for their gardens; two outstanding ones are Cypress Gardens and Busch Gardens, both in Florida. In addition, the San Diego Zoo, in California, is just as remarkable for its botanic collection as it is for its animals.

dens in the United States; their plan copied the symmetry and design typical of major European estates.

Nearby, on the same highway (South Carolina 61), is another equally impressive plantation: Magnolia Plantation and Gardens, claimed to contain the oldest major (but not formal) gardens in the United States. These gardens follow and enhance the natural contours and beauty of the land. Their exact age is not known, but documentation proves that by 1716 they had already covered more than 10 acres. They have been a tourist attraction for more than a hundred years. In the 1880s they were listed in Baedecker's travel guide as one of the three foremost attractions in the United States, along with the Grand Canyon and Niagara Falls. Many garden experts wrote articles of praise in leading magazines of the day. Novelist and playwright John Galsworthy wrote this description:

> Brilliant with azaleas and magnolias, it centers around a pool of dreamy water overhung by tall trunks wanly festooned with the gray Florida moss. Beyond anything I have ever seen, it is otherworldly. And I went there day after day, drawn as one is drawn in youth by visions.

Galsworthy's description is as accurate today as it was a century ago.

Beautiful gardens have a universal and timeless appeal. On the noted list of Seven Wonders of the Ancient World were the Hanging Gardens of Babylon, a series of landscaped terraces created in the desert by King Nebuchadrezzar in about the sixth century B.C.

There are hundreds of gardens open to the public in every sector of the United States: botanic gardens, or arboretums, estate or plantation gardens such as the two described above, nature preserves, and commercial attractions. Some are tiny gems less than an acre in size; some extend over several square miles. The Place Profiles for this chapter list about 160 leading botanic gardens, found in 62 Vacation Places.

Two of the largest and most lavishly planted are the gardens of the Biltmore estate, in Asheville, North Carolina; and Callaway Gardens, in Pine Mountain, Georgia, southwest of Atlanta. The recently completed John A. Sibley Horticultural Center at Callaway is a dramatic combination greenhouse-garden that employs brand-new design and engineering concepts to bring indoors and outdoors together. Fans of the program "The Victory Garden," shown on public television, will recognize Callaway as the Victory Garden South.

Both of these estates are important laboratories for botanical and horticultural research and experimentation as well as places of beauty to be enjoyed. Their original owners, George Vanderbilt and Cason Callaway, were both intensely interested in the land and forests and in helping educate the farmers of the southeastern United States to improve their agricultural methods.

Longwood Gardens, Kennett Square, Pennsylvania, (in the Philadelphia area), occupies part of a huge arboretum originally established about 1800. Among the huge old trees are fountains, ponds, shrubs, topiary gardens, and year-round blooms. Bellingrath Gardens, east of Mobile in Theodore, Alabama, has displays of some 250,000 strikingly brilliant azaleas, in bloom from January to April.

Some small gardens are as memorable and inspiring as those spreading over many acres. Longue Vue Gardens, New Orleans, Louisiana, has four formal gardens, one of which is laid out in Spanish style, and one wild garden with trees and shrubs native to the Gulf area—all on eight acres. And in Portland, Oregon, the stunning five-acre Japanese Garden is on top of a hill in Washington Park.

Not all botanic gardens emphasize flowering plants. In Tucson, Arizona, the Arizona–Sonora Desert Museum consists of 12 acres of desert plants and others native to the state. The Corkscrew Swamp Sanctuary near Naples, Florida, is maintained by the Audubon Society; its emphasis is on native Floridian plants. A mile-long boardwalk leads through a swamp and past a huge stand of gigantic bald-cypress trees. Morton Arboretum, in Lisle, Illinois, has miles and miles of wooded roads. Self-guided driving tours through the groves are especially popular in spring when lilac and crab-apple trees are in bloom and during the leaf-turning days of October.

## PLANETARIUMS

Perhaps within the next century some vacationers will be able to take a trip into outer space and explore the far reaches of the Solar System. Until then, the best

---

### The Leading Planetariums

Of the approximately 80 planetariums listed in the Place Profiles, found in about half of the Vacation Places, 11 have more than 250 seats and offer major programs. Several of them have an astronomical museum, an observatory, or both on the premises, or are a part of a large science museum. Here are the 11 leaders:

Adler Planetarium, Chicago, IL
Albert Einstein Spacearium, Washington, DC
Charles Hayden Planetarium, Boston, MA
Fels Planetarium, Philadelphia, PA
Fernbank Science Center, Atlanta, GA
Hayden Planetarium, New York, NY
McDonnell Planetarium, St. Louis, MO
Morrison Planetarium, San Francisco, CA
Reuben H. Fleet Space Theater, San Diego, CA
Science Center Planetarium, Baton Rouge, LA
Space Transit Planetarium, Miami, FL

---

**Award-winning Zoos: Breeders of Rare Species**

Each year the American Association of Zoological Parks and Aquariums recognizes accomplishments in the breeding of rare specimens of animal life. Listed here are some of the zoos that have received this award since 1980 and the species for which they were honored.

**Buffalo** (NY) **Zoological Gardens:** Red-eyed tree frog

**Cincinnati** (OH) **Zoo:** Texas blind salamander

**Houston** (TX) **Zoological Gardens:** Angolan python

**Metrozoo** (Miami, FL): Crocodile

**National Zoological Park** (Washington, DC) and the **New York** (NY) **Zoological Park:** Chinese alligator

**New York** (NY) **Zoological Park:** White-naped crane

**The Seattle** (WA) **Aquarium:** Coho salmon

**Sea World** (San Diego, CA): Emperor penguin

---

and most pleasant way to learn about that new frontier is to visit a planetarium. Unlike gardens, museums, and zoos—all of which have been around since the dawn of civilization—planetariums are a modern invention. Ancient people in several parts of the world knew about the movements of the planets and stars, but it was not until this century that methods and machinery were developed to demonstrate and reproduce these extremely complicated motions accurately.

The first modern planetarium was built in Germany in the 1920s. The earliest one constructed in the United States was the Adler Planetarium, in Chicago, completed in 1930. Most planetariums are in schools and are used to aid the formal teaching of astronomy, but there are scores in science museums, parks, and on campuses that produce programs for public enjoyment on a regular basis.

In a planetarium show, a reproduction of the Solar System—or another part of the universe—is projected on the inside of a huge dome. The movements of the heavenly bodies are sped up, translating years into minutes and seconds, so that the audience can see what happens over time. Special programs illustrate such phenomena as the appearance of Halley's comet or a reproduction of the sky as it was in Bethlehem at the time of the birth of Jesus. Other presentations may represent the Solar System as it appears from hundreds of thousands of miles out in space—or the earth as it is seen from a spaceship.

## ZOOS AND AQUARIUMS

The earliest known zoo belonged to Queen Hatshepsut of Egypt and was built in about 1500 B.C. Other ancient rulers kept collections of exotic animals on display. Modern zoos have been around for about 150 years; the first one in the United States was founded in 1859 in Philadelphia.

Zoos are among the most popular attractions for viewers of all ages. The average visitor may be only slightly aware of the serious scientific research being carried on behind the scenes, where a professional staff studies the habits and needs of all its animals. Zoos are also preserves for the breeding and protection of rare and endangered species.

The word *zoo* is a short form of either *zoological park* or *zoological garden,* and most zoos are landscaped with decorative plantings. Frequently the vegetation and contours of each section of the park are planned to duplicate insofar as possible the native habitat of the species kept in that area.

Monkeys are always popular in zoos; visitors love to watch them use gestures like those of humans and go through childlike capers. Another favorite feature is the petting area set aside in a number of zoos, where people are encouraged to play with lambs, kids, and other small animals.

Public aquariums, including oceanariums, are buildings or complexes that serve as zoos for marine life. In older aquariums the specimens are exhibited in a series of tanks similar to the small glass tanks people purchase in pet stores. Newer, more modern complexes have huge, elaborate display tanks with windows in the sides so that viewers can see the underwater environment and activity. A large aquarium has collections of both freshwater and saltwater fish, shell-

---

**The Best Zoos and Aquariums**

Zoos have been steadily improving their methods of housing and caring for animals. Roadside menageries, run by private parties who are not trained professionals, are rapidly disappearing. Public opinion has been influential in persuading a number of publicly owned zoos to clean up their acts. Twelve of the largest zoos and aquariums were accredited by the American Association of Zoological Parks and Aquariums as of 1984. They are as follows:

John G. Shedd Aquarium, Chicago, IL
Lincoln Park Zoological Garden, Chicago, IL
Marine World/Africa USA, Redwood City, CA
National Zoological Park, Washington, DC
New York Zoological Park, Bronx, NY
Philadelphia (PA) Zoological Gardens
St. Louis (MO) Zoological Park
San Diego (CA) Wild Animal Park
San Diego (CA) Zoo
Sea World, San Diego, CA
Sea World of Florida, Orlando, FL
Washington Park Zoo, Portland, OR

## Types of Museums

The following list illustrates the wide variety of public museums in the United States. The different types appeal to people of many different interests, specialties, and hobbies. This list, which does not include history museums, is excerpted from the index to *The Official Museum Directory*.

**Art**
Art museums and galleries
Arts and crafts museums
China, glass, and silver museums
Civic art and cultural centers
Decorative arts museums
Folk art museums
Textile museums

**Children's and junior**

**College and university**

**Company**

**Exhibit areas**

**Nature centers**

**Park museums and visitor centers**

**Science**
Aeronautics and space museums
Anthropology, ethnology, and Indian museums
Aquariums, marine museums, and oceanariums
Arboretums
Archeology museums and sites
Aviaries and ornithology museums
Botanical and aquatic gardens and conservatories
Entomology museums and insect collections
Geology, mineralogy, and paleontology museums
Herbariums
Herpetology museums
Medical, dental, health, pharmacology, apothecary, and psychiatry museums
Natural history and natural science museums
Planetariums, observatories, and astronomy museums
Science museums (general science and physical science)
Wildlife refuges and bird sanctuaries
Zoology museums
Zoos and children's zoos

**Specialized**
Agriculture museums
Antiques museums
Architecture museums
Audiovisual and film museums
Circus museums
Communications museums
Costume museums
Crime museums
Electricity museums
Fire-fighting museums
Forestry museums
Furniture museums
Gun museums
Hobby museums
Horological museums
Industrial museums
Lapidary arts museums
Logging and lumber museums
Mapparia
Mining museums
Money and numismatics museums
Musical instruments museums
Philatelic museums
Religious museums
Scouting museums
Sports museums
Technology museums
Theater museums
Toy and doll museums
Transportation museums
Typography museums
Village museums
Wax museums
Whaling museums
Wood-carving museums

fish, seals, sea lions, otters, walruses, dolphins, and whales. Several oceanariums present regularly scheduled shows featuring trained dolphins, whales, and other aquatic animals; they do synchronized swimming, jump through hoops, and obey simple commands. Another popular feature in many aquariums is the "touch and feel" tank, where visitors are encouraged to pat and stroke some of the water creatures.

The professional watchdog for zoos in the United States is the American Association of Zoological Parks and Aquariums. It was formed in 1924, originally as a branch of the American Institute of Park Executives. In the 1950s and 1960s, zoos and aquariums enjoyed greatly increased popularity as the public in general became more aware of and interested in conservation.

The association became an independent organization in 1972 and immediately began to set up an accreditation program. Today it represents nearly every major zoological park, aquarium, wildlife park, and oceanarium in North America, and by the end of 1985 accreditation was required as a condition of membership.

## MUSEUMS

The earliest colonists came to the Americas with few possessions—only those things most essential for survival in the wilderness. These first settlers were followed soon afterward by wealthier landowners who came with the intention of establishing the same kinds of grand estates their families had owned in Europe.

## The Leading Museums

Thirty-five Vacation Places had one or more major museums that qualified for the highest possible score in that category—800 points. There are 71 of these leading museums: Washington, DC, leads the list with seven; San Francisco, California, has five; Chicago, Illinois, Dallas–Fort Worth, Texas, Minneapolis–St. Paul, Minnesota–Wisconsin, New York City, New York, and Philadelphia, Pennsylvania–Delaware–New Jersey each have four. Listed below are the 70 top museums in the Vacation Places.

**Albuquerque–Santa Fe–Taos, NM**
Museum of New Mexico, Santa Fe

**Boston, MA**
Fogg Art Museum, Cambridge
Museum of Fine Arts, Boston

**Chicago, IL**
The Art Institute of Chicago
Field Museum of Natural History, Chicago
Museum of Contemporary Art, Chicago
Museum of Science and Industry, Chicago

**Cincinnati, OH–KY**
Cincinnati Art Museum
Dayton Art Institute
Dayton Museum of Natural History

**Dallas–Fort Worth, TX**
Dallas Museum of Art
Dallas Museum of Natural History
Fort Worth Museum of Science and History
Kimbell Art Museum, Fort Worth

**Denver–Rocky Mountain National Park, CO**
Denver Museum of Natural History

**Finger Lakes, NY**
Corning Museum of Glass

**Grand Canyon Country, AZ**
Museum of Northern Arizona, Flagstaff

**Hawaii**
Bishop Museum, Honolulu
Honolulu Academy of Arts

**Houston–Galveston, TX**
Museum of Fine Arts, Houston

**Lexington–Bluegrass Country, KY**
J. B. Speed Art Museum, Louisville

**Long Island, NY**
The Museums at Stony Brook

**Los Angeles, CA**
J. Paul Getty Museum, Malibu
Los Angeles County Museum of Art

**Memphis, TN–AR–MS**
Memphis Brooks Museum of Art

**Minneapolis–St. Paul, MN–WI**
Minneapolis Institute of Arts
Minnesota Museum of Art, St. Paul
Science Museum of Minnesota, St. Paul
Walker Art Center, Minneapolis

**New Orleans, LA**
New Orleans Museum of Arts

**New York City, NY**
American Museum of Natural History, New York
Brooklyn Museum
Metropolitan Museum of Art, New York
The Solomon R. Guggenheim Museum, New York
Whitney Museum of Art, New York

**Niagara Falls–Western New York, NY**
Albright-Knox Art Gallery, Buffalo
Buffalo Museum of Science

**Oklahoma City–Cherokee Strip, OK**
Stovall Museum of Science and History, Norman

**Pennsylvania Dutch Country, PA**
The State Museum of Pennsylvania, Harrisburg

**Philadelphia, PA–DE–NJ**
Academy of Natural Science of Philadelphia
The Pennsylvania Academy of the Fine Arts, Philadelphia
Philadelphia Museum of Art
The University Museum, University of Pennsylvania, Philadelphia

**Put-in-Bay–Lake Erie Shore, OH**
Toledo Museum of Art

**Richmond–Fredericksburg, VA**
Virginia Museum of Fine Arts, Richmond

**St. Augustine–Northeast Coast, FL**
Jacksonville Museum of Arts and Sciences

**St. Louis–Mark Twain Country, MO–IL**
St. Louis Art Museum

**Salt Lake City, UT**
Utah Museum of Fine Arts, Salt Lake City

**San Diego, CA**
Natural History Museum, San Diego
San Diego Museums of Art

**San Francisco, CA**
Asian Art Museum, San Francisco
California Academy of Sciences, San Francisco
Fine Arts Museum of San Francisco
The Oakland Museum
University Art Museum, Berkeley

**Santa Barbara–San Simeon, CA**
Santa Barbara Museum of Art

**Seattle–Mount Rainier–North Cascades, WA**
Museum of History and Industry, Seattle
Seattle Art Museum
Thomas Burke Memorial Washington State Museum, Seattle

**Tampa Bay–Southwest Coast, FL**
John and Mable Ringling Museum of Art, Sarasota

**Tucson, AZ**
Arizona-Sonora Desert Museum, Tucson
University of Arizona Museum of Art, Tucson

**Washington, DC–MD–VA**
Hirshhorn Museum and Sculpture Garden—Smithsonian, Washington
National Gallery of Art—Smithsonian, Washington
National Museum of African Art—Smithsonian, Washington
National Museum of American Art—Smithsonian, Washington
National Museum of Natural History—Smithsonian, Washington
National Portrait Gallery—Smithsonian, Washington
The Phillips Collection, Washington

**White Mountains, NH**
Hood Museum of Art, Hanover

**Williamsburg–Colonial Triangle, VA**
The Chrysler Museum, Norfolk

They brought with them the fine household furnishings, art objects, and even plants, that had graced their former luxurious homes.

They also brought a tradition of support of the arts and of education, which soon led to the establishment of public museums in which to store collections of books, documents, paintings, sculpture, archeological finds, furniture, furnishings, and other valuable objects. Before 1800 public museums had been opened in Charleston, South Carolina, and Salem, Massachusetts, that still exist today.

Today's museums use the latest technological methods of audio and visual dramatization to educate and entertain; they are far from the static displays of objects in dusty glass cages that many of them used to be, and the subjects treated are of fascinating variety.

Fans and professionals with an interest in several of the major sports have established museums called *halls of fame* to honor the history of the sport and its heroes. Two of the best known are the National Baseball Hall of Fame, Cooperstown, New York, and the Basketball Hall of Fame, Springfield, Massachusetts. Horse racing is honored at the National Museum of Racing, Saratoga Springs, New York, and the Kentucky Derby Museum, Louisville, Kentucky.

Art museums may be huge, with collections from many different artists and periods, or they may specialize in the work of one artist or type of art. The Metropolitan Museum of Art, New York City, and the National Gallery of Art, Washington, DC, are examples of the largest and finest. The Salvador Dali Museum, in St. Petersburg, Florida, exhibits only the works of the Spanish surrealist. The Amon Carter Museum, in Forth Worth, Texas, is a lovely small museum featuring primarily American artists—its collection of paintings of the American West by Frederic Remington and Charles Russell is especially impressive.

Brookgreen Gardens, Murrells Inlet, South Carolina, is a delightful and most unusual outdoor museum. It is three museums in one: botanic garden, zoo, and sculpture collection. More than 350 pieces of sculpture by American artists are displayed in a 300-acre garden adjacent to a wildlife park that is an accredited zoo. There are fountains, walkways, pools, and seating areas shaded by moss-draped trees and flowering shrubs. As its founders intended, it represents "a quiet joining of hands between science and art."

A few museums have collections related to an important craft or product of an area, such as the glass collections in Sandwich, Massachusetts, and Toledo, Ohio, and the excellent display of wood products in the Western Forestry Center in Portland, Oregon.

The Computer Museum in Boston may well be a forerunner of technological exhibits of the future. Collections trace the history and development of computers; the museum also sponsors programs in which people can employ highly sophisticated hardware and software to delve into and solve varied problems.

Collections of antique toys are popular; an outstanding one is the Perelman Antique Toy Museum in Philadelphia. Antique automobiles are another favorite. One of the best-known car collections is Harrah's, in Reno, Nevada. There is a Museum of Vintage Fashion in Lafayette, California, a Horseless Carriage Museum in Rapid City, South Dakota, and a Museum of the Circus in Sarasota, Florida.

Ethnic-art museums are plentiful in New York City and San Francisco. Outstanding science museums, such as the Museum of Science and Industry in Chicago, the Natural History Museum in San Diego, and the Denver Museum of Natural History are always crowded with visitors.

## SPECIAL ATTRACTIONS

The heading of Special Attractions in this chapter is a catchall for anything man-made, as opposed to the attractions of nature, that doesn't fit neatly into the other classifications. Most numerous in the Place Profile listings are guided sightseeing tours. Any such tour of a city or area, whether by bus, train, trolley, horse-drawn carriage, boat, or airplane, is an excellent means of getting a fast overall knowledge of the place. Individual guides vary widely in their ability to impart accurate and entertaining information, but in almost every case you will learn something new and interesting, and at best you'll come away feeling you have really become well acquainted with the locality.

Other special attractions include ghost towns in Colorado and Nevada; industrial tours and exhibits; the formerly seafaring luxury liner *Queen Mary* (now docked and used as a hotel) and Howard Hughes's airplane, the *Spruce Goose*, both on display in Long Beach, California; and a couple of collections of weird, fantasylike structures on opposite sides of the country —the Watts Towers in Los Angeles and the Coral Castle in Miami. Both of these creations were the work of highly talented, eccentric, individualistic artists.

# SCORING: Feeding the Mind and Spirit

This chapter compares the availability of various attractions that bring sightseers to the 107 Vacation Places: botanic gardens, planetariums, zoos and aquariums, museums (other than museums primarily concerned with history), and other special sites and services.

The number of points awarded by *Vacation Places Rated* to each attraction was based on the various factors explained below. In all cases the scores indicate which attractions have the most appeal for the largest number of people and where the average vacationer will want to spend the most time. Such factors as size, magnitude of annual budgets, extent of programs and services, and accreditation by professional societies were used as indicators of the importance of an institution.

The attractions in some of the categories in this chapter were assigned a rating of AA, A, B, or C, depending on some measure of their size. The nature of this measure varied among the different types of attractions. Points were then awarded on the basis of the letter rating. The letter ratings appear in the Place Profiles.

Many sites that were included in the scoring of this chapter were not strictly within the boundaries of the Vacation Places. These attractions were given half the comparable score of those sites within the boundaries. They are printed in the Place Profiles in italics.

## Botanic Gardens

Each botanic garden received a base score of 50 points. Additional points were awarded based on the number of acres in cultivation.

Sixty-two Vacation Places have one or more botanic gardens. Philadelphia ranks first, with 14 gardens and a score of 1,255.

### Top Ten for Botanic Gardens

|   | | Botanic Gardens | Points |
|---|---|---|---|
| 1. | Philadelphia, PA–DE–NJ | 14 | 1,255 |
| 2. | Washington, DC–MD–VA | 10 | 903 |
| 3. | Catskill Mountains, NY | 6 | 847 |
| 4. | Los Angeles, CA | 9 | 803 |
| 5. | Chicago, IL | 5 | 709 |
| 6. | New York City, NY | 7 | 653 |
| 7. | San Francisco, CA | 6 | 611 |
| 8. | Cincinnati, OH–KY | 5 | 602 |
| 9. | Tampa Bay–Southwest Coast, FL | 5 | 593 |
| 10. | Long Island, NY | 5 | 565 |

## Planetariums

There are more than 1,000 planetariums in the United States—a large proportion of which are in schools and colleges. Only those open to the general public, with auditoriums and a schedule of public programs, were scored and included in the Place Profiles. Each planetarium was assigned a rating of A, B, or C to indicate its seating capacity. Scoring was as follows:

| A planetarium received a rating of: | And a score of: | If it had: |
|---|---|---|
| A | 300 | 250 or more seats |
| B | 250 | 100 to 249 seats |
| C | 200 | 100 or fewer seats |

The Washington, DC, area has eight planetariums, yielding a score of 1,600. Eight other Vacation Places received 550 or more points; five places tied for tenth place.

### Top Nine for Planetariums

|   | | Planetariums | Points |
|---|---|---|---|
| 1. | Washington, DC–MD–VA | 8 | 1,600 |
| 2. | Atlanta, GA | 4 | 1,050 |
| 3. | Miami–Gold Coast–Keys, FL | 4 | 1,000 |
| 4. | St. Augustine–Northeast Coast, FL | 3 | 700 |
| 5. | Long Island, NY | 3 | 650 |
| 6. | Boston, MA | 3 | 625 |
| 7. | New York City, NY | 2 | 550 |
| 7. | San Francisco, CA | 2 | 550 |
| 7. | Vicksburg–Natchez– Baton Rouge, MS–LA | 2 | 550 |

## Zoos and Aquariums

The A, B, and C ratings for zoos and aquariums were based on the annual budgets of the institutions. In addition, about 45 of the more than 80 zoos and aquariums listed in the Place Profiles were accredited by the American Association of Zoological Parks and Aquariums as of 1984, and an asterisk (*) appears after their letter ratings. Scoring was as follows:

| A zoo received a rating of: | And a score of: | If its budget was: |
|---|---|---|
| A | 600 | $5 million or more |
| B | 500 | between $2 million and $5 million |
| C | 400 | less than $2 million |

Bonus points for accreditation: 200

| An aquarium received a rating of: | And a score of: | If its budget was: |
|---|---|---|
| A | 500 | $3 million or more |
| B | 400 | between $1 million and $3 million |
| C | 300 | less than $1 million |

Bonus points for accreditation: 100

A combination zoo and aquarium was scored as a zoo.

San Diego, California, with two zoos and an aquarium, all of which were category A and accredited, tied for first place with Seattle–Mount Rainier–North Cascades, Washington, with three zoos and an aquarium. Each of these top two received 2,200 points. The next eight in rank for zoos and aquariums had three attractions each.

## Top Eleven for Zoos and Aquariums

| | Zoos and Aquariums | Points |
|---|---|---|
| 1. San Diego, CA | 3 | 2,200 |
| 1. Seattle–Mount Rainier–North Cascades, WA | 4 | 2,200 |
| 3. Chicago, IL | 3 | 2,000 |
| 4. San Francisco, CA | 3 | 1,900 |
| 5. Los Angeles, CA | 3 | 1,600 |
| 5. New York City, NY | 3 | 1,600 |
| 5. Orlando–Space Coast, FL | 3 | 1,600 |
| 8. Dallas–Fort Worth, TX | 3 | 1,400 |
| 8. Pennsylvania Dutch Country, PA | 3 | 1,400 |
| 10. Boston, MA | 3 | 1,300 |
| 10. Cincinnati, OH–KY | 2 | 1,300 |

## Museums

Museums were given a rating of AA, A, B, or C, according to the type and extent of collections and programs. Bonus points were awarded for accreditation by the American Association of Museums, and recipients of these bonus points were marked with an asterisk (*) in the Place Profiles. Museums primarily devoted to history were not included, since they appeared in the previous chapter. Some general museums contain major collections of several types—history, natural history, and art, for example. A few such museums were listed in both chapters. Those institutions whose collections were of extremely limited interest to the general public were not scored.

| A museum received a rating of: | And a score of: | If it had: |
|---|---|---|
| AA | 600 | six or more collections, activities, and publication programs and a staff of ten or more in *The Official Museum Directory* |
| A | 500 | three or more collections and *both* an activities and a publication program |
| B | 400 | more than two collections plus a varied activities program *or* a publications program |
| C | 200 | one or two collections or no special programs or activities |

Bonus points for accreditation: 200

To have qualified for scoring, activities programs must have included lectures, concerts, formal educational programs, or other functions beyond exhibits and gallery talks. Publications programs must have included regular newsletters or several books.

## Top Ten for Museums

| | Museums* | Points |
|---|---|---|
| 1. New York City, NY | 47 | 21,400 |
| 2. Boston, MA | 28 | 13,600 |
| 3. Philadelphia, PA–DE–NJ | 32 | 13,100 |
| 4. Los Angeles, CA | 29 | 13,000 |
| 5. Washington, DC–MD–VA | 23 | 12,100 |
| 6. San Francisco, CA | 18 | 9,700 |
| 7. Dallas–Fort Worth, TX | 15 | 7,000 |
| 8. Long Island, NY | 14 | 6,800 |
| 9. Miami–Gold Coast–Keys, FL | 14 | 6,400 |
| 10. Minneapolis–St. Paul, MN–WI | 12 | 6,200 |

*Figures do not include history museums.

New York City was the runaway leader for its museums, receiving a score more than 50 percent higher than Boston, which ranked second. There were 47 qualifying museums in New York. Minneapolis, in tenth place, had 12.

## Special Attractions

Special attractions were also marked AA, A, B, or C, based on how appealing this kind of place or activity was generally considered to be to large numbers of people. The types of attraction included in each category are as follows:

| A special attraction received a rating of: | And a score of: | If it had: |
|---|---|---|
| AA | 800 | a unique point of interest or activity around which an entire vacation is often planned |
| A | 600 | a hands-on museum primarily for youngsters, a sightseeing tour, or a point of interest worth several hours of exploration |
| B | 400 | a miscellaneous tour or sightseeing ride, an observatory or observation deck, or another unique man-made attraction |
| C | 200 | a point of interest or activity of casual interest to average vacationers or of interest primarily to specialists or hobbyists |

Special man-made attractions can be found almost everywhere; no one section of the United States dominated this category. Los Angeles, California, which leads the list with 8,000 points, draws tourists with famous sites that range from tours of movie studios and broadcasting stations to the fossil exhibits at the La Brea Tar Pits. Miami–Gold Coast–Keys, Florida, and Tampa Bay–Southwest Coast, Florida, in second and third place, have a number of gardens, animal sanctuaries, and attractions related to their proximity to the ocean.

## Top Ten for Special Attractions

| | Special Attractions | Points |
|---|---|---|
| 1. Los Angeles, CA | 20 | 8,000 |
| 2. Miami–Gold Coast–Keys, FL | 16 | 7,200 |
| 3. Tampa Bay–Southwest Coast, FL | 14 | 6,400 |
| 4. Niagara Falls–Western New York, NY | 10 | 5,400 |
| 5. San Francisco, CA | 10 | 5,200 |
| 6. Lexington–Bluegrass Country, KY | 11 | 4,800 |
| 6. Mystic Seaport–Connecticut Valley, CT | 8 | 4,800 |
| 6. Washington, DC–MD–VA | 11 | 4,800 |
| 9. Seattle–Mount Rainier–North Cascades, WA | 11 | 4,600 |
| 10. New York City, NY | 7 | 4,400 |

# 🏛 PLACE PROFILES: Feeding the Mind and Spirit

In these pages, sightseeing points of interest in the following categories are listed for the 107 Vacation Places: Botanic Gardens, Planetariums, Zoos and Aquariums, Museums, and Special Attractions. The figures that appear in parentheses following the categories indicate point value.

As in other chapters, certain listings nearby but not precisely within the area defined as the Vacation Place are printed in italics. These are included because they are easily accessible and important or interesting enough to be worth a short side trip; they were given one-half the point score of similar listings within the Vacation Place boundaries.

See the scoring section for an explanation of the AA, A, B, and C ratings. An asterisk (*) following the rating indicates accreditation by the American Association of Museums or the American Association of Zoological Parks and Aquariums.

A star (★) preceding a Vacation Place highlights that place as one of the top ten in this chapter.

## Adirondack Mountains, NY

|  | Rating |
|---|---|
| **Planetariums (200)** | |
| Buces (Herkimer) | C |
| **Zoos (200)** | |
| *Utica Zoo (Utica)* | C |
| **Museums (1,250)** | |
| Adirondack Museum: general (Blue Mountain Lake) | C* |
| The Hyde Collection: art (Glens Falls) | A |
| *National Museum of Racing (Saratoga Springs)* | C |
| *Children's Museum (Utica)* | A |
| **Special Attractions (2,800)** | |
| Boat ride through Ausable Chasm | A |
| Cruise on Lake George | A |
| Cruise on Lake Placid | A |
| Tours of garnet mines (North Creek) | B |
| Cruises on Lake Champlain (Plattsburgh) | A |
| Places Rated Score: 4,450   Places Rated Rank: 53 | |

## Albuquerque–Santa Fe–Taos, NM

|  | Rating |
|---|---|
| **Planetariums (200)** | |
| Eugene E. Carl (Albuquerque) | C |
| **Zoos (600)** | |
| Rio Grande Zoological Park (Albuquerque) | C* |
| **Museums (4,600)** | |
| Albuquerque Museum: art, science, history (Albuquerque) | A |
| Institute of Meteoritics Meteorite Museum (Albuquerque) | B |
| Jonson Gallery: art (Albuquerque) | C |
| National Atomic Museum: nuclear energy, weapons (Albuquerque) | C |
| University Art Museum (Albuquerque) | A |
| Bradbury Science Museum (Los Alamos) | C |
| Governor's Gallery (Santa Fe) | C |
| Institute of American Indian Arts Museum (Santa Fe) | A |
| Museum of New Mexico: general (Santa Fe) | AA* |
| Wheelwright Museum of the American Indian (Santa Fe) | A |
| Millicent Rogers Museum: art, anthropology (Taos) | AA |
| **Special Attractions (2,200)** | |
| Indian Pueblo Cultural Center (Albuquerque) | B |
| Pottery making (San Ildefonso Pueblo) | B |
| Sightseeing bus tours (Santa Fe) | A |
| Stables Art Center of the Taos Art Assn. (Taos) | B |
| Taos Pueblo (Taos) | B |
| Places Rated Score: 7,600   Places Rated Rank: 25 | |

## Anchorage–Kenai Peninsula, AK

|  | Rating |
|---|---|
| **Planetariums (200)** | |
| Jane W. Mears (Anchorage) | C |
| **Zoos (400)** | |
| Alaska Zoo (Anchorage) | C |
| **Museums (1,600)** | |
| Alaska Wildlife and Natural History Museum (Anchorage) | C |
| Anchorage History and Fine Arts Museum (Anchorage) | A* |
| Pratt Museum of Natural History (Homer) | A* |
| **Special Attractions (1,800)** | |
| Boat rides on Ketchican Bay (Anchorage) | A |
| Flightseeing tours of area (Anchorage) | A |
| Sightseeing bus tours (Anchorage) | A |
| Places Rated Score: 4,000   Places Rated Rank: 59 | |

## Asheville–Smoky Mountains, NC

|  | Rating |
|---|---|
| **Botanic Gardens (405)** | |
| Biltmore House and Gardens: 11,000 acres of grounds; 35 acres of formal gardens (Asheville) | |
| University Gardens: 10 acres (Asheville) | |
| **Museums (1,400)** | |
| Asheville Art Museum (Asheville) | A |
| Biltmore Homespun Shops: textiles (Asheville) | C |
| Estes-Winn Antique Auto Museum (Asheville) | C |
| The Health Adventure (Asheville) | A |
| **Special Attractions (400)** | |
| Folk Art Center of the Southern Highland Handicraft Guild (Asheville) | B |
| Places Rated Score: 2,205   Places Rated Rank: 83 | |

## Aspen–Vail, CO

|  | Rating |
|---|---|
| **Museums (600)** | |
| Aspen Center for the Visual Arts: outdoor sculpture (Aspen) | C |
| Breckenridge Mining Camp Museum (Breckenridge) | C |
| Colorado Ski Museum and Hall of Fame (Vail) | C |
| **Special Attractions (600)** | |
| Ghost towns, near Aspen and Breckenridge | B |
| Tabor Opera House (Leadville) | C |
| Places Rated Score: 1,200   Places Rated Rank: 98 | |

## Atlanta, GA

|  | Rating |
|---|---|
| **Botanic Gardens (400)** | |
| Fernbank Science Center (Atlanta) | |
| Callaway Gardens: 2,500 acres (Pine Mountain) | |
| **Planetariums (1,050)** | |
| Fernbank Science Center (Atlanta) | A |
| Fulton (Atlanta) | B |
| Harper (Atlanta) | B |
| Northside (Atlanta) | B |
| **Zoos (400)** | |
| Atlanta Zoo (Atlanta) | C |
| **Museums (2,200)** | |
| Emory University Museum of Art and Architecture (Atlanta) | C |
| Fernbank Science Center (Atlanta) | A |
| Georgia State Museum of Science and Industry (Atlanta) | C |
| The High Museum of Art (Atlanta) | A* |
| Photographic Investments Gallery (Atlanta) | C |
| Cobb County Youth Museum (Marietta) | B |

|  | Rating |
|---|---|
| **Special Attractions (1,800)** | |
| Fox Theater (Atlanta) | C |
| Sightseeing bus tours (Atlanta) | A |
| Stone Mountain Park | B |
| Gold panning (Dahlonega) | C |
| "Alpine" village (Helen) | B |
| Places Rated Score: 5,850    Places Rated Rank: 38 | |

### Atlantic City, NJ
| | |
|---|---|
| **Museums (900)** | |
| Mid-Atlantic Center for the Arts (Cape May) | A |
| Noyes Museum: art (Oceanville) | B |
| **Special Attractions (800)** | |
| Boardwalk (Atlantic City) | B |
| Winery tour (Egg Harbor City) | B |
| Places Rated Score: 1,700    Places Rated Rank: 92 | |

### Austin–Hill Country, TX
| | |
|---|---|
| **Museums (1,900)** | |
| Archer M. Huntington Art Gallery (Austin) | A |
| Laguna Gloria Art Museum (Austin) | AA |
| Texas Memorial Museum: natural science, history (Austin) | AA |
| Cowboy Artists of America Museum (Kerrville) | C |
| **Special Attractions (600)** | |
| Sightseeing bus tours (Austin) | A |
| Places Rated Score: 2,500    Places Rated Rank: 78 | |

### Baltimore–Chesapeake Bay, MD
| | |
|---|---|
| **Botanic Gardens (240)** | |
| William Paca Garden: 2 acres (Annapolis) | |
| Cylburn Park: 40 acres (Baltimore) | |
| London Town Publik House and Gardens: 11 acres (Edgewater) | |
| Ladew Topiary Garden: 25 acres (Monkton) | |
| **Planetariums (450)** | |
| Davis (Baltimore) | B |
| St. Michaels (St. Michaels) | C |
| **Zoos and Aquariums (1,100)** | |
| Baltimore Zoo (Baltimore) | C* |
| National Aquarium (Baltimore) | A |
| **Museums (3,900)** | |
| Baltimore Museum of Art—nine centers (Baltimore) | AA |
| Baltimore Streetcar Museum (Baltimore) | B |
| Gallery of Art (Baltimore) | B |
| Lacrosse Foundation: sports (Baltimore) | C |
| Maryland Academy of Sciences (Baltimore) | A |
| Walters Art Gallery (Baltimore) | A* |
| Maryland Museum of African Art (Columbia) | C |
| Ellicott City B & O Railroad Station Museum (Ellicott City) | C |
| Chesapeake Bay Maritime Museum (St. Michaels) | A* |
| **Special Attractions (1,200)** | |
| Harbor cruises (Annapolis) | A |
| Harbor cruises (Baltimore) | A |
| Places Rated Score: 6,890    Places Rated Rank: 30 | |

### Bar Harbor–Acadia, ME
| | |
|---|---|
| **Botanic Gardens (100)** | |
| Wild Gardens of Acadia (Bar Harbor) | |
| Asticou Terraces (Northeast Harbor) | |
| **Museums (1,600)** | |
| Owl Head Transportation Museum (Rockland) | C |
| Shore Village Museum; Maine's Lighthouse Museum (Rockland) | B |
| William A. Farnsworth Library and Art Museum (Rockland) | B* |
| Penobscot Marine Museum (Searsport) | C |
| Wendell Gilley Museum: folk art, woodcarving (Southwest Harbor) | C |
| **Special Attractions (2,800)** | |
| Ferry service to Nova Scotia (Bar Harbor) | A |
| Industrial tours, pottery factories (Blue Hill) | B |
| Sightseeing cruises, Penobscot Bay (Camden) | A |

|  | Rating |
|---|---|
| Windjammer cruises (Camden) | A |
| Sightseeing cruises (Deer Isle) | A |
| Places Rated Score: 4,500    Places Rated Rank: 49 | |

### Bend–Cascade Mountains, OR
| | |
|---|---|
| **Museums (400)** | |
| Oregon High Desert Museum: natural science (Bend) | B |
| **Special Attractions (800)** | |
| Newberry Crater (Deschutes National Forest) | B |
| University of Oregon's Pine Mountain Observatory (Millican) | B |
| Places Rated Score: 1,200    Places Rated Rank: 98 | |

### Berkshire Hills–Pioneer Valley, MA
| | |
|---|---|
| **Botanic Gardens (204)** | |
| Smith College Botanic Garden: 200 acres (Northampton) | |
| Berkshire Garden Center: 8 acres (Stockbridge) | |
| **Planetariums (250)** | |
| Seymour (Springfield) | B |
| **Museums (4,000)** | |
| Holyoke Museum: art (Holyoke) | B |
| Smith College Museum of Art (Northampton) | B |
| Berkshire Museum: art, natural history, history (Pittsfield) | B |
| Basketball Hall of Fame (Springfield) | C |
| George Walter Vincent Smith Art Museum (Springfield) | A |
| Museum of Fine Arts (Springfield) | B |
| Springfield Science Museum (Springfield) | B |
| Norman Rockwell Museum (Stockbridge) | C |
| Sterling and Francine Clark Art Institute (Williamstown) | A* |
| Williams College Museum of Art (Williamstown) | B |
| Places Rated Score: 4,454    Places Rated Rank: 51 | |

### Black Hills, SD
| | |
|---|---|
| **Zoos (400)** | |
| Bear Country USA (Rapid City) | C |
| **Museums (1,200)** | |
| Ledbetter Antique Car Museum (Custer) | C |
| Western Woodcarvings (Custer) | C |
| Mammoth Site of Hot Springs: paleontology (Hot Springs) | C |
| Parade of Presidents Wax Museum (Keystone) | C |
| Horseless Carriage Museum (Rapid City) | C |
| Museum of Geology, South Dakota School of Mines (Rapid City) | C |
| **Special Attractions (2,200)** | |
| Mount Rushmore National Memorial (Keystone) | AA |
| Ranch tours, chuckwagon suppers (Rapid City) | A |
| Sightseeing bus tours (Rapid City) | A |
| Wall Drug Store (Wall) | C |
| Places Rated Score: 3,800    Places Rated Rank: 62 | |

### Blue Ridge Mountains, VA
| | |
|---|---|
| **Botanic Gardens (112)** | |
| O. E. White Arboretum: 123 acres (Boyce) | |
| **Planetariums (200)** | |
| M. T. Brackbill (Harrisonburg) | C |
| **Museums (400)** | |
| University of Virginia Art Museum (Charlottesville) | B |
| **Special Attractions (1,600)** | |
| Blue Ridge Parkway | A |
| Skyline Drive | A |
| Shenandoah Visitor Center (Luray) | B |
| Places Rated Score: 2,312    Places Rated Rank: 82 | |

### Boise–Sun Valley, ID
| | |
|---|---|
| **Planetariums (200)** | |
| T. C. Bird (Boise) | C |
| **Zoos (400)** | |
| Boise City Zoo (Boise) | C |
| **Museums (500)** | |
| Boise Gallery of Art (Boise) | A |
| Places Rated Score: 1,100    Places Rated Rank: 100 | |

Rating

## Boone–High Country, NC
Museums (700)
  Wilkes Art Gallery (North Wilkesboro)    **A**
  Museum of North Carolina Minerals (Spruce Pine)    **C**
Special Attractions (400)
  Frescoes, Holy Trinity Church (Glendale Springs)    **B**
Places Rated Score: 1,100    Places Rated Rank: 100

## ★ Boston, MA
Botanic Gardens (500)
  Mount Auburn Cemetery: 165 acres (Cambridge)
  Will C. Curtis Garden in the Woods: 15 acres
    (Framingham)
  Arnold Arboretum: 265 acres (Jamaica Plain)
  Walter Hunnewell Pinetum; 40 acres (Wellesley)
  Case Estates of the Arnold Arboretum: 11 acres
    (Weston)
Planetariums (625)
  Charles Hayden (Boston)    **A**
  *Alice G. Wallace (Fitchburg)*    **B**
  Plymouth-Carver (Plymouth)    **C**
Zoos and Aquariums (1,300)
  Franklin Park Zoo (Boston)    **C**
  New England Aquarium (Boston)    **B***
  Walter D. Stone Memorial Zoo (Stoneham)    **C**
Museums (13,600)
  Addison Gallery of American Art (Andover)    **B***
  The Old Schwamb Mill: industrial history (Arlington)    **B**
  Boston University Art Gallery (Boston)    **B**
  Children's Art Center (Boston)    **C**
  Children's Museum (Boston)    **A***
  Computer Museum (Boston)    **C**
  Institute of Contemporary Art (Boston)    **AA**
  Isabella Stewart Gardner Museum: art (Boston)    **B***
  Museum of Fine Arts (Boston)    **AA***
  Museum of the National Center of Afro-American
    Artists (Boston)    **A***
  Museum of Science (Boston)    **A***
  The Brockton Art Museum (Brockton)    **A***
  Bush-Reisinger Museum: art (Cambridge)    **B***
  Fogg Art Museum (Cambridge)    **AA***
  Francis Russell Hart Nautical Museum
    (Cambridge)    **C**
  The M.I.T. Museum: history of science and
    technology (Cambridge)    **C**
  Peabody Museum of Archaeology and Ethnology
    (Cambridge)    **A***
  Cohasset Maritime Museum (Cohasset)    **C**
  Art Complex Museum (Duxbury)    **A**
  Essex Shipbuilding Museum (Essex)    **C**
  De Cordova and Dane Museum and Park: art
    (Lincoln)    **A***
  The China Trade Museum: decorative arts
    (Milton)    **C***
  The Custom House Maritime Museum
    (Newburyport)    **B**
  Merrimac Valley Textile Museum: industrial history
    (North Andover)    **C***
  Mount Holyoke College Art Museum (South Hadley)    **A**
  Rose Art Museum, Brandeis University (Waltham)    **B**
  The Wellesley College Museum: art (Wellesley)    **B**
  Cardinal Spellman Philatelic Museum (Weston)    **C***
Special Attractions (2,000)
  Boston Public Library: extensive art collection
    (Boston)    **B**
  Harbor cruises (Boston)    **A**
  Mapparium, Christian Science Center (Boston)    **C**
  Sightseeing tours (Boston)    **A**
  Swan boat rides, on the Common (Boston)    **C**
Places Rated Score: 18,025    Places Rated Rank: 4

## Brownsville–Rio Grande Valley, TX
Botanic Gardens (60)
  Valley Botanical Garden: 20 acres (McAllen)
Zoos (600)
  Gladys Porter Zoo (Brownsville)    **C***

Rating

Museums (600)
  McAllen International Museum: art (McAllen)    **B**
  Old Clock Museum (Pharr)    **C**
Special Attractions (600)
  Shopping in Mexican border towns    **A**
Places Rated Score: 1,860    Places Rated Rank: 87

## Cape Cod–The Islands, MA
Botanic Gardens (88)
  Heritage Plantation of Sandwich: 76 acres (Sandwich)
Museums (2,000)
  Cape Cod Museum of Natural History (Brewster)    **A**
  Provincetown Art Association and Museum of Art
    (Provincetown)    **B**
  Heritage Plantation of Sandwich: general
    (Sandwich)    **A***
  Sandwich Glass Museum (Sandwich)    **C**
  Yesteryears: dolls (Sandwich)    **C**
Special Attractions (400)
  The Nantucket Maria Mitchell Association:
    observatories and natural science (Nantucket)    **B**
Places Rated Score: 2,488    Places Rated Rank: 79

## Catskill Mountains, NY
Botanic Gardens (847)
  George Landis Arboretum: 100 acres (Esperance)
  Boscobel Restoration: 16 acres (Garrison)
  Vanderbilt Mansion: 211 acres (Hyde Park)
  Cary Arboretum: 700 acres (Millbrook)
  Innisfree Garden: 150 acres (Millbrook)
  Mohonk Gardens: 15 acres (New Paltz)
Planetariums (200)
  Gustafson (Fishkill)    **C**
Zoos (400)
  Catskill Game Farm (Catskill)    **C**
Museums (2,900)
  Albany Institute of History and Art (Albany)    **C***
  Museum of Early American Decoration (Albany)    **C**
  University Art Gallery, State University of New York
    (Albany)    **C**
  *Farmers' Museum (Cooperstown)*    **B***
  Museum of the Hudson Highlands: natural history,
    art (Cornwall-on-Hudson)    **A**
  Hall of Fame of the Trotter (Goshen)    **C**
  American Museum of Fire Fighting (Hudson)    **C**
  Storm King Art Center (Mountainville)    **C**
  College Art Gallery, the College at New Paltz
    (New Paltz)    **C**
  Rensselaer County Junior Museum (Troy)    **A**
Special Attractions (1,100)
  *National Baseball Hall of Fame (Cooperstown)*    **A**
  Winery tour (New Paltz)    **B**
  Reptile Institute (Rhinebeck)    **C**
  Proctor's Theater (Schenectady)    **C**
Places Rated Score: 5,447    Places Rated Rank: 41

## Charleston, SC
Botanic Gardens (277)
  Magnolia Gardens: 25 acres (Charleston)
  Middleton Place: 65 acres (Charleston)
  Cypress Gardens: 162 acres (Oakley)
Museums (1,800)
  Avery Institute of Afro-American History and
    Culture (Charleston)    **C**
  Charleston Museum (Charleston)    **A***
  Gibbes Art Gallery (Charleston)    **A***
  The Old Slave Mart Museum: art gallery and
    cultural history (Charleston)    **C**
Special Attractions (600)
  Guided tours by trolley or horse-drawn carriage
    (Charleston)    **A**
Places Rated Score: 2,677    Places Rated Rank: 75

## Chattanooga–Huntsville, TN–AL–GA
Botanic Gardens (75)
  Reflection Riding: 50 acres (Chattanooga, TN)

|  | Rating |
|---|---|
| **Museums (1,800)** | |
| Houston Antique Museum (Chattanooga) | C |
| Hunter Museum of Art (Chattanooga) | A* |
| Tennessee Valley Railroad Museum (Chattanooga) | C |
| Huntsville Museum of Art (Huntsville, AL) | A* |
| **Special Attractions (1,200)** | |
| Rock City (Chattanooga) | A |
| Alabama Space and Rocket Center (Huntsville) | A |

Places Rated Score: 3,075    Places Rated Rank: 73

## ★ Chicago, IL

**Botanic Gardens (709)**
Garfield Park Conservatory: 4 acres (Chicago)
Lincoln Park Conservatory: 3 acres (Chicago)
Chicago Horticultural Society Botanic Garden: 300 acres (Glencoe)
Morton Arboretum: 600 acres (Lisle)
Cantigny, Robert R. McCormick Gardens: 10 acres (Wheaton)

|  | Rating |
|---|---|
| **Planetariums (300)** | |
| Adler (Chicago) | A |
| **Zoos and Aquariums (2,000)** | |
| Chicago Zoological Park (Brookfield) | A |
| John G. Shedd Aquarium (Chicago) | A* |
| Lincoln Park Zoological Garden (Chicago) | A* |
| **Museums (6,000)** | |
| The Art Institute of Chicago (Chicago) | AA* |
| Chicago Academy of Science, Museum of Ecology (Chicago) | A* |
| The David and Alfred Smart Gallery, University of Chicago: art (Chicago) | A |
| Field Museum of Natural History (Chicago) | AA* |
| Museum of Contemporary Art (Chicago) | AA* |
| Museum of Science and Industry (Chicago) | AA* |
| Oriental Institute, University of Chicago (Chicago) | A |
| Spertus Museum of Judaica (Chicago) | A* |
| Terra Museum of American Art (Evanston) | B |
| **Special Attractions (2,000)** | |
| Cruises on Lake Michigan and Chicago River (Chicago) | A |
| Guided walks conducted by Chicago Architecture Foundation (Chicago) | B |
| Observation deck, Sears Tower–world's tallest building (Chicago) | B |
| Sightseeing bus tours (Chicago) | A |

Places Rated Score: 11,009    Places Rated Rank: 10

## Cincinnati, OH–KY

**Botanic Gardens (602)**
Cemetery of Spring Grove: 400 acres (Cincinnati)
Cox Arboretum: 20 acres (Cincinnati)
Irwin M. Krohn Conservatory (Cincinnati)
Mt. Airy Arboretum: 120 acres (Cincinnati)
Stanley M. Rowe Arboretum: 164 acres (Cincinnati)

|  | Rating |
|---|---|
| **Planetariums (450)** | |
| Museum of Natural History (Cincinnati) | C |
| Dayton Museum of Natural History (Dayton) | B |
| **Zoos (1,300)** | |
| Cincinnati Zoo (Cincinnati) | B* |
| Wild Animal Habitat (Cincinnati) | C* |
| **Museums (4,600)** | |
| Cincinnati Art Museum (Cincinnati) | AA* |
| Cincinnati Fire Museum (Cincinnati) | C |
| Cincinnati Museum of Natural History (Cincinnati) | A |
| Contemporary Arts Center (Cincinnati) | B |
| Taft Museum: art (Cincinnati) | B* |
| Aullwood Audubon Center and Farm (Dayton) | A |
| Dayton Art Institute (Dayton) | AA* |
| Dayton Museum of Natural History (Dayton) | AA* |
| **Special Attractions (1,000)** | |
| Cruises on Ohio River (Cincinnati) | A |
| Carillon Park: transportation exhibits (Dayton) | B |

Places Rated Score: 7,952    Places Rated Rank: 23

## Colorado Springs, CO

|  | Rating |
|---|---|
| **Zoos (600)** | |
| Cheyenne Mountain Zoological Park (Colorado Springs) | C* |
| **Museums (1,300)** | |
| Colorado Springs Fine Arts Center (Colorado Springs) | A* |
| Museum of the American Numismatic Association (Colorado Springs) | C |
| Western Museum of Mining and Industry (Colorado Springs) | C* |
| **Special Attractions (1,400)** | |
| Royal Gorge Incline Railway (Canon City) | A |
| Chapel, U.S. Air Force Academy (Colorado Springs) | C |
| Cog Railway to top of Pike's Peak (Colorado Springs | A |

Places Rated Score: 3,300    Places Rated Rank: 70

## Coos Bay–South Coast, OR

|  | Rating |
|---|---|
| **Museums (500)** | |
| Coos Art Museum (Coos Bay) | A |
| **Special Attractions (600)** | |
| Mail-boat rides up the Rogue River (Gold Beach) | A |

Places Rated Score: 1,100    Places Rated Rank: 100

## Corpus Christi–Padre Island, TX

|  | Rating |
|---|---|
| **Museums (2,200)** | |
| Art Museum of South Texas (Corpus Christi) | B* |
| Corpus Christi Museum: general (Corpus Christi) | A* |
| Museum of Oriental Cultures (Corpus Christi) | A |
| Welder Wildlife Foundation: natural history (Sinton) | B |
| **Special Attractions (1,800)** | |
| Boat cruises (Corpus Christi) | A |
| Sightseeing tours (Corpus Christi) | A |
| Boat cruises (Rockport) | A |

Places Rated Score: 4,000    Places Rated Rank: 59

## Crater Lake–Klamath Falls, OR

|  | Rating |
|---|---|
| **Zoos (400)** | |
| Wildlife Safari (Winston) | C |
| **Museums (1,800)** | |
| Collier State Park Logging Museum (Chiloquin) | C |
| University of Oregon Museum of Art (Eugene) | B* |
| Willamette Science and Technology Center (Eugene) | B |
| Grants Pass Museum of Art (Grants Pass) | C |
| Favell Museum of Western Art and Indian Artifacts (Klamath Falls) | B |

Places Rated Score: 2,200    Places Rated Rank: 84

## Dallas–Fort Worth, TX

**Botanic Gardens (161)**
Dallas Civic Garden Center: 7½ acres (Dallas)
Fort Worth Botanic Gardens: 114 acres (Fort Worth)

|  | Rating |
|---|---|
| **Planetariums (200)** | |
| Noble (Fort Worth) | C |
| **Zoos and Aquariums (1,400)** | |
| Dallas Aquarium (Dallas) | C |
| Dallas Zoo (Dallas) | B |
| Fort Worth Zoological Park (Fort Worth) | C* |
| **Museums (7,000)** | |
| Age of Steam Railroad Museum (Dallas) | C |
| Biblical Arts Center (Dallas) | C |
| Dallas Museum of Art (Dallas) | AA* |
| Dallas Museum of Natural History (Dallas) | AA* |
| McCord Theater Collection (Dallas) | C |
| Meadows Museum: art (Dallas) | B |
| Southwest Museum of Science and Technology (Dallas) | B* |
| Amon Carter Museum (Fort Worth) | A* |
| Fort Worth Art Museum (Fort Worth) | A* |
| Fort Worth Museum of Science and History (Fort Worth) | AA* |
| Kimbell Art Museum (Forth Worth) | AA* |
| Pate Museum of Transportation (Fort Worth) | C |
| Southwest Aerospace Museum (Fort Worth) | C |

| | Rating |
|---|---|
| Western Company Museum: science and technology (Fort Worth) | C |
| Texas Sports Hall of Fame (Grand Prairie) | C |
| Special Attractions (1,400) | |
| Sightseeing tours (Dallas) | A |
| Southfork Ranch (Dallas) | C |
| Sightseeing tours (Fort Worth) | A |
| Places Rated Score: 10,161    Places Rated Rank: 13 | |

## Denver–Rocky Mountain National Park, CO

Botanic Gardens (135)
  Denver Botanic Gardens: 170 acres (Denver)
Planetariums (250)

| | Rating |
|---|---|
| Gates (Denver) | B |
| Zoos (700) | |
| Denver Zoological Gardens (Denver) | B* |
| Museums (4,200) | |
| University of Colorado Museum: natural science and art (Boulder) | AA |
| Children's Museum of Denver (Denver) | A |
| Colorado Science Center (Denver) | A |
| Denver Art Museum (Denver) | B* |
| Denver Museum of Natural History (Denver) | AA* |
| Fornay Transportation Museum (Denver) | C |
| Museum of Western Art (Denver) | B |
| Colorado Railroad Museum (Golden) | C |
| Colorado School of Mines Geology Museum (Golden) | C |
| Lafayette Miners Museum (Lafayette) | C |
| Special Attractions (1,800) | |
| Aerial tramway (Estes Park) | B |
| Georgetown Loop Railroad (Georgetown) | A |
| Industrial tour, Adolph Coors Company (Golden) | B |
| Argo Town gold mine (Idaho Springs) | B |
| Places Rated Score: 7,085    Places Rated Rank: 29 | |

## Door County, WI

| | Rating |
|---|---|
| Museums (1,150) | |
| Chief Oshkosh Museum (Egg Harbor) | C |
| Door County Maritime Museum (Gills Rock) | C |
| *Green Bay Packer Hall of Fame: sports museum (Green Bay)* | C |
| *National Railroad Museum (Green Bay)* | C |
| *Neville Public Museum of Brown County (Green Bay)* | A* |
| Sturgeon Bay Marine Museum (Sturgeon Bay) | C |
| Special Attractions (200) | |
| Bjorklunden Chapel (Baileys Harbor) | C |
| Places Rated Score: 1,350    Places Rated Rank: 97 | |

## Eastern Shore, VA

| | Rating |
|---|---|
| Museums (200) | |
| Oyster Museum of Chinco: natural science (Chincoteague) | C |
| Special Attractions (1,200) | |
| Chesapeake Bay Bridge–Tunnel (Cape Charles) | C |
| Chincoteague Miniature Pony Farm (Chincoteague) | B |
| Excursions to Tangier Island | A |
| Places Rated Score: 1,400    Places Rated Rank: 96 | |

## Finger Lakes, NY

Botanic Gardens (200)
  Sonnenberg Gardens: 50 acres (Canandaigua)
  The Cornell Plantations: 150 acres (Ithaca)

| | Rating |
|---|---|
| Museums (4,550) | |
| Cayuga County Agricultural Museum (Auburn) | C |
| Corning Museum of Glass (Corning) | AA* |
| *Arnot Art Museum (Elmira)* | A* |
| *National Soaring Museum: aeronautics (Elmira)* | C |
| Glen H. Curtiss Museum of Local History: aeronautics (Hammondsport) | C |
| Grayton H.Taylor Wine Museum (Hammondsport) | C |
| Herbert F. Johnson Museum of Art (Ithaca) | A* |
| National Women's Hall of Fame (Seneca Falls) | B |
| Discovery Center of Science and Technology (Syracuse) | A |
| Everson Museum of Art (Syracuse) | A* |
| Joe and Emily Low Art Gallery (Syracuse) | B |

| | Rating |
|---|---|
| Special Attractions (2,800) | |
| Winery tours (Hammondsport) | B |
| Winery tours (Penn Yan) | B |
| Cruises on Lake Skaneateles (Skaneateles) | A |
| Cruises on Erie Canal (Syracuse) | A |
| Landmark Theatre (Syracuse) | C |
| Cruises on Seneca Lake (Watkins Glen) | A |
| Places Rated Score: 7,550    Places Rated Rank: 26 | |

## Flaming Gorge, UT–WY–CO

| | Rating |
|---|---|
| Museums (400) | |
| Community Fine Arts Center (Rock Springs, WY) | B |
| Special Attractions (200) | |
| Dinosaur Natural History State Park (Vernal, UT) | C |
| Places Rated Score: 600    Places Rated Rank: 104 | |

## Glacier National Park–Flathead Lake, MT

| | Rating |
|---|---|
| Museums (1,400) | |
| Museum of the Plains Indian (Browning) | B |
| Scriver Museum of Montana Wildlife (Browning) | A |
| Hockaday Center for the Arts (Kalispell) | A |
| Special Attractions (400) | |
| Hungry Horse Dam and Power Plant (Whitefish) | B |
| Places Rated Score: 1,800    Places Rated Rank: 88 | |

## Grand Canyon Country, AZ

| | Rating |
|---|---|
| Museums (1,600) | |
| Museum of Northern Arizona: natural history (Flagstaff) | AA* |
| Northern Arizona University Art Gallery (Flagstaff) | B |
| Museum of Astrogeology, Meteor Crater (Winslow) | B |
| Special Attractions (2,200) | |
| Lowell Observatory (Flagstaff) | B |
| Flightseeing trips (Grand Canyon) | A |
| Sightseeing bus trips (Grand Canyon) | A |
| Backcountry jeep tours (Sedona) | A |
| Places Rated Score: 3,800    Places Rated Rank: 62 | |

## Green Mountains, VT

| | Rating |
|---|---|
| Museums (3,300) | |
| Robert Hull Fleming Museum: art (Burlington) | B |
| Discovery Museum: children's museum (Essex Junction) | A |
| Johnson Gallery of Middlebury College: art (Middlebury) | B |
| Sheldon Museum: Vermontiana (Middlebury) | C |
| New England Maple Museum (Rutland) | C |
| Norman Rockwell Museum (Rutland) | C |
| Fairbanks Museum: general (St. Johnsbury) | A* |
| Maple Museum (St. Johnsbury) | C |
| Shelburne Museum: general (Shelburne) | A |
| Special Attractions (2,800) | |
| Industrial tour, Rock of Ages Quarry and Craftsman Center (Barre) | B |
| Ferryboat rides on Lake Champlain (Burlington) | A |
| Paddlewheeler cruises on Lake Champlain (Burlington) | A |
| Morgan Horse Farm (Middlebury) | C |
| Vermont Marble Exhibit (Rutland) | B |
| Shelburne Farms (Shelburne) | B |
| Mount Mansfield Gondola (Stowe) | C |
| Places Rated Score: 6,100    Places Rated Rank: 36 | |

## Hawaii

Botanic Gardens (260)
  Waimea Arboretum: 100 acres (Haleiwa, Hawaii)
  Foster Botanic Garden: 20 acres (Honolulu)
  Harold L. Lyon Arboretum (Honolulu)
  Pacific Tropical Botanical Garden (Lawai, Kauai)

| | Rating |
|---|---|
| Planetariums (250) | |
| Bishop (Honolulu) | B |
| Zoos and Aquariums (1,200) | |
| Honolulu Zoo (Honolulu) | C |
| Waikiki Aquarium (Waikiki) | C* |
| Sea Life Park (Waimanalo) | B |

| Museums (2,200) | Rating |
|---|---|
| Bishop Museum: cultural and natural history (Honolulu) | AA* |
| Honolulu Academy of Arts (Honolulu) | AA* |
| Kauai Museum: history and art (Lihue) | B |
| Pacific Whaling Museum (Waimanulo) | C |

| Special Attractions (3,800) | |
|---|---|
| Industrial tour, Mauna Loa Macadamia Nut Plant (Hilo, Hawaii) | B |
| Lahaina–Kaanapali & Pacific Railroad (Lahaina, Maui) | A |
| Parker Ranch Visitor Center (Waimea, Hawaii) | B |
| Sightseeing cruises (Island of Hawaii) | A |
| Sightseeing cruises (Island of Kauai) | A |
| Sightseeing cruises (Island of Maui) | A |
| Sightseeing cruises (Island of Oahu) | A |

Places Rated Score: 7,710    Places Rated Rank: 24

## Hilton Head, SC

| Museums (200) | |
|---|---|
| Beaufort Museum: general (Beaufort) | C |

Places Rated Score: 200    Places Rated Rank: 106

## Holland–Lake Michigan Shore, MI

| Botanic Gardens (95) | |
|---|---|
| Fernwood, Inc.: 90 acres (Niles) | |

| Planetariums (200) | |
|---|---|
| Roger B. Chaffee (Grand Rapids) | C |

| Zoos (600) | |
|---|---|
| John Ball Zoological Gardens (Grand Rapids) | C* |

| Museums (4,600) | |
|---|---|
| Grand Rapids Art Museum (Grand Rapids) | A* |
| Grand Rapids Public Museum: general (Grand Rapids) | A* |
| Netherlands Museum: Dutch folklore, Delftware (Holland) | C |
| Kalamazoo Institute of Art (Kalamazoo) | A* |
| Kalamazoo Public Museum: general (Kalamazoo) | B |
| Great Lakes Marine Museum (Muskegon) | C |
| Muskegon County Museum: general (Muskegon) | B |
| Muskegon Museum of Art (Muskegon) | B |
| Krasl Art Center (St. Joseph) | A* |
| Lake Michigan Maritime Museum (South Haven) | C |

| Special Attractions (1,800) | |
|---|---|
| Windmill Island (Holland) | B |
| Industrial tour, General Motors Corp.–Fisher Body Division (Kalamazoo) | B |
| Industrial tour, Upjohn Company (Kalamazoo) | B |
| Sightseeing cruises (Saugatuck) | A |

Places Rated Score: 7,295    Places Rated Rank: 27

## Houston–Galveston, TX

| Botanic Gardens (183) | |
|---|---|
| Houston Arboretum and Botanical Garden: 265 acres (Houston) | |

| Planetariums (250) | |
|---|---|
| Burke Baker (Houston) | B |

| Zoos (400) | |
|---|---|
| Houston Zoological Gardens (Houston) | C |

| Museums (4,700) | |
|---|---|
| Beaumont Art Museum (Beaumont) | AA |
| Antique Dollhouse Museum (Galveston) | C |
| Rosenberg Library: general museum and library (Galveston) | A |
| Contemporary Arts Museum (Houston) | B |
| Environmental Science Center (Houston) | B |
| Houston Museum of National Science (Houston) | AA |
| Houston Police Museum (Houston) | C |
| Museum of American Architecture and Decorative Arts (Houston) | B |
| Museum of Fine Arts (Houston) | AA* |
| Sarah Campbell Blaffer Gallery (Houston) | B |
| Texas Forestry Museum (Lufkin) | C |

| Special Attractions (3,200) | |
|---|---|
| Paddlewheeler cruises (Beaumont) | A |
| Industrial tour, Port Authority docks (Brazosport) | B |
| NASA Lyndon B. Johnson Space Center (Clear Lake City) | A |
| Sightseeing trolley tours (Galveston) | A |
| Astrodome (Houston) | B |

| | Rating |
|---|---|
| Nederland Windmill Museum (Port Arthur) | C |
| Pleasure Island (Port Arthur) | B |

Places Rated Score: 8,733    Places Rated Rank: 18

## Jersey Shore, NJ

| Botanic Gardens (61) | |
|---|---|
| Holmdel Arboretum: 22 acres (Holmdel) | |

Places Rated Score: 61    Places Rated Rank: 107

## Knoxville–Smoky Mountains, TN

| Botanic Gardens (93) | |
|---|---|
| University of Tennessee Arboretum: 85 acres (Oak Ridge) | |

| Zoos (600) | |
|---|---|
| Knoxville Zoological Park (Knoxville) | C* |

| Museums (2,700) | |
|---|---|
| Dulin Gallery of Art (Knoxville) | B |
| Frank H. McClung Museum: general (Knoxville) | B* |
| Students' Museum: natural history (Knoxville) | A* |
| American Museum of Science and Energy (Oak Ridge) | A |
| Children's Museum of Oak Ridge (Oak Ridge) | A |

| Special Attractions (1,800) | |
|---|---|
| Xanadu: The Home of the Future (Gatlinburg) | C |
| Sightseeing chair lift and gondola (Gatlinburg) | B |
| Sightseeing bus tours (Gatlinburg) | A |
| Norris Dam: first TVA dam (Norris) | B |
| Smoky Mountain Car Museum (Pigeon Forge) | C |

Places Rated Score: 5,193    Places Rated Rank: 42

## Lake of the Ozarks, MO

| Museums (500) | |
|---|---|
| Kilsey's Antique Cars (Camdenton) | C |
| Missouri Veterinary Medical Foundation Museum (Jefferson City) | C |
| Memoryville, USA: antique cars (Rolla) | C |

| Special Attractions (2,800) | |
|---|---|
| Osage Power Plant (Bagnell Dam) | B |
| Fantasy World Caverns (Lake of the Ozarks) | B |
| Lake cruises (Lake of the Ozarks) | A |
| Seaplane rides (Lake of the Ozarks) | A |
| Indian Burial Cave: boat ride on underground river (Osage Beach) | B |
| Winery tours (Rolla) | B |

Places Rated Score: 3,300    Places Rated Rank: 70

## Lake Powell–Glen Canyon, AZ–UT

| Special Attractions (3,400) | |
|---|---|
| Guided tours of Monument Valley (Kayenta, AZ) | A |
| Guided tours of southeast Utah (Bluff and Mexican Hat, UT) | A |
| Guided tours of Canyonlands (Moab, UT) | A |
| Boat trips on Lake Powell (Page, AZ) | A |
| Scenic flights over area (Page) | A |
| Glen Canyon Visitor Center (Page) | B |

Places Rated Score: 3,400    Places Rated Rank: 68

## Lake Tahoe–Reno, NV–CA

| Museums (400) | |
|---|---|
| Harrah's Automobile Collection (Reno, NV) | C |
| Mackay School of Mines Museum (Reno) | C |

| Special Attractions (1,400) | |
|---|---|
| Ponderosa Ranch (Crystal Bay, NV) | C |
| Ghost towns (Hawthorne, NV) | A |
| Sightseeing tours (Reno) | A |

Places Rated Score: 1,800    Places Rated Rank: 88

## Las Vegas–Lake Mead, NV–AZ

| Museums (800) | |
|---|---|
| Liberace Museum (Las Vegas, NV) | C |
| Museum of Natural History (Las Vegas) | B |
| Colorado River Indian Tribes Museum (Parker, AZ) | C |

| Special Attractions (1,600) | |
|---|---|
| Ghost town of Searchlight (Henderson, NV) | B |
| Ghost town of Oatman (Kingman, AZ) | B |

Rating

London Bridge (Lake Havasu City, AZ)    C
Several ghost towns (Las Vegas)    A
Places Rated Score: 2,400    Places Rated Rank: 80

## Lexington–Bluegrass Country, KY
Botanic Gardens (215)
    Bernheim Forest: 225 acres (Clermont)
    Lexington Cemetery: 4 acres (Lexington)
Planetariums (250)
    Rauch Memorial (Louisville)    B
Zoos (600)
    Louisville Zoological Gardens (Louisville)    C*
Museums (4,700)
    Berea College Museum (Berea)    B*
    Headley-Whitney Museum (Lexington)    C
    International Museum of the Horse (Lexington)    C
    Living Arts and Science Center: children's
      museum (Lexington)    A
    Photographic Archives, University of Kentucky
      (Lexington)    C
    University of Kentucky Art Museums (Lexington)    C*
    American Saddle Horse Museum (Louisville)    C
    J. B. Speed Art Museum (Louisville)    AA*
    Kentucky Derby Museum (Louisville)    C
    Kentucky Railway Museum (Louisville)    C
    Louisville Art Gallery: art for children (Louisville)    A
    Museum of History and Science (Louisville)    A
    Photographic Archives, University of Louisville (Louisville)    C
Special Attractions (4,800)
    Industrial tours of distilleries (Frankfort)    B
    Industrial tour, Old Harrodsburg Pottery (Harrodsburg)    B
    Kentucky Horse Center (Lexington)    C
    Kentucky Horse Park (Lexington)    C
    Tours of horse farms (Lexington)    A
    Sightseeing bus tours (Lexington)    A
    Churchill Downs and Kentucky Derby Museum
      (Louisville)    B
    Kentucky Center for the Performing Arts (Louisville)    C
    Riverboat excursions (Louisville)    A
    Several industrial tours (Louisville)    A
    Sightseeing bus tours (Louisville)    A
Places Rated Score: 10,565    Places Rated Rank: 12

## Long Island, NY
Botanic Gardens (565)
    Fanny Dwight Clark Garden: 12 acres (Albertson)
    Bailey Arboretum: 42 acres (Locust Valley)
    Bayard-Cutting Arboretum: 150 acres (Oakdale)
    Old Westbury Gardens: 15 acres (Old Westbury)
    Planting Fields Arboretum: 409 acres (Oyster Bay)
Planetariums (650)
    Vanderbilt (Centerport)    B
    Packard (North Massapequa)    C
    Sayville (Sayville)    C
Museums (6,800)
    East Hampton Town Marine Museum (Amagansett)    C
    Whaling Museum Society (Cold Spring Harbor)    A
    Guildhall Museum (East Hampton)    A*
    Hillwood Art Gallery (Greenvale)    C
    Emily Low Gallery (Hempstead)    A
    Fine Arts Museum of Long Island (Hempstead)    A
    The Gregory Museum; Long Island Earth Science Center
      (Hicksville)    B
    Heckscher Museum (Huntington)    A*
    Science Museum of Long Island (Manhasset)    A
    Nassau County Museum of Fine Art (Roslyn Harbor)    B
    The Parrish Art Museum (Southampton)    A*
    Museum of Long Island Natural Sciences (Stony Brook)    A
    The Museums at Stony Brook (Stony Brook)    AA*
    Suffolk Marine Museum (West Sayville)    C
Special Attractions (1,600)
    Ferryboat rides to New London, CT (Orient Point)    A
    Ferryboat rides to Bridgeport, CT (Port Jefferson)    A
    Brookhaven National Laboratory Exhibit Center
      (Riverhead)    B
Places Rated Score: 9,615    Places Rated Rank: 15

Rating

## ★ Los Angeles, CA
Botanic Gardens (803)
    Los Angeles State and County Arboretum: 127 acres
      (Arcadia)
    Wrigley Memorial and Botanical Garden: 38 acres
      (Avalon)
    Rancho Santa Ana Botanic Garden: 83 acres
      (Claremont)
    Sherman Foundation Garden: 2 acres (Corona del Mar)
    Descanso Gardens: 150 acres (La Canada)
    UCLA Botanical Garden: 8 acres (Los Angeles)
    South Coast Botanic Garden: 87 acres (Palos Verdes)
    Huntington Botanical Gardens: 207 acres (San Marino)
    Gregor Mendel Garden (Thousand Oaks)
Planetariums (250)
    Tessman (Santa Ana)    B
Zoos and Aquariums (1,600)
    California Alligator Farm (Buena Park)    C
    Los Angeles Zoo (Los Angeles)    B*
    Marineland (Rancho Palos Verdes)    A
Museums (13,000)
    Galleries of the Claremont Colleges (Claremont)    B
    Raymond M. Alf Museum (natural history) (Claremont)    A
    Downey Museum of Art (Downey)    B
    La Habra Children's Museum (La Habra)    A
    Laguna Beach Museum of Art (Laguna Beach)    C
    CSU Long Beach, University Art Museum (Long Beach)    B
    Long Beach Museum of Art (Long Beach)    A*
    California Museum of Science and Industry (Los
      Angeles)    A*
    Craft and Folk Art Museum (Los Angeles)    A
    Fisher Gallery USC (Los Angeles)    A
    Frederick S. Wight Art Gallery of UCLA (Los Angeles)    B
    Grunwald Center for the Graphic Arts (Los Angeles)    B
    Hebrew Union College Skirball Museum: religious history
      and art (Los Angeles)    B*
    Los Angeles Center for Photographic Studies (Los
      Angeles)    C
    Los Angeles Children's Museum (Los Angeles)    A
    Los Angeles County Museum of Art (Los Angeles)    AA*
    Museum of African-American Art (Los Angeles)    A
    Museum of Contemporary Art (Los Angeles)    C
    Museum of Neon Art (Los Angeles)    C
    Natural History Museum of Los Angeles County (Los
      Angeles)    A*
    J. Paul Getty Museum: art (Malibu)    AA*
    Newport Harbor Art Museum (Newport Beach)    A*
    Museum of Dentistry (Orange)    C
    Carnegie Cultural Arts Center (Oxnard)    B
    Kidspace; children's museum (Pasadena)    A
    Norton Simon Museum of Art (Pasadena)    C
    Pacific Asia Museum (Pasadena)    A
    Cabrillo Marine Museum (San Pedro)    C
    California Oil Museum (Santa Paula)    C
Special Attractions (8,000)
    Sightseeing bus tours (Anaheim)    A
    Sightseeing boat and bus tours (Catalina Island)    A
    Crystal Cathedral (Garden Grove)    C
    Hollywood Memorial Park Cemetery (Hollywood)    C
    Hollywood Wax Museum (Hollywood)    B
    Mann's Chinese Theatre (Hollywood)    C
    Walk of Fame (Hollywood)    C
    Ocean liner Queen Mary (Long Beach)    B
    Spruce Goose (Long Beach)    B
    Sightseeing cruises (Long Beach)    A
    Griffith Observatory (Los Angeles)    B
    Industrial tour, Lawry's Foods (Los Angeles)    B
    La Brea Tar Pits (Los Angeles)    B
    Watts Towers Arts Center (Los Angeles)    A
    Tours of broadcasting stations (Los Angeles)    B
    Tour of Universal Studios (Los Angeles)    B
    Winery tour (Los Angeles)    B
    Sightseeing bus tours (Los Angeles)    B
    Douglas Aerospace Museum (Santa Monica)    C
    Channel Islands tours (Ventura)    A
Places Rated Score: 23,653    Places Rated Rank: 2

Rating

## Mackinac Island–Sault Ste. Marie, MI
### Special Attractions (2,800)
| | |
|---|---|
| Carriage tours: no cars on island (Mackinac Island) | **A** |
| Ferryboat rides to St. Ignace (Mackinac Island) | **A** |
| The "Soo" Locks, observation towers (Sault Ste. Marie) | **B** |
| Boat excursions through locks (Sault Ste. Marie) | **A** |
| Sightseeing train tours (Sault Ste. Marie) | **A** |

Places Rated Score: 2,800     Places Rated Rank: 74

## Memphis, TN–AR–MS
### Botanic Gardens (150)
Dixon Gallery and Gardens (Memphis)
Memphis Botanic Garden: 100 acres (Memphis)
### Planetariums (250)
| | |
|---|---|
| Craigmont (Memphis) | **B** |

### Zoos and Aquariums (700)
| | |
|---|---|
| Memphis Zoological Garden and Aquarium (Memphis) | **B**\* |

### Museums (2,600)
| | |
|---|---|
| Dixon Gallery and Gardens (Memphis) | **A**\* |
| Memphis Brooks Museum of Art (Memphis) | **AA**\* |
| Memphis Pink Palace Museum: general (Memphis) | **A**\* |
| The University Gallery (Memphis) | **B** |

### Special Attractions (2,500)
| | |
|---|---|
| *Casey Jones Home and Railroad Museum (Jackson)* | **C** |
| Elvis Presley Museum (Memphis) | **C** |
| Graceland (Memphis) | **C** |
| Industrial tour, Stroh's Brewing Company (Memphis) | **B** |
| Mississippi River Museum at Mud Island (Memphis) | **B** |
| Mississippi River cruises (Memphis) | **A** |
| Sightseeing bus tours (Memphis) | **A** |

Places Rated Score: 6,200     Places Rated Rank: 35

## ★ Miami–Gold Coast–Keys, FL
### Botanic Gardens (315)
Fairchild Tropical Garden: 83 acres
(Coral Gables)
Orchid Jungle: 23 acres (Homestead)
Redland Fruit and Spice Park: 20 acres
(Homestead)
Japanese Garden: 1 acre (Miami)
Miami Beach Garden Center and Conservatory
(Miami Beach)
### Planetariums (1,000)
| | |
|---|---|
| Buehler (Fort Lauderdale) | **B** |
| Richard E. Lear (Miami) | **C** |
| Space Transit (Miami) | **A** |
| Science Museum (West Palm Beach) | **B** |

### Zoos (1,000)
| | |
|---|---|
| Metrozoo (Miami) | **A** |
| Monkey Jungle (Miami) | **C** |

### Museums (6,400)
| | |
|---|---|
| Boca Raton Museum of Arts (Boca Raton) | **C** |
| Lowe Art Museum (Coral Gables) | **B**\* |
| Morikami Museum of Japanese Culture (Delray Beach) | **A** |
| Discovery Center, Inc.: art, science, history (Fort Lauderdale) | **A** |
| International Swimming Hall of Fame (Fort Lauderdale) | **C** |
| Museum of Art (Fort Lauderdale) | **A**\* |
| Art and Culture Center of Hollywood (Hollywood) | **A** |
| Center for the Fine Arts (Miami) | **C** |
| Museum of Science (Miami) | **A** |
| Visual Arts Gallery, Florida International University (Miami) | **C** |
| Bass Museum of Art (Miami Beach) | **B** |
| Society of the Four Arts (Palm Beach) | **B**\* |
| Norton Gallery and School of Art (West Palm Beach) | **B**\* |
| Science Museum of Palm Beach County (West Palm Beach) | **A**\* |

### Special Attractions (7,200)
| | |
|---|---|
| Cruises of harbor and waterways (Fort Lauderdale) | **A** |
| Sightseeing train tours (Fort Lauderdale) | **A** |
| Heinlein Fruit and Spice Park (Homestead) | **C** |

Rating

| | |
|---|---|
| Boat trips over coral reef (Key Largo) | **A** |
| Conch Train tour (Key West) | **A** |
| Reef cruises (Key West) | **A** |
| Coral Castle (Miami) | **C** |
| Parrot Jungle (Miami) | **C** |
| Planet Ocean: marine science (Miami) | **A** |
| Sightseeing cruises (Miami) | **A** |
| Sightseeing helicopter rides (Miami) | **A** |
| Sightseeing bus tours (Miami) | **A** |
| Ancient Spanish Monastery of St. Bernard de Clairvaux Cloister (North Miami Beach) | **B** |
| World of Miniature Horses (Pompano Beach) | **C** |
| Paddlewheeler cruises (Riviera Beach) | **A** |

Places Rated Score: 15,915     Places Rated Rank: 7

## Minneapolis–St. Paul, MN–WI
### Botanic Gardens (442)
University of Minnesota Landscape Arboretum:
580 acres (Chaska, MN)
Eloise Butler Wild Flower Garden
(Minneapolis, MN)
Como Park Conservatory: 3 acres (St. Paul, MN)
### Planetariums (250)
| | |
|---|---|
| Science Museum (Minneapolis) | **B** |

### Zoos (600)
| | |
|---|---|
| Minnesota Zoological Garden (Apple Valley, MN) | **A** |

### Museums (6,200)
| | |
|---|---|
| Minnesota Transportation Museum (Hopkins, MN) | **C** |
| African-American Museum of Art and History (Minneapolis) | **A** |
| African Swedish Institute (Minneapolis) | **A** |
| Bakkem Library of Electricity in Life (Minneapolis) | **C** |
| The Children's Museum (Minneapolis) | **A** |
| James Ford Bell Museum of Natural History (Minneapolis) | **A** |
| Minneapolis Institute of Arts (Minneapolis) | **AA**\* |
| University Art Museum (Minneapolis) | **B** |
| Walker Art Center (Minneapolis) | **AA**\* |
| Goldstein Gallery, University of Minnesota (St. Paul) | **C** |
| Minnesota Museum of Art (St. Paul) | **AA**\* |
| Science Museum of Minnesota (St. Paul) | **AA**\* |

### Special Attractions (2,400)
| | |
|---|---|
| Sightseeing bus tours (Minneapolis) | **A** |
| Sternwheeler river cruises (St. Paul) | **A** |
| Sightseeing bus tours (Taylors Falls, MN) | **A** |
| Paddleboat river cruises (Winona, MN) | **A** |

Places Rated Score: 9,892     Places Rated Rank: 14

## Mobile Bay–Gulfport, AL–MS
### Botanic Gardens (83)
Bellingrath Gardens: 65 acres (Theodore, AL)
### Museums (1,100)
| | |
|---|---|
| J. L. Scott Marine Education Center (Biloxi, MS) | **A** |
| Eastern Shore Art Association (Gulf Shores, AL) | **C** |
| Fine Arts Museum of the South (Mobile, AL) | **B** |

### Special Attractions (1,200)
| | |
|---|---|
| Cruises to West Ship Island (Biloxi and Gulfport, MS) | **A** |
| Sightseeing bus tours (Mobile, AL) | **A** |

Places Rated Score: 2,383     Places Rated Rank: 81

## Monterey–Big Sur, CA
### Botanic Gardens (53)
Saratoga Horticultural Foundation: 6 acres
(Saratoga)
### Planetariums (450)
| | |
|---|---|
| Minolta (Cupertino) | **C** |
| Rosicrucian (San Jose) | **B** |

### Zoos (400)
| | |
|---|---|
| San Jose Zoo (San Jose) | **C** |

### Museums (4,000)
| | |
|---|---|
| Big Basin Redwoods State Park: natural history (Big Basin) | **C** |
| Allen Knight Maritime Museum (Monterey) | **C** |

|  | Rating |
|---|---|
| Monterey Peninsula Museum of Art (Monterey) | A* |
| San Carlos Cathedral Art Museum (Monterey) | C |
| Pacific Grove Museum of Natural History (Pacific Grove) | C* |
| Rosicrucian Egyptian Museum and Art Gallery (San Jose) | A |
| San Jose Museum of Art (San Jose) | B |
| de Saisset Museum: art (Santa Clara) | A* |
| Santa Cruz City Museum: general (Santa Cruz) | A* |

**Special Attractions (4,000)**

|  |  |
|---|---|
| Biblical Garden (Carmel) | C |
| Seventeen Mile Drive: scenic toll road (Carmel) | A |
| Sightseeing bus tours (Carmel) | A |
| Winery tours (Gilroy) | B |
| Winery tours (Los Gatos) | B |
| Sightseeing bus tours (Monterey) | A |
| Winchester Mystery House (San Jose) | C |
| World of Miniatures (San Jose) | C |
| Winery tours (San Jose) | B |
| Paul Masson Vineyard tour (Saratoga) | B |

Places Rated Score: 8,903     Places Rated Rank: 17

## Myrtle Beach–Grand Strand, SC

**Botanic Gardens (200)**
Brookgreen Gardens: 300 acres (Murrells Inlet)

**Zoos (600)**

|  |  |
|---|---|
| Brookgreen Gardens (Murrells Inlet) | C* |

**Museums (400)**

|  |  |
|---|---|
| Brookgreen Gardens: sculpture garden (Murrells Inlet) | B |

**Special Attractions (600)**

|  |  |
|---|---|
| Sightseeing train tours (Georgetown) | A |

Places Rated Score: 1,800     Places Rated Rank: 88

## Mystic Seaport–Connecticut Valley, CT

**Botanic Gardens (308)**
Rose Garden, Elizabeth Park (Hartford)
Connecticut Arboretum: 415 acres (New London)

**Planetariums (250)**

|  |  |
|---|---|
| Mystic Seaport (Mystic) | B |

**Museums (5,300)**

|  |  |
|---|---|
| Children's Museum of Hartford (Hartford) | A |
| Davison Art Center, Wesleyan University (Middletown) | C |
| Memory Lane Doll and Toy Museum (Mystic) | C |
| Mystic Seaport Museum (Mystic) | A* |
| New Britain Museum of American Art (New Britain) | A* |
| New Britain Youth Museum (New Britain) | A* |
| Lyman Allyn Museum: art (New London) | A* |
| Tale of the Whale Museum (New London) | C |
| Thames Science Center (New London) | A |
| Florence Griswold Museum: art (Old Lyme) | C* |
| Science Museum of Greater Hartford: art (West Hartford) | A |

**Special Attractions (4,800)**

|  |  |
|---|---|
| Valley Railroad tours (Essex) | A |
| Harbor cruises (Groton) | A |
| Sightseeing bus tours (Hartford) | A |
| Mystic Marinelife Aquarium (Mystic) | A |
| Windjammer cruises (Mystic) | A |
| Sightseeing bus tours (Mystic) | A |
| Ferryboat rides to Long Island (New London) | A |
| Sightseeing bus tours (New London) | A |

Places Rated Score: 10,658     Places Rated Rank: 11

## Nashville, TN

**Botanic Gardens (78)**
Tennessee Botanical Gardens and Fine Arts Center, Cheekwood: 55 acres (Nashville)

**Planetariums (250)**

|  |  |
|---|---|
| Sudekum (Nashville) | B |

**Museums (2,900)**

|  |  |
|---|---|
| Cheekwood Fine Arts Center (Nashville) | AA |
| Country Music Hall of Fame and Museum (Nashville) | AA |
| Cumberland Museum and Science Center (Nashville) | AA |
| Fisk University Museum of Art (Nashville) | A |
| Museum of Tobacco Art and History (Nashville) | C |
| Nashville Parthenon (Nashville) | C |
| RCA's Original Studio B (Nashville) | C |

**Special Attractions (1,400)**

|  |  |
|---|---|
| *Loretta Lynn's Dude Ranch (Hurricane Mills)* | B |
| Riverboat cruises (Nashville) | A |
| Sightseeing bus tours (Nashville) | A |

Places Rated Score: 4,628     Places Rated Rank: 47

## New Orleans, LA

**Botanic Gardens (54)**
Longue Vue Gardens: 8 acres (New Orleans)

**Planetariums (200)**

|  |  |
|---|---|
| Frank J. Lewis (New Orleans) | C |

**Zoos (700)**

|  |  |
|---|---|
| Audubon Park and Zoological Gardens (New Orleans) | B* |

**Museums (2,100)**

|  |  |
|---|---|
| Gallier House: decorative arts (New Orleans) | A* |
| Louisiana Nature and Science Center (New Orleans) | AA |
| New Orleans Museum of Arts (New Orleans) | AA* |

**Special Attractions (2,400)**

|  |  |
|---|---|
| Boat trips through wild swamp and marshlands (Houma) | A |
| Vieux Carré (New Orleans) | A |
| Sternwheeler river cruises (New Orleans) | A |
| Sightseeing bus tours (New Orleans) | A |

Places Rated Score: 5,454     Places Rated Rank: 40

## ★ New York City, NY

**Botanic Gardens (653)**
New York Botanical Garden: 239 acres (Bronx)
Wave Hill Center for Environmental Studies: 28 acres (Bronx)
Brooklyn Botanic Garden: 50 acres (Brooklyn)
Meyer Arboretum: 175 acres (Cross River)
Oriental Stroll Gardens, Hammond Museum: 3½ acres (North Salem)
Queens Botanical Garden: 39 acres (Queens)
Lyndhurst: 67 acres (Tarrytown)

**Planetariums (550)**

|  |  |
|---|---|
| Hayden (New York City) | A |
| Andrus Space Theater (Yonkers) | B |

**Zoos and Aquariums (1,600)**

|  |  |
|---|---|
| New York Zoological Park (Bronx) | A* |
| New York Aquarium (New York City) | B |
| Staten Island Zoo (Staten Island) | C |

**Museums (21,400)**

|  |  |
|---|---|
| American Museum of the Moving Image (Astoria) | B |
| Bronx Museum of the Arts (Bronx) | B |
| Brooklyn Children's Museum (Brooklyn) | A |
| Brooklyn Museum: art (Brooklyn) | AA* |
| New York Hall of Science and Technology (Corona) | A* |
| Frances Godwin and Joseph Ternbach Museum: art (Flushing) | A |
| The Queens Museum: art (Flushing) | A |
| The Store Front Museum–Paul Robeson Theater: Afro-American and African Art (Jamaica) | B |
| Caramoor Center for Music and the Arts (Katonah) | C |
| American Academy and Institute of Arts and Letters (New York City) | C |
| American Crafts Museum (New York City) | C* |
| American Museum of Natural History (New York City) | AA* |
| The American Numismatic Society (New York City) | C* |
| Asia Society Gallery (New York City) | C |
| Center for Inter-American Relations Art Gallery (New York City) | C |
| The Cloisters (New York City) | AA |

| | Rating |
|---|---|
| Cooper-Hewitt Museum—The Smithsonian Institution's National Museum of Design (New York City) | AA |
| El Museo del Barrio: ethnic art (New York City) | C |
| Franklin Furnace Archive: art (New York City) | C |
| The Frick Collection: art (New York City) | A* |
| Gallery of Prehistoric Art (New York City) | A |
| The Hispanic Society of America: art (New York City) | AA |
| International Center of Photography (New York City) | AA |
| Intrepid Sea–Air–Space (New York City) | B |
| Japan House Gallery (New York City) | B |
| The Jewish Museum (New York City) | A* |
| Metropolitan Museum of Art (New York City) | AA* |
| Museum of American Folk Art (New York City) | AA |
| Museum of American Illustration (New York City) | C |
| Museum of the American Indian (New York City) | A* |
| Museum of Broadcasting (New York City) | A |
| Museum of Holography (New York City) | C |
| Museum of Modern Art (New York City) | A* |
| National Academy of Design (New York City) | C |
| New Museum of Contemporary Art (New York City) | C |
| New York City Police Academy Museum (New York City) | C |
| Nicholas Roerich Museum: art (New York City) | C |
| The Pierpont Morgan Library (New York City) | B* |
| Scalamandre Museum of Textiles (New York City) | C |
| Shelby Cullom Davis Museum: theater (New York City) | B* |
| The Solomon R. Guggenheim Museum: art (New York City) | AA* |
| The Studio Museum in Harlem: African, Afro-American, and Haitian art (New York City) | B |
| The Ukrainian Museum (New York City) | C |
| Whitney Museum of Art (New York City) | AA* |
| Yeshiva University Museum (New York City) | A |
| Jacques Marchais Center of Tibetan Art (Staten Island) | C |
| Staten Island Children's Museum (Staten Island) | A |
| **Special Attractions (4,400)** | |
| Views from observation decks: | |
|   Empire State Building (New York City) | A |
|   RCA Building (New York City) | A |
|   World Trade Center (New York City) | A |
| United Nations complex (New York City) | AA |
| Sightseeing boat tours (New York City) | A |
| Sightseeing helicopter rides (New York City) | A |
| Sightseeing bus tours (New York City) | A |

Places Rated Score: 28,603      Places Rated Rank: 1

## Niagara Falls–Western New York, NY

| | Rating |
|---|---|
| **Planetariums (200)** | |
| Niagara Falls (Niagara Falls) | C |
| **Zoos (400)** | |
| Buffalo Zoological Gardens (Buffalo) | C |
| **Museums (2,300)** | |
| Albright-Knox Art Gallery (Buffalo) | AA* |
| Buffalo Museum of Science (Buffalo) | AA* |
| Native American Center for the Living Arts (Niagara Falls) | A |
| Schoellkopf Geological Museum (Niagara Falls) | C |
| **Special Attractions (5,400)** | |
| Shea's Buffalo Theater (Buffalo) | C |
| Cruises, Niagara River and Lake Erie (Buffalo) | A |
| Sightseeing bus tours (Buffalo) | A |
| Chautauqua Institution (Chautauqua) | A |
| Boat cruises (Chautauqua) | A |
| Winery tours (Dunkirk) | B |
| Artpark (Niagara Falls) | A |
| Boat rides under falls (Niagara Falls) | A |
| Sightseeing helicopter rides (Niagara Falls) | A |
| Sightseeing train rides (Niagara Falls) | A |

Places Rated Score: 8,300      Places Rated Rank: 20

## North Woods–Land O'Lakes, WI

| | Rating |
|---|---|
| **Museums (700)** | |
| Apostle Islands National Lakeshore: maritime museum (Bayfield) | C |
| Old Town Hall Museum: logging and lumber (Fifield) | C |
| National Fresh Water Fishing Hall of Fame: outboard motors, mounted fish, tackle (Hayward) | C |
| Camp Five Museum: logging museum and blacksmith shop (Laona) | C |
| Rhinelander Logging Museum (Rhinelander) | C |

Places Rated Score: 700      Places Rated Rank: 103

## Oklahoma City–Cherokee Strip, OK

| | Rating |
|---|---|
| **Botanic Gardens (112)** | |
| Martin Park Nature Center (Edmond) | |
| Will Rogers Horticulture Garden: 23 acres (Oklahoma City) | |
| **Planetariums (250)** | |
| Kirkpatrick (Oklahoma City) | B |
| **Zoos (700)** | |
| Oklahoma City Zoo (Oklahoma City) | B* |
| **Museums (3,700)** | |
| Southern Plains Indian Museum and Craft Center (Anadarko) | C |
| Cimarron Valley Railroad Museum (Cushing) | C |
| Museum of Art, University of Oklahoma (Norman) | B* |
| Stovall Museum of Science and History (Norman) | AA* |
| National Cowboy Hall of Fame (Oklahoma City) | C |
| National Softball Hall of Fame (Oklahoma City) | C |
| Oklahoma Art Center (Oklahoma City) | A* |
| Oklahoma Firefighters Museum (Oklahoma City) | C |
| Oklahoma Museum of Art (Oklahoma City) | B |
| Oklahoma State University Museum of Natural and Cultural History (Stillwater) | C |

Places Rated Score: 4,762      Places Rated Rank: 46

## Olympic Peninsula, WA

| | Rating |
|---|---|
| **Museums (200)** | |
| Evergreen Galleries (Olympia) | C |
| **Special Attractions (2,000)** | |
| Industrial tour, Pacific Power and Light Co. (Centralia) | B |
| Industrial tour, Olympia Brewery (Olympia) | B |
| Ferryboat to Victoria, British Columbia (Port Angeles) | A |
| Sightseeing bus tours (Port Angeles) | A |

Places Rated Score: 2,200      Places Rated Rank: 84

## Orlando–Space Coast, FL

| | Rating |
|---|---|
| **Botanic Gardens (120)** | |
| Florida Cypress Gardens: 140 acres (Cypress Gardens) | |
| **Planetariums (250)** | |
| John Young (Orlando) | B |
| **Zoos and Aquariums (1,600)** | |
| Discovery Island, Walt Disney World (Lake Buena Vista) | C* |
| Central Florida Zoological Park (Lake Monroe) | C |
| Sea World of Florida (Orlando) | A* |
| **Museums (3,600)** | |
| Brevard Museum: history, science (Cocoa Beach) | C |
| Polk Public Museum: art (Lakeland) | A* |
| Brevard Art Center and Museum (Melbourne) | A |
| Lock Haven Art Center (Orlando) | A* |
| Orlando Science Center (Orlando) | A |
| Museum of Old Dolls and Toys (Winter Haven) | C |
| Water Ski Museum and Hall of Fame (Winter Haven) | C |
| Cornell Fine Arts Center (Winter Park) | C* |
| Morse Gallery of Art: Tiffany glass artworks (Winter Park) | C |
| **Special Attractions (3,000)** | |
| Kennedy Space Center (Kennedy Space Center) | AA |
| The Bok Tower Gardens (Lake Wales) | A |

| | Rating |
|---|---|
| Six Flags, Stars Hall of Fame (Orlando) | B |
| Sightseeing bus tours (Orlando) | A |
| Boat cruises on Lake Osceola (Winter Park) | A |

Places Rated Score: 8,570      Places Rated Rank: 19

## Outer Banks, NC
**Botanic Gardens (52)**
Tryon Palace: 3 acres (New Bern)
**Museums (600)**

| | Rating |
|---|---|
| North Carolina Maritime Museum (Beaufort) | C |
| North Carolina Marine Resources Center (Manteo) | C |
| New Bern Firemen's Museum (New Bern) | C |

**Special Attractions (800)**

| | Rating |
|---|---|
| Bank of the Arts (New Bern) | C |
| Ferryboat rides (Ocracoke) | A |

Places Rated Score: 1,452      Places Rated Rank: 95

## Ozarks–Eureka Springs, AR–MO
**Zoos (400)**

| | Rating |
|---|---|
| Dickerson Park Zoo (Springfield, MO) | C |

**Museums (1,600)**

| | Rating |
|---|---|
| Gay Nineties Button and Doll Museum (Eureka Springs, AR) | C |
| Geuther Doll Museum (Eureka Springs) | C |
| Miles Musical Museum (Eureka Springs) | C |
| Spiva Art Center (Joplin, MO) | C |
| Tri-State Mineral Museum (Joplin) | C |
| Springfield Art Museum (Springfield) | B* |

**Special Attractions (2,100)**

| | Rating |
|---|---|
| Scenic amphibious tours (Branson, MO) | A |
| Excursion train rides (Eureka Springs) | A |
| Sightseeing bus tours (Eureka Springs) | A |
| *Ozark Folk Center (Mountain View, AR)* | A |

Places Rated Score: 4,100      Places Rated Rank: 55

## Palm Springs–Desert Playgrounds, CA
**Botanic Gardens (68)**
University Botanic Gardens: 35 acres (Riverside)
**Planetariums (200)**

| | Rating |
|---|---|
| Daniel B. Millikan (Alta Loma) | C |

**Zoos (600)**

| | Rating |
|---|---|
| Living Desert Reserve (Palm Springs) | C* |

**Museums (4,400)**

| | Rating |
|---|---|
| Edward Dean Museum of Decorative Arts (Cherry Valley) | B* |
| Living Desert Museum (Palm Desert) | A |
| Palm Springs Desert Museum: art, natural history (Palm Springs) | A* |
| Orange Empire Railroad Museum (Perris) | C |
| San Bernardino County Museum: natural history (San Bernardino) | A* |
| California Museum of Photography (Riverside) | C |
| Riverside Art Center (Riverside) | A |
| Riverside Municipal Museum: general (Riverside) | B* |
| Hi-Desert Nature Museum (Yucca Valley) | B |

**Special Attractions (1,600)**

| | Rating |
|---|---|
| Cabot's Old Indian Pueblo and Museum (Desert Hot Springs) | C |
| Brookside Wine Museum (Ontario) | B |
| Palm Springs Aerial Tramway (Palm Springs) | B |
| Sightseeing bus tours (Palm Springs) | A |

Places Rated Score: 6,868      Places Rated Rank: 31

## Panhandle, FL
**Planetariums (200)**

| | Rating |
|---|---|
| E. G. Owens (Pensacola) | C |

**Museums (800)**

| | Rating |
|---|---|
| Pensacola Museum of Art (Pensacola) | B* |
| University of West Florida Art Gallery (Pensacola) | C |

**Special Attractions (600)**

| | Rating |
|---|---|
| Sightseeing cruises (Fort Walton Beach) | A |

Places Rated Score: 1,600      Places Rated Rank: 93

## Pennsylvania Dutch Country, PA
**Botanic Gardens (125)**
Hershey Rose Gardens and Arboretum: 23 acres (Hershey)
Reading Public Museum Botanical Garden: 25 acres (Reading)
**Planetariums (250)**

| | Rating |
|---|---|
| William Penn Memorial (Harrisburg) | B |

**Zoos (1,400)**

| | Rating |
|---|---|
| Gettysburg Game Park (Fairfield) | C |
| Lake Tobias Zoo and Animal Haven (Halifax) | C |
| Zoo America at Hersheypark (Hershey) | C* |

**Museums (3,500)**

| | Rating |
|---|---|
| The Trout Art Gallery (Carlisle) | A |
| The National Assn. of Watch and Clock Collectors Museum: horology (Columbia) | C |
| Cornwall Iron Furnace: industrial museum (Cornwall) | C |
| The State Museum of Pennsylvania: fine arts, natural science (Harrisburg) | AA* |
| Hershey Museum of American Life: decorative arts (Hershey) | C |
| Community Gallery of Lancaster (Lancaster) | C |
| Heritage Center of Lancaster County: decorative arts (Lancaster) | C |
| The North Museum of Franklin and Marshall College: general museum (Lancaster) | C |
| Reading Public Museum and Art Gallery (Reading) | B* |
| Railroad Museum of Pennsylvania (Strasburg) | C |
| Toy Train Museum (Strasburg) | C |

**Special Attractions (2,800)**

| | Rating |
|---|---|
| National Tower: view of battlefield (Gettysburg) | C |
| Sightseeing helicopter tours (Gettysburg) | A |
| Steam train excursions (Gettysburg) | A |
| Sightseeing bus tours (Lancaster) | A |
| Koziar's Christmas Village (Reading) | C |
| Steam train rides (Strasburg) | A |

Places Rated Score: 8,075      Places Rated Rank: 21

## ★ Philadelphia, PA–DE–NJ
**Botanic Gardens (1,255)**
Henry Foundation for Botanical Research: 27 acres (Gladwyne, PA)
Longwood Gardens: 285 acres (Kennett Square, PA)
John J. Tyler Arboretum: 60 acres (Lima, PA)
Swiss Pines: 20 acres (Malvern)
Arboretum of the Barnes Foundation: 12 acres (Philadelphia, PA)
John Bartram's Garden: 27 acres (Philadelphia)
Morris Arboretum: 175 acres (Philadelphia)
Pennsylvania Horticultural Society's 18th Century Garden: 2 acres (Philadelphia)
Arthur Hoyt Scott Horticultural Foundation: 300 acres (Swarthmore, PA)
Taylor Memorial Arboretum: 32 acres (Wallingford, PA)
Bowman's Hill Wild Flower Preserve: 100 acres (Washington Crossing, PA)
Westtown School Arboretum (Westtown, PA)
Eleutherian Mills, Hagley Museum: 2 acres (Wilmington, DE)
Winterthur Gardens: 64 acres (Winterthur, DE)
**Planetariums (300)**

| | Rating |
|---|---|
| Fels (Philadelphia) | A |

**Zoos (800)**

| | Rating |
|---|---|
| Philadelphia Zoological Gardens (Philadelphia) | A* |

**Museums (13,100)**

| | Rating |
|---|---|
| Boyertown Vehicle Museum (Boyertown, PA) | C |
| The Brandywine River Museum: art (Chadds Ford, PA) | A* |
| Merritt's Museum of Childhood (Douglassville, PA) | C |
| Mercer Museum: technology, folk art (Doylestown, PA) | A |
| Buten Museum: ceramics, especially Wedgwood (Merion Station, PA) | C* |

| | Rating |
|---|---|
| The Wharton Escherick Museum: art, woodcarving (Paoli, PA) | C |
| Academy of Natural Science of Philadelphia (Philadelphia) | AA* |
| Afro American Historical and Cultural Museum (Philadelphia) | A |
| Athenaeum of Philadelphia: library with art collection (Philadelphia) | B |
| The Balch Institute for Ethnic Studies (Philadelphia) | A |
| Franklin Institute: science (Philadelphia) | A* |
| Goldie Paley Design Center (Philadelphia) | C |
| Institute of Contemporary Art, University of Pennsylvania (Philadelphia) | A |
| LaSalle College Art Museum (Philadelphia) | C |
| The Pennsylvania Academy of the Fine Arts (Philadelphia) | AA* |
| Perelman Antique Toy Museum (Philadelphia) | C |
| The Philadelphia Art Alliance (Philadelphia) | A |
| Philadelphia College of Art (Philadelphia) | B |
| Philadelphia Maritime Museum (Philadelphia) | A* |
| Philadelphia Mummers Museum: audiovisuals, film, costumes (Philadelphia) | C |
| Philadelphia Museum of Art (Philadelphia) | AA* |
| Please Touch Museum: children's (Philadelphia) | A |
| Rodin Museum: art (Philadelphia) | C* |
| Signa Museum and Art Collection: company museum (Philadelphia) | C |
| Temple University Film Museum (Philadelphia) | C |
| The University Museum, University of Pennsylvania: natural history and science (Philadelphia) | AA* |
| Wagner Free Institute of Science (Philadelphia) | B |
| The Woodmere Art Museum (Philadelphia) | C |
| Wilmar Lapidary Museum (Pineville, PA) | C |
| Pollock Auto Showcase (Pottstown, PA) | C |
| Museum of Art, Pennsylvania State University (University Park, PA) | C |
| The All-College Museums, West Chester University: natural history (West Chester, PA) | C |
| **Special Attractions (2,000)** | |
| Vineyard and winery tours (New Hope, PA) | B |
| Japanese Exhibition House (Philadelphia) | B |
| Sightseeing bus tours (Philadelphia) | A |
| Sightseeing bus tours (Valley Forge, PA) | A |
| Places Rated Score: 17,455    Places Rated Rank: 6 | |

## Phoenix–Valley of the Sun, AZ

| | |
|---|---|
| **Botanic Gardens (126)** | |
| Desert Botanical Garden: 16 acres (Phoenix) | |
| Boyce Thompson Southwestern Arboretum: 35 acres (Superior) | |
| **Zoos (700)** | |
| Phoenix Zoo (Phoenix) | B* |
| **Museums (1,700)** | |
| Museum for Youth: children's art center (Mesa) | A |
| The Heard Museum (Phoenix) | B* |
| Center for Meteorite Studies (Tempe) | C |
| University Art Collections, Arizona State University (Tempe) | B |
| **Special Attractions (1,200)** | |
| *Arcosanti: avant garde prototype town (Cortes Junction)* | B |
| Mystery Castle (Phoenix) | C |
| Sightseeing bus tours (Phoenix) | A |
| Taliesin West (Scottsdale) | C |
| Places Rated Score: 3,726    Places Rated Rank: 65 | |

## Pocono Mountains, PA

| | |
|---|---|
| **Museums (3,200)** | |
| Allentown Art Museum (Allentown) | B |
| Annie S. Kemerer Museum: general (Bethlehem) | B* |
| Lehigh University Art Galleries (Bethlehem) | C |
| Lehigh Valley Antique Fire Museum (Bethlehem) | C |
| Moravian Museum of Bethlehem: religious (Bethlehem) | C |

| | Rating |
|---|---|
| Children's Museum of Northeastern Pennsylvania (Forty Fort) | A |
| Everhart Museum: art, science, natural history (Scranton) | A |
| Scranton Anthracite Museum (Scranton) | C |
| Steamtown Foundation: railroad Americana (Scranton) | C |
| The Sordoni Art Gallery (Wilkes-Barre) | C |
| **Special Attractions (1,600)** | |
| Industrial tour, Holley Ross Pottery (Cresco) | B |
| Steam train rides (Hamburg) | A |
| Eckley Miners' Village (Hazelton) | C |
| Roadside America (Shartlesville) | B |
| Places Rated Score: 4,800    Places Rated Rank: 45 | |

## Portland, ME

| | |
|---|---|
| **Planetariums (400)** | |
| Ream Traveling Planetarium (Auburn) | C |
| Southworth (Portland) | C |
| **Museums (3,400)** | |
| Boothbay Railway Village (Boothbay) | C |
| Boothbay Theater Museum (Boothbay) | C |
| Grand Banks Schooner Museum (Boothbay) | C |
| Boothbay Region Art Gallery (Boothbay Harbor) | C |
| Bowdoin College Museum of Art (Brunswick) | B* |
| Jones Gallery of Glass and Ceramics (East Sebago) | C |
| Children's Museum of Maine (Portland) | A |
| Joan Whitney Payson Gallery of Art (Portland) | C |
| Portland Museum of Art (Portland) | A |
| State of Maine Marine Resources Laboratory (West Boothbay Harbor) | B |
| Music Museum (Wiscasset) | C |
| **Special Attractions (3,400)** | |
| Harbor cruises (Boothbay Harbor) | A |
| L.L. Bean headquarters (Freeport) | B |
| Boat excursions (Monhegan Island) | A |
| Harbor cruises (Portland) | A |
| Ferryboat service to Nova Scotia (Portland) | A |
| Sightseeing bus tours (Portland) | A |
| Places Rated Score: 7,200    Places Rated Rank: 28 | |

## Portland–Columbia River, OR

| | |
|---|---|
| **Botanic Gardens (310)** | |
| Crystal Springs Rhododendron Garden: 6 acres (Portland) | |
| Hoyt Arboretum: 214 acres (Portland) | |
| International Rose Test Garden (Portland) | |
| Japanese Garden (Portland) | |
| **Planetariums (250)** | |
| H. C. Kendall (Portland) | B |
| **Zoos (800)** | |
| Washington Park Zoo (Portland) | A* |
| **Museums (3,200)** | |
| Columbia River Maritime Museum (Astoria) | B* |
| Hatfield Marine Science Center (Newport) | C |
| Contemporary Crafts Association (Portland) | C |
| Oregon Museum of Science and Industry (Portland) | A* |
| Portland Art Museum (Portland) | B* |
| Portland Children's Museum (Portland) | A |
| Western Forestry Center (Portland) | B |
| **Special Attractions (2,000)** | |
| Industrial tour, Pendleton Woolen Mills (Portland) | B |
| Sightseeing bus tours (Portland) | A |
| Winery tours (Salem) | B |
| The Dalles Dam (The Dalles) | B |
| Camp Perpetua Visitor Center: oceanography, natural science (Yachats) | C |
| Places Rated Score: 6,560    Places Rated Rank: 32 | |

## Portsmouth–Kennebunk, NH–ME

| | |
|---|---|
| **Botanic Gardens (51)** | |
| Fuller Gardens: 2 acres (North Hampton, NH) | |
| **Museums (800)** | |
| University Art Galleries (Durham, NH) | C |

| | Rating |
|---|---|
| Seashore Trolley Museum (Kennebunkport, ME) | C |
| York Institute Museum (Saco, ME) | C |
| Wells Auto Museum (Wells, ME) | C |
| **Special Attractions (2,800)** | |
| Ruggles Mine (Franklin, NH) | B |
| Amoskeag Mills (Manchester, NH) | C |
| Industrial tour, Anheuser-Busch, Inc. (Nashua, NH) | B |
| Harbor cruises (Portsmouth, NH) | A |
| Sightseeing bus tours (Portsmouth) | A |
| Steam train rides (Wolfeboro, NH) | A |

Places Rated Score: 3,651    Places Rated Rank: 67

### Providence–Newport, RI

| | Rating |
|---|---|
| **Botanic Gardens (54)** | |
| Green Animals: 7 acres (Portsmouth) | |
| **Planetariums (200)** | |
| Maribelle Curmack (Providence) | C |
| **Zoos (400)** | |
| Roger Williams Park Zoo (Providence) | C |
| **Museums (2,200)** | |
| New England Wireless and Steam Museum: industrial (East Greenwich) | C |
| International Tennis Hall of Fame (Newport) | C |
| Newport Art Museum (Newport) | C |
| Children's Museum of Rhode Island (Pawtucket) | A |
| Museum of Art, Rhode Island School of Design (Providence) | A* |
| Roger Williams Park Museum: natural history (Providence) | B |
| **Special Attractions (1,600)** | |
| Ferryboats to Block Island (Newport and Providence) | A |
| Sightseeing bus tours (Newport) | A |
| The Arcade (Providence) | C |
| Walking tours, conducted by the Providence Preservation Society (Providence) | C |

Places Rated Score: 4,454    Places Rated Rank: 51

### Put-in-Bay–Lake Erie Shore, OH

| | Rating |
|---|---|
| **Botanic Gardens (375)** | |
| Secor Park Arboretum: 500 acres (Berkey) | |
| Crosby Gardens: 50 acres (Toledo) | |
| **Planetariums (450)** | |
| Hedrick (Toledo) | C |
| Ritter (Toledo) | B |
| **Zoos (700)** | |
| Toledo Zoological Gardens (Toledo) | B* |
| **Museums (1,500)** | |
| Blair Museum (lithophanes and wax carvings) (Toledo) | C |
| Toledo Museum of Art (Toledo) | AA* |
| Toledo Museum of Natural Sciences (Toledo) | A |
| **Special Attractions (1,000)** | |
| View of Lake Erie from observation platform, Perry Memorial (Put-in-Bay) | B |
| Ferry service to Kelleys Island and Canada (Sandusky) | A |

Places Rated Score: 4,025    Places Rated Rank: 58

### Rangeley Lakes, ME

| | Rating |
|---|---|
| **Museums (200)** | |
| Wilhelm Reich Museum: science, art (Rangeley) | C |
| **Special Attractions (200)** | |
| Gondola rides, Sugarloaf Mountain (Kingfield) | C |

Places Rated Score: 400    Places Rated Rank: 105

### Redwoods–Shasta–Lassen, CA

| | Rating |
|---|---|
| **Museums (200)** | |
| Pacific Lumber Company Museum: logging (Scotia) | C |
| **Special Attractions (1,600)** | |
| Harbor cruises (Eureka) | A |
| Sightseeing bus tours (Eureka) | A |
| Klamath National Forest Interpretive Museum (Yreka) | B |

Places Rated Score: 1,800    Places Rated Rank: 88

### Richmond–Fredericksburg, VA

| | Rating |
|---|---|
| **Planetariums (400)** | |
| Steele (Richmond) | C |
| Thomas Jefferson (Richmond) | C |
| **Zoos (400)** | |
| Kings Dominion (Doswell) | C |
| **Museums (1,800)** | |
| *Longwood Fine Arts Center (Farmville)* | C* |
| Belmont, the Gari Merchers Memorial Gallery (Fredericksburg) | C |
| Meadow Farm Museum: agriculture (Glen Allen) | C |
| Science Museum of Virginia (Richmond) | B |
| Virginia Museum of Fine Arts (Richmond) | AA* |
| **Special Attractions (600)** | |
| Sightseeing bus tours (Fredericksburg) | A |

Places Rated Score: 3,200    Places Rated Rank: 72

### Sacramento–Gold Rush Towns, CA

| | Rating |
|---|---|
| **Botanic Gardens (53)** | |
| C.M. Goethe Arboretum: 5 acres (Sacramento) | |
| **Zoos (600)** | |
| Sacramento Zoo (Sacramento) | C* |
| **Museums (1,300)** | |
| California State Railroad Museum (Sacramento) | C |
| Crocker Art Museum (Sacramento) | B* |
| Sacramento Science Center and Junior Museum (Sacramento) | A |
| **Special Attractions (2,000)** | |
| *Ghost towns (Lodi)* | B |
| *Winery tour (Lodi)* | B |
| Oroville Chinese Temple (Oroville) | C |
| Gold Bug Mine (Placerville) | B |
| Industrial tour, California Almond Growers (Sacramento) | B |
| Sightseeing bus tours (Sacramento) | A |

Places Rated Score: 3,953    Places Rated Rank: 61

### St. Augustine–Northeast Coast, FL

| | Rating |
|---|---|
| **Planetariums (700)** | |
| Museum of Arts and Sciences (Daytona Beach) | B |
| Alexander Brest (Jacksonville) | B |
| Fountain of Youth (St. Augustine) | C |
| **Zoos (400)** | |
| Jacksonville Zoological Park (Jacksonville) | C |
| **Museums (3,500)** | |
| Museum of Arts and Sciences (Daytona Beach) | A |
| De Land Museum: art (De Land) | A |
| Cummer Gallery of Art (Jacksonville) | B* |
| Jacksonville Art Museum (Jacksonville) | A* |
| Jacksonville Museum of Arts and Sciences (Jacksonville) | AA* |
| Lightner Museum: decorative arts (St. Augustine) | B |
| **Special Attractions (1,800)** | |
| Daytona International Speedway (Daytona Beach) | C |
| Industrial tour, Anheuser Busch Brewery (Jacksonville) | B |
| Scenic waterfront cruises (St. Augustine) | A |
| Sightseeing train and carriage tours (St. Augustine) | A |

Places Rated Score: 6,400    Places Rated Rank: 33

### St. Louis–Mark Twain Country, MO–IL

| | Rating |
|---|---|
| **Botanic Gardens (88)** | |
| Missouri Botanical Garden: 75 acres (St. Louis) | |
| **Planetariums (300)** | |
| McDonnell (St. Louis) | A |
| **Zoos (800)** | |
| St. Louis Zoological Park (St. Louis) | A* |
| **Museums (2,300)** | |
| National Bowling Hall of Fame (St. Louis) | C |
| National Museum of Transport (St. Louis) | C |
| St. Louis Art Museum (St. Louis) | AA* |
| St. Louis Center Museum of Science and Natural History (St. Louis) | A* |
| Washington University Gallery of Art (St. Louis) | C |
| Laumeier Sculpture Park and Gallery (Sunset Hills) | C |

| | Rating |
|---|---|
| **Special Attractions (2,800)** | |
| Riverboat excursions (Hannibal) | A |
| Train ride (Hannibal) | B |
| Winery tours (Hermann) | B |
| Industrial tour, Anheuser-Busch Brewery (St. Louis) | B |
| Industrial tour, Bardenheier's Wine Cellars (St. Louis) | B |
| Sightseeing bus tours (St. Louis) | A |
| Places Rated Score: 6,288   Places Rated Rank: 34 | |

## Salt Lake City, UT

| | Rating |
|---|---|
| **Planetariums (250)** | |
| Hansen (Salt Lake City) | B |
| **Zoos (600)** | |
| Hogle Zoological Gardens (Salt Lake City) | C* |
| **Museums (2,800)** | |
| John Hutchings Museum of Natural History (Lehi) | B |
| Salt Lake Art Center (Salt Lake City) | A |
| Springville Museum of Art (Salt Lake City) | B |
| Utah Museum of Fine Arts (Salt Lake City) | AA* |
| Utah Museum of Natural History (Salt Lake City) | A* |
| **Special Attractions (1,400)** | |
| Egyptian Theatre (Park City) | C |
| Osmond Studios (Provo) | C |
| Temple Square (Salt Lake City) | B |
| Sightseeing bus tours (Salt Lake City) | A |
| Places Rated Score: 5,050   Places Rated Rank: 43 | |

## San Antonio, TX

| | Rating |
|---|---|
| **Zoos and Aquariums (700)** | |
| San Antonio Zoological Gardens and Aquarium (San Antonio) | B* |
| **Museums (1,700)** | |
| Marion Koogler McNay Art Museum (San Antonio) | A* |
| San Antonio Museum of Art (San Antonio) | B |
| San Antonio Museum of Science–Technology–Transportation (San Antonio) | C |
| Southwest Craft Center (San Antonio) | C |
| Fiedler Memorial Museum: geology (Seguin) | C |
| **Special Attractions (2,200)** | |
| Buckhorn Hall of Horns (San Antonio) | C |
| Hertzberg Circus Collection (San Antonio) | C |
| Institute of Texas Cultures (San Antonio) | A |
| Majestic Performing Arts Center (San Antonio) | C |
| Observation floor, Tower of the Americas (San Antonio) | B |
| Sightseeing bus tours (San Antonio) | A |
| Places Rated Score: 4,600   Places Rated Rank: 48 | |

## San Diego, CA

| | Rating |
|---|---|
| **Botanic Gardens (64)** | |
| Quail Botanic Gardens: 27 acres (Encinitas) | |
| **Planetariums (300)** | |
| Reuben H. Fleet Space Theater (San Diego) | A |
| **Zoos and Aquariums (2,200)** | |
| San Diego Wild Animal Park (San Diego) | A* |
| San Diego Zoo (San Diego) | A* |
| Sea World (San Diego) | A* |
| **Museums (3,600)** | |
| La Jolla Museum of Contemporary Art (La Jolla) | B |
| Mingei International Museum of World Folk Art (La Jolla) | C |
| Natural History Museum (San Diego) | AA* |
| San Diego Aero-Space Museum (San Diego) | C |
| San Diego Hall of Champions: sports (San Diego) | C |
| San Diego Maritime Museum: ships (San Diego) | C |
| San Diego Museums of Art (San Diego) | AA* |
| San Diego Museum of Man (San Diego) | B* |
| Timken Art Gallery (San Diego) | C |
| **Special Attractions (2,800)** | |
| Lawrence Welk Theater–Museum (Escondido) | C |
| Palomar Observatory (Escondido) | B |
| Winery tours (Escondido) | B |

| | Rating |
|---|---|
| Simon Edison Center for the Performing Arts (San Diego) | C |
| Harbor excursions (San Diego) | A |
| "Tijuana Trolley" (San Diego) | B |
| Sightseeing bus tours (San Diego) | A |
| Places Rated Score: 8,964   Places Rated Rank: 16 | |

## ★ San Francisco, CA

| | Rating |
|---|---|
| **Botanic Gardens (611)** | |
| Regional Parks Botanic Garden: 7 acres (Berkeley) | |
| University of California Botanical Garden: 25 acres (Berkeley) | |
| Muir Woods National Monument: 500 acres (Mill Valley) | |
| Japanese Tea Garden (San Francisco) | |
| Strybing Arboretum and Botanical Gardens: 70 acres (San Francisco) | |
| Filoli Gardens: 17 acres (Woodside) | |
| **Planetariums (550)** | |
| Rotary Chabot (Oakland) | B |
| Morrison (San Francisco) | A |
| **Zoos and Aquariums (1,900)** | |
| Knowland Park Zoo (Oakland) | C |
| Marine World/Africa USA (Redwood City) | A* |
| San Francisco Zoological Gardens (San Francisco) | B* |
| **Museums (9,700)** | |
| Lawrence Hall of Science, University of California (Berkeley) | AA |
| University Art Museum (Berkeley) | AA* |
| Museum of Vintage Fashion (Lafayette) | C |
| The Oakland Museum (Oakland) | A* |
| Richmond Art Center (Richmond) | C |
| Asian Art Museum (San Francisco) | AA* |
| California Academy of Sciences (San Francisco) | AA* |
| The Exploratorium: science (San Francisco) | A |
| Fine Arts Museum of San Francisco (San Francisco) | AA* |
| Josephine D. Randall Junior Museum (San Francisco) | A |
| The Mexican Museum: fine arts (San Francisco) | B |
| National Maritime Museum: ships (San Francisco) | A |
| Old Mint Museum: money, numismatics (San Francisco) | C |
| San Francisco Fire Dept. Museum (San Francisco) | C |
| San Francisco Museum of Modern Art (San Francisco) | B* |
| Coyote Point Museum for Environmental Education (San Mateo) | A* |
| Stanford University Museum: art (Stanford) | B |
| Alexander Lindsay Junior Museum (Walnut Creek) | A* |
| **Special Attractions (5,200)** | |
| Winery tours (Livermore) | B |
| Sightseeing bus tours (Oakland) | A |
| Chinatown (San Francisco) | AA |
| Chinese Culture Center (San Francisco) | B |
| Cow Palace (San Francisco) | B |
| Fisherman's Wharf (San Francisco) | A |
| Industrial tour, Acres of Orchids (San Francisco) | B |
| Japan Center (San Francisco) | B |
| Cruises on San Francisco Bay (San Francisco) | A |
| Sightseeing bus tours (San Francisco) | A |
| Places Rated Score: 17,961   Places Rated Rank: 5 | |

## Santa Barbara–San Simeon, CA

| | Rating |
|---|---|
| **Botanic Gardens (183)** | |
| Hearst San Simeon State Historical Monument: 100 acres (San Simeon) | |
| Santa Barbara Botanic Garden: 65 acres (Santa Barbara) | |
| **Planetariums (200)** | |
| Gladwin (Santa Barbara) | C |
| **Zoos (1,000)** | |
| Charles Paddock Zoo (Atascadero) | C |

| | Rating |
|---|---|
| Santa Barbara Zoological Gardens (Santa Barbara) | C* |
| Museums (2,200) | |
| Santa Barbara Museum of Art (Santa Barbara) | AA* |
| Santa Barbara Museum of Natural History (Santa Barbara) | A* |
| University Art Museum (Santa Barbara) | A* |
| Special Attractions (600) | |
| Harbor cruises (Morro Bay) | A |
| Places Rated Score: 4,183    Places Rated Rank: 54 | |

### Savannah–Golden Isles, GA

| | |
|---|---|
| Museums (1,900) | |
| Museum of Antique Dolls (Savannah) | C |
| Oatland Island Educational Center: environmental nature center (Savannah) | B |
| Savannah Science Museum (Savannah) | A |
| Ships of the Sea Maritime Museum (Savannah) | C |
| Telfair Academy of Arts and Sciences (Savannah) | B* |
| Special Attractions (1,800) | |
| Sightseeing cruises (Brunswick) | A |
| Harbor cruises (Savannah) | A |
| Sightseeing bus tours (Savannah) | A |
| Places Rated Score: 3,700    Places Rated Rank: 66 | |

### ★ Seattle–Mount Rainier–North Cascades, WA

| | |
|---|---|
| Botanic Gardens (225) | |
| University of Washington Arboretum in Washington Park: 200 acres (Seattle) | |
| Point Defiance Park: 50 acres (Tacoma) | |
| Planetariums (200) | |
| Starlab (Seattle) | C |
| Zoos and Aquariums (2,200) | |
| Northwest Trek Wildlife Park (Eatonville) | C |
| The Seattle Aquarium (Seattle) | B* |
| Woodland Park Zoological Garden (Seattle) | B* |
| Point Defiance Zoo and Aquarium (Tacoma) | C* |
| Museums (5,700) | |
| Bellevue Art Museum (Bellevue) | B |
| Whatcom Museum of History and Art (Bellingham) | A* |
| The Whale Museum (Friday Harbor) | C |
| Henry Art Gallery Textile Collection (Seattle) | C |
| Museum of Flight (Seattle) | C |
| Museum of History and Industry (Seattle) | AA* |
| Pacific Science Center (Seattle) | A |
| Seattle Art Museum (Seattle) | AA* |
| Thomas Burke Memorial Washington State Museum (Seattle) | AA* |
| Puget Sound Railroad Museum (Snoqualmie) | C |
| Tacoma Art Museum (Tacoma) | A* |
| University of Puget Sound Museum of Natural History (Tacoma) | C |
| Special Attractions (4,600) | |
| Industrial tour, Boeing 747/767 Division (Everett) | B |
| Industrial tour, Walker Tree Nursery and Forest Research Center (Port Gamble) | B |
| Chinatown (Seattle) | A |
| Kingdome (Seattle) | C |
| Space Needle (Seattle) | B |
| Winery and brewery tours (Seattle) | B |
| Ferryboat trips to Olympic Peninsula (Seattle) | A |
| Harbor tours (Seattle) | A |
| Sightseeing bus tours (Seattle) | A |
| Trolley, diesel, and steam train rides (Snoqualmie) | B |
| Places Rated Score: 12,925    Places Rated Rank: 8 | |

### Spokane–Coeur d'Alene, WA–ID

| | |
|---|---|
| Botanic Gardens (83) | |
| John A. Finch Arboretum: 65 acres (Spokane, WA) | |
| Museums (1,100) | |
| Cheney Cowles Memorial Museum: general (Spokane) | A* |
| Museum of Native American Cultures (Spokane) | C |
| Coeur d'Alene District Mining Museum (Wallace, ID) | C |

| | Rating |
|---|---|
| Special Attractions (2,600) | |
| Lake cruises (Coeur d'Alene, ID) | A |
| Winery tours (Spokane) | B |
| Sightseeing train tours (Spokane) | A |
| Sightseeing bus tours (Spokane) | A |
| Mine tours (Wallace) | B |
| Places Rated Score: 3,783    Places Rated Rank: 64 | |

### ★ Tampa Bay–Southwest Coast, FL

| | |
|---|---|
| Botanic Gardens (593) | |
| Thomas A. Edison Winter Home Botanical Gardens: 14 acres (Fort Myers) | |
| Suncoast Botanical Garden: 60 acres (Largo) | |
| Corkscrew Swamp Sanctuary: 11,000 acres (Naples) | |
| Marie Selby Botanical Gardens: 11 acres (Sarasota) | |
| Busch Gardens (Tampa) | |
| Planetariums (450) | |
| Bishop Space Transit (Bradenton) | B |
| Pinellas County (St. Petersburg) | C |
| Zoos (500) | |
| Busch Gardens (Tampa) | B |
| Museums (3,700) | |
| Museum of Fine Arts of St. Petersburg (St. Petersburg) | A* |
| Salvador Dali Museum (St. Petersburg) | C |
| The Science Center of Pinellas County (St. Petersburg) | A |
| John and Mable Ringling Museum of Art (Sarasota) | AA* |
| Museum of the Circus (Sarasota) | C |
| H. B. Plant Museum: antiques (Tampa) | C |
| Museum of Science and Industry (Tampa) | AA |
| Tampa Museum: art (Tampa) | A |
| Special Attractions (6,400) | |
| Sightseeing cruises (Clearwater) | A |
| Sightseeing bus tours (Clearwater) | A |
| Tiki Gardens (Clearwater Beach) | B |
| Shell Factory (Fort Myers) | C |
| Suncoast Seabird Sanctuary (Indian Shores) | C |
| London Wax Museum (St. Petersburg) | C |
| MGM'S *Bounty* (St. Petersburg) | B |
| Sightseeing cruises (St. Petersburg) | A |
| Sightseeing bus tours (St. Petersburg) | A |
| Sarasota Jungle Gardens (Sarasota) | B |
| Sightseeing cruises (Sarasota) | A |
| Industrial tours, breweries, cigar factories (Tampa) | B |
| Ybor City (Tampa) | A |
| Sightseeing bus tours (Tampa) | A |
| Places Rated Score: 11,643    Places Rated Rank: 9 | |

### Traverse City–Petoskey, MI

| | |
|---|---|
| Museums (600) | |
| Sleeping Bear Point Maritime Museum (Glen Haven) | C |
| Con Foster Museum: general (Traverse City) | C |
| Great Lakes Area Paleontological Museum (Traverse City) | C |
| Special Attractions (2,000) | |
| Lake cruises (Charlevoix) | A |
| Cruises to Manitou Islands (Leland) | A |
| Winery tours (Leland) | B |
| Winery tours (Traverse City) | B |
| Places Rated Score: 2,600    Places Rated Rank: 76 | |

### Tucson, AZ

| | |
|---|---|
| Botanic Gardens (56) | |
| Arizona–Sonora Desert Museum: 12 acres (Tucson) | |
| Zoos (1,100) | |
| Arizona–Sonora Desert Museum (Tucson) | B |
| Gene Reid Zoological Park (Tucson) | C* |
| Museums (3,200) | |
| Cochise Fine Arts (Bisbee) | C |
| The Aquary Museum (Tucson) | C |

|  | Rating |
|---|---|
| Arizona-Sonora Desert Museum (Tucson) | AA* |
| Center for Creative Photography (Tucson) | C |
| Old West Wax Museum (Tucson) | C |
| Pima Air Museum (Tucson) | C |
| Tucson Museum of Art (Tucson) | B* |
| University of Arizona Museum of Art (Tucson) | AA* |
| **Special Attractions (600)** | |
| Sightseeing bus tours (Tucson) | A |

Places Rated Score: 4,956          Places Rated Rank: 44

## Tulsa–Lake O' The Cherokees, OK

| **Botanic Gardens (50)** | |
|---|---|
| Tulsa Garden Center and Arboretum (Tulsa) | |
| **Zoos (600)** | |
| Tulsa Zoological Park (Tulsa) | C* |
| **Museums (2,500)** | |
| Woolaroc Museum: art, history (Bartlesville) | B* |
| Treasure House Doll Museum (Claremore) | C |
| Antiques, Inc., Car Museum (Muskogee) | C |
| Five Civilized Tribes Museum: Indian art (Muskogee) | C |
| Philbrook Art Center (Tulsa) | AA |
| Thomas Gilcrease Institute of American History and Art (Tulsa) | A* |
| **Special Attractions (2,400)** | |
| Tom Mix Museum (Bartlesville) | C |
| Lake cruises (Grand Lake) | A |
| Cherokee Heritage Center (Talequah) | A |
| Industrial tour, Frankoma Pottery (Tulsa) | B |
| Sightseeing bus tours (Tulsa) | A |

Places Rated Score: 5,550          Places Rated Rank: 39

## Vicksburg–Natchez–Baton Rouge, MS–LA

| **Botanic Gardens (68)** | |
|---|---|
| Rosedown Plantation and Gardens: 35 acres (St. Francisville, LA) | |
| **Planetariums (550)** | |
| Science Center (Baton Rouge, LA) | A |
| R. C. Davis (Jackson, MS) | B |
| **Zoos (600)** | |
| Greater Baton Rouge Zoo (Baton Rouge) | C* |
| **Museums (1,500)** | |
| Anglo American Art Museum (Baton Rouge) | B |
| Louisiana Arts and Science Center (Baton Rouge) | A* |
| Louisiana State University Museum of Geoscience (Baton Rouge) | B |
| **Special Attractions (600)** | |
| Riverboat cruises (Vicksburg, MS) | A |

Places Rated Score: 3,318          Places Rated Rank: 69

## ★ Washington, DC–MD–VA

| **Botanic Gardens (903)** | |
|---|---|
| Oatlands: 3 acres (Leesburg, VA) | |
| Gunston Hall Plantation Gardens: 556 acres (Lorton, VA) | |
| Kitchen Garden, Mount Vernon Restoration (Mount Vernon, VA) | |
| Woodlawn Plantation: 127 acres (Mount Vernon, VA) | |
| Bishop's Garden, Washington National Cathedral: 3 acres (Washington, DC) | |
| Dumbarton Oaks: 17 acres (Washington) | |
| Smithsonian Institution Pleasure Gardens: 20 acres (Washington) | |
| U.S. Botanic Garden Conservatory (Washington) | |
| U.S. National Arboretum: 50 acres (Washington) | |
| Brookside Botanical Garden: 25 acres (Wheaton, MD) | |
| **Planetariums (1,600)** | |
| Hayfield (Alexandria, VA) | C |
| Earth and Space (Frederick, MD) | C |
| NASA–Goddard Space Flight (Greenbelt, MD) | C |
| Washington County (Hagerstown) | C |
| Prince Georges County (Lanham, MD) | C |
| Albert Einstein Spacearium (Washington) | A |

|  | Rating |
|---|---|
| Brookmont (Washington) | C |
| Rock Creek (Washington) | C |
| **Zoos (800)** | |
| National Zoological Park (Washington) | A* |
| **Museums (12,100)** | |
| The Art Gallery at the University of Maryland (College Park, MD) | C* |
| Rose Hill Manor Children's Museum (Frederick) | A |
| Anacostia Neighborhood Museum–Smithsonian: Afro-American arts et al. (Washington) | C |
| Capital Children's Museum (Washington) | A |
| The Children's Museum of Washington (Washington) | A |
| The Corcoran Gallery of Art (Washington) | B* |
| D.A.R. Museum (Washington) | B* |
| Dumbarton Oaks Collection: art (Washington) | B |
| Freer Gallery of Art—Smithsonian (Washington) | AA |
| Hirshhorn Museum and Sculpture Garden—Smithsonian (Washington) | AA* |
| Museum of the Society of the Cincinnati: art, decorative arts (Washington) | C |
| National Air and Space Museum—Smithsonian (Washington) | A |
| National Gallery of Art—Smithsonian (Washington) | AA* |
| National Museum of African Art—Smithsonian (Washington) | AA* |
| National Museum of American Art—Smithsonian (Washington) | AA* |
| National Museum of Natural History—Smithsonian (Washington) | AA* |
| National Portrait Gallery—Smithsonian (Washington) | AA* |
| National Rifle Association Firearms Museum (Washington) | C |
| The Phillips Collection: art (Washington) | AA* |
| Renwick Gallery of the National Museum of American Art—Smithsonian: design, crafts, and decorative arts (Washington) | C |
| Rock Creek Nature Center (Washington) | A |
| The Textile Museum (Washington) | C* |
| Washington Dolls' House and Toy Museum (Washington) | C |
| **Special Attractions (4,800)** | |
| Folger Shakespeare Library (Washington) | B |
| Jefferson Memorial (Washington) | B |
| John F. Kennedy Center for the Performing Arts (Washington) | B |
| Lincoln Memorial (Washington) | B |
| Theodore Roosevelt Memorial (Washington) | B |
| Vietnam Veterans Memorial (Washington) | B |
| Washington Monument (Washington) | B |
| Washington National Cathedral (Washington) | B |
| The White House (Washington) | B |
| Cruises to Mount Vernon (Washington) | A |
| Sightseeing bus tours (Washington) | A |

Places Rated Score: 20,203          Places Rated Rank: 3

## White Mountains, NH

| **Museums (1,500)** | |
|---|---|
| Hood Museum of Art (Hanover) | AA* |
| Mountshire Museum of Science (Hanover) | A |
| Mount Washington Summit Museum (Mount Washington) | C |
| **Special Attractions (2,600)** | |
| League of New Hampshire Craftsmen (Hanover) | B |
| Flightseeing over White Mountains (North Conway) | A |
| Steam train rides (North Conway) | B |
| Cog railway to top of Mount Washington (Twin Mountain) | A |
| Cruises on Lake Winnipesaukee (Weirs Beach) | A |

Places Rated Score: 4,100          Places Rated Rank: 55

## Williamsburg–Colonial Triangle, VA

| **Botanic Gardens (160)** | |
|---|---|
| Norfolk Botanical Gardens: 220 acres (Norfolk) | |

|  | Rating |
|---|---|
| Planetariums (400) | |
| Peninsula Nature and Science Center (Newport News) | C |
| Portsmouth (Portsmouth) | C |
| Zoos (400) | |
| Lafayette Zoological Park (Norfolk) | C |
| Museums (4,800) | |
| Virginia Institute of Marine Science (Gloucester Point) | C |
| The College Museum, Hampton Institute (Hampton) | B |
| The Mariners' Museum (Newport News) | A* |
| Peninsula Nature and Science Center (Newport News) | A* |
| The Chrysler Museum (Norfolk) | AA* |
| Hermitage Foundation Museum: art (Norfolk) | C |
| Children's Museum (Portsmouth) | A |
| Portsmouth Community Arts Center (Portsmouth) | A |
| Virginia Beach Arts Center (Virginia Beach) | B |
| Abby Aldrich Rockefeller Folk Art Center (Williamsburg) | C |
| Muscarelle Museum of Art, College of William and Mary (Williamsburg) | C |
| Special Attractions (2,200) | |
| Harbor cruises (Newport News) | A |
| Norfolk School of Boatbuilding (Norfolk) | B |
| Harbor cruises (Norfolk) | A |
| Sightseeing bus tours (Norfolk) | A |
| Places Rated Score: 7,960    Places Rated Rank: 22 | |

### Wilmington–Cape Fear, NC

| Botanic Gardens (60) | |
|---|---|
| Orton Plantation Gardens: 20 acres (Wilmington) | |
| Museums (800) | |
| North Carolina Marine Resources Center (Kure Beach) | C |
| St. John's Museum of Art (Wilmington) | B* |
| Special Attractions (1,200) | |
| Chandlers Wharf (Wilmington) | B |
| Cotton Exchange (Wilmington) | C |
| Harbor and river cruises (Wilmington) | A |
| Places Rated Score: 2,060    Places Rated Rank: 86 | |

### Wine Country, CA

| Botanic Gardens (74) | |
|---|---|
| Mendocino Coast Botanical Gardens: 47 acres (Fort Bragg) | |
| Museums (400) | |
| Codding Museum of Natural History (Santa Rosa) | C |
| Silverado Museum (St. Helena) | C |
| Special Attractions (3,600) | |
| California Railway Museum (Fairfield) | C |
| Scenic rail excursions (Fort Bragg) | A |
| Winery tours (Guerneville) | B |
| Winery tours ((Healdsburg) | B |
| Winery tours (St. Helena) | B |
| Winery tours (Santa Rosa) | B |
| Winery tours (Sonoma) | B |
| Winery tours (Ukiah) | B |
| Winery tours (Yountville) | B |
| Places Rated Score: 4,074    Places Rated Rank: 57 | |

### Wisconsin Dells, WI

| Botanic Gardens (405) | |
|---|---|
| Louis R. Head Arboretum: 10 acres (Madison) | |
| University of Wisconsin Arboretum: 1,200 acres (Madison) | |
| Zoos (600) | |
| Henry Vilas Park Zoo (Madison) | C* |

|  | Rating |
|---|---|
| Museums (2,600) | |
| Circus World Museum (Baraboo) | C |
| International Crane Foundation: aviary and ornithology (Baraboo) | C |
| Theodore Lyman Wright Art Center (Beloit) | A |
| Elvehjem Museum of Art (Madison) | B* |
| Helen Allen Textile Collection (Madison) | C |
| Mid-Continent Railway Museum (North Freedom) | C |
| Platteville Mining Museum (Platteville) | C |
| MacKenzie Environmental Education Center (Poynette) | B |
| Badger Mine and Museum (Shullsburg) | C |
| Special Attractions (2,400) | |
| Little Norway (Mount Horeb) | B |
| Chalet of the Golden Fleece (New Glarus) | B |
| The House on the Rock (Spring Green) | B |
| Taliesin Fellowship Buildings (Spring Green) | B |
| Scenic Dells Boat Tours (Wisconsin Dells) | A |
| Xanadu (futuristic home) (Wisconsin Dells) | C |
| Places Rated Score: 6,005    Places Rated Rank: 37 | |

### Yellowstone–Jackson–Tetons, WY–MT–ID

| Museums (900) | |
|---|---|
| Lava Hot Springs Museum (Lava Hot Springs, ID) | C |
| Teton Flood Museum (Rexburg, ID) | C |
| Beaverhead County Museum (Dillon, MT) | C |
| Dale Warren's Wild Life Exhibit (Dubois, ID) | C |
| Fremont Count Museums: logging and lumber (Dubois) | C |
| Special Attractions (3,600) | |
| Aerial Tramway to top of Rendezvous Mountain (Jackson, WY) | B |
| Covered wagon trips through Grand Tetons (Jackson) | A |
| Scenic float trips on Snake River (Jackson) | A |
| Guided snowcoach tours (West Yellowstone, MT) | A |
| Sightseeing bus tours (West Yellowstone) | A |
| Visitor centers: five centers (Yellowstone National Park, WY) | AA |
| Places Rated Score: 4,500    Places Rated Rank: 49 | |

### Yosemite–Sequoia–Death Valley, CA

| Museums (1,000) | |
|---|---|
| Laws Railroad Museum (Bishop) | C |
| Death Valley Museum of Natural History (Death Valley) | B |
| Yosemite Collection, National Park Service (Yosemite Visitor Center) | B |
| Special Attractions (1,600) | |
| Narrow-gauge steam train excursions (Bass Lake) | A |
| Scotty's Castle (Death Valley) | C |
| Death Valley Visitor Center (Furnace Creek) | C |
| Grant Grove and Lodgepole visitor centers (Sequoia and Kings Canyon National Parks) | A |
| Places Rated Score: 2,600    Places Rated Rank: 76 | |

### Zion–Bryce Canyon, UT

| Museums (400) | |
|---|---|
| Braithwaite Fine Arts Gallery (Cedar City) | B |
| Special Attractions (1,200) | |
| Bryce Canyon Visitor Center (Bryce Canyon National Park) | C |
| Cedar Breaks Visitor Center (Cedar Breaks National Monument) | C |
| Flightseeing trips over area (Cedar City) | A |
| Zion Visitor Center (Zion National Park) | C |
| Places Rated Score: 1,600    Places Rated Rank: 93 | |

# RANKINGS: Feeding the Mind and Spirit

Five criteria were evaluated to determine the scores in this chapter: (1) botanic gardens, (2) planetariums, (3) zoos and aquariums, (4) museums (other than history museums, which were included in the previous chapter, entitled Discovering Our Heritage), and (5) special attractions.

Vacation Places that receive tie scores are given the same rank and are listed in alphabetic order.

## Vacation Places from First to Last

| Places Rated Rank | Places Rated Score | Places Rated Rank | Places Rated Score | Places Rated Rank | Places Rated Score |
|---|---|---|---|---|---|
| 1. New York City, NY | 28,603 | 37. Wisconsin Dells, WI | 6,005 | 72. Richmond–Fredericksburg, VA | 3,200 |
| 2. Los Angeles, CA | 23,653 | 38. Atlanta, GA | 5,850 | 73. Chattanooga–Huntsville, TN–AL–GA | 3,075 |
| 3. Washington, DC–MD–VA | 20,203 | 39. Tulsa–Lake O' The Cherokees, OK | 5,550 | 74. Mackinac Island–Sault Ste. Marie, MI | 2,800 |
| 4. Boston, MA | 18,025 | 40. New Orleans, LA | 5,454 | 75. Charleston, SC | 2,677 |
| 5. San Francisco, CA | 17,961 | 41. Catskill Mountains, NY | 5,447 | |  |
| 6. Philadelphia, PA–DE–NJ | 17,455 | 42. Knoxville–Smoky Mountains, TN | 5,193 | 76. Traverse City–Petoskey, MI | 2,600 |
| 7. Miami–Gold Coast–Keys, FL | 15,915 | 43. Salt Lake City, UT | 5,050 | 76. Yosemite–Sequoia–Death Valley, CA | 2,600 |
| 8. Seattle–Mount Rainier–North Cascades, WA | 12,925 | 44. Tucson, AZ | 4,956 | 78. Austin–Hill Country, TX | 2,500 |
| 9. Tampa Bay–Southwest Coast, FL | 11,643 | 45. Pocono Mountains, PA | 4,800 | 79. Cape Cod–The Islands, MA | 2,488 |
| 10. Chicago, IL | 11,009 | 46. Oklahoma City–Cherokee Strip, OK | 4,762 | 80. Las Vegas–Lake Mead, NV–AZ | 2,400 |
| 11. Mystic Seaport–Connecticut Valley, CT | 10,658 | 47. Nashville, TN | 4,628 | 81. Mobile Bay–Gulfport, AL–MS | 2,383 |
| 12. Lexington–Bluegrass Country, KY | 10,565 | 48. San Antonio, TX | 4,600 | 82. Blue Ridge Mountains, VA | 2,312 |
| 13. Dallas–Fort Worth, TX | 10,161 | 49. Bar Harbor–Acadia. ME | 4.500 | 83. Asheville–Smoky Mountains, NC | 2,205 |
| 14. Minneapolis–St. Paul, MN–WI | 9,892 | 49. Yellowstone–Jackson–Tetons, WY–ID–MT | 4,500 | 84. Crater Lake–Klamath Falls, OR | 2,200 |
| 15. Long Island, NY | 9,615 | 51. Berkshire Hills–Pioneer Valley, MA | 4,454 | 84. Olympic Peninsula, WA | 2,200 |
| 16. San Diego, CA | 8,964 | 51. Providence–Newport, RI | 4,454 | |  |
| 17. Monterey–Big Sur, CA | 8,903 | 53. Adirondack Mountains, NY | 4,450 | 86. Wilmington–Cape Fear, NC | 2,060 |
| 18. Houston–Galveston, TX | 8,733 | 54. Santa Barbara–San Simeon, CA | 4,183 | 87. Brownsville–Rio Grande Valley, TX | 1,860 |
| 19. Orlando–Space Coast, FL | 8,570 | 55. Ozarks–Eureka Springs, AR–MO | 4,100 | 88. Glacier National Park–Flathead Lake, MT | 1,800 |
| 20. Niagara Falls–Western New York, NY | 8,300 | 55. White Mountains, NH | 4,100 | 88. Lake Tahoe–Reno, NV–CA | 1,800 |
| 21. Pennsylvania Dutch Country, PA | 8,075 | 57. Wine Country, CA | 4,074 | 88. Myrtle Beach–Grand Strand, SC | 1,800 |
| 22. Williamsburg–Colonial Triangle, VA | 7,960 | 58. Put-in-Bay–Lake Erie Shore, OH | 4,025 | 88. Redwoods–Shasta–Lassen, CA | 1,800 |
| 23. Cincinnati, OH–KY | 7,952 | 59. Anchorage–Kenai Peninsula, AK | 4,000 | 92. Atlantic City, NJ | 1,700 |
| 24. Hawaii | 7,710 | 59. Corpus Christi–Padre Island, TX | 4,000 | 93. Panhandle, FL | 1,600 |
| 25. Albuquerque–Santa Fe–Taos, NM | 7,600 | | | 93. Zion–Bryce Canyon, UT | 1,600 |
| | | 61. Sacramento–Gold Rush Towns, CA | 3,953 | 95. Outer Banks, NC | 1,452 |
| 26. Finger Lakes, NY | 7,550 | 62. Black Hills, SD | 3,800 | |  |
| 27. Holland–Lake Michigan Shore, MI | 7,295 | 62. Grand Canyon Country, AZ | 3,800 | 96. Eastern Shore, VA | 1,400 |
| 28. Portland, ME | 7,200 | 64. Spokane–Coeur d'Alene, WA–ID | 3,783 | 97. Door County, WI | 1,350 |
| 29. Denver–Rocky Mountain National Park, CO | 7,085 | 65. Phoenix–Valley of the Sun, AZ | 3,726 | 98. Aspen–Vail, CO | 1,200 |
| 30. Baltimore–Chesapeake Bay, MD | 6,890 | 66. Savannah–Golden Isles, GA | 3,700 | 98. Bend–Cascade Mountains, OR | 1,200 |
| 31. Palm Springs–Desert Playgrounds, CA | 6,868 | 67. Portsmouth–Kennebunk, NH–ME | 3,651 | 100. Boise–Sun Valley, ID | 1,100 |
| 32. Portland–Columbia River, OR | 6,560 | 68. Lake Powell–Glen Canyon, AZ–UT | 3,400 | 100. Boone–High Country, NC | 1,100 |
| 33. St. Augustine–Northeast Coast, FL | 6,400 | 69. Vicksburg–Natchez–Baton Rouge, MS–LA | 3,318 | 100. Coos Bay–South Coast, OR | 1,100 |
| 34. St. Louis–Mark Twain Country, MO–IL | 6,288 | 70. Colorado Springs, CO | 3,300 | 103. North Woods–Land O'Lakes, WI | 700 |
| 35. Memphis, TN–AR–MS | 6,200 | 70. Lake of the Ozarks, MO | 3,300 | 104. Flaming Gorge, UT–WY–CO | 600 |
| 36. Green Mountains, VT | 6,100 | | | 105. Rangeley Lakes, ME | 400 |
| | | | | 106. Hilton Head, SC | 200 |
| | | | | 107. Jersey Shore, NJ | 61 |

## Vacation Places Listed Alphabetically

| Vacation Place | Places Rated Rank | | Places Rated Rank | | Places Rated Score | | Places Rated Rank | Places Rated Score |
|---|---|---|---|---|---|---|---|---|
| Adirondack Mountains, NY | 53 | | Hawaii | 24 | | Phoenix–Valley of the Sun, AZ | 65 |
| Albuquerque–Santa Fe–Taos, NM | 25 | | Hilton Head, SC | 106 | | Pocono Mountains, PA | 45 |
| Anchorage–Kenai Peninsula, AK | 59 | | Holland–Lake Michigan Shore, MI | 27 | | Portland, ME | 28 |
| Asheville–Smoky Mountains, NC | 83 | | | | | | |
| Aspen–Vail, CO | 98 | | Houston–Galveston, TX | 18 | | Portland–Columbia River, OR | 32 |
| | | | Jersey Shore, NJ | 107 | | Portsmouth–Kennebunk, NH–ME | 67 |
| Atlanta, GA | 38 | | Knoxville–Smoky Mountains, TN | 42 | | Providence–Newport, RI | 51 |
| Atlantic City, NJ | 92 | | Lake of the Ozarks, MO | 70 | | Put-in-Bay–Lake Erie Shore, OH | 58 |
| Austin–Hill Country, TX | 78 | | Lake Powell–Glen Canyon, AZ–UT | 68 | | Rangeley Lakes, ME | 105 |
| Baltimore–Chesapeake Bay, MD | 30 | | | | | | |
| Bar Harbor–Acadia, ME | 49 | | Lake Tahoe–Reno, NV–CA | 88 | | Redwoods–Shasta–Lassen, CA | 88 |
| | | | Las Vegas–Lake Mead, NV–AZ | 80 | | Richmond–Fredericksburg, VA | 72 |
| Bend–Cascade Mountains, OR | 98 | | Lexington–Bluegrass Country, KY | 12 | | Sacramento–Gold Rush Towns, CA | 61 |
| Berkshire Hills–Pioneer Valley, MA | 51 | | Long Island, NY | 15 | | St. Augustine–Northeast Coast, FL | 33 |
| Black Hills, SD | 62 | | Los Angeles, CA | 2 | | St. Louis–Mark Twain Country, MO–IL | 34 |
| Blue Ridge Mountains, VA | 82 | | | | | | |
| Boise–Sun Valley, ID | 100 | | Mackinac Island–Sault Ste. Marie, MI | 74 | | Salt Lake City, UT | 43 |
| | | | Memphis, TN–AR–MS | 35 | | San Antonio, TX | 48 |
| Boone–High Country, NC | 100 | | Miami–Gold Coast–Keys, FL | 7 | | San Diego, CA | 16 |
| Boston, MA | 4 | | Minneapolis–St. Paul, MN–WI | 14 | | San Francisco, CA | 5 |
| Brownsville–Rio Grande Valley, TX | 87 | | Mobile Bay–Gulfport, AL–MS | 81 | | Santa Barbara–San Simeon, CA | 54 |
| Cape Cod–The Islands, MA | 79 | | | | | | |
| Catskill Mountains, NY | 41 | | Monterey–Big Sur, CA | 17 | | Savannah–Golden Isles, GA | 66 |
| | | | Myrtle Beach–Grand Strand, SC | 88 | | Seattle–Mount Rainier–North Cascades, WA | 8 |
| Charleston, SC | 75 | | Mystic Seaport–Connecticut Valley, CT | 11 | | Spokane–Coeur d'Alene, WA–ID | 64 |
| Chattanooga–Huntsville, TN–AL–GA | 73 | | Nashville, TN | 47 | | Tampa Bay–Southwest Coast, FL | 9 |
| Chicago, IL | 10 | | New Orleans, LA | 40 | | Traverse City–Petoskey, MI | 76 |
| Cincinnati, OH–KY | 23 | | | | | | |
| Colorado Springs, CO | 70 | | New York City, NY | 1 | | Tucson, AZ | 44 |
| | | | Niagara Falls–Western New York, NY | 20 | | Tulsa–Lake O' The Cherokees, OK | 39 |
| Coos Bay–South Coast, OR | 100 | | North Woods–Land O'Lakes, WI | 103 | | Vicksburg–Natchez–Baton Rouge, MS–LA | 69 |
| Corpus Christi–Padre Island, TX | 59 | | Oklahoma City–Cherokee Strip, OK | 46 | | Washington, DC–MD–VA | 3 |
| Crater Lake–Klamath Falls, OR | 84 | | Olympic Peninsula, WA | 84 | | White Mountains, NH | 55 |
| Dallas–Fort Worth, TX | 13 | | | | | | |
| Denver–Rocky Mountain National Park, CO | 29 | | Orlando–Space Coast, FL | 19 | | Williamsburg–Colonial Triangle, VA | 22 |
| | | | Outer Banks, NC | 95 | | Wilmington–Cape Fear, NC | 86 |
| Door County, WI | 97 | | Ozarks–Eureka Springs, AR–MO | 55 | | Wine Country, CA | 57 |
| Eastern Shore, VA | 96 | | Palm Springs–Desert Playgrounds, CA | 31 | | Wisconsin Dells, WI | 37 |
| Finger Lakes, NY | 26 | | Panhandle, FL | 93 | | Yellowstone–Jackson–Tetons, WY–ID–MT | 49 |
| Flaming Gorge, UT–WY–CO | 104 | | | | | | |
| Glacier National Park–Flathead Lake, MT | 88 | | Pennsylvania Dutch Country, PA | 21 | | Yosemite–Sequoia–Death Valley, CA | 76 |
| | | | Philadelphia, PA–DE–NJ | 6 | | Zion–Bryce Canyon, UT | 93 |
| Grand Canyon Country, AZ | 62 | | | | | | |
| Green Mountains, VT | 36 | | | | | | |

# TOP TEN: Feeding the Mind and Spirit

Unlike the distribution of the highest-scoring Vacation Places in some of the other chapters, in which one part of the United States dominates the top ten, the highest scorers in this chapter are distributed across the country. Six are scattered down the East Coast, from Boston to Miami and Tampa; Chicago represents the center of the country; the western cities of Seattle, San Francisco, and Los Angeles are the other three. Not surprisingly, large metro areas claim the leading ranks, as urban areas are where investment money for the arts and sciences is usually more readily available.

|  | Places Rated Score |
|---|---|
| 1. New York City, NY | 28,603 |
| 2. Los Angeles, CA | 23,653 |
| 3. Washington, DC–MD–VA | 20,203 |
| 4. Boston, MA | 18,025 |
| 5. San Francisco, CA | 17,961 |
| 6. Philadelphia, PA–DE–NJ | 17,455 |
| 7. Miami–Gold Coast–Keys, FL | 15,915 |
| 8. Seattle–Mount Rainier–North Cascades, WA | 12,925 |
| 9. Tampa Bay–Southwest Coast, FL | 11,643 |
| 10. Chicago, IL | 11,009 |

## 1. New York City, NY

New York's first-place position in the number, size, and appeal of its 47 qualifying museums is the major component of its total score in this chapter. In addition, this Vacation Place is among the top ten in all categories: its botanic gardens rank sixth; its planetariums, seventh; and its special attractions, tenth. Sightseers in the Big Apple enjoy the views from observation decks atop its tallest buildings, the World Trade Center and the Empire State Building; boat rides to Staten Island, the Statue of Liberty, and around Manhattan Island; and a variety of sightseeing bus tours. New York City is a good place for sightseeing on foot; many of its major points of interest are in central Manhattan and within walking distance of one another. Others can easily be reached by public transportation. First-time or infrequent visitors will find it well worthwhile to stop at the information center of the New York Convention and Visitors Bureau at 2 Columbus Circle to pick up free maps and other information about sightseeing in the city.

## 2. Los Angeles, CA

Los Angeles is a much younger city than those on the East Coast; it was incorporated as a city in 1850, and at the turn of this century it had only 100,000 inhabitants. By 1920 the number of residents had grown to half a million, and by the mid-1980s its population had surpassed that of Chicago, making it the second largest city in the United States. The list of attractions that makes it an important tourist city has kept pace with its growth. It ranks first among Vacation Places in its special attractions, with many one-of-a-kind places to see. One of its major attractions is the movie industry, and the tour of Universal Studios is among the most popular of the many unusual sightseeing tours available in the area. Unlike New York City, where most, though not all, of the important points of interest are in the central part of the city, the attractions of Los Angeles are spread to many outlying areas. Among the most important of these are Hollywood, Pasadena, and Long Beach. The Los Angeles area ranks fourth for its botanic gardens and for its museums, fifth for its zoos.

## 3. Washington, DC–MD–VA

Washington ranks first in the chapter that covers historic sightseeing, and its high ranks for other types of museums and special attractions are proof that there is a great deal more to be seen here as well. Its many botanic gardens are spectacular; only Philadelphia garners more points in this category. The Washington area's planetariums rank first; its museums, fifth; and its special attractions, sixth. Its National Zoological Park is world famous; its many museums filled with collections of paintings, sculpture, decorative arts, and ethnic arts are among the finest in any country. The Smithsonian Institution consists of several museums, each of them first class; among the most popular is the National Air and Space Museum. Among the most photographed sites in the nation are Washington's three presidential shrines: the Jefferson, Lincoln, and Washington memorials.

## 4. Boston, MA

Second only to New York in museums, Boston also places sixth among the 107 Vacation Places for planetariums and tenth for zoos. Some of the oldest museum collections in the country are in or near Boston. Its many educational institutions have contributed to the richness of the area's art and science exhibits. Harvard's Peabody Museum of Archaeology and Ethnology in Cambridge has collections of early Mexican and Native American artistic achievements that are second to none in the United States. There is a huge collection of museum-quality art in the Boston Public Library. A most unusual exhibit is the Mapparium in Boston's Christian Science Center, where visitors can walk through a huge globe that replicates the earth. The continents and seas are represented on the inside of the globe, and the view from the earth's center affords a uniquely graphic idea of geographic relationships.

## 5. San Francisco, CA

San Francisco's rank for zoos is fourth, fifth for special attractions, seventh for botanic gardens, and tied for seventh for planetariums. Two of its most unusual special attractions are the Chinese Culture Center and the Japan Center, where galleries of Oriental arts are complemented by gift shops, restaurants, and ethnic entertainment. Other Oriental exhibits are in the Asian Art Museum. Cable-car rides and visits to Fisherman's Wharf and to Golden Gate Park are traditional musts for San Francisco's visitors.

## 6. Philadelphia, PA–DE–NJ

Fourteen qualifying botanic gardens earned 1,255 points for Philadelphia, first of all Vacation Places for this category. It ranks third for museums, following New York and Boston. Specialized museum collections in the Philadelphia area include ceramics, toys, films, gems, and automobiles. The University Museum has extensive and breathtaking collections from all the continents; touring its Egyptology collection is almost like a trip to the museums and tombs along the Nile.

## 7. Miami–Gold Coast–Keys, FL

The Miami area finished second for special attractions, third for planetariums, and ninth for museums. Among its unusual museums are the Morikami Museum of Japanese Culture at Delray Beach, bequeathed to the city by the last survivor of a colony of Japanese pineapple growers, and the International Swimming Hall of Fame at Fort Lauderdale. The Norton Gallery in West Palm Beach is a fine small art museum. Popular special attractions in the area include Orchid Jungle, Coral Castle, Monkey Jungle, and Planet Ocean.

## 8. Seattle–Mount Rainier–North Cascades, WA

This northwestern city is tied with San Diego for first place in zoos and ranks ninth for its special attractions. There is a good variety of museums, including the Whale Museum, the Museum of Flight, and the Puget Sound Railroad Museum, along with the more usual art, science, and natural-history collections. Visitors can tour the Boeing plant, a tree nursery, a winery, and breweries.

## 9. Tampa Bay–Southwest Coast, FL

The Tampa area ranks third for special attractions and ninth for botanic gardens, which represent many widely differing kinds of vegetation. The Suncoast Seabird Sanctuary in Indian Shores is an open-air refuge and hospital for injured birds, especially peli-

---

### Author's Favorites

**Aquariums**
National Aquarium, Baltimore, MD
Sea World of Florida, Orlando, FL

**Art Museums**
The Art Institute of Chicago, Chicago, IL
The Corcoran Gallery of Art, Washington, DC
Metropolitan Museum of Art, New York, NY
National Gallery of Art—Smithsonian, Washington, DC

**Botanic Gardens**
Arizona–Sonora Desert Museum, Tucson, AZ
Brookgreen Gardens, Murrells Inlet, SC
Callaway Gardens, Pine Mountain, GA
Japanese Garden, Washington Park, Portland, OR

**Children's Museums**
Children's Museum, Indianapolis, IN

**General Museums**
Memphis Pink Palace Museum, Memphis, TN
Tennessee State Museum, Nashville, TN

**Natural History Museums**
Museum of Northern Arizona, Flagstaff, AZ
Peabody Museum of Archaeology and Ethnology, Cambridge, MA
The University Museum, University of Pennsylvania, Philadelphia, PA

**Science Museums**
Museum of Science and Industry, Chicago, IL

**Sightseeing Tours**
Conch Train tour, Key West, FL
Cruises on Lake Michigan, Chicago, IL
Sightseeing bus tours, Anchorage, AK
Sightseeing bus tours, New Orleans, LA

**Small Museums**
The College Museum, Hampton Institute, Hampton, VA
The Heard Museum, Phoenix, AZ

**Specialized Museums**
North Carolina Maritime Museum, Beaufort, NC
Western Forestry Center, Portland, OR

**Zoos**
Busch Gardens, Tampa, FL
Lincoln Park Zoological Park, Chicago, IL
San Diego Zoo, San Diego, CA

---

cans, that is worth a visit. Ybor City, a neighborhood settled in the 19th century by Cuban cigar makers, is a charming and interesting area. Circus fans find the Museum of the Circus in Sarasota fascinating.

## 10. Chicago, IL

Chicago ranks third among the Vacation Places for zoos and fifth for botanic gardens. In addition, four of its museums received the *Places Rated* AA rating and were accredited; thus they received the maximum score. They are The Art Institute of Chicago, the Field Museum of Natural History, the Museum of Contemporary Art, and the Museum of Science and Industry.

# Entertainment for All

Family Parks, Performing Arts, Spectator Sports, and Special Events

# INTRODUCTION: Entertainment for All

"Build a better mousetrap, and the world will beat a path to your door," your teachers have told you. But who has ever heard of a big-time mousetrap builder? Entertainers are far more likely to find fame and fortune.

Take Walt Disney, for example. He didn't invent a new mousetrap, he invented a new mouse. And today, two decades after his death, his name is known everywhere and the world is still beating a path to the doors of Disneyland, Walt Disney World, and theaters showing Disney movies.

The Disney name is a giant in the field of entertainment; not many can match Disney's record of successes. But those who entertain the public well certainly do earn a place in history. Phineas T. Barnum and John Ringling, Cecil B. deMille and Samuel Goldwyn, Buffalo Bill Cody, Elvis Presley and John Lennon; these names are at least as familiar to millions of people as those of prominent political personalities.

Specific fashions in entertainment and leisure-time activities are notoriously transient and difficult to forecast. "In a nutshell," reported Standard & Poors in an industry survey of leisure time published in late 1984, "it is impossible to predict the popularity or longevity of the fads or trends to which most of this industry is subject."

The popularity of movies has its ups and downs—right now it appears to be on an upswing, despite booming cable television and videocassette-recorder sales. The number of motion-picture screens in the United States has steadily increased over the past dozen years; there are now more than 18,000. Nearly 2 billion movie tickets were sold in 1983. Going to the movies is an activity many vacationers enjoy and take for granted; however, since motion-picture theaters are available nearly everywhere (except in the most remote and sparsely populated spots), the cinema is not a type of entertainment that has an important effect on the choice of a vacation destination.

The same thing is true for big-name, single-performance concerts. Today's most popular entertainers draw capacity crowds in large concert halls and arenas, and fans often travel long distances to see and hear them, but whole vacations are not normally planned around this type of entertainment.

When star-studded entertainment is coupled with casino gambling, however, the combined appeal is powerful. Thousands of vacationers flock to the few places in the United States—notably Atlantic City, Las Vegas, and the Reno–Lake Tahoe area—that offer both attractions. Casino gambling rakes in even more money than the movies; the total take of wagers minus payouts was around $5 billion in 1984.

## FROM CIRCUSES TO THEME PARKS

Fairs and circuses are two of the oldest types of popular entertainment, and they are the most important ancestors of modern forms of fun. Both have a history of thousands of years; they have changed a bit over the years, but many of the original features survive.

Fairs were originally gatherings where traders met to exchange their goods. Often the date chosen for a fair had a religious significance, and the word was derived from the Latin *feria*, meaning holiday (or holy day). Even rival clans and tribes agreed to truces in order to carry on trade, and the "fair ground" was regarded as a neutral zone.

Fairs and festivals were held in ancient Greece and Rome, in the Middle East and the Far East, in all of medieval Europe, and in pre-Columbian Mexico. Athletic competitions and other contests, shows, and various kinds of games created an atmosphere of entertainment to accompany the serious business that took place.

Circuses—complete with parades, races, competitions, and extravagant shows—also began in ancient Roman times, when huge arenas were built to seat the spectators. In the United States, circuses became a major form of entertainment in the 19th century.

Phineas T. Barnum organized his Greatest Show on Earth in 1871; at the time his was one of several major circuses that toured the cities and small towns of the United States. In 1907 the Ringling Brothers, who had been Barnum's chief competitors since 1884, bought the Barnum (by then the Barnum and Bailey) show and eventually merged the two into the Ringling Brothers and Barnum & Bailey Circus.

Since 1956 the circus has performed indoors. Gone are the huge tents and parades featuring dozens of gaily painted horse-drawn wagons. The circus doesn't go to small towns anymore. But along with the ancient fair, the circus has spawned many descendants: carnivals and rodeos, boardwalks and amusement parks, world expositions and modern theme parks all belong to the same venerable family. Carnivals and rodeos carry on the traveling tradition of the circus; boardwalks, amusement parks, and theme parks have been established in permanent locations; large, modern state fairs and a number of major expositions maintain the ancient tradition of fairs—they are held in the same fairgrounds at approximately the same season each year but are not year-round events.

The popularity of amusement parks in the United States developed simultaneously with that of such seaside resorts as Coney Island and Atlantic City.

## The 25 Most Popular Theme Parks

| Park (Opening Year) | Operating Schedule | Annual Visitors | Park (Opening Year) | Operating Schedule | Annual Visitors |
|---|---|---|---|---|---|
| 1. **Walt Disney World & Epcot Center** (1971)—Orlando, FL | 365 days | 12,560,000 | 14. **Opryland USA** (1972) Nashville, TN | 140 days | 2,290,000 |
| 2. **Disneyland** (1954) Anaheim, CA | 303 days | 10,420,000 | 15. **Six Flags Over Georgia** (1967)—Atlanta, GA | 148 days | 2,180,000 |
| 3. **Knott's Berry Farm** (1920) Buena Park, CA | 365 days | 4,000,000 | 16. **Busch Gardens—The Old Country** (1975) Williamsburg, VA | 137 days | 1,920,000 |
| 4. **Universal Studios Tour** (1964)—Los Angeles, CA | 365 days | 3,450,000 | 17. **Marriott's Great America** (1976)—Santa Clara, CA | 141 days | 1,760,000 |
| 5. **Busch Gardens—The Dark Continent** (1959)—Tampa, FL | 365 days | 3,080,000 | 18. **Astroworld** (1968) Houston, TX | 159 days | 1,660,000 |
| 6. **Sea World of Florida** (1973) Orlando, FL | 365 days | 3,000,000 | 19. **Hersheypark** (1907) Hershey, PA | 120 days | 1,480,000 |
| 7. **Six Flags Great Adventure** (1974)—Jackson, NJ | 163 days | 2,760,000 | 20. **Worlds of Fun** (1973) Kansas City, MO | 140 days | 1,400,000 |
| 8. **Cedar Point** (1960) Sandusky, OH | 119 days | 2,630,000 | 21. **Sea World of Ohio** (1970) Aurora, OH | 100 days | 1,170,000 |
| 9. **Kings Island** (1972) Cincinnati, OH | 126 days | 2,601,000 | 22. **Six Flags Over Mid-America** (1971)—St. Louis, MO | 140 days | 1,120,000 |
| 10. **Six Flags Magic Mountain** (1971)—Valencia, CA | 185 days | 2,570,000 | 23. **Carowinds** (1973) Charlotte, NC | 121 days | 1,113,000 |
| 11. **Sea World of California** (1964)—San Diego, CA | 365 days | 2,560,000 | 24. **Cypress Gardens** (1936) Winter Haven, FL | 365 days | 1,112,000 |
| 12. **Six Flags Great America** (1976)—Gurnee, IL | 120 days | 2,370,000 | 25. **Kings Dominion** (1975) Richmond, VA | 121 days | 1,011,000 |
| 13. **Six Flags Over Texas** (1961) Arlington, TX | 146 days | 2,330,000 | | | |

Source: Kings Entertainment Company, 1984, and Merrill Lynch, *Theme Park Industry Survey*, 1983.

Vendors and entertainers followed the crowds in search of customers, and various kinds of rides were built for amusement. As the emphasis turned more and more to the rides, the parks became known within the industry as iron parks. The carousel, or merry-go-round, was imported to this country from Europe, where it was invented in the late 1700s or early 1800s. Another popular ride, the Ferris wheel, was invented for use at the World's Columbian Exposition in Chicago in 1893. Soon rides proliferated to include everything from slow and gentle kiddie cars to wild and thrilling contraptions that gave the riders sudden breathtaking drops through space and hurtled them around in whip-cracking spins.

When Walt Disney established Disneyland in Anaheim, California, he created a new type of family entertainment center. Amusement parks before that had a somewhat unsavory reputation—they were known for hard-sell hawkers selling cheap merchandise, con men and shills ready to take advantage of unwary customers, tawdry sideshows displaying unfortunate humans as freaks, and a generally unsanitary atmosphere. Disneyland, on the other hand, emphasized cleanliness; courtesy; wholesomeness; and high-quality food, merchandise, and entertainment. Especially entertainment—all the singers, danc-

ers, and other performers were professionals of Hollywood-level skill. The rides were still there—taller, more thrilling, more elaborately conceived than ever—but the emphasis was, and still is, entertainment, or show business. An illustration of this philosophy is this: no one is "hired" to work at a Disney park; all employees are "cast" for certain roles—including those who work behind the food counters or usher customers on and off the rides.

The popularity of Disneyland and its successor, Walt Disney World, has sparked many variations of theme parks. These two are still the pacesetters; they are the most popular commercial tourist attractions in the world. Some two dozen other major theme parks have followed their lead. Knott's Berry Farm, in Buena Park, California; Hersheypark, in Hershey, Pennsylvania; and Cypress Gardens, in Winter Haven, Florida, had been around for quite a while before Disneyland, but their focus and format changed with Disney's success; they too began to market themselves as theme parks.

Busch Gardens, in Tampa, Florida, and Williamsburg, Virginia, concentrate heavily on two themes—travel and animals. The Florida park has an African theme, and its collection of exotic animals makes it one of the leading zoos in the country as well as a premiere theme park; Williamsburg's theme is European travel. Three of the country's most popular theme parks are also oceanariums: Sea World of Florida, Sea World of California, and Sea World of Ohio.

Opryland USA, in Nashville, Tennessee, took a slightly different tack. Based on the huge, fantastic, long-lasting loyalty of fans to the Grand Ole Opry show produced in Nashville, Opryland USA was created as a theme park with a concentration on live entertainment that even exceeded that of its predecessors.

Walt Disney started an important trend when he established Disneyland in 1954; theme parks still have hot-dog, popcorn, and ice-cream stands, but today they also have health-food stands and salad bars, sit-down restaurants featuring floor shows, and beer gardens with oompah bands. They are no longer thought of as spots where local and summer residents go for a pleasant day's outing; they have become an important part of the leisure-time industry, and they have a major impact on vacation decision making.

## SPECTATOR SPORTS

Athletic contests performed for the enjoyment of spectators are another branch of the venerable fair-circus family. Today's chariot races are performed on auto racetracks; today's versions of jousting tournaments are games played by teams of people in padded uniforms struggling for possession of a ball or puck.

### Racing

Major racing contests in 20th-century America are Thoroughbred, harness, greyhound, and auto races; betting on the outcome is a prime ingredient of the excitement for most spectators.

There are many times more racetracks for auto racing than for horse racing and greyhound racing; most of them are small, not sanctioned by one of the three national racing organizations, and largely of interest to local audiences only. On the other hand, such nationally known events as the Indianapolis 500, the Sebring, Florida, 12-hour race, and several of the annual racing events at Daytona Beach, Florida, draw spectators in the hundreds of thousands, many of whom have planned their vacations or long weekends to coincide with the event.

Horse racing also lures vacationers who go to races only rarely as well as more habitual racing fans. The three big events in horse racing, known as the Triple Crown, are the Kentucky Derby, in Louisville, Kentucky; the Preakness, run at Pimlico Race Course in Baltimore; and the Belmont Stakes, held at Belmont Park just outside Queens, New York.

Some racetracks are tourist attractions in themselves, and they are open to visitors at times when races are not being run. Churchill Downs, home of the Kentucky Derby, has museum exhibits related to the history of racing, the Derby, and the breeding of Thoroughbred horses. Hialeah Park, in the Miami metropolitan area, is a beautiful area with tropical gardens and a flamingo colony; a collection of carriages and stagecoaches is also on display.

Harness racing does not draw as many followers nationally as Thoroughbred racing, but there are harness tracks in 13 states, and in some areas—notably Delaware, Michigan, upstate New York, and the Chi-

### The Ten Most Popular Thoroughbred Tracks

|  | Average Daily Attendance | Average Bet |
|---|---|---|
| 1. Santa Anita Park (Arcadia, CA) | 32,013 | $163 |
| 2. Hollywood Park (Inglewood, CA) | 28,891 | 180 |
| 3. Saratoga (Saratoga Springs, NY) | 26,644 | 112 |
| 4. Oaklawn Jockey Club (Hot Springs, AR) | 23,271 | 129 |
| 5. Del Mar (Del Mar, CA) | 19,584 | 167 |
| 6. Belmont Park (Elmont, NY) | 19,530 | 177 |
| 7. Aqueduct (New York) | 14,749 | 204 |
| 8. Meadowlands (East Rutherford, NJ) | 14,233 | 151 |
| 9. Gulfstream Park (Hallandale, FL) | 14,074 | 151 |
| 10. Ak-Sar-Ben (Omaha) | 13,655 | 118 |

Source: Daily Racing Form, March 26, 1984, and Thoroughbred Racing Associations of North America, Inc., Directory and Record Book, 1984.

### The Ten Most Popular Harness Tracks

|  | Average Daily Attendance | Average Bet |
|---|---|---|
| 1. Meadowlands (East Rutherford, NJ) | 16,010 | $145 |
| 2. Sportsman's Park (Cicero, IL) | 8,988 | 132 |
| 3. Roosevelt Raceway (Westbury, NY) | 7,873 | 168 |
| 4. Hollywood Park (Inglewood, CA) | 7,805 | 127 |
| 5. Hawthorne (Cicero, IL) | 7,179 | 150 |
| 6. Yonkers Raceway (Yonkers, NY) | 6,441 | 204 |
| 7. Maywood Park (Maywood, IL) | 6,135 | 139 |
| 8. Los Alamitos (Cypress, CA) | 5,499 | 150 |
| 9. Pompano Park (Pompano Beach, FL) | 5,492 | 88 |
| 10. Hazel Park (Hazel Park, MI) | 5,200 | 140 |

Source: U.S. Trotting Association, Trotting and Pacing Guide, 1984.

### The Ten Most Popular Greyhound Tracks

|  | Average Daily Attendance | Average Bet |
|---|---|---|
| 1. Wonderland (Revere, MA) | 1,247,653 | $119 |
| 2. Southland Greyhound Park (West Memphis, AR) | 1,189,108 | 108 |
| 3. Lincoln Greyhound Park (Lincoln, RI) | 1,159,070 | 101 |
| 4. St. Petersburg Kennel Club (St. Petersburg) | 1,045,078 | 92 |
| 5. Hollywood Greyhound Track (Hallandale, FL) | 1,043,201 | 108 |
| 6. Wheeling Downs Greyhound Park (Wheeling, WV) | 929,243 | 118 |
| 7. Plainfield Greyhound Park (Plainfield, CT) | 867,773 | 131 |
| 8. Biscayne Greyhound Park (Miami, FL) | 832,963 | 125 |
| 9. Tampa Greyhound Park (Tampa) | 749,318 | 114 |
| 10. Mobile Greyhound Park (Mobile) | 728,305 | 106 |

Source: American Greyhound Track Operators Association, Directory, 1984.

cago metro area—it is even more popular than Thoroughbred racing. State and local fairs often feature harness racing, usually without legalized betting.

Dog racing is a much younger spectator sport than horse racing; it has developed to its present form in the United States during the 20th century. There are 45 greyhound tracks in the United States.

## Team Sports

The popularity of all professional sports has increased greatly in the past few years. In 1983 more than 84 million tickets were sold to major-league baseball, basketball, football, soccer, and hockey games.

Avid baseball fans follow their favorite athletes to spring training; many a football devotee, if given the choice, would rather be given a season ticket than a raise in pay.

Golf and tennis tournaments are also becoming more important as spectator sports. Doubtless the list of popular athletic competitons will continue to grow in the future.

### Trends in Sports
#### Attendance in Thousands

|  | 1970 | 1980 | 1981 | 1982 | 1983 |
|---|---|---|---|---|---|
| Baseball (AL and NL) | 29,191 | 43,746 | 27,285* | 45,415 | 46,269 |
| Basketball (NBA) | 4,912 | 10,967 | 10,235 | 10,732 | 10,262 |
| Football (NFL) | 10,071 | 14,092 | 14,326 | 8,504* | 13,953 |
| Hockey (NHL) | 5,992 | 10,534 | 10,726 | 10,710 | 11,021 |
| Soccer (NASL) | n.a. | 6,194 | 5,429 | 3,251 | 2,675 |

Source: U.S. Bureau of the Census, *Statistical Abstract of the United States: 1985.*

*Season was interrupted by strike.

---

### Which Sports Have the Largest Attendance?

In 1983, according to the statistics reported in this table, horse racing was still the most popular spectator sport in America. However, the figures include major-league baseball attendance only. If minor-league games had been included, the picture would have been different. *Business Week* reported, ". . . the sport of kings [horse racing] no longer is the king of sports. Last year [1983], baseball unseated it as America's best attended spectator sport."

|  | Yearly Attendance (in thousands) |
|---|---|
| 1. Horse racing | 75,693 |
| 2. Baseball | 46,269 |
| 3. Football, college | 36,302 |
| 4. Basketball, college | 31,471 |
| 5. Greyhound racing | 22,140 |
| 6. Football, National League | 13,953 |
| 7. Hockey, National League | 12,027 |
| 8. Basketball, professional | 10,262 |
| 9. Soccer, North American League | 2,675 |

Source: U.S. Bureau of the Census, *Statistical Abstract of the United States: 1985.*

Figures reflect 1983 data.

---

## MUSIC

Symphony orchestras and opera companies sell fewer tickets annually than do the major spectator sports— horse racing, baseball, football, and basketball—but the growth in popularity of these musical events has been phenomenal in recent years. Symphony concerts attracted a total audience of some 22 million in 1983— an increase of 73 percent over 1970 figures. The increase in opera attendance is even more impressive: 12.7 million in 1983—176 percent more than 1970's total of 4.6 million.

Major summer music festivals draw huge crowds every year.

The Boston Symphony Orchestra performs from late June to late August each year at the Berkshire Music Festival at Tanglewood, Lenox, Massachusetts. In Highland Park, Illinois, north of Chicago, the Chicago Symphony Orchestra and other artists give concerts all summer (late June to mid-September) at the Ravinia Festival. Interlochen, Michigan, is the home of the National Music Camp, where talented students and guest professionals present programs from late June to late August. The Minnesota Orchestra gives an annual concert series in connection with Somerfest, in July and August, on the mall in downtown Minneapolis. In Hollywood, the Los Angeles Philharmonic presents "Symphony Under the Stars" at the Hollywood Bowl, a program of several concerts a week from July 4 to September. Daily chamber music and orchestral concerts are given during July and August at the Aspen Music Festival and School in Aspen, Colorado. These are some of the most renowned, but they are only a sample of hundreds of alfresco musical programs enjoyed throughout the country.

Operas have been performed in the United States since the 1700s. New York City is the most important opera center, and the Metropolitan is the premiere opera company, but nationwide there are about 130 opera companies with annual budgets of more than $100,000. There are a number of delightful outdoor settings for summer opera performances; one of the most prominent is Wolf Trap Farm Park in Vienna, Virginia.

Other types of music draw fans to countless festivals throughout the country. Bluegrass, country and western, folk, and Cajun concerts and festivals abound in Arkansas, Tennessee, Kentucky, and Virginia, but these types of music are also heard and celebrated in many other areas—from Maine to California. The sounds of jazz, ragtime, blues, and rhythm and blues echo up and down the Mississippi River as well as in New York City and elsewhere.

## THEATER

Tell a friend you are going to New York City for a vacation, and nine times out of ten you'll be asked, Are you going to see any shows? If your destination is Cape Cod or the coast of Maine and your friend has been there before you, the subject of summer theater will probably arise.

These are the traditional theater centers, but residents of Chicago, Minneapolis, and Los Angeles are quick to brag about the extent, variety, and artistic innovation of the theaters of their cities.

The Actors Theatre of Louisville, Kentucky, is proud of the work it does in introducing the plays of new writers. The Oregon Shakespeare Festival in Ashland, Oregon, is world famous for its performances of the works of the Bard. In the Berkshire Hills of Massachusetts, the Williamstown Theatre Festival enjoys a reputation that brings many of the biggest stars of stage, screen, and television to perform there each summer.

In the Black Hills of South Dakota, vacationers can choose among several productions put on each summer—a Passion play, a couple of melodramas, and a historical drama—or they can enjoy them all.

## SPECIAL EVENTS

The variety of festivals and special events, found not only in popular vacation destinations but in virtually every nook and cranny of every state, is nearly infinite. Almost every known crop—from watermelons to popcorn—is celebrated with a harvest festival. Churches, colleges, charitable organizations, and municipalities all seize on the idea of a fair as a method of raising money while publicizing their causes and promoting fun and friendship. Can you think of a historic event we can commemorate with an anniversary party? Let's have a festival. Interested in arts and crafts? Arts and crafts fairs always go over well.

For local color, for a good sense of what a certain part of the country is really all about, vacationers should take part in these festivities. From sugaring-off parties (to celebrate the maple-syrup crop) in New England to logrolling contests in Washington and Oregon; from Mexican fiestas in Arizona and Texas to a pirate invasion in Tampa, Florida—festivals represent some of the best of Americana.

---

### Major U.S. Symphony Orchestras

Vacation trips or long weekends are often planned around special entertainment events and opportunities to see certain star performers in person.

Symphony fans may be, on average, a little older, a bit more affluent, or a tinge more conservative than fans of leading rock stars, but they are no less enthusiastic. Symphony buffs are just as thrilled to meet, talk with, and get the autographs of their favorite conductors as any other groupies.

Following is a list of the major (based on annual income or budget) U.S. symphony orchestras and their current music directors.

| | |
|---|---|
| Atlanta Symphony (GA) | Robert Shaw |
| Baltimore Symphony (MD) | David Zinman |
| Boston Symphony (MA) | Seiji Ozawa |
| Buffalo Philharmonic (NY) | Semyon Bychkov |
| Chicago Symphony (IL) | Georg Solti |
| Cincinnati Symphony (OH) | Michael Gielen |
| Cleveland Orchestra (OH) | Christoph von Dohnányi |
| Dallas Symphony (TX) | Eduardo Mata |
| Denver Symphony (CO) | Gaetano Delogu |
| Detroit Symphony (MI) | Gunther Herbig |
| Houston Symphony (TX) | Sergiu Comissiona |
| Indianapolis Symphony (IN) | John Nelson |
| Los Angeles Philharmonic (CA) | André Previn |
| Milwaukee Symphony (WI) | Lukas Foss |
| Minnesota Orchestra (Minneapolis) | Neville Marriner |
| National Symphony (Washington, DC) | Mstislav Rostropovich |
| New Orleans Philharmonic Symphony Orchestra (LA) | Maxim Shostakovich |
| New York Philharmonic (New York City) | Zubin Mehta |
| Oregon Symphony (Portland) | James DePreist |
| Philadelphia Orchestra (PA) | Ricardo Muti |
| Pittsburgh Symphony (PA) | Lorin Maazel |
| Rochester Philharmonic (NY) | Jerzy Semkow |
| St. Louis Symphony (MO) | Leonard Slatkin |
| St. Paul Chamber Orchestra (MN) | Pinchas Zukerman |
| San Antonio Symphony (TX) | Vacant |
| San Diego Symphony (CA) | David Atherton |
| San Francisco Symphony (CA) | Herbert Blomstedt |
| Seattle Symphony (WA) | Gerard Schwarz |
| Syracuse Symphony (NY) | Kazuyoshi Akiyama |
| Utah Symphony (Salt Lake City) | Joseph Silverstein |

*Source:* American Symphony Orchestra League.

# SCORING: Entertainment for All

Entertainment is often an important factor in the choice of a vacation destination, and frequently the type of entertainment that leads the vacationer to choose one destination over another is something not easily available during nonvacation periods at home. Watching television and going to movies may be the diversions you enjoy most frequently during the rest of the year, but the availability of movie theaters and television sets probably doesn't even occur to you when you are planning your vacation.

The forms of entertainment listed in the Place Profiles and used as factors in scoring are popular with vacationers and often have an influence on the choice of where to go. Baseball fans in the family want to follow their home team to the spring-training grounds; theater buffs are anxious to see several first-run plays; young children in a family are clamoring to visit a famous theme park; country music fans want to see a live performance of Grand Ole Opry.

The four categories of entertainment used as factors were Family Entertainment Parks, Music and Theater, Professional Sports, and Special Annual Events. In addition, a few Vacation Places received bonus points for unusual and outstanding entertainment opportunities not covered in those classifications. These categories are by no means a complete inventory of entertainment facilities in any location, but they are indicative of the importance any Vacation Place has in the world of entertainment.

As in other chapters, certain attractions nearby but not precisely within the area defined as the Vacation Place are printed in italics in the Place Profiles. These were included because they are easily accessible and have a wide appeal that makes them worth a short side trip; they were given one-half the point score of listings within the Vacation Place boundaries.

## Family Entertainment Parks

Major theme parks draw visitors from a wide geographic area. In many cases the choice of a vacation spot is based at least partially on the presence of one of the huge modern theme parks, such as Disney World, Busch Gardens, or Knott's Berry Farm. And a few minutes of people-watching at one of these major attractions demonstrate that the appeal is not just for children. Gray hair is seen as commonly as blond or black. Honeymooners are drawn to the theme parks along with teenagers.

The International Association of Amusement Parks and Attractions publishes an annual directory of parks, which lists information about the number of major rides, kiddie rides, water-oriented rides, games,

restaurants, and other features. These data were used in scoring family entertainment parks; the more a park had to offer, the higher the score. A small amusement pier or kiddie park may keep some members of a family occupied for a couple of hours, while a major theme park, appealing to all ages, can be enjoyed for two or three days.

Theme parks drawing an average annual attendance of 1 million or more were given 700 points each. All of these parks draw a national (actually an international) audience and are based on a central theme that is played upon throughout the park. The entertainment includes both strolling performances and stage shows; sit-down restaurants are available as well as fast-food outlets; and there are major shopping areas. In several cases the parks have zoos or oceanariums and trained animal or bird acts in addition to the other attractions. And of course there are numerous major rides.

Smaller theme parks and amusement parks with both major rides and kiddie rides received 500 points. Parks designated kiddie parks, waterparks, and amusement piers were given 200 points.

Waterparks are a fairly new type of amusement park. As the name implies, the emphasis is on activities in water. The parks have wave pools, water slides, water-oriented rides, and swimming areas.

### Top Ten for Family Entertainment Parks

| | Parks | Points |
|---|---|---|
| 1. Los Angeles, CA | 4 | 2,800 |
| 2. Atlantic City, NJ | 6 | 2,100 |
| 2. Orlando–Space Coast, FL | 3 | 2,100 |
| 4. Cincinnati, OH–KY | 4 | 1,900 |
| 5. Chicago, IL | 5 | 1,800 |
| 5. Jersey Shore, NJ | 5 | 1,800 |
| 7. Pocono Mountains, PA | 4 | 1,700 |
| 7. Portsmouth–Kennebunk, NH–ME | 4 | 1,700 |
| 9. Ozarks–Eureka Springs, AR–MO | 3 | 1,500 |
| 9. Philadelphia, PA–DE–NJ | 3 | 1,500 |

Of the 107 Vacation Places, about 60 had one or more family entertainment parks. Los Angeles topped the list; its four major parks each earned a score of 700 points. This is the only Vacation Place among the top ten that is in a western state. Atlantic City, with three 500-point parks and three at 200, tied for second place with Orlando, with its three major parks.

## Music and Theater

Music and theater are major attractions for vacationers and weekenders. Summer theaters and summer music festivals flourish in resort areas. Major orchestras, opera companies, and repertory theaters with substantial budgets and good-sized annual attendances are listed in the Place Profiles. Scoring was based on the assumption that in general larger companies with larger budgets have the means to hire the best artists and stage the most impressive performances. The best-known theaters attract the largest audiences and are most apt to have an influence on decisions about vacations.

Point scores were calculated as follows: the top score of 400 points was given to orchestras with annual budgets of $900,000 or more; opera companies with annual budgets of $1 million or more; major, nationally known summer music festivals; and repertory theater companies with an annual attendance of more than 100,000.

The next class, at 200 points, included orchestras whose budgets were between $250,000 and $900,000; opera companies with budgets between $500,000 and $1 million; summer music festivals not quite so well known nationally as those above but held for a period longer than two weeks; repertory theater companies with an annual attendance between 40,000 and 100,000; summer theaters, regularly presented historical dramas, and Passion plays.

Receiving 100 points each were orchestras with annual budgets between $115,000 and $250,000; opera companies with budgets between $100,000 and $500,000; and repertory companies with an annual attendance of fewer than 40,000.

**Top Ten for Music and Theater**

| | Companies | Points |
|---|---|---|
| 1. New York City, NY | 56 | 10,400 |
| 2. Boston, MA | 16 | 3,700 |
| 3. Chicago, IL | 16 | 3,400 |
| 4. Catskill Mountains, NY | 16 | 3,300 |
| 5. Los Angeles, CA | 15 | 3,200 |
| 6. Berkshire Hills–Pioneer Valley, MA | 12 | 3,000 |
| 7. Philadelphia, PA–DE–NJ | 13 | 2,800 |
| 7. San Francisco, CA | 12 | 2,800 |
| 9. Minneapolis–St. Paul, MN–WI | 8 | 2,400 |
| 10. Washington, DC–MD–VA | 9 | 2,300 |

About 90 of the 107 Vacation Places had at least one music or theater company. New York City lived up to its reputation as an entertainment center; it topped the list with more than twice as high a score as Boston, which finished second. Six of the top ten scorers were in the East, two in the Midwest, and two in California.

## Professional Sports

Major-league sports teams draw big crowds of both local residents and out-of-towners wherever they play. People plan for weeks ahead to travel to see their favorites play; when tickets are particularly hard to get the planning is months, not just weeks. Avid fans travel south in late winter to watch baseball teams in spring training.

Professional teams were awarded either 400 or 300 points: 400 for the presence of an American League or National League baseball team, National Football League team, or National Basketball Association team; 300 points for Major Indoor Soccer League, National Hockey League, or North American Soccer League team, or major-league baseball spring-training location. This allocation of scores was determined after several conferences with sports writers and fans and represents the consensus that those teams scored at 400 points have somewhat more appeal for vacationers, whether or not they attract more fans year-round, than those scored at 300 points.

About 30 of the 107 Vacation Places had one or more major-league teams. Of the top ten, New York City placed first, with 3,250 points, followed by the Tampa Bay area with 3,100. Five Vacation Places tied for seventh place. All sections of the country were represented.

**Top Eleven for Professional Sports**

| | Teams | Points |
|---|---|---|
| 1. New York City, NY | 10 | 3,250 |
| 2. Tampa Bay–Southwest Coast, FL | 10 | 3,100 |
| 3. Los Angeles, CA | 8 | 3,000 |
| 4. Chicago, IL | 6 | 2,200 |
| 5. Phoenix–Valley of the Sun, AZ | 7 | 2,050 |
| 6. Miami–Gold Coast–Keys, FL | 6 | 1,900 |
| 7. Boston, MA | 4 | 1,500 |
| 7. Dallas–Fort Worth, TX | 4 | 1,500 |
| 7. Orlando–Space Coast, FL | 5 | 1,500 |
| 7. Philadelphia, PA–DE–NJ | 4 | 1,500 |
| 7. Seattle–Mount Rainier–North Cascades, WA | 4 | 1,500 |

## Special Annual Events

Every Vacation Place has at least one special annual event that draws crowds. Some are of interest primarily to area residents; some are enjoyed by vacationers as well; some are of such importance that people come from long distances just to attend the event.

The American Bus Association has for the past few years published a list of the Top 100 Events in North America. The organization represents approximately 1,000 intercity bus carriers, some of which are among the nation's largest producers of chartered and packaged vacation tours. Nominations of events are submitted to a committee which acts as a panel of judges.

A few events, such as Mardi Gras in New Orleans and the Rose Bowl Parade and game in Pasadena, have been given permanent status by the association as *annual super events*.

Because this group has a unique opportunity to examine the merits of the most popular and impressive events in North America, its lists were used in scoring, as follows: annual super events were given 300 points; events listed in 1984 or 1985 received 150 points. Other nationally known celebrations and state fairs also received 150 points; annual football bowl games not named by the association, rodeos, and unique festivals of general interest were given 100 points. A few events that were primarily of local interest were listed and given 50 points; these were celebrations that reflected local color and heritage and were considered well worth visiting.

### Top Eleven for Special Annual Events

| | Events | Points |
|---|---|---|
| 1. New Orleans, LA | 3 | 750 |
| 1. Washington, DC–MD–VA | 4 | 750 |
| 3. Baltimore–Chesapeake Bay, MD | 5 | 700 |
| 4. Minneapolis–St. Paul, MN–WI | 5 | 650 |
| 5. Boston, MA | 5 | 600 |
| 6. Boise–Sun Valley, ID | 5 | 550 |
| 7. New York City, NY | 4 | 525 |
| 7. St. Louis–Mark Twain Country, MO–IL | 4 | 525 |
| 9. Albuquerque–Santa Fe–Taos, NM | 4 | 500 |
| 9. Cincinnati, OH–KY | 4 | 500 |
| 9. Oklahoma City–Cherokee Strip, OK | 5 | 500 |

Even though New Orleans had only three special events listed in the Place Profiles, it tied for first place with Washington, DC, (with four events) because of the high interest these events generated. The 11 Vacation Places that received 500 points or more (3 places tied for ninth place) were distributed throughout the country.

## Bonus Points

Five Vacation Places received 500 bonus points each because of the unusual entertainment they offered and because of their special interest to many vacationers: Atlantic City, New Jersey, Lake Tahoe–Reno, Nevada–California, and Las Vegas–Lake Mead, Nevada–Arizona, for their casinos and the lavish stage shows presented at the casinos; New Orleans, Louisiana, for its many opportunities to hear excellent live jazz; and Nashville, Tennessee, for its many musicians that provide entertainment in restaurants, taverns, and lounges.

# PLACE PROFILES: Entertainment for All

In these pages, entertainment opportunities are listed for the 107 Vacation Places. The listings include family entertainment parks, music and theater, professional sports, and special annual events. Figures shown in parentheses indicate point value.

One flag (◄) to the left of a listing in the Place Profiles means that the attraction or event is worth going out of your way to visit. Two flags (◄ ◄) indicate that the particular attraction is one of the best of its kind in the United States.

Points of interest are listed in alphabetic order first by town, then within the town.

Vacation Places have been given one-half the normal score for attractions that are close by but not within the defined boundaries of the area. These points of interest and events are printed in italics.

A star (★) preceding a Vacation Place highlights that place as one of the top ten in this chapter.

**Adirondack Mountains, NY**
Family Entertainment Parks (1,400)
   The Great Escape (Lake George)
   Waterslide World (Lake George)
   Santa's Workshop (North Pole)
   Enchanted Forest of the Adirondacks (Old Forge)
Music and Theater (900)
   Lake George Opera Festival, summer (Glens Falls)
   Lake George Dinner Theatre, summer (Lake George)
   Summer Music Theater (Lake Placid)
   Music Theater North, summer (Potsdam)
   *Performing Arts Center's Little Theater, summer (Saratoga Springs)*
Special Annual Events (50)
   Spring Festival of the Arts (Potsdam)
Places Rated Score: 2,350        Places Rated Rank: 34

**Albuquerque–Santa Fe–Taos, NM**
Family Entertainment Parks (500)
   Uncle Cliffs Familyland (Albuquerque)
Music and Theater (900)
   Albuquerque Opera Theater (Albuquerque)
   New Mexico Symphony Orchestra (Albuquerque)
   Santa Fe Opera
   New Mexico Music Festival at Taos
Special Annual Events (500)
◄ Indian National Finals Rodeo, late fall (Albuquerque)
◄ International Hot Air Balloon Fiesta, fall (Albuquerque)
   Santa Fe Harvest Festival
   Taos Rodeo, summer
Places Rated Score: 1,900        Places Rated Rank: 43

**Anchorage–Kenai Peninsula, AK**
Music and Theater (500)
   Alaska Repertory Theatre (Anchorage)
   Anchorage Civic Opera (Anchorage)
   Anchorage Symphony Orchestra (Anchorage)
Special Annual Events (300)
◄ Alaska Festival of Music and Native Arts, late summer (Anchorage)
◄ Fur Rendezvous, winter (Anchorage)
Places Rated Score: 800        Places Rated Rank: 68

**Asheville–Smoky Mountains, NC**
Family Entertainment Parks (600)
   Magic Waters (Cherokee)
   Santa's Land, Inc. (Cherokee)
   Ghost Town in the Sky (Maggie Valley)
Music and Theater (1,000)
   Asheville Community Theater (Asheville)
   Shakespeare in the Park, summer (Asheville)
◄ Shindig-on-the-Green, summer (Asheville)
◄ *Unto These Hills*, historical drama, summer (Cherokee)
   *Flat Rock Playhouse, summer (Flat Rock)*
◄ International Folk Festival, summer (Maggie Valley)

Special Annual Events (250)
◄ Christmas at Biltmore (Asheville)
   Mountain Dance and Folk Festival, summer (Asheville)
Places Rated Score: 1,850        Places Rated Rank: 44

**Aspen–Vail, CO**
Music and Theater (800)
◄ Aspen Music Festival (Aspen)
   Pilgrim Theater (Aspen)
   Snowmass Theater Festival, winter and summer (Snowmass Village)
Special Annual Events (300)
   Ullr Fest Winter Carnival (Breckenridge)
   Coors International Bicycle Classic, summer (Vail)
Places Rated Score: 1,100        Places Rated Rank: 58

**Atlanta, GA**
Family Entertainment Parks (700)
◄ ◄ Six Flags Over Georgia (Atlanta)
Music and Theater (500)
   Atlanta Civic Opera (Atlanta)
◄ Atlanta Symphony Orchestra (Atlanta)
Professional Sports (1,200)
   Atlanta Braves, NL baseball
   Atlanta Falcons, football
   Atlanta Hawks, basketball
Special Annual Events (250)
◄ Peach Bowl football classic (Atlanta)
   Oktoberfest (Helen)
Places Rated Score: 2,650        Places Rated Rank: 28

**Atlantic City, NJ**
Family Entertainment Parks (2,100)
   Morey's Pier (North Wildwood)
   S & T Amusement Pier (Ocean City)
   Wonderland Pier (Ocean City)
   Hunt's Amusement Park (Wildwood)
   Marine West Amusement Pier (Wildwood)
   Mariner's Landing Amusement Pier (Wildwood)
Music and Theater (400)
   Mid-Atlantic Stage, summer (Cape May)
   Concerts at Music Pier, summer (Ocean City)
Special Annual Events (300)
◄ Miss America Pageant, late summer (Atlantic City)
Bonus Points (500)
   The gambling casinos and the elaborate shows they put on are a major entertainment draw for this destination.
Places Rated Score: 3,300        Places Rated Rank: 22

**Austin–Hill Country, TX**
Family Entertainment Parks (200)
   Pioneer Town (Wimberley)
Music and Theater (600)
   Austin Symphony Orchestra (Austin)
   *Point Theater, summer (Ingram)*
   Summer music festivals at Quiet Valley Ranch (Kerrville)

Special Annual Events (150)
Fair and Rodeo, summer (Burnet)
Easter Fires Pageant (Fredericksburg)
Places Rated Score: 950   Places Rated Rank: 65

**Baltimore–Chesapeake Bay, MD**
Music and Theater (1,400)
Annapolis Summer Garden Theatre (Annapolis)
◄ Baltimore Opera (Baltimore)
◄ Baltimore Symphony Orchestra (Baltimore)
Center Stage (Baltimore)
Cockpit in Court Summer Theatre (Baltimore)
Professional Sports (700)
Baltimore Blast, indoor soccer
Baltimore Orioles, AL baseball
Special Annual Events (700)
Christmas in Annapolis celebration (Annapolis)
◄ Preakness Race Festival, spring (Baltimore)
Showcase of Nations, summer (Baltimore)
The Waterfowl Festival, fall (Easton)
Maryland Renaissance Festival, fall (Ellicott City)
Places Rated Score: 2,800   Places Rated Rank: 26

**Bar Harbor–Acadia, ME**
Music and Theater (400)
Bar Harbor Festival, summer (Bar Harbor)
Shakespeare Company, summer (Camden)
Special Annual Events (200)
Song of the Sea Gaelic Festival, summer (Bar Harbor)
Maine Seafood Festival, summer (Rockland)
Places Rated Score: 600   Places Rated Rank: 79

**Bend–Cascade Mountains, OR**
Special Annual Events (200)
Crooked River Roundup and Races, summer (Prineville)
Deschutes County Fair and Rodeo, summer (Redmond)
Places Rated Score: 200   Places Rated Rank: 96

**Berkshire Hills–Pioneer Valley, MA**
Family Entertainment Parks (900)
Riverside Park (Agawam)
Mountain Park (Holyoke)
Mt. Tom Great Slide Show (Holyoke)
Music and Theater (3,000)
A Question of Place, historical drama, summer (Deerfield)
◄ Jacob's Pillow Dance Festival, summer (Lee)
◄◄ Berkshire Music Festival, Tanglewood, summer (Lenox)
◄ Shakespeare and Company, summer (Lenox)
Berkshire Public Theater, summer (Pittsfield)
South Mountain concerts, late summer and early fall (Pittsfield)
Mount Holyoke College summer theater (South Hadley)
◄ Springfield Symphony Orchestra (Springfield)
◄ Berkshire Theatre Festival, summer (Stockbridge)
Stage West (West Springfield)
Shaker Mill Tavern Backstage, summer (West Stockbridge)
◄◄ Williamstown Theatre Festival (Williamstown)
Special Annual Events (300)
Eastern States Exposition, summer (Springfield)
ACC Craft Fair, summer (West Springfield)
Places Rated Score: 4,200   Places Rated Rank: 13

**Black Hills, SD**
Music and Theater (700)
Trial of Jack McCall, historical drama, summer (Deadwood)
Black Hills Passion Play (Spearfish)
The Phantom of Matthews' Opera House, summer (Spearfish)
Dakota Musical, historical drama, summer (Wall)
Special Annual Events (325)
Black Hills Roundup, rodeo, summer (Belle Fourche)
Gold Discovery Days, summer (Custer)
Sioux Fair and Pow Wow, summer (Rosebud)
Places Rated Score: 1,025   Places Rated Rank: 64

**Blue Ridge Mountains, VA**
Music and Theater (400)
Heritage Repertory Theater, summer (Charlottesville)
Festival Theater, summer (Lexington)
Special Annual Events (100)
Reenactment of the Battle of New Market, spring (New Market)
Places Rated Score: 500   Places Rated Rank: 82

**Boise–Sun Valley, ID**
Music and Theater (400)
Boise Philharmonic (Boise)
Idaho Shakespeare Festival, summer (Boise)
Special Annual Events (550)
Music Week, spring (Boise)
Snake River Stampede, summer (Nampa)
Old Time Fiddlers' Jamboree, summer (Shoshone)
Twin Falls County Fair and Rodeo, late summer (Twin Falls)
◄ National Old time Fiddlers' Contest, early summer (Weiser)
Places Rated Score: 950   Places Rated Rank: 65

**Boone–High Country, NC**
Music and Theater (200)
Horn in the West, historical drama, summer (Boone)
Special Annual Events (250)
Grandfather Mountain Highland Games and Gathering of Scottish Clans, summer (Linville)
◄ Masters of Hang Gliding Championship, late summer (Linville)
Places Rated Score: 450   Places Rated Rank: 85

**★ Boston, MA**
Family Entertainment Parks (200)
Amusement Park (Salisbury Beach)
Music and Theater (3,700)
North Shore Music Theater, summer (Beverly)
Boston Concert Opera (Boston)
Boston Lyric Opera (Boston)
◄◄ Boston Pops Concerts (Boston)
◄ Boston Shakespeare Company (Boston)
◄ Boston Symphony Orchestra (Boston)
Next Move Theatre (Boston)
◄ Opera Company of Boston (Boston)
Opera New England (Boston)
◄ American Repertory Theater (Cambridge)
Peoples Theatre (Cambridge)
South Shore Music Circus, summer (Cohasset)
High Tor Summer Theatre, summer (Fitchburg)
Gloucester Stage Company, summer (Gloucester)
Merrimack Regional Theatre (Lowell)
Priscilla Beach Theater, summer (Plymouth)
Professional Sports (1,500)
Boston Bruins, hockey
Boston Celtics, basketball
Boston Red Sox, AL baseball
New England Patriots, football (Foxboro)
Special Annual Events (600)
Boston Harborfest, summer (Boston)
Boston Marathon, spring
First Night, January 1 (Boston)
Early 19th Century Fourth of July (Sturbridge)
Thanksgiving at Old Sturbridge Village (Sturbridge)
Places Rated Score: 6,000   Places Rated Rank: 5

**Brownsville–Rio Grande Valley, TX**
Family Entertainment Parks (200)
Jeremiah's Landing (South Padre Island)
Special Annual Events (150)
◄ Confederate Air Force Annual Air Show, fall (Harlingen)
Rio Grande Music Festival, spring (Harlingen)
Places Rated Score: 350   Places Rated Rank: 90

**Cape Cod–The Islands, MA**
Family Entertainment Parks (600)
Sealand of Cape Cod (Brewster)
Cartland of Cape Cod (Buzzards Bay)
Aqua Circus (West Yarmouth)

Music and Theater (1,500)
  Monomoy Theater, summer (Chatham)
  The Cape Playhouse, summer (Dennis)
  College Light Opera (Falmouth)
  Falmouth Playhouse, summer (Falmouth)
  Cape Cod Melody Tent, summer (Hyannis)
  Academy Playhouse, summer (Orleans)
  Outer Cape Performance Company, summer (Wellfleet)
  Harwich Junior Theater, summer (West Harwich)
Special Annual Events (50)
  Barnstable County Fair, summer (Falmouth)
Places Rated Score: 2,150      Places Rated Rank: 37

**Catskill Mountains, NY**
Family Entertainment Parks (400)
  Hillside Resort, waterpark (Narrowsburg)
  Hoffman's Playland (Newtonville)
Music and Theater (3,300)
  Mac-Haydn Theater, summer (Chatham)
  Hyde Park Festival Theater, summer (Hyde Park)
  Sullivan Festival, summer (Loch Sheldrake)
  Forestburgh Playhouse, summer (Monticello)
◀◀ New York Periwinkle Productions (Monticello)
  New Paltz Summer Repertory Theater (New Paltz)
  New Way Repertory Company, summer (New Paltz)
  SUNY Oneonta Summer Theater (Oneonta)
  Interarts, summer (Palenville)
  Traverse Opera Ltd. (Palenville)
  Hudson Valley Philharmonic Orchestra (Poughkeepsie)
  Powerhouse Double Image Theater, summer (Poughkeepsie)
  Ulster County Community College Quimby Theater, summer
    (Stone Ridge)
  Penguin Repertory Company, summer (Stony Point)
  New York Renaissance Festival, summer (Tuxedo)
  Woodstock Playhouse, summer (Woodstock)
Special Annual Events (150)
  Hunter County Music Festival, summer (Hunter)
  Mountain Eagle Indian Festival, late summer (Hunter)
Places Rated Score: 3,850      Places Rated Rank: 17

**Charleston, SC**
Music and Theater (200)
  Charleston Symphony Orchestra (Charleston)
Special Annual Events (300)
◀◀ Spoleto USA, late spring (Charleston)
Places Rated Score: 500      Places Rated Rank: 82

**Chattanooga–Huntsville, TN–AL–GA**
Music and Theater (300)
  Chattanooga Opera Association (Chattanooga, TN)
  Chattanooga Symphony Orchestra (Chattanooga)
Special Annual Events (150)
  Riverbend Festival, summer (Chattanooga)
Places Rated Score: 450      Places Rated Rank: 85

**★ Chicago, IL**
Family Entertainment Parks (1,800)
  Three Worlds of Santa's Village (Dundee)
◀◀ Six Flags Great America (Gurnee)
  MacNeal's Holiday Park, waterpark (Ingleside)
  Hillcrest Park (Lake Zurich)
  Kiddie Park (Melrose Park)
Music and Theater (3,400)
  Body Politic (Chicago)
  Chicago Chamber Orchestra (Chicago)
◀◀ Chicago Symphony Orchestra (Chicago)
◀◀ Goodman Theatre (Chicago)
  Grant Park concerts, summer (Chicago)
  Lithuanian Opera Company (Chicago)
◀◀ Lyric Opera of Chicago (Chicago)
  Performance Community (Chicago)
  St. Nicholas Theater Company (Chicago)
  Steppenwolf Theatre (Chicago)
  Theater on the Lake, summer (Chicago)
  Victory Gardens Theater (Chicago)
  Wisdom Bridge Theater (Chicago)
  North Light Repertory Company (Evanston)

◀◀ Ravinia Festival (Highland Park)
  Hinsdale Opera Theater (Hinsdale)
Professional Sports (2,200)
  Chicago Bears, football
  Chicago Blackhawks, hockey
  Chicago Bulls, basketball
  Chicago Cubs, NL baseball
  Chicago Sting, soccer
  Chicago White Sox, AL baseball
Special Annual Events (300)
  Chicago International Film Festival, fall (Chicago)
  Christmas Around the World (Museum of Science and
    Industry, Chicago)
Places Rated Score: 7,700      Places Rated Rank: 3

**★ Cincinnati, OH–KY**
Family Entertainment Parks (1,900)
◀ Kings Island (Cincinnati)
  The Beach, waterpark (Mason)
  Americana Amusement Park (Middletown)
  Fantasy Farm Amusement Park (Middletown)
Music and Theater (1,700)
◀ Cincinnati Opera Association (Cincinnati)
◀ Cincinnati Playhouse in the Park (Cincinnati)
◀ Cincinnati Symphony Orchestra (Cincinnati)
  Showboat Majestic (Cincinnati)
  Dayton Opera Association
  Dayton Philharmonic Orchestra
Professional Sports (800)
  Cincinnati Bengals, football
  Cincinnati Reds, NL baseball
Special Annual Events (500)
  Ohio Kool Jazz Festival, summer (Cincinnati)
  Riverfest, late summer (Cincinnati and Covington, KY)
  Oktoberfest (Covington)
  Dayton International Airshow, summer
Places Rated Score: 4,900      Places Rated Rank: 8

**Colorado Springs, CO**
Family Entertainment Parks (500)
  Santa's Workshop (North Pole)
Music and Theater (400)
  Colorado Opera Festival, summer (Colorado Springs)
  Colorado Springs Symphony Orchestra (Colorado Springs)
Special Annual Events (150)
  Garden of the Gods Easter Sunrise Service (Colorado
    Springs)
Places Rated Score: 1,050      Places Rated Rank: 61

**Coos Bay–South Coast, OR**
Special Annual Events (100)
  Azalea Festival, late spring (Brookings)
  Port Orford Jubilee Celebration, summer
Places Rated Score: 100      Places Rated Rank: 102

**Corpus Christi–Padre Island, TX**
Family Entertainment Parks (500)
  Magic Isles (Corpus Christi)
Music and Theater (200)
  Corpus Christi Symphony Orchestra (Corpus Christi)
Special Annual Events (150)
  Bayfest, early fall (Corpus Christi)
  Buccaneer Days, spring (Corpus Christi)
  Texas A & I National Intercollegiate Rodeo, early spring
    (Kingsville)
Places Rated Score: 850      Places Rated Rank: 67

**Crater Lake–Klamath Falls, OR**
Music and Theater (700)
◀◀ Oregon Shakespeare Festival (Ashland)
  Eugene Opera (Eugene)
  Eugene Symphony Orchestra (Eugene)
Special Annual Events (100)
  Peter Britt Gardens Music and Arts Festival, summer
    (Medford)
Places Rated Score: 800      Places Rated Rank: 68

## ★ Dallas–Fort Worth, TX
Family Entertainment Parks (1,300)
◄ ◄ Six Flags Over Texas (Arlington)
    Wet 'N Wild, waterpark (Arlington)
    White Water, waterpark (Dallas)
    International Wildlife Park (Grand Prairie)
Music and Theater (1,200)
◄ Dallas Symphony Orchestra (Dallas)
    Dallas Theater Center (Dallas)
    Theatre Three (Dallas)
◄ Fort Worth Symphony Orchestra (Fort Worth)
Professional Sports (1,500)
    Texas Rangers, AL baseball (Arlington)
    Dallas Cowboys, football
    Dallas Mavericks, basketball
    Dallas Sidekicks, indoor soccer
Special Annual Events (450)
◄ ◄ Cotton Bowl Parade and Football Classic (Dallas)
    State Fair of Texas, fall (Dallas)
Places Rated Score: 4,450    Places Rated Rank: 9

## Denver–Rocky Mountain National Park, CO
Family Entertainment Parks (700)
    Elitch Gardens (Denver)
    Hyland Hills Waterpark (Denver)
Music and Theater (1,800)
    Colorado Music Festival (Boulder)
    Shakespeare Festival (Boulder)
    Central City Opera House Assn. (Denver)
    The Changing Scene (Denver)
◄ Denver Symphony Orchestra (Denver)
    Denver Theatre Company (Denver)
    Germinal Stage Denver (Denver)
    Opera Colorado (Denver)
    Boulder Repertory Company, summer (Estes Park)
    Colorado Philharmonic (Evergreen)
Professional Sports (800)
    Denver Broncos, football
    Denver Nuggets, basketball
Special Annual Events (100)
    National Western Livestock Show, Horse Show, and Rodeo,
      winter (Denver)
Places Rated Score: 3,400    Places Rated Rank: 21

## Door County, WI
Family Entertainment Parks (200)
    Thumb Fun (Fish Creek)
Music and Theater (300)
    Birch Creek Music Center, summer concerts (Egg Harbor)
    Peninsula Players, summer theater (Fish Creek)
Special Annual Events (50)
    Fyr-Bal Fest, early summer (Ephraim)
Places Rated Score: 550    Places Rated Rank: 80

## Eastern Shore, VA
Special Annual Events (100)
    Pony Penning, roundup of wild ponies and carnival, summer
      (Chincoteague)
Places Rated Score: 100    Places Rated Rank: 102

## Finger Lakes, NY
Family Entertainment Parks (500)
    Roseland Park (Canandaigua)
Music and Theater (2,000)
    Auburn Civic Theater, summer (Auburn)
    Corning Summer Theater (Corning)
    Cortland Repertory Theater, summer (Cortland)
    The Hangar Theater, summer (Ithaca)
    The Bristol Valley Playhouse, summer (Naples)
    Hill Cumorah Pageant, summer (Palmyra)
    Opera Theater of Syracuse (Syracuse)
    Syracuse Stage (Syracuse)
◄ Syracuse Symphony Orchestra (Syracuse)
Special Annual Events (100)
    New York State Fair, late summer (Syracuse)
Places Rated Score: 2,600    Places Rated Rank: 30

## Flaming Gorge, UT–WY–CO
Special Annual Events (150)
    *Cowboy Days, late summer (Evanston, WY)*
    *Winter Carnival (Evanston)*
    Flaming Gorge Days, summer (Green River, WY)
Places Rated Score: 150    Places Rated Rank: 99

## Glacier National Park–Flathead Lake, MT
Family Entertainment Parks (200)
    Big Sky Waterslide (Columbia Falls)
Music and Theater (200)
    Bigfork Summer Playhouse (Bigfork)
Special Annual Events (250)
    Art in the Park, summer (Kalispell)
    Northwest Montana Fair and Rodeo, summer (Kalispell)
    Montana State Fiddlers' Contest, summer (Polson)
Places Rated Score: 650    Places Rated Rank: 74

## Grand Canyon Country, AZ
Special Annual Events (100)
    Flagstaff Festival of the Arts, summer
    Old Fashioned Mellerdrammar, summer (Sedona)
Places Rated Score: 100    Places Rated Rank: 102

## Green Mountains, VT
Music and Theater (1,200)
    Champlain Shakespeare Festival, summer (Burlington)
    Vermont Mozart Festival (Burlington and other locations)
    Vermont Symphony Orchestra (Burlington)
    Vermont Ensemble Theater, summer (Middlebury)
    SummerStage (Stowe)
    St. Michael's Playhouse, summer (Winooski)
Special Annual Events (350)
    National Traditional Old Time Fiddlers' Contest, late summer
      (Barre)
    Lake Champlain Discovery Festival, late spring (Burlington)
◄ Stowe Winter Carnival (Stowe)
Places Rated Score: 1,550    Places Rated Rank: 48

## Hawaii
Music and Theater (1,000)
    Hawaiian Festival of Music, spring (Honolulu)
    Hawaii Opera Theater (Honolulu)
◄ Honolulu Symphony Orchestra (Honolulu)
◄ Honolulu Theatre for Youth (Honolulu)
Special Annual Events (200)
    Hula Bowl Football Classic (Honolulu)
    Ukelele Festival, summer (Waikiki Beach, Honolulu)
    Queen Kaahumanu Festival, summer (Wailuku, Maui)
Places Rated Score: 1,200    Places Rated Rank: 55

## Hilton Head, SC
Special Annual Events (150)
    Springfest (Hilton Head)
Places Rated Score: 150    Places Rated Rank: 99

## Holland–Lake Michigan Shore, MI
Family Entertainment Parks (500)
    Deer Park Funland (Muskegon)
Music and Theater (500)
◄ Grand Rapids Symphony Orchestra (Grand Rapids)
    Opera Grand Rapids (Grand Rapids)
Special Annual Events (225)
    *World Hot-Air Balloon Championship, summer (Battle Creek)*
◄ Tulip Time Festival (Holland)
Places Rated Score: 1,225    Places Rated Rank: 54

## Houston–Galveston, TX
Family Entertainment Parks (900)
◄ Astroworld (Houston)
    Ski Trek, waterpark (Houston)
Music and Theater (1,200)
◄ Alley Theatre (Houston)
◄ Houston Grand Opera Association (Houston)
◄ Houston Symphony Orchestra (Houston)

Professional Sports (1,200)
Houston Astros, baseball
Houston Oilers, football
Houston Rockets, basketball
Special Annual Events (150)
Bluebonnet Bowl Football Classic (Houston)
The Houston Festival, spring (Houston)
Places Rated Score: 3,450 Places Rated Rank: 20

**Jersey Shore, NJ**
Family Entertainment Parks (1,800)
Fantasy Island Amusement Park (Beach Haven)
◄ Six Flags Great Adventure (Jackson)
Long Branch Amusement Pier (Long Branch)
Casino Pier (Seaside Heights)
Rainbow Rapids Waterslide (Toms River)
Music and Theater (200)
Surflight Summer Theater (Beach Haven)
Special Annual Events (50)
Band concerts on the Boardwalk, summer (Asbury Park)
Places Rated Score: 2,050 Places Rated Rank: 40

**Knoxville–Smoky Mountains, TN**
Family Entertainment Parks (900)
Ogle's Water Park (Pigeon Forge)
Silver Dollar City (Pigeon Forge)
Water Ski Shows (Pigeon Forge)
Music and Theater (800)
The Road Company (Johnson City)
Knoxville Symphony Orchestra (Knoxville)
The Play Group (Knoxville)
National Mountain Music Festival (Pigeon Forge)
Special Annual Events (150)
Dulcimer Convention, summer (Cosby)
National Storytelling Festival, early fall (Jonesborough)
Places Rated Score: 1,850 Places Rated Rank: 44

**Lake of the Ozarks, MO**
Family Entertainment Parks (500)
Fort Funtier Land (Osage Beach)
Music and Theater (100)
Arrow Rock Lyceum Theater, summer (Arrow Rock)
Special Annual Events (50)
Central Missouri Regional Fair, summer (Rolla)
Ozark Extravaganza, late summer (Rolla)
Places Rated Score: 650 Places Rated Rank: 74

**Lake Powell–Glen Canyon, AZ–UT**
Special Annual Events (200)
Bluff Indian Day, late spring (Bluff, UT)
Big Dam Rodeo, spring (Page, AZ)
Places Rated Score: 200 Places Rated Rank: 96

**Lake Tahoe–Reno, NV–CA**
Music and Theater (200)
Shakespeare at the Lake (Incline Village, Lake Tahoe, NV)
Special Annual Events (350)
International Jazz Festival, spring (Reno, NV)
National Championship Air Races, late summer (Reno)
Reno Rodeo, summer (Reno)
Bonus Points (500)
The gambling casinos and the elaborate shows they present
are a major entertainment draw for this destination.
Places Rated Score: 1,050 Places Rated Rank: 61

**Las Vegas–Lake Mead, NV–AZ**
Special Annual Events (200)
Contemporary Music Festival, winter (Las Vegas, NV)
Elks Helldorado Days, spring (Las Vegas)
Bonus Points (500)
The gambling casinos and the elaborate shows they present
are a major entertainment draw for this destination.
Places Rated Score: 700 Places Rated Rank: 71

**Lexington–Bluegrass Country, KY**
Music and Theater (1,800)
Lexington Philharmonic Orchestra (Lexington)

◄◄ Actors Theatre of Louisville (Louisville)
Humana Festival of New American Plays, spring (Louisville)
Kentucky Opera Assn. (Louisville)
◄ Louisville Orchestra (Louisville)
Shakespeare-in-the-Park, summer (Louisville)
Stage One: The Louisville Children's Theatre (Louisville)
Special Annual Events (400)
◄◄ Kentucky Derby Festival, spring (Louisville)
Kentucky Fried Chicken Bluegrass Music Festival, late
summer (Louisville)
Places Rated Score: 2,200 Places Rated Rank: 36

**Long Island, NY**
Family Entertainment Parks (500)
Adventureland (Farmingdale)
Music and Theater (2,000)
Gateway Playhouse, summer (Bellport)
Arena Players Repertory, summer (East Farmingdale)
John Drew Theater, summer (East Hampton)
Broadhollow Theater, summer (Farmingdale)
Post Summer Theater (Greenvale)
The Harry Chapin Theatre Center (Huntington Station)
Studio Theater, summer (Lindenhurst)
Long Island Philharmonic (Melville)
Stony Brook Theater Festival, summer (Stony Brook)
Westbury Music Fair, summer (Westbury)
Professional Sports (300)
New York Islanders, hockey
Special Annual Events (100)
Summer Arts Festival (Huntington)
Pow Wow, late summer (Southampton)
Places Rated Score: 2,900 Places Rated Rank: 25

**★ Los Angeles, CA**
Family Entertainment Parks (2,800)
◄◄ Disneyland (Anaheim)
◄◄ Knott's Berry Farm (Buena Park)
◄◄ Universal Studios Tour and Entertainment Center (Los
Angeles)
◄◄ Six Flags Magic Mountain (Valencia)
Music and Theater (3,200)
◄ South Coast Repertory (Costa Mesa)
Fullerton Civic Light Opera (Fullerton)
American Theatre Arts (Hollywood)
East West Players (Los Angeles)
Los Angeles Actors' Theatre (Los Angeles)
◄ Los Angeles Chamber Orchestra (Los Angeles)
Los Angeles Opera Repertory Theater (Los Angeles)
◄ Los Angeles Philharmonic (Los Angeles)
Los Angeles Public Theatre (Los Angeles)
Los Angeles Theatre Works (Los Angeles)
◄ Mark Taper Forum (Los Angeles)
Odyssey Theatre Ensemble (Los Angeles)
Provisional Theatre (Los Angeles)
Long Beach Grand Opera (Long Beach)
◄ Long Beach Symphony Orchestra (Long Beach)
Professional Sports (3,000)
California Angels, AL baseball (Anaheim)
Los Angeles Rams, football (Anaheim)
Los Angeles Clippers, basketball
Los Angeles Dodgers, NL baseball
Los Angeles Kings, hockey
Los Angeles Lakers, basketball
Los Angeles Lazers, indoor soccer
Los Angeles Raiders, football
Special Annual Events (300)
Festival of Arts and Pageant of the Masters, summer (Laguna
Beach)
◄◄ Tournament of Roses Parade and Football Classic (Pasadena)
Places Rated Score: 9,300 Places Rated Rank: 2

**Mackinac Island–Sault Ste. Marie, MI**
Special Annual Events (50)
Fort Michilimackinac Pageant, spring (Mackinaw City)
Places Rated Score: 50 Places Rated Rank: 107

## Memphis, TN–AR–MS
Family Entertainment Parks (500)
  Libertyland (Memphis, TN)
Music and Theater (1,000)
  Cotton Carnival Musicfest, spring (Memphis)
◄ Memphis Symphony Orchestra (Memphis)
  Opera Memphis (Memphis)
  Playhouse on the Square (Memphis)
Professional Sports (300)
  Memphis Americans, indoor soccer
Special Annual Events (250)
  Elvis International Tribute Week, summer (Memphis)
  Liberty Bowl Football Classic (Memphis)
Places Rated Score: 2,050      Places Rated Rank: 40

## Miami–Gold Coast–Keys, FL
Family Entertainment Parks (400)
  Herman's Ocean Amusement Rides (Fort Lauderdale)
  Six Flags Atlantis, waterpark (Hollywood)
Music and Theater (1,700)
  Florida Atlantic University Theater, summer (Boca Raton)
◄ Players State Theatre (Coconut Grove)
  The Ring Theater, summer (Coral Gables)
  Fort Lauderdale Symphony Orchestra (Fort Lauderdale)
◄ Greater Miami Opera Association (Miami)
  Shakespeare by the Sea, summer (Miami Beach)
  Palm Beach Opera (Palm Beach)
Professional Sports (1,900)
  New York Yankees, spring baseball (Fort Lauderdale)
  Baltimore Orioles, spring baseball (Miami)
  Miami Dolphins, football
  Texas Rangers, spring baseball (Pompano Beach)
  Atlanta Braves, spring baseball (West Palm Beach)
  Montreal Expos, spring baseball (West Palm Beach)
Special Annual Events (300)
◄◄ Orange Bowl Festival and Football Classic (Miami)
Places Rated Score: 4,300      Places Rated Rank: 12

## ★ Minneapolis–St. Paul, MN–WI
Family Entertainment Parks (700)
  Lilli Putt Amusement Park (Anoka)
  Valleyfair (Shakopee)
Music and Theater (2,400)
◄ The Children's Theatre Company (Minneapolis)
  Cricket Theatre (Minneapolis)
◄◄ The Guthrie Theatre (Minneapolis)
◄ Minnesota Opera (Minneapolis)
◄ Minnesota Orchestra (Minneapolis)
  Playwrights' Center (Minneapolis)
  Actors Theatre of St. Paul (St. Paul)
◄ St. Paul Chamber Orchestra (St. Paul)
Professional Sports (1,400)
  Minnesota North Stars, hockey
  Minnesota Strikers, soccer
  Minnesota Twins, AL baseball
  Minnesota Vikings, football
Special Annual Events (650)
  Minneapolis Aquatennial, summer (Minneapolis)
  Winter Carnival Polka and Music Festival (Mounds View)
  Festival of Nations, spring (St. Paul)
  St. Paul Winter Carnival
  Rennaissance Festival, late summer (Shakopee)
Places Rated Score: 5,150      Places Rated Rank: 7

## Mobile Bay–Gulfport, AL–MS
Family Entertainment Parks (400)
  Beach Amusement Park (Long Beach, MS)
  Water Resort (Robertsdale, AL)
Music and Theater (300)
  Festival of American Music and Theater, summer (Mobile, AL)
  Mobile Opera (Mobile)
Special Annual Events (450)
  National Shrimp Festival, fall (Gulf Shores, AL)
◄ Mardi Gras (Mobile)
  Mums Extravaganza, fall (Theodore, AL)
Places Rated Score: 1,150      Places Rated Rank: 56

## Monterey–Big Sur, CA
Family Entertainment Parks (700)
◄◄ Marriott's Great America (Santa Clara)
Music and Theater (1,000)
  Carmel Bach Festival, summer (Carmel)
◄ San Jose Symphony Orchestra (San Jose)
  El Teatro Campesino (San Juan Bautista)
  Montalvo Summer Music Festival (Saratoga)
Professional Sports (300)
  Golden Bay Earthquakes, soccer (San Jose)
Special Annual Events (50)
  Monterey Jazz Festival, late summer (Monterey)
Places Rated Score: 2,050      Places Rated Rank: 40

## Myrtle Beach–Grand Strand, SC
Family Entertainment Parks (600)
  Water Sports, waterpark (Conway)
  Magic Harbor (Myrtle Beach)
  Myrtle Beach Pavilion and Amusement Park (Myrtle Beach)
Special Annual Events (150)
  Canadian-American Days, spring (Myrtle Beach)
Places Rated Score: 750      Places Rated Rank: 70

## Mystic Seaport–Connecticut Valley, CT
Music and Theater (1,800)
  Goodspeed Opera House (East Haddam)
  Connecticut Opera (Hartford)
◄ Hartford Stage Company (Hartford)
◄ Hartford Symphony Orchestra
  Ivoryton Playhouse, summer (Ivoryton)
  American Musical Theater, summer (Stonington)
  O'Neill Theatre Center, summer (Waterford)
Professional Sports (300)
  Hartford Whalers, hockey
Special Annual Events (200)
  New England Fiddle Contest, spring (Hartford)
◄ Christmas at Mystic Seaport
Places Rated Score: 2,300      Places Rated Rank: 35

## Nashville, TN
Family Entertainment Parks (700)
◄◄ Opryland, USA (Nashville)
Music and Theater (800)
◄ Grand Ole Opry (Nashville)
◄ Nashville Symphony Orchestra (Nashville)
Special Annual Events (150)
  International Country Music Fan Fair, late spring (Nashville)
Bonus Points (500)
  Nashville is full of talented artists who come to seek fame and fortune in the recording industry. Most bars and lounges in the city feature good live entertainment.
Places Rated Score: 2,150      Places Rated Rank: 37

## New Orleans, LA
Family Entertainment Parks (200)
  Mart Amusement Park (New Orleans)
Music and Theater (600)
  New Orleans Opera Association (New Orleans)
◄ New Orleans Philharmonic Symphony Orchestra (New Orleans)
Professional Sports (400)
  New Orleans Saints, football
Special Annual Events (750)
◄◄ Mardi Gras (New Orleans)
  New Orleans Jazz and Heritage Festival, spring (New Orleans)
  Sugar Bowl Football Classic (New Orleans)
Bonus Points (500)
  Many places in New Orleans offer excellent jazz and Dixieland music. One of the best known is Preservation Hall.
Places Rated Score: 2,450      Places Rated Rank: 32

## ★ New York City, NY
Family Entertainment Parks (1,000)
  Astroland Amusement Park (Brooklyn)
  Nellie Bly Park (Brooklyn)

Music and Theater (10,400)
  Bronx Arts Ensemble Chamber Orchestra (Bronx)
◄ BAM Theater Company (Brooklyn)
  Brooklyn Philharmonic Symphony Orchestra (Brooklyn)
  Caramoor Music Festival, summer (Katonah)
◄ The Acting Company (Manhattan)
  AMAS Theatre (Manhattan)
  American Place Theatre (Manhattan)
◄ American Symphony Orchestra (Manhattan)
  Chamber Opera Company of New York (Manhattan)
  Children's Free Opera of New York (Manhattan)
◄ Circle in the Square (Manhattan)
  Circle Repertory Company (Manhattan)
  CSC Repertory (Manhattan)
  Eastern Opera Theater of New York (Manhattan)
  Encompass Music Theater (Manhattan)
  Ensemble Studio Theatre (Manhattan)
  The First All Children's Theatre (Manhattan)
◄ Goldovsky Opera Institute and Theater (Manhattan)
  Guggenheim Concerts, summer (Manhattan)
  Hudson Guild Theatre (Manhattan)
  INTAR (Manhattan)
  Interart Theatre (Manhattan)
  Jean Cocteau Repertory (Manhattan)
  Light Opera of Manhattan (Manhattan)
  Mabou Mines (Manhattan)
  Manhattan Theatre Club (Manhattan)
  Medicine Show Theatre Ensemble (Manhattan)
◄◄ Metropolitan Opera (Manhattan)
  Music Theatre Group (Manhattan)
  National Black Theatre (Manhattan)
  National Opera Touring Company, Lincoln Center (Manhattan)
◄ National Shakespeare Company (Manhattan)
  Negro Ensemble Company (Manhattan)
  New Dramatists (Manhattan)
  New Federal Theatre (Manhattan)
  New York City Opera, Lincoln Center (Manhattan)
  New York Gilbert and Sullivan Players (Manhattan)
  New York Lyric Opera (Manhattan)
◄◄ New York Philharmonic (Manhattan)
◄◄ New York Shakespeare Festival (Manhattan)
  Opera Ensemble of New York (Manhattan)
◄ Paper Bag Players (Manhattan)
  Phoenix Theatre (Manhattan)
  Playwrights' Horizons (Manhattan)
  Repertorio Español (Manhattan)
  The Ridiculous Theatrical Company (Manhattan)
◄ Roundabout Theatre Company (Manhattan)
◄ Shakespeare in Central Park (Manhattan)
  Soho Repertory Theatre (Manhattan)
  Theater for the New City (Manhattan)
  Theater of the Open Eye (Manhattan)
  Pelham Theater Workshop, summer (Pelham)
  PepsiCo Summerfare (Purchase)
  Queens Symphony Orchestra (Rego Park)
  County Symphony of Westchester (Scarsdale)
  The Street Theater (White Plains)
Professional Sports (3,250)
  *New Jersey Nets, basketball (East Rutherford, NJ)*
  *New Jersey Devils, hockey (East Rutherford)*
  New York Arrows, indoor soccer
  New York Cosmos, soccer
  New York Giants, football
  New York Jets, football
  New York Knickerbockers, basketball
  New York Mets, NL baseball
  New York Rangers, hockey
  New York Yankees, AL baseball
Special Annual Events (525)
  *The Hambletonian, summer (East Rutherford)*
  Kool Jazz Festival, summer (New York City)
◄◄ Macy's Thanksgiving Day Parade (New York City)
  New York Women's Jazz Festival, summer (New York City)
Places Rated Score: 15,175    Places Rated Rank: 1

**Niagara Falls–Western New York, NY**
Family Entertainment Parks (200)
  Midway Park (Maple Springs)
Music and Theater (1,700)
◄ Buffalo Philharmonic Orchestra (Buffalo)
  Shakespeare in Delaware Park, summer (Buffalo)
◄ Studio Arena Theatre (Buffalo)
◄ Chautauqua Institution, summer theater (Chautauqua)
  Chautauqua Opera Company (Chautauqua)
  Chautauqua Symphony Orchestra (Chautauqua)
  Artpark, summer (Lewiston)
Professional Sports (700)
  Buffalo Bills, football
  Buffalo Sabres, hockey
Special Annual Events (150)
  Niagara Festival of Lights, Thanksgiving until the New Year (Niagara Falls)
Places Rated Score: 2,750    Places Rated Rank: 27

**North Woods–Land O'Lakes, WI**
Family Entertainment Parks (200)
  Eagle Pass Amusement Park (Eagle River)
Special Annual Events (200)
  World Championship Snowmobile Derby, winter (Eagle River)
  Hodag Country Festival, summer (Rhinelander)
Places Rated Score: 400    Places Rated Rank: 89

**Oklahoma City–Cherokee Strip, OK**
Family Entertainment Parks (500)
  Frontier City (Oklahoma City)
Music and Theater (400)
◄ Oklahoma Symphony Orchestra (Oklahoma City)
Special Annual Events (500)
◄ National Finals Rodeo, late fall (Oklahoma City)
  Oklahoma City Festival of the Arts, spring (Oklahoma City)
  State Fair of Oklahoma, early fall (Oklahoma City)
◄ World Championship Quarter Horse Show, fall (Oklahoma City)
  World Series of Fiddling and Bluegrass Festival, late spring (Oklahoma City)
Places Rated Score: 1,400    Places Rated Rank: 51

**Olympic Peninsula, WA**
Special Annual Events (100)
  Tumwater Bluegrass Festival, spring (Olympia)
  Angeles Art in Action, summer (Port Angeles)
Places Rated Score: 100    Places Rated Rank: 102

★ **Orlando–Space Coast, FL**
Family Entertainment Parks (2,100)
◄◄ Sea World of Florida (Orlando)
◄◄ Walt Disney World and Epcot Center (Orlando)
◄◄ Cypress Gardens (Winter Haven)
Music and Theater (700)
  Passion Play, Lenten season (Lake Wales)
◄ Florida Symphony Orchestra (Orlando)
  Orlando Opera Company (Orlando)
Professional Sports (1,500)
  Houston Astros, spring baseball (Kissimmee)
  Detroit Tigers, spring baseball (Lakeland)
  Minnesota Twins, spring baseball (Orlando)
  Los Angeles Dodgers, spring baseball (Vero Beach)
  Boston Red Sox, spring baseball (Winter Haven)
Special Annual Events (100)
  Florida Citrus Bowl football classic (Orlando)
Places Rated Score: 4,400    Places Rated Rank: 10

**Outer Banks, NC**
Music and Theater (200)
  *The Lost Colony*, outdoor drama (Manteo)
Special Annual Events (100)
  Hang Gliding Spectacular, spring (Nags Head)
Places Rated Score: 300    Places Rated Rank: 92

**Ozarks–Eureka Springs, AR–MO**
Family Entertainment Parks (1,500)
  McCall Amusement Park (Branson, MO)

Silver Dollar City (Branson)
Dogpatch USA (Dogpatch, AR)
**Music and Theater (300)**
 Passion Play, summer (Eureka Springs, AR)
 Springfield Symphony Orchestra (Springfield, MO)
**Special Annual Events (300)**
 Mountain Folks' Music Festival, summer (Silver Dollar City, Branson)
 Parade of Barbershop Harmony, late summer (Dogpatch)
 Original Ozark Folk Festival, fall (Eureka Springs)
 *Old-Time Fiddlers State Championship, late summer (Ozark Folk Center, Mountain View, AR)*
**Places Rated Score: 2,100      Places Rated Rank: 39**

### Palm Springs–Desert Playgrounds, CA
**Music and Theater (100)**
 Idyllwild Festival Music Concert, summer (Idyllwild)
**Professional Sports (300)**
 Los Angeles Angels, spring baseball (Palm Springs)
**Special Annual Events (100)**
 National Date Festival, winter (Indio)
 Mounted Police Rodeo and Parade, winter (Palm Springs)
**Places Rated Score: 500      Places Rated Rank: 82**

### Panhandle, FL
**Family Entertainment Parks (900)**
 Gator Race Track (Panama City)
 Miracle Strip Amusement Park (Panama City)
 Lafitte's Landing (Pensacola)
**Music and Theater (100)**
 Greater Pensacola Symphony Orchestra (Pensacola)
**Special Annual Events (50)**
 Pensacola Interstate Fair, fall (Pensacola)
**Places Rated Score: 1,050      Places Rated Rank: 61**

### Pennsylvania Dutch Country, PA
**Family Entertainment Parks (1,200)**
◄◄ Hersheypark (Hershey)
 Dutch Wonderland (Lancaster)
**Music and Theater (1,100)**
 Allenberry Playhouse, summer (Boiling Springs)
 Gettysburg Theater Festival, summer (Gettysburg)
 Host Inn Dinner Theater, summer (Harrisburg)
 Harrisburg Symphony Orchestra
 Host Farm Resort Dinner Theater, summer (Lancaster)
 The Independent Eye (Lancaster)
**Special Annual Events (300)**
 Gettysburg Civil War Heritage Days, early summer
 Pennsylvania State Farm Show, winter (Harrisburg)
**Places Rated Score: 2,600      Places Rated Rank: 30**

### ★ Philadelphia, PA–DE–NJ
**Family Entertainment Parks (1,500)**
 Sesame Place (Langhorne, PA)
 Lakeview Amusement Park (Royersford, PA)
 West Point Park (West Point, PA)
**Music and Theater (2,800)**
 Valley Forge Music Fair, summer (Devon)
 Peoples Light and Theatre Company (Malvern, PA)
◄ Bucks County Playhouse, summer (New Hope, PA)
 Barn Playhouse, summer (Norristown, PA)
 Concerto Soloists of Philadelphia (Philadelphia)
 LaSalle Music Theater, summer (Philadelphia)
◄ Opera Company of Philadelphia (Philadelphia)
 Opera Ebony (Philadelphia)
 Pennsylvania Opera Theater (Philadelphia)
 Philadelphia Drama Guild (Philadelphia)
◄ Philadelphia Orchestra (Philadelphia)
 Villanova Summer Theater (Villanova)
 Delaware Symphony (Wilmington, DE)
**Professional Sports (1,500)**
 Philadelphia Eagles, football
 Philadelphia Flyers, hockey
 Philadelphia Phillies, NL baseball
 Philadelphia 76ers, basketball

**Special Annual Events (300)**
◄ Mummers Parade, New Year's Day (Philadelphia)
 Philadelphia Flower and Garden Show, spring (Philadelphia)
**Places Rated Score: 6,100      Places Rated Rank: 4**

### Phoenix–Valley of the Sun, AZ
**Family Entertainment Parks (200)**
 Marine Life (Scottsdale)
**Music and Theater (400)**
◄ Phoenix Symphony Orchestra (Phoenix)
**Professional Sports (2,050)**
 Chicago Cubs, spring baseball (Mesa)
 Phoenix Suns, basketball
 Oakland A's, spring baseball (Scottsdale)
 San Francisco Giants, spring baseball (Scottsdale)
 Milwaukee Brewers, spring baseball (Sun City)
 Seattle Mariners, spring baseball (Tempe)
 *San Diego Padres, spring baseball (Yuma)*
**Special Annual Events (300)**
 Fiesta Bowl Football Classic (Tempe)
**Places Rated Score: 2,950      Places Rated Rank: 23**

### Pocono Mountains, PA
**Family Entertainment Parks (1,700)**
 Dorney Park (Allentown)
 Bushkill Park (Easton)
 Angela Park (Hazleton)
 Rocky Glen Park (Wilkes-Barre)
**Music and Theater (800)**
 Muhlenberg College Theater Festival, summer (Allentown)
 Pennsylvania Stage Company (Allentown)
 Dale Snow Theater, summer (East Stroudsburg)
 Gennetti Dinner Playhouse, summer (Hazleton)
**Special Annual Events (150)**
 Pocono Winter Carnival (Stroudsburg area)
**Places Rated Score: 2,650      Places Rated Rank: 28**

### Portland, ME
**Family Entertainment Parks (200)**
 Palace Playland (Old Orchard Beach)
**Music and Theater (900)**
 North Country Productions at Pleasant Mountain, summer (Bridgton)
 Brunswick Music Theater, summer (Brunswick)
 Russell Square Players, summer (Gorham)
 Portland Stage Company (Portland)
 Portland Symphony Orchestra (Portland)
**Special Annual Events (50)**
 Maine Festival of the Arts, summer (Brunswick)
**Places Rated Score: 1,150      Places Rated Rank: 56**

### Portland–Columbia River, OR
**Music and Theater (800)**
◄ Oregon Symphony Orchestra (Portland)
◄ Portland Opera Association (Portland)
**Professional Sports (400)**
 Portland Trail Blazers, basketball
**Special Annual Events (300)**
◄ Portland Rose Festival, late spring (Portland)
**Places Rated Score: 1,500      Places Rated Rank: 50**

### Portsmouth–Kennebunk, NH–ME
**Family Entertainment Parks (1,700)**
 Benson's Animal Park (Hudson, NH)
 Funtown U.S.A. (Saco, ME)
 Canobie Lake Park (Salem, NH)
 York's Wild Kingdom (York Beach, ME)
**Music and Theater (1,800)**
 Hackmatack Playhouse, summer (Berwick, ME)
 The Hampton Playhouse, summer (Hampton, NH)
 American Stage Festival, summer (Milford, NH)
 Ogunquit Playhouse, summer (Ogunquit, ME)
 Peterborough Players, summer (Peterborough, NH)
◄ Theatre by the Sea (Portsmouth, NH)
 Town & Country Playhouse, summer (Salem)

Special Annual Events (250)
　　Summer Band Festival (Concord, NH)
　　Holiday Tours of Strawberry Banke, Christmas season
　　　(Portsmouth)
Places Rated Score: 3,750　　　Places Rated Rank: 18

## Providence–Newport, RI
Family Entertainment Parks (500)
　　Rocky Point Park (Warwick)
Music and Theater (2,000)
　　Theater by the Sea, summer (Matunuck)
◄ Newport Music Festival (Newport)
　　The Rhode Island Shakespeare Theater, summer (Newport)
　　Brown Summer Theater (Providence)
　　Looking Glass Theatre (Providence)
◄ Trinity Square Repertory Company (Providence)
　　Warwick Musical Theater, summer (Warwick)
　　*Colonial Theater, summer (Westerly)*
Special Annual Events (450)
　　Bristol Fourth of July Parade (Bristol)
　　Christmas in Newport (Newport)
　　Festival of Historic Houses, spring (Providence)
Places Rated Score: 2,950　　　Places Rated Rank: 23

## Put-in-Bay–Lake Erie Shore, OH
Family Entertainment Parks (700)
◄ Cedar Point (Sandusky)
Music and Theater (500)
　　Toledo Opera Association (Toledo)
　　Toledo Symphony Orchestra (Toledo)
Special Annual Events (100)
　　Erie County Fair, summer (Sandusky)
　　International Festival, spring (Toledo)
Places Rated Score: 1,300　　　Places Rated Rank: 53

## Rangeley Lakes, ME
Special Annual Events (250)
　　Sled Dog Races, winter (Rangeley)
　　Skowhegan State Fair, summer (Skowhegan)
Places Rated Score: 250　　　Places Rated Rank: 95

## Redwoods–Shasta–Lassen, CA
Music and Theater (100)
　　Dell'Arte Players Company (Arcata)
Special Annual Events (175)
　　Rodeo Week, spring (Redding)
　　Siskiyou Golden Fair, summer (Yreka)
Places Rated Score: 275　　　Places Rated Rank: 94

## Richmond–Fredericksburg, VA
Family Entertainment Parks (700)
◄ Kings Dominion (Doswell)
Music and Theater (1,000)
◄ Richmond Symphony Orchestra (Richmond)
　　Virginia Museum Theatre (Richmond)
◄ Virginia Opera Association (Richmond)
Special Annual Events (150)
　　June Jubilee (Richmond)
　　Virginia State Fair, early fall (Richmond)
Places Rated Score: 1,850　　　Places Rated Rank: 44

## Sacramento–Gold Rush Towns, CA
Music and Theater (500)
　　Sacramento Opera (Sacramento)
◄ Sacramento Symphony Orchestra (Sacramento)
Special Annual Events (150)
　　Sacramento Dixieland Jubilee, spring
Places Rated Score: 650　　　Places Rated Rank: 74

## St. Augustine–Northeast Coast, FL
Music and Theater (600)
◄ Jacksonville Symphony Orchestra (Jacksonville)
　　*Cross and Sword,* historical drama (St. Augustine)
Special Annual Events (100)
　　Gator Bowl Festival and Football Classic (Jacksonville)
Places Rated Score: 700　　　Places Rated Rank: 71

## St. Louis–Mark Twain Country, MO–IL
Family Entertainment Parks (700)
◄ Six Flags Over Mid-America (Eureka)
Music and Theater (1,400)
◄ Opera Theater of St. Louis (St. Louis)
◄ Repertory Theatre of St. Louis (St. Louis)
◄ St. Louis Symphony Orchestra (St. Louis)
　　Theatre Project Company (St. Louis)
Professional Sports (1,400)
　　St. Louis Blues, hockey
　　St. Louis Cardinals, NL baseball
　　St. Louis Cardinals, football
　　St. Louis Steamers, indoor soccer
Special Annual Events (525)
　　*Way of Lights, Thanksgiving to January (Belleville, IL)*
　　National Tom Sawyer Days, early summer (Hannibal, MO)
　　National Ragtime and Traditional Jazz Festival, late spring
　　　(St. Louis)
　　Veiled Prophet Fair, summer (St. Louis)
Places Rated Score: 4,025　　　Places Rated Rank: 16

## Salt Lake City, UT
Family Entertainment Parks (700)
　　Lagoon Amusement Park (Farmington)
　　Surf Amusement, waterslide (Ogden)
Music and Theater (1,000)
◄ Pioneer Memorial Theater (Salt Lake City)
　　Utah Opera Company (Salt Lake City)
◄ Utah Symphony Orchestra (Salt Lake City)
Professional Sports (400)
　　Utah Jazz, basketball
Special Annual Events (300)
　　Festival of the American West, summer (Logan)
　　Days of '47 Pioneer Celebration, summer (Salt Lake City)
Places Rated Score: 2,400　　　Places Rated Rank: 33

## San Antonio, TX
Family Entertainment Parks (200)
　　Camp Warnecke, waterpark (New Braunfels)
Music and Theater (500)
　　San Antonio Grand Opera (San Antonio)
◄ San Antonio Symphony Orchestra (San Antonio)
Professional Sports (400)
　　San Antonio Spurs, basketball
Special Annual Events (300)
　　Wurstfest, fall (New Braunfels)
◄ Fiesta San Antonio, spring (San Antonio)
Places Rated Score: 1,400　　　Places Rated Rank: 51

## San Diego, CA
Family Entertainment Parks (900)
　　Raging Waters, waterpark (Carlsbad)
◄ Sea World of California (San Diego)
Music and Theater (1,600)
　　La Jolla Playhouse, summer (La Jolla)
◄ Old Globe Theatre (San Diego)
◄ San Diego Opera (San Diego)
　　San Diego Repertory Theatre (San Diego)
◄ San Diego Symphony Orchestra (San Diego)
Professional Sports (1,100)
　　San Diego Chargers, football
　　San Diego Padres, NL baseball
　　San Diego Sockers, soccer
Special Annual Events (100)
　　Holiday Bowl football classic (San Diego)
Places Rated Score: 3,700　　　Places Rated Rank: 19

## San Francisco, CA
Family Entertainment Parks (200)
　　Marine World Africa USA (Redwood City)
Music and Theater (2,800)
◄ Berkeley Repertory Theatre (Berkeley)
　　Berkeley Stage Company (Berkeley)
◄ Oakland Symphony Orchestra (Oakland)
◄ American Conservatory Theatre (San Francisco)
　　Julian Theatre (San Francisco)

Lamplighters/Opera West (San Francisco)
Magic Theatre (San Francisco)
One Act Theatre Company of San Francisco (San Francisco)
Pocket Opera (San Francisco)
◀ San Francisco Opera Association (San Francisco)
◀ San Francisco Symphony (San Francisco)
Western Opera Theater (San Francisco)
Professional Sports (1,200)
Oakland A's, AL baseball
San Francisco 49ers, football
San Francisco Giants, NL baseball
Special Annual Events (150)
Chinese New Year Celebration, winter (San Francisco)
Places Rated Score: 4,350      Places Rated Rank: 11

### Santa Barbara–San Simeon, CA
Music and Theater (200)
Santa Barbara Symphony Orchestra (Santa Barbara)
Special Annual Events (100)
Mozart Festival, summer (San Luis Obispo)
Santa Barbara Arts Festival, spring (Santa Barbara)
Places Rated Score: 300      Places Rated Rank: 92

### Savannah–Golden Isles, GA
Music and Theater (400)
Jekyll Island Musical Comedy Festival, summer (Jekyll Island)
Savannah Symphony Orchestra (Savannah)
Special Annual Events (150)
Christmas in Savannah (Savannah)
Places Rated Score: 550      Places Rated Rank: 80

### Seattle–Mount Rainier–North Cascades, WA
Family Entertainment Parks (700)
Waterworks Park, waterpark (Bellevue)
Enchanted Village (Federal Way)
Music and Theater (1,700)
Empty Space Theatre (Seattle)
Intimate Theatre Company (Seattle)
Northwest Chamber Orchestra (Seattle)
◀ Seattle Opera Association (Seattle)
◀ Seattle Repertory Theatre (Seattle)
Seattle Symphony Orchestra (Seattle)
Tacoma Actors Guild (Tacoma)
Professional Sports (1,500)
Seattle Mariners, AL baseball
Seattle Seahawks, football
Seattle SuperSonics, basketball
Tacoma Stars, indoor soccer
Special Annual Events (300)
Washington State International Air Fair, summer (Everett)
Seafair, summer (Seattle)
Places Rated Score: 4,200      Places Rated Rank: 13

### Spokane–Coeur d'Alene, WA–ID
Family Entertainment Parks (500)
Riverfront Park (Spokane, WA)
Music and Theater (400)
◀ Spokane Symphony Orchestra (Spokane)
Special Annual Events (200)
Diamond Spur Rodeo, spring (Spokane)
Spokane Interstate Fair, late summer (Spokane)
Places Rated Score: 1,100      Places Rated Rank: 58

### ★ Tampa Bay–Southwest Coast, FL
Family Entertainment Parks (900)
Jungle Larry's African Safari Park (Naples)
◀◀ Busch Gardens—The Dark Continent (Tampa)
Music and Theater (1,500)
Florida Opera West (St. Petersburg)
◀ Palisades Theatre Company (St. Petersburg)
Asolo Opera Company (Sarasota)
◀ Asolo State Theater (Sarasota)
Florida Studio Theatre (Sarasota)
◀ Florida Gulf Coast Symphony Orchestra (Tampa)

Professional Sports (3,100)
Pittsburgh Pirates, spring baseball (Bradenton)
Philadelphia Phillies, spring baseball (Clearwater)
Toronto Blue Jays, spring baseball (Dunedin)
Kansas City Royals, spring baseball (Fort Myers)
New York Mets, spring baseball (St. Petersburg)
St. Louis Cardinals, spring baseball (St. Petersburg)
Chicago White Sox, spring baseball (Sarasota)
Cincinnati Reds, spring baseball (Tampa)
Tampa Bay Buccaneers, football
Tampa Bay Rowdies, soccer
Special Annual Events (150)
Gasparilla Pirate Invasion Parade and State Fair, winter (Tampa)
Places Rated Score: 5,650      Places Rated Rank: 6

### Traverse City–Petoskey, MI
Music and Theater (600)
◀◀ National Music Camp (Interlochen)
Cherry County Playhouse, summer (Traverse City)
Special Annual Events (100)
Indian Pow-Wow, summer (Cross Village)
Places Rated Score: 700      Places Rated Rank: 71

### Tucson, AZ
Music and Theater (900)
◀ Arizona Opera Company (Tucson)
Arizona Theatre Company (Tucson)
Invisible Theatre (Tucson)
Tucson Symphony Orchestra (Tucson)
Special Annual Events (200)
La Fiesta de los Vaqueros, winter (Tucson)
Tucson Festival, early spring (Tucson)
Places Rated Score: 1,100      Places Rated Rank: 58

### Tulsa–Lake O' The Cherokees, OK
Music and Theater (1,200)
*Trail of Tears* outdoor historic drama (Tahlequah)
American Theatre Company (Tulsa)
◀ Tulsa Opera Inc. (Tulsa)
◀ Tulsa Philharmonic Orchestra (Tulsa)
Professional Sports (300)
Tulsa Roughnecks, soccer
Special Annual Events (350)
Will Rogers Rodeo, summer (Claremore)
Muskogee State Fair, late summer (Muskogee)
Discoveryland's *Oklahoma,* summer (Tulsa)
Places Rated Score: 1,850      Places Rated Rank: 44

### Vicksburg–Natchez–Baton Rouge, MS–LA
Music and Theater (400)
Baton Rouge Symphony Orchestra (Baton Rouge, LA)
Jackson Symphony Orchestra (Jackson, MS)
Special Annual Events (250)
LSU Festival of Contemporary Music, spring (Baton Rouge)
Natchez Pilgrimage, spring (Natchez, MS)
Places Rated Score: 650      Places Rated Rank: 74

### Washington, DC–MD–VA
Music and Theater (2,300)
Olney Theater, summer (Olney, MD)
Round House Theatre (Silver Spring, MD)
◀ Arena Stage (Washington)
◀ Folger Theatre Group (Washington)
Living Stage Theatre Company (Washington)
◀ National Symphony Orchestra (Washington)
New Playwright's Theatre (Washington)
◀ Washington Opera (Washington)
Wolf Trap Company (Vienna, VA)
Professional Sports (1,100)
Washington Bullets, basketball
Washington Capitals, hockey
Washington Redskins, football

Special Annual Events (750)
Virginia Wine Festival, summer (Middleburg area, VA)
◄ Cherry Blossom Festival, spring (Washington)
Festival of American Folklife, summer (Washington)
Fourth of July Celebration (Washington)
Places Rated Score: 4,150    Places Rated Rank: 15

**White Mountains, NH**
Music and Theater (400)
New Hampshire Music Festival (Center Harbor)
Weathervane Theater, summer (Whitefield)
Special Annual Events (50)
Winterfest (North Conway)
Places Rated Score: 450    Places Rated Rank: 85

**Williamsburg–Colonial Triangle, VA**
Family Entertainment Parks (700)
◄◄ Busch Gardens—The Old Country (Williamsburg)
Music and Theater (500)
◄ Virginia Orchestra Group (Norfolk)
Virginia Stage Company (Norfolk)
Special Annual Events (350)
Hampton Jazz Festival, early summer (Hampton)
Harborfest, summer (Norfolk)
Grand Illumination, December (Williamsburg)
Places Rated Score: 1,550    Places Rated Rank: 48

**Wilmington–Cape Fear, NC**
Music and Theater (200)
*The Immortal Showboat,* summer (Wilmington)
Special Annual Events (150)
Celebration of the Arts, spring (Wilmington)
Indian Dance Festival, spring (Wilmington)
Old Wilmington Riverfest, fall (Wilmington)
Places Rated Score: 350    Places Rated Rank: 90

**Wine Country, CA**
Music and Theater (200)
Russian River Jazz Festival (Guerneville)
Special Annual Events (450)
Russian River Rodeo, late spring (Guerneville)
Russian River Wine Fest, spring (Healdsburg)
Lake County Rodeo, summer (Lakeport)
Sonoma-Marin Fair, summer (Petaluma)
Sonoma County Fair, summer (Santa Rosa)
Mendocino Coast Music Festival, winter (Ukiah)
Places Rated Score: 650    Places Rated Rank: 74

**Wisconsin Dells, WI**
Music and Theater (100)
Madison Civic Opera Association (Madison)
Special Annual Events (100)
Great Wisconsin Dells Balloon Rally, summer (Wisconsin Dells)
Places Rated Score: 200    Places Rated Rank: 96

**Yellowstone–Jackson–Tetons, WY–ID–MT**
Special Annual Events (450)
College National Finals Rodeo, late spring (Bozeman, MT)
Festival of Nations, summer (Red Lodge, MT)
Grand Teton Music Festival, summer (Teton Village, WY)
Places Rated Score: 450    Places Rated Rank: 85

**Yosemite–Sequoia–Death Valley, CA**
Special Annual Events (100)
Sierra Summer Festival (Mammoth Lakes)
Places Rated Score: 100    Places Rated Rank: 102

**Zion–Bryce Canyon, UT**
Special Annual Events (150)
Utah Shakespearean Festival, summer (Cedar City)
Places Rated Score: 150    Places Rated Rank: 99

# RANKINGS: Entertainment for All

Four criteria were used to determine the scores in this chapter: (1) family entertainment parks; (2) music and theater—including symphony orchestras, opera companies, repertory theater companies, summer theaters, and summer music festivals; (3) professional sports—including resident professional, big-league baseball, basketball, football, soccer, and hockey teams; (4) special annual events. In addition, bonus points were given to the Vacation Places for certain unique types of entertainment.

Places that receive tie scores are given the same rank and are listed in alphabetic order.

## Vacation Places from First to Last

| Places Rated Rank | Places Rated Score |
|---|---|
| 1. New York City, NY | 15,175 |
| 2. Los Angeles, CA | 9,300 |
| 3. Chicago, IL | 7,700 |
| 4. Philadelphia, PA–DE–NJ | 6,100 |
| 5. Boston, MA | 6,000 |
| 6. Tampa Bay–Southwest Coast, FL | 5,650 |
| 7. Minneapolis–St. Paul, MN | 5,150 |
| 8. Cincinnati, OH–KY | 4,900 |
| 9. Dallas–Fort Worth, TX | 4,450 |
| 10. Orlando–Space Coast, FL | 4,400 |
| 11. San Francisco, CA | 4,350 |
| 12. Miami–Gold Coast–Keys, FL | 4,300 |
| 13. Berkshire Hills–Pioneer Valley, MA | 4,200 |
| 13. Seattle–Mount Rainier–North Cascades, WA | 4,200 |
| 15. Washington, DC–MD–VA | 4,150 |
| 16. St. Louis–Mark Twain Country, MO–IL | 4,025 |
| 17. Catskill Mountains, NY | 3,850 |
| 18. Portsmouth–Kennebunk, NH–ME | 3,750 |
| 19. San Diego, CA | 3,700 |
| 20. Houston–Galveston, TX | 3,450 |
| 21. Denver–Rocky Mountain National Park, CO | 3,400 |
| 22. Atlantic City, NJ | 3,300 |
| 23. Phoenix–Valley of the Sun, AZ | 2,950 |
| 23. Providence–Newport, RI | 2,950 |
| 25. Long Island, NY | 2,900 |
| 26. Baltimore–Chesapeake Bay, MD | 2,800 |
| 27. Niagara Falls–Western New York, NY | 2,750 |
| 28. Atlanta, GA | 2,650 |
| 28. Pocono Mountains, PA | 2,650 |
| 30. Finger Lakes, NY | 2,600 |
| 30. Pennsylvania Dutch Country, PA | 2,600 |
| 32. New Orleans, LA | 2,450 |
| 33. Salt Lake City, UT | 2,400 |
| 34. Adirondack Mountains, NY | 2,350 |
| 35. Mystic Seaport–Connecticut Valley, CT | 2,300 |
| 36. Lexington–Bluegrass Country, KY | 2,200 |
| 37. Cape Cod–The Islands, MA | 2,150 |

| Places Rated Rank | Places Rated Score |
|---|---|
| 37. Nashville, TN | 2,150 |
| 39. Ozarks–Eureka Springs, AR–MO | 2,100 |
| 40. Jersey Shore, NJ | 2,050 |
| 40. Memphis, TN–AR–MS | 2,050 |
| 40. Monterey–Big Sur, CA | 2,050 |
| 43. Albuquerque–Santa Fe–Taos, NM | 1,900 |
| 44. Asheville–Smoky Mountains, NC | 1,850 |
| 44. Knoxville–Smoky Mountains, TN | 1,850 |
| 44. Richmond–Fredericksburg, VA | 1,850 |
| 44. Tulsa–Lake O' The Cherokees, OK | 1,850 |
| 48. Green Mountains, VT | 1,550 |
| 48. Williamsburg–Colonial Triangle, VA | 1,550 |
| 50. Portland–Columbia River, OR | 1,500 |
| 51. Oklahoma City–Cherokee Strip, OK | 1,400 |
| 51. San Antonio, TX | 1,400 |
| 53. Put-in-Bay–Lake Erie Shore, OH | 1,300 |
| 54. Holland–Lake Michigan Shore, MI | 1,225 |
| 55. Hawaii | 1,200 |
| 56. Mobile Bay–Gulfport, AL–MS | 1,150 |
| 56. Portland, ME | 1,150 |
| 58. Aspen–Vail, CO | 1,100 |
| 58. Spokane–Coeur d'Alene, WA–ID | 1,100 |
| 58. Tucson, AZ | 1,100 |
| 61. Colorado Springs, CO | 1,050 |
| 61. Lake Tahoe–Reno, NV–CA | 1,050 |
| 61. Panhandle, FL | 1,050 |
| 64. Black Hills, SD | 1,025 |
| 65. Austin–Hill Country, TX | 950 |
| 65. Boise–Sun Valley, ID | 950 |
| 67. Corpus Christi–Padre Island, TX | 850 |
| 68. Anchorage–Kenai Peninsula, AK | 800 |
| 68. Crater Lake–Klamath Falls, OR | 800 |
| 70. Myrtle Beach–Grand Strand, SC | 750 |
| 71. Las Vegas–Lake Mead, NV–AZ | 700 |

| Places Rated Rank | Places Rated Score |
|---|---|
| 71. St. Augustine–Northeast Coast, FL | 700 |
| 71. Traverse City–Petoskey, MI | 700 |
| 74. Glacier National Park–Flathead Lake, MT | 650 |
| 74. Lake of the Ozarks, MO | 650 |
| 74. Sacramento–Gold Rush Towns, CA | 650 |
| 74. Vicksburg–Natchez–Baton Rouge, MS–LA | 650 |
| 74. Wine Country, CA | 650 |
| 79. Bar Harbor–Acadia, ME | 600 |
| 80. Door County, WI | 550 |
| 80. Savannah–Golden Isles, GA | 550 |
| 82. Blue Ridge Mountains, VA | 500 |
| 82. Charleston, SC | 500 |
| 82. Palm Springs–Desert Playgrounds, CA | 500 |
| 85. Boone–High Country, NC | 450 |
| 85. Chattanooga–Huntsville, TN–AL–GA | 450 |
| 85. White Mountains, NH | 450 |
| 85. Yellowstone–Jackson–Tetons, WY–ID–MT | 450 |
| 89. North Woods–Land O'Lakes, WI | 400 |
| 90. Brownsville–Rio Grande Valley, TX | 350 |
| 90. Wilmington–Cape Fear, NC | 350 |
| 92. Outer Banks, NC | 300 |
| 92. Santa Barbara–San Simeon, CA | 300 |
| 94. Redwoods–Shasta–Lassen, CA | 275 |
| 95. Rangeley Lakes, ME | 250 |
| 96. Bend–Cascade Mountains, OR | 200 |
| 96. Lake Powell–Glen Canyon, AZ–UT | 200 |
| 96. Wisconsin Dells, WI | 200 |
| 99. Flaming Gorge, UT–WY–CO | 150 |
| 99. Hilton Head, NC | 150 |
| 99. Zion–Bryce Canyon, UT | 150 |
| 102. Coos Bay–South Coast, OR | 100 |
| 102. Eastern Shore, VA | 100 |
| 102. Grand Canyon Country, AZ | 100 |
| 102. Olympic Peninsula, WA | 100 |
| 102. Yosemite–Sequoia–Death Valley, CA | 100 |
| 107. Mackinac Island–Sault Ste. Marie, MI | 50 |

## Vacation Places Listed Alphabetically

| Vacation Place | Places Rated Rank | Vacation Place | Places Rated Rank | Vacation Place | Places Rated Rank |
|---|---|---|---|---|---|
| Adirondack Mountains, NY | 34 | Hawaii | 55 | Pocono Mountains, PA | 28 |
| Albuquerque–Santa Fe–Taos, NM | 43 | Hilton Head, SC | 99 | Portland, ME | 56 |
| Anchorage–Kenai Peninsula, AK | 68 | Holland–Lake Michigan Shore, MI | 54 | | |
| Asheville–Smoky Mountains, NC | 44 | | | Portland–Columbia River, OR | 50 |
| Aspen–Vail, CO | 58 | Houston–Galveston, TX | 20 | Portsmouth-Kennebunk, NH–ME | 18 |
| | | Jersey Shore, NJ | 40 | Providence–Newport, RI | 23 |
| Atlanta, GA | 28 | Knoxville–Smoky Mountains, TN | 44 | Put-in-Bay–Lake Erie Shore, OH | 53 |
| Atlantic City, NJ | 22 | Lake of the Ozarks, MO | 74 | Rangeley Lakes, ME | 95 |
| Austin–Hill Country, TX | 65 | Lake Powell–Glen Canyon, AZ–UT | 96 | | |
| Baltimore–Chesapeake Bay, MD | 26 | | | Redwoods–Shasta–Lassen, CA | 94 |
| Bar Harbor–Acadia, ME | 79 | Lake Tahoe–Reno, NV-CA | 61 | Richmond–Fredericksburg, VA | 44 |
| | | Las Vegas–Lake Mead, NV–AZ | 71 | Sacramento–Gold Rush Towns, CA | 74 |
| Bend–Cascade Mountains, OR | 96 | Lexington–Bluegrass Country, KY | 36 | St. Augustine–Northeast Coast, FL | 71 |
| Berkshire Hills–Pioneer Valley, MA | 13 | Long Island, NY | 25 | St. Louis–Mark Twain Country, | |
| Black Hills, SD | 64 | Los Angeles, CA | 2 | MO–IL | 16 |
| Blue Ridge Mountains, VA | 82 | | | | |
| Boise–Sun Valley, ID | 65 | Mackinac Island–Sault Ste. Marie, | | Salt Lake City, UT | 33 |
| | | MI | 107 | San Antonio, TX | 51 |
| Boone–High Country, NC | 85 | Memphis, TN–AR–MS | 40 | San Diego, CA | 19 |
| Boston, MA | 5 | Miami–Gold Coast–Keys, FL | 12 | San Francisco, CA | 11 |
| Brownsville–Rio Grande Valley, TX | 90 | Minneapolis–St. Paul, MN–WI | 7 | Santa Barbara–San Simeon, CA | 92 |
| Cape Cod–The Islands, MA | 37 | Mobile Bay–Gulfport, AL–MS | 56 | | |
| Catskill Mountains, NY | 17 | | | Savannah–Golden Isles, GA | 80 |
| | | Monterey–Big Sur, CA | 40 | Seattle–Mount Rainier–North | |
| Charleston, SC | 82 | Myrtle Beach–Grand Strand, SC | 70 | Cascades, WA | 13 |
| Chattanooga–Huntsville, TN–AL–GA | 85 | Mystic Seaport–Connecticut Valley, | | Spokane–Coeur d'Alene, WA–ID | 58 |
| Chicago, IL | 3 | CT | 35 | Tampa Bay–Southwest Coast, FL | 6 |
| Cincinnati, OH–KY | 8 | Nashville, TN | 37 | Traverse City–Petoskey, MI | 71 |
| Colorado Springs, CO | 61 | New Orleans, LA | 32 | | |
| | | | | Tucson, AZ | 58 |
| Coos Bay–South Coast, OR | 102 | New York City, NY | 1 | Tulsa–Lake O' The Cherokees, OK | 44 |
| Corpus Christi–Padre Island, TX | 67 | Niagara Falls–Western New York, | | Vicksburg–Natchez–Baton Rouge, | |
| Crater Lake–Klamath Falls, OR | 68 | NY | 27 | MS–LA | 74 |
| Dallas–Fort Worth, TX | 9 | North Woods–Land O'Lakes, WI | 89 | Washington, DC–MD–VA | 15 |
| Denver–Rocky Mountain National | | Oklahoma City–Cherokee Strip, OK | 51 | White Mountains, NH | 85 |
| Park, CO | 21 | Olympic Peninsula, WA | 102 | | |
| | | | | Williamsburg–Colonial Triangle, VA | 48 |
| Door County, WI | 80 | Orlando–Space Coast, FL | 10 | Wilmington–Cape Fear, NC | 90 |
| Eastern Shore, VA | 102 | Outer Banks, NC | 92 | Wine Country, CA | 74 |
| Finger Lakes, NY | 30 | Ozarks–Eureka Springs, AR–MO | 39 | Wisconsin Dells, WI | 96 |
| Flaming Gorge, UT–WY–CO | 99 | Palm Springs–Desert Playgrounds, | | Yellowstone–Jackson–Tetons, | |
| Glacier National Park–Flathead | | CA | 82 | WY–ID–MT | 85 |
| Lake, MT | 74 | Panhandle, FL | 61 | | |
| | | | | Yosemite–Sequoia–Death Valley, | |
| Grand Canyon Country, AZ | 102 | Pennsylvania Dutch Country, PA | 30 | CA | 102 |
| Green Mountains, VT | 48 | Philadelphia, PA–DE–NJ | 4 | Zion–Bryce Canyon, UT | 99 |
| | | Phoenix–Valley of the Sun, AZ | 23 | | |

**TOP TEN:** Entertainment for All

All of the top ten Vacation Places ranked for entertainment are metropolitan areas containing large cities. Five of them, not unexpectedly, are among the seven largest cities in the United States.

| | Places Rated Score |
|---|---|
| 1. New York City, NY | 15,175 |
| 2. Los Angeles, CA | 9,300 |
| 3. Chicago, IL | 7,700 |
| 4. Philadelphia, PA–DE–NJ | 6,100 |
| 5. Boston, MA | 6,000 |
| 6. Tampa Bay–Southwest Coast, FL | 5,650 |
| 7. Minneapolis–St. Paul, MN–WI | 5,150 |
| 8. Cincinnati, OH–KY | 4,900 |
| 9. Dallas–Fort Worth, TX | 4,450 |
| 10. Orlando–Space Coast, FL | 4,400 |

## 1. New York City, NY

Theater in New York means the bright lights of Broadway to most out of towners, but Broadway is only a part of it. In Manhattan alone, more than two dozen professional repertory theaters present regular seasons of performances. Many of these companies are innovative in their approach to the theater; they take chances on new ideas that the commercial Broadway theaters are not willing to take. More than half a dozen opera companies in addition to the Metropolitan and several symphony orchestras add to the entertainment fare available year-round in the city. In the summer the New York Philharmonic, the Metropolitan Opera, and the New York Shakespeare Festival all present free performances in Central Park.

New York places first among all the Vacation Places for its professional sports and for music and theater, and seventh for special annual events. Both baseball leagues are represented here, as are basketball, football, soccer, and hockey.

For the latest information on what is going on in the city, phone the New York Convention and Visitors Bureau at (212) 397-8222 or go to their center at 2 Columbus Circle, where free maps, brochures, and twofers (two tickets for the price of one) to some shows are available. If you are looking for free entertainment, phone (212) 755-4100 for a list of current happenings. There are three locations where tickets for same-day performances are put on sale for half price: at the Times Square Ticket Center, 47th Street and Broadway; at 2 World Trade Center, mezzanine level; and at the Fulton Mall, DeKalb Avenue, in Brooklyn.

## 2. Los Angeles, CA

The parks of the Los Angeles area are major draws for vacationers: Disneyland, Knott's Berry Farm, the Universal Studios Tour and Entertainment Center, and Six Flags Magic Mountain all rank among the 25 most popular theme parks in the United States.

The first-class theaters, orchestras, and opera companies listed in this chapter's Place Profiles compose only a small part of the entertainment possibilities in this star-struck city. Actors Equity, the union to which virtually all professional actors and actresses belong, has a waiver rule that allows members to work with aspiring performers (even if they are nonmembers) in theaters of fewer than 100 seats. This waiver makes it possible for many small and developing theaters to present excellent shows.

Both baseball leagues and all four of the other major professional sports considered by *Vacation Places Rated* are represented in the Los Angeles area.

Watching the annual Tournament of Roses Parade and Football Classic is a New Year's Day habit for millions of television watchers throughout the United States. The American Bus Association has awarded it the designation of annual super event.

## 3. Chicago, IL

The Chicago metropolitan area has one major theme park, Six Flags Great America, and several smaller amusement areas.

Chicagoans are justly proud of the Chicago Symphony Orchestra, which has a worldwide reputation, as well as of the Goodman Theatre and the Lyric Opera. The Ravinia Festival, a summer-long program of musical performances ranging from symphony to folk music, is especially appreciated. Hundreds of the people who attend Ravinia concerts arrive with picnic baskets; some bring elegant accessories for their outdoor suppers, such as white tablecloths, candles in silver candelabras and crystal champagne glasses.

The five professional sports considered for the scoring are represented in Chicago. The Chicago Cubs, the city's National League baseball team, have become favorites in many other parts of the country in recent years whether or not they are on a winning streak, because their home games are telecast nationally.

## 4. Philadelphia, PA–DE–NJ

Philadelphia's amusement parks are not of major size, but there are three of them in the vicinity. Sesame Place, in Langhorne, Pennsylvania, is based on the television show, "Sesame Street."

The Philadelphia Orchestra is outstanding; it performs under the stars in Fairmount Park in summer. A few miles north of the city, in New Hope, the Bucks County Playhouse presents a summer program of Broadway hits in an old mill.

Professional sports teams include National League baseball, basketball, football, and hockey.

## 5. Boston, MA

Five repertory theaters, four opera companies, a world-class symphony orchestra, and half a dozen summer-theater and concert programs earn Boston second place for its music and theater. Entertainment opportunities in Boston are not limited to professional presentations; there are more than 50 colleges and universities within 20 miles of the State House that offer hundreds of student performances of concerts and plays.

For its professional sports teams Boston is tied with four other Vacation Places for seventh place. The metro area has American League baseball, basketball, hockey, and football teams.

Several exceptional annual events earn Boston fifth place in this classification. One of the most exciting is Harborfest, a week-long celebration of the city's historic maritime past held around the Fourth of July.

## 6. Tampa Bay–Southwest Coast, FL

This Vacation Place is in second place for its professional sports. Eight big-league baseball teams have their spring-training headquarters here; Tampa also has professional football and soccer teams.

Busch Gardens—The Dark Continent is second only to Disney World as a major Florida tourist attraction. In addition to the entertainment, rides, food outlets, and shops characteristic of modern theme parks, Busch Gardens is one of the largest zoological parks in the country.

In Sarasota, the Asolo State Theater performs on the John Ringling estate. The interior decor of the beautiful building, originally part of a castle near Venice, Italy, was purchased by the state of Florida and reassembled here.

Tampa holds a unique festival each February called the Gasparilla Pirate Invasion.

## 7. Minneapolis–St. Paul, MN–WI

The Twin Cities rank ninth among Vacation Places for their music and theater, placing them above many metropolitan areas of much larger population. There are six musical and theatrical companies in Minneapolis, two in St. Paul. The magnificent Minnesota Orchestra performs in a hall that is acclaimed as acoustically perfect; the orchestra's winter season is complemented by a series of free summer concerts. St. Paul has what is claimed to be the only full-time professional chamber orchestra in the United States. The Guthrie Theatre is known from coast to coast for its excellence; in 1982 it was given a Tony Award for outstanding contribution to American theater.

Professional baseball, football, soccer, and hockey teams call the Twin Cities home.

Several outstanding annual events earned fourth place in this category for the Twin Cities, among them the St. Paul Winter Carnival and the midsummer Minneapolis Aquatennial.

## 8. Cincinnati, OH–KY

Cincinnati ranks fourth for its family entertainment parks; the area has one major and three smaller amusement centers.

Four special annual events give it ninth place (tied with two other Vacation Places) in this category.

While not among the top ten in either of the other two entertainment classifications, orchestras and opera companies in Cincinnati and Dayton plus Cincinnati's baseball and football teams add to the overall score for entertainment opportunities.

## 9. Dallas–Fort Worth, TX

Professional baseball, basketball, football, and soccer teams give the Dallas–Fort Worth area seventh place in this type of entertainment.

The two-city Vacation Place also has a major theme park and three smaller amusement parks, two orchestras, and two repertory theaters. The Cotton Bowl Parade and Football Classic is on the American Bus Assocation's list of annual super events.

## 10. Orlando–Space Coast, FL

The Orlando area's three nationally known family entertainment parks give this Vacation Place half of second place (tied with Atlantic City, New Jersey) in this category. The area also includes the spring-training grounds for five major-league baseball teams, giving it seventh place (tied with four others) for professional sports. These assets, along with the enviable winter climate, play a large part in the popularity of central Florida as a vacation destination.

# Putting It All Together

Finding the Best Vacation Places in America

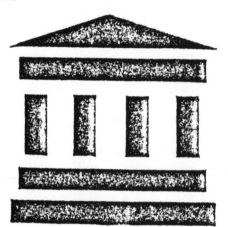

**INTRODUCTION:** Putting It All Together

If you are already familiar with the preceding six chapters, you know that *Vacation Places Rated*, like the first two studies in this series—*Places Rated Almanac* and *Retirement Places Rated*—has ranked all the selected areas according to a variety of criteria. Naturally, very few people would give equal weight to all the measurements in this book; therefore, in the chapter Ranking Your Own Vacation Places we'll show you how to use our information to arrive at your own best choices for vacation destinations.

All the same, any writer, editor, or publisher who plays the rating game is expected to come up with a final list of the top-ranking places. So here goes. This is where we figure out who are the hosts with the most to offer.

This book has examined positive factors for vacation enjoyment. Information on such factors as pos-sible tourist traps, the likelihood of encountering extremes of weather, crime, pollution, and so forth is not included.

Many of the ratings in *Vacation Places Rated* were based primarily upon the availability of the elements that were scored. For instance, the number of hotels, motels, and restaurants within a Vacation Place determined to a great extent that place's score in the chapter entitled Basic Necessities. Some judgments of quality were included, however. In the same chapter, for example, points were also given for award-winning hotels and restaurants. Every effort was made to obtain respected and well-researched sources for these quality judgments, and the sources at times included the careful evaluations of the author.

Insofar as possible, prior opinions about a Vacation Place did not influence the ratings. No one involved in

---

### Do You Read the Last Page of the Mystery First?

If you have skipped ahead to this chapter in order to find out which Vacation Places have been judged the best, you may be surprised at what you see.

Those who think vacations have to include warm weather and beaches will be astounded to find such Vacation Places as Boston, Massachusetts; Chicago, Illinois; New York City, New York; and Philadelphia, Pennsylvania–Delaware–New Jersey among the top twenty.

If you're an outdoors person who can't imagine spending precious vacation time in the big city, the high ranks earned by Los Angeles, California, and Miami–Gold Coast–Keys, Florida, may make you raise your eyebrows. But if you have read the scoring sections of each of the preceding chapters, you'll understand how the calculations were done.

Your particular preferences may cause you to disagree with the choice of criteria used in scoring, but the same criteria, covering many elements deemed desirable in a vacation destination, have been applied consistently to all 107 Vacation Places.

Let's take a look at Lake Tahoe–Reno, Nevada–California—surely a beautiful section of the country and a popular resort area as well. Yet it ties with Yellowstone–Jackson–Tetons, Wyoming–Idaho–Montana (also known to be a super spot for a vacation) for 54th place, right at the midpoint of the total list. Why, you are probably wondering, didn't it come out closer to the top?

If you have read the chapter entitled Fun in the Great Outdoors, you know that Lake Tahoe–Reno,

Nevada–California, ranked number one in that chapter. The mystery plot thickens. Shouldn't that have brought the total rank up? It just wasn't enough. Even with one first-place rank, one average showing and four others below average resulted in a final rank of only 54.

Despite the great beauty of the lake itself and the mountains around it, Lake Tahoe–Reno, Nevada–California, ranked only 50 in Blessings of Nature. With many of the most spectacular places in the country as competition, this one came in only slightly above the midpoint.

In the other four chapters, Vacation Places are judged mainly on the availability of facilities and attractions that are, in general, more common in metropolitan areas than in the wide open spaces. Lake Tahoe–Reno, Nevada–California, was number 65 in Basic Necessities, 75 in Discovering Our Heritage, 88 in Feeding the Mind and Spirit, and 61 in Entertainment for All.

Despite these rankings, it is indisputable that this area is an exceptionally attractive vacation destination. Its winter-sports facilities are among the finest and most numerous in the nation; it has a large supply of federal recreation lands (four national forests, three Bureau of Land Management areas, five Bureau of Reclamation areas, and one Corps of Engineers area); its hotels and casinos offer gambling and big-name entertainment. If these things are important to you in choosing a vacation area, Lake Tahoe–Reno, Nevada –California, may be just your cup of tea.

## Honor Roll

Each of the 34 Vacation Places listed in this table has been ranked among the top ten in one or more of the preceding chapters. Thus they represent the destinations that would be most appreciated by vacationers who put one type of attraction or activity above all others.

| | Rank in Blessings of Nature | Rank in Fun in the Great Outdoors | Rank in Basic Necessities | Rank in Discovering Our Heritage | Rank in Feeding the Mind and Spirit | Rank in Entertainment for All |
|---|---|---|---|---|---|---|
| Anchorage–Kenai Peninsula, AK | 2 | | | | | |
| Bar Harbor–Acadia, ME | 8 | | | | | |
| Boston, MA | | | 5 | 2 | 4 | 5 |
| Cape Cod–The Islands, MA | | | 9 | | | |
| Catskill Mountains, NY | | | | 4 | | |
| Chicago, IL | | | 3 | | 10 | 3 |
| Cincinnati, OH–KY | | | 10 | | | 8 |
| Crater Lake–Klamath Falls, OR | 6 | 10 | | | | |
| Dallas–Fort Worth, TX | | | | | | 9 |
| Hawaii | 5 | 3 | | | | |
| Lake Tahoe–Reno, NV–CA | | 1 | | | | |
| Lexington–Bluegrass Country, KY | | | | 7 | | |
| Long Island, NY | | | 6 | | | |
| Los Angeles, CA | | 5 | 4 | | 2 | 2 |
| Miami–Gold Coast–Keys, FL | | 2 | | | 7 | |
| Minneapolis–St. Paul, MN–WI | | | | | | 7 |
| New York City, NY | | | 1 | 8 | 1 | 1 |
| Olympic Peninsula, WA | 3 | | | | | |
| Orlando–Space Coast, FL | | | | | | 10 |
| Pennsylvania Dutch Country, PA | | | | 9 | | |
| Philadelphia, PA–DE–NJ | | | 7 | 3 | 6 | 4 |
| Portland–Columbia River, OR | | 4 | | | | |
| Providence–Newport, RI | | | 8 | 5 | | |
| Redwoods–Shasta–Lassen, CA | 1 | 9 | | | | |
| Richmond–Fredericksburg, VA | | | | 6 | | |
| Salt Lake City, UT | | 7 | | | | |
| San Francisco, CA | | | 2 | | 5 | |
| Seattle–Mount Rainier–North Cascades, WA | 3 | 6 | | | 8 | |
| Tampa Bay–Southwest Coast, FL | | | | | 9 | 6 |
| Washington, DC–MD–VA | | | | 1 | 3 | |
| Williamsburg–Colonial Triangle, VA | | | | 10 | | |
| Yellowstone–Jackson–Tetons, WY–ID–MT | 10 | 8 | | | | |
| Yosemite–Sequoia–Death Valley, CA | 7 | | | | | |
| Zion–Bryce Canyon, UT | 9 | | | | | |

any part of the research, writing, or editing had any inkling of the final rankings until all the components were calculated. Finally, it must be remembered that there are no "bad" Vacation Places among the 107 in *Vacation Places Rated.*

## THERE ARE NO REAL LOSERS

Of the 107 places studied, 34, or nearly one-third of the total, placed in the top ten in one of the six chapters: Blessings of Nature, Fun in the Great Outdoors, Basic Necessities, Discovering Our Heritage, Feeding the Mind and Spirit, or Entertainment for All. These 34, together with their positions among the top ten in each chapter, are listed in the Honor Roll table.

Even more significant and interesting is that about three-fourths of the Vacation Places were among the ten highest scorers in one or more of the criteria that were used to determine the rankings in each chapter.

---

### Mostly Wide Open Spaces

Twenty-four of the Vacation Places consist of large areas of open space; they have an overall population density of fewer than 40 people per square mile. Any vacationer looking for an area in which to enjoy the outdoors to the exclusion of attractions found in large cities should consider one of these.

The population density is based on year-round residence. Some of the places listed below have within their boundaries a number of developed and popular resort areas; during peak tourist seasons the population is greatly increased.

| | Population Density (per square mile) |
|---|---|
| Adirondack Mountains, NY | 34.0 |
| Anchorage–Kenai Peninsula, AK | 11.2 |
| Aspen–Vail, CO | 11.3 |
| Bar Harbor–Acadia, ME | 39.1 |
| Bend–Cascade Mountains, OR | 11.1 |
| Black Hills, SD | 12.0 |
| Boise–Sun Valley, ID | 26.9 |
| Coos Bay–South Coast, OR | 27.7 |
| Crater Lake–Klamath Falls, OR | 24.7 |
| Flaming Gorge, UT–WY–CO | 5.8 |
| Glacier National Park–Flathead Lake, MT | 8.5 |
| Grand Canyon Country, AZ | 4.6 |
| Lake of the Ozarks, MO | 22.7 |
| Lake Powell–Glen Canyon, AZ–UT | 1.8 |
| Lake Tahoe–Reno, NV–CA | 32.7 |
| Mackinac Island–Sault Ste. Marie, MI | 17.9 |
| North Woods–Land O'Lakes, WI | 16.9 |
| Rangeley Lakes, ME | 5.3 |
| Redwoods–Shasta–Lassen, CA | 16.5 |
| Spokane–Coeur d'Alene, WA–ID | 37.5 |
| White Mountains, NH | 28.9 |
| Yellowstone–Jackson–Tetons, WY–ID–MT | 4.7 |
| Yosemite–Sequoia–Death Valley, CA | 3.7 |
| Zion–Bryce Canyon, UT | 4.8 |

---

### Top 21 for Outdoor Vacations

| | Rank in Blessings of Nature | Rank in Fun in the Great Outdoors | Combined Rank |
|---|---|---|---|
| 1. Hawaii | 5 | 3 | 8 |
| 2. Seattle–Mount Rainier–North Cascades, WA | 3 | 6 | 9 |
| 3. Redwoods–Shasta–Lassen, CA | 1 | 9 | 10 |
| 4. Crater Lake–Klamath Falls, OR | 6 | 10 | 16 |
| 5. Portland–Columbia River, OR | 14 | 4 | 18 |
| 5. Yellowstone–Jackson–Tetons, WY–ID–MT | 10 | 8 | 18 |
| 7. Yosemite–Sequoia–Death Valley, CA | 7 | 16 | 23 |
| 8. Salt Lake City, UT | 19 | 7 | 26 |
| 9. Olympic Peninsula, WA | 3 | 26 | 29 |
| 10. Lake Powell–Glen Canyon, AZ–UT | 13 | 17 | 30 |
| 11. Grand Canyon Country, AZ | 11 | 20 | 31 |
| 12. Albuquerque–Santa Fe–Taos, NM | 24 | 14 | 38 |
| 13. Wine Country, CA | 16 | 25 | 41 |
| 14. Aspen–Vail, CO | 19 | 24 | 43 |
| 15. Zion–Bryce Canyon, UT | 9 | 35 | 44 |
| 16. Spokane–Coeur d'Alene, WA–ID | 21 | 28 | 49 |
| 17. Lake Tahoe–Reno, NV–CA | 50 | 1 | 51 |
| 18. Monterey–Big Sur, CA | 37 | 15 | 52 |
| 19. Anchorage–Kenai Peninsula, AK | 2 | 53 | 55 |
| 20. Coos Bay–South Coast, OR | 17 | 43 | 60 |
| 20. Miami–Gold Coast–Keys, FL | 58 | 2 | 60 |

---

And what about the rest? What about the places that did not come off as outstanding for any one type of vacation attraction or activity?

First of all, as pointed out earlier, the 107 Vacation Places represent only a small part of the total United States. Each of these 107 is a superior place, greatly loved by thousands of visitors, many of whom return year after year.

Some of those not among the top ten in any of the criteria are near misses, placing 11th or 12th. Others are charming places not yet discovered by large throngs from every corner of the globe. These are destinations whose lack of wide popularity is exactly what many people find most enjoyable about them. Some are quiet, off the beaten path, friendly, simple, and unpretentious. Because they do not attract huge crowds, they are not highly commercialized and do not have as many of the tourist attractions that were counted as plus factors in some of the chapters, and

## Top 20 for City Vacations

| | Rank in Basic Necessities | Rank in Discovering Our Heritage | Rank in Feeding the Mind and Spirit | Rank in Entertainment for All | Combined Rank |
|---|---|---|---|---|---|
| 1. New York City, NY | 1 | 8 | 1 | 1 | 11 |
| 2. Boston, MA | 5 | 2 | 4 | 5 | 16 |
| 3. Philadelphia, PA–DE–NJ | 7 | 3 | 6 | 4 | 20 |
| 4. Chicago, IL | 3 | 12 | 10 | 3 | 28 |
| 5. Los Angeles, CA | 4 | 21 | 2 | 2 | 29 |
| 6. Washington, DC–MD–VA | 14 | 1 | 3 | 15 | 33 |
| 7. Tampa Bay–Southwest Coast, FL | 15 | 45 | 9 | 6 | 75 |
| 8. Minneapolis–St. Paul, MN–WI | 32 | 24 | 14 | 7 | 77 |
| 9. San Francisco, CA | 2 | 61 | 5 | 11 | 79 |
| 10. Houston–Galveston, TX | 22 | 22 | 18 | 20 | 82 |
| 10. Long Island, NY | 6 | 36 | 15 | 25 | 82 |
| 12. Baltimore–Chesapeake Bay, MD | 16 | 13 | 30 | 26 | 85 |
| 13. Dallas–Fort Worth, TX | 17 | 48 | 13 | 9 | 87 |
| 13. Providence–Newport, RI | 8 | 5 | 51 | 23 | 87 |
| 15. Pennsylvania Dutch Country, PA | 30 | 9 | 21 | 30 | 90 |
| 16. Seattle–Mount Rainier–North Cascades, WA | 28 | 44 | 8 | 13 | 93 |
| 17. Lexington–Bluegrass Country, KY | 39 | 7 | 12 | 36 | 94 |
| 17. Miami–Gold Coast–Keys, FL | 12 | 63 | 7 | 12 | 94 |
| 17. St. Louis–Mark Twain Country, MO–IL | 29 | 15 | 34 | 16 | 94 |
| 20. Mystic Seaport–Connecticut Valley, CT | 24 | 28 | 11 | 35 | 98 |

their most loyal fans would prefer to keep them as they are.

One small family resort in New England used to place tiny ads in the Boston papers, boasting, "Nothing whatever to do." That says it best—that's the appeal some vacation destinations have in greatest measure.

## WIDE OPEN SPACES AND BRIGHT LIGHTS

Of the many factors that make up a vacation experience, some are of vital importance to one vacationer and mean nothing at all to another. The thrill of discovering and exploring something new is so exciting and satisfying to one person that comfort and luxury are at the bottom of the priority list. For another, the major desires are luxurious quarters, excellent service, fine meals, and plenty of sunshine. A third person will save and plan all year in order to enjoy two weeks of entertainment and sightseeing in a big city.

Hikers who want to explore a wilderness, do some fishing, and snap pictures of birds and animals are not likely to want to include museum visits on the same vacation. City couples looking for relaxation in a quiet lakefront cottage may want to escape everything that reminds them of home, even though they are avid fans of plays, concerts, and gourmet restaurants during the rest of the year. Young and affluent professionals may envision a perfect vacation as one spent at a luxury resort complete with golf courses, health club, tennis courts, and a sandy beach. Families whose members have widely varying interests may find themselves debating the relative merits of Disney World and Yosemite National Park or trying to decide between a sightseeing trip to Washington, DC, and a skiing trip to the Rockies.

Often the first decision to be made concerns the type of destination. Shall it be a rural or urban vacation; the bright lights of a metropolis or the wide open spaces of the countryside?

Rankings calculated in the first two chapters, Blessings of Nature and Fun in the Great Outdoors, were based on factors important to those interested in a primarily rural vacation; factors that determined the rankings in the last four chapters were the attractions and activities found more frequently in the big cities.

The list on the previous page, Top 21 for Outdoor Vacations, consists of the top 21 Vacation Places that emerge when the rankings of the first two chapters are added together; thus they represent the best destinations in terms of what nature and the outdoors have to offer. Most of them are in the West, where the mountains are higher, the canyons are deeper, the cities are fewer, and the national parks are larger.

The criteria for ranking the Vacation Places in the other four chapters are found in much greater numbers in heavily populated—and for the most part older—metropolitan areas.

The 20 best places for city vacations range from coast to coast: twelve are in the East, five in the central part of the country, and three in the West.

Some of the smaller cities represented in these Vacation Places—such as Minneapolis, Minnesota; Louisville, Kentucky; and Hartford, Connecticut—have an impressive array of sightseeing and entertainment opportunities beyond what might be expected in places of their size.

## FINDING THE BEST VACATION PLACES IN AMERICA

This volume follows the method of the earlier books in the *Places Rated* series, *Places Rated Almanac* and *Retirement Places Rated*, for arriving at an overall rank: the ranks earned by each Vacation Place in the six preceding chapters are added together. For example, Portland–Columbia River, Oregon, is 14th in Blessings of Nature, 4th in Fun in the Great Outdoors, 42nd in Basic Necessities, 54th in Discovering Our Heritage, 32nd in Feeding the Mind and Spirit, and 50th in Entertainment for All. The total of these ranks—14 + 4 + 42 + 54 + 32 + 50—equals 196. Because this system is based on ranks, the lower the total of the ranks, the better the Vacation Place is judged to be overall. The total rank of 196 gives Portland–Columbia River, Oregon, an overall rank of 14 among all the Vacation Places.

Following is a list of the 20 places that have the most to offer vacationers.

### America's Top 20 Vacation Places

| | Total of Ranks |
|---|---|
| 1. Seattle–Mount Rainier–North Cascades, WA | 102 |
| 2. Los Angeles, CA | 106 |
| 3. Hawaii | 143 |
| 4. Miami–Gold Coast–Keys, FL | 154 |
| 5. San Francisco, CA | 158 |
| 6. Boston, MA | 163 |
| 7. Chicago, IL | 174 |
| 7. Denver–Rocky Mountain National Park, CO | 174 |
| 7. New York City, NY | 174 |
| 10. Tampa Bay–Southwest Coast, FL | 176 |
| 11. Philadelphia, PA–DE–NJ | 180 |
| 12. Monterey–Big Sur, CA | 186 |
| 13. Catskill Mountains, NY | 194 |
| 14. Portland–Columbia River, OR | 196 |
| 15. Minneapolis–St. Paul, MN–WI | 200 |
| 16. Albuquerque–Santa Fe–Taos, NM | 201 |
| 17. Washington, DC–MD–VA | 203 |
| 18. Salt Lake City, UT | 204 |
| 19. Providence–Newport, RI | 209 |
| 20. San Diego, CA | 218 |

The overall ranks in this chapter should be regarded as informational indicators of the opportunities available for different kinds of recreational enjoyment, not as critical reviews presented for the purpose of stirring up rivalries and controversy.

Vacations ought to be a time for building up stores of happy memories. Too often they are spoiled by unfulfilled expectations and family arguments over what to do and where to go. Good planning, based on accurate information, usually eliminates the major causes of disappointment.

## THE BEST VACATION PLACES IN AMERICA

Cities are predominant in the Vacation Places at the top of the overall list simply because they have more of the kinds of tourist attractions counted in the scoring than do less populated areas. It should be no surprise that such traditionally popular vacation destinations as Hawaii, southeastern and southwestern Florida, and southern California rank among the highest.

Somewhat less expected, perhaps, is the winner of first place—though it will come as no surprise to the people who know it well: Seattle–Mount Rainier–North Cascades, Washington. This excellent vacation destination has an enviable combination of assets, ranging from beautiful natural areas and opportunities for outdoor recreation to an abundance of city advantages.

Following the Seattle area in overall rank are: Los Angeles, California, second; Hawaii, third; Miami–Gold Coast–Keys, Florida, fourth; San Francisco, California, fifth; Boston, Massachusetts, sixth; Chicago, Illinois, Denver–Rocky Mountain National Park, Colorado, and New York City, New York, tied for seventh; and Tampa Bay–Southwest Coast, Florida, tenth.

# Rankings: Putting It All Together

The following table shows the rank of every Vacation Place for each of the six preceding *Vacation Places Rated* chapters.

The sum of these ranks is also shown, as is the overall rank. To use Portland–Columbia River, Oregon, as an example, the total of all ranks was 196, which was the 14th lowest among the Vacation Places, so the overall rank is 14. If a place were to rank first in all six chapters, its total of all the ranks would be six and its overall rank would be one.

| | Rank in Blessings of Nature | Rank in Fun in the Great Outdoors | Rank in Basic Necessities | Rank in Discovering Our Heritage | Rank in Feeding the Mind and Spirit | Rank in Entertainment for All | Total of Ranks | Overall Rank |
|---|---|---|---|---|---|---|---|---|
| Adirondack Mountains, NY | 34 | 40 | 76 | 31 | 53 | 34 | 268 | 39 |
| Albuquerque–Santa Fe–Taos, NM | 24 | 14 | 81 | 14 | 25 | 43 | 201 | 16 |
| Anchorage–Kenai Peninsula, AK | 2 | 53 | 102 | 84 | 59 | 68 | 368 | 65 |
| Asheville–Smoky Mountains, NC | 23 | 46 | 70 | 59 | 83 | 44 | 325 | 49 |
| Aspen–Vail, CO | 19 | 24 | 71 | 80 | 98 | 58 | 350 | 57 |
| Atlanta, GA | 85 | 30 | 34 | 32 | 38 | 28 | 247 | 26 |
| Atlantic City, NJ | 64 | 104 | 13 | 79 | 92 | 22 | 374 | 69 |
| Austin–Hill Country, TX | 90 | 72 | 62 | 35 | 78 | 65 | 402 | 84 |
| Baltimore–Chesapeake Bay, MD | 74 | 95 | 16 | 13 | 30 | 26 | 254 | 28 |
| Bar Harbor–Acadia, ME | 8 | 83 | 87 | 76 | 49 | 79 | 382 | 76 |
| Bend–Cascade Mountains, OR | 25 | 38 | 98 | 107 | 98 | 96 | 462 | 99 |
| Berkshire Hills–Pioneer Valley, MA | 60 | 44 | 33 | 27 | 51 | 13 | 228 | 22 |
| Black Hills, SD | 40 | 37 | 101 | 78 | 62 | 64 | 382 | 76 |
| Blue Ridge Mountains, VA | 35 | 59 | 94 | 33 | 82 | 82 | 385 | 78 |
| Boise–Sun Valley, ID | 36 | 33 | 96 | 73 | 100 | 65 | 403 | 85 |
| Boone–High Country, NC | 56 | 64 | 82 | 97 | 100 | 85 | 484 | 101 |
| Boston, MA | 100 | 47 | 5 | 2 | 4 | 5 | 163 | 6 |
| Brownsville–Rio Grande Valley, TX | 80 | 101 | 55 | 94 | 87 | 90 | 507 | 103 |
| Cape Cod–The Islands, MA | 32 | 80 | 9 | 56 | 79 | 37 | 293 | 44 |
| Catskill Mountains, NY | 66 | 23 | 43 | 4 | 41 | 17 | 194 | 13 |
| Charleston, SC | 63 | 76 | 64 | 16 | 75 | 82 | 376 | 73 |
| Chattanooga–Huntsville, TN–AL–GA | 78 | 49 | 72 | 72 | 73 | 85 | 429 | 92 |
| Chicago, IL | 107 | 39 | 3 | 12 | 10 | 3 | 174 | 7 |
| Cincinnati, OH–KY | 104 | 77 | 10 | 62 | 23 | 8 | 284 | 43 |
| Colorado Springs, CO | 48 | 61 | 73 | 60 | 70 | 61 | 373 | 68 |
| Coos Bay–South Coast, OR | 17 | 43 | 93 | 98 | 100 | 102 | 453 | 97 |
| Corpus Christi–Padre Island, TX | 81 | 98 | 66 | 88 | 59 | 67 | 459 | 98 |

| | Rank in Blessings of Nature | Rank in Fun in the Great Outdoors | Rank in Basic Necessities | Rank in Our Heritage | Rank in Discovering the Mind and Spirit | Rank in Feeding for All | Rank in Entertainment | Total of Ranks | Overall Rank |
|---|---|---|---|---|---|---|---|---|---|
| Crater Lake–Klamath Falls, OR | 6 | 10 | 89 | 69 | 84 | 68 | | 326 | 50 |
| Dallas–Forth Worth, TX | 106 | 75 | 17 | 48 | 13 | 9 | | 268 | 39 |
| Denver–Rocky Mountain National Park, CO | 42 | 19 | 21 | 42 | 29 | 21 | | 174 | 7 |
| Door County, WI | 69 | 99 | 50 | 96 | 97 | 80 | | 491 | 102 |
| Eastern Shore, VA | 27 | 107 | 84 | 95 | 96 | 102 | | 511 | 104 |
| Finger Lakes, NY | 74 | 34 | 48 | 43 | 26 | 30 | | 255 | 30 |
| Flaming Gorge, UT–WY–CO | 29 | 73 | 104 | 102 | 104 | 99 | | 511 | 104 |
| Glacier National Park–Flathead Lake, MT | 12 | 50 | 100 | 106 | 88 | 74 | | 430 | 93 |
| Grand Canyon Country, AZ | 11 | 20 | 103 | 58 | 62 | 102 | | 356 | 63 |
| Green Mountains, VT | 57 | 12 | 52 | 30 | 36 | 48 | | 235 | 23 |
| Hawaii | 5 | 3 | 36 | 20 | 24 | 55 | | 143 | 3 |
| Hilton Head, SC | 68 | 63 | 57 | 82 | 106 | 99 | | 475 | 100 |
| Holland–Lake Michigan Shore, MI | 95 | 60 | 53 | 85 | 27 | 54 | | 374 | 69 |
| Houston–Galveston, TX | 85 | 74 | 22 | 22 | 18 | 20 | | 241 | 25 |
| Jersey Shore, NJ | 71 | 86 | 11 | 99 | 107 | 40 | | 414 | 88 |
| Knoxville–Smoky Mountains, TN | 52 | 41 | 51 | 19 | 42 | 44 | | 249 | 27 |
| Lake of the Ozarks, MO | 45 | 90 | 92 | 52 | 70 | 74 | | 423 | 90 |
| Lake Powell–Glen Canyon, AZ–UT | 13 | 17 | 107 | 92 | 68 | 96 | | 393 | 83 |
| Lake Tahoe–Reno, NV–CA | 50 | 1 | 65 | 75 | 88 | 61 | | 340 | 54 |
| Las Vegas–Lake Mead, NV–AZ | 53 | 48 | 79 | 89 | 80 | 71 | | 420 | 89 |
| Lexington–Bluegrass Country, KY | 94 | 70 | 39 | 7 | 12 | 36 | | 258 | 32 |
| Long Island, NY | 61 | 82 | 6 | 36 | 15 | 25 | | 225 | 21 |
| Los Angeles, CA | 72 | 5 | 4 | 21 | 2 | 2 | | 106 | 2 |
| Mackinac Island–Sault Ste. Marie, MI | 22 | 68 | 83 | 83 | 74 | 107 | | 437 | 95 |
| Memphis, TN–AR–MS | 99 | 105 | 37 | 64 | 35 | 40 | | 380 | 75 |
| Miami–Gold Coast–Keys, FL | 58 | 2 | 12 | 63 | 7 | 12 | | 154 | 4 |
| Minneapolis–St. Paul, MN–WI | 92 | 31 | 32 | 24 | 14 | 7 | | 200 | 15 |
| Mobile Bay–Gulfport, AL–MS | 55 | 85 | 60 | 55 | 81 | 56 | | 392 | 82 |
| Monterey–Big Sur, CA | 37 | 15 | 26 | 51 | 17 | 40 | | 186 | 12 |
| Myrtle Beach–Grand Strand, SC | 44 | 84 | 40 | 101 | 88 | 70 | | 427 | 91 |
| Mystic Seaport–Connecticut Valley, CT | 79 | 93 | 24 | 28 | 11 | 35 | | 270 | 42 |
| Nashville, TN | 97 | 91 | 45 | 34 | 47 | 37 | | 351 | 58 |
| New Orleans, LA | 89 | 97 | 27 | 17 | 40 | 32 | | 302 | 45 |
| New York City, NY | 98 | 65 | 1 | 8 | 1 | 1 | | 174 | 7 |
| Niagara Falls–Western New York, NY | 73 | 54 | 23 | 66 | 20 | 27 | | 263 | 34 |
| North Woods–Land O'Lakes, WI | 32 | 92 | 90 | 105 | 103 | 89 | | 511 | 104 |

| | Rank in Blessings of Nature | Rank in Fun in the Great Outdoors | Rank in Basic Necessities | Rank in Discovering Our Heritage | Rank in Feeding the Mind and Spirit | Rank in Entertainment for All | Total of Ranks | Overall Rank |
|---|---|---|---|---|---|---|---|---|
| Oklahoma City–Cherokee Strip, OK | 100 | 71 | 58 | 29 | 46 | 51 | 355 | 62 |
| Olympic Peninsula, WA | 3 | 26 | 86 | 65 | 84 | 102 | 366 | 64 |
| Orlando–Space Coast, FL | 46 | 32 | 41 | 91 | 19 | 10 | 239 | 24 |
| Outer Banks, NC | 14 | 79 | 85 | 39 | 95 | 92 | 404 | 86 |
| Ozarks–Eureka Springs, AR–MO | 42 | 62 | 88 | 46 | 55 | 39 | 332 | 51 |
| Palm Springs–Desert Playgrounds, CA | 50 | 13 | 61 | 87 | 31 | 82 | 324 | 48 |
| Panhandle, FL | 39 | 56 | 67 | 38 | 93 | 61 | 354 | 60 |
| Pennsylvania Dutch Country, PA | 96 | 68 | 30 | 9 | 21 | 30 | 254 | 28 |
| Philadelphia, PA–DE–NJ | 105 | 55 | 7 | 3 | 6 | 4 | 180 | 11 |
| Phoenix–Valley of the Sun, AZ | 76 | 18 | 47 | 37 | 65 | 23 | 266 | 36 |
| Pocono Mountains, PA | 76 | 22 | 35 | 49 | 45 | 28 | 255 | 30 |
| Portland, ME | 31 | 81 | 46 | 23 | 28 | 56 | 265 | 35 |
| Portland–Columbia River, OR | 14 | 4 | 42 | 54 | 32 | 50 | 196 | 14 |
| Portsmouth–Kennebunk, NH–ME | 58 | 78 | 30 | 18 | 67 | 18 | 269 | 41 |
| Providence–Newport, RI | 70 | 52 | 8 | 5 | 51 | 23 | 209 | 19 |
| Put-in-Bay–Lake Erie Shore, OH | 88 | 89 | 25 | 41 | 58 | 53 | 354 | 60 |
| Rangeley Lakes, ME | 18 | 102 | 105 | 104 | 105 | 95 | 529 | 107 |
| Redwoods–Shasta–Lassen, CA | 1 | 9 | 97 | 81 | 88 | 94 | 370 | 67 |
| Richmond–Fredericksburg, VA | 83 | 100 | 69 | 6 | 72 | 44 | 374 | 69 |
| Sacramento–Gold Rush Towns, CA | 62 | 51 | 44 | 57 | 61 | 74 | 349 | 56 |
| St. Augustine–Northeast Coast, FL | 54 | 45 | 38 | 25 | 33 | 71 | 266 | 36 |
| St. Louis–Mark Twain Country, MO–IL | 84 | 88 | 29 | 15 | 34 | 16 | 266 | 36 |
| Salt Lake City, UT | 19 | 7 | 49 | 53 | 43 | 33 | 204 | 18 |
| San Antonio, TX | 100 | 106 | 20 | 50 | 48 | 51 | 375 | 72 |
| San Diego, CA | 66 | 29 | 18 | 70 | 16 | 19 | 218 | 20 |
| San Francisco, CA | 37 | 42 | 2 | 61 | 5 | 11 | 158 | 5 |
| Santa Barbara–San Simeon, CA | 48 | 58 | 59 | 77 | 54 | 92 | 388 | 81 |
| Savannah–Golden Isles, GA | 30 | 87 | 63 | 26 | 66 | 80 | 352 | 59 |
| Seattle–Mount Rainier–North Cascades, WA | 3 | 6 | 28 | 44 | 8 | 13 | 102 | 1 |
| Spokane–Coeur d'Alene, WA–ID | 21 | 28 | 91 | 86 | 64 | 58 | 348 | 55 |
| Tampa Bay–Southwest Coast, FL | 90 | 11 | 15 | 45 | 9 | 6 | 176 | 10 |
| Traverse City–Petoskey, MI | 26 | 36 | 75 | 103 | 76 | 71 | 387 | 80 |
| Tucson, AZ | 27 | 57 | 80 | 71 | 44 | 58 | 337 | 52 |
| Tulsa–Lake O' The Cherokees, OK | 87 | 27 | 74 | 46 | 39 | 44 | 317 | 47 |
| Vicksburg–Natchez–Baton Rouge, MS–LA | 82 | 96 | 77 | 11 | 69 | 74 | 409 | 87 |
| Washington, DC–MD–VA | 103 | 67 | 14 | 1 | 3 | 15 | 203 | 17 |

| | Rank in Blessings of Nature | Rank in Fun in the Great Outdoors | Rank in Basic Necessities | Rank in Discovering Our Heritage | Rank in Feeding the Mind and Spirit | Rank in Entertainment for All | Total of Ranks | Overall Rank |
|---|---|---|---|---|---|---|---|---|
| White Mountains, NH | 40 | 21 | 77 | 100 | 55 | 85 | 378 | 74 |
| Williamsburg–Colonial Triangle, VA | 65 | 94 | 19 | 10 | 22 | 48 | 258 | 32 |
| Wilmington–Cape Fear, NC | 47 | 103 | 56 | 67 | 86 | 90 | 449 | 96 |
| Wine Country, CA | 16 | 25 | 68 | 74 | 57 | 74 | 314 | 46 |
| Wisconsin Dells, WI | 93 | 66 | 54 | 40 | 37 | 96 | 386 | 79 |
| Yellowstone–Jackson–Tetons, WY–ID–MT | 10 | 8 | 95 | 90 | 49 | 85 | 337 | 52 |
| Yosemite–Sequoia–Death Valley, CA | 7 | 16 | 99 | 68 | 76 | 102 | 368 | 65 |
| Zion–Bryce Canyon, UT | 9 | 35 | 106 | 93 | 93 | 99 | 435 | 94 |

# TOP TEN: Putting It All Together

| | Total of Ranks |
|---|---|
| 1. Seattle–Mount Rainier–North Cascades, WA | 102 |
| 2. Los Angeles, CA | 106 |
| 3. Hawaii | 143 |
| 4. Miami–Gold Coast–Keys, FL | 154 |
| 5. San Francisco, CA | 158 |
| 6. Boston, MA | 163 |
| 7. Chicago, IL | 174 |
| 7. Denver–Rocky Mountain National Park, CO | 174 |
| 7. New York City, NY | 174 |
| 10. Tampa Bay–Southwest Coast, FL | 176 |

## 1. Seattle–Mount Rainier–North Cascades, WA

This Vacation Place is blessed with both bright lights and open spaces. The Seattle area placed in the top ten in three chapters: it tied for third place in Blessings of Nature, placed sixth in Fun in the Great Outdoors, and came in eighth in Feeding the Mind and Spirit. It was second only to Hawaii in a combined score for outdoor vacations, number 16 as a destination for city vacations.

This comparatively young metro area (the city was founded in 1852) has a fiercely loyal population. Newcomers sing its praises as loudly as the natives. The residents tell you that no place else can compare with Seattle in terms of the easy accessibility of outdoor recreation.

Nature has been especially kind to this little corner of the world; among its natural assets are the salt waters of Puget Sound and Elliott Bay; Lake Washington, a 24-mile-long body of fresh water; two mountain ranges—the Olympics to the west and the Cascades to the east; deep forests almost at the city's doorstep; and two spectacular national parks.

It is interesting to note that the research done for *Places Rated Almanac* found Seattle to be the top metropolitan area for recreation, even though the combination of factors used in scoring was quite different from that employed for this volume. Authors Boyer and Savageau noted that in recent years Seattle has placed near the top of every list that ranked American cities or metro areas.

Seattle had a population of 490,000 as of 1983, according to Rand McNally estimates, giving it 24th place in size among American cities.

Vacationers can have the best of most worlds in the Seattle area; they can go sailing in the morning and watch one of four big-league sports teams play in the afternoon or evening; fish for salmon and play golf during the day and attend a first-class performance of a Wagnerian opera at night; stay in an award-winning hotel or camp out in the wilderness.

The Seattle area has 64 municipal and daily-fee golf courses; it placed tenth among the Vacation Places for this criterion. Its wealth of public recreational lands gave it seventh place for federal parks and tenth for state parks and beaches.

Seattle has 27 award-winning hotels and motels, more than any other city of its size; it won fourth place for this criterion. The four zoos in Seattle and surrounding areas yielded a score that tied with San Diego for first place. The city's four professional sports teams made it seventh in this category, and many varied sightseeing tours gave it ninth place for special attractions.

Mount Rainier stands guard over northwestern Washington; its snow-topped peak can be seen for miles in all directions. Passengers approaching Seattle by air look forward to spotting the familiar landmark in the same way that people flying into New York City try to spot the Statue of Liberty. Another landmark, the Space Needle, has been a symbol of the city since the Seattle World's Fair of 1962.

Nearly a million square miles of forests, meadows, mountain peaks, glaciers, lakes, rivers, and waterfalls are contained within the boundaries of the national parks and national recreation areas lying along the Cascade Range northeast and southeast of Seattle. North Cascades National Park is adjoined by Ross Lake and Lake Chelan national recreation areas. Both lakes for which the areas are named lie some 1,600 feet above sea level; the deep, cold bodies of water are fed by glaciers. Ross Lake, created by a dam on the Skagit River, is surrounded by steep walls of rock.

Mount Rainier National Park is one of the older units of the National Park Service; it was established in 1899. The broadly domed mountain, fifth highest peak in the 48 contiguous states, is covered with glaciers, some of them several miles long. Hiking, backpacking, and mountain climbing are popular activities. One marked trail winds for 93 miles all around the mountain.

The park's wildlife checklist reports that more than 50 species of animals and nearly 150 kinds of birds have been spotted here. Mountain meadows bloom profusely with wildflowers in spring and summer. Fishing is good at lower elevations during the summer, but streams and lakes at higher altitudes are too cold for most fish.

Seattle Center, site of the World's Fair of 1962, is the region's entertainment hub. It houses the city's performing-arts companies, the Seattle Art Museum pavilion, and the Pacific Science Center. Murals, sculptures, and fountains beautify the 74 acres of grounds. There are shops, restaurants, and a children's park.

## 2. Los Angeles, CA

Glamour—the glamour of Hollywood and the stars, of Beverly Hills and its superrich residents, of tanned surfers riding the waves of the blue Pacific, of year-round near-perfect weather—the glamour of Los Angeles has been attracting visitors for more than half a century.

Los Angeles is in a basin ringed by hills and mountains. Royal palm trees line the broad avenues of the city; brilliant flowering bushes surround homes and public buildings; the sun shines brightly nearly every day. The city's dozens of suburbs climb over hills and scramble down canyon walls. West of the basin, sugary sand beaches line the oceanfront; to the east, beyond the mountains, lie lush valleys and arid deserts.

The Los Angeles area, composed of Los Angeles, Orange, and Ventura counties, ranked a very close second to Seattle as a Vacation Place, only four points lower in the total of all the ranks. In four chapters—Fun in the Great Outdoors, Basic Necessities, Feeding the Mind and Spirit, and Entertainment for All—Los Angeles placed in the top ten; it ranked fifth as a place for city vacations. The Los Angeles area finished in the top 10 in half of the 26 criteria tabulated in the preceding chapters.

Among the recreational assets of this Vacation Place are 130 municipal and daily-fee golf courses, 2 national forests and a national recreation area, 7 Corps of Engineers recreational areas, and 15 state parks and beaches. Its award-winning hotels and restaurants are the haunts of the rich and famous—visitors sit in such places as the Beverly Hills Hotel's Polo Lounge in the hope of spotting a movie or television idol; personnel of all the leading hotels are quick to reel off the names of celebrities who have stayed with them.

Much of the central part of Los Angeles has been rebuilt in the past decade or so; shiny skyscrapers, plazas, ultramodern hotels, underground malls, and raised walkways have replaced older, crumbling neighborhoods. The Atlantic Richfield Plaza, a beautiful resting place with sculptures and a pool, sits above what is claimed to be the largest underground shopping center in the United States. The Bonaventure Hotel is a space-age fantasy of stone and glass; visitors either love it or hate it, but they can't ignore it.

Other major attractions in the city itself are the splendid Dorothy Chandler Pavilion, where opera, ballet, symphony, and musical comedy are presented; El Pueblo de Los Angeles State Historical Park, the oldest part of the city, including the famous Mexican market of Olvera Street; Little Tokyo; and Chinatown. In Hollywood sightseers flock to Mann's Chinese Theatre to see the footprints of movie stars set in a concrete walk; in Beverly Hills a favorite sight is the fabulous shopping area of Rodeo Drive, reputedly the most expensive strip of stores in the country. Other suburbs have their own world-famous attractions: Pas-adena has its Rose Bowl; Anaheim is the home of Disneyland; Long Beach offers the *Queen Mary* and Howard Hughes's *Spruce Goose*; Santa Monica is famous for its white beaches and for the Santa Monica Mountains; Venice is an artists' colony.

Nine botanic gardens, 3 zoos, 29 qualifying museums, and more than a score of special attractions contributed to a second-place ranking for Los Angeles in Feeding the Mind and Spirit.

Touring television and movie studios is an especially popular activity unique to this area. Foremost among available tours is the Universal Studios tour, which has developed from a sightseeing trek into a major theme park. There are several guided bus tours past the homes of the stars.

Entertainment abounds in Los Angeles and its environs; there are four top-notch theme parks, eight professional sports teams, several orchestras and opera companies, and nine repertory theaters.

## 3. Hawaii

The only tropical state of the 50 United States, the islands of Hawaii spell romance and beauty to all but the most hardened cynics. With a rank of five in Blessings of Nature and three in Fun in the Great Outdoors, Hawaii took first place for outdoor vacations.

Tourists are of prime importance to the economy of Hawaii, and gorgeous hotels and resorts on the islands of Hawaii, Kauai, Maui, Molokai, and Oahu have been built to accommodate them. Hawaii ranked ninth among the 107 Vacation Places for the number of award-winning hotels, seventh for award-winning restaurants. The cuisines are varied and interesting, spiced with the culinary arts of several Oriental and Pacific cultures. Seafood and tropical fruits are plentiful; they are rushed from ocean waters and local orchards to the table.

The Mauna Kea Beach Hotel, on the island of Hawaii, is one of the world's most luxurious resorts. Its gardens and priceless collection of Far Eastern and African art objects are more spectacular than the exhibits in many museums.

The weather of Hawaii ranges from nearly universal sunshine in Honolulu to the world's wettest spot, a forest on Mount Waialeale on the island of Kauai. Rainfall is also very heavy in Hilo, on the eastern side of the island of Hawaii, while it is nearly nonexistent in the vicinity of Kailua-Kona, on the western coast.

Honolulu, Hawaii's major city, is on the island of Oahu. This is where the visitors congregate to enjoy the sands of Waikiki Beach; catch a glimpse of the famous Diamond Head, a small and extinct volcanic crater that is the island's most familiar landmark; and visit Queen Emma's Summer Palace to be reminded that this part of the United States was once a monarchy.

Here in Honolulu American citizens represent a

wide and fascinating variety of ethnic backgrounds—Japanese, Chinese, Polynesian, and dozens of other groups share a Hawaiian history that goes back for several generations.

Several points of interest on Oahu should be visited in order to appreciate the richness of this state's past. The collection of native Hawaiian art objects on display at the Bishop Museum is without compare. The Polynesian Cultural Center, at Laie, is an authentic recreation of villages from several South Seas islands; arts, crafts, and sports of the islands are demonstrated, and an entertainment program features native dances and comedy.

At Pearl Harbor the submerged U.S.S. *Arizona*, sunk with more than 1,100 men aboard on December 7, 1941, is a solemn reminder of one of the saddest hours in American history.

Two giant volcanic mountains dominate the interior of the Big Island of Hawaii—Mauna Loa (13,679 feet) and Mauna Kea (13,796 feet)—along with a few smaller ones. Mauna Kea has not erupted in modern times, and Hualalai has been quiet since 1801, but Mauna Loa and Kilauea, both within Hawaii Volcanoes National Park, put on spectacular shows fairly frequently. When they do erupt, these volcanoes are not life-threatening, as the lava flow is relatively slow and sightseers can enjoy the fireworks without fear of being engulfed.

Maui, the Valley Island, has its own active volcano, Haleakala. This, too, is within a national park. Maui's popularity as a vacation destination has grown enormously in recent years. It is also a productive agricultural spot; farmers grow pineapples, sugarcane, flowers, and truck crops and raise cattle and Thoroughbred horses.

The islands of Kauai and Molokai are somewhat less built-up with hotels and resorts than the other three, but they too attract many visitors. Molokai was for many years dominated by pineapple growers. Kauai, the Garden Island, is a gem of natural beauty; among its attractions are the beach where scenes from *South Pacific* were filmed and Waimea Canyon, a ten-mile series of colorful cuts in the red earth and black volcanic rock.

Over and above the tropical beauty, Hawaii's greatest appeal, according to its many fans, is what Hawaiians call the Aloha Spirit—the warm and gentle friendliness of its people.

## 4. Miami–Gold Coast–Keys, FL

Sun, surf, and sand bring visitors by the thousands to bask on the beaches of Florida's Gold Coast and Keys. This was not always true, however. Before the turn of this century, more alligators than people inhabited southeastern Florida. It took a lot of imagination on the part of a number of people to create a modern city and a string of hugely popular resort communities in this hot and muggy former swampland.

Development of the Gold Coast started in the 1890s, really took off in the years following World War I, and suffered a collapse in the late twenties. Since the Second World War, southeastern Florida has really boomed; the oceanfront is an almost unbroken strip of homes, hotels, beach parks, and marinas. Populated areas used to extend only about ten miles west from the ocean, but the urbanized corridor is constantly expanding.

Miami Beach has undergone a revitalization during the past few years. The beach itself had eroded badly, but today, thanks to the work of the U.S. Army Corps of Engineers, a new beach, 10 miles long and 300 feet deep, has been created with sand dredged from the floor of the ocean. A new pedestrian boardwalk parallels the beach; it provides access for people in wheelchairs. Several of the hotels built in the 1920s have been rehabilitated, giving Miami Beach a revitalized and attractive art-deco district.

This Vacation Place ranked first for availability of tennis resorts and second for municipal and daily-fee golf courses. These facilities plus its two national parks and nine state parks and beaches earned it second place in Fun in the Great Outdoors. Other popular sports, especially in the Keys, are scuba diving, boating, and deep-sea fishing.

There are many, many fine hotels, restaurants, and other facilities for vacationers throughout southeastern Florida; the rank for availability of hotels and motels was six, for award-winning hotels was six, and for award-winning restaurants was six. Two of the very finest older elegant resorts, the Boca Raton Hotel and Club and The Breakers, in Palm Beach, are in this area.

Key West, 155 miles by car from Miami, is an entirely different world—relaxed, colorful, and a bit quaint. Many of the homes are of a distinctive style imported from the Bahamas; they are adorned with the gingerbread trim characteristic of the Victorian era.

A recently improved and widened highway connects the Keys with the mainland; it is possible to make the trip in just about three hours without breaking speed limits. But there are many things worth stopping for along the way; a relaxed vacationer should plan to take a whole day for the drive. John Pennekamp State Park, off the shores of Key Largo, consists of a colorful reef made up of 50 kinds of coral; those who don't care to dive to the reef can enjoy it from the comfortable seats of a glass-bottomed boat. Nature preserves farther down along the Keys are the habitats of herons, cormorants, anhingas, roseate spoonbills, pelicans, and ospreys. The National Key Deer Refuge protects the environment of the rare, tiny animal for which it is named—if you are lucky, you may be able to spot one.

Five major-league baseball teams come to southeastern Florida for spring training. Other available spectator sports include horse racing, greyhound racing, jai alai, polo, and golf and tennis exhibitions. On

New Year's Day Miami's Orange Bowl Festival and Football Classic attracts nationwide attention.

## 5. San Francisco, CA

San Francisco's reputation as an exotic, exciting city is equaled by only a handful of the world's cities. Who has not heard of its charms? Its colorful history has been chronicled in dozens of movies and television shows. Everyone has seen pictures of its dramatic setting on a group of hills overlooking the Golden Gate Bridge and the stunning San Francisco Bay. The cable cars, the brightly colored Victorian houses, the steep and crooked streets, are familiar symbols of San Francisco to millions of people who have never even visited the city. What makes San Francisco so special? The beauty of the location is a part of its appeal, but many other cities are physically attractive without possessing the excitement of this one. One important element is its cosmopolitan population—people of many cultures have come here from all corners of the earth. Another is the waterfront, where the National Maritime Museum has six vessels on display in addition to its museum building, and where tourists throng to Fisherman's Wharf to shop and munch on boiled shrimp and other delicacies. Nearby Ghirardelli Square is an old chocolate factory, an architecturally delightful building now converted into a lively complex of shops, galleries, restaurants, and plazas.

The National Maritime Museum is within the 38,000-acre Golden Gate National Recreation Area, which also takes in beach areas, lagoons, marshes, a redwood forest, and a beautiful oceanfront promenade. Popular activities include biking, hiking, fishing, and guided boat trips to the former penitentiary on Alcatraz Island. North of San Francisco Bay is Point Reyes National Seashore, on a peninsula marked by cliffs and ridges, dunes, lagoons, and long beaches. Visitors enjoy watching the activities of large colonies of birds and sea lions offshore.

San Francisco has so many special and attractive neighborhoods to explore, it's hard to know where to start: Chinatown, Nob Hill, Telegraph Hill, North Beach, Golden Gate Park, The Presidio, and many more. If your time in the city is very limited, you may want to take the 49-mile self-guided scenic drive, marked by blue-and-white signs identified by the number 49 and a seagull. Other fast introductions to the area can be had through bus tours or harbor cruises.

San Francisco is superbly equipped to take care of visitors; it ranked second in Basic Necessities, fifth in Feeding the Mind and Spirit, and eleventh in Entertainment for All, giving it ninth place overall as a place for a city vacation.

Its hotels and restaurants are numerous and good. San Francisco earned fourth place for the availability of both hotels and restaurants, second in the number of award-winning hotels, and third in the number of award-winning restaurants. In many cities, top-notch restaurants are limited to those serving a French or Continental cuisine; in San Francisco some of the finest are Oriental. Several famous hotels on Nob Hill are worth visiting to enjoy the view from the upper floors and to admire the sumptuous appointments.

Because the Oriental influence is so strong in San Francisco, one cannot get the full flavor of the city without seeing such places as the Chinese Culture Center, the Japan Center, and the Asian Art Museum. These are a few of the facilities, along with 6 botanic gardens, 2 planetariums, 3 zoos and aquariums, and 18 qualifying museums, that earned fifth place for San Francisco in Feeding the Mind and Spirit.

San Francisco's eleventh place in Entertainment for All was based on good music, theater, and professional sports teams; there are also dozens of supper clubs and nightclubs—some of them featuring top stars. Types of entertainment are far-reaching: comedy, jazz, revues, and female impersonation.

## 6. Boston, MA

This historic city and its surroundings offer many opportunities to those who choose to visit a major city. Its rank as a destination for a city vacation was second only to New York City; it placed fifth among all Vacation Places in Basic Necessities, second in Discovering Our Heritage, fourth in Feeding the Mind and Spirit, and fifth in Entertainment for All.

There are enough sightseeing attractions in this corner of New England to please the most curious travelers for weeks on end. History is Boston's most obvious strong point, but its many golf courses, restaurants, planetariums, museums, and zoos and aquariums, as well as its impressive array of entertainment opportunities, provide plenty of variety for anyone indifferent to its historic attractions.

Boston itself has a historic landmark on nearly every corner, but it is also surrounded by other cities of great historic significance. The earliest colony in what is now the northeastern United States was established at Plymouth. The American Revolution began with the battles fought in 1775 in Lexington and Concord. Some 75 years later, Concord was the home of several literary giants of their time—Ralph Waldo Emerson; Nathaniel Hawthorne; Louisa May Alcott and her father, Bronson Alcott; and Henry David Thoreau. Several of the homes occupied by these famous Americans are open to the public.

Early maritime history is memorialized in Salem, at the Salem Maritime National Historic Site. Eighteenth-century warehouses and wharves have been preserved along with a custom house built in 1819, where Nathaniel Hawthorne was once employed. The National Park Service conducts guided tours and boat trips.

The earliest days of America's Industrial Revolution come alive in nearby Lowell, this country's first planned industrial city. Visitors take guided tours by trolley, canal boat, and on foot, and costumed interpreters explain the beginnings of the factory system and describe the life-styles of the workers involved in early large-scale manufacture of cotton cloth.

Boston is a small city in area, and one in which some of the most satisfactory sightseeing is done on foot. There are comfortable and attractive places to rest—the Public Garden, Boston Common, Copley Square, Waterfront Park, and Faneuil Hall Marketplace, to name a few. For a view of the city from on high, visit the observation floor of the Prudential or John Hancock tower. Louisburg Square, on Beacon Hill, is a small and beautiful residential enclave that has not changed in appearance for generations.

Across the Charles River is Cambridge, home of Harvard University and the Massachusetts Institute of Technology, a city with many famous landmarks of its own.

Boston is an old city, but the presence of thousands of students helps it maintain a vibrant, ageless atmosphere. Along with the dozens of time-honored and serious attractions, visitors can enjoy college football games, boat races on the Charles River, contemporary theater, and dozens of trendy shops and restaurants.

## 7. Chicago, IL

A vacation in Chicago is not apt to include much in the way of outdoor activities—though the city does offer more municipal and daily-fee golf courses than any other Vacation Place. But as a city vacation destination, Chicago ranked 4th, the result of 3rd place in Basic Necessities, 12th in Discovering Our Heritage, 10th in Feeding the Mind and Spirit, and 3rd in Entertainment for All.

Chicago's greatest physical asset is its long frontage on Lake Michigan. Thanks to the farsighted advice given by architect and city planner Daniel Burnham in 1906, many parks have been developed along the shore. Lake Shore Drive skirts much of the city's 29 miles of open lakefront, offering views of beaches, harbors, and green spaces. Jogging and biking trails, paths, golf courses, and tennis courts; a zoo, a conservatory, a bandshell, a planetarium, and an aquarium; and several world-class museums are near the lake. From mid-June to Labor Day, 21 public bathing beaches are crowded with swimmers and sunbathers, while hundreds of sailboats, motorboats, and sightseeing cruise boats ply the waters. Fishing is good in Lake Michigan, and there is a year-round season for salmon, perch, and trout. Out-of-town visitors can purchase either a one-day or a ten-day fishing license.

Chicago's rankings in Basic Necessities are proof that this is a city ready to take very good care of visitors: fifth in availability of hotels and motels, second in eating and drinking places, sixth in the number of award-winning hotels, and fourth in award-winning restaurants.

As a city to which many waves of immigrants have come over many decades, there are dozens of interesting ethnic neighborhoods, restaurants, and museums.

Chicago has always had an above-average reputation for the quality of its theater, and this reputation has become even more well established and widespread in recent seasons. Several major commercial theaters bring Broadway and first-run shows to town, and dozens of repertory companies are flourishing. The Hot Tix booth, at 24 South State Street, offers same-day half-priced tickets to many performances. There are other booths in the suburbs of Oak Park and Evanston. For theater information, phone Curtain Call at (312) 977-1755.

The Chicago Symphony Orchestra, under the direction of Sir Georg Solti, has a worldwide reputation that has been enhanced by several foreign tours.

Chicagoans are enthusiastic sports fans. South Siders root for the American League's White Sox; North Siders follow the fortunes of the National League's Cubs; all sections of the city are represented in the stands at games played by the Bears, Blackhawks, Bulls, and Sting.

## 7. Denver–Rocky Mountain National Park, CO

Denver was the only one of the final top ten Vacation Places that did not place among the top ten in any of the six preceding chapters. On the other hand, it did not do poorly in any of the chapters either; thus the total of the ranks earned seventh place for the Mile High City.

Denver, the capital of Colorado, is a city of about half a million people, with another million residing in the metropolitan area. More than half the state's total population lives in these environs. It is a metro area surrounded by beautiful scenery and hundreds of square miles of open space. Ten miles west of downtown rise the lofty Rocky Mountains, a stunning backdrop for the city.

Denver was founded in 1858; it served as a gateway and provisioning center for people seeking their fortunes in the gold mines of central Colorado. Since then it has become an important city in its own right, but it is still a gateway—for vacationers heading for wilderness areas and ski slopes. Rocky Mountain National Park, Arapaho National Recreation Area, Roosevelt National Forest, and a dozen other federal recreational areas are beloved by hikers, mountain climbers, campers, fishers, and every other type of outdoors lover.

Within the city, sightseers enjoy exploring Larimer Square, a group of beautifully preserved buildings dating from the Victorian era, now used as restaurants and galleries. Another landmark of that period is the Brown Palace Hotel, built in 1892.

Denver has a famous and unique theater, the Boettcher Concert Hall, where the Denver Symphony Orchestra performs in the round. Twelve miles southwest of the city is Red Rocks Amphitheater, a 10,000-seat performance center surrounded by gigantic red rocks. The acoustics in this natural setting are amazing; Easter sunrise services held here have often been aired on nationwide broadcasts.

Central City and Georgetown are two small villages west of Denver that were boomtowns during Colorado's gold rush days. Visitors can take a scenic ride on the partially reconstructed Georgetown Loop, a narrow-gauge railroad opened in 1884. The original run looped around three and one-half circles and crossed four bridges in order to climb a total of 638 feet in altitude. Tours of historic mine areas are available in both Georgetown and Central City.

The 263,790 acres in Rocky Mountain National Park contain some of the loftiest territory in the United States. The highest mountain is Longs Peak, 14,255 feet in altitude. First-time visitors to the mountains should remember that thin mountain air can cause problems—difficulty in breathing, rapid heartbeat, even severe nausea—for some people. Also, be sure to bring along warm clothing; temperatures can drop drastically as you reach the higher elevations.

## 7. New York City, NY

The Big Apple captured first place as a city vacation destination, the result of its first-place standing for Basic Necessities, Feeding the Mind and Spirit, and Entertainment for All, along with an eighth-place rank for Discovering Our Heritage. When the ranks for the Blessings of Nature and Fun in the Great Outdoors are considered, the final rank for New York City is seven, tied with Chicago, Illinois, and Denver-Rocky Mountain National Park, Colorado.

New York City is big, it's crowded, it's noisy, and everyone seems to be in a hurry. To a first-time visitor it may be almost overwhelming. But it is also a glittering, glamorous, exciting place. This is where you go to see the latest fashions—in clothes, entertainment, and food. This is the first stopping place for most foreign visitors, and people in exotic costumes from every country can be seen enjoying the city's restaurants, museums, and theaters. The city hosts more than 2 million overseas visitors each year, along with more than 14 million American guests.

There are intimate little bistros and tiny neighborhood theaters, and there's Madison Square Garden, where 20,000 people can congregate for a major concert or sports event.

Habitual shoppers find New York City without equal. In addition to the world-class department stores, exclusive boutiques, discount stores, and specialty shops without end, New York's many museum gift shops have art objects and souvenirs that can't be duplicated anywhere else.

Among New York City's hundreds of attractions for the vacationer, here are a few of the most popular:

The Statue of Liberty, repaired and refurbished for its 100th birthday in 1986, is one of the nation's most beloved landmarks.

The United Nations complex is unique. Guided tours are conducted throughout each day, and free tickets for meetings of the General Assembly and councils are available on a first-come, first-served basis.

The skyscrapers, especially the Empire State Building and the twin towers of the World Trade Center, give visitors a chance to view New York's skyline from above.

Lincoln Center is a group of beautiful buildings housing facilities for opera, symphony, dance, and theater.

Rockefeller Center includes Radio City Music Hall, the famous ice-skating rink and gigantic Christmas tree in winter, and outdoor dining in summer.

Times Square, the center of everything in the Big Apple, is enjoying a rebirth; new theaters, movie houses, and shops have given it a new look.

Greenwich Village is still a picturesque neighborhood of homes, shops, and art galleries.

Central Park is the city's prime playground, with 840 landscaped acres. It is also the setting for many festivals and entertainment events in summer.

## 10. Tampa Bay–Southwest Coast, FL

The city of Tampa is a major industrial metropolis and a popular vacation destination. Across Tampa Bay is Pinellas County, a peninsula covered with a huge concentration of popular resort communities. The sun shines nearly every day in this part of the state and the Gulf waters are usually a serene expanse of aquamarine, but occasionally a nasty hurricane sends everyone scurrying for cover. Golf, tennis, shuffleboard, swimming, deep-sea fishing, and pier fishing—every imaginable warm-weather sport is enjoyed here.

Florida leads the United States in the number and variety of its tourist attractions, and the majority of the best-known ones are easily accessible to vacationers staying in this area. Busch Gardens—The Dark Continent is the most popular draw in this locality; it is a theme park and also one of the nation's largest zoos. You can ride in a gondola over the heads of exotic animals—giraffes, lions, rare white Bengal tigers, Grevy zebras, and black rhinoceroses, among others. You can walk past pools where an all-white peacock spreads his feathers and dips his head at you.

A Tampa neighborhood known as Ybor City is a little Cuba in appearance and history. Cuban immigrants came here in the late 1800s to work in the cigar factories, and it was here that Teddy Roosevelt organized his Roughriders to work with Cuban freedom fighters to gain independence for Cuba. The old cigar-factory buildings have been restored and given a new use as a shopping and entertainment center. Excellent restaurants serve sumptuous Cuban meals.

Northwest of Tampa is Tarpon Springs, a village settled by Greek sponge fishermen. Here the Greek influence on food and custom is as strong as the Cuban is in Ybor City. St. Nicholas Greek Orthodox church is beautifully adorned with sculptured marble and stained glass.

There is a great variety of interesting things to see and do along Florida's southwestern coast. An unusual stop in Indian Shores is at the Suncoast Seabird Sanctuary. Not really a tourist attraction but open to the public, the sanctuary is a hospital and retirement home for wounded and disabled seabirds, primarily pelicans.

St. Petersburg has a small museum devoted exclusively to the works of Spanish artist Salvador Dali.

In Sarasota visitors can enjoy an entire day exploring the Ringling Museum complex. Ca'd'zan was the sumptuous home of circus king John Ringling. It is a large museumlike Italian villa filled with art objects. Also on the grounds are the John and Mable Ringling Museum of Art, the Museum of the Circus, and the Asolo State Theater.

Much more modest but just as interesting is Thomas Edison's winter home in Fort Myers. Edison's experimental gardens surround the house; also on the grounds is a small museum where his laboratory and some of his inventions are on display.

# Ranking Your Own Vacation Places

## Do-It-Yourself Scoresheets

| Vacation Place | Blessings of Nature | | | Fun in the Great Outdoors | | | Basic Necessities | | | Discovering Our Heritage | | | Feeding the Mind & Spirit | | | Entertainment for All | | | Cumulative Total | My Final Rank | Comments |
|---|---|---|---|---|---|---|---|---|---|---|---|---|---|---|---|---|---|---|---|---|
| | Vacation Places Rank | My Rank | Importance Factor | Vacation Places Rank | My Rank | Importance Factor | Vacation Places Rank | My Rank | Importance Factor | Vacation Places Rank | My Rank | Importance Factor | Vacation Places Rank | My Rank | Importance Factor | Vacation Places Rank | My Rank | Importance Factor | | | |
| | | | | | | | | | | | | | | | | | | | | | |
| | | | | | | | | | | | | | | | | | | | | | |
| | | | | | | | | | | | | | | | | | | | | | |
| | | | | | | | | | | | | | | | | | | | | | |
| | | | | | | | | | | | | | | | | | | | | | |
| | | | | | | | | | | | | | | | | | | | | | |
| | | | | | | | | | | | | | | | | | | | | | |
| | | | | | | | | | | | | | | | | | | | | | |
| | | | | | | | | | | | | | | | | | | | | | |
| | | | | | | | | | | | | | | | | | | | | | |
| | | | | | | | | | | | | | | | | | | | | | |
| | | | | | | | | | | | | | | | | | | | | | |
| | | | | | | | | | | | | | | | | | | | | | |

"All things being equal" . . . but they never are, of course. If all the criteria used in this book for scoring were the same ones you would use, and if all of them had equal importance in your mind, every one of you would head for Seattle, or Los Angeles, or Hawaii for your next vacation. But since, thank goodness, we don't all share the same tastes, you will make your vacation choices for your own unique reasons—to fulfill your own desires and those of the people you choose to take with you.

*Vacation Places Rated* can help you, even so. You can use the research in this book and the scoresheets in this chapter to assist you in finding the places that will give you what you want.

## HOW TO USE THE SCORESHEETS

First of all, if you have not already made a firm choice of where to go, you have probably made a few broad decisions. "It's got to have beaches and warm winter weather," "We can't go more than 1,000 miles from home," or "I want great golf and the family wants good entertainment," for example.

### Step One: Narrow Down Your Choices

If you have decided on a certain section of the United States, list the Vacation Places in that section in the far left-hand column of a scoresheet. Or if you are interested most of all in outdoor recreation and are willing to go anywhere as long as the place is one of the best in that category, list the top ten from Fun in the Great Outdoors. Or you can use other reasons to narrow your selection of Vacation Places.

Each of the six chapters whose titles are listed across the top of the scoresheet rates a specific aspect of vacationing. (Blessings of Nature, Fun in the Great Outdoors, Basic Necessities, Discovering Our Heritage, Feeding the Mind and Spirit, and Entertainment for All). If any of these do not matter at all to you, simply cross out that column and ignore it.

### Step Two: List the Ranks

Using the table entitled Putting It All Together, find the rank your selected Vacation Places received in each of the chapters that you decided to use in your rankings. Copy each of these ranks in the columns headed Vacation Places Rank.

### Step Three: Rank Your Own List

In the column headed My Rank, rerank your Vacation Places using consecutive numbers and basing them on the Vacation Places Rank: 1 for the lowest number in the Vacation Places Rank column, 2 for the next lowest, and so on.

### Step Four: Determine the Importance Factor

Now is the time to decide which aspects of a vacation mean the most to you and, if you are not going alone, what matters to your companion(s). On a piece of scrap paper, list the titles of all the chapters you have not eliminated, ranked in order of the importance of their topics to you (1 for the most important, up to 6 for the least important). If two chapters seem equally important, give them the same number.

Enter these ranks in the boxes at the top of the columns headed Importance Factor and multiply this factor by the ranks in the columns headed My Rank. Put the totals in the Importance Factor columns.

### Step Five: Calculate the Cumulative Total

Add together the scores in each of the six columns headed Importance Factor and enter the result in the column Cumulative Total.

### Step Six: Find Your Final Rank

Your final rank, from 1 to 10, can now be entered in the

## Sample Scoresheet

| Vacation Place | Blessings of Nature | | | Fun in the Great Outdoors | | | Basic Necessities | | | Discovering Our Heritage | | | Feeding the Mind & Spirit | | | Entertainment for All | | | Cumulative Total | My Final Rank | Comments |
|---|---|---|---|---|---|---|---|---|---|---|---|---|---|---|---|---|---|---|---|---|---|
| | Vacation Places Rank | My Rank | Importance Factor | Vacation Places Rank | My Rank | Importance Factor | Vacation Places Rank | My Rank | Importance Factor | Vacation Places Rank | My Rank | Importance Factor | Vacation Places Rank | My Rank | Importance Factor | Vacation Places Rank | My Rank | Importance Factor | | | |
| | | | | | | | | | | | | | | | | | | | | | |
| | | | | | | | | | | | | | | | | | | | | | |
| | | | | | | | | | | | | | | | | | | | | | |
| | | | | | | | | | | | | | | | | | | | | | |

last column, starting with the lowest cumulative total, which becomes your own number one Vacation Place.

### Step Seven: The Decision

Last of all, let the people involved write down any comments they have about the place they really want most to visit. This may lead to a decision based on actual preferences that may or may not coincide with the mathematical results of your own rankings.

In any case, going through this do-it-yourself ranking procedure should clarify the reasons you want to spend your vacation in a certain place.

### TWO EXAMPLES

Let's go through the self-ranking procedure as it might be done by two couples, the Bookbuyers and the Loves.

### Example One: The Bookbuyers

Mr. and Mrs. Bookbuyer have narrowed down their choices on the basis of geography; they have decided

that this summer they want to go to the Southwest—to New Mexico, Arizona, or southern California. They selected ten Vacation Places in that part of the country, entered them on a scoresheet (step one), and copied the ranks from the Putting It All Together table (step two). Next they filled in the My Rank column (step three).

In step four, the Bookbuyers decided that their importance factors were as follows:

1. Fun in the Great Outdoors
2. Entertainment for All
3. Discovering Our Heritage
4. Blessings of Nature
5. Basic Necessities
6. Feeding the Mind and Spirit

Then they followed through with the rest of the steps and finally added their personal comments.

The Los Angeles area was number two in the original *Vacation Places Rated* rank, and because this rank was the result of very high placement in four of the six chapters, Los Angeles also finished first among

## Example One: The Bookbuyers

| Vacation Place | Blessings of Nature | | | Fun in the Great Outdoors | | | Basic Necessities | | | Discovering Our Heritage | | | Feeding the Mind & Spirit | | | Entertainment for All | | | Cumulative Total | My Final Rank | Comments |
|---|---|---|---|---|---|---|---|---|---|---|---|---|---|---|---|---|---|---|---|---|---|
| | Vacation Places Rank | My Rank | Importance Factor 4 | Vacation Places Rank | My Rank | Importance Factor 1 | Vacation Places Rank | My Rank | Importance Factor 5 | Vacation Places Rank | My Rank | Importance Factor 3 | Vacation Places Rank | My Rank | Importance Factor 6 | Vacation Places Rank | My Rank | Importance Factor 2 | | | |
| Albuquerque | 24 | 3 | 12 | 14 | 3 | 3 | 81 | 8 | 40 | 14 | 1 | 3 | 25 | 3 | 18 | 43 | 4 | 8 | 84 | 3 | me too! |
| Grand Canyon | 11 | 1 | 4 | 20 | 6 | 6 | 103 | 9 | 45 | 58 | 4 | 12 | 62 | 7 | 42 | 102 | 10 | 20 | 129 | 8 | I've always wanted to see the Grand Canyon! |
| Lake Powell | 13 | 2 | 8 | 17 | 4 | 4 | 107 | 10 | 50 | 92 | 10 | 30 | 68 | 9 | 54 | 96 | 9 | 18 | 164 | 9 | |
| Las Vegas | 53 | 7 | 28 | 48 | 8 | 8 | 79 | 6 | 30 | 89 | 9 | 27 | 80 | 10 | 60 | 71 | 6 | 12 | 165 | 10 | A day at the casinos could be fun. |
| Los Angeles | 72 | 9 | 36 | 5 | 1 | 1 | 4 | 1 | 5 | 21 | 2 | 6 | 2 | 1 | 6 | 2 | 1 | 2 | 56 | 1 | How about Hollywood? And Disneyland? |
| Palm Springs | 50 | 6 | 24 | 13 | 2 | 2 | 61 | 5 | 25 | 87 | 8 | 24 | 31 | 4 | 24 | 82 | 7 | 14 | 113 | 4 | |
| Phoenix | 76 | 10 | 40 | 18 | 5 | 5 | 47 | 3 | 15 | 37 | 3 | 9 | 65 | 8 | 48 | 23 | 3 | 6 | 123 | 6 | |
| San Diego | 66 | 8 | 32 | 29 | 7 | 7 | 18 | 2 | 10 | 70 | 5 | 15 | 16 | 2 | 12 | 19 | 2 | 4 | 80 | 2 | |
| Santa Barbara | 48 | 5 | 20 | 58 | 10 | 10 | 59 | 4 | 20 | 77 | 7 | 21 | 54 | 6 | 36 | 92 | 8 | 16 | 123 | 6 | |
| Tucson | 27 | 4 | 16 | 57 | 9 | 9 | 80 | 7 | 35 | 71 | 6 | 18 | 44 | 5 | 30 | 58 | 5 | 10 | 118 | 5 | |

## Example Two: The Loves

| Vacation Place | Blessings of Nature | | | Fun in the Great Outdoors | | | Basic Necessities | | | Discovering Our Heritage | | | Feeding the Mind & Spirit | | | Entertainment for All | | | Cumulative Total | My Final Rank | Comments |
|---|---|---|---|---|---|---|---|---|---|---|---|---|---|---|---|---|---|---|---|---|---|
| | Vacation Places Rank | My Rank | Importance Factor 4 | Vacation Places Rank | My Rank | Importance Factor 6 | Vacation Places Rank | My Rank | Importance Factor 3 | Vacation Places Rank | My Rank | Importance Factor 1 | Vacation Places Rank | My Rank | Importance Factor 2 | Vacation Places Rank | My Rank | Importance Factor 5 | | | |
| Boston | 100 | 8 | 32 | 47 | 2 | 12 | 5 | 2 | 6 | 2 | 2 | 2 | 4 | 3 | 6 | 5 | 3 | 15 | 73 | 1 | Boston sounds great! |
| Catskills | 66 | 2 | 8 | 23 | 1 | 6 | 43 | 9 | 27 | 4 | 4 | 4 | 41 | 8 | 16 | 17 | 5 | 25 | 86 | 2 | I hoped it would be Boston! |
| Lexington | 94 | 5 | 20 | 70 | 7 | 42 | 39 | 8 | 24 | 7 | 7 | 7 | 12 | 5 | 10 | 36 | 8 | 40 | 143 | 8 | |
| New York | 98 | 7 | 28 | 65 | 8 | 48 | 1 | 1 | 3 | 8 | 8 | 8 | 1 | 1 | 2 | 1 | 1 | 5 | 94 | 3 | |
| Pennsylvania Dutch | 96 | 6 | 24 | 68 | 6 | 36 | 30 | 7 | 21 | 9 | 9 | 9 | 21 | 6 | 12 | 30 | 7 | 35 | 137 | 7 | |
| Philadelphia | 105 | 10 | 40 | 55 | 4 | 24 | 7 | 3 | 9 | 3 | 3 | 3 | 6 | 4 | 8 | 4 | 2 | 10 | 94 | 3 | |
| Providence | 70 | 3 | 12 | 52 | 3 | 18 | 8 | 4 | 12 | 5 | 5 | 5 | 51 | 9 | 18 | 23 | 6 | 30 | 95 | 5 | |
| Richmond | 83 | 4 | 16 | 100 | 10 | 60 | 69 | 10 | 30 | 6 | 6 | 6 | 72 | 10 | 20 | 44 | 9 | 45 | 177 | 10 | |
| Washington | 103 | 9 | 36 | 67 | 5 | 30 | 14 | 5 | 15 | 1 | 1 | 1 | 3 | 2 | 4 | 15 | 4 | 20 | 106 | 6 | Washington next time, OK? |
| Williamsburg | 65 | 1 | 4 | 94 | 9 | 54 | 19 | 6 | 18 | 10 | 10 | 10 | 22 | 7 | 14 | 48 | 10 | 50 | 150 | 9 | |

the ten places in the Southwest for the Bookbuyers. But by applying their own individual criteria, they discovered that Albuquerque–Santa Fe–Taos, New Mexico, was a third choice and the San Diego area was second, while *Vacation Places Rated* had ranked them 16 and 20, respectively, among all 107 places.

After adding their comments in the last column and discussing their vacation desires at length, the Book-buyers decided that what they really wanted most was to see the Grand Canyon and do some hiking, after which, maybe, they'd take in the sights of Las Vegas or Los Angeles.

### Example Two: The Loves

The Loves are a young couple, both of whom majored in history in college but have never done much traveling in the eastern part of the United States. They decided to choose from among the top ten Vacation Places in Discovering Our Heritage. Their importance factors, they decided, were as follows:

1. Discovering Our Heritage
2. Feeding the Mind and Spirit
3. Basic Necessities
4. Blessings of Nature
5. Entertainment for All
6. Fun in the Great Outdoors

When Boston turned out to be number one according to the Love's own rankings, they were both delighted and confessed that each had really wanted to spend their vacation there.

# Scoresheet

| Vacation Place | Blessings of Nature | | | Fun in the Great Outdoors | | | Basic Necessities | | | Discovering Our Heritage | | | Feeding the Mind & Spirit | | | Entertainment for All | | | Cumulative Total | My Final Rank | Comments |
|---|---|---|---|---|---|---|---|---|---|---|---|---|---|---|---|---|---|---|---|---|---|
| | Vacation Places Rank | My Rank | Importance Factor | Vacation Places Rank | My Rank | Importance Factor | Vacation Places Rank | My Rank | Importance Factor | Vacation Places Rank | My Rank | Importance Factor | Vacation Places Rank | My Rank | Importance Factor | Vacation Places Rank | My Rank | Importance Factor | | | |
| | | | | | | | | | | | | | | | | | | | | | |
| | | | | | | | | | | | | | | | | | | | | | |
| | | | | | | | | | | | | | | | | | | | | | |
| | | | | | | | | | | | | | | | | | | | | | |
| | | | | | | | | | | | | | | | | | | | | | |
| | | | | | | | | | | | | | | | | | | | | | |
| | | | | | | | | | | | | | | | | | | | | | |
| | | | | | | | | | | | | | | | | | | | | | |
| | | | | | | | | | | | | | | | | | | | | | |
| | | | | | | | | | | | | | | | | | | | | | |
| | | | | | | | | | | | | | | | | | | | | | |
| | | | | | | | | | | | | | | | | | | | | | |
| | | | | | | | | | | | | | | | | | | | | | |
| | | | | | | | | | | | | | | | | | | | | | |
| | | | | | | | | | | | | | | | | | | | | | |
| | | | | | | | | | | | | | | | | | | | | | |
| | | | | | | | | | | | | | | | | | | | | | |
| | | | | | | | | | | | | | | | | | | | | | |
| | | | | | | | | | | | | | | | | | | | | | |
| | | | | | | | | | | | | | | | | | | | | | |
| | | | | | | | | | | | | | | | | | | | | | |

# Scoresheet

| Vacation Place | Blessings of Nature | | | Fun in the Great Outdoors | | | Basic Necessities | | | Discovering Our Heritage | | | Feeding the Mind & Spirit | | | Entertainment for All | | | Cumulative Total | My Final Rank | Comments |
|---|---|---|---|---|---|---|---|---|---|---|---|---|---|---|---|---|---|---|---|---|---|
| | Vacation Places Rank | My Rank | Importance Factor | Vacation Places Rank | My Rank | Importance Factor | Vacation Places Rank | My Rank | Importance Factor | Vacation Places Rank | My Rank | Importance Factor | Vacation Places Rank | My Rank | Importance Factor | Vacation Places Rank | My Rank | Importance Factor | | | |
| | | | | | | | | | | | | | | | | | | | | | |
| | | | | | | | | | | | | | | | | | | | | | |
| | | | | | | | | | | | | | | | | | | | | | |
| | | | | | | | | | | | | | | | | | | | | | |
| | | | | | | | | | | | | | | | | | | | | | |
| | | | | | | | | | | | | | | | | | | | | | |
| | | | | | | | | | | | | | | | | | | | | | |
| | | | | | | | | | | | | | | | | | | | | | |
| | | | | | | | | | | | | | | | | | | | | | |
| | | | | | | | | | | | | | | | | | | | | | |
| | | | | | | | | | | | | | | | | | | | | | |
| | | | | | | | | | | | | | | | | | | | | | |
| | | | | | | | | | | | | | | | | | | | | | |
| | | | | | | | | | | | | | | | | | | | | | |
| | | | | | | | | | | | | | | | | | | | | | |
| | | | | | | | | | | | | | | | | | | | | | |
| | | | | | | | | | | | | | | | | | | | | | |
| | | | | | | | | | | | | | | | | | | | | | |
| | | | | | | | | | | | | | | | | | | | | | |
| | | | | | | | | | | | | | | | | | | | | | |
| | | | | | | | | | | | | | | | | | | | | | |
| | | | | | | | | | | | | | | | | | | | | | |
| | | | | | | | | | | | | | | | | | | | | | |
| | | | | | | | | | | | | | | | | | | | | | |
| | | | | | | | | | | | | | | | | | | | | | |
| | | | | | | | | | | | | | | | | | | | | | |

# Scoresheet

| Vacation Place | Blessings of Nature | | | Fun in the Great Outdoors | | | Basic Necessities | | | Discovering Our Heritage | | | Feeding the Mind & Spirit | | | Entertainment for All | | | Cumulative Total | My Final Rank | Comments |
|---|---|---|---|---|---|---|---|---|---|---|---|---|---|---|---|---|---|---|---|---|---|
| | Vacation Places Rank | My Rank | Importance Factor | Vacation Places Rank | My Rank | Importance Factor | Vacation Places Rank | My Rank | Importance Factor | Vacation Places Rank | My Rank | Importance Factor | Vacation Places Rank | My Rank | Importance Factor | Vacation Places Rank | My Rank | Importance Factor | | | |
| | | | | | | | | | | | | | | | | | | | | | |
| | | | | | | | | | | | | | | | | | | | | | |
| | | | | | | | | | | | | | | | | | | | | | |
| | | | | | | | | | | | | | | | | | | | | | |
| | | | | | | | | | | | | | | | | | | | | | |
| | | | | | | | | | | | | | | | | | | | | | |
| | | | | | | | | | | | | | | | | | | | | | |
| | | | | | | | | | | | | | | | | | | | | | |
| | | | | | | | | | | | | | | | | | | | | | |
| | | | | | | | | | | | | | | | | | | | | | |
| | | | | | | | | | | | | | | | | | | | | | |
| | | | | | | | | | | | | | | | | | | | | | |
| | | | | | | | | | | | | | | | | | | | | | |
| | | | | | | | | | | | | | | | | | | | | | |
| | | | | | | | | | | | | | | | | | | | | | |
| | | | | | | | | | | | | | | | | | | | | | |
| | | | | | | | | | | | | | | | | | | | | | |
| | | | | | | | | | | | | | | | | | | | | | |
| | | | | | | | | | | | | | | | | | | | | | |
| | | | | | | | | | | | | | | | | | | | | | |
| | | | | | | | | | | | | | | | | | | | | | |
| | | | | | | | | | | | | | | | | | | | | | |

# Appendix

## More Information on Vacation Places

**Adirondack Mountains, NY**
Adirondack Association
Adirondack, NY 12808
(518) 494-2515

Central Adirondack Association
Old Forge, NY 13420
(315) 369-6983

**Albuquerque–Santa Fe–Taos, NM**
Albuquerque Convention & Visitors Bureau
202 Central S.E., Suite 301
Albuquerque, NM 87102
(505) 243-3696

**Anchorage–Kenai Peninsula, AK**
Anchorage Convention & Visitors Bureau
201 E. Third Ave.
Anchorage, AK 99501
(907) 276-4118

**Asheville–Smoky Mountains, NC**
Asheville Area Convention & Visitors Bureau
151 Haywood St.
P.O. Box 1011
Asheville, NC 28802
(704) 258-3916

**Aspen–Vail, CO**
Aspen Resort Association
303 E. Main St.
Aspen, CO 81611
(303) 925-1940

Aspen Visitors Center
Wheeler Opera Center
Mill & Hyman Sts.
Aspen, CO 81611

Vail Resort Association
241 E. Meadow Dr.
Vail, CO 81657
(303) 476-1000

**Atlanta, GA**
Atlanta Convention & Visitors Bureau
233 Peachtree St. N.E., Suite 200
Atlanta, GA 30043
(404) 521-6600

**Atlantic City, NJ**
Atlantic City Convention & Visitors Bureau
16 Central Pier
Atlantic City, NJ 08401
(609) 345-7536

**Austin–Hill Country, TX**
Austin Convention & Visitors Bureau
901 W. Riverside
P.O. Box 1967
Austin, TX 78767
(512) 478-9383

**Baltimore–Chesapeake Bay, MD**
Baltimore Office of Promotion & Tourism
34 Market Pl., Suite 310
Baltimore, MD 21202
(301) 752-8632 or 837-4636

**Bar Harbor–Acadia, ME**
Bar Harbor Chamber of Commerce
P.O. Box 158
Bar Harbor, ME 04609

**Bend–Cascade Mountains, OR**
Bend Chamber of Commerce
164 N.W. Hawthorne
Bend, OR 97701
(503) 382-3221

**Berkshire Hills–Pioneer Valley, MA**
Berkshire Hills Conference
Berkshire Common, Plaza Level
Pittsfield, MA 01201
(413) 443-9186

Pioneer Valley Convention & Visitors Bureau
1500 Main St., 6th Floor
Springfield, MA 01115
(413) 787-1548

**Black Hills, SD**
Rapid City Area Convention & Visitors
  Bureau
444 Mt. Rushmore Rd. N.
P.O. Box 747
Rapid City, SD 57709
(605) 343-1744

**Blue Ridge Mountains, VA**
Thomas Jefferson Visitors Bureau
P.O. Box 161
Charlottesville, VA 22902
(804) 977-1783

**Boise–Sun Valley, ID**
Boise Convention & Visitors Bureau
P.O. Box 2106
Boise, ID 83701
(208) 344-7777

**Boone–High Country, NC**
North Carolina High Country Host
701 Blowing Rock Rd.
Boone, NC 28607
(800) 438-7500

**Boston, MA**
Greater Boston Convention & Visitors
  Bureau
Prudential Plaza
P.O. Box 490
Boston, MA 02199
(617) 536-4100

**Brownsville–Rio Grande Valley, TX**
Brownsville Chamber of Commerce
P.O. Box 752
Brownsville, TX 78522-0752
(512) 542-4341

McAllen Chamber of Commerce
P.O. Box 790
McAllen, TX 78502
(512) 682-2871

**Cape Cod–The Islands, MA**
Cape Cod Chamber of Commerce
Junction Routes 6 & 132
Hyannis, MA 02601
(617) 362-3225

**Catskill Mountains, NY**
Delaware County Chamber of Commerce
56 Main St.
Delhi, NY 13753
(607) 746-2281

Greene County Promotion Department
P.O. Box 467 (Thruway Exit 21)
Catskill, NY 12414
(518) 943-3223

**Charleston, SC**
Charleston Chamber of Commerce
P.O. Box 975
Charleston, SC 29402
(803) 722-8338

**Chattanooga–Huntsville, TN–AL–GA**
Chattanooga Area Convention & Visitors
  Bureau
1001 Market St.
Chattanooga, TN 37402
(615) 756-2121
Huntsville Convention & Visitors Bureau
700 Monroe St.
Huntsville, AL 35801
(205) 533-5723

**Chicago, IL**
Chicago Convention & Tourism Bureau
McCormick Place on the Lake
Chicago, IL 60616
(312) 225-5000

**Cincinnati, OH–KY**
Greater Cincinnati Convention & Visitors
  Bureau
501 Vine St.
Cincinnati, OH 45202
(513) 621-2142

**Colorado Springs, CO**
Colorado Springs Convention & Visitors
   Bureau
801 South Tejon
Colorado Springs, CO 80903
(303) 635-7506

**Coos Bay–South Coast, OR**
Bay Area Chamber of Commerce
P.O. Box 210
Coos Bay, OR 97420
(503) 269-0215

**Corpus Christi–Padre Island, TX**
Corpus Christi Area Convention & Tourist
   Bureau
P.O. Box 2664
Corpus Christi, TX 78403
(512) 882-5603

**Crater Lake–Klamath Falls, OR**
Klamath County Visitors & Convention
   Bureau
125 N. 8th St.
Klamath Falls, OR 97601
(503) 884-5193

**Dallas–Fort Worth, TX**
Dallas Chamber of Commerce
1507 Pacific Ave.
Dallas, TX 75201
(214) 954-1111

Fort Worth Convention & Visitors Bureau
700 Throckmorton
Fort Worth, TX 76102
(817) 336-8791

**Denver–Rocky Mountain
National Park, CO**
Denver & Colorado Convention & Visitors
   Bureau
225 W. Colfax Ave.
Denver, CO 80202
(303) 892-1112

**Door County, WI**
Door County Chamber of Commerce
P.O. Box 219
Sturgeon Bay, WI 54235
(414) 743-4456

**Eastern Shore, VA**
Eastern Shore Tourism Commission
1 Court House Ave.
P.O. Box 147
Accomac, VA 23301
(804) 787-2460

**Finger Lakes, NY**
Finger Lakes Association
309 Lake St.
Penn Yan, NY 14527
(315) 536-7488

**Flaming Gorge, UT–WY–CO**
Vernal Area Chamber of Commerce
50 E. Main St.
Vernal, UT 84078
(801) 789-1352

**Glacier National Park–
Flathead Lake, MT**
Glacier Country
P.O. Box 35
Whitefish, MT 59937
(406) 862-5957
Attn.: Greg Bryan

**Grand Canyon Country, AZ**
Flagstaff Chamber of Commerce
101 W. Santa Fe
Flagstaff, AZ 86001
(602) 774-4505

**Green Mountains, VT**
Stowe Area Association
P.O. Box 1230
Stowe, VT 05672
(802) 253-7321

Vermont Travel Division
134 State St.
Montpelier, VT 05602
(802) 828-3236

**Hawaii**
Hawaii Visitors Bureau
2270 Kalakaua Ave., Suite 801
Honolulu, HI 96815
(808) 923-1811

**Hilton Head, SC**
Hilton Head Island Visitor & Convention
   Bureau
P.O. Box 5647
Hilton Head Island, SC 29938
(803) 785-3673

**Holland–Lake Michigan Shore, MI**
West Michigan Tourist Association
136 Fulton E.
Grand Rapids, MI 49503
(616) 456-8557

**Houston-Galveston, TX**
Galveston Convention & Visitors Bureau
2106 Seawall Blvd.
Galveston, TX 77550
(409) 763-4311

Greater Houston Convention & Visitors
   Council
3300 Main St.
Houston, TX 77002
(713) 523-5050

**Jersey Shore, NJ**
Shore Regional Tourism Council
c/o MODC
P.O. Box 2443
Farmingdale, NJ 07727
(201) 938-2222

**Knoxville–Smoky Mountains, TN**
Knoxville Area Council for Conventions &
   Visitors
P.O. Box 15012
Knoxville, TN 37901
(615) 523-7263

**Lake of the Ozarks, MO**
Lake of the Ozarks Association
P.O. Box 98
Lake Ozark, MO 65049
(314) 365-3371

**Lake Powell–Glen Canyon, AZ–UT**
Utah's Canyonlands Region
P.O. Box 550
Moab, UT 84532
(801) 259-8825

**Lake Tahoe–Reno, NV–CA**
Reno Convention/Visitors Authority
P.O. Box 837
Reno, NV 89504

**Las Vegas–Lake Mead, NV–AZ**
Las Vegas Convention & Visitors Authority
Convention Center
3150 Paradise Rd.
Las Vegas, NV 89109
(702) 733-2323

**Lexington–Bluegrass Country, KY**
Greater Lexington Convention & Visitors
   Bureau
430 W. Vine St., Suite 363
Lexington, KY 40507
(606) 233-1221

Louisville Convention & Visitors Bureau
501 S. Third St.
Louisville, KY 40202
(800) 626-5646

**Long Island, NY**
Long Island Tourism & Convention
   Commission
213 Carleton Ave.
Central Islip, NY 11722
(516) 234-4959

**Los Angeles, CA**
Greater Los Angeles Visitors & Convention
   Bureau
505 S. Flower St.
Los Angeles, CA 90071
(213) 239-0200

Long Beach Area Convention & Visitors
   Council, Inc.
180 E. Ocean Blvd., Suite 150
Long Beach, CA 90802
(213) 436-3645

**Mackinac Island–Sault
Ste. Marie, MI**
Mackinac Island Chamber of Commerce
P.O. Box 451
Mackinac Island, MI 49757
(906) 847-3783 (May 10–November 4)
(616) 436-5513 (winter)

Sault Ste. Marie Chamber of Commerce
2581 I-75 Business Spur
Sault Ste. Marie, MI 49783
(906) 632-3301

**Memphis, TN–AR–MS**
Convention & Visitors Bureau of Memphis
12 S. Main St.
Memphis, TN 38103
(901) 526-1919

**Miami–Gold Coast–Keys, FL**
Greater Miami Convention & Visitors Bureau
4770 Biscayne Blvd., Penthouse A
Miami, FL 33137
(305) 573-4300

**Minneapolis–St. Paul, MN–WI**
Minneapolis Convention & Visitors
   Commission
15 S. Fifth St.
Minneapolis, MN 55402
(612) 348-4330

St. Paul Convention Bureau
600 N. Central Tower
St. Paul, MN 55101
(612) 292-4360

**Mobile Bay–Gulfport, AL–MS**
Mississippi Gulf Coast Convention & Visitors
  Bureau
P.O. Box 4554
Biloxi, MS 39531
(601) 388-8000

Mobile Area Chamber of Commerce
Convention & Visitor Department
P.O. Box 2187
Mobile, AL 36652
(205) 433-6951

**Monterey–Big Sur, CA**
Monterey Peninsula Chamber of Commerce
  & Visitors and Convention Bureau
P.O. Box 1770
Monterey, CA 93942-1770
(408) 649-1770

**Myrtle Beach–Grand Strand, SC**
Myrtle Beach Area Convention Bureau
P.O. Box 2115
Myrtle Beach, SC 29578
(803) 448-1629

**Mystic Seaport–Connecticut
Valley, CT**
Mystic Chamber of Commerce
P.O. Box 143
Mystic, CT 06355
(203) 536-8559

**Nashville, TN**
Nashville Area Chamber of Commerce
C & V Division
161 Fourth Ave. N.
Nashville, TN 37219
(615) 259-3900

**New Orleans, LA**
Greater New Orleans Tourist & Convention
  Commission
1520 Sugar Bowl Dr.
New Orleans, LA 70112
(504) 566-5011

**New York City, NY**
New York Convention & Visitors Bureau
2 Columbus Circle
New York, NY 10019
(212) 397-8200

**Niagara Falls–Western
New York, NY**
Niagara Falls Convention & Visitors Bureau
345 Third St.
Niagara Falls, NY 14303
(716) 278-8010

**North Woods–Land O'Lakes, WI**
Wisconsin North Woods Council
Rhinelander–Oneida County Airport
P.O. Box 1167
Rhinelander, WI 54501
(715) 369-2330

**Oklahoma City–Cherokee Strip, OK**
Oklahoma City Convention & Tourism
  Center
4 Santa Fe Plaza
Oklahoma City, OK 73102
(405) 278-8912

**Olympic Peninsula, WA**
Clallam County Economic Development
  Council
P.O. Box 1085
Port Angeles, WA 98362
(206) 452-7831
Attn.: Ted Gage

**Orlando–Space Coast, FL**
Orlando/Orange County Convention &
  Visitors Bureau
7600 Dr. Phillips Blvd., Suite 6
Orlando, FL 32819
(305) 345-8882

**Outer Banks, NC**
Dare County Tourist Bureau
P.O. Box 399
Manteo, NC 27954
(919) 473-2138

**Ozarks–Eureka Springs, AR–MO**
Branson Lakes Area Chamber of Commerce
P.O. Box 220
Branson, MO 65616
(417) 334-4136

Northwest Arkansas Recreation Association
P.O. Box 412
Eureka Springs, AR 72632
(501) 253-8737

Springfield Convention & Visitors Bureau
P.O. Box 1687
Springfield, MO 65805
(417) 862-5501

**Palm Springs–Desert
Playgrounds, CA**
Palm Springs Convention & Visitors Bureau
255 N. El Cielo Rd., Suite 315
Palm Springs, CA 92262
(619) 327-8411

**Panhandle, FL**
Greater Fort Walton Beach Chamber of
  Commerce
P.O. Drawer 640
Fort Walton Beach, FL 32549
(904) 244-8191

Pensacola Area Chamber of Commerce
P.O. Box 550
Pensacola, FL 32593
(904) 438-4081

**Pennsylvania Dutch Country, PA**
Pennsylvania Dutch Visitors Bureau
1799 Hempstead Rd.
Lancaster, PA 17601
(717) 299-8901

**Philadelphia, PA–DE–NJ**
Philadelphia Convention & Visitors Bureau
3 Penn Center Plaza
Philadelphia, PA 19102
(215) 636-3300

**Phoenix–Valley of the Sun, AZ**
Phoenix & Valley of the Sun
  Convention & Visitors Bureau
505 N. Second St., Suite #300
Phoenix, AZ 85004
(602) 254-6500

Scottsdale Chamber of Commerce
  Convention/Tourism Department
P.O. Box 130
Scottsdale, AZ 85252
(602) 945-8481

**Pocono Mountains, PA**
Pocono Mountains Vacation Bureau
Chamber of Commerce
1004 Main St.
Stroudsburg, PA 18360
(717) 421-5791

**Portland, ME**
Convention & Visitors Bureau of Greater
  Portland
142 Free St.
Portland, ME 04101
(207) 772-4994

**Portland–Columbia River, OR**
Greater Portland Convention & Visitors
  Association, Inc.
26 S.W. Salmon St.
Portland, OR 97204-3299
(503) 222-2223

**Portsmouth–Kennebunk, NH–ME**
Greater Portsmouth Chamber of Commerce
P.O. Box 239
Portsmouth, NH 03801
(603) 436-1118

**Providence–Newport, RI**
Greater Providence Convention & Visitors
  Bureau
30 Exchange Terrace
Providence, RI 02903
(401) 274-1636

**Put-in-Bay–Lake Erie Shore, OH**
Greater Toledo Office of Tourism &
  Conventions, Inc.
218 Huron St.
Toledo, OH 43604
(419) 243-8191

**Rangeley Lakes, ME**
Chamber of Commerce
P.O. Box 317
Rangeley, ME 04970
(207) 864-5571

**Redwoods–Shasta–Lassen, CA**
Eureka/Humboldt County Convention &
  Visitors Bureau
1034 Second St.
Eureka, CA 95501
(707) 443-5097

Redwood Empire Association
Spear Street Tower
1 Market Plaza
San Francisco, CA 94105
(415) 543-8334

Trinity County Chamber of Commerce
P.O. Box 517
Weaverville, CA 96093
(916) 623-6101

**Richmond–Fredericksburg, VA**
Metropolitan Richmond Chamber of
  Commerce
300 E. Main St.
Richmond, VA 23219
(804) 782-2777

**Sacramento–Gold Rush Towns, CA**
Sacramento Convention & Visitors Bureau
1311 "I" St.
Sacramento, CA 95814
(916) 442-5542

**St. Augustine–Northeast Coast, FL**
Convention & Visitors Bureau
  of Jacksonville and Its Beaches
33 S. Hogan St., Suite 250
Jacksonville, FL 32202
(904) 353-9736

**St. Louis–Mark Twain Country, MO–IL**
Hannibal Visitors & Convention Bureau
P.O. Box 624
Hannibal, MO 63401
(314) 221-2477

St. Louis Convention & Visitors Commission
10 S. Broadway, Suite 300
St. Louis, MO 63102
(314) 421-1023

**Salt Lake City, UT**
Salt Lake Convention & Visitors Bureau
180 S. W. Temple St.
Salt Lake City, UT 84101
(801) 521-2822

**San Antonio, TX**
San Antonio Convention & Visitors Bureau
P.O. Box 2277
San Antonio, TX 78298
(800) 531-5700 or (512) 270-8700

**San Diego, CA**
San Diego Convention & Visitors Bureau
1200 Third Ave., Suite 824
San Diego, CA 92101
(619) 232-3101

**San Francisco, CA**
San Francisco Convention & Visitors Bureau
201 Third St., Suite 900
San Francisco, CA 94103
(415) 974-6900

**Santa Barbara–San Simeon, CA**
San Simeon Chamber of Commerce
P.O. Box 1
San Simeon, CA 93452
(805) 927-3500

Santa Barbara Conference & Visitors Bureau
P.O. Box 299
Santa Barbara, CA 93102
(805) 965-3023

**Savannah–Golden Isles, GA**
Savannah Area Convention & Visitors
  Bureau
301 W. Broad St.
Savannah, GA 31499
(912) 233-6651

**Seattle–Mount Rainier–North Cascades, WA**
Seattle/King County Convention & Visitors
  Bureau
Visitor Information
666 Stewart
Seattle, WA 98101
(206) 447-4240

**Spokane–Coeur d'Alene, WA–ID**
Spokane Regional Convention & Visitors
  Bureau
301 W. Main
Spokane, WA 99201
(509) 624-1341

**Tampa Bay–Southwest Coast, FL**
Greater Tampa Chamber of Commerce
801 E. Kennedy
P.O. Box 420
Tampa, FL 33601
(813) 228-7777

**Traverse City–Petoskey, MI**
Grand Traverse Convention & Visitors
  Bureau
900 E. Front St., Suite 100
Traverse City, MI 49684
(616) 947-1120

**Tucson, AZ**
Metropolitan Tucson Convention & Visitors
  Bureau
450 W. Paseo Redondo, Suite 110
Tucson, AZ 85705
(602) 624-1817

**Tulsa–Lake O' The Cherokees, OK**
Tulsa Convention & Visitors Bureau
616 S. Boston Ave.
Tulsa, OK 74119
(918) 585-1201

**Vicksburg–Natchez–Baton Rouge, MS–LA**
Baton Rouge Area Convention & Visitors
  Bureau
P.O. Drawer 4149
Baton Rouge, LA 70821
(504) 383-1827

Natchez Convention & Visitors Commission
P.O. Box 794
Natchez, MS 39120
(601) 446-6345

Vicksburg/Warren County Tourist Promotion
  Commission
P.O. Box 110
Vicksburg, MS 39180
(601) 636-9421

**Washington, DC–MD–VA**
Washington, DC, Convention & Visitors
  Association
1575 Eye St. N.W., Suite 250
Washington, DC 20005
(202) 789-7000

**White Mountains, NH**
Littleton Area Chamber of Commerce
P.O. Box 105
Littleton, NH 03561
(603) 444-6561

**Williamsburg–Colonial Triangle, VA**
Norfolk Convention & Visitors Bureau
Monticello Arcade
208 E. Plume St.
Norfolk, VA 23510
(804) 441-5266

Williamsburg Area Tourism & Conference
  Bureau
P.O. Drawer GB
Williamsburg, VA 23187
(800) 368-6511 or (804) 253-0192

**Wilmington–Cape Fear, NC**
Greater Wilmington Chamber of Commerce
P.O. Box 330
Wilmington, NC 28402
(919) 762-2611

**Wine Country, CA**
Sonoma Valley Chamber of Commerce
453 First St. E.
Sonoma, CA 95476
(707) 996-1033

**Wisconsin Dells, WI**
Wisconsin Dells Visitor & Convention Bureau
115 Wisconsin Ave.
P.O. Box 390
Wisconsin Dells, WI 53965
(800) 223-3557 or (608) 254-8088

**Yellowstone–Jackson–Tetons, WY–ID–MT**
Jackson Hole Chamber of Commerce
P.O. Box E
Jackson, WY 83001
(307) 733-3316

**Yosemite–Sequoia–Death Valley, CA**
Mammoth Lakes Resort Association
P.O. Box 123
Mammoth Lakes, CA 93546
(619) 934-2712

Superintendent
Death Valley National Monument
Death Valley, CA 92328

Superintendent
Sequoia and Kings Canyon National Parks
Three Rivers, CA 93271
(209) 565-3341

Superintendent
P.O. Box 577
Yosemite National Park, CA 95389
(209) 372-4454

**Zion–Bryce Canyon, UT**
Cedar City Chamber of Commerce
286 N. Main
Cedar City, UT 84720
(801) 586-4484

St. George Area Chamber of Commerce
97 E. St. George Blvd.
St. George, UT 84770
(801) 628-1658

# State Offices of Tourism

**Alabama**
Alabama Bureau of Tourism & Travel
532 S. Perry St.
Montgomery, AL 36104-4614
(205) 261-4169
(800) 392-8096 (in state)
(800) ALA-BAMA (out of state)

**Alaska**
Alaska Division of Tourism
Pouch E
Juneau, AK 99811
(907) 465-2010

**Arizona**
Arizona Office of Tourism
1480 E. Bethany Home Rd., Suite 180
Phoenix, AZ 85014
(602) 255-3618

**Arkansas**
Arkansas Department of Parks & Tourism
1 Capitol Mall
Little Rock, AR 72201
(501) 371-7777 or 371-1511
(800) 482-9999 (in state)
(800) 643-8383 (out of state)

**California**
California Office of Tourism
1121 L St., Suite 103
Sacramento, CA 95814
(916) 322-1396

**Colorado**
Colorado Tourism Board
5500 S. Syracuse Circle, #267
Englewood, CO 80111
(303) 779-1067
(800) 255-5550 (out of state)

**Connecticut**
Connecticut Department of Economic
    Development
Tourist Division
210 Washington St.
Hartford, CT 06106
(203) 566-3948
1-800-842-7492 (in state)
1-800-243-1685 (ME to VA)

**Delaware**
Delaware Tourism Office
99 Kings Highway
P.O. Box 1401
Dover, DE 19903
(302) 736-4254
1-800-282-8667 (in state)
1-800-441-8846 (out of state)

**Florida**
Florida Division of Tourism
Collins Building
Tallahassee, FL 32301
(904) 488-5606

**Georgia**
Georgia Department of Industry & Trade
Tourist Division
230 Peachtree St. N.W., Suite 700
Atlanta, GA 30303
(404) 656-3545

**Hawaii**
Hawaii Visitors Bureau
2270 Kalakaua Ave., Suite 801
Honolulu, HI 96815
(808) 923-1811

**Idaho**
Idaho Travel Council
Division of Economic & Community Affairs
Capitol Building, Room 108
Boise, ID 83720
(208) 334-2470
(800) 635-7820

**Illinois**
Illinois Office of Tourism
Department of Commerce & Community
    Affairs
310 S. Michigan Ave., Suite 108
Chicago, IL 60604
(312) 793-2094
(800) 252-8987 (in state)
(800) 637-8560 (out of state)

**Indiana**
Indiana Tourism Development Division
Indiana Commerce Center
1 N. Capitol Ave., #700
Indianapolis, IN 46204-2243
(317) 232-8860
(800) 622-4464 (in state)
(800) 858-8073 (IL, IA, KY, MI, MO, OH, TN,
    WI)

**Iowa**
Iowa Development Commission
Division of Tourism & Travel
Capitol Center
600 E. Court Ave., Suite A
Des Moines, IA 50309
(515) 281-3100

**Kansas**
Kansas Department of Economic
    Development
Travel & Tourism Division
503 Kansas Ave., 6th Floor
Topeka, KS 66603
(913) 296-2009

**Kentucky**
Kentucky Department of Travel Development
Capital Plaza Tower, 22nd Floor
Frankfort, KY 40601
(502) 564-4930
(800) 225-8747 (excluding far western states
    and ME)

**Louisiana**
Louisiana Department of Culture,
    Recreation, & Tourism
Office of Tourism
P.O. Box 74291
Baton Rouge, LA 70804-9291
(504) 925-3850
(800) 231-4730 (out of state)

**Maine**
Maine State Development Office
Division of Tourism
189 State St.
Augusta, ME 04333
(207) 289-5710

**Maryland**
Maryland Office of Tourist Development
45 Calvert St.
Annapolis, MD 21401
(301) 269-3517

**Massachusetts**
Massachusetts Department of Commerce &
    Development
Division of Tourism
100 Cambridge St., 13th Floor
Boston, MA 02202
(617) 727-3201

**Michigan**
Michigan Department of Commerce
Travel Bureau
Town Center Building
333 S. Capitol Ave., Suite F
Lansing, MI 48933
(517) 373-0620
(800) 292-2570 (in state)
(800) 248-5700 (CT, DE, DC, IL, IN, IA, KY,
    MD, MA, MN, MO, NC, NH, NJ, NY, OH,
    PA, RI, SD, TN, VT, VA, WV, WI)

**Minnesota**
Minnesota Department of Energy &
    Economic Development
Office of Tourism
240 Bremer Building
419 N. Robert St.
St. Paul, MN 55101
(612) 296-5029
(800) 652-9747 (in state)
(800) 328-1461 (out of state)

**Mississippi**
Mississippi Department of Economic
    Development
Division of Tourism
P.O. Box 22825
Jackson, MS 39205
(601) 359-3414
(800) 962-2346 (in state)
(800) 647-2290 (out of state)

**Missouri**
Missouri Division of Tourism
P.O. Box 1055
Jefferson City, MO 65102
(314) 751-4133

**Montana**
Montana Travel Promotion Division
1424 Ninth Ave.
Helena, MT 59620-0411
(406) 444-2654
(800) 548-3390 (out of state)

**Nebraska**
Nebraska Department of Economic
    Development
Division of Travel & Tourism
301 Centennial Mall South
P.O. Box 94666
Lincoln, NE 68509
(402) 471-3796
(800) 742-7595 (in state)
(800) 228-4307 (out of state)

**Nevada**
Nevada Commission on Tourism
Capitol Complex
Carson City, NV 89710
(702) 885-4322

**New Hampshire**
New Hampshire Office of Vacation Travel
P.O. Box 856
Concord, NH 03301
(603) 271-2666
(800) 258-3608 (New England, northern NJ,
    eastern NY, northern PA)

**New Jersey**
New Jersey Division of Travel & Tourism
CN 826
Trenton, NJ 08625
(609) 292-2470

**New Mexico**
New Mexico Economic Development &
    Tourism Department
Bataan Memorial Building
Santa Fe, NM 87503
(505) 827-6230
(800) 545-2040 (out of state)

**New York**
New York State Department of Commerce
Division of Tourism
1 Commerce Plaza
Albany, NY 12245
(518) 474-4116
(800) CAL-LNYS (New England, north of VA,
    east of MI)

**North Carolina**
North Carolina Department of Commerce
Division of Travel & Tourism
430 N. Salisbury St.
Raleigh, NC 27611
(919) 733-4171
(800) VIS-ITNC

**North Dakota**
North Dakota Tourism Promotion
Capitol Grounds
Bismarck, ND 58505
(701) 224-2525
(800) 472-2100 (in state)
(800) 437-2077 (out of state)

**Ohio**
Office of Travel & Tourism
Department of Development
P.O. Box 1001
Columbus, OH 43216
(614) 466-8844
(800) BUC-KEYE

**Oklahoma**
Oklahoma Tourism & Recreation Department
Literature Distribution Center
215 N.E. 28th St.
Oklahoma City, OK 73105
(405) 521-2409
(800) 652-6552 (AR, CO, KS, MO, NM, TX
    outside area code 512)

**Oregon**
Oregon Economic Development Department
Tourism Division
595 Cottage St. N.E.
Salem, OR 97310
(503) 378-3451
(800) 233-3306 (in state)
(800) 547-7842 (out of state)

**Pennsylvania**
Pennsylvania Department of Commerce
Bureau of Travel Development
Forum Building, Room 416
Harrisburg, PA 17120
(717) 787-5453
(800) VIS-ITPA

**Rhode Island**
Rhode Island Department of Economic
    Development
7 Jackson Walkway
Providence, RI 02903
(401) 277-2601
(800) 556-2484 (ME to VA)

**South Carolina**
South Carolina Department of Parks,
    Recreation, & Tourism
Division of Tourism
P.O. Box 71
Columbia, SC 29202
(803) 758-2279

**South Dakota**
South Dakota Department of State
    Development
Division of Tourism
711 Wells Ave., P.O. Box 6000
Pierre, SD 57501
(605) 773-3301
(800) 952-3625 (in state)
(800) 843-8000 (out of state)

**Tennessee**
Tennessee Department of Tourist
    Development
P.O. Box 23170
Nashville, TN 37202
(615) 741-2158

**Texas**
Texas Department of Highways & Public
    Transportation
Capitol Tourist Bureau
P.O. Box 12374
Austin, TX 78701
(512) 475-2877

**Utah**
Utah Travel Council
Council Hall/Capitol Hill
Salt Lake City, UT 84114
(801) 533-5681

**Vermont**
Vermont Travel Division
Agency of Development & Community Affairs
134 State St.
Montpelier, VT 05602
(802) 828-3236

**Virginia**
Virginia Division of Tourism
202 N. Ninth St., Suite 500
Richmond, VA 23219
(804) 786-4484

**Washington**
Washington Department of Trade &
    Economic Development
Tourism Development Division
101 General Administration Building
Olympia, WA 98504
(206) 753-5600
(800) 562-4570 (in state)
(800) 541-WASH (out of state)

**West Virginia**
West Virginia Department of Commerce
Tourism Division
Capitol Complex, Room B-564
Charleston, WV 25305
(304) 348-2286
(800) 624-9110 (out of state)

**Wisconsin**
Wisconsin Division of Tourism
Department of Development
123 W. Washington Ave.
Madison, WI 53702
(608) 266-2161
(800) ESC-APES (IL, IA, MI, MN, WI)

**Wyoming**
Wyoming Travel Commission
Frank Norris, Jr. Travel Center
Cheyenne, WY 82002
(307) 777-7777
(800) 443-2784 (out of state)

# Sources

Information used to calculate the scores in this book was gathered from the sources listed below, along with hundreds of guidebooks, maps, brochures, and news releases published by various federal agencies and state and local tourism organizations. Every effort was made to verify all of the information listed in the Place Profiles in more than one source. Responsibility for the scores rests with the author and publisher, not with any of the sources consulted.

All unpublished and undated data cited were furnished to the author by the sources in 1984 and 1985.

ABC Leisure Magazines, *Musical America, 1983 International Directory of the Performing Arts*

American Association of Zoological Parks and Aquariums, *Zoological Parks and Aquariums in the Americas*, 1984

American Automobile Association, *AAA TourBook* (20 volumes), 1984

American Bus Association, *The Top 100 Events in North America*, 1984 and 1985

Brooklyn Botanic Garden, *American Gardens: A Traveler's Guide*, 1977

Business Research Division, University of Colorado, and U.S. Travel Data Center, *Tourism's Top Twenty*, 1984

Gale Research Company, *The Lively Arts Information Directory* , 1985

Gall Publications, *Astronomical Directory*, 1982

Golf Digest/Tennis, *Tennis, 1985 Yearbook*

Houghton Mifflin Company, *The 1986 Information Please Almanac*

International Association of Amusement Parks and Attractions, *IAAPA 1985 Directory and Guide*

International Union for Conservation of Nature and Natural Resources, *The World's Greatest Natural Areas*, 1982

Inter-Ski Services, *The White Book of Ski Areas*, Robert G. Enzel, 1983

Marquis Professional Publications, *Music Industry Directory*, 1983

Murdoch Publications, *Meetings and Conventions 1984 Gold Key Award*

National Golf Foundation, unpublished data

National Oceanographic and Atmospheric Administration, unpublished data

National Park Service, unpublished data, 1982

National Register Publishing Company, *The Official Museum Directory*, 1985

New American Library, *Fisher Annotated Travel Guides* (4 volumes), 1985

Newspaper Enterprise Association, *The World Almanac and Book of Facts,* 1985

*New York Times*, June 16, 1985

Rand McNally and Company, *Commercial Atlas,* 1985

Rand McNally and Company, *Mobil Travel Guide,* (7 volumes), 1985

Rand McNally and Company, *National Park Guide*, Michael Frome, 1985

Rand McNally and Company, *Places Rated Almanac,* Richard Boyer and David Savageau, 1985

Ringold and Clark, *The Coastal Almanac*, 1980

Theater Communications Group, *Theater Profiles/6,* 1984

Travel Magazine, *Travel-Holiday*, December 1984

U.S. Bureau of the Census, unpublished data

U.S. Department of the Interior Geological Survey, *The National Atlas of the United States of America*, 1970

U.S. Department of the Interior Geological Survey, unpublished data

U.S. Government Printing Office, *Index 1982, National Park System and Related Areas*

U.S. Government Printing Office, *National Wildlife Refuges, A Visitor's Guide*, 1982

U.S. Secretary of the Interior, unpublished data, 1982

## About the Author

Sylvia McNair is a free-lance writer who specializes in travel and children's nonfiction. She is a former Rand McNally travel guide editor and the author of several guidebooks and travel articles.

McNair is active in the Society of American Travel Writers, an organization in which she has served as chapter chair and national board member. In 1975 she was invited to be a member of a 35-person delegation authorized by the White House and the U.S. Travel Service to make a round-the-world trip to promote U.S. tourism and publicize the American Revolution Bicentennial.

Other professional affiliations include Chicago Women in Publishing, of which she is a charter member, the American Society of Journalists and Authors, and Midwest Travel Writers Association.

Other Useful

# VACATION

Publications from Rand McNally

Many excellent travel books and guides to all sections of the United States are available in bookstores, drug and discount stores, and other retail outlets. Following is a list of useful books published by Rand McNally and Company:

★ **1986 Road Atlas** ($5.95)
The country's best-selling road atlas.

**Are We There Yet?** ($2.95)
More than 80 activities to pass time while traveling.

**Best Travel Activity Book Ever** ($5.95)
Familiarizes children with the U.S. through varied activities.

**Rand McNally Travel Fun Kit** ($9.95)
Hours of on-the-go fun for the whole family. Activity books, crayons, audio cassette of original songs, and songsheet—all in a reusable plastic tote bag.

★ **Campground & Trailer Park Directory**
The directories preferred by America's campers.

★ **City & Highway Road Atlas** ($3.95)
The road atlas that fits your map compartment perfectly!

★ **Family Adventure Road Atlas** ($7.95)
The *1986 Road Atlas* with travel information on action vacations and special-events vacations.

★ **Glove Compartment Guide to Emergency Car Repair** ($4.95)
An essential glove compartment item for the layperson—easy to use problem/solution format with many illustrations.

**Map Set**
Regional map sets, with city and state titles in a handy pack.
  **California & Las Vegas** ($9.95)
  **Central Plains** ($8.95)
  **Florida & the Southeast** ($8.95)
  **Great Lakes** ($9.95)
  **Middle Atlantic** ($6.95)
  **The Northeast** ($6.95)
  **The Pacific Coast** ($8.95)
  **Rocky Mountain States** ($7.95)
  **The Southwest** ($9.95)

★ **Mobil Travel Guide** ($8.95 each)
America's most reliable quality ratings of lodgings and restaurants, in seven regional editions.

★ **National Park Guide** ($10.95)
The leading guide to America's national parks.

**The National Parks** ($45.00)
Text and over 120 photographs capture all the beauty and diversity of all the national parks.

**This Great Land** ($40.00)
Text and 130 photographs portray the natural wonders of America.

*Look for these titles in your favorite store. Many stores can also order any titles for you.*

# IMPORTANT!   IMPORTANT!
## Please fill out and return within the next 10 days.

Please complete and return this *postage paid* card to Rand McNally. The information on you and your travel habits will help us develop more products to better serve you in the future. THANK YOU!!

**1.** 1. ☐ Mr.  2. ☐ Mrs.  3. ☐ Ms.  4. ☐ Miss                    **73-L**

First Name                    Initial    Last Name

Street                                                              Apt. No.

City                                    State        Zip

**2.** Date of Purchase:    Month    Day    Year        Area Code        Telephone

**3.** Where did you make this purchase?
1. ☐ Received as Gift
2. ☐ Department Store
3. ☐ Chain Bookstore (Waldenbooks, B. Dalton, Crown, etc.)
4. ☐ Independent Bookstore
5. ☐ Book Club
6. ☐ Discount Store (K Mart, etc.)
7. ☐ Mail Order
8. ☐ Office Supply/Stationery Store
9. ☐ Drugstore
10. ☐ Supermarket
11. ☐ Other:_____

**4.** What are the *two* (2) most important uses for Vacation Places Rated?
1. ☐ Vacation (week or more) Planning
2. ☐ Short Trip (less than a week) Planning
3. ☐ Business Trip Planning
4. ☐ Take Along on Vacation
5. ☐ Browsing/Arm Chair Travel
6. ☐ Other:_____

**5.** Please check the *three* (3) features of the Vacation Places Rated that will be the most useful to you.
1. ☐ General Chapter Introduction
2. ☐ Specific Scoring Criteria
3. ☐ Vacation Place Profiles
4. ☐ Numerical Ranking List
5. ☐ Alphabetical Ranking List
6. ☐ Top Ten Listing
7. ☐ Author's Favorite Listings
8. ☐ Putting It All Together Chapter
9. ☐ The Do-It-Yourself Scoresheet

**6.** Which of the following reference materials do you own? (Check all that apply)
1. ☐ Encyclopedia
2. ☐ Dictionary
3. ☐ Bible Dictionary/Atlas
4. ☐ Thesaurus
5. ☐ Almanac
6. ☐ Places Rated Almanac
7. ☐ Globe
8. ☐ Wall Map
9. ☐ World Atlas
10. ☐ Road Atlas
11. ☐ Places Rated Retirement Guide
12. ☐ Other:_____

**7.** How many round trips of 200 miles or more have you taken within the past year for pleasure travel?
1. ☐ None
2. ☐ 1-2 Trips
3. ☐ 3-5 Trips
4. ☐ 6-10 Trips
5. ☐ 11-19 Trips
6. ☐ 20 or More Trips

**8.** On the following scale, please indicate whether you agree or disagree with these statements:

| | Disagree Strongly | | Agree Strongly | |
|---|---|---|---|---|
| 1. I would buy a book that rates jobs and their locations. | 1☐ | 2☐ | 3☐ | 4☐ |
| 2. Addresses of hotels in this book would be helpful. | 1☐ | 2☐ | 3☐ | 4☐ |
| 3. Addresses of restaurants in this book would be helpful. | 1☐ | 2☐ | 3☐ | 4☐ |
| 4. I would buy a $6.95 world atlas that lists major events of the year. | 1☐ | 2☐ | 3☐ | 4☐ |
| 5. Coupons for reduced admissions to places in this book would make me question its validity. | 1☐ | 2☐ | 3☐ | 4☐ |
| 6. I would buy a book that rates areas on sports activities. | 1☐ | 2☐ | 3☐ | 4☐ |
| 7. Addresses of where to write for more information would make this book more useful. | 1☐ | 2☐ | 3☐ | 4☐ |

**9.** Date of birth of person whose name appears above:
Month    Year    1  9

**10.** Marital Status:
1. ☐ Married
2. ☐ Divorced/Separated
3. ☐ Widowed
4. ☐ Single/Never Married

**11.** Occupation:

| | You | Your Spouse |
|---|---|---|
| Homemaker | 1. ☐ | 1. ☐ |
| Teacher/Educator | 2. ☐ | 2. ☐ |
| Professional/Technical | 3. ☐ | 3. ☐ |
| Executive/Administrator | 4. ☐ | 4. ☐ |
| Middle Management | 5. ☐ | 5. ☐ |
| Sales/Marketing | 6. ☐ | 6. ☐ |
| Clerical | 7. ☐ | 7. ☐ |
| Craftsworker | 8. ☐ | 8. ☐ |
| Machine Oper./Laborer | 9. ☐ | 9. ☐ |
| Service Worker | 10. ☐ | 10. ☐ |
| Retired | 11. ☐ | 11. ☐ |
| Student | 12. ☐ | 12. ☐ |

**12.** Do you have any children living at home in any of the following age groups?
1. ☐ None
2. ☐ Baby Under 6 months
3. ☐ Baby 6 to 12 months
4. ☐ Age 1
5. ☐ Age 2-4
6. ☐ Age 5-7
7. ☐ Age 8-10
8. ☐ Age 11-12
9. ☐ Age 13-15
10. ☐ Age 16-18

**13.** Which group describes your annual family income?
1. ☐ Under $10,000
2. ☐ $10,000-$14,999
3. ☐ $15,000-$19,999
4. ☐ $20,000-$24,999
5. ☐ $25,000-$29,999
6. ☐ $30,000-$34,999
7. ☐ $35,000-$39,999
8. ☐ $40,000-$44,999
9. ☐ $45,000-$49,999
10. ☐ $50,000-$54,999
11. ☐ $55,000-$59,999
12. ☐ $60,000 & Over

**14.** Which types of credit cards do you use regularly?
1. ☐ American Express, Diners Club, Carte Blanche
2. ☐ Bank Card (MasterCard, Visa)
3. ☐ Gas, Department Store, etc.
4. ☐ None of the Above

**15.** For your primary residence, do you:
1. ☐ Own a house?
2. ☐ Rent a house or apartment?
3. ☐ Own a townhouse or condominium?

(over)

73-L
vacation places rated

# Business Reply Mail

FIRST CLASS   PERMIT NO. 388   CHICAGO, IL

POSTAGE WILL BE PAID BY ADDRESSEE

 **Rand McNally & Company**
P.O. Box 172001
Denver, CO 80217-9830

**please do not send any products or correspondence to this address**

(Please fold here)

16. To help us understand our customers' lifestyles, please indicate the interests and activities in which *you* or *your spouse* enjoy participating on a *regular* basis:

| | | |
|---|---|---|
| 1. ☐ Golf | 19. ☐ Home Workshop/ Do-It-Yourself | 34. ☐ Collectibles/ Collections |
| 2. ☐ Physical Fitness/Exercise | 20. ☐ Photography | 35. ☐ Fine Art/Antiques |
| 3. ☐ Running/Jogging | 21. ☐ Stereo, Records & Tapes | 36. ☐ Real Estate Investments |
| 4. ☐ Skiing Frequently | 22. ☐ Avid Book Reading | 37. ☐ Stock/Bond Investments |
| 5. ☐ Tennis Frequently | 23. ☐ Bible/Devotional Reading | 38. ☐ Entering Sweepstakes |
| 6. ☐ Bicycle Touring/Racing | 24. ☐ Crafts | 39. ☐ Health Foods/Vitamins |
| 7. ☐ Boating/Sailing | 25. ☐ Needlework/Knitting | 40. ☐ Money Making Opportunities |
| 8. ☐ Gardening | 26. ☐ Sewing | |
| 9. ☐ Grandchildren | 27. ☐ Attending Cultural/ Arts Events | 41. ☐ Our Nation's Heritage |
| 10. ☐ Household Pets (dogs, cats, etc.) | 28. ☐ Community/Civic Activities | 42. ☐ Wildlife/Environmental Issues |
| 11. ☐ Camping/Hiking | | 43. ☐ Science/New Technology |
| 12. ☐ Fishing Frequently | 29. ☐ Fashion Clothing | 44. ☐ Personal/Home Computer |
| 13. ☐ Hunting/Shooting | 30. ☐ Foreign Travel | |
| 14. ☐ Motorcycles | 31. ☐ Gourmet Cooking/ Fine Foods | 45. ☐ Home Video Games |
| 15. ☐ Recreational Vehicle | | 46. ☐ Videocassette Recording (VCR) |
| 16. ☐ CB Radio | 32. ☐ Wines | 47. ☐ Cable TV Viewing |
| 17. ☐ Automotive Work | 33. ☐ Coin/Stamp Collecting | 48. ☐ Watching Sports on TV |
| 18. ☐ Electronics | | |

Thanks for taking the time to fill out this questionnaire. Your answers will be used for market research studies and reports – and will help us better serve you in the future. They will also allow you to receive important mailings and special offers from a number of fine companies whose products and services relate directly to the specific interests, hobbies and other information indicated above. Through this selective program, you will be able to obtain more information about activities in which you are involved and less about those in which you are not. Please check here if, for some reason, you would prefer not to participate in this opportunity. ☐

If you have comments or suggestions about our products, please write to:

Customer Service
Rand McNally & Company

8255 North Central Park Avenue
Skokie, Illinois 60076

**Fold in half and tape (or seal) for mailing. Do not staple.**